D0099252

INVISIBLE ARMIES

✦✦✦

ALSO BY MAX BOOT

War Made New: Technology, Warfare, and the Course of History, 1500 to Today

✦

The Savage Wars of Peace: Small Wars and the Rise of American Power

INVISIBLE ARMIES

An Epic History of Guerrilla Warfare from Ancient Times to the Present

MAX BOOT

LIVERIGHT PUBLISHING CORPORATION

A Division of W. W. Norton & Company

New York • London

Copyright © 2013 by Max Boot

All rights reserved
Printed in the United States of America
First Edition

For information about permission to reproduce selections from this book,
write to Permissions, Liveright Publishing Corporation,
a division of W. W. Norton & Company, Inc.,
500 Fifth Avenue, New York, NY 10110

For information about special discounts for bulk purchases, please contact
W. W. Norton Special Sales at specialsales@wwnorton.com or 800-233-4830

Manufacturing by RR Donnelley, Harrisonburg
Book design by Ellen Cipriano
Production manager: Devon Zahn

Library of Congress Cataloging-in-Publication Data

Boot, Max, 1968–
Invisible armies : an epic history of guerrilla warfare from ancient times to the present /
Max Boot. — 1st ed.
p. cm.
Includes bibliographical references and index.
ISBN 978-0-87140-424-4 (hardcover)
1. Guerrilla warfare—History. I. Title.
U240.B656 2012
355.02'1809—dc23
2012028522

Liveright Publishing Corporation
500 Fifth Avenue, New York, N.Y. 10110
www.wwnorton.com

W. W. Norton & Company Ltd.
Castle House, 75/76 Wells Street, London W1T 3QT

1 2 3 4 5 6 7 8 9 0

To the Council on Foreign Relations,

for making this book possible;

✦

And to Victoria, Abigail, and William Boot,

for the good fortune of being their father.

CONTENTS

BOOK II

LIBERTY OR DEATH

The Rise of the Liberal Revolutionaries

✦

BOOK III

THE SPREADING OIL SPOT
The Wars of Empire

✦

BOOK IV

THE BOMB THROWERS

The First Age of International Terrorism

✦

BOOK V

THE SIDESHOWS

Guerrillas and Commandos in the World Wars

✦

BOOK VI

THE END OF EMPIRE

The Wars of "National Liberation"

✦

BOOK VIII

GOD'S KILLERS
The Rise of Radical Islam

✦

"An invisible army spread itself out over nearly the whole of Spain like a net from whose meshes there was no escape for the French soldier who for a moment left his column or his garrison. Without uniforms and without weapons, apparently the guerilleros escaped easily from the columns that pursued them, and it frequently happened that the troops sent out to do battle with them, passed through their midst without perceiving them."

—COUNT MIOT DE MELITO (1858)[1]

✦

"We . . . attack an enemy who is invisible, fluid, uncatchable."

—COLONEL ROGER TRINQUIER (1961)[2]

PROLOGUE

BAGHDAD PATROL, APRIL 9, 2007

LIKE PREDATORS READY for the hunt, the paratroopers came out of their "hootches," their quarters, as twilight began to fall, their tan desert boots crunching softly on the silvery gravel spread over the barren soil of their compound. On went their gear: Kevlar helmets, M-4 assault rifles, 9-millimeter pistols, fire-retardant gloves, night-vision goggles, first-aid kits, ammunition pouches, walkie-talkies, and much else besides. The most unwieldy implement was their body armor, complete with shoulder and crotch coverings and SAPI plates (small arms protective inserts) in front, back, and around the sides. At least sixty pounds of added weight in all—about the same weight that a Roman legionnaire would have carried.

A short mission brief, then onto an unarmored truck that would spare them the half-mile walk to the front gate of Forward Operating Base Justice. After a brief drive, they hopped off. Four feet down from the rear of the truck. Out the gate. Into the warm spring air. Into the toxic smells drifting across the nearby Tigris River.

Monday, April 9, 2007. The Kadhimiya neighborhood of northwestern Baghdad.

This was the anniversary of the fall of Saddam Hussein's regime. Although American troops had no trouble toppling the Iraqi army and Republican Guard, which fought exactly the kind of positional warfare that all conventional militaries prefer, they had found themselves stymied by armed groups ranging from Sunni jihadists to Shiite militias. Using simple weapons—AK-47s, rocket-propelled grenades, and, above all, the bombs that the American military dubbed IEDs (improvised explosive devices)—a variety of militants had already killed over 3,300 Americans and wounded 25,000 more. Another 1,184 would die over the next four years and eight months. The death toll among Iraqis was far more horrific, eventually reaching more than 80,000 dead.[1] Just a few months earlier, the terrible bloodletting in Baghdad had brought the country to the brink of all-out civil war.

American troops found their tactics and technology, still designed to defeat an opponent like the now defunct Red Army, woefully inadequate to deal with these new threats. In this sort of war, there were no flanks to turn, few bastions to storm, no capitals to seize. Only the grim daily challenge of battling an unseen foe that was everywhere and nowhere. A foe that struck with ruthless abandon and then melted into the population. A foe that hoped to goad the Americans into savage reprisals that would turn the population against them. This was the kind of enemy that Americans have battled before, from the jungles of the Philippines in the early 1900s to the rice paddies of Vietnam in the 1960s, but it is not an enemy that most soldiers feel comfortable in confronting.

Not until the end of 2006—almost four years after the beginning of the Iraq War—did the Army and Marine Corps finally release their first new field manual in decades (FM 3-24) dealing specifically with counterinsurgency operations. When General David H. Petraeus, who oversaw the writing of FM 3-24, was appointed the American commander in Iraq in early 2007, he began to implement its prescriptions. More troops were dispatched to Iraq and more of them began to move out of their remote Forward Operating Bases, where miles of concertina wire and concrete cut them off from contact with the society they were supposed to be pacifying. Troops began to take up residence in Joint Security Stations and Combat Outposts, where they could live and work alongside Iraqis. The emphasis began to shift from drive-bys in heavily armored Humvees to foot patrols that allow the soldiers to get out among the people and to gather the intelligence they need to hunt down insurgents.

Captain David Brunais, newly promoted from the rank of first lieutenant but still in command of a platoon, was a small part of this shift in strategy as he led eleven enlisted men and a sergeant from the Eighty-Second Airborne Division onto the darkened streets of Kadhimiya. This was their third patrol of the day in a heavily Shiite area where the few Sunni residents had been chased out months before. It was home to many sympathizers of Moqtada al Sadr's Jaish al Mahdi (Mahdist Army), an extremist Shiite group, as well as to a revered Shiite shrine heavily protected by local security forces. Much like the Mafia in John Gotti's neighborhood, the Mahdists preferred to keep their own area quiet while exporting violence elsewhere. So this neighborhood was relatively secure by Iraqi terms. But that did not mean much. Shocking violence could erupt with no notice practically anywhere in this lawless land. Not even the Green Zone at the center of the city was secure. In a few days' time, a suicide bomber would penetrate the Iraqi parliament in the Green Zone and kill a lawmaker in a heavily publicized attack.

The paratroopers fanned out on either side of the street, keeping a vigilant eye for trouble with night-vision goggles that turn the darkness into a glowing, green-tinted version of daylight, communicating in low tones over microphones strapped to their helmets. The only problem they encountered was a bad traffic accident: a taxi flipped upside down. Brunais stopped to chat with an Iraqi Army major to ask whether he needed any help, but the Iraqis seemed to have the situation well in hand. The paratroopers kept on walking until they got to an outdoor café where half a dozen middle-aged men were smoking hookah pipes. Brunais had gotten to know them in the month that he had been patrolling this neighborhood. He stopped to chat, sitting down in a cheap plastic lawn chair.

The men displayed the invariable Arab hospitality, offering Brunais a water pipe, which he declined, and a Pepsi, which he accepted. Sometimes an English-speaking Iraqi was among the hookah smokers, but not today, so Brunais called his interpreter over—an Iraqi man wearing a ski mask to hide his identity in order to avoid insurgent retaliation. Through his "terp," Brunais conducted a stilted if friendly conversation that began with jokes about playing dominoes and soccer and proceeded to an explanation from the captain of why the government of Iraq had decided to close the capital to vehicular traffic on this symbolic day. The men complained good-naturedly about this interruption in their daily routines which they said was bad for business. Brunais pointed out that car bombs were even worse for business.

The conversation lasted but a few minutes. Then, with protestations of friendship on both sides, Brunais and his men were on their way, walking slowly back to where they started from. An hour and a half after having left their base, they were back, spent, tired, and sweaty, ready to sack out and do it all over again in the morning.[2]

✦ ✦ ✦

THERE WAS NOTHING exceptional about what these soldiers from the Eighty-Second Airborne Division did on this balmy Baghdad night. And that is precisely the point. They were undertaking the sort of modest, tedious, mundane intelligence gathering and security operations that have been a cornerstone of counterinsurgency operations since the days of Alexander the Great and Julius Caesar. They were part of a long continuum of soldiers who have struggled to master the rigors of unconventional warfare, just as their enemies were part of an even longer continuum of irregular warriors who have always given conventional armies fits.

Time and again, guerrilla warfare seemed to be superseded by the "new new thing"—industrial warfare in the 1910s, aerial warfare in the 1930s, nuclear warfare in the 1950s, network-centric warfare in the 1990s. And yet each time it reasserted itself with a vengeance.

Since World War II, insurgency and terrorism have become the dominant forms of conflict—a trend likely to continue into the foreseeable future. Even as conventional interstate clashes dwindle, the number of guerrilla and terrorist groups continues to grow, the latter even faster than the former.[3] One study found that in the 1990s over 90 percent of all wartime deaths occurred in civil wars fought primarily by irregulars; the figure was undoubtedly just as high in the first decade of the twenty-first century.[4]

It is not hard to see why this mode of warfare has become so prevalent. For one thing, it is cheap and easy: waging guerrilla warfare does not require procuring expensive weapons systems or building an elaborate bureaucracy. And it works. At least sometimes. From Algeria and Vietnam to Afghanistan, Chechnya, Lebanon, Somalia, and Iraq, insurgents have shown a consistent ability to humble great powers. Americans got an unwelcome reminder of how potent irregular tactics could be on September 11, 2001, and in the wars that ensued. Suddenly understanding the nature of guerrilla warfare, and its close cousin, terrorism, was no longer the stuff of musty academic studies from the era of flower power. It had become a matter of life and death.

Yet there was no accessible and up-to-date account to trace the evolution of guerrilla warfare and terrorism over the ages.[5] The aim of *Invisible Armies* is to deliver precisely such a narrative, telling the story of irregular warfare from its origins in the prehistoric world to the contemporary conflicts in Iraq, Afghanistan, and beyond. The aim is to show low-intensity conflict in its most important variations and manifestations over the centuries. The primary focus is on the last two centuries, but the first part of the book examines guerrilla warfare in the ancient and medieval worlds in order to place more recent developments in perspective.

This book is intended to serve as a one-stop destination, as it were, for a general reading public interested in this subject. But I had no intention of producing an encyclopedia. My goal has been to pen an account that is as engrossing as it is instructive. Instead of trying to chronicle every occurrence of guerrilla warfare and terrorism—something that is impossible, in any case—I aim to draw out the main trends and to illustrate them with well-chosen and well-told stories. In the interests of concision, I have had to omit or abbreviate discussion of many wars. Those in search of greater detail on a particular topic should turn to the endnotes for suggested reading.

In the narrative that follows, I place considerable emphasis on the views and personalities of notable commanders. Not only are the quirks of personality inherently interesting, but they are also important in determining the course of events—especially in insurgencies. Guerrilla armies, which lack the organizational structure of regular forces, are often the reflection of one forceful personality such as Robert the Bruce, Giuseppe Garibaldi, Orde Wingate, or Mao Zedong. Likewise, the most successful guerrilla fighters—men such as Hubert Lyautey, Edward Lansdale, and David Petraeus—are often mavericks at odds with their own military establishments.

✦ ✦ ✦

THE FIRST DIFFICULTY inherent in a work of this sort is that there is no commonly accepted definition of words like "guerrilla" and "terrorist." As the saying has it, one man's terrorist is another man's freedom fighter. Walter Laqueur complains, with a great deal of justification, that "the term 'terrorism' (like 'guerrilla') has been used in so many different senses as to become almost meaningless."[6] It is precisely because such terms are so hard to define that *Invisible Armies* covers both terrorists and guerrillas; leaving either one out would present a distorted picture.

For purposes of this book, *terrorism* describes the use of violence by nonstate actors directed primarily against noncombatants (mostly civilians but also including government officials, policemen, and off-duty soldiers) in order to intimidate or coerce them and change their government's policies or composition. Typically the political or psychological effect desired by terrorists is out of all proportion to the actual destruction they inflict. The nineteenth-century slogan "Propaganda by the Deed" still applies today: terrorism is primarily a psychological weapon. The use of violence by the state against civilians is excluded from our definition, because the common meaning of "terrorism" has changed considerably since the French Revolution's Reign of Terror in 1793–94 unleashed what Edmund Burke dubbed "those Hell-hounds called Terrorists."[7] Our focus is on bottom-up, not top-down, terrorism, although the boundaries blur because of the prevalence of terrorist groups that receive covert state support.

Guerrilla literally means "small war"; the name derives from the struggles of Spanish irregulars against Napoleon from 1808 to 1814, but the practice is as ancient as mankind. Here it will be used to describe the use of hit-and-run tactics by an armed group directed primarily against a government and its security forces for political or religious reasons. Bandits in search of nothing more than lucre are excluded; they are usually not interested in shaking up the established order, just in profiting from it. Most guerrillas belong to nonstate groups, but some are part of formal military units (nowadays known as Special Operations Forces) that are dispatched to operate behind enemy lines. Other irregulars may cooperate closely with conventional armies even if they are not formally enrolled in their ranks. At the lowest level, guerrilla war has much in common with the small-unit tactics of conventional armies: both rely on ambush and rapid movement. The difference is that guerrilla warfare lacks front lines and large-scale, set-piece battles—the defining characteristics of conventional conflict.

It is sometimes said that terrorists are "urban guerrillas," but this is an oversimplification; urban areas have seen both guerrilla and terrorist operations, just as rural areas have. Moreover, few armed uprisings have ever confined their violence strictly to noncombatants (terrorism) or combatants (guerrilla warfare). The Vietcong, for instance, killed significant numbers of South Vietnamese civilians as well as South Vietnamese and American soldiers. Similarly, the Irish Republican Army targeted stores and pubs as well as British army patrols and barracks. Usually it's a matter of emphasis, with, for example, the Boers in the early twentieth century emphasizing guerrilla tactics and, a century later, Al Qaeda emphasizing terrorism.

A few other salient differences are worth noting: guerrillas often try to hold territory, however briefly; terrorists do not. Guerrilla armies often number in the tens of thousands; most terrorist organizations have never had more than a few hundred adherents. Guerrillas usually limit their operations to a well-recognized war zone; terrorists focus their attacks on the home front where no formal state of war exists. Guerrillas seek to physically defeat or at least wear down the enemy; terrorists hope with a few spectacular attacks to trigger a revolution. In the continuum of armed conflict, terrorists are at the bottom, next are guerrillas, then conventional forces, and finally nuclear weapons and other weapons of mass destruction.

To further muddy the issue, their enemies usually try to brand all "guerrillas" or "insurgents" (fairly laudatory titles) as "terrorists" or other terms of abuse such as "criminals," "bandits," "traitors," or "dead-enders." Those who carry out such attacks naturally prefer to label themselves as "freedom fighters," "holy warriors," "patriots," "soldiers," or some other term with positive connotations. Perhaps nothing better illustrates the elasticity of these descriptions than a directive the British government was said to have issued in 1944 after switching its support in Yugoslavia from Mihailović's Chetniks to Tito's Partisans: "In future Mihailovitch forces will be described not as patriots but as terrorist gangs: we shall also drop the phrase 'red bandits' as applied to partisans, and substitute 'freedom fighter.' "[8] The Nazis might not have agreed on much with the British, but they agreed on the inadvisability of ceding the semantic edge to their enemies. Heinrich Himmler issued a directive in 1941 that, "for psychological reasons," the term "partisan" was to be replaced by "bandit."[9]

Whatever you call them, fighters resort to terrorist or guerrilla tactics for one reason only: they are too weak to employ conventional methods. As the political scientist Samuel Huntington noted in 1962, "Guerrilla warfare is a form of warfare by which the strategically weaker side assumes the tactical offensive in selected forms, times, and places."[10] Virtually any armed group would prefer to wage conventional warfare, because it has traditionally had a higher probability of success. Conventional armies can try to carry out a strategy of annihilation, seeking to destroy the enemy's armed forces as quickly as possible. Irregular forces are compelled to undertake a strategy of attrition, trying to wear down the enemy's will to fight. This is invariably a costly, protracted, difficult affair, and one that no belligerents in their right minds would voluntarily undertake if there were any credible alternative. Guerrilla and terrorist tactics, therefore, always have been the resort of the weak against the strong. That is why insurgents wage war from the shadows; if they fought in the open, like a regular army, they would be annihilated.

The strong are not, of course, above terrible acts of violence. Far more people have been killed by just three states (Hitler's Germany, Stalin's Russia, and Mao's China) than by all terrorists and guerrillas in history put together, but their acts lie outside the scope of this study, except insofar as they were directed against guerrilla foes or utilized guerrilla tactics.

Guerrilla and terrorist tactics fall under such broad categories as low-intensity, irregular, asymmetric, complex, hybrid, or unconventional warfare—what was known in an earlier era as *la petite guerre* or "small war." All those categories are hard to define but, like pornography, most analysts know them when they see them. Their dimensions will, I hope, become more apparent as this work progresses.

✦ ✦ ✦

I WROTE *INVISIBLE ARMIES* neither to praise guerrillas and terrorists nor to bury them. Some have been commendable, others not. Which is which depends on your own worldview. Weakness does not necessarily produce virtue any more than strength does. My aim is not polemical. It is simply to tell a story that has never been well told and to tell it as engagingly and evenhandedly as possible.

The first part of this book looks at the origins of the oldest form of warfare, beginning in the mists of time with prehistoric tribal warfare, continuing to ancient Mesopotamia, Rome, and China, and concluding with the medieval skirmishes between the Scots and the English.

Then we move on to the guerrilla campaigns that resulted from the liberal revolutions that swept the world from roughly the 1770s to the 1870s. Particular emphasis is placed not only on the American War of Independence but on the Spanish struggle against Napoleon, the Haitian slave revolt, the Greek War of Independence against the Ottomans, and Garibaldi's campaigns for Italian unification. Many of these campaigns are as revealing as the U.S. Revolution, and yet in recent years they have received far less attention than they deserve—an omission that this book attempts to address.

The third part of the book examines another facet of nineteenth-century guerrilla warfare—the campaigns waged by Europeans to suppress "native" resistance to imperial rule. The focus will be on the American Indian wars, the Russian war in Chechnya and Dagestan against Muslim rebels, the First Afghan War and subsequent campaigns pitting Britons against Pashtuns on the Northwest Frontier of India, the French pacification of Morocco, and, lastly, the Boer War, which revealed the first signs of the frailty of European rule.

Next we move away from guerrilla warfare per se to look at the closely related growth of terrorism. The initial focus is on one of the first terrorist campaigns ever, waged by the Assassins in the medieval Middle East. Then, jumping ahead, we look at two terrorist campaigns in nineteenth-century America that were among the most successful ever but are often neglected in discussions of the subject—namely, John Brown's attacks on proslavery interests and the Ku Klux Klan's efforts to undermine Reconstruction. The narrative then switches to Europe, specifically the attacks by Russian Nihilists and socialists on the tsarist state and by the IRA on British rule in Ireland.

The fifth part of the book examines the guerrilla campaigns that arose out of World Wars I and II, focusing on T. E. Lawrence, Orde Wingate, and Josip Broz Tito—all extraordinary leaders of irregulars who left a large mark on the postwar world.

With a focus on the Asian and African theaters, the sixth part chronicles the Chinese revolution as well as the post-1945 decolonization struggles in Indochina, Algeria, and Malaya that were inspired by Mao Zedong's example.

Our next subject is leftist guerrilla and terrorist groups since the 1950s. The focus is first on the Huks in the Philippines and the Vietcong in Vietnam. This is followed by Fidel Castro's uprising in Cuba and Che Guevara's failed efforts to spread the Cuban revolution elsewhere. Then comes an examination of the terrorist groups of the 1970s, such as the Baader-Meinhof Gang, and, finally, the long, up-and-down career of Yasser Arafat and of the organization he led, the PLO.

The last part of the narrative deals with the rise of Islamist militancy, which circa 1979 displaced leftist ideology as the prime motivating force for the guerrillas and terrorists who inspired the most dread in the West. We look at the efforts of the mujahideen to drive the Red Army out of Afghanistan, then at the emergence of Hezbollah and Al Qaeda, and conclude with the rise and fall of Al Qaeda in Iraq.

Out of this five-thousand-year historical narrative some important and provocative themes emerge. They will be explored more fully in the Implications chapter, which looks at twelve lessons of history. The appendix provides a more statistical approach to learning from the past—it presents the findings of a database of insurgencies since 1775 compiled for this book.

As you read what follows, five major points are worth keeping in mind:

First, low-intensity conflict has been ubiquitous throughout history and of vital importance in shaping the world.

Second, political organizing and propaganda have been rising in importance as factors in low-intensity warfare over the past two centuries. Modern guerrillas tend to be intensely ideological and focused on winning the "battle of narrative," while their ancient forerunners were largely apolitical and tribal. As a result modern governments have to pay much greater attention to establishing their popular legitimacy and managing their public image than did their premodern predecessors.

Third, in a related development, guerrillas and terrorists have been growing more successful since 1945, in large part because of their ability to play on public opinion, a relatively new factor in warfare. Most insurgencies, however, still fail.

Fourth, outside assistance—whether in the form of arms supplies and safe havens or, even better, the provision of conventional forces to operate in conjunction with guerrillas—has been one of the most important factors in the success of insurgent campaigns. The absence of outside backing is not necessarily fatal, but its existence is a big plus for any guerrilla or terrorist organization.

Fifth, and finally, "population-centric" counterinsurgency, more popularly if inaccurately known as winning "hearts and minds," has been an essential part of most successful counterguerrilla campaigns. While scorched-earth tactics and "search and destroy" missions have worked on occasion, especially when the insurgents were utterly isolated from outside support, more often they have bred such resentment that they sowed the seeds of their own defeat. The population-centric approach has worked better, but it is not as "touchy-feely" as popularly supposed. While it does try to address the population's social and political needs, it is primarily focused on establishing security and involves a substantial measure of force, albeit more tightly focused and more intelligently targeted than the blunderbuss approach common to more conventional campaigns.

✦ ✦ ✦

MOST OF THIS account is based on written sources, both published and archival, in which I have immersed myself for years. But it is also informed by my own experience with guerrilla warfare and terrorism. I first became interested in the subject in the late 1990s, the period when American troops were being sent to places such as Haiti and Bosnia on "peacekeeping" missions to fight wars that dared not speak the name. The result of my initial interest was *The Savage Wars of Peace: Small Wars and the Rise of American Power* (2002).

As *The Savage Wars of Peace* was in its final stages, I happened to be going to my day job as an editor at the *Wall Street Journal* on the morning of September 11, 2001. On the Metro-North commuter train into New York City I heard ominous rumors that an airplane had struck the World Trade Center. I imagined a Cessna accidentally flying into one of the buildings. Curious to learn more, I proceeded downtown on what turned out to be the last subway train still running. By the time I stepped out of the City Hall station, it was clear that this was no minor aviation accident. Walking through white clouds of dust as sirens wailed, I caught sight of one of the Twin Towers. I could see the flames at the top and people jumping to their deaths. Then the building collapsed and a white cloud came roaring down the narrow avenue. Along with the other dazed, incredulous onlookers, I fled in horror. Thus was America launched into what became known as the war on terror.

Before long American troops would be fighting in Afghanistan and Iraq. I followed in their wake as a Council on Foreign Relations senior fellow who served as a commentator and adviser to American military commanders. I first visited Iraq in August 2003, when the post-invasion reverie was just wearing off and a long deadly insurgency was just beginning. I got a small taste of what was in the offing when a Marine Force Reconnaissance strike team with which I was riding was attacked with an IED south of Baghdad. I vividly remember the marines scrambling to identify the bomber as gunships buzzed overhead. An Iraqi man approached a marine and me while we were standing beside a Light Armored Vehicle and tried to tell us something. But he did not speak English and we did not speak Arabic, and in those days American units had few if any interpreters. It was a mutually incomprehensible conversation—a fitting symbol of how lost the American armed forces were in Mesopotamia.

Another portent of looming problems occurred when the marines finally detained a suspect, a young man in a track suit. He was placed in the armored vehicle next to me, his hands manacled behind his back with plastic handcuffs. Because there were not enough marines present—an indicator, I would come to understand, of inadequate troop numbers in the country as a whole—a corporal handed me his sidearm and asked me to "cover" the suspect before he was transferred to another vehicle. This I did, albeit a bit nervously: I am more used to think tanks than battle tanks.

I would return regularly to Iraq thereafter, meeting with senior American and Iraqi commanders and ordinary grunts while traveling around the country for a week or two at a time. As the situation deteriorated, I drove in heavily "up-armored" vehicles that resembled urban submarines through neighborhoods that had been turned into veritable ghost towns. In one such area of Mosul in 2008, I was caught in what the military calls a "complex ambush" when the Humvee in front of me hit an IED submerged in a puddle and the entire convoy came under automatic weapons fire. Luckily no one in our group was seriously hurt, although a Humvee was wrecked and a poor bystander had his arm sliced off by flying shrapnel.

Mosul was the last remaining stronghold of Al Qaeda in Iraq. By that time, thanks to the unexpected success of the "surge," this deadly insurgent group had already been driven out of its other major safe havens—cities such as Ramadi, the capital of Anbar Province, which I visited in the spring of 2007.

Ramadi summoned up images from Berlin in 1945. Rubble was everywhere. Entire buildings had collapsed. The streets were flooded because the water mains had been destroyed by so many underground bomb blasts. Yet the guns suddenly had gone quiet. A few months earlier American soldiers and marines had been fighting for their lives simply to hold on to the government center. Now I could wander around without getting shot at thanks to the recent implementation of the ancient principles of counterinsurgency. Everywhere I went I saw scruffy guards, often with bandoleers of ammunition slung across their chests like extras from a bad war movie. These were the Sons of Iraq, the Sunni militia whose defection from the insurgency had sealed Al Qaeda's doom in Iraq.

By 2008 the war in Iraq was winding down, and I began to turn my attention to Afghanistan, traveling there regularly to assess the situation under a succession of American commanders. I was, for example, part of a small "directed telescope" team of advisors that General Petraeus convened in Kabul in the summer of 2010 when he first took command. I have also traveled to see other irregular conflicts for myself. I have been to Israel (I met with Yasser Arafat in 1998 and was present for both the war against Hezbollah in 2006 and the war against Hamas in 2009, and I returned again in 2011 to spend a week interviewing Israeli officers); to Lebanon (in 2009 I visited Beirut and the Bekaa Valley, where Hezbollah was born); to the Philippines (in 2009 and 2011 I traveled with U.S. Special Operations Forces assisting the Philippine armed forces in the fight against Islamist rebels); and to Colombia (in 2008 I went to see how the fight against FARC was progressing).

I am fully cognizant of how coddled I was as a visitor, and I always left in awe of the dedication and professionalism of the soldiers I met who had to endure hardship and danger unimaginable to most civilians. Nonetheless I believe there is real value in the forays I have made "down range." By leaving my book-lined office in New York, I have been better able to understand what insurgency and counterinsurgency look like, smell like, feel like—not just in retrospect (the historian's usual vantage point) but while fighting is still going on and the outcome remains uncertain.

I have benefited immensely from these trips. Yet the more I learned, the more I realized how much I still did not know. Bumper-sticker certitudes are easy to propound from thousands of miles away. The closer I got, the more questions I had. In 2006 I began an extended search for answers by starting to research the history of guerrilla warfare and terrorism. The result is *Invisible Armies*.

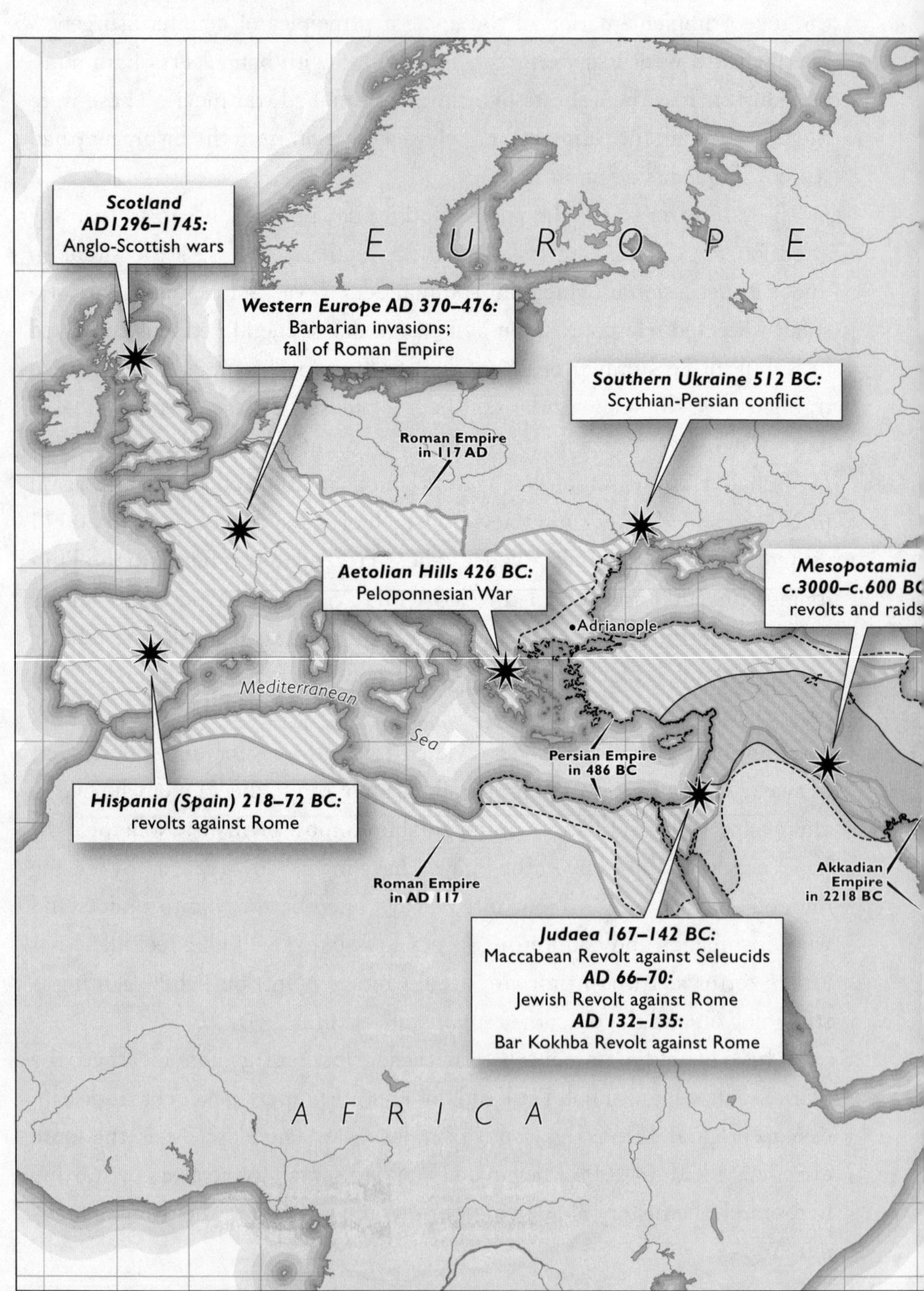

Scotland
AD1296–1745:
Anglo-Scottish wars
E U R O P E
Western Europe AD 370–476:
Barbarian invasions;
fall of Roman Empire
Southern Ukraine 512 BC:
Scythian-Persian conflict
Roman Empire
in 117 AD
Aetolian Hills 426 BC:
Peloponnesian War
Mesopotamia
c.3000–c.600 BC
revolts and raids
Adrianople
Mediterranean
Sea
Persian Empire
in 486 BC
Hispania (Spain) 218–72 BC:
revolts against Rome
Roman Empire
in AD 117
Akkadian
Empire
in 2218 BC
Judaea 167–142 BC:
Maccabean Revolt against Seleucids
AD 66–70:
Jewish Revolt against Rome
AD 132–135:
Bar Kokhba Revolt against Rome
A F R I C A

BOOK I

BARBARIANS AT THE GATE

The Origins of Guerrilla Warfare

A S I A

Afghanistan and Central Asia
329–327 BC:
campaigns of Alexander the Great

Persian Empire
in 486 BC

Han Empire
in first century BC

Northern China
200 BC–AD 51:
Xiongnu attacks

Ch'ang-an

Arabian Sea

Bay of
Bengal

South China Sea

INDIAN OCEAN

INVISIBLE ARMIES

✦ ✦ ✦

1.

AMBUSH AT BETH-HORON

Romans vs. Jews, AD 66

THE RETREAT BEGAN in November. The year was AD 66.[1] A Roman army more than thirty thousand strong had marched south from Syria into the province of Judaea to suppress an incipient uprising. The soldiers slaughtered Jews and burned towns as they advanced. Finally the legionnaires arrived at Jerusalem. From their camp on Mount Scopus, the imperial authorities sent emissaries to tell the rebels that they would be forgiven if they would throw away their arms and surrender. The Jews delivered their answer by killing one emissary and wounding the other. The legions then mounted five days of attacks on the capital. They captured the suburbs and were about to assault the inner city when, for reasons that remain mysterious, their commander, Cestius Gallus, the governor of Syria, decided to call off the offensive.

The Roman-Jewish historian Flavius Josephus, who was himself a rebel before being captured and is the primary source for these events, was convinced that had Cestius "but continued the siege a little longer [he] certainly would have taken the city." But perhaps in the heat of battle Cestius was not sure of success and was worried about being cut off from his supply lines with winter approaching. Or perhaps he thought that he had already made his point and that the Jewish rebels, having gotten a taste of Roman fury, would now come to their senses. If so, he was mistaken. Fatally mistaken.

Far from being cowed, the Jews were emboldened by "this unexpected retreat" and fell with a vengeance upon the retreating ranks.

With its superior training, discipline, and cohesion, the Roman army was the most formidable military force in the ancient world—but only if it met its enemies in open battle. Roman infantrymen advanced into battle silently and slowly in a checkerboard formation, their polished armor and helmets gleaming in the sun. When they got to within less than thirty yards of the enemy, they would toss their *pilum*, a seven-foot javelin. Then the legionnaires would let out a terrifying scream and charge the enemy lines, already thrown off balance by the heavy javelins, to punch their foes in the face with their *scutum*, a rectangular shield weighing approximately sixteen pounds, and to stab them in the belly with their *gladius*, a short double-edged sword that gave its name to gladiators. This initial wave of legionnaires would be supported in the rear by two reserve lines of infantry and on the flanks by cavalry and foreign auxiliaries armed with missile weapons such as bows and slings. Also available would be specialists in such fields as mechanical artillery, fortifications, road building, surveying, bridging, and logistics. Roman soldiers were sworn to follow their eagle standards to the gates of Hades if necessary, and if they failed they knew they could be subject to "decimation" by their own officers: every tenth man in a unit that disgraced itself could be flogged to death. There was no more formidable a military force in the ancient world.[2]

But all of this military might could be negated if the legions were caught in treacherous terrain and harassed by skillful, determined guerrillas. That is precisely what happened to Cestius Gallus's army as it marched along narrow, winding mountain paths from Jerusalem heading for the Roman-held cities of the Mediterranean coast. The legionnaires and their local allies were beset by lightly armed Jewish fighters who would fire their slingshots or javelins from above and dash down to pick off stragglers with swords and knives. With their heavy armor and equipment, weighing up to a hundred pounds per man, the legionnaires were too slow to catch these nimble harassers. Among those killed early on was the commander of the Sixth Legion, a unit roughly five thousand strong, equivalent to a modern U.S. Army brigade. Much of the baggage train had to be abandoned and the pack animals killed.

Three days after setting out, the Romans had to march through a narrow pass next to the village of Beth-horon, adjacent to the modern Israeli town of Beit Horon in the West Bank. Already Beth-horon had been the site of a notable victory by Jewish guerrillas against an occupying force—it had been where the Maccabees had defeated the Greco-Syrian Seleucid army in 166 BC, exactly two hundred years before. Now history was about to repeat itself. The Jewish rebels had gathered here, noted Josephus, "and covered the Roman army with their darts." There was no escape for the beleaguered, exhausted soldiery. Above them on the hillsides their enemies were as thick as olive groves. Below were steep precipices down which the cavalrymen on their frightened horses "frequently fell." "[T[here was neither place for their flight," Josephus wrote, "nor any contrivance . . . for their defense." All they could do was cower under their shields and pray to their deities. Josephus believed that the Jews would have "taken Cestius's entire army prisoners, had not the night come on."

Under cover of darkness, Cestius managed to escape with the remainder of his command. He left behind four hundred of his "most courageous" men with orders to fly their colors and pretend that the whole of the army was still at Beth-horon. When morning came, the Jews discovered the ruse and immediately killed the four hundred soldiers before setting off in pursuit of Cestius. Even though they did not catch up with the retreating legions, Cestius had suffered a humiliating defeat. More than 5,700 of his soldiers had perished, and he had been forced to leave behind not only his baggage and his siege engines but also—even more galling to a legionnaire—an eagle standard.[3]

2.

CLASSICAL CONFLICTS

The Peloponnesian War, Alexander the Great in Central Asia, the Maccabees, and the Bar Kokhba Revolt, 426 BC–AD 132

The Roman legions returned four years later, in AD 70, under the emperor's son and future emperor, Titus Flavius Vespasianus, to conquer Jerusalem. By the time they were done, the Jewish Temple lay in ruins and, wrote Josephus, no doubt with some poetic license, the streets were piled so high with corpses that "the ground did nowhere appear visible" and "the whole city [did] run with blood." Captured rebels were crucified or sold into slavery.[4]

Although unsuccessful, the Jewish Revolt showed the vulnerability of even ancient empires to irregular tactics. The Jews were among the most successful practitioners of guerrilla warfare in the classical world, but they were far from alone. The surviving literature of this period amply attests to the power of guerrillas, even if the word itself would not be coined for millennia to come. A few famous examples make the point, starting with the most influential account of war and politics ever written.

Most of Thucydides's *History of the Peloponnesian War* recounts a conventional conflict between Athens and Sparta, but there were also many clashes of irregulars. During a war lasting almost three decades, there were only fifty-five major battles, whereas just in the first few years the Athenians alone staged hundreds of low-level attacks on various locations. "This was raiding and killing," writes the historian Victor Davis Hanson, "not formal war as previously defined by the Greeks."[5] The less-than-heroic side of this iconic conflict was best captured in Thucydides's description of a civil war on the island of Corfu in 427 BC pitting pro-Spartan "oligarchs" against pro-Athenian "democrats": "There was death in every shape and form. And, as usually happens in such situations, people went to every extreme and beyond it. There were fathers who killed their sons; men were dragged from the temples or butchered on the very altars; some were actually walled up in the temples of Dionysus and died there."[6]

This was far from the lone instance of unconventional warfare in the Peloponnesian War. Consider, for example, Thucydides's account of how in 426 BC the "fast moving and light armed" natives of the Aetolian hills in northwestern Greece decimated a ponderous force of armored hoplites from Athens. The Athenian commander, Demosthenes, had been convinced that "the Aetolians were an easy conquest." Like other generals from city-states located on a plain, he preferred whenever possible to seek victory by sending densely packed phalanxes of infantry, as many as fifty men deep, each of them equipped with a bronze helmet and heavy armor, crashing into an enemy similarly equipped and arrayed. But the Aetolians' "asymmetric" tactics made that impossible. They would fall back "whenever the Athenian army advanced" and advance again "as soon as it retired." Only allied archers saved the Athenians from disaster initially, but as soon as their arrows ran out, the rout was on. The Athenians tried to flee, but, in a scene reminiscent of the later slaughter at Beth-horon, "a great many were overtaken" by the Aetolians "and fell beneath their javelins." Others plunged "into pathless gullies and places that they were unacquainted with" and "thus perished." The remainder fled into a forest, which the Aetolians set on fire. One can only imagine the agony of these hoplites being roasted alive in their cumbersome armor or else being asphyxiated as they tried desperately with fumbling hands to strip off their breastplates and helmets. "The Athenian army," Thucydides concluded, "fell victims to death in every form, and suffered all the vicissitudes of flight."[7]

The Athenians might have taken some comfort at their misfortune if they could have known that the greatest Greek conqueror of them all—Alexander the Great—would experience similar frustrations at the hands of supposedly inferior foes. Arrian's *The Campaigns of Alexander*, Plutarch's

The Life of Alexander the Great, and Quintus Curtius Rufus's *The History of Alexander*, among other sources, recount the difficulties that the Macedonian king experienced in Bactria, Sogdiana, and Scythia—modern-day Afghanistan and Central Asia. Alexander had already defeated the mighty Persian Empire, but it took him another two years (329–327 BC) to subdue the fierce tribes of this frontier region. Entire Macedonian detachments were lost in ambushes, and Alexander himself was wounded twice. In one battle his leg was shattered by an arrow; in another he was struck in the neck and head by a stone, causing diminished eyesight and nearly blindness. The harsh terrain, ranging from the towering peaks of the Hindu Kush to the arid deserts of Central Asia, added to the Macedonians' difficulties. Plutarch later compared fighting this decentralized uprising led by numerous petty warlords to "cutting off the heads of the Hydra, which always grow back twice as thick." To supplement his military countermeasures, which included sending his soldiers to scale snowy, rock-bound peaks where the rebels were ensconced, Alexander had to undertake diplomatic outreach, his most successful initiative being his agreement to marry Roxane, the beautiful daughter of a rebellious baron named Oxyartes. By the time Alexander finally moved on to India, he had been thoroughly drained by his exertions and did not have long to live.[8]

After Alexander's death, his empire was carved up among various successor states. The greatest was the Seleucid kingdom, which came to control much of the Middle East. One of its kings, Antiochus IV, overreached himself, however, when he erected a statue of Zeus in the Jewish Temple in Jerusalem, ordered Jews to sacrifice pigs, and generally tried to ban at spear point the practice of the Jews' own religion. Josephus's *Jewish Antiquities* and the Bible's two Books of Maccabees tell the story of the resulting revolt launched in 167 BC by the priestly Hasmonean clan to reclaim independence for Judaea. Under the leadership first of Judas Maccabeus ("Judas the Hammer") and then, after he was killed, of his brothers, the Jewish rebels used ambush and surprise to wear down and defeat the more powerful occupation army with its intimidating armored elephants. By 142 BC, after more than two decades of warfare, they had driven the Seleucids out and established their own dynasty in one of antiquity's most successful insurgencies.[9]

The Maccabees had less than a century of independence before their state fell under the sway of an empire far mightier than the Seleucids'—and one that, as we have already seen, had far greater success in crushing another Jewish revolt. Yet even the devastating Roman response to the uprising of AD 66–70 was not sufficient to extinguish the Jewish desire for independence. As recounted by Cassius Dio in his *Roman History*, the Jews rebelled twice more against Roman authority. A revolt among Diaspora Jews living in the Middle East occurred in AD 115 and a revolt among Jews in the Holy Land in AD 132. The latter uprising was led by a self-proclaimed messiah known as Simon bar Kokhba ("Son of the Star"), whose followers scurried out of caves in the Judean desert to harass the Roman garrison. Both uprisings were ultimately crushed, but their suppression required several years in each case and the dispatch of many thousands of Roman troops. After the Bar Kokhba revolt, Judaea was renamed Syria Palaestina—hence the origin of "Palestine."[10]

3.

UNCIVILIZED WARFARE

Tribal Wars of Mass Destruction

IF WE ARE to understand the type of war waged by modern guerrillas and terrorists, it is highly illuminating to immerse ourselves in the past. In particular it is essential to grasp the basics of guerrilla warfare in the ancient and medieval worlds, a time when such tactics were adopted by groups ranging from the Jews of the Holy Land to the nomads of Inner Asia and the clansmen of the Scottish Highlands. All of the great empires of antiquity, whether in the West or the East, had to devote considerable resources to combating this scourge. And many ultimately failed. Ancient guerrillas may have been primitive by modern lights—they lacked weapons such as the AK-47 capable of inflicting mass slaughter, they did not answer to a Politburo, they did not solicit funds from sympathizers abroad, and seldom did they issue bombastic communiqués to justify their existence—but nevertheless they could be exceedingly effective. As we shall see, they brought down the empires of Mesopotamia and Rome, and they overran significant parts of the Chinese Empire. No polity in the world was safe from the predations of terrifying and ruthless raiders, bound together not by political or religious ideology, like many modern-day insurgents, but simply by ties of tribe and kinship. Revolts against imperial authority were also common in conquered lands. Ancient sovereigns, even in undemocratic polities, had to learn to temper the harshness of their response by delivering benefits to those they governed to forestall future revolts. Thus was born what is today known as counterinsurgency.

Classical history was well known in the eighteenth and nineteenth centuries, yet these invaluable lessons in the power and ubiquity of low-intensity conflict had been all but forgotten—or, if remembered, discarded as relics of a primitive age with little application to the modern world. Writers as distinguished as Clausewitz and Jomini imagined that guerrilla warfare was more novel than it actually was; they were shocked and dismayed when they encountered it. Even today there is a tendency to think that there is something new about guerrilla tactics—that they are a departure from the norm, which is assumed to be state-on-state conflict.

Nothing could be further from the truth. While there are many novel aspects of low-intensity warfare as it has developed since antiquity, the essential concept itself was already well established by the time that David, one of the first guerrillas whose name we know, became king of Israel around 1000 BC. (David's credentials as a guerrilla were established not in his legendary combat with the Philistine champion Goliath but rather in subsequent years after he had been forced to flee the jealous wrath of his own king, Saul, and took to leading an outlaw band in raids on Amalekite and Philistine settlements in the Judaean wilderness.)[11]

Guerrilla warfare is as old as mankind. Conventional warfare is, by contrast, a relatively recent invention. It was made possible by the development of the first agricultural societies after untold millennia in which the hunter-gatherer reigned supreme. Farming communities for the first time produced enough surplus wealth and population to allow for the creation of specially designed fortifications and weapons as well as the hiring of specialists to operate them. That process began after 10,000 BC in the Middle East and a few thousand years later in the Americas, Europe, and East Asia. The first genuine armies—commanded by a strict hierarchy, composed of trained soldiers, disciplined with threats of punishment, divided into different specialties (spearmen, bowmen, charioteers, engineers), deployed in formations, supported by a logistics service—arose after 3100 BC in Egypt and Mesopotamia.[12] The first full-scale battle between two such armies of which we have a detailed account occurred in 1468 BC near Megiddo, a town eighteen miles southeast of the modern Israeli city of Haifa. It pitted perhaps five thousand soldiers from Egypt against two thousand soldiers from a coalition of local city-states.[13]

Considering that *Homo sapiens* has been roaming the earth for at least a hundred fifty thousand years and his hominid ancestors for millions of years before that, the era of conventional conflict is the blink of an eye in historical terms.[14] Moreover, the process of state formation and with it army formation took considerably longer in other parts of the world. "Even as late as 1492," notes the geographer and historian Jared Diamond, "all of North America, sub-Saharan Africa, Australia, New Guinea, and the Pacific islands, and most of Central and South America didn't have states."[15] In some of those places, states emerged only during the past century, and their ability to carry out such basic functions as maintaining an army is tenuous at best. Somalia today represents one of the most extreme examples of such state failure, but many other territories are not far behind.

Throughout most of our species' long and bloody slog, both before the development of urban civilization and since, warfare has been carried out primarily by bands of loosely organized, ill-disciplined, lightly armed volunteers who disdain open battle. They prefer to employ stealth, surprise, and rapid movement to harass, ambush, massacre, and terrorize their enemies while trying to minimize their own casualties through rapid retreat when confronted by equal or stronger forces. These are the primary features both of modern guerrilla warfare and of primitive, prestate warfare whose origins are lost in the mists of prehistoric time and which has only recently been extinguished in the remote jungles of Amazonia and the highlands of Papua New Guinea. Guerrillas therefore may be said to engage in the world's second-oldest profession, behind only hunting, which draws on the same skill set.

Since at least the days of the Greeks and Romans, primitive warfare and by extension guerrilla warfare has seldom been accorded much respect by Western soldiers and scholars, who have tended to view it as an "irregular," "unmanly," even "dastardly" activity and to label its practitioners barbarians, criminals, or savages.[16] To take a typical example, Massachusetts colonists in the 1600s complained that Indians fought "in a secret, skulking manner, lying in abushment, thickets, and swamps by the way side, and so killing people in a base and ignoble manner."[17]

It is not hard to see why prejudice against guerrillas has been so pervasive. Prestate warriors are, in the words of John Keegan, "cruel to the weak and cowardly in the face of the brave"[18]—precisely the opposite of what professional soldiers have always been taught to revere. They refuse to grapple face-to-face with a strong foe until one side or the other is annihilated in the kind of warfare immortalized, if not invented, by the Greeks.

Battles among nonstate peoples have often consisted of nothing more than two lines of warriors decked out in elaborate paint shouting insults at one another, making rude gestures, and then discharging spears, darts, or arrows from such long range that they inflict few casualties. Primitive societies lack an organizational structure that can force men on pain of punishment to engage in costly close-quarters combat in defiance of a basic instinct for self-preservation. This has led some observers to suggest that nonstate peoples do not engage in warfare at all but rather in "feuds" or "vendettas" that are for the most part ceremonial and have little in common with "true" war as practiced at Cannae, Agincourt, or Gettysburg. After moving to Massachusetts in the seventeenth century, for example, a professional English soldier wrote with scorn that Indians "might fight seven years and not kill seven men" because "this fight is more for pastime, than to conquer and subdue enemies."[19]

What such critics overlook is that battles constitute only a small part of primitive warfare. Most casualties are inflicted not in these carefully choreographed encounters but in what comes before and after—in the stealthy forays of warriors into the territory of their neighbors. The anthropologist Lawrence Keeley writes, "One common raiding technique (favored by groups as diverse as the Bering Straits Eskimo and the Mae Enga of New Guinea) consisted of quietly surrounding enemy houses just before dawn and killing the occupants by thrusting spears through the flimsy walls, shooting arrows through doorways and smoke holes, or firing as the victims emerged after the structure had been set afire."[20]

Following such an attack, the raiders might disperse before large numbers of enemy warriors could arrive, only to return a few days later, hoping to catch another enemy village unawares. All adult men participate in this type of warfare, and quarter is seldom asked or given. Surrender for warriors is not an option; if they suffer the dishonor of defeat, they are either killed on the spot or, as was common among the Iroquois Indians of northeastern North America, they might be tortured to death and then partially eaten. At the end of such an encounter, the victor rapes the loser's women, enslaves them and their children, burns crops, steals livestock, destroys the village.

Primitive warfare has been consistently deadlier than civilized warfare—not in total numbers killed (tribal societies are tiny compared with urban civilizations) but in the *percentage* killed. The Dani tribesmen of New Guinea, the Dinka of northeast Africa, the Modoc Indians of California, the Kalinga headhunters of the Philippines, and other nonstate peoples studied by ethnographers over the past two centuries suffered considerably higher death rates from warfare annually (sometimes five hundred times higher) than did the most war-ravaged European countries, such as twentieth-century Germany and Russia. The average tribal society loses 0.5 percent of its population in combat every year.[21] If the United States suffered commensurately today, that would translate into 1.5 million deaths, or five hundred 9/11's a year. Archaeological evidence confirms that such losses are no modern anomaly: at one early burial site in the Sudan, Djebel Sahaba, which was used sometime between 12,000 and 10,000 BC, 40 percent of the skeletons showed evidence of stone arrowheads; many had multiple wounds.[22] That shows the ubiquity and deadliness of warfare at a time when, to the modern eye, guerrillas would have been barely distinguishable in intellectual sophistication from gorillas.

There was little ideology or strategy behind the kind of war waged among tribal warriors in prerecorded times or even more recently. They did not employ "lightning raids by ad hoc companies,"[23] in the words of one modern scholar, because they concluded, after careful consideration of all the alternatives, that this was the surest way to hurt their foes. They fought as they did simply because it was the way their fathers had always fought, and their grandfathers before them. It was all they knew. That sort of instinctual guerrilla warfare remained the commonest kind until recent centuries.

What changed with the coming of the first civilizations is the kind of foes that tribal warriors confronted. Before circa 3000 BC, tribal guerrillas fought exclusively against other tribal guerrillas. While that type of tribe-on-tribe warfare continued long after 3000 BC, it was supplemented and sometimes supplanted by warfare pitting tribes and rebels against newly formed states. The history of ancient Mesopotamia—a time long before the events described in the Bible or the *Iliad*—is replete with struggles between guerrilla-style raiders and the world's first states. It is not much of a stretch to describe these conflicts as the world's first insurgencies and counterinsurgencies.

4.

AKKAD AND THE ORIGINS OF INSURGENCY

Mesopotamia, 2334–2005 BC

THE VERY FIRST empire on record and, not coincidentally, the first standing army were built by Sargon, an early-day Saddam Hussein whose capital was Akkad, a city believed to have been located near modern-day Baghdad. According to legend, his was an early rags-to-riches tale. He was said to have begun life like Moses, an orphan who was sent floating in a wicker basket on the river and was found by a farmer. He rose from being cupbearer to the king of the city-state of Kish to being king of all he surveyed. Between 2334 and 2279 BC, he subdued what is now southern Iraq along with western Iran, northern Syria, and southern Turkey. Victorious in thirty-four battles, he called himself "king of the world."

The secret of Akkad's military success is unclear, but it may have been its possession of a powerful composite bow tipped with bronze arrowheads, whose impact has been called "as revolutionary, in its day . . . as the discovery of gunpowder thousands of years later." Other weapons included the lance, spear, javelin, mace, and battle-ax. Just as important was the maintenance of an extensive bureaucracy to fund and sustain Akkad's army, providing soldiers with such essentials as "bread and beer."

This military machine was kept fully employed not only in seizing new domains but also in holding on to those already conquered. Defeated cities constantly rose up to resist imperial control. The Akkadians responded with what a modern scholar describes as "mass slaughter, enslavement, and deportation of defeated enemies, and the total annihilation of their cities." Calling himself a "raging lion," Sargon was faithful to the injunction of one of his gods, Enlil, who instructed him to show "mercy to no one." One city after another was left, in the words of the ancient tablets, a "ruin heap."

Sargon did not entirely neglect the need to win over his subjects, especially the Sumerians, who lived in Mesopotamia. He spread the Akkadian language and offered patronage to the arts. His daughter, Enheduanna, a princess, poet, and priestess who is often considered the world's first author, wrote cuneiform verse celebrating the unity of Sumerian and Akkadian gods. This was intended to buttress Sargon's legitimacy as a Semite to rule over Sumerians.

But after Sargon's death, revolts rippled across the empire, and they were only temporarily suppressed by Sargon's son Rimush, who "annihilated" rebellious cities. Rimush's older brother, Manishtushu, who may have usurped his throne and murdered him, found that "all the lands . . . which my father Sargon left had in enmity revolted against me."

Weakened by incessant uprisings, Akkad was finally brought down around 2190 BC by neighboring mountain peoples, including the Hurrians, Lullubi, Elamites, and Amorites. The most devastating were the Gutians from the Zagros Mountains of southwestern Iran, who have been described as "fierce and lawless barbarians." Mesopotamian inscriptions described the highlanders, who may be said to have been the first successful guerrillas on record, in terms that would be instantly familiar to Europeans or Chinese of a later age as "the fanged serpent of the mountain, who acted with violence against the gods . . . who took away the wife from the one who had a wife, who took away the child from the one who had a child, who put wickedness and evil in the land of Sumer." Such has ever been the reaction of settled farmers ravaged by rootless "barbarians."[24]

After the fall of Akkad, nomads who moved on foot, not on horseback (domestication of horses and camels was just beginning), swarmed all over Mesopotamia, Syria, and Palestine for two hundred years. Brigands and pirates came in their wake, there being no imperial authority to keep the peace. The city dwellers of Sumeria looked with fear and loathing upon these outsiders—so capable militarily, so uncouth culturally. They were described as a "ravaging people, with the instincts of a beast, like wolves," and they were denigrated as "men who ate not fish, men who ate not onions," men who "stunk of camelthorn and urine." (Camelthorn is a noxious weed native to Asia.)

In 2059 BC, the empire of Ur in southern Iraq erected a "Wall Facing the Highland" to keep nomads out of central Mesopotamia. This construction project wound up running over time and over budget because its builders were constantly harassed by Amorite nomads ("tent dwellers . . . [who] from ancient times have known no cities"), and in the end it could not provide lasting security any more than could the Great Wall of China or the Morice Line erected by the French in Algeria in the 1950s. In 2005 BC the Elamites, "the enemy from the highlands," sacked Ur, turning the great city into a "ruined mound." They left "corpses floating in the Euphrates" and reduced the survivors to refugees who, according to Mesopotamian tablets, were "like stampeding goats, chased by dogs."[25]

5.
CATCH ME IF YOU CAN

Persians vs. Scythians, 512 BC

THE ANCIENT CITY-STATES of Mesopotamia were the first polities to be ravaged by nomadic guerrillas. They were far from the last. Nomads would become history's most pervasive and successful guerrillas.

The essential problem that confronted their enemies is simple to state but hard to resolve: How do you catch raiders? Unencumbered by elaborate equipment or lengthy supply trains, they have almost always been able to move faster than conventional military units. Their motto might as well be a modern phrase as simple as "Catch me if you can." Most pursuers have failed. Notable early failures may be found in ancient Persia under the Achaemenid dynasty.

This was one of the greatest empires of the ancient world, with its capital first in Pasargadae and then in Persepolis. From colossal stone buildings ringed by imposing columns, bureaucrats presided over a vast realm broken down into provinces governed by satraps (governors), ruled according to a complex body of law, funded with an efficient system of tax collection and some of the world's first banks, linked together by all-weather highways and a horse-borne postal system, and defended by a crack army whose elite were known as the "Immortals."

The architect of Persia's rise was King Cyrus II ("the Great"), of whom the Greek soldier-scholar Xenophon wrote in glowing terms that he "struck all men with terror and no one tried to withstand him; and he was able to awaken in all so lively a desire to please him that they always wished to be guided by his will."[26] Sadly, Cyrus's magic did not work with the nomads of the steppe. He met his end in 529 BC, apparently while campaigning against Massagetae tribesmen in Central Asia.[27]

He was succeeded by a young lance bearer, Darius, who seized the throne from one of Cyrus's sons. Darius, also styled "the Great," was more fortunate than his predecessor, but not much more successful in his clashes with the Scythians, another race of steppe nomads who were closely related to the Massagetae. The Scythians and Massagetae were cut from essentially the same cloth as all of the horse-riding nomads or seminomads—Huns, Xiongnu, Avars, Bulgars, Magyars, Seljuks, Mongols, Tatars, Manchus—who would terrorize the Eurasian plain until the eighteenth century AD. They also had more than a bit in common with the Sioux, Cheyenne, Apache, and other tribes that would attack American settlements in the trans-Mississippi West in the nineteenth century. All of the Eurasian tribes migrated with their herds of sheep, goats, horses, cattle, camels, and sometimes yaks across the grasslands of Asia in search of suitable pasture. They survived on whatever their livestock could provide—from meat and milk for their diet to leather and hides for their clothing and dung for their fires—and they lived in tents known as yurts. Their hard way of life made them expert horsemen and archers far more adept at warfare than most of the sedentary peoples they encountered. Every man was a warrior, and the average warrior's ferocity was legendary. The world's first historian, Herodotus, wrote in the fifth century BC that the "Scythian soldier drinks the blood of the first man he overthrows in battle" and makes a drinking cup out of the skull. Some Scythians, Herodotus claimed, even flayed "the right arms of their dead enemies" and made capes or quiver covers out of their skin.[28]

Darius decided to punish these ferocious raiders for their raids into his territory. Around 512 BC, he crossed the Bosporus over a pontoon bridge—an impressive feat of military engineering—and advanced with hundreds of thousands of soldiers through the Balkans into what is today southern Ukraine. Much to Darius's frustration, the Scythians refused to stand and fight. Knowing they were too weak to counter the Persians in open battle, the Scythians chose to retreat, Herodotus wrote in his *Histories*, "driving off their herds, choking up all the wells and springs as they retreated, and leaving the whole country bare of forage."[29] Darius became so frustrated that he sent a plaintive message to Idanthyrsus, the king of the Scythians, demanding, "Thou strange man, why dost thou keep on flying before me. . . . [C]ome, let us engage in battle."

Idanthyrsus sent back a disdainful reply: "That is my way, Persian. . . . We Scythians have neither towns nor cultivated lands, which might induce us, through fear of their being taken or ravaged, to be in any hurry to fight with you. . . . [W]e shall not join battle, unless it pleases us."[30]

This illuminating exchange neatly summarizes the gulf of incomprehension that separates "regular" armies from their "irregular" foes. It could have taken place between virtually any civilized king and nomad chieftain in the ancient or medieval world or between many a president or prime minister and guerrilla or terrorist leader today. At least Darius was smarter than many commanders who have been in his sandals. He knew when he was beaten. He trudged back to Persia with his army still intact.

6.

"CREATE A DESERT"

The Origins of Counterinsurgency in Assyria and Rome, 1100 BC–AD 212

Most ancient empires responded to the threat of guerrilla warfare, whether waged by nomads from the outside or rebels from the inside, with the same strategy. It can be boiled down to one simple word: *terror.* Ancient monarchs sought to inflict as much suffering as possible to put down and deter armed challenges. Since, with a few exceptions such as Athens and the Roman Republic, ancient polities were monarchies or warrior states, rather than constitutional republics, they seldom felt bound by any moral scruples or by any need to appease public opinion—neither "public opinion" nor "human rights" being concepts that they would have understood. (The former phrase was not coined until the eighteenth century, the latter not until the twentieth, although the ideas they describe have been traced back to ancient Greece.)

The Assyrians, who starting in 1100 BC conquered a domain stretching a thousand miles from Persia to Egypt, were particularly grisly in their infliction of terror. King Ashurnasirpal II (r. 883–859 BC) had inscribed on his royal residence an account of what he did after recapturing the rebellious city of Suru:

> I built a pillar over against [the] city gate, and I flayed all the chief men who had revolted, and I covered the pillar with their skins; some I walled

> up within the pillar, some I impaled upon the pillar on stakes, and others I bound to stakes round about the pillar; many within the border of my own land I flayed, and I spread their skins upon the walls; and I cut off the limbs of the officers, of the royal officers, who had rebelled.[31]

The Mongols would later become famous for equally grotesque displays designed to frighten adversaries into acquiescence. But even at a time when there were no human-rights lobbies and no free press, this strategy was far from invariably successful. Often it backfired by simply creating more enemies. Wracked by civil war, Assyria was helpless in the end to suppress a revolt by the Babylonians, inhabitants of a city previously sacked by the Assyrians, and the Medes, a tribe dwelling in modern-day Iran. They pooled their resources to fight their mutual oppressors. In 612 BC they managed to conquer the imperial capital and, as Herodotus put it, "to shake off the yoke of servitude, and to become a free people."[32]

✦ ✦ ✦

THE ROMAN EMPIRE, which faced and suppressed more rebellions than most of its predecessors or successors, developed a more sophisticated approach to counterinsurgency. But then it had to, because it faced more sophisticated insurgents—not just the type of primitive nomads that Akkad confronted but also rebellions led by men such as Quintus Sertorius, Arminius, Jugurtha, Tacfarinas, Spartacus, and Julius Civilis who had previously fought with the Romans or lived among them and knew how to exploit their weaknesses. Quintus Sertorius was sui generis, having once been a Roman general and governor of Spain. He became the leader of Lusitanian rebels fighting Roman rule in Spain after having been on the losing side of Rome's first civil war, in 87–86 BC. The others were originally "barbarians" who were Romanized to some degree, typically through military service. Yet, being foreign born, they were usually not able to share in the full fruits of Roman citizenship. This privation was especially severe in the case of Spartacus, a slave from the Balkans who escaped from a gladiator training school in Capua and eventually led an army of ninety thousand freed slaves who briefly overran much of southern Italy.[33] Not only Spartacus but many other semi-Romanized barbarians built up a lifetime's worth of perceived slights and grudges. They also sympathized with the plight of their native countrymen, who were often exploited by Roman overlords. As is the case with many modern terrorists such as Khalid Sheikh Mohammed, their familiarity with the West bred a volatile mixture of admiration, jealousy, and resentment.

The resulting tensions exploded in some of the worst revolts that Rome faced. Entire legions could be lost in the resulting wars. This happened most famously in AD 9, when three legions comprising fifteen thousand soldiers and auxiliaries were wiped out in the Teutoburg Forest by Germanic tribesmen, the Cherusci, led by their chief, Arminius, who had previously attained Roman citizenship and equestrian (or aristocratic) rank. The remains of this annihilating ambush were not found by another Roman army until six years later. When they finally arrived at the site of the battle, the historian Tacitus recounted, the legionnaires found a plain full of "bleaching bones, scattered or in little heaps, as the men had fallen, fleeing or standing fast." Nearby were "splintered spears and limbs of horses, while human skulls were nailed prominently on the tree-trunks." Florus, another Roman historian, reported on the mistreatment of Roman captives: "They put out the eyes of some of them and cut off the hands of others; they sewed up the mouth of one of them after first cutting out his tongue, exclaiming, 'At last, you viper, you have ceased to hiss.' " The Romans came back to conquer after many other defeats, but this one was decisive. Never again would Rome try to permanently extend its rule east of the Rhine River.[34]

In response to such insurrections, the Romans could be just as savage and bloodthirsty as the Akkadians or Assyrians. Witness the destruction of Carthage in 146 BC or of Jerusalem in AD 70 and again in 135. The Greek historian Polybius noted that in towns taken by the legions "one may often see not only the corpses of human beings, but dogs cut in half, and the dismembered limbs of other animals. . . . They do this, I think, to inspire terror."[35] To deter would-be rebels, the Romans spread news of their merciless conquests far and wide. After the fall of Jerusalem in AD 70, for example, new coins were minted all over the empire with the legend "Judaea Conquered," showing "a Roman soldier with a spear standing over a mourning Jew."[36] As a result, Roman counterinsurgency warfare has understandably, if unfairly, come to be associated with the famous words attributed to a British tribal chief by Tacitus: "They create a desert, and call it peace."[37]

In reality, the Romans often relied on subtler tactics—for example, the type of targeted assassinations employed in recent years by the Israelis against Hamas and by the Americans against Al Qaeda. In 139 BC the Romans arranged for the murder of one of the most troublesome rebel leaders in Hispania (Spain), which they valued for its silver and gold mines. Viriathus, a shepherd who became the leader of a guerrilla army, had inflicted one setback after another on the legions during the preceding eight years. Operating from mountain strongholds, he perfected a tactic beloved of primitive warriors everywhere: he would pretend to flee before Roman forces in order to draw them into an ambush. This stratagem paid off in 146 BC when his Lusitanian tribesmen, armed with spears and curved swords, managed to kill four thousand Romans out of an army of ten thousand. The dead included the portly Roman praetor (governor) Gaius Vetilius. Vetilius's successor, Gaius Plautius, proved just as foolhardy, losing another four thousand soldiers in futile pursuit of Viriathus. Catching the rebel leader proved impossible. He and his men traveled light on "very agile horses," the Greek historian Appian wrote, "while the Romans were unable to pursue him in the same way because of the weight of their armor, their ignorance of the routes and the inferiority of their horses."

Perhaps growing weary of never-ending conflict, Viriathus sent three of his friends in 139 BC to negotiate with the praetor Servilius Caepio. But instead of settling on terms for Viriathus's surrender, Caepio corrupted the envoys and persuaded them to kill their chief in return for a handsome reward. The rebel leader was so vigilant that he slept in full armor, so his assassins stabbed him in the only unprotected part of his body—the throat. The turncoats then escaped back to the Roman camp, where they were disappointed to find their blood money not forthcoming.[38]

Decapitation strategies often fail. Al Qaeda in Iraq, for instance, was not significantly hindered by the killing of its leader, Abu Musab al-Zarqawi, in 2006. But in ancient Spain the Roman strategy paid off, at least temporarily. Viriathus's followers lost heart after their leader's death and soon surrendered. Unfortunately for the Romans, however, there would soon be fresh rebellions in Hispania.

Besides targeted assassinations, the Romans also employed psychological warfare. During the siege of Jerusalem, for instance, the Roman commander, Titus, interrupted his attacks on at least two occasions. After he had demolished the first city wall, he tried to awe the defenders into surrender by parading his army in front of them. The legionnaires, Josephus wrote, "opened the cases wherein their arms before lay covered, and marched with their breastplates on, as did the horsemen lead the horses in their fine trappings." The whole north side of the city wall was crowded with spectators who felt "very great dismay" upon beholding the size of the army as well as "the fineness of their arms, and the good order of their men." On another occasion, Titus sent Josephus to tell his compatriots to follow his example by defecting to the Roman camp. Josephus walked around the walls of Jerusalem, he later wrote, "to find a place that was out of the reach of their darts, and yet within their hearing and begged them, in many words, to spare themselves, to spare their country and their temple."[39] The gambit failed. Josephus was greeted with catcalls and missiles rather than cries of surrender. But that it was tried at all showed the importance the Romans attached to undermining the will of the enemy.

Those who praise the Romans for their ferocity in putting down revolts should realize that this was only part of the story. Rome's enemies were not always slain. Often they were accommodated. A succession of emperors maintained stability on the frontiers by reaching understandings with "barbarian" tribes, often greased by trade and what would now be called "foreign aid." Neighboring kings became Roman clients, and many of their followers were paid to defend the empire or at least not to attack it. The Romans, like most successful imperialists, were skilled at exploiting political divisions among their enemies and using gold as a weapon.

Rome's ruling elites also spun a complex web of social and financial connections that bound them closely with local elites both inside and outside the empire. Typical was Herod the Great's situation. The king of Judaea (r. 37–4 BC) was a Hellenized Jew who was supported by such influential friends in Rome as Mark Antony and Augustus, and he in turn offered them support in their own power struggles, deftly transferring his allegiance from one to the other as events dictated. Herod's help made it unnecessary for the Romans to deploy scarce legions to Judaea.[40] These sorts of relationships allowed the ramshackle Roman state, with an army of less than half a million men and revenues amounting to less than 10 percent of gross domestic product (compared with over 40 percent for most modern states), to control an empire of sixty million to seventy million inhabitants.[41]

If the Roman Empire had offered nothing but death and desolation to those it ruled, it could never have survived as long as it did: Rome ruled most of western Europe, the Balkans, Anatolia, and northern Africa for 450 years. The secret to the empire's longevity was that while the Romans punished revolts harshly, they generally ruled with a light touch. Even Judaea before the Jewish Revolt was "emphatically not a police state," writes a modern authority.[42] The Romans may have offended Jewish sensitivities in various ways (during one Passover, a legionnaire mooned the assembled worshippers and let out a sound not unlike flatulence),[43] but the Jews were largely allowed to run their own affairs and to freely practice their religion, no matter how bizarre the Romans found monotheism to be. Only three thousand Roman troops were normally stationed in Judaea. (Titus later charged, in a plaint echoed by countless other imperial rulers over the centuries, that the Jews had mistaken Roman "kindness" and "humanity" for "weakness.")[44]

Indeed, one recent book argues that Rome was, like modern America, an "empire of trust" that was built and maintained with the implicit consent of its subjects.[45] Another scholar suggests that Roman imperialism was primarily a "diplomatic and even social" phenomenon, not "only or mainly" a military undertaking, and that it was the result of "complex negotiation . . . in which the subjects' agenda was as important as that of the conqueror."[46] The Roman Senate even occasionally punished its own soldiers and envoys for dealing too treacherously or cruelly with subject peoples.[47] As well it should have: the Roman legions could barely have functioned without the manpower and supplies provided by vanquished foes converted into allies.

As assimilation accelerated, internal revolts began to fall off, although they never ceased entirely. Roman citizenship was granted to all Italians in 90 BC to end an uprising among Rome's allies known as the Social War. In AD 212, citizenship was extended to all free inhabitants of the empire, making them, in theory at least, equals before the law. This was one of the most effective counterinsurgency initiatives the Romans ever took, because it gave their subjects a stake in the empire's survival. For most of its subjects, the benefits of the Pax Romana dulled the urge for independence. The greatest benefit of all was deliverance from the fear of tribal guerrillas and bandits, invasion and civil war—from the conditions that were endemic throughout Europe and North Africa before the rise of the Roman Empire and after its collapse. Security made prosperity possible.

The Jews, with their strong sense of identity, which long predated the rise of Greco-Roman civilization, were an obvious exception, but many other conquered peoples were successfully absorbed into the empire. Their elites learned Greek and Latin, employed Roman coins, built Roman-style towns, traveled on Roman-built roads, enjoyed baths and circuses, wore togas, drank wine, cooked with olive oil, and joined in the practice of Roman religious cults (and later Rome's new religion, Christianity). In the countryside, most people continued to cling to their old customs. Still, the eighteenth-century historian Edward Gibbon was right to note, "The gentle but powerful influence of laws and manners had gradually cemented the union of the provinces."[48]

A more recent historian, Adrian Goldsworthy, observes the lack of independence movements in the provinces: "Quite simply there were no equivalents in the Roman period of Gandhi and Nehru, Washington or Bolivar, Kenyatta or Mugabe."[49] When Roman rule did end, it was due to external invasion, not internal revolt.

Thus Rome exemplified the yin and yang of successful counterinsurgency warfare—chastisement *and* attraction. It was no proto-Stalinist state.

7.

ROME'S DOWNFALL

The Barbarian Invasions, AD 370–476

THERE IS STILL considerable debate over the extent to which Rome's collapse was brought about by growing corruption, dissension, tax avoidance, currency depreciation, and other types of internal decay. Traditional accounts such as Gibbon's *The Decline and Fall of the Roman Empire* have emphasized the shortcomings, moral and otherwise, of the later Roman Empire. Writing of the excesses of one Syrian-born emperor in the third century AD ("He was drawn in his sacerdotal robes of silk and gold, after the loose flowing fashion of the Medes and Phoenicians; his head was covered with a lofty tiara, his numerous collars and bracelets were adorned with gems of inestimable value. His eyebrows were tinged with black, and his cheeks painted with an artificial red and white"), Gibbon acerbically concluded that "Rome was at length humbled beneath the effeminate luxury of Oriental despotism."[50]

More recent scholarship, however, suggests that the empire was vibrant enough to survive absent a string of military defeats.[51] Those defeats were delivered by a variety of "barbarians." Some, notably the Germanic tribes, fought on foot and farmed; others, notably the Huns, fought on horseback and disdained agriculture. On occasion they could mobilize large armies and engage in major battles; Rome suffered a major disaster at Adrianople in AD 378 near the present-day Turkish city of Edirne. Here the Goths wiped out a Roman army and killed the emperor Valens in a battle in which both sides had roughly fifteen thousand soldiers engaged.[52] But this clash in the open was the exception, not the rule. More often the barbarians campaigned as small groups of raiders—essentially guerrillas. At least at first, writes the historian John Ellis, "their tactics were very much of the guerrilla mode."[53]

Thus Rome, as much as ancient Mesopotamia, was a victim of the type of hit-and-run warfare practiced by nomadic guerrillas. One of the precipitating events in its cataclysmic collapse was the appearance of the Huns, a nomadic horse people migrating from Central Asia. They showed up in Europe around AD 370—just before the battle at Adrianople that did so much to weaken Roman power in the West. Not only did the Huns do great damage themselves with their subsequent invasion of western Europe, but the knock-on effects of their savagery also pushed other, more sedentary tribes into Roman territory in an attempt to escape from them.

Little is known about the Huns. Since they were illiterate, they left no records. We are not even sure what language they spoke or where they came from, although one popular theory holds that they migrated from China's northern border. What we do know is that, like other steppe nomads, they were ferocious and fearless, supremely skilled in the use of composite bows on horseback (notwithstanding their apparent lack of stirrups), capable of moving great distances at high speed, and able to endure immense hardships.

The fourth-century Roman historian Ammianus Marcellinus summed up many of these qualities in a description of these "brute beasts," at turns admiring and horrified, that echoed the Mesopotamian tablets' descriptions of the Gutians, Elamites, and other "tent dwellers" who had terrorized Sumeria. "The people called Huns . . . are a savage race beyond all parallel. . . ." Ammianus wrote.

> They are certainly in the shape of men, however uncouth, but are so hardy that they neither require fire nor well-flavoured food, but live on the roots of such herbs as they get in the fields, or on the half-raw flesh of any animal, which they merely warm rapidly by placing it between their own thighs and the backs of their horses. . . .
>
> They never shelter themselves under roofed houses. . . . [B]ut

> they wander about, roaming over the mountains and the woods, and accustom themselves to bear frost and hunger and thirst from their very cradles.

As for their methods of warfare, Ammianus reported that they employed guerrilla-like tactics:

> They are very quick in their operations, of exceeding speed, and fond of surprising their enemies. With a view to this, they suddenly disperse, then reunite, and again, after having inflicted vast loss upon the enemy, scatter themselves over the whole plain in irregular formations: always avoiding a fort or an entrenchment.

Perhaps for this reason, the sixth-century Gothic historian Jordanes wrote, "The Huns do not overthrow nations by means of war, where there is an equal chance, but assail them by treachery, which is a greater cause for anxiety." That is a curious comment to make about such a notoriously warlike people who were hardly noted for their subtlety. It makes sense only if one assumes that "treachery" is simply a pejorative way of referring to "guerrilla warfare"—a term that did not then exist.

It was not easy to wield such an "active and indomitable race" into a coherent military force. That required the rare talents of Attila the Hun. The legendary leader of the Huns initially ruled for a decade in conjunction with his brother, Bleda, but in 444 or 445 he murdered his sibling and assumed sole control. "The Scourge of God" was described by a Roman envoy who met him as short and squat, with a broad chest, small eyes, a thin, gray-flecked beard, flat nose, and "swarthy complexion." He spoke "a confused jumble of Latin, Hunnic, and Gothic." He dressed simply and disdained the finery, decorative gems, and golden goblets that his chief lieutenants came to favor. A clean garment, an unadorned sword, and a wooden cup were always good enough for Attila. Yet for all his lack of pretense, which anticipated Genghis Khan's manner, the great Hun's aura of power was unmistakable: "He was haughty in his walk, rolling his eyes hither and thither, so that the power of his proud spirit appeared in the movement of his body."

During the 440s Attila cut a swath of destruction through eastern

Europe before moving west. Impalement, the act of driving a wooden stake through the victim's anus, was a favorite method of execution as well as a source of merriment. The Christian scholar Saint Jerome wrote of how "terror-struck" the Roman world was by the advance of these "wild beasts": "Everywhere their approach was unexpected, they outstripped rumor in speed, and, when they came, they spared neither religion nor rank nor age, even for wailing infants they felt no pity. Children were made to die before it can be said that they had begun to live. . . . How many of God's matrons and virgins, virtuous and noble ladies, have been made the sport of these brutes!"

In the past disciplined Roman armies would have made short work of the rapacious but disorganized Huns. But by the fifth century Rome had been weakened by centuries of incessant infighting, with multiple imperial usurpers competing for power and Roman military units regularly fighting one another, often with the help of tribal allies. As one recent history notes, "After 217 there were only a handful of decades without a violent struggle for power within the Roman Empire." The once mighty legions were so weak that the Huns were not stopped until 451, when a mixed force of Romans, Franks, Saxons, and Visigoths barely managed to repulse them near the French town of Troyes. Two years after this defeat, Attila died, an apparent victim of excessive drinking on his wedding night, hardly his first, to a German maiden. With its polygamous conqueror gone, the Hunnic empire collapsed within a few years.[54]

By then, however, it was too late to save Rome. By 452 much of Britain, Spain, North Africa, and parts of Gaul had been overrun by assorted barbarians. The lost tax revenues from those rich provinces made it impossible to keep the central machinery of the empire going, setting off a death spiral.[55] Rome was sacked by the Visigoths in 410 and by the Vandals in 455. The last Western emperor was deposed in 476.

A recent historical study estimates that the mightiest of empires was ultimately brought down by no more than 110,000 to 120,000 invaders. That might seem like a paltry figure given that as late as AD 375 the Roman army was estimated to total at least 300,000 men and possibly many more. But most of those troops were tied down either confronting the Persian Empire, engaging in Roman civil wars, or guarding thousands of miles of frontier against raiders or guerrillas. That left only 90,000 men in the field armies deployed in the west to confront the barbarian onslaught.[56] Not nearly enough. Guerrilla-style raiders thus became a crucial contributing factor in Rome's downfall, although we should not neglect the important role played by domestic disunity and disorganization—a major factor in the success of more recent insurgents, too, from Chiang Kai-shek's China to Batista's Cuba. As Adrian Goldsworthy notes, Rome "may well have been 'murdered' by barbarian invaders, but these struck at a body made vulnerable by prolonged decay."[57]

With Roman control gone, European unity and security would also disappear. For centuries to come the continent would be at the mercy of sanguinary raiders who fought for the most part in guerrilla-like fashion. From the north came Vikings; from the south, Arabs; from the east, Avars, Bulgars, Magyars, Mongols, and Turks. Tales of their predations would echo those of the Huns'. It would take a millennium for a polyglot array of weak polities to cohere into states strong enough to safeguard their own frontiers. The Eastern empire was longer lived: it would continue to rule at Constantinople (modern Istanbul) for another thousand years, but over the centuries its culture would become less and less Roman.

8.

AN EASTERN WAY OF WAR?

Ancient Chinese Warfare beyond Sun Tzu

ROMAN LEGIONS OFTEN fought guerrillas but did not practice guerrilla tactics themselves. What about their counterparts in Asia? There is a widespread belief that a distinctly "Oriental" or "Eastern Way of War" placed particular emphasis, in John Keegan's words, on "evasion, delay and indirectness"[58]—the skills of the guerrilla. This is usually contrasted with the kind of toe-to-toe fight to the death that has supposedly characterized the "Western Way of War" since the days of classical Greece.[59] This interpretation became especially popular after the success of Chinese and Vietnamese communists in guerrilla struggles in the twentieth century. Many concluded that Mao Zedong and Ho Chi Minh were the direct heirs of Sun Tzu and other ancient Confucian strategists who had supposedly placed a greater emphasis than their Western counterparts on strategies designed to circumvent the main forces of the enemy. Thus Keegan writes that " 'the Chinese Way of Warfare' would, in the twentieth century, inflict on Western armies and their commanders, schooled in [Clausewitz's] teachings, a painful and long-drawn-out humiliation."[60]

This interpretation is given superficial support by the fact that China's foremost military philosopher, Sun Tzu, famously counseled that "attaining one hundred victories in one hundred battles is not the pinnacle of excellence. Subjugating the enemy's army without fighting is the true pinnacle of excellence." Another widely cited passage of his masterpiece, *The Art of War*, holds, "Warfare is the Way (Tao) of deception. Thus although [you are] capable display incapability to them. When committed to employing your forces, feign inactivity. When [your objective] is nearby, make it appear as if distant; when far away, create the illusion of being nearby."[61] Mao would later echo this advice almost verbatim.

But *The Art of War* was only one of the "Seven Military Classics" of ancient China. Other tomes, which are less quoted today, suggested a more direct approach. For instance, there was the *Wei Liao-tzu*, written by an official named Wei Liao during the same Warring States period (403–221 BC) that produced *The Art of War*. Wei Liao was as concerned with drill, discipline, and formation as any Roman drillmaster. He laid out an elaborate procedure utilizing "gongs, drums, bells, and flags" to control and maneuver formations in battle down to the level of a five-man squad: "When the drums sound, the army should advance; when the drums are beat again, they should attack. When the gongs sound, they should stop; when the gongs are struck again, they should withdraw. Bells are used to transmit orders. When the flags point to the left, [the army should] go left; when the flags point to the right, then to the right."

Those who failed to heed these elaborate instructions could expect a fate that makes the Roman practice of decimation seem lenient by comparison. If the soldiers in a squad "lose members without capturing [or killing] equal numbers of the enemy, they will be killed and their families will be exterminated." So too "anyone who loses his emblem will be executed." Even the poor drummers were in peril: "If a drummer misses a beat he is executed."

All of these injunctions presumably were designed to produce an army that in good Clausewitzian fashion was capable of defeating the main forces of the enemy. Rather than preaching indirectness, the *Wei Liao-tzu* holds, "If the enemy is in the mountains, climb up after him. If the enemy is in the depths, plunge in after him. Seek the enemy as if searching for a lost child, follow him without any doubt. In this way you will be able to defeat the enemy and control his fate."[62]

Although definitive evidence is lacking, ancient Chinese and Indian warfare seemed to conform more closely to Wei Lao's conventional injunctions than to Sun Tzu's indirect approach. Certainly both cultures produced vast armies that would have been of little use for evasive maneuvers. In the third century BC, at a time when China was divided like Greece into numerous warring polities, the weaker states were said to field armies of a hundred thousand men. The largest states supposedly had armies of nearly a million men. Even allowing for inevitable exaggeration by contemporary chroniclers, that is indisputably a lot of soldiers. Most were conscripted peasants who fought on foot, wore armor, and were equipped with swords, spears, halberds, and crossbows. As in the Roman army, these infantrymen were supplemented by experts in such fields as mechanical artillery and siege works. Note that the army of more than six thousand life-size terracotta soldiers and horses discovered in 1974 at the burial place of China's first emperor, Shi Huangdi (r. 221–210 BC), was arranged in elaborate formations and grouped by type of weapon. The odds are that China saw many clashes between such armies.[63]

In sum, any attempt to suggest that Europeans have an inherent predilection toward infantry battle in the open field, whereas Asians prefer to fight in guerrilla-like ways, does not stand up to scrutiny. As two scholars of Chinese military history write, "The difference between premodern warfare in China and the West was probably not as great as prescriptive texts such as the Chinese military classics might lead us to believe. Despite the literary emphasis on caution and avoidance of the risks of battle, battle was no less common an occurrence in imperial China than it was in the ancient Mediterranean world or in medieval Europe."[64]

Guerrilla warfare, then, is not the product of an "Eastern (or Oriental) culture"—itself a misnomer, since Asia has more than one culture. It is the last resort of all those over time, of whatever culture, forced to fight a stronger foe. Generally, whenever any group was strong enough to field a conventional army, it did so. But this required the creation of a strong, centralized state, and this was usually beyond the capabilities of tribal societies.

9.

NOMADS AND MANDARINS

Xiongnu vs. Han, 200 BC–AD 48

If there was any group that had a particular predilection for guerrilla warfare, it was not the great states of Asia but rather the stateless nomads that preyed on them—just as they preyed on the Roman Empire and its predecessors and successors in the West. In 135–134 BC, a major debate broke out in the Han imperial court over how to deal with one particularly dangerous group of nomads: the Xiongnu.[65]

The godlike emperors of the Han dynasty, styled as the Sons of Heaven, ruled over some 50 million people with the help of 120,000 mandarins who were educated in an elite academy and tested for competence. The imperial capital was Ch'ang-an in present-day Shaanxi Province. With a population of over 500,000, it was one of the biggest cities in the world, rivaled only by Rome, and had a variety of impressive structures, ranging from the emperor's palace to a vast marketplace said to be bigger than any mall in the United States today. The wealthy drove through its streets in fine carriages, wearing beautiful silk robes. To keep them entertained, there were orchestras, jugglers, and acrobats, and elaborate banquets featuring exquisitely prepared delicacies served in lacquer dishes.[66]

Very different were the Xiongnu—herdsmen and hunters who were known as "Mountain Barbarians" to the Han Chinese. They came from Inner Asia, a term that usually takes in, at a minimum, Mongolia, the modern Chinese province of Xinxiang, and Central Asia,[67] but, like the Huns to whom they may have been related, they remain figures of mystery. One theory has it that they were of Mongolian stock, but no one knows for sure. What little we know of them comes from Chinese sources, and it was not flattering. One Confucian scholar likened them to "all manner of insects, reptiles, snakes and lizards,"[68] while the Han court historian Sima Qian regarded them "as beasts to be pastured, not as members of the human race."[69] He was shocked that "these people know nothing of the elegance of hats and girdles, nor of the rituals of the court!"[70]

What the Xiongnu did know was war, and in this field their superiority to the more settled Chinese was unquestioned. They had mastered a style of archery on horseback that was alien to a Han army composed primarily of infantrymen supplemented by charioteers. Thus time after time they were able to inflict humiliating defeats on the Chinese, even though their entire population of 1 million to 3.5 million people would hardly have amounted to one province of the Celestial Empire.[71] A mandarin named Zhao Zuo wrote ruefully, "On dangerous roads and sloping narrow passages they can both ride and shoot arrows; Chinese mounted soldiers cannot match that. They can withstand the wind and rain, fatigue, hunger and thirst; Chinese soldiers are not as good."[72]

When Chinese forces got close, the Xiongnu simply retreated, sometimes clear across the Gobi Desert, and the Chinese armies, with their cumbersome supply requirements, lacked the ability to keep up. Sounding very much like his Western counterparts, Sima Qian complained, "If the battle is going well for them they will advance, but if not, they will retreat, for they do not consider it a disgrace to run away. Their only concern is self-advantage, and they know nothing of propriety and righteousness."[73] (This passage provides further evidence that the Chinese, like the Greeks and Romans, elevated face-to-face infantry battle to the pinnacle of warfare and frowned upon tactical retreat.)

The first emperor of the Han dynasty, Gaozu, discovered for himself just how formidable the Mountain Barbarians were. He mounted a major expedition against them in 200 BC which turned into a fiasco. First his forces, said to be more than 300,000-strong, ran into cold weather that caused a third of his men to lose fingers to frostbite. Then they stumbled onto what they thought was a weak Xiongnu detachment. The Chinese vanguard mounted pursuit, only to run into an ambush; they were not familiar with the tried-and-true nomadic tactic of "feigned retreat." The entire Han army was surrounded and allowed to withdraw only after offering "generous gifts," essentially bribes, to Modun, the powerful Chanyu, or chieftain, of the Xiongnu confederation.[74]

Making the best of a bad situation, Gaozu entered into a supposedly equal arrangement of "brothers" with Modun that was in fact anything but equal. In return for peace, in 198 BC China agreed to send to the Xiongnu a Chinese princess in marriage along with annual shipments of grain, silk, and wine—all goods that the nomads coveted but could not make for themselves. The subsidies, which increased over time, included 200,000 liters of wine a year and 92,400 meters of silk.[75] The wise men of the Han court hoped to use these luxury goods to sap the ferocity of their rivals as part of what became known as the "five baits" policy and what would today be called foreign aid: "elaborate clothes and carriages to corrupt their eyes; fine food to corrupt their mouths; music to corrupt their ears; lofty buildings, granaries, and slaves to corrupt their stomachs; gifts and favors for Xiongnu who surrendered."[76]

The Xiongnu, like the modern North Koreans, proved hard to corrupt. The initial shipments only whetted their appetite for more, and they knew that by raiding they could either carry away what they wanted or force the Chinese to increase the size of their tribute. Even if the Chanyu wanted to honor the terms of his treaty with the emperor, moreover, he had only limited power to control individual tribes in his confederation. (Much the same problem would later confront early American leaders trying to cut deals with Indian chiefs.) As a result, the frontier remained turbulent and unsettled. The Xiongnu, "greedy as ever" in the eyes of the Chinese, continued to carry out "innumerable plundering raids."[77]

Hence the debate that took place in 135–134 BC in the court of the young emperor Wu. How, his mandarins wondered, should they deal with the Xiongnu? Continue the *he-qin* (peace and kinship) policy? Or take up arms for the first time in more than half a century?

Dovish officials argued that it was hopeless to fight the Xiongnu. One of them cited the arguments that a predecessor had made to Emperor Gaozu, Wu's great-grandfather, against launching his own ill-fated expedition:

> They move from place to place like flocks of birds and are just as difficult to catch and control. . . . Even if we were to seize control of the Xiongnu lands, they would bring us no profit, and even if we were to win over their people, we could never administer and keep control of them. . . . Therefore we would only be wearing out the strength of China in an attempt to have our way with the Xiongnu. Surely this is not a wise policy!"[78]

But more hawkish advisers argued that it was useless to make any agreements with the Xiongnu, because they had shown themselves to be untrustworthy. One official likened them to "an abscess which must be burst open with strong crossbows and arrows, and absolutely should not be left to fester."[79] Others argued that the Han Chinese had an obligation to establish a "universal empire" that would bring "the poor, backward, and uncultured barbarians . . . into civilization."[80]

The emperor was just twenty-one years old and had been on the throne for five years. He was the tenth son of the preceding emperor, and his mother had been merely a middle-ranking concubine when he was born. But she had been successful enough at palace intrigue to displace the elder empress and win the throne for her son. Wu remained dominated in his early years by his mother, the empress dowager. He was also a bisexual with two prominent male lovers, one of whom was killed by his mother over his protests; the other he killed himself in a fit of jealous rage. Having grown up in an atmosphere of insecurity and intrigue, Wu became brutal and aggressive. He killed five of his seven chancellors and several of his children and wives on suspicion of plotting against him. Anxious to establish greater security for his realm as well as for his person and to "avenge the difficulties" suffered by his great-grandfather Gaozu, he was readily won over to calls to attack the Xiongnu.[81]

Wu knew that a prerequisite for any offensive was to assemble enough horses to track down the elusive raiders. Horse-breeding stations were established along the frontier, and costly military expeditions were dispatched all the way to the vicinity of modern Uzbekistan to capture more mounts.[82] Horses in hand, the Han expanded their cavalry ranks, even going so far as to dress some of their soldiers in the "barbarian" manner, meaning in trousers and short jackets as opposed to the traditional Chinese long coats. Wu also expanded his links with the Xiongnu's nomadic neighbors, enlisting many of their horsemen in his own ranks as part of the time-honored policy, also beloved of the Romans, of "using barbarians to control the barbarians."[83]

This was part of a broader transformation of the Chinese army, which came to number 700,000 men.[84] The need to send troops to distant frontiers for extended periods necessitated an end of reliance on peasant conscripts serving one- or two-year tours—not enough time to master horsemanship or the crossbow. Instead the army came to be composed, in the words of the historian Mark Edward Lewis, of "professionals, nomads, and criminals."[85] Much the same transformation was occurring in the Roman army at the same time and for the same reason—the demands of imperial pacification made it impractical to rely on citizen-soldiers called away temporarily from their farms.[86] Thus professional armies may be said to have arisen in both Europe and Asia in response to the threat posed by guerrillas.

When Wu, soon to be known as the "martial emperor," finally sent his armies marching into the lands of the Xiongnu in 129 BC, they scored some successes and killed large numbers of nomads. But, like most armies through the ages undertaking large-scale maneuvers against guerrillas, they had trouble finishing off the resilient and elusive Xiongnu. In his attempts to annihilate them, Wu wound up exhausting his own resources, causing "extreme hardship to the empire." One campaign alone consumed more than half of his annual revenues. Within a few years, wrote Sima Qian, "there was not enough money left to support the troops," and "the common people were exhausted and began to look for some clever way to evade the [tax] laws." Coinage became so debased that the emperor had to kill his own white deer and use their hides, cut into one-foot squares, as "hide currency."[87]

Following two defeats at the hands of the Xiongnu and with Wu's strength fading (he would die three years later), the Han court finally gave up the offensive in 90 BC and reverted to defensive measures such as erecting walls to keep out the barbarians. Over the preceding forty years, more than two million soldiers and ten million support personnel had been mobilized to mount twenty-one separate offensives against the Xiongnu and their allies.[88] They had greatly expanded the emperor's domains, but they had not delivered real security. The improvements were mostly cosmetic. The Xiongnu had agreed to become "tributaries" of the Celestial Empire. But in return for token tribute, the emperor annually gave the Chanyu "gifts" that were worth far more. This was a continuation of the previous policy of appeasement dressed up in rhetoric more pleasing to Chinese ears.[89]

The Xiongnu confederation eventually collapsed, but this was due more to civil wars that broke out in 57 BC and AD 48 than to external pressure. Many of the nomads moved south to be absorbed into the Chinese Empire. Others fled west where, according to one theory, they later materialized as the Huns who helped bring down the Roman Empire.[90]

The Xiongnu had not brought down the Chinese Empire, but that was never their purpose; they were interested in raiding, not in occupying land or overthrowing the ruling dynasty. Perhaps because their ambitions were modest, they were able to survive longer than any other nomadic empire, including those of the Mongols and Huns, which are far better known in the West. For 250 years the Xiongnu dominated the steppe, and for 500 years they were a major irritant to their southern neighbors. The failure of the mighty Chinese Empire to decisively defeat the relatively small number of "Mountain Barbarians" demonstrates once again the difficulties that guerrilla-style tactics caused for armies in both East and West.

✦ ✦ ✦

THE MIDDLE KINGDOM'S problems with nomads did not end with the extinction of the Xiongnu threat. New waves of horse-borne invaders materialized to harass China's northern frontier. The nomadic threat did not disappear until AD 1750, when the Manchu dynasty exterminated the Zunghars, or Western Mongols, the last of the great nomadic confederations, in a genocidal campaign made possible by the development of firearms and vastly improved logistics.[91] Dealing with external attacks was all the harder for many emperors because of the frequency of peasant uprisings orchestrated by secret societies such as the Red Eyebrows, the Yellow Turbans, and later the Taipings and Boxers. These rebels, too, often employed guerrilla tactics and, even if unsuccessful, sapped the energy of the imperial government.

Dynasties were more likely to launch punitive expeditions early in their tenure when they were more vigorous. As they became more decrepit, they usually resorted to buying off the nomads and erecting fortifications to block their advance. This strategy culminated in the construction of the Great Wall of China, one of the great engineering feats in world history, under the Ming dynasty in the fifteenth and sixteenth centuries AD.[92]

None of these measures worked all that well. China saw a succession of "conquest" dynasties rule its northern territory, while domestic dynasties continued to survive in the south. The Mongols in the thirteenth century and the Manchus in the seventeenth managed to conquer the entire empire. It may be doubted, however, whether they were truly guerrillas. Far from being a loose-flowing horde of tribesmen, the Mongol army was a disciplined military force that was trained to operate in units of 10, 100, 1,000, and 10,000. At their peak the Mongols may have had a million men under arms.[93] The size and discipline of their armies put them on a different plane from other nomads and elevated them out of the realm of purely guerrilla warfare.

However one classifies the invaders, their impact was clear: In the last 1,003 years of Chinese imperial history, ending in 1911, alien regimes established by steppe nomads or seminomads ruled over all or part of Chinese territory for 730 years.[94] The Chinese over the long run showed a remarkable ability to absorb their conquerors rather than be absorbed by them, thereby preserving their ancient heritage. Much the same thing happened in Europe, where local populations gradually assimilated waves of invaders from the east, north, and south; the Normans, for instance, first appeared in France in the eighth century AD as feared Viking raiders and ended up adopting the French language and Christian religion. But the eventual triumph of their native culture was scant comfort to countless generations of Chinese peasants terrorized by the horse archers from the steppe, just as it would have been scant comfort to French peasants of the Dark Ages terrorized by seaborne marauders from Scandinavia.

10.

THE GUERRILLA PARADOX

Why the Weak Beat the Strong

THE SUCCESS OF various raiders in attacking states from ancient Rome to medieval China gives rise to what one historian has called the "nomad paradox." "In the history of warfare it has generally been the case that military superiority lies with the wealthiest states and those with the most developed administrations," Hugh Kennedy notes. Yet nomads going back to the days of Akkad managed to bring down far richer and more advanced empires, even though "they did not have states and administrative apparatus, they were often dirt poor and entirely unversed in the arts of civilized living."

Kennedy explains this paradox by citing all the military advantages enjoyed by nomads, many of which we have already noted. First, they were more mobile than their enemies and better able to thrive in harsh terrain without need of supply trains. Second, in nomadic societies every adult male was a warrior, thus allowing the nomads to mobilize a higher portion of the population than in sedentary societies. Third, many of the nomads, such as the Huns, Xiongnu, and Mongols, excelled in a distinctive technique of fighting—mounted archery—that was alien to their enemies. Fourth, in nomadic societies "leadership was based on skill and wisdom in warfare and hunting." By contrast, many settled societies appointed army commanders based more on political considerations than on military merit. We might add a fifth and final advantage: having no cities, crops, or other fixed targets to defend, nomads had little cause to worry about enemy attacks, making them hard to deter. Thus it should be no surprise that on numerous occasions nomads bested their agrarian adversaries.[95]

But impressive as the nomads' military success was, it was hardly unique. The nomads' victories become less mysterious and more explicable if they are seen as part of the long continuum of guerrilla warfare. After all, even in the last two centuries, when states were far more powerful than in the ancient or medieval periods, guerrillas were able to humble superpowers. Think of the Vietnamese defeating France and the United States or the Afghans defeating Great Britain and the Soviet Union. The factors that made these modern guerrillas so formidable were not exactly the same as those of the ancient nomads, but there was considerable overlap. Both groups relied on superior mobility, cunning leadership, the ability to mobilize a large portion of society, and mastery of a style of a war different from that of their enemies. Thus the "nomad paradox" is really the guerrilla paradox: how the weak can defeat the strong. The answer lies largely in the use of hit-and-run tactics emphasizing mobility and surprise, which makes it difficult for the stronger state to bring its full weight to bear.

There is a further paradox to contemplate: even the most successful raiders were prone to switch to conventional tactics once they had gained the ability to do so. We have already noted the example of the Mongols, who turned into a semiregular army under Genghis Khan. The Arabs underwent a similar transformation. They fought in traditional Bedouin style while spreading Islam across the Middle East in the century after Muhammad's death, in AD 632. The result of their conquests was the creation of the Umayyad and Abbasid caliphates, two of the greatest states of the medieval world, which were defended by conventional forces composed of expert foreign soldiers such as the Mamluks in Egypt, mainly slaves or former slaves. The Turks, too, arose out of the raiding culture of the steppes but built a formidable conventional army, with their highly disciplined slave-soldiers, the janissaries, replacing the tribal levies known as *ghazis*. The new Ottoman army conquered Constantinople in a famous siege in 1453 and went on within less than a century to advance to the gates of Vienna.[96]

Why would groups so adept at guerrilla tactics resort to positional warfare? In the first place professional armed forces, with infantry, artillery, armorers, sappers, and other experts, gave them the ability to fight on ground not suitable for cavalry and, most important of all, to batter down city walls. Nomadic archers could not have taken Constantinople; this feat required a battery of sixty-nine cannons, including two monstrous guns that were twenty-seven feet long and fired stone balls weighing more than half a ton. Nor were fast-moving tribal levies of much use in defending, administering, and policing newly conquered states. This, too, required a professional standing army.

A further factor dictated the transformation of nomads into regulars: the style of fighting practiced by the mounted archers was so difficult and demanding that it required constant practice from childhood to maintain proficiency. Just try twisting around in the saddle while riding at full gallop to fire an arrow behind you—the famous "Parthian shot." Once they were living among more sedentary peoples, notes one historian, "nomads easily lost their superior individual talents and unit cohesion."[97] This was a trade-off most former nomads, or at least their children and grandchildren, were happy to make because a more settled life was so much safer and easier than their previous existence. In the end, no one chooses to fight as a guerrilla, a lifestyle that has always come with great hardships, if there is any alternative.

11.

THE TARTAN REBELLIONS

Scotland vs. England, 1296–1746

IN THE WEST, following the fall of the Roman Empire, there was, in fact, no other choice. It would take more than a thousand years before strong states emerged across Europe. In the meantime, the continent was broken up into petty statelets and fiefdoms that lacked the resources to field disciplined standing armies as Rome had done. That required the support of an elaborate administrative infrastructure, which no longer existed. Feudal armies were made up of nobles, retainers, and mercenaries who would come together for a few months to fight a single battle or campaign and then disperse afterward. Kings had to rely on the goodwill of powerful magnates to assemble their forces, and if that goodwill was lost the soldiers were liable to walk off the job. If guerrilla warfare is the war of the weak, then during the Middle Ages practically every European polity was weak enough to resort to it.

It is easy to lose sight of this elemental truth because of the great myth of the Middle Ages—the clash of knights on horseback. This would seem to be the very antithesis of stealthy, low-intensity conflict. But such battles did not happen nearly as often in real life as they did in the epics of the period.[98] Siege warfare was more important. So was the raid, or to use the French name popular at the time, the *chevauchée* ("ride"). That innocuous term connoted something far more ominous: roaming the enemy's countryside, burning, stealing, raping, kidnapping, and killing at will. The flavor of one of these operations can be gleaned from a letter written home to England by Sir John Wingfield, steward to Edward of Woodstock, better known to posterity as the Black Prince, during his eight-week *chevauchée* through France in 1355. "And, my lord," Wingfield wrote to the bishop of Winchester, on December 23, 1355, "you will be glad to know that my Lord has raided the county of Armagnac and taken several walled towns there, burning and destroying them, except for certain towns which he garrisoned. Then he went to the viscounty of Rivière, and took a good town called Plaisance, the chief town of the area, and burnt it and laid waste the surrounding countryside. Then he went into the county of Astarac. . . ." Well, it is not hard to imagine what the Black Prince did there, or in succeeding towns that the English force, five thousand strong, entered. They left a swath of devastation in their wake, stretching from Bordeaux to Toulouse, a distance of 150 miles. Wingfield boasted that "the countryside and towns which have been destroyed in this raid produced more revenue for the King of France in aid of his wars than half his kingdom."[99]

Sometimes the *chevauchée* was a tactic used to draw the enemy's armed forces into battle. More often, as in the case of the Black Prince, it was designed to avoid battle against a superior foe. The *chevauchée* was hardly a European invention—it was also endemic under different names in Arabia, North Africa, Central Asia, and many other areas. The Bedouin of the Arabian Peninsula were particular masters of what came to be known as the *razzia*, which would make them, as T. E. Lawrence was to discover many centuries later, highly skilled guerrillas.

Unlike the Bedouin or the Xiongnu, the Europeans of the Middle Ages did not have any particular cultural affinity for a raiding style of warfare; indeed they esteemed face-to-face battle above all. They adopted the *chevauchée* for purely practical reasons. The spread of castles made set-piece battles a rarity and, when they did occur, made them less decisive, for the defeated side could usually retreat to the safety of its castles. But while fortified castles were hard to penetrate until the spread of cannons in the fifteenth century, the tendency to seek refuge inside them left much of the surrounding countryside lightly defended and vulnerable to enemy raiders. The *chevauchée* had the advantage of being both easy to carry out and lucrative. The spoils gained thereby could provide sustenance for fighters who could not expect a salary from a paymaster or a meal from a commissariat. It also offered a convenient excuse for bandits and deserters to prey on helpless peasants: they could claim to be fighting for some larger cause when their only interest was in enriching themselves.

When carried out, as it often was, by relatively small groups ranging in size from a few dozen men to a few thousand, the raid was akin to what we would call guerrilla warfare. When undertaken by larger armies of tens of thousands of soldiers, it was closer to a conventional military operation, especially if the invaders intended to occupy territory, instead of simply grabbing loot.

The *chevauchée* was above all a tactic of attrition designed to instill fear in the enemy's population and wear down its will to resist. As with other manifestations of low-intensity warfare, the practitioners of the *chevauchée* could not expect fast results. It would take many years of suffering before the issue could be settled. Thus the length of Europe's wars during the Middle Ages, Renaissance, and Reformation, which strike the modern observer as perverse. Typical conflicts included the Hundred Years' War (England vs. France), the Eighty Years' War (Netherlands vs. Spain), and the Thirty Years' War (Protestants vs. Catholics in Germany).

The Anglo-Scottish struggle lasted even longer: 450 years from the first invasion of Scotland by King Edward I in 1296 to the failure of the last Scottish uprising in 1746. The Tartan Rebellions, as we may dub them, show why guerrilla tactics were so pervasive in the Middle Ages—and so indecisive.

✦ ✦ ✦

EIGHT HUNDRED SOLDIERS were on his trail, all "valiant and active men," in the words of the great Scottish poet John Barbour, and they had a secret weapon: "a sleuth hound so good that it would turn aside for nothing." It was said that Robert the Bruce had raised the dog himself, so that it knew his scent and would follow it unerringly. The pursuers were led by a fellow Scottish nobleman, John of Lorne. He was serving the king of England, Edward I, but he had a more personal reason to track down the fugitive and his "rebel accomplices." He was a relative of Sir John "the Red" Comyn, whom Bruce, the thirty-three-year-old earl of Carrick, had murdered the preceding year in a bid to establish his own claim to the throne of Scotland.

Bruce had indeed been crowned on March 25, 1306, six weeks after Comyn's death, but ever since he had been on the run from the English troops and their Scottish allies. His attempts to meet the more numerous English army in open battle had led to a shattering defeat at Methven, followed by another repulse at Dalry.[100] Almost bereft of followers, he was forced to seek shelter in the countryside amid what a modern historian describes as the "wide wastes of moor and bog" where wolves and wild boars still roamed and roads and bridges were "few and far between."[101]

The inhabitants of this rough land were poor but extraordinarily tough and hardy. They fought with spears, long-handled Lochaber axes, and two-handed broadswords more than five feet in length.[102] The men of the Highlands wore a kilt, which today has become a decorative item of clothing but in those days was quite practical. Since, as one historian notes, "men were frequently wading deep in water and travelling long distances through days of rain," it made sense to wear the "loose kilted plaid," which "allowed quick drying, and could easily be stripped off and wrung," rather than breeches which "stuck to and galled the skin or induced rheumatism and other ills by keeping the legs constantly wet and cold."[103] Wearing a kilt and carrying a sword, Bruce's few followers could travel long distances with nothing more to sustain them than a little water and a bag of oatmeal.

Often Bruce himself did not have even that much. A contemporary chronicler, John of Fordun, described Bruce as "passing a whole fortnight without food of any kind to live upon, but raw herbs and water." Sometimes he had to walk barefoot because his shoes "became old and worn out," and he had to sleep in caves to avoid detection. He was "an outcast among the nobles," most of whom had accepted English rule—as Bruce himself had done for four years before making his own bid for power. "And thus," wrote John, "he became a byword and a laughing-stock for all, both near and far to hiss at."

In desperation Bruce was forced to undertake a mode of warfare that could not have come easily to a great feudal lord. He had been brought up to view the cavalry charge as the epitome of combat—to dream of leading a great host with heraldic banners flying. He was inclined to agree with a nephew who counseled him, "Ye should endeavor to make good your right in open battle, and not by stratagem and craft." But Bruce was wise enough to see that "he could in nowise harry his foes with equal forces," so he turned to stratagem after all. "Speed, surprise, mobility, small-scale engagements, scorched earth and dismantling of fortresses—these were to be the hallmarks of his campaigns," writes Bruce's foremost modern biographer, Geoffrey Barrow. He adds that for the would-be king to act "based on his belief in the supreme virtue of guerrilla warfare . . . was not only a revolutionary decision, it was proof of his genius and imagination." But could it possibly work?

William Wallace, the leader of an earlier Scottish insurrection in which Bruce had played a minor and ambiguous part, had tried similar stratagems, and, notwithstanding some initial successes, he had failed miserably. In 1305 he was captured and sent to London, where he was given the standard punishment for treason: he was briefly hanged, then cut down "half-living" to have his genitals sliced off and internal organs ripped out of his chest before he was decapitated and his body hacked into pieces. His head was placed on London Bridge, and his quartered remains were sent to four different cities.[104] Bruce knew he risked a similar fate. Already his family members had paid a steep price for his effrontery: his sister and daughter were imprisoned in cages, and three brothers had been executed. But to hang this "Scottish traitor," the English would first have to catch him. And that was no easy matter.

In 1307, when the bloodhound got on his trail, the guerrilla king was hiding near Cumnock, south of Glasgow. He had but three hundred men and thus had no intention of risking battle against John of Lorne's forces. He decided to break up his men into three different groups to facilitate their escape. But the hound was not fooled. He ignored the other two groups and kept on Bruce's track. Bruce then divided his followers again into parties of three—and again the dog held a "straight course" after his former master. Bruce now decided it was every man for himself and set off accompanied only by his foster brother. The hound still followed him "without wavering." Seeing which way the dog went, John of Lorne ordered five of his speediest men to race ahead and cut off the fugitives. Knowing there was no escape, Bruce turned and stood his ground, great sword in hand. John Barbour described what happened next in his epic poem, *The Brus* (The Bruce), completed in 1376:

> Soon the five came in the greatest haste, with mighty clamour and menace. Three of them went at the king, and the other two, sword in hand, made stoutly at his man [the foster brother]. The king met the three . . . and dealt such a blow at the first that he shore through ear and cheek

> and neck to the shoulder. The man sank down dizzily, and the two, seeing their fellow's sudden fall, were affrighted, and started back a little. With that the king glanced aside and saw the other two making full sturdy battle against his man. He left his own two, and leapt lightly at them that fought with his man, and smote off the head of one of them. Then he went to meet his own assailants, who were coming at him right boldly. He met the first so eagerly that with the edge of his sword he hewed the arm from the body.
>
> . . . [S]o fairly it fell out that the king, though he had a struggle and difficulty, slew four of his foemen. Soon afterwards his foster-brother ended the days of the fifth.[105]

Bruce was "drenched in sweat," but he had no time to exult in this small victory. He saw John of Lorne's men coming up fast with their bloodhound. He and his foster brother had to run off into the woods. From 1306 to 1314 that is mostly what he did—run and run some more. During what were literally his wilderness years, he persevered through what John of Fordun summed up as "mishaps, flights and dangers; hardships and weariness; hunger and thirst; watchings, and fastings; nakedness, and cold; snares, and banishment; the seizing, imprisoning, slaughter and downfall of his near ones"[106]—and gradually, despite all that, he gained the upper hand. He started to push the English out of their captured territory, even raiding into northern England on occasion.

The key obstacles were the English castles that dotted the Scottish countryside. Since the Scottish rebels lacked proper siege engines, they had to resort to daring commando raids. On one occasion, Bruce's men even donned black capes and walked on their hands and knees in the dark pretending to be cows in order to get close enough to clamber up rope ladders and seize a redoubt.[107]

✦ ✦ ✦

By 1314 the Scots felt strong enough to challenge the English, now led by Edward I's ineffectual son, Edward II, in open battle at Bannockburn. Bannockburn was a glorious Scottish victory and, in the words of a medieval chronicle, "an evil, miserable, and calamitous day for the English."[108] Yet it no more determined the outcome of the war than had previous clashes at Stirling

Bridge and Falkirk. The war ground on, ceaselessly, remorselessly, unendingly, interrupted only by brief "peaces" and "truces" that were inevitably violated.

Bruce and his successors would launch repeated *chevauchées* into northern England, where, according to a medieval chronicle, they "ravaged and burnt."[109] They also stole everything they could carry away, and extorted protection money from the locals. The English army moved too slowly to stop them, but attacks on a sparsely settled frontier region could not bring England to heel. In desperation, Bruce tried other tactics, such as invading Ireland to harass its English occupiers and even attempting to kidnap the queen of England from her home in York.[110] However bold and imaginative, these ploys failed.

King Robert I died in 1329 with his country still facing the constant threat of English invasion. Scotland was simply too small and too poor to defeat its southern neighbor. Its population in the early fourteenth century was less than a million; England's was 5.5 million.[111] But it was too tough and prickly to be subdued.

For their part, English monarchs lacked sufficient resources or willpower to pacify the sprawling Scottish countryside. Most of their invasions followed a pattern: after an initial victory or two, the English army would be forced to slink home because the Scots' scorched-earth tactics made it impossible to stay in the field. During one such expedition in 1322, the ravenous English foragers were said to have found only one lame cow in the entire Lothian region.[112] Those today who imagine that long-running conflicts—say, over Kashmir or Palestine—can be resolved neatly and expeditiously through negotiations ignore the lesson of the Anglo-Scottish wars: conflicts of blood and soil, fought as a series of skirmishes between guerrillas and regulars, can drag on for centuries even among peoples far closer in religion and outlook than the Indians and Pakistanis or the Israelis and Palestinians.

Organized warfare between Scotland and England finally petered out in the sixteenth century, although the final clash between Scottish insurgents and English armies did not occur until the Jacobite rising of 1745–46 aimed at restoring the Catholic Stuarts to the throne of Great Britain. For centuries before that the frontier was unsettled by the attacks of border reivers (from the Old English word meaning robbers), who chose to cloak their thievery in a nationalistic guise.

✦ ✦ ✦

THE HISTORIAN Eric Hobsbawm coined the term "social bandits" to describe "peasant outlaws" who "are considered by their people as heroes, as champions, avengers, fighters for justice, perhaps even leaders of liberation, and in any case as men to be admired, helped and supported." The mythical archetype was Robin Hood. Rob Roy MacGregor in Scotland (1671–1734), Jesse James in America (1847–1882), Ned Kelly in Australia (1855–1880), and Pancho Villa in Mexico (1878–1923) were real-life examples. Less famous but more significant were the klephts and haiduks, the Christian bandits who battled Ottoman overlords in the Balkans for five hundred years. Hobsbawm notes that the prevalence of such men "is one of the most universal social phenomena known to history"; they flourish wherever social order has broken down, including today in such areas as the triborder region of South America. In years past rough badlands such as Scotland, Corsica, Sicily, Spain, and the Balkans were particularly fertile pastures for social bandits until the state became too strong to resist.[113]

In most of the wars fought in Europe between the fall of Rome and the rise of nation-states in the seventeenth century, it was not easy to tell "social bandits" from soldiers, regulars from irregulars. All victimized hapless peasants in equally savage fashion for their own benefit. Friedrich Schiller, the eighteenth-century poet, playwright, and historian, wrote with great feeling of how during the Thirty Years' War in the preceding century his native Germany "was laid waste by the desolating bands" of various captains and "lay exhausted, bleeding, wasted, and sighing for repose."[114] This was the guerrilla version of total war, a struggle of all against all, and it was the natural result of the decline of nation-states and conventional armies in the millennium after the fall of Rome.

All that was about to change, at least in the West. The years after 1648, when the Peace of Westphalia ended the Thirty Years' War, would see the rise of increasingly powerful and sophisticated states—and also the rise of increasingly powerful and sophisticated insurgent groups to challenge their power. That is one of the most enduring dynamics in the history of warfare: as a state becomes more capable in its defense, so guerrillas become more capable in their offense.

12.

WAR BY THE BOOK

The Counterinsurgents' Advantage

A LOOK AT the ancient and medieval worlds suggests yet another paradoxical conclusion: the most primitive guerrillas were the most successful. There were a few notable insurgents such as Judas Maccabeus and Robert the Bruce who operated with a fair degree of sophistication and managed to achieve a fair degree of success. They were sensitive to the need to build political support and to establish political institutions to replace those of their enemies. But such successes were rare, in no small part because ancient rebels lacked the ability to appeal to a hostile population over the head of its leader—and, in those days when autocracy was the dominant form of government, few populations could do much anyway to sway the decisions of their emperor, king, or chief. Most insurgents suffered the fate of Viriathus, Quintus Sertorius, Spartacus, Vercingetorix, Boudicca, and others who died battling Roman power. Lacking the ability to call in outside aid or state their case to the mass media (which did not yet exist), ancient insurgents were generally on their own to face the pitiless power of a pagan polity.

The most successful guerrillas of the ancient world were the nomads who brought down the Roman Empire and seized large chunks of the Chinese Empire and other Eurasian states. They did not try to organize a revolution within a state, a notoriously difficult undertaking. Rather they chipped away at the state's outer defenses until, in some cases, the entire edifice collapsed. The nomads' achievement, while great, was almost wholly negative: with the exception of the Arabs, Turks, Moguls, and Manchus, who blended with more-settled societies, nomads could not build lasting institutions. Nomadic empires generally crumbled after a generation or two. But, as long as they were around, nomads had few equals in their ability to inflict catastrophic costs on established states through the use of hit-and-run tactics. All of the great commanders of antiquity—Alexander, Caesar, Hannibal, Scipio—grappled with the problem. Many of them discovered, as did Alexander the Great during his Central Asian campaign in 329–327 BC, that fleet nomads were harder to defeat than massive conventional armies.

While the nomadic menace had once been of overriding, indeed existential, importance to the world's greatest states, by the seventeenth century it was becoming a historical curiosity. The rise of the gunpowder empires (British, French, Russian, Prussian, Turkish, Indian, Chinese), with powerful bureaucracies able to marshal vast resources, was creating a new world order. Potent in the age of bows and arrows, nomads could not compete with large armies equipped with guns and supported by extensive logistical establishments. Among other problems, nomadic societies were severely limited in size because of their limited food resources. (There are only so many livestock that you can herd before you run out of grasslands.) In the long run they would be overwhelmed by the greater wealth and resources of industrial societies.

Primitive guerrilla warfare of the kind practiced by groups as disparate as the haiduks, the Pashtuns, and the Sioux would continue to flourish until the twentieth century on the periphery of the Western world. A vestige of this type of warfare still exists today in such ungoverned spaces as Somalia and the Pakistan frontier, albeit in considerably modified form. In Book III we will examine the resulting conflicts as primitive guerrillas were defeated by Western armies from the plains of the American Midwest to the crags of the Caucasus. But the eighteenth and nineteenth centuries would also see the rise of increasingly sophisticated guerrillas thoroughly steeped in the political ideologies and military tactics of the West. They were not so easy to defeat, because they made use of many of the same weapons and techniques that made modern armies so potent.

One of the greatest advantages enjoyed by modern, as opposed to ancient or medieval, guerrillas was the ability to learn from their predecessors. Before the twentieth century, literacy levels were low, books rare, long-distance travel difficult. Most people led isolated lives. In this environment, it was hard for rebels to learn from one another, much less to cooperate in the way that twenty-first century jihadist groups seek to do by embracing the Internet. Simon bar Gioras, leader of the Jewish Revolt against Rome, undoubtedly was familiar with the experience of Judas Maccabeus and King David, two earlier Jewish guerrilla leaders. But it is doubtful that he knew much if anything of Viriathus, who resisted Roman authority in Spain, and even less likely that the illiterate Viriathus was familiar with the exploits of Spitamenes, who fought Alexander the Great in Central Asia, much less with Modun, leader of the Xiongnu who fought the Chinese Empire. Once printed books and periodicals began to spread and literacy to rise, insurgents were able to study their predecessors' experiences and puzzle out more potent techniques to bring powerful empires to their knees.

Counterinsurgents were able to learn from their predecessors much earlier. Counterinsurgency manuals have been common at least since the Byzantine emperor Maurice produced his *Strategikon* around AD 600. It offered advice on how to battle Slavs, Avars, and other "undisciplined, disorganized peoples" who "prefer to prevail over their enemies not so much by force as by deceit, surprise attacks, and cutting off supplies." Maurice offered an early warning against the sort of blundering "search and destroy" missions that would prove a failure centuries later for, among others, German forces in Yugoslavia, American forces in Vietnam, and Russian forces in Afghanistan. "[I]n warring against them one must avoid engaging in pitched battles, especially in the early stages," he wrote. "Instead, make use of well-planned ambushes, sneak attacks, and stratagems."[115] Even earlier Greek and Roman manuals of military science, such as Aeneas Tacticus's fourth-century BC work, *How to Survive under Siege*, offered guidance on how to combat revolutionaries and subversives (the enemy within the city walls), while battles against "barbarian" tribes (the enemy without) formed a substantial part of Herodotus's *Histories*, Caesar's *Gallic War*, and other famous narratives of ancient military history.

But accounts written from the insurgents' perspective were practically nonexistent until the modern era because most ancient and medieval insurgents were unlettered. Insurgent manuals did not become common until the nineteenth century. By then the spread of the printed word had made it easier for guerrillas to appeal for popular support, thereby elevating the role of propaganda and psychological warfare, the distinguishing features of contemporary guerrilla warfare. In the modern age, the printing press would become as important a weapon in the insurgents' arsenal as the rifle and the bomb. In a related development, the growing ease of communications would expand the range of motivations for insurgencies. Whereas in the past most of those who adopted guerrilla tactics did so for elemental tribal or religious reasons, in the years ahead secular ideologies such as nationalism, liberalism, and socialism were to be added to the volatile mix, thereby attracting more recruits to insurgent ranks. The Enlightenment ushered in a new epoch not only in the history of the West but also in the history of guerrilla warfare. That is the subject of Book II.

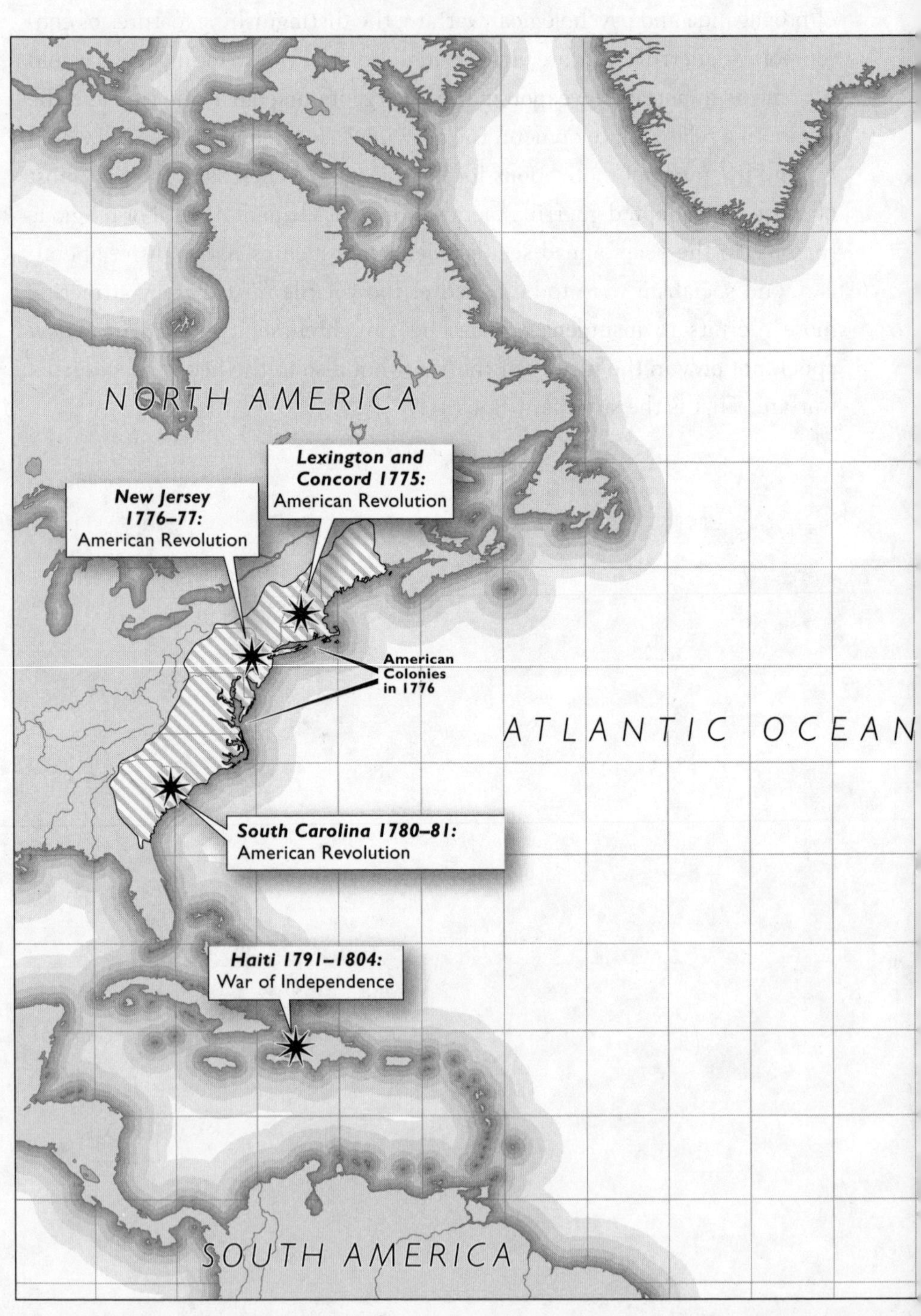
NORTH AMERICA
Lexington and Concord 1775: American Revolution
New Jersey 1776–77: American Revolution
American Colonies in 1776
ATLANTIC OCEAN
South Carolina 1780–81: American Revolution
Haiti 1791–1804: War of Independence
SOUTH AMERICA

BOOK II
LIBERTY OR DEATH
The Rise of the Liberal Revolutionaries

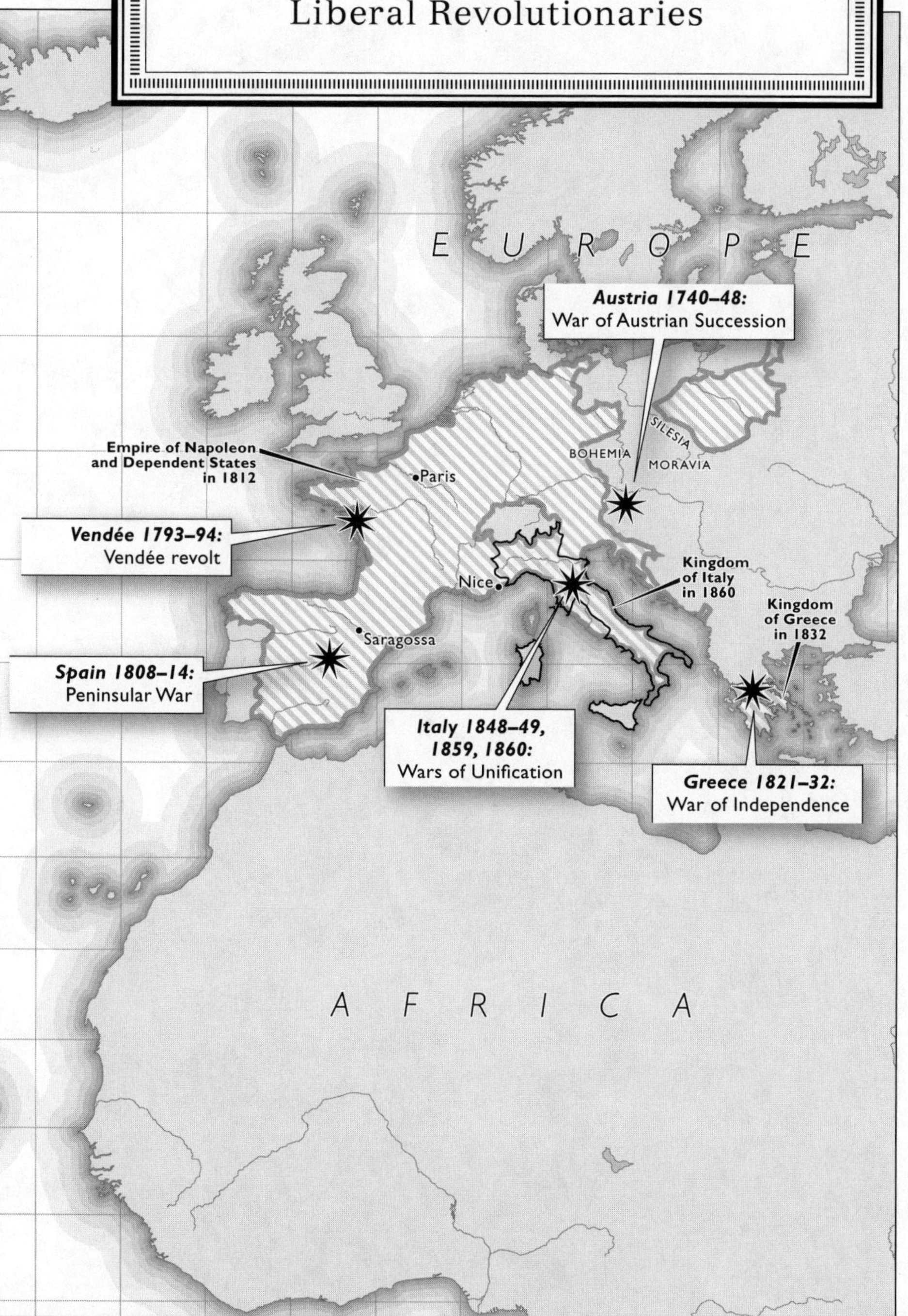

13.

IRREGULARS IN THE AGE OF REASON

Hussars, Pandours, and Rangers, 1648–1775

NOTHING DEMONSTRATED THE importance of ideology, propaganda, and other relatively new elements of guerrilla warfare more powerfully than the revolution that broke out in Britain's North American colonies in 1775. This was the first in a series of liberal upheavals, many of which would involve considerable guerrilla fighting, that would flare across Europe and its settler colonies for a century—from the late 1700s to the late 1800s. This book examines not only the skirmishes of American rebels, which are well covered in American history texts, but also less-familiar struggles—Spaniards and Haitians fighting French troops, Greeks fighting the Ottomans, and Italians fighting Habsburgs and Bourbons. But before we get to these wars, it is important to understand how the 1648 Peace of Westphalia transformed European warfare.

The dividing line between regular and irregular warfare, which became so blurred as to almost vanish during the Middle Ages, was to grow more distinct after the end of the Thirty Years' War with the spread of standing, national armies. That process, which went hand in hand with the growth of nation-states, reached a critical mass in the second half of the seventeenth century. This period saw the spread of barracks to house soldiers, drillmasters to train them, professional officers to lead them, logistical services to supply them, factories to clothe and equip them, and hospitals and retirement homes to take care of them in times of distress. By 1700 France alone had 400,000 men under arms year-round.

Western warfare reached stylized heights in the eighteenth century seldom seen before or since, with monarchical armies fighting in roughly similar style and abiding by roughly similar rules of conduct. (Those limitations on warfare would not survive into the more ideological age of conflict to come, when conventional armies were often pitted against irregulars who fought by their own rules.) Just as in ancient Greece, elaborate procedures were concocted to guide every aspect of warfare, from besieging fortresses to marching cross-country, thereby bringing to the battlefield the scientific, or, more accurately, pseudo-scientific, ethos so beloved of contemporary *philosophes*. The ultimate result was to send brightly clad lines of troops marching into battle at a slow, steady pace without making any attempt at concealment. Soldiers were taught to cultivate an air of nonchalance as bullets whizzed around them. Ducking was considered bad form.[1]

No change was more important symbolically than the adoption of standardized uniforms—scarlet red for the English, white for the French, dark blue for the Prussians, pearl gray for the Austrians. The advent of uniforms meant that the difference between soldiers and civilians could be glimpsed in an instant. Fighters who insisted on making war without uniforms therefore became more distinctive. In time they would become known as guerrillas. It is not a perfect definition, because some guerrillas have adopted uniforms, too, and some regular units have fought in the style of guerrillas or have worn out their uniforms, but by and large the principle of "clothes make the man" applies. As does as its obverse: lack of a uniform makes an armed man a bandit, spy, or guerrilla, not a proper soldier entitled to all the protections of the laws of war, which began to be codified and intermittently observed in European warfare starting in the seventeenth century.

Since the Spanish term for "guerrilla war" had not been coined yet, the practice was referred to by its French and German equivalents: *petite guerre* and *kleine Krieg* ("small war"). Its practitioners were known as partizans. The importance of such troops, after declining for a century, began to grow again during the War of the Austrian Succession (1740–48), a multifaceted conflict pitting Austria, Britain, Hanover, Hesse, and the Dutch Netherlands against Bavaria, France, Prussia, Saxony, and Spain. Austria lost the war's early battles, allowing foreign troops to occupy a substantial portion of its territory. The Austrian comeback was spearheaded by the so-called wild men from the fringes of the empire—hussars from Hungary and Croats, pandours, and other Christians from the Balkans who had been fighting the Turks for centuries. These irregulars dealt mercilessly with small French or Prussian units in the Austrian provinces of Silesia, Bohemia, and Moravia, seldom giving quarter and sometimes even chopping off heads. Once Austria went on the offensive, these tribal marauders were at the forefront, burning villages and killing peasants. An Austrian prince described their war making as "setting fire to houses, pillaging churches, cutting off ears and eyes, murdering citizens and raping women," while a nineteenth-century author lamented that "Bavaria was overrun and almost destroyed by the terrible swarms of barbarian pandours and all the rabble of the Turkish border."[2]

Frederick the Great and other generals denounced these raiders as "savages."[3] But as soon as they saw the irregulars' effectiveness, the other rulers of Europe, Frederick among them, copied the Austrian example. Some of the newly recruited irregulars, such as the Prussian hussars or the Russian Cossacks, were drawn from lawless areas on the periphery of Europe. Others, such as the Hessian jägers or the French chasseurs, were hunters or gamekeepers skilled in the use of a rifle, which was slower to load than the smoothbore musket employed by troops of the line but more accurate. Gradually regular troops were detailed for light infantry duty to perform such tasks as screening the regulars' march, scouting, and disrupting enemy supply lines. By the 1770s light troops made up 20 percent of most European armies.[4]

In North America the British army came increasingly to rely on a new variety of light infantry known as rangers. Precursors to today's "special forces"—troops trained in guerrilla tactics and enjoying more leeway than normal infantry but still subject to greater discipline than stateless fighters—they were raised for "wood service" against French colonial troops, the *Troupes de la Marine*, and their Indian allies. The most famous were Rogers's Rangers, led by Major Robert Rogers, a strapping Scotch-Irish frontiersman from New Hampshire, a "very resolute" man "of few words" whose face bore the scars of a lifetime of combat. He had been battling, and sometimes cooperating with, Indians since the age of fourteen while growing up in a small town on what was then the edge of British settlement. Upon joining a colonial army regiment when he was twenty-four, in 1755, he was charged with scouting and similar missions. He was so successful that within a year he had been asked to raise "an independent company of Rangers" who were "well acquainted with the woods" and would, in the words of a British officer, "dress and live like the Indians."

Much of what Rogers did sounds like a *chevauchée* transported straight from the Middle Ages. When he stumbled upon a lightly defended French village, Rogers wrote, "we employed ourselves . . . in setting fire to the houses and barns in the village, with which were consumed large quantities of wheat, and other grain; we also killed about fifty cattle, and then retired, leaving the whole village in flames." Rogers was not above scalping the odd Frenchman who crossed his path, murdering a prisoner too badly wounded to walk, or even massacring an entire Indian village. In 1759 he and his rangers killed at least thirty Abenaki Indians, including women and children, in the village of Saint Francis, whose warriors were notorious for their raids into New England. Such ruthlessness earned Rogers the sobriquet "white devil" among the Indians. He later grew to be reviled by his own countrymen because he sided with Britain in the War of Independence. It was not until many years later that he became enshrined in the pantheon of American heroes.

His most lasting legacy was the twenty-eight rules "to be observed in the Ranging service" that he compiled to train his men. They included:

> If the enemy is so superior that you are in danger of being surrounded by them, let the whole body disperse, and every one take a different road to the place of rendezvous appointed for that evening. . . .
>
> [Y]ou should not attack them till the evening, as then they will not know your numbers, and if you are repulsed, your retreat will be facilitated by the darkness of the night. . . .
>
> If the enemy pursue your rear, take a circle till you come to your own tracks, and there form an ambush to receive them, and give them the first fire.

These rules have stood the test of time; they are still issued in modified form to U.S. Army Rangers today. But, as one of Rogers's biographers notes, their "simplicity" is "deceiving": "they actually could be applied only by expert woodsmen."[5]

Besides Rogers's rules, which he published in his *Journals*, light infantry tactics were discussed in general military manuals such as Marshal de Saxe's *Reveries* as well as in numerous specialized monographs. A typical example was *La petite guerre* (1756), written by a French officer who counseled, "It is therefore necessary to admit the necessity of light troops against an enemy that has them. . . . The advantage of an army with many light troops is even clearer against an army that lacks them." There were so many books on this subject that in his own *Treatise on Partisan Warfare* published in 1785, the Hessian officer Johann von Ewald conceded, "I know that I am not writing anything new."[6]

One of the cherished myths of American history is that independence from Great Britain was won by plucky Yankees armed with rifles who picked off befuddled redcoats too dense to deviate from the ritualistic parade-ground warfare of Europe. That is an exaggeration. By the time the revolution broke out, the British had had considerable experience of irregular warfare, not only in Europe with Austrian pandours and Scottish Highlanders but also in the Caribbean with Jamaican maroons and in North America with Indians and rangers. Redcoats certainly knew enough to break ranks and seek cover in battle when possible, rather than, in the words of one historian, "remaining inert and vulnerable to enemy fire."[7]

But many other lessons of frontier fighting were forgotten by the time the American Revolution broke out. Much like the U.S. Army with its post-Vietnam amnesia about counterinsurgency, which helped lead to the early disasters in Iraq, the British army was to pay a steep price for forgetting how to fight on an unconventional battlefield. The redcoats' difficulties were compounded because in the war to come they would encounter not only the kind of traditional hit-and-run tactics employed by tribesmen but also a new factor in guerrilla warfare—the power of public opinion. This new weapon was to prove even deadlier and harder to cope with than a tomahawk in the back.

14.

THE AMERICAN HORNETS

The Revolution against Britain, 1775–1783

Over the generations countless security forces have tried to prevent or abort revolts by arresting suspected ringleaders and confiscating their arms. Such operations were successful on numerous occasions in Italy, Ireland, and Poland in the eighteenth and nineteenth centuries—countries where revolutionary conspiracies against foreign occupiers were always in the works. The same might be said of the West Bank and Gaza Strip from 1967 to 1987, a period when Israeli security forces had considerable success with preemptive raids against Palestinian nationalists. In all such cases, the authorities must have calculated that "it's easier to crush evils in their infancy than when grown to maturity."

Those words were written on March 28, 1775, by General Thomas Gage, commander in chief of British North America, who faced an incipient revolt of his own. Disturbances such as the Boston Tea Party in 1773, when radicals dumped a load of English tea into Boston Bay to protest a tea tax, made that clear enough. To preserve order, Gage ordered a series of preemptive strikes whose template was established on September 1, 1774, when a column of 260 soldiers marched six miles outside Boston, confiscated 250 half barrels of gunpowder, and returned to base without a shot being fired. Yet in all such operations, no matter how successful, there is always a significant element of risk. A raid can go disastrously awry, as American Special

Operations Forces were to discover in Mogadishu in 1993 during the "Black Hawk Down" battle. The redcoats were to learn a similar if even more costly lesson on the outskirts of Boston on April 19, 1775. In the process they were to precipitate the very thing they most wanted to avoid: a full-blown revolution.

Gage hoped that day to confiscate a substantial store of munitions that, according to his spies, was to be found in the town of Concord, twenty miles north of Boston. He also wanted to arrest the notorious agitators John Hancock and Samuel Adams, who were hiding in the nearby village of Lexington. A picked force of more than eight hundred light infantrymen and grenadiers was detailed for this mission—elite troops all. Even before they set off, however, their plan had been revealed to the American radicals by informers who may have included Gage's own American-born wife. Two express riders, William Dawes and Paul Revere, galloped off beneath a bright moon on the chilly spring evening of Tuesday, April 18, to sound the alarm. Legend has it they shouted "the British are coming," but that is unlikely—as the historian David Hackett Fischer points out, they considered themselves to be British too. What they actually said was, "The Regulars are coming out!"

As those regulars marched across the countryside in the predawn darkness, they could hear an ominous clamor of church bells ringing, drums pounding, and signal guns firing. By the time the advance guard reached Lexington Common at 4:30 a.m. on Wednesday, April 19, they found a company of militia waiting for them. The two groups of armed men—240 British regulars in their red coats and white breeches, 60 or 70 local farmers in their work clothes—confronted each other in the early-morning half-light, loaded muskets in hand, just seventy yards apart.

A British officer growled, "Disperse, you damned rebels! Lay down your arms and disperse!"

The militia commander, Captain John Parker, was acutely conscious of the need to keep the moral advantage—to make the British fire the first shot. He instructed his own men, "Don't fire unless fired upon! But if they want to have a war let it begin here." Then, as the militia were beginning to disperse, someone fired a shot, perhaps by accident. The frightened and frustrated British soldiers unleashed a "roar of musketry" in response. Seventeen Lexington men fell over. Eight of them lay dead or were dying.

By the time the British column reached Concord around 8 a.m., hundreds of militiamen were converging on the area. Soon there would be thousands, including the famous "minutemen" who were supposed to be ready "at a minute's notice." The British did not think much of the fighting qualities of these "country people"—"the most absolute cowards on the face of the earth," a captain of the Fourth Regiment ("King's Own") sneered—but they were about to acquire newfound respect for these lightly regarded foes. Although not professional soldiers, many of the Massachusetts militiamen were veterans of frontier fighting against Indians, and this day they showed what they had learned.[8] In the process they would deliver a sobering lesson in the dangers of hubris for future generations of soldiers, including their own offspring who would one day police the far corners of the globe as the British were doing in the eighteenth century.

Before long the fire from the militiamen became so heavy that more than a hundred regulars were driven "in the greatest disorder and confusion" from Concord's North Bridge. Starting at noon, after a long, grueling morning, with many men already wounded, the grenadiers and light infantry began to march back to Boston along a single, narrow lane. The militia was hard upon their heels. The Americans seldom got close enough for the regulars to mow them down with disciplined volleys. Instead the farmers and tradesmen in arms moved around their flanks "in a very scattered, irregular manner," making use of hills, houses, stone walls, and fruit orchards to conceal their firing positions. A British soldier later said, "We could not see above ten in a body." The "Yankey scoundrels" slithered on their bellies like deadly vipers and picked off officers who were clearly visible because of their bright scarlet uniforms and the shiny metal gorgets around their necks. "They did not fight us like a regular army, only like savages behind trees & stone walls, and out of the woods & fields," wrote a wounded soldier. Another complained, "They would never engage us properly."

The British soldiers, "enraged at suffering from an unseen enemy," stormed into houses from which they were taking fire and "put to death all those found in them." But this did nothing to end the agony. The initial British column would have suffered "inevitable destruction," according to Lord Hugh Percy, had not a brigade of reinforcements under his command arrived in Lexington by 2 p.m. Even with two field pieces and almost 2,000 men, including the remnants of the original column, the British were hard put to get back to Boston under what many officers described as "an incessant fire all around us." They suffered 65 dead and 207 wounded or missing that day, compared with 49 Americans killed and 44 wounded or missing.

This was a vindication of the approach advocated by the self-described "very corpulent and bald-headed" militia commander, Brigadier General William Heath, who arrived to take command in the early afternoon. An amiable, well-to-do farmer and amateur strategist, he had studied books on irregular warfare as conducted in both Europe and America—"every military treatise in the English language which was obtainable." Convinced that skirmishing was the mode of fighting best suited to the New England landscape, he was determined to turn his militia into what a fellow rebel described as "Colonist Hussars."

On April 19, 1775, the day that a revolution broke out and an empire began to crumble, that strategy worked to perfection. The Battle of Lexington and Concord was a textbook example of what civilians in arms could do even against crack soldiers if they fought in the guerrilla style. Even Lord Percy was compelled to concede, "They have among amongst them men who know very well what they are about having been employed as Rangers against the Indians & Canadians, and this country being much covered with wood, and hilly, is very advantageous for their method of fighting."[9]

✦ ✦ ✦

George Washington was less impressed by the "embattled farmers" who, as Ralph Waldo Emerson was to write, had fired "the shot heard round the world."[10] Having served with British regulars in the French and Indian War, he was determined to imitate their mode of warfare. When the newly appointed general arrived in Boston on July 2, 1775, to take command at the behest of the Continental Congress—following not only the Battle of Lexington and Concord but also the Battle of Bunker Hill, where the Massachusetts militia had killed or wounded half of the attacking redcoats—he was appalled to find "provincials under very little command, discipline, or order." This aristocratic Virginian derided the militiamen as "exceeding dirty & nasty people," and lamented "an unaccountable kind of stupidity in the lower class of these people." He saw his chief role as "introducing proper discipline & subordination," and concluded, "To place any dependence upon militia, is, assuredly, resting upon a broken staff."[11]

Washington rejected the suggestions of Major General Charles Lee, the third-ranking officer in the Continental army, who advocated a *petite guerre* strategy in which small detachments of armed rebels would avoid pitched battles and harass the enemy forces until they were exhausted. Lee was a former British officer and a self-professed "eccentric" who had more than a little in common with two future visionaries of irregular warfare, Orde Wingate and T. E. Lawrence. Like them, he amused, alarmed, and alienated his fellow officers in equal measure.[12] He argued that it was a mistake for the Americans to maintain an army on the "European Plan" and that a "plan of defense, harassing, and impeding can alone succeed." Washington, on the other hand, preferred to create a disciplined army that would be able to beat the British regulars at their own game. The historian John Shy suggests that Washington and other rebel leaders "stressed a regular army . . . because they felt a need to be seen as cultivated, honorable, respectable men, not savages leading other savages in a howling wilderness."[13]

But even though the Continental army would become the mainstay of the revolution, state militias performed such vital functions as suppressing Loyalist uprisings, gathering intelligence, and impeding enemy movements.[14] On occasion they even played a leading role. And for all his antipathy to the militia, Washington was enough of a pragmatist that he was willing to take advantage of their efforts when they proved their worth.

Militiamen played an especially vital role in driving the British out of New Jersey after they had occupied the state in November–December 1776. Many of the state's 120,000 inhabitants were soon inflamed by lurid tales, spread by rebel newspapers and pamphlets, of redcoats stealing everything from looking glasses to frying pans, cutting down fruit orchards, burning houses, even "ravishing" women as young as ten and as old as seventy.[15] The militiamen began to fight back in what started as a largely spontaneous uprising. They focused their ire on small parties of British soldiers on foraging or scouting expeditions. Sir William Howe, the British commander, himself nearly fell victim to an ambush while traveling with a bodyguard of twenty cavalrymen.[16]

He responded by ordering soldiers to travel only in large convoys and threatening to hang on the spot anyone in civilian clothes caught committing an act of war. These measures' impact, or lack thereof, can be gauged by the complaint of a Hessian officer, Captain Friedrich von Muenchhausen, who wrote on December 14, 1776, "It is now very unsafe for us to travel in Jersey. The rascal peasants meet our men alone or in small unarmed groups. They have their rifles hidden in the bushes, or ditches, and the like. When they believe they are sure of success and they see one or several men belonging to our army, they shoot them in the head, then quickly hide their rifles and pretend they know nothing."[17]

Echoing the lament of counterinsurgents since ancient times, Muenchhausen added, "Everyone in our army wishes that the rebels would do us the favor to take their chances in regular battle. We would surely defeat them." But the British were to be disappointed in their desire for "regular battle." After being chased out of Long Island and Manhattan in the fall of 1776, Washington was careful not to hazard the bulk of the Continental army in a frontal battle that could have led to its annihilation. Most of the time, the redcoats were left to punch at the air, unable, in a British cabinet minister's lament, "to bring Mr. Washington to a general and decisive action."[18] Washington was pursuing a Fabian strategy of keeping his army in existence as a symbol of resistance, avoiding battle except on favorable terms, and relying on the militia, supplemented by a small stiffening of regulars, to wear down his pursuers. In New Jersey, for example, he detached 2,500 Continental soldiers to "annoy and harass" the enemy in cooperation with the militia.[19]

Their raids and ambushes made it impossible for the army of occupation to supply itself. At the end of June 1777 the redcoats were forced to pull out of New Jersey after having suffered almost three thousand casualties. Some of those losses were inflicted during Washington's surprise attacks on Trenton (December 25, 1776) and Princeton (January 3, 1777), following his celebrated crossing of the Delaware River, but many more were caused by swarms of militiamen, dubbed "American hornets" by one rebel officer, who buzzed around the redcoats' flanks.[20] The British commander Sir Henry Clinton later complained, after his forces briefly reentered New Jersey, that "the whole country was now in arms." This "most unfortunate *contretemps*," as Clinton described it,[21] made it impossible for the British to extend their authority beyond gunshot range of Newport and New York, their principal northern citadels after their evacuation of Boston.

✦ ✦ ✦

IRREGULARS WERE TO play an even more important role in the South, where the British had decided to concentrate their efforts after having all but lost the war in the North following their disastrous defeat at Saratoga in 1777. The strategy began to unfold with the capture of Savannah at the end of 1778. The focus then shifted to the Carolinas. On May 12, 1780, Charleston, the richest and largest city in the South, capitulated. It was the biggest British success of the entire war. Major cities such as Philadelphia and New York had fallen before, but their garrisons had escaped. This time, all 5,500 defenders surrendered.[22] Lord Cornwallis, the British commander, then routed the remaining Continental forces in South Carolina at the Battle of Camden on August 16.

Cornwallis has gotten a bad press from the colonialists and their descendants. But, like many other senior British commanders, including Sir Henry Clinton, Thomas Gage, Sir William Howe, and his brother, Admiral Lord Howe, Cornwallis was a liberal Whig aristocrat committed to a policy of conciliation. He was sympathetic to the rebels' complaints, convinced that most Americans remained loyal to the king, and determined to woo the colonists rather than to terrorize them into acquiescence. In an anticipation of the sort of tactics that would be advocated by British generals battling insurgencies in Malaya, Aden, Cyprus, Iraq, Afghanistan, and other countries in the late twentieth and early twenty-first centuries, he wanted to use the "gentlest methods which the nature of this business will admit of."[23] His superior, General Clinton, was of the same mindset. He blamed obstinate British officials and "overzealous loyalists" for spreading "the demon of discord" by ignoring the colonialists' legitimate complaints. He coined a famous phrase when he wrote in early 1776 of the need "to gain the hearts and subdue the minds of America,"[24] making this the first recorded use of "hearts and minds" in a counterinsurgency context. This phrase would later come to be emblematic of a certain school of "population-centric" counterinsurgency, favored particularly by liberal states such as Britain and the United States. Like later advocates of this approach, from the French field marshal Hubert Lyautey to the British field marshal Gerald Templer and the American adviser Edward Lansdale, Clinton believed that the "future peace, dignity, and happiness of both countries" depended not on iron repression but on finding a "path to reconciliation." He and his fellow generals wanted British troops to act not as conquerors but as liberators spreading the "blessings that attend British liberty."[25]

Unfortunately Clinton's and Cornwallis's admonitions against "irregularities" were ignored by their most vigorous and enterprising subordinate. The son of a wealthy Liverpool merchant and a onetime student at Oxford, Banastre Tarleton was a young rake who had squandered his inheritance on fashionable amusements in London and had no choice but to volunteer for the British army in 1775. The very next year he distinguished himself by taking part in the capture of Major General Charles Lee in a New Jersey tavern. By the time of Charleston's fall, Tarleton, still only twenty-six, was already a lieutenant colonel commanding the British Legion, a green-coated group of more than five hundred infantry and cavalry recruited primarily from recent Scottish and Irish immigrants in the northern colonies. A messenger who met the dashing cavalryman described him as being "rather below the middle height . . . with a face almost femininely beautiful . . . [and] elegance of proportion." But there was nothing soft about "Ban" Tarleton. He had earned the favor of his superiors by being "cool and intrepid in action."

Tarleton was hardly the monster depicted in Mel Gibson's 2000 movie, *The Patriot*, which has "Colonel William Tavington" burning down a church full of men, women, and children. That never happened. But the real-life Tarleton was part of a faction of British officers, known as the "fire and sword men," who believed that it was necessary to "strike terror into the inhabitants." No doubt he would have agreed with the sentiments of a British army captain who wrote, "The Natives are such a leveling, underbred, artful race of people that . . . I frequently long to shove a soup ladle down their throat." Although Tarleton did not kill women and children, he and other British troops did burn plantations, loot houses, ransack churches, slaughter livestock, kill rebels asking for quarter, and, perhaps most disturbing to white Carolinians, liberate black slaves in the hope of turning them against their masters. One resident of the backwoods complained that he had been "stripped naked" by British troops who stole "horses, cows, sheep, clothing of all sorts, money, pewter, tins, knives."[26]

Such methods, even if tame by earlier Mesopotamian or later Nazi standards, sparked a backlash among the liberty-loving residents of South Carolina, who were used to being lightly governed. Since there was no Continental army left in the state, resistance was led by loose-knit partisan units whose most notable leaders were Thomas Sumter ("the Gamecock"),[27] Francis Marion ("the Swamp Fox"), and Andrew Pickens[28] (who, sadly for his historical reputation, never acquired a memorable nickname). All were men in their forties and of some standing in their communities. Sumter was a wealthy planter and a justice of the peace, Marion a planter and a member of the provincial congress, Pickens a Presbyterian elder. All were also veterans of the Cherokee War (1759–61), when South Carolina's militia had fought a ruthless campaign against a large Indian tribe in the western part of the state. Along the way, they had learned not only regular soldiering but also the more freewheeling style employed by the Indians. They now applied those lessons in the forbidding swamps and dense forests of the South Carolina backcountry.

Marion became the most celebrated of the three. A Continental army officer recalled that he "was about forty-eight years of age, small in stature, hard in visage, healthy, abstemious, and taciturn." He dressed in simple "homespun" clothes, with a leather cap that had a silver crescent inscribed with the words "Liberty or Death." One of his men noted that "his frame was capable of enduring fatigue and every privation necessary for a partisan."

Born in 1732 to a family of French Huguenots in the South Carolina low country, he never had much education; he remained barely literate throughout his life. He began his military career as a twenty-five-year-old militiaman. In the battles against the Cherokees he revealed himself to be, in the words of his commanding officer, "an active, brave, and hardy soldier, and an excellent partisan officer." In 1775, after years as a planter, he joined a Continental regiment being raised in South Carolina. Rising through the ranks, he became its colonel and commander. His unit did not survive the British capture of Charleston, but Marion escaped the disaster while nursing a broken ankle at home. He went into hiding in the backcountry, where he organized a band of partisans to prey on British communications between Charleston and Camden.[29]

Marion's band sometimes swelled to several hundred men before shrinking again, as its members returned home to tend their crops. But even when he had just "five and twenty men" and "three or four rounds to a man,"[30] he would continue to stage lightning raids on Loyalist and British detachments, often around midnight, while carefully avoiding battle with superior forces. "I have had great fatigues, but I surmount every difficulty," Marion wrote in October 1780 to his Continental army superior, General Horatio Gates, adding proudly (note his dodgy grammar and spelling), "The Toreys are so affrighted with my little excursions that many is moving off to Georgia with their effects others are rund into swamps."[31]

The British found it impossible to get accurate intelligence on Marion's whereabouts because, as Cornwallis noted ruefully, "there was scarcely an inhabitant between the Sentee and Pedee [Rivers] that was not in arms against us."[32] Marion was also careful to elude the redcoats; he advised his men "not to sleep in any house or stay above an hour at any plantation."[33] After one fruitless foray in pursuit, Banastre Tarleton was said to have exclaimed, "Come, my boys! Let us go back, and we will find the Gamecock. But as for this damned old fox, the devil himself could not catch him." This was later modified into "Swamp Fox," apparently by Parson Weems, the prolific mythologizer who invented the tale of Washington's chopping down a cherry tree and who also wrote a biography of Marion.[34]

Marion's favorite hideout was on Snow's Island, at the confluence of the Pee Dee River and Lynch's Creek. Amid the Spanish moss and oak and pine groves, he and his followers built crude huts to protect themselves against wind and rain and storage bins to hold their scanty provisions. "They slept in the open air, according to their means, either with or without a blanket," wrote a member of the band. "They had nothing but water to drink. They fed chiefly upon sweet potatoes, either with or without fresh beef. And they submitted to this without a murmur; but all sighed for salt! for salt! That first article of necessity for the human race." Marion won his men's gratitude by distributing the coveted condiment when he had some available. A British column managed to capture Snow's Island in March 1781, but it made little difference. Marion and most of his men were gone at the time, and they could always pitch camp elsewhere; unlike a regular army, they did not have permanent bases or supply depots they had to defend.[35]

Washington realized that while these irregulars could make life miserable for the British, they could not by themselves liberate the state. Therefore he replaced Horatio Gates, the failed head of the Continental army's Southern Department (and a rumored rival for his own position), with Nathanael Greene, a lapsed Quaker from Rhode Island who had started the war as a self-taught militiaman but had swiftly risen to become one of Washington's most trusted generals. Major General Greene's job was to rebuild the battered Continental force in North Carolina and lead it into South Carolina. Greene found, he wrote, "but the shadow of an army without clothing, tents, and provisions." Realizing that "we have it not in our power to attempt any thing . . . but some little partizan strokes," he split his regular forces and ordered them to operate with militia units to "keep up a partizan war" on a slightly larger scale than before.[36] Marion, by now a brigadier general, was paired with a Continental cavalry regiment under Lieutenant Colonel "Light-Horse" Harry Lee of Virginia, who would father the future Confederate general Robert E. Lee.

The Americans continued to fare poorly in conventional encounters with British forces. They won the Battles of King's Mountain (October 7, 1780) and Cowpens (January 17, 1781), but they lost at Guilford Courthouse (March 15, 1781), Hobkirk Hill (April 25, 1781), and Eutaw Springs (September 8, 1781). Whatever the outcome, however, the British suffered heavy casualties, and the Americans survived to fight another day. Greene, a canny strategist, summed up his philosophy when he said, "We fight, get beat, rise, and fight again."[37] Because the Americans were able to make up their losses more easily than the British (more Carolinians were willing to fight for the rebels than for the royalists), they got the better of this war of attrition.

By the spring of 1781, Cornwallis despaired of winning in South Carolina. Complaining that "the perpetual risings in different parts of this province . . . keep the whole country in continual alarm,"[38] he shifted the bulk of his force first to North Carolina and then to Virginia, where he entrenched at Yorktown on the Chesapeake coast. The surrender of this redoubt to a Franco-American army on October 19, 1781, after the French navy had prevented resupply from the sea, would mark the effective end of the Revolutionary War. While the final victory was won by regular troops, their triumph would not have been possible without the efforts of the bedraggled South Carolina irregulars who tied down and slowly bled Cornwallis's army at a time when its success in the South seemed assured. A recent history of the revolutionary struggle concludes that this "was where the war was won."[39]

✦ ✦ ✦

WHAT GETS OVERLOOKED in most accounts of the American Revolution is that even after Yorktown the British could have continued fighting. They had lost only eight thousand men. Their remaining troops in North America, more than thirty-four thousand strong, still outnumbered the combined Franco-American forces, and more could always have been raised from a British population of twelve million or purchased from the German states that had already provided so much manpower.[40] If the Americans had been resisting the Roman Empire, there is little doubt that a fresh army would have been raised and George Washington and other leading insurgents would have been crucified. But such a response was unthinkable, given the state of British "public opinion"—a phrase that first saw print in Gibbon's *Decline and Fall*, the first volume of which appeared, by a fateful coincidence, in 1776.[41] This was a new and hugely important development in the long history of guerrilla warfare: a parliamentary government could not prosecute a war that did not enjoy popular backing. Insurgents' ability to manipulate popular sentiment—to break the enemy's will to resist—helped to offset some of the advantages enjoyed by an incumbent regime and gave them a greater chance of success. Public opinion would play an even larger role in future wars as Britain and the United States, which still restricted the franchise in the eighteenth century, became more democratic and as similar political systems spread around the world. Future insurgents, from nineteenth-century Greece to twenty-first-century Lebanon, would make full use of this potent new weapon wielded so expertly by the American rebels.

Initially the British people had supported the effort to suppress the American Revolution. A contemporary memoirist wrote that there "does not perhaps occur in the annals of Britain a single instance of a war more popular at its commencement."[42] But from the start there had been a substantial undercurrent of opposition. The Whig party, whose ranks included such eloquent spokesmen as Edmund Burke and Charles James Fox, had argued for a policy of conciliation rather than confrontation. Many of these Whigs saw the Americans' struggle as a continuation of their own efforts to limit overweening royal power. Speaking on the floor of the House of Commons in 1775, one member of Parliament called the war "a butchery of his fellow subjects, to which his conscience forbad him to give his consent."[43] The antiwar ranks included prominent military men such as Vice Admiral Augustus Keppel and Lieutenant General Sir Jeffrey Amherst, who made clear that they would not fight their "American brethren."[44] They had the support of most major newspapers, such as the *Evening Post*, which called the war "unnatural, unconstitutional, unnecessary, unjust, dangerous, hazardous, and unprofitable."[45]

The rebels skillfully and shamelessly played on this sentiment. As early as 1772 the Boston radicals Samuel Adams and Joseph Warren had started a Committee of Correspondence to plead their case, an example that was emulated throughout the colonies.[46] After every major event, the revolutionaries raced to get out their version of events. An American account of the Battle of Lexington and Concord, addressed to the "Inhabitants of Great Britain," reached London two full weeks before the official dispatches.[47] The Declaration of Independence, written out of "a decent respect to the opinions of mankind," was a supremely successful weapon in this propaganda struggle. It was reprinted verbatim in every major British newspaper.[48] Just as effective was Thomas Paine's best-selling pamphlet *Common Sense* (1776), which was widely read not only in America but also in Britain and France. Benjamin Franklin was another successful propagandist. His work in Paris starting in December 1776, which included numerous letters and essays in *Affaires de l'Angleterre et de l'Amérique*, a newspaper covertly financed by the French government, helped to win the rebels their most important foreign ally.[49]

The Tory prime minister, Lord North, tried to get out his side of the story through the official government mouthpiece, the *London Gazette*. He even gave secret subsidies to a popular scandal sheet, the *Morning Post*, thereby converting it from a critic to a supporter of the war effort.[50] Initially the government line—that the revolutionaries had "been compelled to take up arms against their sovereign & country under false pretenses"[51] and would soon be defeated—was accepted by many, perhaps most, in Britain and North America. But as the war dragged on, with few victories and many casualties, support sagged. The British defeat at Saratoga in 1777 caused a spike in opposition, with the London *Gazetteer* describing America as the "Grave of Englishmen" and writing that it would now be "national suicide" to continue the war. After Yorktown the cries of "enough of war," "enough of slaughter" became deafening. "Everybody seems really sick of carrying on ye American war," wrote one parliamentarian in late 1781.[52]

On February 28, 1782, Parliament voted by a narrow margin, 234 to 215, to discontinue offensive operations. After this stinging rebuke, Lord North had no choice but to resign. He was replaced by a Whig government led by Lord Rockingham, which was committed to peace even at the price of independence. The war finally ended with the signing of the Treaty of Paris in 1783.

✦ ✦ ✦

BESIDES HIGHLIGHTING THE newfound importance of the struggle for "hearts and minds," the American success in winning independence from the world's most powerful empire offers a number of other lessons about the nature of guerrilla warfare.

It demonstrates, first of all, the heavy toll of taking on a superpower. Revolutionary forces lost an estimated 25,674 dead, with disease being the biggest killer. (The British lost even more men—43,000 in all, including naval losses fighting the French, but many of the dead were German mercenaries.) Considering that the population of the thirteen colonies in 1776 was only 2.5 million people, this represents a loss of 1 percent of the entire population, making the Revolutionary War the second-costliest war in American history on a per capita basis, behind only the Civil War, in which 1.6 percent of the population perished.[53] The American patriots, like most other successful insurgents, needed extraordinary willpower to prevail despite such heavy losses.

Even with all the willpower in the world, however, victory would not have been possible, at least not in the early 1780s, without French backing. The war's second major lesson is the importance of such outside support.

The turning point was the American victory at Saratoga, because it persuaded King Louis XVI to enter the conflict. His support made all the difference: first because French supplies did so much to bolster the Continental army (they accounted for 90 percent of all American gunpowder),[54] then because the danger of French attacks on the British Isles and other parts of the empire prevented Britain from concentrating all of its forces in North America, and finally because a French fleet defeated the Royal Navy off the Virginia coast, thereby isolating the British field army at Yorktown.

Third, the outcome of the American war demonstrated the importance of partisans operating in close conjunction with a regular army. If the Americans had lacked an army, they might have been no more successful than the Irish rebels who rose up in 1798 and were put down by Cornwallis. As Nathanael Greene noted, "You may strike a hundred [partizan] strokes, and reap little benefit from them, unless you have a good army to take advantage of your success."[55] But without a guerrilla force to harry them, the British could have concentrated all their resources on crushing the Continental army, and the Americans might have been no more successful than the Scottish rebels who rose up in 1745. As it was, the Americans were able to land a one-two punch, with the irregulars weakening the army of occupation until a conventional force could administer the coup de grâce. This method of fighting—dubbed "hybrid warfare" by twenty-first-century strategists—has usually been the surest road to success for an insurgency.[56]

A fourth lesson is the need for counterinsurgents to have a suitable strategy and unity of command to execute it. The British suffered from terminal confusion as to ends and means, with cabinet officers in London and general officers in North America pushing competing, often incompatible, visions. Was the British goal to terrorize the Americans into restoring the status quo ante? Or was it to reach a liberal accommodation that would maintain only the most tenuous links between the metropolis and the colonies? Conciliatory officers such as Cornwallis issued lenient orders based on the latter assumption, but those orders were often ignored by hard-line subordinates such as Tarleton who operated under the former assumption. The result was a counterproductive muddle. British forces were harsh enough to alienate the Americans but not terrifying enough to bring them to heel.[57]

This failure was closely related to another: the inability or unwillingness to send enough troops to pacify 2.5 million Americans spread over more than twelve hundred miles of the Eastern Seaboard. The need for adequate resources to fight an insurgency constitutes the war's fifth major lesson. Britain began the war with only 8,500 soldiers in North America, a figure that briefly swelled to 50,000 in 1778 before falling again to 30,000–35,000 for the remainder of the conflict.[58] British commanders had only enough men to garrison a few enclaves along the coast (Savannah, Charleston, New York, Newport), where they could be resupplied by the Royal Navy. The vast interior was always beyond their grasp. They hoped that native allies would hem in the Americans, but the Indians got the worst of this savage struggle. Nor did enough Tories sign up for the struggle against their American compatriots. The British compounded their difficulties with questionable troop deployments—for instance, leaving 15,000 men in New York during the southern campaign. A U.S. Marine Corps officer who has studied the campaign suggests that New York could have been defended with a force a third the size, while the rest should have been sent to reinforce the 8,500 redcoats in the South.[59]

But none of these failings need have proven fatal if the British public had retained the desire to continue fighting, no matter the cost. The average American today probably thinks that the Vietnam War was the first time that a counterinsurgency was fatally undermined on the home front. A citizen of France would probably cite the Algerian War. But the American War of Independence long predated either conflict, and it was effectively decided not at Yorktown, as most historians would have it, but in Westminster. The battlefield success of George Washington's soldiers was not irrelevant, but neither was it decisive. Public opinion in Britain was. This was a lesson that future generations of guerrillas could study and apply.

15.

WAR TO THE KNIFE

The Peninsular War, 1808–1814

THE AGE OF ideological struggles ushered in by the American Revolution would cast aside the limitations on warfare created in the century after the 1648 Peace of Westphalia. Few counterinsurgents would display the kind of restraint shown by the British in North America. Even the British themselves would show less restraint in repressing uprisings in Ireland in 1798 and India in 1857. But then the Irish and Indians were not "Englishmen."

A more savage approach to counterinsurgency was displayed by the French revolutionary regime that took power in a popular revolt and that by 1793–94 was under the control of the radical Jacobins of the Committee of Public Safety, led by the pitiless Maximilien de Robespierre. Their growing tyranny sparked uprisings in Bordeaux, Brittany, Lyon, Marseilles, Toulon, and other areas. The republican regime responded with the kind of scorched-earth tactics practiced in ancient times by Akkad and Assyria and in the modern day by Nazi Germany, Baathist Iraq, and the Soviet Union. Such policies can succeed but only if the insurgents are devoid of outside support and if the counterinsurgents have some degree of popular legitimacy, if they can muster overwhelming force, and if they are willing to engage in mass murder on a scale that would be intolerable to a more liberal regime. The Jacobins succeeded in establishing their control because revolutionary France met all these conditions.

More than 16,000 "enemies of the revolution" were formally executed during the Reign of Terror in 1793–94; many more perished without any judicial proceeding at all. The repression of the Vendée in western France, where the makeshift Catholic and Royal Army arose to challenge the revolution, was particularly brutal. A republican general reported in 1793, "I crushed the children beneath the horses' hooves, massacred the women who . . . will bear no more brigands. I have not a single prisoner to reproach myself with. I exterminated them all." Almost 250,000 people, more than a third of the Vendéans, were killed before the revolution's "infernal columns" were finally disbanded in May 1794. The Catholic and Royal Army might have had more success in fighting back if it had received arms and other supplies from Britain or other powers, but no such support was forthcoming.[60]

There were also uprisings in parts of Europe conquered by the French, including Calabria, the southernmost portion of Italy,[61] and the Tyrol, an Alpine region that had been under Austrian control.[62] The rebels in all these cases were not radicals like the American or French revolutionaries. They were conservative peasants like the Vendéans who wanted nothing to do with Napoleon's social engineering. In putting down these revolts, the French army was helped by the fact that they were much more confined, geographically and demographically, and much closer to home than the uprising the British had faced in North America. Moreover, like the Vendéans but unlike the Americans, none of these rebel groups received any meaningful external aid.

Although willing to be just as brutal in Spain, the French would find that they simply lacked the resources to be equally successful when faced with an uprising that was much larger and that received much more external aid. Scale matters in guerrilla warfare: what works in a single isolated region may not work across an entire country.

✦ ✦ ✦

EMBLEMATIC OF THE relentlessly conventional and bloody-minded French approach to counterinsurgency was the assault on Zaragoza, known to the English-speaking world as Saragossa, in northern Spain. The bombardment began on the night of July 31–August 1, 1808, and grew worse by the day. Sixty French guns belched shot night and day. "The firing was infernal," wrote an early Spanish historian, "no idea can be formed of it." Among the structures severely damaged was the hospital that housed the mentally as well as the physically ill. Many were still confined in their cells as masonry and splinters began to fly. Their voices "raving or singing in paroxysms of wilder madness, or crying in vain to be set free, were heard amid the confusion of dreadful sounds." Some lunatics escaped and capered past burning buildings, singing and laughing, even dancing on corpses. Other patients who tried to get away were literally blown to bits. Their body parts littered the streets along with reddened bandages and crutches. "Hell opened its gates that day," said a witness.

By the afternoon of August 4, the artillery had blasted a hole nearly three hundred yards wide in the city wall, and thousands of infantrymen in their blue coats, white breeches, and black shako hats prepared to pour through the breach. Surely now, the French commanders must have reasoned, they would finally eliminate this troublesome obstacle and its fanatical defenders.

In truth, Zaragoza should have fallen much sooner. This city of 60,000 people was garrisoned by just 1,500 Spanish troops. Its adobe walls were old and decrepit. Under the rules of "civilized warfare," it should have surrendered with no more than a perfunctory resistance. But on June 15, 1808, the initial French assault had been bloodily repulsed—not by the Spanish troops but by the Spanish people. "Foaming with rage," the people grabbed knives, sticks, hatchets, scissors, old blunderbusses, whatever was at hand, and rushed to the barricades. A squadron of Polish lancers, pennants flying, advanced into the city only to be picked off by concealed sniper fire and pelted by stones tossed from rooftops and balconies. They were finished off by the assaults of ordinary residents who pulled the riders off their horses and bludgeoned them to death.

Nominally the defenders were under the command of José de Palafox, an aristocratic army officer. He was "a perfectly well-bred man," but he had an unfortunate habit of leaving the city on one pretext or another when the fighting was at its heaviest. No matter. The workers, peasants, craftsmen, and priests carried on by themselves under their own elected leaders.

Even the women joined in, rushing supplies to the fighters and succoring the wounded. On July 2 a dark-haired young woman with a "mild and feminine countenance" witnessed French fire kill all of the gunners manning a battery of antiquated cannons at one of the city gates. French troops with fixed bayonets were only moments away from streaming into the city. Before that could happen, Agustina Zaragoza rushed through the smoke and scorching heat, grabbed a still-smoldering linstock from one of the dead gunners (said to be her lover), and fired the cannon at point-blank range. The densely packed assault force crumpled before her grapeshot. "The Maid of Zaragoza" became an army lieutenant and a legend celebrated by Lord Byron, among others. Her example inspired Zaragoza's residents to fight with what a French officer described as "incredible fury." So incredible that, as the attackers discovered, resistance would not crumble even after an unrelenting, three-day artillery barrage.

On August 4, after an all-out offensive had begun, the French commander, General Jean-Antoine Verdier, who had already been wounded by a musket ball, sent a message under a flag of truce demanding "peace and capitulation." A pointed answer came back: "War even to the knife."

One of Napoleon's Polish officers who took part in a subsequent assault on Zaragoza left a vivid description of what "war to the knife" looked like in the narrow, winding lanes of the city. He could just as easily have been describing the experiences of Romans in first-century Jerusalem, Germans in twentieth-century Warsaw, or Americans in twenty-first-century Fallujah:

> The more we advanced the more dogged resistance became. We knew that in order not to be killed . . . we would have to take each and every one of these houses converted into redoubts and where death lurked in the cellars, behind doors and shutters—in fact, everywhere. . . . Often as we were securing one floor we would be shot at from point blank range from the floor above through loopholes in the floorboards. All the nooks and crannies of these old-fashioned houses aided such deadly ambushes. We also had to maintain a good watch on the rooftops. With their light sandals, the Aragonese could move with the ease of and as silently as a cat and were thus able to make surprise incursions well behind the front line. It was indeed aerial combat. We would be sitting

> peacefully around a fire, in a house occupied for some days, when suddenly shots would come through some window just as though they had come from the sky itself. . . .
>
> Sometimes we would burst into a house . . . [t]hen suddenly there would be an explosion and the whole obstacle would tumble down like a pack of cards. . . . Even when they were at last forced to abandon a building, they would scatter resin soaked faggots everywhere and set them alight. The ensuing fires would not destroy the stone buildings but served to give the besieged time to prepare their defenses in neighboring houses.

Suddenly on the morning of August 14, 1808, all was quiet—as quiet as a cemetery. The French troops had disappeared after having lost 3,500 killed and wounded out of a total force of 15,000 men. They had no choice but to withdraw because of the devastating defeat a French corps had suffered in the province of Andalusia: 17,000 troops had been captured and 2,000 killed or wounded in a battle with Spanish regulars at Bailén on July 19. Almost all the French troops in Spain, including those besieging Zaragoza, were removed to defensive positions in the northernmost part of the country.[63]

✦ ✦ ✦

By then it was hard to believe how smoothly the initial French invasion had gone—as smoothly in its own way as the future German occupation of Yugoslavia, the Russian occupation of Afghanistan, and the American occupation of Iraq, all of which were destined to become notable guerrilla battlegrounds. French armies had first entered Spain the preceding autumn, on October 18, 1807, following a deal between Napoleon and the Spanish prime minister to allow French troops free passage to attack Portugal. Napoleon's secretary called it "an armed promenade and not a war."[64] Things began to go awry after Napoleon deposed the ruling Bourbon royal family and installed his older brother, Joseph, on the throne. On May 2, 1808, a spontaneous rebellion broke out in Madrid. Shouting, "Death to the French," residents armed with clubs and scissors and blunderbusses attacked the army of occupation. The uprising was quelled within hours by 30,000 French troops who wheeled cannons into the streets and killed perhaps 400 Spaniards. But tales of the *Dos de Mayo*, immortalized by court painter Francisco de Goya, resonated across the Peninsula and sparked a more general uprising that included the successful defense of Zaragoza.[65]

Having almost been pushed off the Peninsula, Napoleon set out to retrieve his fortunes with a series of lightning thrusts employing 250,000 veterans from his *grande armée* hastily redeployed from central Europe. Leading his soldiers in person, the emperor routed all opposition in just four weeks and entered Madrid on December 4, 1808. Even Zaragoza, that heroic citadel, finally fell on February 20, 1809, after a second siege involving 45,000 soldiers. Portugal still held out with British help, but most of Iberia appeared to be firmly in the emperor's grasp. His success seemed to vindicate his boast to Joseph: "I shall find in Spain the Pillars of Hercules, but not the limits of my power."[66] (The Pillars of Hercules is the ancient name for the promontories on either side of the Strait of Gibraltar.)

Those limits, however, became apparent when the Spanish did not stop fighting. With their regular army defeated, the Spanish turned to a people's resistance that would give rise to the word "guerrilla." The first recorded use of the term (also spelled "guerilla") dates to 1611, when it referred to "a quarrel between private citizens . . . that causes them to split into rival bands." Its use to refer to a form of warfare dates from the eighteenth century. Originally "guerrilla" referred to the war as a whole ("They are taking part in a guerrilla . . ."). Its practitioners were known as *guerrilleros* or *partidas de guerrilla* (guerrilla bands), and they would come to the forefront in Spain in 1809.[67]

Although some Spaniards, primarily from the upper classes, were willing to collaborate with Joseph's regime (they were known derisively as the *afrancesados*, "the Frenchified"), the majority were not. A revolutionary government called the Central Junta, or council, took refuge in the southwestern city of Seville while local juntas arose in the provinces. In 1810, following the French capture of Seville, the junta was replaced by a parliament, or Cortes, in the peninsular stronghold of Cadiz. This regime, ruling in the name of King Ferdinand VII (who was in captivity in France), issued decrees calling for popular resistance against "these ferocious animals . . . this damnable race of monsters."[68] Spanish clerics did their best to transform the insurgency into a holy war against the French, whom they accused "of being Jews, heretics, sorcerers." In their eyes, Napoleon was the Antichrist, his generals were "Satan's emissaries," and heaven was to be attained by killing their minions.[69] Popular legitimacy, so important in any revolutionary struggle, lay on the side of the insurgents.

The British helped by sending everything from cash to shirts, shoes, and camp kettles. In the uprising's first six months alone, they provided 160,000 muskets, with more to come.[70] Their bases in Portugal and Gibraltar gave the British beachheads from which they could resupply Spanish forces and conduct amphibious raids against the French.

As in the wars waged by Viriathus and Sertorius against the Romans almost two millennia before, the difficult topography of the Iberian Peninsula, with its many mountains and ravines, also aided the revolt. "No country in the world is more favorable to partisan warfare than Spain," wrote a French officer.[71]

✦ ✦ ✦

THE GUERRILLA BANDS operated with little if any central direction under the leadership of charismatic captains who became known by such evocative aliases as El Empecinado (the Rustic), El Mozo (the Lad), and El Caracol (the Snail). The most successful of all was Francisco Espoz y Mina, who would come to dominate the Basque-speaking province of Navarre, adjacent to France.

He initially joined the uprising in 1809 as part of a small band organized by his nephew, Martin Javier Mina y Larrea, an eighteen-year-old seminary student. In 1810 the French captured Javier Mina. His command dispersed, but its banner was picked up by Francisco Espoz Illundain, the twenty-nine-year-old son of a wealthy peasant who renamed himself Francisco Espoz y Mina to establish his legitimacy to succeed his captured nephew. Because initially he had just six followers, his immediate goal was to take over larger *partidas* that had broken away. Within a few months he commanded more men than his nephew ever had.

This was a stunning testament to the leadership qualities of this country bumpkin—described as "a man of average, slightly blond looks, well-built, about five foot one inch in height, and of few but direct words"—who could neither read nor write Spanish and barely learned to spell his own name. He made up for this deficiency with a surplus of cunning, bravery, and bluff. On one occasion he was surprised alone by a French cavalry detachment. As the French were breaking through the door of his lodgings, he boldly shouted, "Lancers, to the rear! Cavalry sergeant, take the first squadron to the left!" Thinking that Espoz y Mina had a substantial force, the French backed off just long enough for him to escape.

By 1812, having survived numerous setbacks, Espoz y Mina commanded thirteen thousand men in the Division of Navarre. He took over the customs posts in Navarre, making his division largely self-financing; created covert factories to manufacture uniforms and weapons; and ran his own hospitals and even his own court system. Thus Espoz y Mina became the "little king" of Navarre as well as part of neighboring Aragon.

The French were driven out of Navarre's countryside and blockaded for twenty-two months inside Pamplona, the provincial capital, where they slowly starved under the watchful eyes of Mina's pickets. To enforce the blockade, the *guerrilleros* did not hesitate to hang a lemon seller who sought to do business with the occupiers. French attempts to venture out in search of provisions resulted in heavy losses. In 1812 alone the Division of Navarre killed 5,500 French troops. By the following year Espoz y Mina was stronger still, using artillery landed by the British to take the remaining French strongholds.[72]

✦ ✦ ✦

THE NECESSITY OF dealing with such "invisible armies," which by 1811 numbered more than 50,000 men across the entire country, siphoned off valuable French forces that could have been used to crush 80,000 British and Portuguese regulars. The French kept more than 350,000 men in Iberia between 1810 and 1812. Most were detailed for antiguerrilla duty. Seventy thousand troops alone were required to maintain communications between Madrid and the French border. Thus the French were never able to assemble more than 60,000 men for a single battle, allowing the allied commander, the duke of Wellington, to fight on roughly equal terms.[73]

Unable to post troops everywhere, the occupiers fanned out from a few large garrisons in futile forays that could seldom pin down the elusive insurgents. Marshal Louis-Gabriel Suchet complained, "On the approach of our troops, these bands withdrew without fighting, so that they made their appearance at every spot we did not occupy, and offered no opportunity for making a serious attack upon them in any position."[74] The result, as a lower-ranking French officer confessed, was that "we always managed to harass the enemy but never to destroy him completely."[75]

The inherent difficulties of conducting counterinsurgency in a nation of eleven million people were compounded by the inefficient French command structure and a muddled strategy reminiscent of British difficulties in the American Revolution. Although Joseph Bonaparte was nominally king of Spain, real authority rested with various marshals who oversaw military governments in the provinces and reported directly to Napoleon. The northern Spanish provinces were even annexed to France, leaving Joseph with no real responsibility beyond Madrid and its environs. His younger brother, the emperor, did not appoint any other official to oversee a countrywide pacification campaign. As a result there was little practical coordination between different French armies. The situation grew so bad that rebels could often escape pursuit by heading into a neighboring province.[76]

To compound his woes, Napoleon made scant attempt to win over the population. He never provided an incentive for Spaniards to side with France, consistently undercutting Joseph's attempts to conciliate the population by the promulgation of a liberal constitution and the construction of schools and hospitals. The habitual murder of civilians and prisoners by the imperial forces, and their widespread looting and raping, cost them many potential friends. A French cavalryman, in a plaint echoed by counterinsurgents ranging from the Assyrians to the Nazis, lamented that "violent measures, far from keeping down the inhabitants, only sharpened their hatred of the French, and, what always happens in a country where there is patriotism, violent measures led to reprisals still more violent. Squadrons, entire battalions, were annihilated by the peasants in the course of a night."[77]

The French lost further ground in 1812 when troop levels in Spain fell to 250,000 as Napoleon siphoned off men for his ill-fated invasion of Russia. In Russia, too, he encountered partisans operating in conjunction with regular forces, but they never attained the same size or importance.[78]

Once the forces opposing him had been depleted, Wellington was able to surge out of his stronghold in Portugal and win a series of victories culminating in the capture of Madrid on August 12, 1812. His offensive stalled out in the fall of 1812, forcing the British to retreat temporarily, but Wellington marched deep into Spain again in 1813—this time to stay. Thanks in part to the aid he received from the Spanish irregulars, whose "boldness and activity are increasing [he wrote] and [whose] operations against the enemy are becoming daily more important,"[79] he inflicted a final crushing defeat on the French at Vitoria on June 21, 1813. Espoz y Mina alone claimed to have diverted 28,000 French troops who might otherwise have faced Wellington.[80] That fall the British crossed France's southern frontier while Austrian, Prussian, and Russian armies marched from the east. Napoleon abdicated on April 12, 1814, thereby ending, at least for the time being, the greatest war the world had yet known.

✦ ✦ ✦

ON A FAR bigger scale than the American Revolution, the Peninsular War showed how regular and irregular forces could work together, making it impossible for a powerful army of occupation to focus on either threat. In North America the regulars did the bulk of the fighting. In Spain it was the irregulars. Their activities accounted for the majority of the casualties suffered by the French during six years of war. (As many as 180,000 French soldiers perished.)[81] Few would dispute the conclusion of Suchet, one of Napoleon's best field marshals, that the *guerrilleros* "defended the country in a far more effectual manner than the regular war carried on by disciplined armies."[82]

While Spaniards could take pride in their contribution to Napoleon's downfall, the cost was considerable. "All authority has been annihilated in Spain," Wellington wrote at the end of 1813.[83] Many of the men who had spent years fighting the French would not go back voluntarily to being poor and powerless once the war was over. Some continued to prey on the population as outlaws. Others, including Espoz y Mina, fought against the restoration of Bourbon absolutism. The well-known guerrilla leader El Empecinado (Juan Martin Díaz) would be hanged by King Ferdinand VII, while Espoz y Mina would seek refuge in, of all places, France.

With central authority virtually nonexistent, Spain was plagued by decades of banditry and political turmoil. From the 1820s to the 1870s, the country was torn apart by civil wars pitting urban liberals against rural conservatives. Since the liberals ruled in Madrid, the conservatives, or Carlists, resorted to guerrilla warfare. This struggle culminated well over a century later in the Spanish Civil War of 1936–39. Such rending of the social fabric occurs in most prolonged insurgencies, and it was precisely why a landed gentleman such as George Washington had recoiled from employing this method of resistance on his native soil. Robert E. Lee, another southern aristocrat, would refuse for similar reasons to wage guerrilla resistance in 1865 after the surrender of the Confederate army at Appomattox.

✦ ✦ ✦

"THE PENINSULAR WAR should be carefully studied, to learn all the obstacles which a general and his brave troops may encounter in the occupation or conquest of a country whose people are all in arms." So wrote the Swiss soldier Antoine-Henri de Jomini in his classic text, *Summary of the Art of War* (1838). He knew whereof he spoke. Having served with the French army in Spain and Russia, he wrote with great feeling about the difficulties of an invader who "holds scarcely any ground but that upon which he encamps; outside the limits of his camp every thing is hostile and multiplies a thousandfold the difficulties he meets at every step." But while convinced of the efficacy of people's war, he was aghast at its "terrible" consequences. "As a soldier," he preferred "loyal and chivalrous warfare to organized assassination."[84]

The only military theorist whose fame outstripped Jomini's also described the consequences of "arming the nation" in a small section of a larger work devoted to conventional conflict. In *On War* (1832), the Prussian general Carl von Clausewitz wrote of popular resistance: "Like a slow, gradual fire, it destroys the foundation of the enemy's army." Like Jomini, Clausewitz thought that "people's war" was more novel than it actually was because it represented a departure from the "artificial" warfare of the eighteenth century. But, unlike Jomini, Clausewitz did not shy away from embracing what he erroneously labeled "a phenomenon of the nineteenth century."

"However small and weak a state may be in comparison with its enemy," he wrote, "if it forgoes a last supreme effort, we must say that there is no longer any soul left in it."[85]

During the French Revolutionary and Napoleonic Wars, the Vendée, Calabria, Tyrol, and Spain, among others, all revealed no shortage of "soul." But no nation made a more "supreme effort" to resist French rule than its prize overseas colony. The insurgency in Haiti was the very embodiment of the sort of conflict that Jomini deplored: "wars of extermination."[86] Hard as it may be to believe, on this Caribbean island the French matched and possibly exceeded the savagery they had displayed in the Vendée—but without attaining similar success.

16.

BLACK SPARTACUS

The Haitian War of Independence, 1791–1804

IT BEGAN ON the Noé plantation on the night of August 22, 1791. A dozen or so slaves went to the sugar refinery, seized a young white apprentice, and hacked him to pieces with cutlasses. "His screams," recounted the planter Bryan Edwards, "brought out the overseer whom they instantly shot. The rebels now found their way to the apartment of the refiner, and massacred him in his bed."

Similar outbreaks were occurring at the same time on most of the other plantations spread across the northern plains of Saint-Domingue, as Haiti was then known. Amid the general scenes of horror, a few gory details stood out in the colonists' lurid, and most likely exaggerated, account, which was compiled to galvanize their countrymen back home into coming to their rescue. A carpenter supposedly was seized, bound between two planks, and sawed in half. A policeman supposedly was nailed alive to the gate of a plantation and had his limbs chopped off one by one with an ax. Women and girls supposedly were gang-raped on the still-warm corpses of their husbands, brothers, fathers. Some of the rebels were said to have employed as their emblem the body of a white infant impaled on a stake. "The sword was then exchanged for the torch," related a group of colonists in an appeal for help, "fire was set to the canes, and the buildings soon added to the conflagration. It was the appointed signal; revolt was the word and with the speed of lightning it flamed out on the neighboring plantations."

Whatever the literal truth of these stories, reminiscent of the embellished tales spread by the British in the 1950s to build support for the suppression of the Mau Mau uprising in Kenya, there is no doubt that the slave revolt spread panic among the whites. Nor is there any doubt that this was not a spontaneous outbreak. It had been planned eight days before in a nighttime voodoo ceremony held under a rainy sky in Bois Cayman (Alligator Wood). The participants were the leading slaves from many of the northern plantations—those who exercised some authority over their fellow slaves and enjoyed some autonomy from their masters. Led by a coachman named Boukman, who moonlighted as a voodoo priest, they slaughtered a black pig and drank its blood as they sealed a solemn compact to seek "vengeance" on the *blancs* (whites).

They had much to seek vengeance for. Saint-Domingue was France's wealthiest colony. Its sugar, coffee, cotton, indigo, and cocoa plantations accounted for more than a third of France's foreign trade, 40 percent of Europe's sugar consumption, and 60 percent of its coffee. The elite class of white planters, amounting to a small portion of the forty thousand Europeans, lived a life that was described by a visitor as "imperious and voluptuous." They became devotees of "all the arts of indulgence," with their every whim catered to by legions of slave servants. One of the indulgences of which they freely availed themselves was the sexual exploitation of their female slaves. The result was the creation of a class of thirty thousand mixed-race mulattos who were not slaves but did not enjoy the full liberties of whites either. They became increasingly resentful and ripe for revolt—almost as bitter as the blacks who were literally being worked to death in the fields. Most of them were recently wrenched from Africa and not used to servitude. To keep them in check, they were frequently whipped, with hot pepper, lemon, or salt rubbed in the wounds. More exotic and gruesome punishments were also meted out: some had gunpowder stuffed up the rectum and exploded; others were immersed in boiling sugarcane juice.

On the morning of August 23, 1791, the horrified *blancs* of Cap-Français, the major town of the north, reaped the whirlwind as they watched "a wall of fire" move across the horizon—turning, in the words of Bryan Edwards, "the most fertile and beautiful plains in the world . . . into one vast field of carnage—a wilderness of desolation." More than a thousand plantations were reduced to ashes and more than two thousand whites killed.

In "consternation and terror," the populace of Le Cap, as Cap-Français was called, sent out soldiers to skirmish against the rebels—the "unchained tigers," some of them naked, "some in tatters, and some grotesquely decked," wrote one colonist, "in the rich apparel taken from our wardrobes." They made a "hideous din" by "shrieking" and "beating cauldrons," and they were armed mainly with "guns, knives, sticks, and all the sharp utensils of kitchen and of farm"—hardly a formidable arsenal. But many of the blacks were veterans of African wars and fought in a style different from that expected by the Europeans. As one colonist recounted in a classic, if little-known, description of guerrilla warfare: "Night and day we chased an enemy who never awaited our approach. . . . Each tree, each hole, each piece of rock hid from our unseeing eyes a cowardly assassin, who, if undiscovered, came to pierce our breasts; but who fled or begged for mercy when we found him face to face."

When they did manage to catch rebels, the whites were utterly savage. Edwards reported seeing "two of these unhappy men" executed beneath his window in Le Cap on September 28, 1791. The first died a mercifully quick death. In the case of the other, after the executioner had already broken his legs and arms and was about to finish him off with a blow to the chest, the mob shouted *arretez* (stop) and left him to suffer for forty minutes tied to a cart wheel until "some English seamen, who were spectators of the tragedy, strangled him in mercy." Another white witness recorded the killing of "Negresses who were completely blameless" and "blacks who were chained up in the hospital."[87]

An estimated ten thousand slaves were killed in the initial fighting, as the whites gradually managed to box in the rebellious areas with a series of military outposts, their entrances lined with Negro corpses dangling from the trees. The slave owners eventually might have regained control as they had done after so many previous Caribbean slave revolts had it not been for the extraordinary man who rose to command the insurgents. He announced his appearance in 1793 with a dramatic proclamation: "I am Toussaint Louverture. . . . I want liberty and equality to reign in St-Domingue."[88]

✦ ✦ ✦

HIS ORIGINAL NAME was Toussaint Bréda. He adopted Louverture ("the opening") to signify his new role as a freedom fighter. He had not been prominent in the initial uprising, but he soon rose to the top, helped no doubt by his relatively privileged background, which was reminiscent in some ways of two future Caribbean rebel leaders—Fidel Castro and Che Guevara. Descended from royalty in the west African kingdom of Dahomey, Toussaint retained, in the words of a colonist who met him, "the haughty reserve" of a nobleman. He had been born in the mid-1740s as a slave on a plantation owned by the Bréda family and managed by a benevolent overseer. Unlike most blacks, he was not consigned to punishing labor in the fields. He had started off as a stable hand and had risen to coachman, a relatively privileged position whose holders, notes the historian David Patrick Geggus, had "frequent contacts with their owners and white society."

Toussaint had acquired some education, probably from the Jesuits before their expulsion from Haiti in the mid-1760s. He could speak and read French, albeit with some difficulty, whereas most slaves were illiterate and understood only Creole or African tribal languages. What made Toussaint especially unusual was a fact that was not discovered until the 1970s. It turns out he was a slave owner, not a slave, at the time of the revolution. Since winning his freedom around the age of twenty-five, he had become owner of a plantation worked by a small number of his own slaves. This essential point was obscured because he continued to live on the Bréda estate and because his wife and children remained in bondage.[89]

For a while Toussaint, along with other black soldiers, fought with Spanish forces based in neighboring Santo Domingo, today's Dominican Republic, against the French. In the spring of 1794, following France's abolition of slavery, he defected to the French side along with four thousand followers. With the help of white and mulatto officers, he turned his ex-slaves into the most formidable fighting force in the entire island. "It was remarkable to see these Africans, naked, equipped with nothing but a cartridge belt, a saber and a rifle, providing an example of the most severe discipline," wrote Pamphile Lacroix, a white French general. "To have imposed discipline on these barbarians was the supreme triumph of Toussaint-Louverture . . . that extraordinary man."[90]

Unable to stand against this formidable foe, Spain had to sue for peace in July 1795, ceding control of the entire island to France. Two years later Toussaint was made commander of all French forces. His primary foes were the British. As part of their broader, global war against France, they had occupied a narrow strip of coastal territory running from Môle Saint Nicolas in the north to Jérémie in the south. The redcoats were skillfully harassed by Toussaint's "brigands"—"infinitely the most formidable enemy the British arms have to encounter with," wrote Lieutenant Thomas Phipps Howard of the York Hussars. Their war-making method, he explained, "consists entirely of ambuscades for which the face of the country is particularly calculated. . . . Five hundred European cavalry would destroy five thousand of them in the plain, but the case is much altered when they fight in their own woods & mountain." The heat added to British difficulties, with "men lying on their backs, their tongues lolling out of their mouths & in the agonies of death for want of water." Diseases made the situation truly hellish. Soldiers "absolutely drowned in their own blood, bursting from them at every pore. Some died raving mad."[91]

King George III's army finally pulled out in 1798. In return for a promise that the blacks would not foment a slave revolt in Britain's Caribbean possessions (a promise that Toussaint honored by betraying plans to launch a rising in Jamaica), all of the British troops left the island. Having vanquished various local rivals, Toussaint became governor-for-life of the entire island under a constitution adopted in July 1801.[92]

It was a hard-won achievement for which Toussaint paid, by his own count, with seventeen different wounds. These included "a violent blow on the head from a [British] cannonball, which knocked out the greater part of my teeth, and loosened the rest."[93] This deformity only added to the impression that Toussaint was, as the biographer and novelist Madison Smartt Bell puts it, "funny-looking"—"short and slight," with a disproportionately large head, and a "jockey's build."[94]

Opinions of his character were split. A British officer who had met Toussaint several times and went on to publish a biography of him in 1805 found him "full of the most prepossessing suavity—terrible to an enemy, but inviting to the objects of his friendship or his love. His manners and deportment were elegant when occasion required, but easy and familiar in common."[95] A French author who published an even earlier biography was less impressed: "His character is a strange and frightful mixture of fanaticism and fierce passions. He passes without remorse from the altar to premeditated carnage, and from devotion to the darkest contrivances of perfidy."[96]

Toussaint's conduct once in power provided ample fodder for such differing impressions. He refused to break up existing plantations or drive out erstwhile slave owners. Instead he mandated that former slaves return to their old plantations to work for wages. Those who resisted were whipped or killed. While becoming the scourge of black laborers, Toussaint worked to protect wealthy white landowners, with whom he socialized and with whose women he carried on multiple affairs. He created a "brilliant" court and traveled in "splendor," while, noted a colonist, "applying the lash of his oppressive control to men who didn't show him respect."[97] Before long some blacks grew disenchanted with their "liberator"—although not as disenchanted as his nominal French superiors.

Although Toussaint was careful not to declare outright independence, Saint-Domingue's increasing autonomy irked France's new first consul. Napoleon needed the revenues generated by this colony to fund his war machine. So he dispatched an army to reestablish control. Its commander was Victor Emmanuel Leclerc, a twenty-nine-year-old general married to Napoleon's sister who was known as the "Blond Bonaparte" for his attempts to emulate his brother-in-law. He brought along his four-year-old son and his wife, "the celebrated and beautiful" Pauline,[98] who was gaining a legendary reputation for infidelity. (Her lovers may have included her own brother, the first consul.) While she allegedly experimented with "white and black lovers to see which she preferred,"[99] Leclerc set about executing his grim orders to deport or kill all blacks of any standing. "Rid us of these gilded negroes," Napoleon told him, "and we shall desire nothing more."[100]

The first part of Leclerc's expeditionary force, which would eventually total more than sixty thousand men, arrived off Le Cap on February 2, 1802.[101] Toussaint knew he had scant chance of beating Leclerc's veterans in open battle. Hoping that the invaders eventually would be decimated by tropical diseases, he decided to play for time by resorting to a strategy of "destruction and fire." He ordered his followers to "tear up the roads with shot; throw corpses and horses into all the fountains; burn and annihilate everything, so that those who have come to return us to slavery will always find in front of them the image of the hell they deserve."[102]

Toussaint's men set fire to Cap-Français, Gonaïves, Saint Marc, and other towns and retreated into the mountain wilderness. After three months of costly fighting, however, several of Toussaint's generals lost heart and began surrendering to the French, who offered them amnesty and equivalent positions in their own ranks. Toussaint followed suit on May 6, 1802, accepting a pardon from Leclerc and pledging loyalty to France. Perhaps he hoped to resume the fight at a later date. If so, he never got the chance. Notwithstanding Leclerc's "word of honor" that he would be allowed to live in peace, Toussaint was, in his own words, "surrounded . . . seized . . . bound . . . and conducted . . . on board the frigate *Créole*," which set sail for France. The most famous Negro in the world died in a "frightful dungeon" in France the following year.[103]

✦ ✦ ✦

NOTWITHSTANDING THEIR SUCCESS in eliminating the revolt's leaders, the French found the battle swinging against them, showing the limitations of a "decapitation" strategy when fighting a deep-rooted insurgency—a lesson that would be confirmed centuries later in Israel's wars against Hamas and Hezbollah. Because his European troops were dying at the rate of 130 a day from tropical diseases, Leclerc was left increasingly dependent on black soldiers.[104] Unfortunately for him, many of the blacks went over to the rebels once they realized the French could not be trusted and were bent on reestablishing slavery. The most dangerous defector was Jean-Jacques Dessalines, "a bold, turbulent, and ferocious spirit" who assumed command of the insurgent forces.[105] Born in Africa, "the inhuman Dessalines" was known for massacring whites and mulattoes with equal gusto; he was said to view "white people with the ferocious eyes of a famished tiger." Among them, rumors of his very appearance induced "panic."[106]

Leclerc, derided by Napoleon's secretary as "one of the youngest and least capable of all the generals in the army,"[107] made the situation worse by trying to disarm and arrest all the remaining black soldiers. A thousand black soldiers were loaded onto a ship off Le Cap and thrown overboard to drown with heavy sacks of flour tied around their necks.[108] Leclerc advocated and practiced genocide, writing to Napoleon on October 7, 1802, "We must destroy all the Negroes of the mountains, men and women, and keep only children under twelve years old, destroy half of those of the plain, and not leave in the colony a single man of color who has worn an epaulette."[109]

Less than a month after scribbling those chilling words, Leclerc himself died—a victim of the same diseases that had claimed so many of his men. His successor, the "fat and squat" General Donatien Rochambeau, son of the general who had commanded French forces in the American Revolution, proved to be equally sadistic. He imported attack dogs from Cuba, nourished on blood, to rip black prisoners to shreds. Blacks caught setting fire to a plantation were burned alive. Helpless blacks were even suffocated with sulfur fumes in a makeshift gas chamber constructed in the hold of a ship. An English officer wrote that the air around Le Cap "became tainted by the putrefaction of the bodies." But, as in Spain, these "atrocious acts of horror" simply drove more of the population into the enemy ranks and encouraged them to treat French prisoners with equal inhumanity.[110]

Although many of the rebels had muskets, they also resorted to simple booby traps such as hiding boards studded with nails beneath leaves where French troops would be likely to tread on them.[111] A boy who marched with French troops recalled that "if any unfortunate soldiers, worn out by exhaustion, lagged behind the column, they soon saw a black head with fiery eyes come out of from behind each clump of cactus, and soon these demons sprang on them, their knives in their hands, and carried out their work of destruction in silence."[112]

The French, their ranks dwindling from "the dreadful fever,"[113] found themselves unable to cope with this growing threat. "The enemy held nowhere, and yet never ceased to be the master of the country," complained one of the beleaguered French officers.[114]

The last place the French held was Le Cap. But even this stronghold became untenable when, following the resumption of war between Britain and France, the Royal Navy cut off the garrison from reinforcement or resupply. On November 30, 1803, Rochambeau sailed away with his remaining troops, having "brought about the definite loss of the island by his severity," in the words of Napoleon's secretary.[115]

✦ ✦ ✦

ON JANUARY 1, 1804, independence was proclaimed for "Haiti," the old Arawak Indian name of the island, making it the first black republic in the world and only the second republic in the entire Western Hemisphere. This was the culmination of the only successful slave revolt in history, ancient or modern.[116] Other slaves in the Americas, known as maroons, managed to run away from their plantations and to successfully defend their fugitive communities. The maroons of Jamaica, notes one historian, "developed extraordinary skills in guerrilla warfare" and enjoyed considerable success in beating back British counterattacks for decades.[117] But eventually they were subdued. Only in Haiti did slaves succeed in toppling the entire colonial regime.

A substantial part of their success can be explained by Haiti's tropical climate, which was a breeding ground for mosquitoes that, unbeknownst at the time, spread yellow fever and malaria. These insect warriors, "the most terrible of all enemies,"[118] as a contemporary magazine dubbed them, accounted for the vast majority of casualties among European troops. Also helpful to the rebels was Haiti's location (on the other side of the planet from France), the timing of its revolt (in the middle of the Napoleonic Wars), and the disparity in population between slaves and slave owners (500,000 slaves versus 40,000 whites).[119] But considerable credit for the outcome must go to the former slaves who showed infinite determination born of desperation—and to their extraordinary leader, the Black Spartacus.[120]

The cost of winning independence was sad and staggering. By some estimates the war that ravaged Haiti for thirteen years claimed the lives of 200,000 blacks and mulattos, 25,000 white colonists, 50,000 French soldiers, and 15,000 British soldiers. As one scholar notes, "Six times as many Haitians as Americans died during their respective wars for independence," even though the population of Haiti was one-fourth that of the North American colonies. Few if any people have ever paid a higher price for independence. That France failed to regain control despite its willingness to slaughter without mercy shows that even the most unrestrained counterinsurgency strategies can come up short.[121] This was a lesson that France would learn anew more than two centuries later in Algeria and Indochina.

17.

GREEKS AND THEIR LOVERS

The Greek War of Independence, 1821–1832

THE REVOLUTIONARY SHOCK waves set off by the American and French revolutions did not dissipate with Napoleon's defeat in 1815. Liberal and national revolts continued to occur. Most, however, failed.

Typical was the Irish rebellion against Britain in 1798. It was organized by the Society of United Irishman, an underground movement created by Wolfe Tone, Napper Tandy, Lord Edward Fitzgerald, and other well-to-do Protestants. Unfortunately for the United Irishmen, their ranks were so infiltrated by informers that the government was able to arrest most of its leaders before the revolt began. The use of torture forced conspirators to inform on one another; many suspects were spread-eagled on wooden triangles and flogged, "their flesh cut without mercy," with salt sometimes sprinkled into the wounds to prolong the agony. Those rebels who took up arms—in many cases, nothing more than a pike was available—were crushed by the better-armed and better-organized militia and military. Many prisoners were shot or hanged; others were sent to newly established penal colonies in Australia. (Tone cheated the hangman by cutting his own throat.) The whole rebellion was suppressed within six weeks at a cost of perhaps fifty thousand lives. Revolutionary France had promised to aid the United Irishmen, but French troops did not land in Ireland until it was far too late to affect the outcome. Most of the populace remained loyal to the crown; the military forces that put down the revolt were composed almost entirely of Catholic Irishmen.[122] Further Irish uprisings in 1803, 1848, 1867, and 1916 were just as ill-starred.

At the other end of Europe, the Poles matched the Irish for revolutionary futility. They rebelled in 1794, 1830, 1863, and 1905, and each time they were crushed by the repressive machinery of Austria, Prussia, or, more often, Russia—the three states that had divided Poland between them. There is no point in going into the gory details; one disorganized, doomed uprising is pretty much like another.

More interesting to examine are the few revolts that succeeded and ask why they were exceptions to the rule. How was it, for example, that the Latin American republics managed to win their independence from Spain between 1810 and 1825? Part of the answer has to do with the genius of the leading "liberators," José de San Martín and Simón Bolívar, who, while revolutionaries, were not guerrillas per se. Although they occasionally made use of hit-and-run tactics, their victory was due to their ability to cobble together small conventional armies and to maneuver rapidly to catch the ponderous Spanish defenders off guard. Their ultimate triumph becomes more explicable if one keeps three facts in mind: the Latin American colonies were 50 percent more populous than metropolitan Spain; they were 3,500 miles away; and Spain was distracted by its own war against Napoleon and the chaotic aftermath.[123]

✦ ✦ ✦

HARDER TO UNDERSTAND at first blush is how the Greeks, who constituted a tiny minority within the Ottoman Empire and had never had a unified nation-state during their long history, won their freedom from imperial masters who were located next door. The Ottoman Empire may have been in decline, but it had lasted more than five hundred years and encompassed much of the Middle East and Balkans. During the course of its history it had banished foes far more formidable than the Greeks—including the Byzantium Empire, the heirs of Rome. The Greeks' skill at guerrilla warfare was impressive but not enough to prevail. Their revolt, which broke out in 1821 thanks to the machinations of a secret society of Greek exiles known as the

Philiki Etairia (Society of Friends), would showcase for the first time the importance of "humanitarian intervention" in deciding the outcome of a guerrilla war.

Greeks had a long tradition of low-intensity warfare waged by the klephts, the traditional Christian Greek bandits, as well as by the *armatoli*, who had been recruited by the Ottomans from among former outlaws to keep the klephts in check. Whether klephts or *armatoli*, these hardy warriors were organized into bands ranging in size from a dozen to a few hundred men. Many were kinsmen, and they were invariably led by a ruthless and charismatic captain. The irregular style of fighting practiced by these men left much to be desired from the standpoint of soldiers schooled in modern methods, including the American and European philhellenes ("lovers of Greeks") who flocked to fight in the land where Western civilization had been born. Samuel Gridley Howe, a young doctor from Boston who served with the Greek forces, left a vivid appreciation of their strengths and weaknesses:

> A Greek soldier is intelligent, active, hardy, and frugal; he will march, or rather skip, all day among the rocks, expecting no other food than a biscuit and a few olives, or a raw onion; and at night, lies down content upon the ground, with a flat stone for a pillow, and with only his capote [a hooded cloak], which he carries with him winter and summer, for covering; baggage-wagon and tent he knows nothing of. But he will not work, for he thinks it disgraceful; he will submit to no discipline, for he thinks it makes a slave of him; he will obey no order which does not seem to him a good one, for he holds that in these matters he has a right to be consulted.

Howe went on to note that these Greeks "would be called cowards" in a European army: "They never can be brought to enter a breach, to charge an enemy who has a wall before him, or to stand up and expose themselves to fire." Instead, like most irregulars, their "invariable practice is to conceal their bodies behind a wall, or a rock, and fire from under cover." Howe nevertheless concluded that they were actually "brave, if you will let them fight in their own way, which is like that of our own Indians."[124]

Attempts to make the Greeks conform to conventional military practices did not get very far. There was no chance that klepht chieftains such as Theódoros Kolokotrónis and Odysseus Androutses would cede power to regular army officers, because they knew this would strengthen the hand of the central government at their expense. The klephts literally let European volunteers starve rather than provide them with provisions.

Westernizing Greek leaders created the small nucleus of a conventional army, but it was composed of foreigners and Greek exiles. This force, numbering five hundred regulars, saw its first and last major action on July 16, 1822, when it attempted to defend the hill village of Péta from several thousand Turkish soldiers. The battle began satisfactorily enough from the philhellenes' standpoint: they opened a "regular fire . . . very coolly" and brought down hundreds of attackers. After a couple of hours, the Europeans fancied that victory was theirs. "All of a sudden," one of them wrote, "we heard dreadful cries behind us." Their rear had been secured by a thousand Greek irregulars under a chieftain named Gogol, who had chosen this moment to depart with his men. The philhellenes later charged that he had been bought off by the Turks, but he may simply have been following the dictates of self-preservation. Whatever his motivations, he left the regulars horribly exposed to a flanking attack. "In one moment the Turks rushed upon us like a torrent . . . so that we were compelled to abandon our position," a philhellene later wrote. Only a third of the philhellenes managed to escape this debacle. In its aftermath their battalion was disbanded.[125]

Luckily for the Greeks' cause, the klephts' preferred method of fighting proved more effective. It was certainly better suited to an outnumbered, badly equipped force fighting in mountainous terrain than were the linear formations favored by the well-intentioned but arrogant European volunteers. In 1821–22, one Turkish fortress after another fell to the rebels, and Turkish reinforcements sent from the north to restore order were repulsed with heavy losses through traditional hit-and-run tactics. Macedonia and northern Greece remained in Ottoman hands, but much of central and southern Greece was liberated, and an impressive-sounding constitution and government were proclaimed by a national assembly led by Europeanized Greeks.

The Greeks did not limit their war to land. At sea their primary weapon was the fireship—a nautical car bomb. The crew would ram a small vessel packed full of gunpowder and combustible materials into the target ship, set it afire, and then escape in a rowboat. When everything went according to plan, this could be a devastating tactic. On June 18, 1822, the Turkish fleet was anchored off the Aegean island of Chios, celebrating the end of Ramadan. Just after midnight, a Greek fireship hit the brightly lit flagship. The flames quickly reached the powder store, and the ship exploded. Out of 2,300 people on board, fewer than 200 survived. The dead included the Turkish admiral who was hit on the head by a falling mast as he was trying to get into a lifeboat.[126]

The Ottomans failed to exhibit any of the restraint shown by the British in dealing with American rebels. In retaliation for the firebombing of their flagship, the Turks killed 25,000 Greeks and enslaved another 41,000 on Chios. Many of the dead had their noses, heads, and ears cut off, and these were sent by the sackful to Constantinople as grisly mementos.[127] This was part of a pattern of the Ottomans targeting Greek civilians, including the elderly Greek Orthodox patriarch of Constantinople, who was hanged notwithstanding his opposition to the revolt. After the Ottoman fleet returned to Constantinople, spectators on the docks could see captured Greeks hung by their necks from bowsprits and yardarms, "struggling in the agonies of death."[128]

The Greeks were hardly innocent of such transgressions as they set about ethnically cleansing—a practice scarcely new to the twentieth century—the Peloponnese of all "Mohammedans." Theirs was not only a nationalist struggle; it was also a holy war pitting Christians against Muslims with all the cruelty implicit in wars of religion. After the fall in 1821 of Tripolitza, a wealthy Turkish town, an Italian philhellene recounted, "We found nothing but dead bodies, which lay as food for dogs. What shocked us the most was the sight of the naked bodies of the women and children."[129]

In Europe, however, Greek misconduct barely registered, while Turkish atrocities, real or imagined, loomed large: the Western public had been conditioned by centuries of lurid and often inaccurate tales from "the Orient" to ascribe barbarism to "the Turk" and "Mohammedan" while crediting the Greeks with all the virtues of Pericles and Aristotle. The imbalance was compounded by the fact that Ottomans had no conception of the importance of Western opinion and no plan to marshal it in their favor. Greek exiles were much more cognizant of this new realm of what is today known as information warfare. They were able to take advantage of the inherent sympathy for their cause among Western intellectuals as well as the loathing of "the Turk" and other Middle Easterners that dated back to the ancient wars between Greeks and Persians and had been strengthened by more recent events such as the Ottoman conquest of Byzantium in 1453, the subsequent Ottoman sieges of Vienna in 1529 and 1683, and the capture from the seventeenth to the nineteenth centuries in the Mediterranean and Atlantic of tens of thousands of Western mariners by "Barbary pirates" from North Africa who were nominally subjects of the Ottoman Empire.

Prominent philhellenes included the English philosopher Jeremy Bentham, the American professor and future secretary of state Edward Everett, and the French painter Eugène Delacroix. The most famous Greek lover of all was Lord Byron, the wealthy, scandal-ridden, and priapic English poet who in the summer of 1823 sailed to Greece on his private yacht, the *Hercules*, which carried a retinue of volunteers and servants, including a gondolier and valet, along with horses, medicines, two cannons, and a large bankroll. En route he honed his pistol marksmanship, a companion reported, by shooting at "live poultry" that "was put into a basket" and "hoisted to the main yard-arm."[130] Upon arrival Byron formed his own brigade in Greece, but it accomplished nothing and fell apart after his death from disease in the pestilential port of Missolonghi on April 19, 1824. He had anticipated his fate with a poem completed on his thirty-sixth birthday just a few months before. It ended, "Seek out—less often sought than found— / A Soldier's Grave, for thee the best; / Then look around, and choose thy Ground, / And take thy rest."[131] His romantic demise on his chosen ground caused a sensation back home that anticipated the British reaction to the death of Princess Diana, and further inflamed support for the cause to which he had given his life.

In addition to Byron, twelve hundred other philhellenes eventually reached Greece.[132] Their military significance was negligible. Far more important was the philhellenes' political role in rallying Western support for the Greeks after the Ottomans launched an effective counterattack in 1824. The Turkish forces were led by Mehmet Ali, the Albanian-born ruler of Egypt, and his son Ibrahim Pasha. With the help of European advisers, they created a regular army on the European model that was far more formidable than the antiquated Ottoman janissary corps. The Egyptians' ability to stay in their ranks, suffer losses, and charge home with the bayonet allowed them to shrug off irregular attacks and regain much of the ground the Greeks had won in 1821–22. "The cause of the Greeks is fast declining," commented a British diplomat in 1825.[133]

Only the intervention of Britain, France, and Russia saved the Greek cause. Overcoming the qualms of conservatives such as the duke of Wellington who regarded the Ottomans as a force for stability,[134] the three powers spoke with one voice to demand that the Turks grant the Greeks autonomy. The sultan ignored their demand and paid the price. On October 20, 1827, twenty-four British, French, and Russian warships mauled a larger Ottoman fleet in the Bay of Navarino in the southwestern Peloponnese. In four hours of close-quarters firing, the Ottomans lost sixty of eighty-nine warships, while the allies did not lose one of their own.[135] Because the Ottomans were now unable to resupply their forces by sea, the Battle of Navarino made Greek independence inevitable. Four years later Greece was formally recognized as a unified, independent state for the first time in its long history.

There was nothing novel about outside powers' helping a rebellion. The French had helped the Americans, as well as, less successfully, the Scots and Irish, in their struggles against Britain. The British, in turn, had helped the Spanish guerrillas against France and, before them, the Dutch rebels against the Spanish Habsburgs (1568–1648). But they had done so strictly for strategic reasons, whereas Britain and France, and even to some extent Russia, intervened in Greece in no small measure out of sheer humanitarian instinct. Certainly they had little but moral satisfaction to gain from weakening their ally, the Ottoman Empire. In an echo of modern human-rights campaigners, Vice Admiral Sir Edward Codrington, commander of the allied armada at Navarino, said that his goal was to force Ibrahim Pasha "to discontinue the brutal war of extermination which he has been carrying on."[136]

Although commercial and strategic considerations were not entirely absent and the French covered their bets by also providing surreptitious military assistance to Mehmet Ali,[137] the allied role in the Greek War of Independence was, as argued by the historian Gary Bass, a precursor to the 1990s interventions in Bosnia and Kosovo (and the 2011 intervention in

Libya), with Byron and Delacroix performing the galvanizing role that television networks and human-rights groups would play in the latter conflicts.[138] By publicizing their suffering, the Greeks managed to persuade others to free them. Their strategy of "winning by losing" would be emulated by numerous rebels in the future, most notably by the Cubans who in 1898 persuaded the United States to declare war against their Spanish oppressors.

Theodore Roosevelt, for one, sounded as ardent as any philhellene when he wrote in 1897, "I am a quietly rampant 'Cuba Libra' man," and suggested that "a war with Spain" would be advisable "on the grounds both of humanity and self-interest."[139] The Rough Rider would enjoy more military success in Cuba than the philhellenes had had in Greece, but victory in the Spanish-American War, as in the Greek Revolution, would be secured primarily by naval might—specifically by the U.S. Navy's successes in sinking the Spanish squadrons at the Battles of Manila Bay and Santiago de Cuba.

18.

HERO OF TWO WORLDS

Giuseppe Garibaldi and the Struggle for Italian Unification, 1833–1872

ANOTHER NATION THAT managed to win its freedom and unity was Italy, which before the 1860s had been divided into eight different states dominated by Austria. Its unification was only partially the result of a guerrilla war, but it would give rise to the most famous guerrilla leader of the nineteenth century—one who would remain a prototype for self-styled freedom fighters up to the present day.

It is an oddity of history that many ardent nationalists were not born on the soil of the nation they championed. Napoleon was born in Corsica, not France; Helmuth von Moltke the Elder in the duchy of Mecklenburg-Schwerin, not Prussia; Stalin in Georgia, not Russia; Hitler in Austria, not Germany. Likewise Giuseppe Garibaldi, who would become Italy's leading nationalist, was born in Nice—a city that, at the time of his birth (1807), was occupied by France. After Napoleon's defeat, when Garibaldi was eight, Nice reverted to the kingdom of Piedmont-Sardinia, but it would once again become a part of France in 1860, where it has remained ever since. Garibaldi, born to a poor family of sailors and fishermen, grew up fluent in both French and Italian, yet he always thought of himself as Italian.[140]

He went to sea as a cabin boy at sixteen and spent the next decade plying the waters of the Mediterranean. In 1833, when he was twenty-six, inflamed by "a passionate love of [his] country . . . [as he later wrote] and burning with indignation against her oppressors,"[141] this self-educated sailor joined Young Italy, a secret society founded by another Giuseppe, who was just two years older—the lawyer and propagandist Giuseppe Mazzini, a native of Genoa who was determined to unify the Italian peninsula into one nation-state for the first time in its long history.

Dubbed by Prince Metternich of Austria "the most dangerous man in Europe," Mazzini would inspire liberal revolutionaries across the Continent much as Marx and Engels would later inspire communists. Young Italy would be joined by Young France, Young Austria, and other republican societies, all coordinated by Young Europe. Mazzini believed, "Insurrection—by means of guerrilla bands—is the true method of warfare for all nations desirous of emancipating themselves from a foreign yoke. . . . It is invincible, indestructible." He even published in 1832 an early guerrilla manual, *Rules for the Conduct of Guerrilla Bands*, which in many ways anticipated the writings of Mao Zedong. "Guerrilla war is a war of judicious daring and audacity, active legs, and espionage . . . ," he wrote. "The greatest merit in the commander of regular troops is to know when to fight and conquer; the greatest merit of the guerrilla chief is to contrive constantly to attack, do mischief, and retire."[142]

However sensible his advice, Mazzini was more adept with a pen than a gun, more comfortable in a book-lined study than on a blood-drenched battlefield. The plots that he tried to carry out personally ended in tragedy or farce. Garibaldi discovered that for himself in 1834 when he was assigned to infiltrate the Royal Sardinian Navy to incite a mutiny among its sailors. Mazzini and other exiles were supposed to invade Piedmont from Switzerland to coincide with this sailors' revolt, but the plot fizzled out after Mazzini literally lost his way. Garibaldi, facing a death sentence, was forced to seek refuge in South America.

After trying unsuccessfully to pursue commercial enterprises such as selling macaroni, Garibaldi decided he was "destined for greater things."[143] In 1837 he found his true calling as a soldier when he enlisted on behalf of Rio Grande do Sul, a province trying to break away from Brazil. In 1842 he joined another war in neighboring Uruguay. He would spend the next six years defending its liberal government against an Argentinean dictator and his local allies.

With his seafaring background, it was natural that Garibaldi would be employed at first as a privateer preying on enemy shipping—a guerrilla of the sea. But he also commanded forces on land. Armies were so small and distances so vast in Latin America that Garibaldi frequently campaigned with a few men in the wilderness. Often he was pursued by superior forces, but he seldom hesitated to attack even when badly outnumbered, and his audacity usually carried the day. He exhibited preternatural resilience by marching and riding for long periods, notwithstanding illness, wounds, and supply shortages. Even while combating ruthless enemies who once captured and tortured him, he always observed a "chivalrous" code.[144] If he lacked detention facilities, as he usually did, he would release prisoners rather than kill them, even if he knew they would report his position, and he took care to prevent his soldiers from abusing civilians.[145]

His most notable exploits came in hit-and-run raids at the head of the 800-man Italian Legion, which he organized from among his fellow immigrants in Uruguay—the "brave sons of Columbus," he called them with his typically florid rhetoric.[146] Their uniform became the red shirt after the government discovered a stockpile of these garments, which had been intended for use in slaughterhouses, where the red color would not show blood.[147] Stocky, bearded, and long-haired, with a serene expression and "eyes [that] were steadfast and piercing," wearing a red tunic, black felt hat, and "gaudy handkerchief" around his collar, a cavalry sword dangling from his waist and a pair of pistols in a saddle holster—Garibaldi was, in the words of a British naval officer, "the *beau ideal* of a chief of irregular troops."[148]

Among those enraptured with him was Anna Maria Ribeiro da Silva, a young Brazilian woman whose husband, a shoemaker, was away from home performing his army service. She was living in the town of Laguna when Garibaldi's ship anchored in the harbor. The year was 1839. He was thirty-three, she eighteen. He claimed, perhaps with romantic hindsight, to have first spotted her with a telescope from his quarterdeck while she was standing outside her hilltop home. He immediately disembarked in search of her. His very first words upon meeting her: "Thou oughtest to be mine." Instead of slapping him, she found his "insolence . . . magnetic." Garibaldi could not have been accused of falling for just another pretty face. The homely Anita was never known as a great beauty; she was described by one of Garibaldi's biographers as "a big-busted peasant wench." But, pretty or not, Garibaldi was instantly smitten with her, and she with him. They proverbially sailed away together but were not married until 1842, which, as another biographer notes, was "two years after the birth of their first child."

Anita traveled and fought alongside Garibaldi, sharing the dangers and discomforts of a soldier's life for the next decade while giving birth to four children in all. Their romance, which flew in the face of social convention, added to Garibaldi's growing reputation as a rebel.[149]

✦ ✦ ✦

THANKS IN NO small part to Mazzini's assiduous propagandizing, Garibaldi's exploits were avidly recounted in European newspapers, whose circulation was booming.[150] Thus he was already a national hero when he returned to Italy in June 1848 along with sixty-three of his legionnaires. Liberal, nationalist revolutions were spreading across Italy and other parts of Europe. Austrian troops were compelled to evacuate Milan and Venice. The kingdom of Piedmont-Sardinia chose this moment to declare war against Austria in an attempt to unify the entire peninsula under its own royal family. Italy's Risorgimento (Rising Again) was in full swing. "We had fought gloriously to defend the oppressed in other countries," Garibaldi wrote; "now we were hastening to take up arms for our own beloved motherland."[151]

He first tried to offer his services to Piedmont. But the royal army had little use for this adventurer who had once been convicted of treason. Garibaldi wound up fighting on behalf of the revolutionary committee in Milan, leading fifteen hundred volunteers around Lake Maggiore in Austrian-occupied Lombardy. He hoped, he later wrote, to involve his "fellow-countrymen in a guerrilla war which, in the absence of an organized army, by itself would lead on to the liberation of Italy," but he found few recruits and "any number of traitors and spies among the populace." The Austrians effectively cowed the people with their brutal tactics. Once the Austrians were expelled from a village, Garibaldi recounted, "they ruthlessly set fire to all the surrounding houses all the while bombarding the village itself indiscriminately." He and his small band had to stay on the run. "Almost every night we had to change position in order to elude and deceive the enemy." Finally, after three weeks of skirmishing, he had to seek refuge across the Swiss border, demonstrating not for the first or last time the importance of foreign sanctuaries for hard-pressed guerrillas. Austria had won this round; not only Garibaldi but the regular Piedmontese army had to retreat in disarray.[152]

Garibaldi got another chance to fight when on April 27, 1849, he arrived, atop nothing less than a white horse, at the head of thirteen hundred men from his Italian Legion to defend the newly proclaimed Roman republic against the armies of Austria, Spain, Naples, and France—all Catholic states that wanted to restore papal rule. Garibaldi hoped to wage a guerrilla war from redoubts in the Apennine Mountains. Instead he was forced by Mazzini, the de facto leader of Rome, to conduct a more conventional defense, against hopeless odds. Citizens were mobilized and barricades erected. Fighting "like lions," the Romans managed to check the initial French and Neapolitan onslaught. But before long the Roman revolution, like others across Europe, was on its deathbed.

Garibaldi was recovering from a stomach wound and assorted bruises suffered during the fighting, but he turned down an American diplomat's offer to evacuate him on an American warship. He decided to march out of Rome and continue the fight. His stirring call for volunteers would be echoed by Winston Churchill during the darkest days of World War II: "This is what I have to offer to those who wish to follow me: hunger, cold, the heat of the sun; no wages, no barracks, no ammunition; but continual skirmishes, forced marches, and bayonet-fights. Those of you who love your country and love glory, follow me!"

More than four thousand men heeded his call. So did his wife, pregnant with their fifth child, who came despite his "entreaties that she should remain behind." They marched out of Rome on July 2, 1849, with tens of thousands of soldiers from four nations in pursuit. As their desperate month-long trek progressed, many of Garibaldi's men deserted, while no peasants rallied to his cause, leading him to curse "the timidity and effeminacy of my fellow Italians . . . who were incapable of keeping the field a month without their three meals a day." It was hardly surprising, however, that conservative Catholic peasants would not support a radical republican who denounced the pope as the "Antichrist" and their priests as the "pestilent scum of humanity" and "the prop of every vice, despotism, and corruption to be found on this earth."

While most people wanted nothing to do with him, Garibaldi did find a few republican loyalists who helped him elude his pursuers after some close calls. Once, he recalled, he was lying "on one side of a clump of bushes," while "the Austrians passed on the other" without discovering him.

Although he managed to escape, his beloved Anita was not so lucky. She caught a fever, possibly malaria, and, in spite of being "in a deplorable state of suffering," refused to turn back. She died on August 4, 1849, not far from Ravenna. It was a bitter blow to her devoted husband, but, prefiguring Mao's Long March, Garibaldi's success in eluding capture only added to his luster.[153]

✦ ✦ ✦

AFTER THE END of the 1848–49 revolutions, Garibaldi was in for another long, frustrating period of exile, which took him from New York to Lima, Canton, and London. He supported himself by working jobs ranging from candle maker to captain of a cargo ship carrying guano. In 1856 he moved to the tiny isle of Caprera, near Sardinia, using a small inheritance from his brother to buy half of this "mass of granite, clothed here and there with a thin mass of earth."[154] Here he built with his own hands a four-room stone cottage that would serve as a refuge until the end of his life. Although a lock of his late wife's hair hung in an ebony frame over his bed,[155] Garibaldi did not allow his devotion to her memory to stand in the way of fulfilling his "increasing need" for, as one of his conquests put it, "womanly attentions."[156]

He would marry again in 1860, when he was fifty-two, to an eighteen-year-old Italian aristocrat far more comely than his first wife. At the wedding reception, in a scene that could have come straight from an opera written by his fellow Italian nationalist Giuseppe Verdi, Garibaldi was approached by a man who passed him a note claiming that his bride had spent the preceding night with him, that she was pregnant, and did not love her new husband. He immediately asked her whether the letter was accurate. When she said it was, he loudly called her a *puttana*, declared that she was not really his wife, and never spoke to her again. He did not get a formal divorce and marry again until the end of his life.[157] In 1880 he wed his children's nanny, a simple peasant woman, neither beautiful nor clever, who had already borne him three children during the course of a relationship that began in 1866. Earlier, in 1859, the guerrilla chief had had yet another child with his "small and rather ugly" housekeeper—or at least so she appeared to another jealous girlfriend.[158]

Garibaldi provides an early example of how the nascent mass media, created by the proliferation of cheap books, newspapers, and magazines in rapidly growing cities, could turn a guerrilla into a popular idol, even a sex symbol. Future rebel leaders, from Tito and Mao to Arafat, Nasrallah, and Bin Laden, would benefit from the same phenomenon: a media-driven cult of personality.

✦ ✦ ✦

THE WHOLE TIME he was on Caprera, Garibaldi was a caged lion, impatiently biding his time until "the day," as one of his girlfriends wrote, "when he will be wanted" again by the Risorgimento.[159] That moment arrived in 1858, when the "Lion of Caprera" was recruited for service as an irregular by Count Camillo di Cavour, the calculating aristocrat who was prime minister of Piedmont-Sardinia. Like Prussia's Otto von Bismarck, Cavour wanted to co-opt nationalist sentiment, hitherto a force for liberal revolutions, to create a conservative nation-state under his king, Victor Emmanuel II. As part of this strategy, Cavour had forged an alliance with France's emperor, Louis Napoleon, to wage another war against Austria in order to seize its Italian domains. Cavour wanted to enlist Garibaldi to bolster public enthusiasm for what might otherwise be seen as a disreputable landgrab by two Machiavellian monarchs. Against Mazzini's advice, Garibaldi agreed to help. He was not told that as part of the deal Piedmont had agreed to give his hometown, Nice, back to France.

War duly came in 1859. Garibaldi, newly commissioned a major general in the royal army of Piedmont but still wearing his old poncho and slouch hat, set off once again to wage a guerrilla campaign around Lake Maggiore with three thousand "ill-armed but high-spirited youths" organized into the *Cacciatori delle Alpi* (Hunters of the Alps). He was operating on the left flank of the French and Piedmontese armies, much as T. E. Lawrence would do nearly sixty years later with his Arab irregulars on the right flank of a British army in the Holy Land. Garibaldi's goals included "disorganizing the Austrian Army, disrupting their lines of communications by blowing up bridges, cutting telegraph wires and burning stores." He won a series of victories against the more numerous and better-equipped Austrians by taking advantage of the mountainous terrain to appear where he was not expected, striking at night, and pressing home his attacks with the bayonet. Garibaldi's actions were peripheral to the main event, however, which was a showdown between the Austrian and the Franco-Piedmontese armies. The latter won, and the resulting peace treaty ceded Lombardy to Piedmont while France got Nice and the nearby region of Savoy.[160]

✦ ✦ ✦

GARIBALDI WAS TO play a more central role in the next phase of the Risorgimento, which began when a revolution broke out in Sicily on April 4, 1860, against the Bourbon king of Naples. With Cavour taking a wait-and-see attitude—ready to support Garibaldi if he succeeded and disavow him if he failed[161]—the famous guerrilla chief went to the Sicilians' aid on his own initiative with 1,089 volunteers. They were mostly young professionals, workers, students, and intellectuals from the cities of the north, and they became known as the Thousand or the Redshirts. "Their faith in Garibaldi," commented an observer, amounted almost "to a religion."[162]

This small force departed aboard two steamships from a small port near Genoa on May 5, 1860, and arrived at the Sicilian port of Marsala six days later. It was extraordinarily lucky that two Neopolitan battle cruisers had just left. By the time the warships returned and began bombarding their steamers, the Redshirts had already disembarked. Four days later, under what one of the Redshirts described as a "sky of glory from which a warm light poured down which, blending with the perfumes of the valley, intoxicated us all," they ran into three thousand Bourbon troops atop a hill outside the town of Calatafimi. Because the Redshirts had only "decrepit old rifles," Garibaldi ordered them to fire as little as possible. They charged up the hill "under a hail of bullets" and scattered the enemy with their bayonets. This skirmish, Garibaldi wrote, "had an immeasurable moral result in encouraging the population and demoralizing the hostile army."[163]

Aided by *squadre* (bands) of local guerrillas, the Redshirts advanced on Palermo, a city of 160,000 people held by 20,000 troops. Thousands of enemy soldiers advanced to meet them, but Garibaldi's small force avoided them and slipped into the hills. He staged "incessant feints by night and day," but refused to accept battle in the open. Even Garibaldi's men wondered what he was up to. "What are we waiting for?" one Redshirt wrote on May 23. "What does this circling around Palermo mean, as though we were moths round a lamp?" It meant that Garibaldi was intent on achieving surprise when he finally did attack.

The Redshirts entered Palermo quietly at 2 a.m. on May 27, 1860, catching the garrison unawares. Three days of bitter street fighting ensued, with Neapolitan artillery bombarding the city, creating what one witness described as "frightful . . . carnage"—"those ten-inch shells bringing down houses wholesale, and burying the unfortunate inhabitants in the ruins." The brutality of the Bourbons enraged rather than cowed the populace, which erected barricades to impede the movement of Bourbon infantry. "Many joined us," Garibaldi wrote, "with daggers, knives, roasting spits and iron utensils of all kinds since they didn't have rifles. . . . Every balcony and loggia was covered with mattresses for defense and heaped with stones and projectiles of every description." Seeing this mass mobilization and short on supplies, the Bourbon commander agreed to a truce that allowed him to evacuate his troops. An English naval officer noted that this victory was "won in utter defiance of . . . the rules of war"—rules that Garibaldi, a self-taught soldier, was blissfully unaware of.[164]

Continuing their improbable string of successes, the Redshirts routed the rest of the Bourbon troops in Sicily, then on August 19 crossed the Straits of Messina to land in Calabria, on the toe of the Italian boot. After they bested the first Neapolitan troops they met, many of the rest surrendered or deserted. Garibaldi entered Naples, Italy's largest city, to "an everlasting chorus of *vivas*."[165] The rest of the Bourbon army, totaling fifty thousand men, gathered for a counteroffensive on the Volturno River north of the city. On October 1–2, Garibaldi beat them with thirty thousand troops in the only large-scale engagement that he ever fought. Naturally, a correspondent wrote, Garibaldi was in the thick of the action, "revolver in hand," while "the balls and grape were flying about."[166]

He then briefly ruled southern Italy as its "dictator," not yet a pejorative term, before voluntarily handing over power to Victor Emmanuel II on November 8, 1860, following a plebiscite in which the people of Sicily and Naples agreed to accept the king as their ruler. Garibaldi had more than doubled the king's domains,[167] but he characteristically refused offers of a rich reward, preferring to retire to his frugal existence on Caprera. Such selflessness was one of the secrets of his popularity. An English naval officer who knew him commented, "The irresistible spell which enables him to usurp all hearts may be traced to the simple fact that he is . . . 'an honest man.' "[168]

The kingdom of Italy, the goal toward which Garibaldi had been working his whole life, finally came into existence in 1861. Venice was added in 1866, following a war against Austria by Prussia and Italy. During this conflict Garibaldi once again undertook guerrilla warfare in northern Italy and, although wounded, was more successful than the regular Italian forces. That left only Rome outside the new state. Vowing *Roma o Morte!* (Rome or Death), Garibaldi invaded the pope's domains in 1862 and 1867.[169] Both expeditions failed, and Garibaldi was badly wounded in the former instance. Rome finally would be annexed in 1870 by the Italian army, not by Garibaldi's irregulars.

✦ ✦ ✦

WITH HIS WORLDWIDE fame (more than half a million people thronged the streets of London to greet him in 1864),[170] Garibaldi was often in demand in other people's wars. In 1861 he turned down an offer from Abraham Lincoln to fight in the U.S. Civil War because the Union had not yet committed to abolish slavery—and because he was not offered command of the entire Union army. Garibaldi may have been an idealist, but he also had a healthy ego.[171]

In November 1870, although by now "old and lame,"[172] suffering from rheumatism and old wounds, he was more eager to go to the defense of his erstwhile enemy, France, in its war against Prussia. The regular French armies under Emperor Louis Napoleon were swiftly surrounded and forced to surrender. A republican government then took power and vowed to continue resistance. Now that the "execrable tyrant," Napoleon, had been overthrown, Garibaldi volunteered "what was left of him," explaining, "Whenever an oppressed people struggles against its oppressors, whenever an enslaved people combats for its liberty, my place is in their midst."

In spite of the hostility of conservative Catholics toward this notorious freethinker, the provisional government accepted his services and assigned him to command the irregular Army of the Vosges in eastern France. This was one of many units of *francs-tireurs* ("free shooters") that sprang up across occupied France (roughly a third of its total territory) in response to the republican leader Léon Gambetta's call to "harass the enemy's detachments without pause or relaxation." They sniped at "the Boche" and blew up bridges, railroads, and telegraph lines.

Garibaldi's force, which swelled to over sixteen thousand men, was made up not only of Frenchmen but also of Italians, including his two sons, Poles, Hungarians, and other foreigners dedicated to defending liberty. "In his element once again," writes the foremost student of the *francs-tireurs*, "[Garibaldi] fought the way he knew best, striking, feinting, falling back, and striking again—tactics which were the essence of irregular warfare." His son Ricciotti scored a particularly notable success with his raid on the town of Châtillon-sur-Seine on November 18, 1870, killing or capturing more than three hundred soldiers out of a Prussian garrison of eight hundred. Garibaldi later occupied the city of Dijon and held it for a while against heavy counterattack.

German commanders were exasperated by such setbacks. They ordered their soldiers to shoot captured guerrillas and to impose "harsh reprisals" on towns suspected of aiding them. "They are not soldiers: we are treating them as murderers," Prussia's prime minister, Otto von Bismarck, declared.

This was in keeping with the traditional approach to guerrillas codified in the influential Lieber Code, authored by the German-American law professor Francis Lieber and promulgated by the Union army in 1863 as General Orders No. 100 to deal with Southern "bushwhackers." Lieber's most important contribution was to distinguish between partisans and guerrillas. The former were fighters "wearing the uniform of their army" and "belonging to a corps which acts detached from the main body." They were entitled if captured "to all the privileges of the prisoner of war." But "men, or squads of men, who commit hostilities . . . without being part and portion of the organized hostile army . . . shall be treated summarily as highway robbers or pirates."[173]

This sounds as if it could have been a prescription for mass executions of captured guerrillas. But it was applied much more inconsistently and humanely by Lincoln's soldiers in the South and, in spite of Germany's later reputation for inhumane warfare, by the kaiser's soldiers in France. Both armies were considerably more restrained than French troops had been in the Vendée, Spain, or Haiti. Captured *Garibaldini* were especially well treated, because they wore uniforms and generally obeyed the laws of war. The Germans could afford to be magnanimous. The *francs-tireurs* never seriously threatened to change the outcome of the war, which ended with the fall of Paris in January 1871.

Garibaldi returned home to the jeers of French conservatives. Their vitriol was understandable given that the veteran revolutionary had not worked the miracles that were now expected of him. All of the *francs-tireurs* had killed fewer than a thousand German troops and tied down a hundred thousand more while prolonging the war for just a few months. They had not saved France from a humiliating defeat that included the loss of two provinces. But then the entire conflict had been so short—just six months—that there was no time for the guerrillas to wear down the invaders, as the Spanish had done seven decades earlier.[174]

✦ ✦ ✦

NOTWITHSTANDING THE anticlimactic end of his career, when he died in 1882, at seventy-four, Garibaldi was celebrated far outside his homeland as "the Hero of Two Worlds."[175] The British historian A. J. P. Taylor would reportedly call him "the only wholly admirable figure in modern history."[176] He was the forerunner of all the twentieth-century guerrillas who would become international celebrities. But he was more laudable than most guerrilla chieftains in that he consistently displayed humanity and restraint in his war making and never sought power or riches for himself. In both his sterling conduct and his spectacular results, he set a standard seldom matched before or since.

19.
REVOLUTIONARY CONSEQUENCES

The Liberal Achievement

GARIBALDI'S DEATH, TEN years after Mazzini's, marks a fitting end to this survey of the era of liberal revolutions inaugurated by the minutemen of Massachusetts more than a hundred years earlier. Most future revolutionaries, whether of the right or the left, would be more extreme in their methods and beliefs. But whatever their orientation, generations of rebels to come would learn from the liberals' use of propaganda as a powerful weapon of war. It would continue to grow in importance until the present day when Osama bin Laden would declare, not implausibly, that the "media war" constituted 90 percent of his entire battle.[177] The percentage was lower in the nineteenth century but much higher than it had been in the countless centuries of largely apolitical guerrilla warfare that preceded it.

Liberal insurgents scored their most impressive victories in the New World, where, with a few small exceptions, by 1825 the writ of European colonialists no longer ran. Louis Napoleon tried to install a puppet regime in Mexico in the 1860s, but his chosen ruler, the Austrian archduke Maximilian, was killed and his government overthrown by liberal forces, including guerrillas led by Benito Juárez. In Europe the most successful uprisings were in Greece and Italy. Constitutional monarchies were also established in Belgium and France in 1830, but these upheavals, like the French Revolution of 1789, were the product of "people power" in the streets rather than of guerrilla warfare. There were many more revolutionary failures, from the Chartists in Britain to the Decembrists in Russia. But even unsuccessful revolts could exert a powerful influence by persuading rulers to grant some of the rebels' demands in order to assuage their supporters. Thus most of Europe was moving in a more liberal direction in the nineteenth century—even states such as Russia, Germany, and Austria that remained absolute monarchies.

Ironically the consequences of liberal revolts were in some ways the least satisfactory in the places where they had ostensibly succeeded. The French Revolution started with the Declaration of the Rights of Man and ended in war and terror. The Greek revolt did not usher in a "Great Age" and "another Athens," as imagined by philhellenes such as Shelley, but rather rule by an imported Bavarian prince who was overthrown by a coup in 1862.[178] Haiti's liberation was followed by a "general massacre"[179] of the remaining whites and an instability that persists to the present day. Spain experienced repression and civil war after the expulsion of the French; it would not see the emergence of democracy until the 1970s. Italy was more peaceful, but Garibaldi, increasingly socialistic and pacifistic in his old age, was deeply discontented by the "misery of [his] country," which he attributed to "the base and deceitful conduct of government and priests."[180] Even in the United States, a model of effective governance compared with Greece, Haiti, Italy, or Spain, most of the revolutionaries who had fought for freedom from Britain refused to grant freedom to African-Americans, whose humanity they denied.

José de San Martín and Simón Bolívar, the liberators of Latin America, were even more disenchanted than Garibaldi with the consequences of their struggles. They had hoped to inaugurate an era of "peace, science, art, commerce, and agriculture" overseen by strong central governments operating under liberal constitutions.[181] Instead they gave birth to caudillos, corruption, and civil strife—what Bolívar in his last years denounced as "this fearful anarchy."[182] Hard as it usually is to overthrow a regime, harder still is it to establish an enduring and successful successor. Many revolutionaries have discovered, along with San Martín and Bolívar, that ideals are simpler to fight for than to implement.

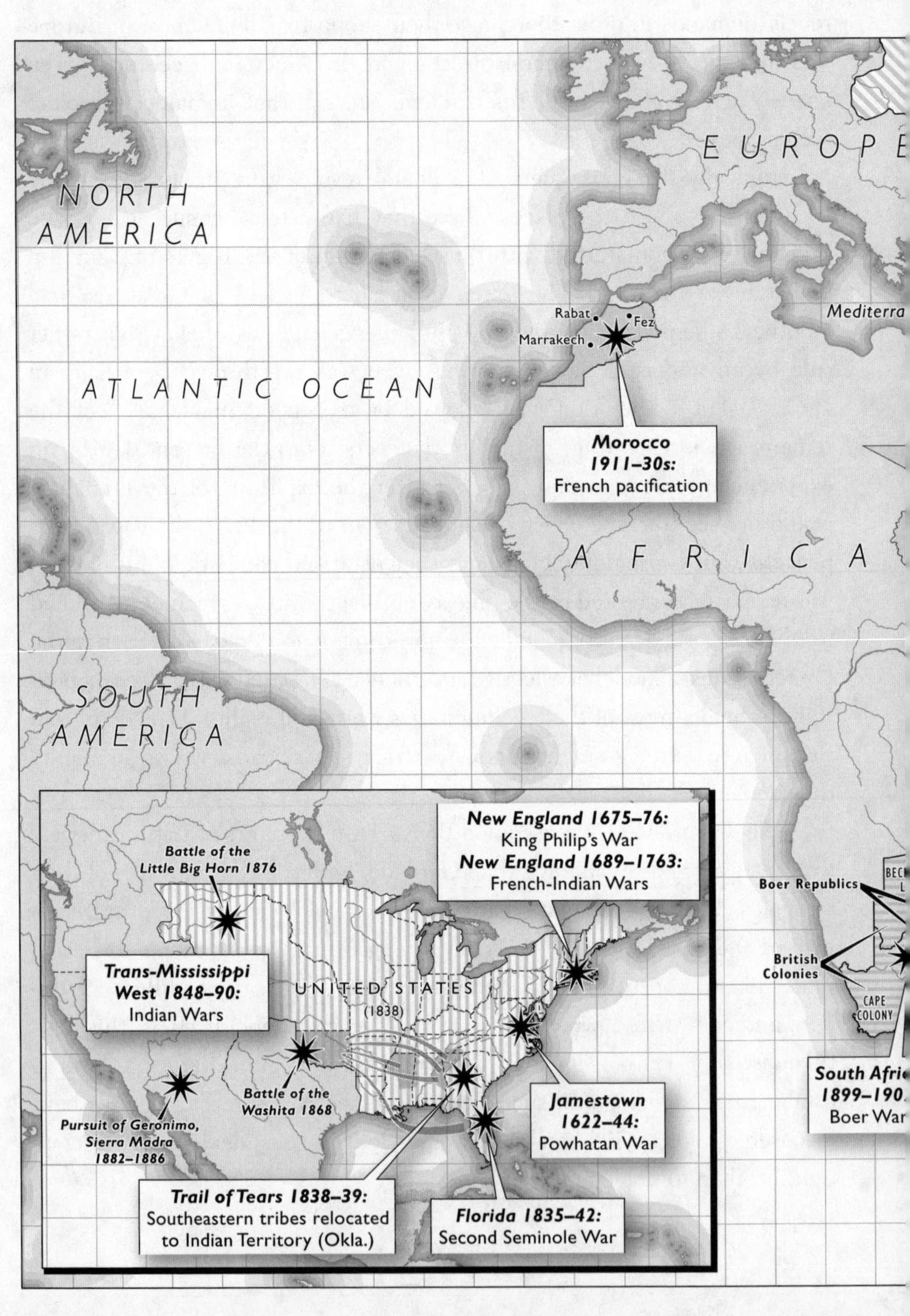

NORTH AMERICA
ATLANTIC OCEAN
SOUTH AMERICA
AFRICA
Rabat
Fez
Marrakech
Morocco 1911–30s: French pacification
New England 1675–76: King Philip's War
New England 1689–1763: French-Indian Wars
Battle of the Little Big Horn 1876
Trans-Mississippi West 1848–90: Indian Wars
UNITED STATES (1838)
Battle of the Washita 1868
Pursuit of Geronimo, Sierra Madra 1882–1886
Jamestown 1622–44: Powhatan War
Trail of Tears 1838–39: Southeastern tribes relocated to Indian Territory (Okla.)
Florida 1835–42: Second Seminole War
Boer Republics
British Colonies
CAPE COLONY

BOOK III
THE SPREADING OIL SPOT

The Wars of Empire

ASIA

Northwest Frontier of India 1849–1945:
Anglo-Pashtun Wars

Chechnya, Dagestan 1829–59:
Holy War

Afghanistan 1839–43:
First Afghan War
_1878–80:_
Second Afghan War
_1919:_
Third Afghan War

Philippines 1899–1902:
Philippine Insurrection

Kabul

BRITISH INDIA
(c.1877)

Bay of Bengal

Madagascar

INDIAN OCEAN

20.

THE WARS THAT WEREN'T

Why Did So Few Guerrillas Resist the European Advance?

AT THE SAME time that Western states were becoming more liberal at home, they were extending their rule across much of the non-European world in decidedly illiberal fashion: at gunpoint. The process of colonization and resistance would do much to shape the modern world as we know it in the twenty-first century. It would also give rise to the most influential counterinsurgency doctrine of all time, "the spreading oil spot," which was the forerunner of the "population-centric" doctrine implemented in the twenty-first century by U.S. forces in Iraq and Afghanistan. This meant slowly pushing out army posts and settlements until indigenous resistance was crushed. Long before the term was coined by the French soldier Hubert Lyautey toward the end of the nineteenth century, the strategy that it described was being employed by Europeans with great success.

The inhabitants of Asia, Africa, and the Americas resisted the white man's advance as best they could. Sometimes they were able to inflict serious setbacks; two famous examples, which will be discussed in this section, were the 1842 British retreat from Kabul and the 1876 Battle of the Little Bighorn. But these were only temporary reverses in the inexorable Westernization of the world. Most of the wars chronicled here were won by the Europeans—whether against the American Indians, Pashtuns, Chechens, Moroccans, or Boers (themselves of European origin). By 1914 Europeans and their offspring controlled 84 percent of the world's landmass—up from 35 percent in 1800, at the beginning of the Industrial Revolution, and just 15 percent in 1450, at the beginning of the Age of Exploration.[1]

That non-Europeans did not have more success in preserving their independence was due in large measure to Europe's growing advantages in military technology and technique. But it also owes something to the fact that most non-Europeans did not adopt the smartest strategies to make use of their limited resources. Few fought as the Haitians did. Instead of attempting to engage in guerrilla warfare—which, even if unsuccessful, might have staved off ultimate defeat for years, if not decades, and inflicted considerable costs on the invaders—most non-Europeans fought precisely as the Europeans wanted them to. That is to say, in conventional, if not particularly effective, fashion.

Westerners thought that most of the areas they conquered were "primitive" and "backward," but in a sense they were too advanced for their own good. By the turn of the nineteenth century, most of Africa and Asia had fallen under the sway of native regimes with standing armies, and their rulers naturally looked for protection to those forces. Sub-Saharan Africa was the least advanced region from a European vantage point, but even here a recent study has found "the presence of state structures, often elaborate ones, in all military organization[s]."[2] Thus in fighting the European onslaught, Africans generally eschewed the sort of tribal tactics—a primitive form of guerrilla warfare—practiced by their ancestors.

To take just one example, the Zulus may have been armed primarily with assegais (stabbing spears) rather than Martini-Henry rifles, but, like the British, their forces were organized into disciplined regiments known as impis, which did not usually fight from cover but rather maneuvered on the battlefield. The Zulus' goal was to annihilate the enemy—not to engage in hit-and-run raiding. Their favorite tactical formation was known as the "horns of the bull." The center, or "chest," of the impi would pin down the enemy while two "horns" on either side raced around to envelop the enemy's flanks. On January 22, 1879, an impi of 20,000 men wiped out a British column at Isandlwana, killing 1,329 British and African troops. But a frontal assault on the nearby British garrison at Rorke's Drift was repulsed by just 120 soldiers, and on March 29 the entire Zulu army was defeated at Kambula. In this decisive but little-known battle, the British lost just 18 soldiers to the Zulus' 2,000. A few months later British troops burned the capital of Zululand and captured its king, Cetshwayo.[3]

The British did not usually lose as many men as they had at Isandlwana, but otherwise this tale of a minor setback followed by decisive triumphs was replicated in many other corners of the queen's domains. The Americans, French, Germans, Russians, and other imperialists had similar experiences. The most daunting obstacles to the Westerners' advance were not native armies but treacherous terrain and deadly diseases. Those difficulties were finally surmounted by advances in medical and transportation technology (quinine, railroads, and steamboats were critical), thereby making possible the "Scramble for Africa" in the late nineteenth century.

Why did so few indigenous regimes resort to guerrilla tactics? Part of the explanation is that most non-Westerners had little idea of the combat power of Western armies until it was too late. Too many empire builders in the developing world imagined that the tactics that had worked against local tribes would work against the white tribe. They were fatally mistaken, but their incomprehension was understandable given how slowly news traveled before the spread of telegraphs, undersea cables, steamships, and railroads—to say nothing of radio, television, airplanes, and the Internet. In the ancient world, Rome's enemies had scant opportunity to learn from one another's experiences. So too in the Victorian world there was little chance that the Zulus could benefit from the experience of the Sioux. By contrast, soldiers from more advanced nations did study each other's campaigns. A spate of military manuals was published in the nineteenth and early twentieth centuries advising Westerners how to win "small wars."

When native rulers did try to learn from past mistakes, their impulse was usually to make their armies more conventional, rather than less, by hiring European advisers and buying European arms. With the notable exception of Japan, the reproductions were seldom as good as the originals, and their inferiority was brutally exposed in battle. Most peoples in the developing world would have been better off reverting to older forms of irregular warfare. The Marathas of India, for example, had a long history as superb horse raiders, but in the late eighteenth century they chose to raise European-style regiments that proved no match for disciplined British regulars under such talented generals as Arthur Wellesley and Gerald Lake.[4] In a very real sense they beat themselves by imbibing the myth then prevalent in European military circles of the superiority of conventional warfare and the ineffectuality of guerrilla resistance.

Such counterproductive behavior is hard to explain unless one realizes that it would have been hard for traditional rulers to give up their palaces and riches without a fight—or to maintain their grip on recalcitrant subjects while hiding in the bush. There was also an onus in many indigenous armies, just as in their Western counterparts, against fighting in a stealthy or underhanded way. It was considered unmanly. Much better, many figured, to fight courageously and die gloriously. Accepting the ascendance of the Europeans was often not that hard in any case, because the new overlords were liable to practice "indirect rule" that kept local elites in place.

Even if there had been more desire to ignite insurgencies, ideological fuel was generally lacking. Most people have always been attached to their homes, but until modern times their primary allegiance was to the family, clan, or tribe, not to the state. Often the rulers of indigenous states were resented as much as Europeans, if not more so, especially by those who belonged to a different tribe or sect. Nationalism was an eighteenth-century European invention that by the nineteenth century had not spread much beyond European settler colonies in the Americas. That helps to explain why most of those colonies achieved independence. The rest of the world lost its independence as much because of a lack of national feeling as because of a lack of modern weapons. The brittle kingdoms of what came to be known as the Third World were wont to collapse after their armies had been defeated on the battlefield. There was seldom prolonged resistance of the kind that occurred in Spain after Napoleon's initial victories.

A partial exception was to be found in Islamic countries where the people were bound together by ties of religion as well as tribe. Some Muslim states also made the mistake of fighting Europeans head-on. The most notorious example was the Battle of Omdurman in 1898 when thousands of Sudanese "dervishes" charged straight at the British lines in broad daylight only to be mown down by machine-gun, artillery, and rifle fire. But other jihadists were clever enough to avoid the full fury of Western firepower.

Chechens, Pashtuns, and Moroccans, among others, would wage protracted insurgencies against European occupiers in the nineteenth century.

Some non-Muslim peoples, notably the Filipinos and Boers, would also inflict serious damage on colonial powers. While painful for the Americans and the British, however, the uprisings in the Philippines and South Africa at the turn of the twentieth century were also relatively brief. Not so the wars of the North American Indians. They would display both the potential and the limitations of guerrilla tactics during a resistance to white rule that lasted almost three centuries.

21.

THE SKULKING WAY OF WAR

The "Forest Wars" in Eastern North America, 1622–1842

THE ACME OF guerrilla skill is to spring an ambush on a completely unsuspecting foe—something that the Indians of North America managed to accomplish on too many occasions to count. The most famous such ambush occurred on July 9, 1755, when a combined force of French soldiers and Indian warriors caught a column of British and colonial soldiers in the woods near Fort Duquesne, the site of present-day Pittsburgh. Some 600 men, out of 1,469, were killed, including the British commander, General Edward Braddock. His aide de camp, a young officer named George Washington, barely escaped this debacle. The massacre at the Monongahela was particularly notable because the Indians' enemies were armed soldiers who should have been ready for battle—but weren't.[5] If even large bodies of troops could be caught unawares, it should not be terribly surprising that farming communities on the frontier were regularly caught by surprise. One of the first and most devastating such attacks occurred near Jamestown, the first permanent English settlement in North America, located near modern-day Williamsburg.

The English colonists suspected nothing amiss on Friday morning, March 22, 1622. Powhatan Indians were showing up in great numbers on the outlying plantations scattered for eighty miles around Jamestown. Those plantations had sprung up in recent years to farm a lucrative new crop—

tobacco. There was nothing unusual about such visits. The Indians would bring deer, turkey, fish, fruit, and fur and in return would get beads and other trinkets that they valued. It was a clash of cultures, with the English in their cumbersome woolen clothes and leather shoes while the Indian men wore nothing but loincloths and moccasins, their faces brightly painted, heads half shaved, and elaborate earrings dangling from their ears. But by then each side was familiar with the other. The Indians were unarmed, so they aroused no suspicion.

Relations between settlers and Indians had been tense initially when the first ships of the Virginia Company had arrived fifteen years earlier carrying a hundred or so settlers to establish what would become the first permanent English colony in North America. Clashes were frequent, and in the early days the English would never have permitted the Indians to roam around their colony as they did in 1622. But peace had generally prevailed since 1614. The preceding year the English had kidnapped Pocahontas, the daughter of Powhatan, founder of an empire of ten thousand Indians stretching around Jamestown like a vast human necklace. Pocahontas converted to Christianity and married a settler, and her father reached an accommodation with his new in-laws.

In 1618 Powhatan died but his successor and half brother, Opechancanough, promised to continue friendly relations. He told the colonists that "he held the peace concluded so firm as the skies should sooner fall than it dissolve." Many of the English believed that they were in "a happy league of peace and amity" with the natives and "that the fear of killing each other is vanished away." Only too late would they realize this was "treacherous dissimulation" on the part of a clever chieftain who nurtured deep-seated hatred of the newcomers, who were encroaching on his lands and trying to convert his people to an alien religion. Opechancanough had concocted an elaborate plot to destroy the invaders before any more ships could arrive to swell their ranks even further.

On the morning of March 22, 1622, all of the Indians appeared to be friendly. Some even sat down to breakfast with their hosts. The colonists were going about their normal routines—planting corn and tobacco, gardening, building, sawing. Without warning, wrote John Smith, one of the founders of the colony, the "cruel beasts . . . slew most barbarously, not sparing either age or sex, man, woman, or child, so sudden in their execution, that few or none discerned the weapon or blow that brought them to destruction . . . most by their own weapons." Those weapons ranged from swords to axes, knives, hammers, and saws. Picking up these crude implements, the Indians went on a marauding rampage, killing every European they could find, including women and children. "And not being content with taking away life alone," an official report noted, "they fell after upon the dead, making as well as they could a fresh murder, defacing, dragging, and mangling the dead carcasses."

Jamestown itself was on guard because it had been warned in advance by a Christian Indian, but the attackers moved so quickly from farm to farm that there was no time to organize a general defense against what one Englishman described as this "viperous brood" and another called "those hell-hounds." The attack wiped out more than one-fourth of the colonists—347 out of 1,240—and put the entire colony on the brink of extinction.

Yet Captain Smith, who had long counseled a hard line against the natives, perceived a chilling bit of good news in this disaster: "Some say [this massacre] will be good for the plantation because now we have just cause to destroy them by all means necessary." Sir Francis Wyatt, governor of Jamestown, agreed on the need to "pursue their extirpation." But he realized that a straightforward assault would be unlikely to succeed. "It is most apparent," he wrote, "that they are an enemy not to be suddenly destroyed with the sword by reason of their swiftness of foot, and advantages of the wood, to which upon all our assaults they retire."

Instead he proposed to wipe them out "by the way of starvings and all other means." Punitive expeditions were sent to burn the Powhatans' towns and steal or destroy their corn, thus bringing them to the brink of starvation the following winter. Two months after the initial attack, on May 22, 1623, a party of Englishmen lured the war-weary Indians for peace talks and served them poisoned wine. The peace negotiators then fired a "volley of shot" into the incapacitated Powhatan, killing two hundred of them. On their way back to the colony, the Englishmen shot fifty more Indians "and brought home part of their heads."

The pattern was set for almost three centuries of what the Virginia Company directors would describe after the Jamestown uprising as "perpetual war without peace or truce." Perpetual it was, but it was not war as understood on the battlefields of Europe. It was a frontier style of fighting that was marked by treachery and surprise and massacre on both sides. In other words, it was guerrilla warfare, a phrase not usually associated with seventeenth- and eighteenth-century colonial history.[6]

✦ ✦ ✦

THE JAMESTOWN SETTLERS were among the first to discover what many Europeans would learn: that Indians excelled at the "skulking style of war." The Indians of eastern North America were not nomads like the tribes of Inner Asia or the tribes that would come to populate the Great Plains. They lived in permanent villages for most of the year, in birch-bark wigwams sometimes ringed by wooden palisades, and grew corn, squash, and other crops.[7] But farming was considered women's work. The men were left free to hunt, fish—and make war. Like many other prestate peoples, their hunting skills made them effective killers whether stalking animals on four legs or two. "However absurd it may appear," wrote George Washington, who as a young man fought with and against Indians on the Virginia frontier, "it is nevertheless certain" that "five hundred Indians" could be a more potent fighting force "than ten times their number of Regulars."[8]

That was only true, however, when the Indians fought in a stealthy manner. In 1492, when the first Europeans landed in the New World, the indigenous peoples did not have horses, wheels, steel, or firearms. They fought on foot with wooden swords, spears, slings, clubs, axes, and bows and arrows tipped with obsidian, flint, or bone. Thus equipped, they could not stand in the open against the Europeans and their "thunder sticks."

The explorer Samuel de Champlain and two other French soldiers had enough firepower between them to rout two hundred Mohawk Indians. Just after daybreak on July 30, 1609, on the shores of what is now Lake Champlain in New York State, Champlain calmly walked in front of a group of his Algonquin and Huron allies who were at war with the Mohawk. They were standing in a tight array, wearing wooden armor and holding shields. Champlain raised his arquebus, a primitive musket that had been loaded with four balls, and fired a single, deafening shot that knocked over three Mohawk at once, two of them chiefs easily recognizable by the feathers they wore on their heads. "As I was loading again," he recalled, "one of my companions fired a shot from the woods, which astonished them anew to such a degree that . . . they lost courage, and took to flight . . . fleeing into the woods, whither I pursued them, killing still more of them."[9]

Not all Indian societies survived such disastrous initial contacts.[10] Some, such as the Caribs and Arawaks of the West Indies, were wiped out altogether by a combination of European weapons and European microbes in what the historian Edmund S. Morgan rightly calls a "tale of horror." (Morgan explains "the fury with which the Spanish assaulted the Arawaks even after they had enslaved them" by arguing that the Indians' innocence and austerity—they required and wanted little in the way of worldly goods—was an affront to "the Europeans' cherished assumption of their own civilized, Christian superiority over naked, heathen barbarians.")[11] Ironically, the most advanced societies—the Aztecs and Incas—suffered the most devastating defeats because, like the Zulus or the South Asians, they were so tightly organized and so hierarchical that they could mass thousands of warriors in the kind of open battle at which Europeans excelled. Moreover, these states were so densely populated that they could transmit smallpox and other plagues "like ink spreading through tissue paper."[12] And they were so centralized that the loss of a few key leaders could immobilize the rest of society. Less centralized, less populous, less sophisticated societies fared better because they had no choice but to place heavy reliance on guile and subterfuge to resist the better-armed newcomers—they employed guerrilla tactics such as the raid on Jamestown orchestrated by Opechancanough.

Indian ambushes became even more formidable once their warriors learned to make use of the guns, horses, and steel introduced by the Europeans, a process that was just beginning in Opechancanough's day. Although colonial authorities tried to keep Indians from getting their hands on firearms, they acquired all they needed through trade or theft. While they never fully gave up the bow and arrow, their marksmanship soon exceeded that of most settlers, who were mainly farmers and craftsmen, not hunters or soldiers.[13] The dense woods of eastern North America greatly abetted the Indians because they made the Europeans' parade-ground formations and volley fire difficult to execute, providing a contrast between the inflexibility of the newcomers, prisoners to imported and inappropriate tactical doctrines, and the shrewdness and adaptability of the natives who developed a way of war ideally suited to their environment. Gliding between the trees, the Indians were able to carry out raids and ambushes that took advantage of what was, to the colonists, unfamiliar terrain. Having no need of cumbersome supply trains, they could survive for extended periods on acorns, nuts, ground-up animal bones, even tree bark, thereby allowing them to move much faster than colonial militias.[14]

Like their settled forebears dating back to ancient Mesopotamia, New England farmers had trouble defending themselves against highly skilled tribal guerrillas. "Scarcely a hamlet of the Massachusetts and New Hampshire borders escaped a visit from the nimble enemy," the nineteenth-century historian Francis Parkman wrote of the French and Indian wars that raged from 1689 to 1759. "[All] were all more or less infested, usually by small scalping parties, hiding in the outskirts, waylaying stragglers, or shooting men at work in the fields, and disappearing as soon as their blow was struck."[15]

✦ ✦ ✦

FOR ALL THEIR skill at the art of ambush, the Indians got the worst of the "forest wars" waged along the Eastern Seaboard in the seventeenth and eighteenth centuries. The outcome may seem inevitable in retrospect, but that was not how it appeared at the time. In Jamestown in 1622 the colonists, not the Indians, seemed to be on the brink of extinction. Why did the Indians lose in the end? Principally because of two critical deficiencies—a lack of population and a lack of unity.

Indians had far outnumbered the initial settlers in North America. (The actual number of Indians, preconquest, has been a source of never-ending debate.)[16] But by the eighteenth century the demographic balance had shifted decisively in favor of the Europeans, who kept arriving in great numbers while Indian populations kept declining. Epidemics in 1616 (possibly bubonic plague) and 1633 (smallpox) killed as many as 95 percent of the New England Indians.[17] Governor William Bradford of Plymouth Plantation left a harrowing account of how the pox struck Indian societies, writing, "They die like rotten sheep."[18] Such calamitous losses—far greater on a proportional basis than those suffered at Hiroshima or in the trench warfare of World War I—left the survivors, one historian notes, "shocked, grief-stricken, and bewildered."[19] In this weakened condition they were easy prey for rapacious Europeans who waged war without mercy.

Sadly typical was the fate of the Wampanoag and other tribes that fought under the leadership of Metacom, the sachem (chief) known to the English as King Philip. King Philip's War (1675–76) was the worst frontier war of the seventeenth century. It damaged half the towns of New England and killed 600 to 800 settlers. But the other side fared far worse. By one estimate, out of 11,600 Indians in the rebel camp, 5,000 died of battle, disease, and starvation, 1,000, including Metacom's nine-year-old son, were sold as slaves, and 2,000 were turned into permanent refugees. There were so few surviving Wampanoag that they would not hold another powwow until 1929—253 years after Metacom's death.[20]

By the end of the eighteenth century, most other northeastern tribes had been similarly devastated. Guerrilla tactics are designed to compensate for inferiority of numbers and firepower, but over the course of many years even the most nimble guerrillas can be ground down by the remorseless, ceaseless, pitiless application of overwhelming resources.

The Indians' demographic disadvantage was compounded by their internal divisions. When Europeans arrived, the natives of North America were split, notes one recent history, among six hundred "autonomous societies" from "twelve quite distinct and apparently unrelated linguistic groups, in some cases more dissimilar than English and Chinese."[21] Each society, in turn, was broken into many tribes, clans, bands, and villages, and these were further split into competing factions, with some favoring accommodation with the whites and others preferring confrontation. Indian culture was so egalitarian that individuals and groups were usually free not to carry out policies they disagreed with. A front of united Native American tribes might have significantly altered the narrative of American history. It was not to be.

Some charismatic chiefs such as Powhatan managed to forge great "nations" or "confederations," but they generally lacked the authority to compel compliance with their wishes. They were similar in this respect to European rulers of the Middle Ages who lacked a bureaucracy to carry out their edicts and thus depended on the goodwill of their nobles to undertake any major enterprise such as a war. And just as in medieval Europe a peasant was apt to think of himself as a "Norman" or a "Burgundian" rather than a Frenchman, much less a European, so too individual Indians were apt to identify with their tribe or clan rather than any larger entity. There was little or no pan-Indian sense of identity that could lead warriors of many different tribes to cooperate with one another. The talented Shawnee chief Tecumseh, one of the greatest orators North America has ever known and brother of a mystical preacher known as the Prophet, came closer than anyone else to uniting disparate tribes in a revolt against the Europeans. But he was defeated and killed in 1813 while fighting alongside British allies against American troops under the command of future president William Henry Harrison. The dream of Indian unity died with him.

Thus in every Indian war, the whites were able to find numerous willing collaborators—either individual Indians willing to serve as scouts and soldiers for pay or entire tribes or factions eager to gain an advantage over traditional rivals. The outcome of King Philip's War was decided in no small measure because the Pequot, Mohawk, and Mohegan, as well as the Christian converts known as "praying Indians," fought alongside the New Englanders against the Wampanoag and their allies. Metacom was ultimately tracked down and killed by a mixed unit of 50 whites and 150 Indians raised by Captain Benjamin Church of Plymouth Colony. Throughout the next half century the French would ally with Algonquin tribes to attack English settlements while English settlers would fight back in league with the Algonquins' historic enemies, the Iroquois. European armies were able to exploit similar divisions across Africa and Asia. Colonialism by a small number of Europeans would have been impossible otherwise.

Just as they could not come together to wage war, so Indians could not reach consensus on making peace. This led whites to make claims of bad faith when chiefs signed treaties but could not enforce them on headstrong young braves eager for battle. Americans had a similar problem: state and federal capitals were often unwilling or unable to control far-flung settlers bent on grabbing Indian lands for themselves. Canada saw fewer clashes with its Indians in part because the British government, less beholden politically to the settlers, had more success in upholding treaties. But the United States, decentralized as it was, was able to achieve a more coherent approach toward the Indians than they were able to achieve toward the United States.

The great innovation of Indian policy in the early nineteenth century was a reversion to what might be called the Assyrian strategy. Over the course of three centuries, the Assyrians deported between four and five million subject peoples, most famously ten tribes of Israelites who were sent to

Mesopotamia in 721 BC and thereby lost their distinctive identity.[22] President Andrew Jackson, an old Indian fighter from Tennessee, had something similar in mind when he schemed to remove all of the remaining Indian tribes from lands in the East that were coveted by settlers. He decided to send them to the wild territory beyond the Mississippi River in modern-day Oklahoma, where he assumed no whites would ever want to live.

Following the passage by Congress of the Indian Removal Act in 1830, seventy thousand Indians were forced to march west along what the Cherokee called the Trail of Tears (1838–39). Many died at the start of their onerous journey in poorly equipped internment camps that suffered from many of the problems that would plague the notorious British concentration camps in the Boer War six decades later. More died en route, especially the young and the old, because of the harsh winter and inadequate provisions, clothing, transportation, medical care, and lodging. A missionary complained that they were treated "very much like brute animals"—"obliged at night to lie down on the naked ground, in the open air, exposed to wind and rain." Some fifteen thousand people perished in this repugnant operation.[23]

The Cherokee, an agrarian, peaceful, and remarkably Americanized tribe with their own written language, tried to resist relocation by legal action—to no avail. More militant tribes, ranging from the Sauk and Fox of Illinois to the Seminole of Florida, resisted with force. They were equally unsuccessful, although they inflicted considerable costs on the American government. The Second Seminole War was particularly costly: lasting seven years (1835–42), it led to the death of nearly 1,500 soldiers, or almost 15 percent of the entire force in Florida, and the expenditure of $30 million—more than the annual federal budget at the time. Hostilities did not end until virtually the entire Seminole nation, originally comprising some four thousand people, had been captured or killed.[24]

Like the Seminole, all the other eastern Indians eventually were clubbed into submission and shipped west. This was one of the darkest chapters in the long, shameful history of European and American mistreatment of indigenous peoples. But it was not the end of the Indian Wars. In the trans-Mississippi West would be written the climactic chapters of the struggle between Americans and Indians.

22.

THE WINNING OF THE WEST

Braves vs. Bluecoats, 1848–1890

IT WAS THE "buffalo trail" that gave the Cheyenne away. On the morning of November 26, 1868, near the Texas border, the Osage Indian scouts found a path in the snow that ran parallel to the stream. Buffalo always went straight for the water and then scattered to graze. So this trail had been made by people.

For the past three days, through falling snow and thick fog, the Seventh U.S. Cavalry Regiment had been on the trail of hostile Indians who had raided settlements in Kansas, killing men, raping women, torching homesteads. Now, deep in "Indian Territory," today's Oklahoma, they had their first solid lead. As the troopers rode on, wrote a captain, they found traces of "a plain fresh trail which had obviously been made in the afternoon of the day previous by a war party of from one to two hundred Indians."

The troopers loaded their Springfield carbines and tested them to make sure they were not frozen. In the evening they rested for an hour, fed their horses and themselves, brewed some coffee, and then mounted up to continue the pursuit. At 1:30 a.m. on Friday, November 27, the Osage scouts reported smelling smoke and hearing faint tinkling sounds in the distance. "Heap Injuns down there," the Osage chief Little Beaver reported. The regiment's commander, Lieutenant Colonel George Armstrong Custer, crawled to the top of a summit with some of his officers to decide on a course of action. He did not know how many Indians were in the village nestled below him in a bend of the Washita River. Nor did he care. For a daring cavalier like Custer—a man with a cast of mind similar to Robert Rogers's and Banastre Tarleton's—there was but one acceptable course of action. He would attack at dawn.

Still only twenty-nine years old, Custer was already a famous war hero, known for his vanity (he sported uniforms of his own design, long golden hair, and an imposing walrus mustache), his reckless courage, and his driving ambition, all of which attracted ardent admiration and perfervid loathing in equal measure. At West Point he had been nearly expelled on more than one occasion and had finished dead last in the class of 1861. Yet so conspicuous was his gallantry as a Union cavalryman that just two years later he vaulted straight from the rank of lieutenant to that of brevet brigadier general at age twenty-three. He ended the Civil War as a brevet major general and a division commander who was celebrated for leading his men from the front and simultaneously criticized for getting so many of them killed or wounded.

Peacetime brought a demotion for the "Boy General," as he was known in the press, and deployment to the western frontier. But Custer never lost his knack for courting controversy. In 1867 he was convicted by a court-martial for deserting his command in order to meet his beloved wife, Libbie, at a distant fort. When a fresh campaign against the Cheyenne, Arapaho, and other tribes beckoned the following year, Major General Phil Sheridan, commander of the Department of the Missouri, cut short Custer's sentence—a year's suspension without pay—and recalled him to duty in the expectation that this swashbuckling officer could wage unremitting war as successfully against Indians as he had against Confederates. Sheridan's confidence would be amply repaid at what became known as the Battle of the Washita, if not on later occasions.

Custer split his seven hundred officers and men into four columns and told them "to get as close as possible to the village without giving any alarm." No talking, no smoking, no cooking. He even ordered the dogs that had accompanied them to be strangled with ropes or "dispatch[ed] with knives" to prevent them from spoiling the surprise attack. "The silence was oppressive," wrote a captain. "Even the horses by their rapid gait showed that they, too, nervously partook of the quiet excitement." The troopers spent "the night in moody meditations," recalled a lieutenant, "broken occasionally by spasmodic shivers and involuntary shakes."

As the warming rays of the sun flickered over the horizon, the soldiers could see the "clustered tepees, situated among wide-branching cottonwood trees." "The hour was so still," recalled a scout, "that a man could almost hear his watch tick." Suddenly a shot rang out. The band struck up "Garry Owen," Custer's favorite martial tune, although the musicians managed to get out only a few bars before their instruments froze. With a thunderous roar the cavalrymen galloped toward the five hundred Indians assembled before them. As they crashed through the frozen snow, "the Indian village rang with unearthly war-whoops, the quick discharge of firearms, the clamorous barking of dogs, the cries of infants and the wailing of women."

The teepees belonged to a band of Cheyenne led by Chief Black Kettle, a tragic figure who counseled peace but could not control the depredations of his young braves. These Cheyenne had already suffered grievously from the white man. Four years earlier, while camped under a white flag along Sand Creek in Colorado, Black Kettle's band was attacked without provocation by seven hundred volunteers under the sanguinary Colonel John M. Chivington. One white witness later recalled that "all manner of depredations were inflicted"—Indians "were scalped, their brains knocked out; the men used their knives, ripped open women, clubbed little children, knocked them in the head with their guns, beat their brains out, mutilated their bodies in every sense of the word." The death toll amounted to two hundred people, two-thirds of them women and children.[25]

Black Kettle survived the Sand Creek Massacre. He would not survive the Washita attack. He was shot off his horse as he was trying to flee. Two of his wives and a daughter were also killed. Many others fell "almost before sleep had left their eyelids." But other Indians overcame their initial surprise and, as Custer wrote, "seized their rifles, bows and arrows, and sprang behind the nearest trees, while some leaped into the stream, nearly waist deep, and using the bank as a rifle-pit, began a vigorous and determined defense." One of his officers noted, "The Indian boys and squaws fought as fiercely as did the bucks"—small wonder, given their previous experience of the white man's brutal way of war.

It took hours to extinguish the last resistance and by then a disconcerting sight was visible on the nearby ridgelines: Indians on ponies, hundreds of them, "gorgeous in war bonnets and paints," some "armed with guns and some with bows and arrows and gaudy shields." A cavalry officer noted how "surprising" it was too see "all the hills . . . alive with mounted warriors." Little did the impetuous Custer, who was undertaking his first Indian campaign, realize when he began the attack that thousands of Apache, Arapaho, Cheyenne, Comanche, and Kiowa were camped a few miles downstream. Already they had killed Major Joel Elliott and seventeen troopers who had become separated from the main body of troops while riding in pursuit of fleeing Cheyenne. A war correspondent who visited the battlefield the next month found their naked corpses frozen solid and covered with numerous bullet and arrow holes. Some were missing their heads; others had their throats cut. "There was not a single body," he reported, "that did not exhibit evidences of fearful mutilation." The entire regiment only narrowly avoided a similar fate.

Rather than risk a battle against "greatly superior numbers," Custer did the prudent thing—for once. He decided to retreat after destroying the Cheyennes' shelters and steeds. Huge bonfires were kindled to burn the seventy-five buffalo-hide tepees and all of their contents. The 650 ponies were harder to eradicate. Initially the men tried to rope the animals and slit their throats, but the poor ponies became so frantic that this plan was abandoned. The troopers spent two exhausting hours firing volley after volley into the moaning and snorting and bleeding animals. As the sun fell behind the snow-covered peaks, the cavalrymen feinted an attack toward nearby Indian villages. This drew off the Indian warriors and allowed the cavalry to march back to its camp as the band played "Ain't I Glad to Get out of the Wilderness."

The results of this "nice little fight," as one officer termed it, would be shrouded in controversy—along with everything else in Custer's life. Some officers accused Custer of leaving Major Elliott and his men to their fate by not making an attempt to rescue them. The Indians, for their part, accused Custer of grossly exaggerating the casualties he had inflicted among their fighting men. He claimed to have killed 103 warriors. The Cheyenne said they had lost fewer than 20 men and a similar number of women and children. There was no doubt that some "squaws" and their "papooses" were shot down in the chaos of battle. Custer had intervened to save the rest, but he was still accused by some of committing a massacre. There were also allegations that he had taken one of the 53 female captives as his mistress. Everything that Custer did prompted denunciation and defense, both in his lifetime and afterward. Of one aspect of the raid, however, there was little doubt. By destroying their village, their food supply, and their ponies, Custer had dealt a severe blow to the Indians. The campaign was not yet over, but it was through the use of such tactics that the Cheyenne and the other proud, warlike tribes would be brought to their knees.[26]

✦ ✦ ✦

THE WARS SURVEYED in the preceding chapter—conflicts fought largely in the forests of the East Coast and on foot against settled tribes of farmers—do not fit the common conception of Indian Wars. The popular stereotype of bluecoats and braves on horseback was forged in the trans-Mississippi West between 1848 and 1890 in clashes such as the Battle of the Washita. Those wars would lead, by a conservative estimate, to the deaths of 1,109 U.S. soldiers, 461 U.S. civilians, and over 5,500 Indians.[27]

The greatest clashes occurred on the Great Plains against the Arapaho, Cheyenne, Comanche, Kiowa, and Sioux. Like the nomads of Inner Asia, these superb horsemen ranged across seas of grass in the post–Civil War era following buffalo herds and warring with neighboring tribes. They lived in portable, buffalo-hide teepees and disdained agriculture. Theirs was a warrior society par excellence where sustenance came from the slaughtering of buffalo, deer, and other animals and the plundering of the possessions, especially the horses, of enemy tribes. Bravery was inculcated from birth; boys joined their first war party as young as eleven. "Better to die on the battlefield than to live to be old": this was the philosophy of the Sioux and other Plains tribes. From their perspective, wrote Royal Hassrick, the foremost student of the Sioux, "courting death" was "as important a part of warfare as victory." The highest honors, in the form of feathers worn in a war bonnet, were reserved for warriors who "counted coup"—that is, struck an enemy in battle, whether that blow caused any injury or not—because this was an inherently dangerous undertaking. Stoicism was another cardinal virtue. "Men on war missions or hunting expeditions," wrote Hassrick, "were noted for their ability to suffer wounds unflinchingly, to experience long periods of hunger and exposure." Plains Indians neither gave nor expected quarter in battle: for a man, the wages of defeat were death, often accompanied by mutilation. Women and children, by contrast, were spared; typically they were adopted into the tribe that had defeated their menfolk.[28]

On a man-to-man basis there is little doubt that the individual Indian was a better warrior—tougher, bolder, braver—than the average U.S. Army soldier. But by the midnineteenth century there were only 270,000 Indians in the West, and many of them had already made their peace with the white man. The "hostile" tribes had fewer than 100,000 people—this in a region that would be the destination for 8 million Americans in the four decades following the California gold strike of 1848. Even the mightiest of tribes, the Sioux, numbered fewer than 30,000 in 1866, which meant that they could probably field no more than 7,000 warriors.[29] Just as in the East, therefore, the tribes could not make good their losses, while the whites could count on seemingly endless reinforcements.

Settlers' militias sometimes pursued a genocidal policy against the Indians, as the Sand Creek Massacre showed. The U.S. Army did not. Although the bluecoats were capable of considerable brutality, their goal was not to exterminate the Indians but to move them onto reservations—a strategy known as "concentration" that would be employed by many other counterinsurgents, including, as we shall see, the British in the Boer War. "For whites," write two leading historians of the West, "concentration offered a happy coincidence of self-interest and noble philanthropy."[30] The self-interest was that Indians could be removed from lands coveted by whites, thereby preventing what the secretary of the interior described in 1873 as "frequent outrages, wrongs, and disturbances of the public peace." The philanthropic part of the enterprise ("the great work of humanity and benevolence") was that Indians were supposed to be taught "the arts of agriculture, and such pursuits as are incident to civilization." In practice, however, Indians were often denied the lands promised to them and taken advantage of by unscrupulous Indian agents. Seldom were these restless hunters happy to settle down as inoffensive farmers. Thus confining Indians on reservations required the constant application of force with, as the secretary of the interior said, "all needed severity."[31]

That was a job for a ragtag American army, which by 1874 numbered just twenty-seven thousand officers and men—smaller than the New York Police Department today.[32] They were a hard-drinking, hard-bitten group of volunteers characterized, unkindly if not inaccurately, by one newspaper as "bummers, loafers, and foreign paupers."[33] Their assignment was to man a series of forts along the trails taken by pioneers heading west. Contrary to the popular impression fostered by nineteenth-century "dime novels" and twentieth-century movies, forts were rarely besieged by Indians; most did not even have stockades or other defenses. Rather they provided a base from which soldiers could fan out in pursuit of hostile warriors, much as the French army was then doing in North Africa and the British army on the Northwest Frontier. In common with the British and French, the American army's most effective tactics were to target, as Custer did in 1868, Indian food stores, pony herds, and teepees, especially in wintertime when tribes were less mobile. Given the Indians' subsistence-level economy, it did not take much to put them on the brink of starvation, giving them no choice but to enter a reservation. In essence tactics had not changed all that much since the seventeenth-century battles between the Jamestown settlers and the Powhatan.

✦ ✦ ✦

THE MOST INNOVATIVE and admirable of the post–Civil War Indian fighters was Major General George Crook, a "straight as a lance," broad-shouldered West Pointer who had fought at Antietam and Chickamauga. He was an avid hunter and a crack shot who stood out in the dissolute postwar army for not drinking alcohol to excess, not smoking, not using profanity, and not gambling. His diary was filled with disapproval, in small, neat handwriting, of all these "vices." His beverage of choice was milk; his preferred hobby cribbage and other card games played only for "pastime," never for money.[34]

"A brilliant strategist,"[35] he made an in-depth study of Indian ways and realized that, as an aide put it, "unless savage should be pitted against savage, the white man would be outwitted, exhausted, circumvented, possibly ambuscaded and destroyed."[36] He therefore made extensive use of Indians as scouts and auxiliaries ("the wildest that I could get") led by officers with "the best physique" and "great patience."

Crook also realized that it would be hard to catch elusive braves with the ponderous wagon trains favored by the army. So he ditched them in favor of more mobile mules, becoming the leading expert on the military uses of these humble pack animals. Mule packing was such a specialized skill that he thought it could only be undertaken by civilian experts who were "paid liberally"—an early form of military contractor. Crook's motto was "the trail must be stuck to and never lost."[37]

While dogged in pursuit of Indians, Crook also tried to be fair in his dealings with them. He instructed subordinates to "deliver justice to all—Indians as well as white men," "to make no promises not in their power to carry out," and not "to become the instruments of oppression."[38] In his diary he recorded his personal creed: "The persons who enjoy the most happiness in this world are those who have the greatest amount of charity for their fellow man."[39] More than most of his contemporaries, he understood that a successful Indian policy had to offer carrots as well as sticks. Unfortunately he had trouble convincing his superiors. They favored a harsher approach.

Crook did not have much success against the Sioux in 1876 on the northern Great Plains. Leading large units was not his strength. He did better employing small, mobile columns against the Paiute of the Pacific Northwest in 1866–68 and against the Apache of the Southwest in 1872–73, 1882–84, and 1885–86. His most notable exploits occurred in 1883 when he routed the famous Apache chief Geronimo out of the forbidding Sierra Madre in northern Mexico by employing a force of 266 mules and 327 men, the largest contingent being friendly Apache. Geronimo was one of the most skilled, dogged, and merciless raiders that any Indian tribe had ever produced. He spent decades terrorizing settlers in northern Mexico and the southwestern United States. But the presence of so many of his own people in the enemy camp demoralized even Geronimo and persuaded him to surrender, at least temporarily. He went off the reservation again, literally, in 1885, only to give up the next year after another relentless pursuit overseen by Crook. Yet, after getting drunk on mescal, Geronimo and a few others (20 men, 13 women) reneged on their promise to surrender. This embarrassing setback stained Crook's reputation and caused him to be relieved of command at his own request.

The honor of capturing Geronimo for the last time fell to Crook's hated rival, Brigadier General Nelson A. Miles. He sent out a picked force of 55 soldiers, 30 mule packers, and 29 Apache scouts. They finally ran down Geronimo and his small band after one of the most arduous operations in the history of the U.S. Army—a 2,500-mile trek through the mountains of northern Mexico, whose government allowed such American forays into its territory much as Pakistan and Yemen in more recent times have given permission for some U.S. counterterrorist operations on their soil.

To prevent any more escapes, Geronimo and the rest of the Warm Springs and Chiricahua Apache, even those who had worked for Crook as scouts, were transported to captivity in Florida. Crook, who died in 1890, spent the last years of his life campaigning for justice for the Apache, who had been promised that they would be allowed to return to Arizona after a short stay in Florida. Geronimo never did live to see his native land again. As close as he ever got was Fort Sill, Oklahoma, where he was moved in 1894 and died in 1909. In his last years he became, improbably enough, a celebrity who appeared at the 1904 world's fair in St. Louis and other events staged by his erstwhile enemies, where he made good money ($2 each) from selling his autographed photograph.[40]

✦ ✦ ✦

TODAY BOTH CROOK and Miles—two of the most illustrious generals of the late nineteenth-century army—have been long forgotten. Just about the only Indian fighter who is still widely remembered shared Crook's aversion to alcohol, tobacco, and cussing but in most other ways was his opposite.[41] The "genial, modest and unassuming" Crook disdained "the slightest pomp or parade."[42] A mule packer who served under him wrote, "In the field, except that everyone knew him, he might have been taken for a Montana miner. The only part of the uniform he wore was an old overcoat."[43] George Armstrong Custer, by contrast, with his flamboyant style and cadre of "embedded" reporters, made sure that everyone knew exactly who he was. He would become a legend by leading his command to annihilation.

As even casual students of history know, on the torrid afternoon of June 25, 1876, Custer rode with 597 officers and men of the Seventh Cavalry Regiment against a giant Indian encampment along the Little Bighorn River in southeastern Montana. There were many more Indians than expected—6,000 to 7,000 in all, of whom 1,000 to 2,000 were warriors—and they were led by superb leaders, including the greatest of them all: Crazy Horse. One army officer left a description of him that suggests the awe in which he was held even by his enemies: "In repose, his face and figure were as clear-cut and classical as a bronze statue of a Greek God. When he moved, he was as lithe and graceful as a panther, and on the war-path, he was as bold as a lion, and as cruel and bloodthirsty as a Bengal tiger."

The Indians had an advantage not only in warrior skill but also in weaponry. Many had Winchester repeating rifles (as well as bows and arrows), while the Seventh Cavalry was equipped with inferior single-shot .45 Colt revolvers and Springfield carbines. The overconfident Custer had refused to take along a battery of Gatling guns (an early machine gun), fearing they would only slow him down. He also split his command prior to the attack, as he had in the Battle of the Washita, confident that the results would be equally satisfactory. Apparently he had forgotten what a near-run thing the Washita had been. He had once declared, "There are not Indians enough in the country to whip the Seventh Cavalry." That day he learned how wrong he was. "Long Hair" and 262 others—soldiers, scouts, civilians—wound up falling after a furious fight.[44]

This spectacular setback eclipsed, then and now, other Indian War catastrophes that were more costly, such as the defeat of the British general Edward Braddock at the Monongahela in 1755, where some six hundred soldiers died, or the defeat of the American general Arthur St. Clair in Ohio in 1791, which also led to the death of over six hundred soldiers.[45] Most of these disasters were the result of the difficult dilemma that confronted commanders not only in the Indian Wars but in most other guerrilla wars: speed versus size. The bigger the column, the safer it was but also the less likely to catch elusive foes. Custer made the wrong choice, choosing speed over size, and paid the ultimate penalty. It was not, however, as unreasonable a choice as it appears in retrospect, given the success that Custer and countless other officers had enjoyed against more numerous Indian foes in battles such as the one at the Washita River eight years earlier.[46]

Moreover, for all its fame, in purely military terms the impact of Custer's Last Stand was negligible: a reality that tends to be slighted in many works of history. All it did was hasten the end of independence for the Sioux and Cheyenne by persuading the "Great Father" in Washington to send more soldiers to their hunting grounds. Focusing on the Little Bighorn, as do a disproportionate number of all books written on the Indian Wars, can give a distorted impression. Such battles were rare. Indians, like all good guerrillas, typically avoided large-scale confrontations. The problem for the U.S. Army was similar to that faced by King Darius of Persia in his war against the Scythians: not defeating the raiders but catching them.

After the Little Bighorn, the star of the pursuit was "Bear Coat"—Colonel Nelson A. Miles, commander of the Fifth Infantry Regiment and George Crook's great rival in the post–Civil War army. A mere store clerk in Boston in 1861, he had earned by the end of the Civil War a temporary promotion to major general and a Medal of Honor (not awarded until decades later) to go along with four different wounds. Following his service at Fredericksburg and Chancellorsville, his corps commander described him as "one of the bravest men in the Army; a soldier by nature." After the war, this nakedly ambitious and exceedingly vain officer—just as talented as Crook but much more self-promoting—stayed in the army and married General William Tecumseh Sherman's niece. Depicted by an admiring general as "a man of untiring and sleepless energy," Miles led his five hundred infantrymen ("walk-a-heaps," the Indians called them) in a relentless pursuit of Custer's killers from October 1876 to January 1877.

Temperatures sometimes hit sixty degrees below zero Fahrenheit—so unbearably frigid that "the men had to stop in the midst of battles to light fires, to warm their fingers, which were no longer able to work the breech-locks." Miles and his men were better prepared than their adversaries for such Arctic conditions. They were bundled up in fur-trimmed greatcoats, mittens, buffalo moccasins, and woolen face masks—making them look, Miles thought, "like a large body of Esquimaux." With his "uncommon talent for fighting battles," possessed (as one superior noted) of "perfect coolness and self-possession," he skillfully deployed his artillery to beat off major attacks even when his command was completely surrounded. "He literally gave the savages no rest," wrote a newspaper correspondent employing the ethnocentric vernacular of the day. The Sioux and Cheyenne who had annihilated the Seventh Cavalry were so disheartened by this "constant pounding" that they either surrendered or fled to Canada.[47]

Miles would go on to become the commanding general of the U.S. Army in 1895. His foes Crazy Horse and Sitting Bull—two of the greatest Indian leaders in history—would in contrast meet a melancholy end, killed while resisting arrest on the reservation. Sitting Bull's demise came in 1890, the year that the Indian Wars officially ended with a one-sided shootout at Wounded Knee Creek in South Dakota that claimed the lives of 25 soldiers and 153 Sioux men, women, and children. It was a fitting conclusion to almost three centuries of relentless slaughter and depravity—as well as considerable heroism and self-sacrifice on both sides.

✦ ✦ ✦

When the Indian Wars are remembered today, it is with cinematic images of whooping Indians and charging cavalrymen. Those stereotypes are not wrong, but they are incomplete. As important to the final outcome was the boom of hunters' guns destroying the buffalo, the buzz of telegraph wires summoning reinforcements, the steady clank of pioneer wagons across the prairie, and the toot-toot of trains traversing the transcontinental railroad completed in 1869. The occupation of their hunting grounds by white settlers doomed the Indians as surely as any battle. Often the application of force was actually counterproductive, encouraging the Indians to resist longer than if they had been better treated.

That should not detract, however, from an appreciation of the skills or the ruthlessness exhibited by George Armstrong Custer, George Crook, Nelson Miles, and other notable Indian fighters. Although the U.S. Army always considered Indian fighting an activity of secondary importance and never developed much doctrine designed specifically for this mission, soldiers stumbled through sheer experimentation upon effective techniques to defeat what one of them called "the best fighters the sun ever shone on."[48] The methods they employed—in particular the use of native scouts, attacks on the enemy's food supplies, and the rounding up of the insurgent population—would play a major part in most successful counterinsurgency campaigns well into the twentieth century. Their Indian adversaries, in turn, showed how to utilize their mobility effectively to evade and hinder more numerous pursuers—and how to fight with great resolution in a doomed cause.

Equal determination would be shown by very different tribesmen fighting a very different sort of empire not in the Wild West but in the even more wild East.

23.

THE WINNING OF THE EAST

The Holy War against Russia in Chechnya and Dagestan, 1829–1859

INSURGENTS DO NOT often set up fortified redoubts; their strengths lie in mobility and invisibility, not in military engineering. But, though relatively rare, rebel strongholds can be devilishly hard to attack if well, meaning inconveniently, situated. One of the first and most famous of all was at Masada, where Herod the Great had built palaces atop a steep mountain in the lion-colored Judean desert, 1,400 feet above the Dead Sea. Here the Jewish Zealot sect, fewer than a thousand in number, held out for three years after the fall of Jerusalem and finally committed mass suicide rather than be captured alive by a Roman army, 15,000 strong, in AD 73. A thousand years later, the medieval Muslim sect known as the Assassins operated out of a nearly impregnable fortress known as Alamut in the Elburz Mountains of northern Persia. Not nearly as well known today, but just as formidable to its besiegers, was the nineteenth-century citadel of Gimri, an *aoul*, or fortified village, built of stone and sun-baked mud, high in the mountains of Dagestan.

"The bare rock face towered up from the valley in unbroken slabs of limestone," wrote one traveler. "There were no trees, no foothold anywhere." Only two tracks led to its entrance, neither one wide enough to let more than one man pass at a time. "A whole regiment could be held at bay by a handful of sharp-shooters." Reaching Gimri was especially difficult when snow was on the ground, as it was in the fall of 1832 when a Russian army approached the site. Yet the Russians were not dissuaded. Their commander, General Alexander Veliaminov, declared, "Could a dog pass? Then that's enough. Where a dog can go, so can a Russian soldier." And he ordered his men upward through a thick mist.

By October 17, 1832, some ten thousand Russian soldiers had surrounded Gimri and were ready to launch an assault. Inside, they knew, was Ghazi Muhammad, the man who three years earlier had proclaimed a *gazavat* (sacred struggle) against them. He became known as the first imam of Dagestan, and his followers were called the murid ("he who seeks" in Arabic). Although they were influenced primarily by the Sufist tradition, their "fanatical puritan movement," wrote two historians, "was in many ways comparable to the contemporary Wahabi movement in Arabia." Ghazi Muhammad managed to make life uncomfortable for the Russians by striking into the neighboring province of Chechnya. In August 1832 he ambushed five hundred Cossacks in a forest, killing more than a hundred of them.

The Russian forces sent out to round up the murids found it a frustrating experience—just as frustrating as it was for American soldiers sent to track down Indian war parties or French soldiers sent to find Haitian or Spanish revolutionaries. General Fedor Fedorovich Tornau left a vivid account of campaigning against this "ferocious, tireless enemy." Each day, he wrote, was pretty much like another—"only at rare intervals" did face-to-face clashes with guerrillas vary "the deadly monotony of the proceedings." More often, Russian troops marched from one campsite to another pursued by an invisible foe. "Fighting went on from beginning to end of each march: there was the chatter of musketry, the hum of bullets; men fell; but no enemy was seen." Soldiers who became separated from the main body, such as sharpshooters who operated in pairs, would suffer a gruesome fate reminiscent of French troops in Haiti: "the Chechens would rise as it were out of the ground, rush at the isolated couples and cut them to pieces before their comrades could come to the rescue." Even in fortified bivouacs there was little security from "the bullets with which the Chechens favored us nearly every night, creeping up to the camp in spite of all precautions."

Russian troops reacted much as American troops did against the Indians: "Small columns were sent out on all sides to ravage the enemy's fields and dwellings. The aouls blaze, the crops are mown down, the musketry rattles, the guns thunder; again the wounded are brought in and the dead."

On those rare occasions when the murids were cornered, they fought with a magnificent disregard for their own lives. In 1832 the Russians stormed the *aoul* of Germentchug, the largest and richest in Chechnya, with over six hundred houses. After the initial assault, only three houses remained in the murids' hands. Under heavy fire, Russian volunteers set fire to the houses and threw grenades down their chimneys. "There was nothing left for the enemy but to surrender or burn," General Tornau wrote. But when an emissary asked for their capitulation, "a half-naked Chechen, black with smoke," emerged to declare, "We want no quarter; the only grace we ask of the Russians is to let our families know that we died as we lived, refusing submission to any foreign yoke." Suddenly the door of a burning house was flung open and a Chechen charged out sword in hand. He was immediately shot down. Five minutes later the same thing happened. By the time the fires had been extinguished, seventy-two murids had died. Not one had been taken alive.

Given such fanatical resistance, which was hardly typical of nineteenth-century imperial campaigns, the Russians were understandably pleased to have cornered Ghazi Muhammad in 1832. Eliminate him, they figured, and his movement would collapse. As usual, the murids fought to the death, but the Russians smashed through their fortifications. As they were about to complete the conquest of Gimri, however, a group of soldiers noticed a man in the doorway of a house just outside the *aoul*. He was "very tall and powerfully built" and was on an elevated stoop. He pulled out his sword, hitched up his robe, and charged through the door. An officer described what happened next:

> Then, suddenly, with the spring of a wild beast, he leapt clean over the heads of the very line of soldiers about to fire on him, and landing behind them, whirling his sword in his left hand he cut down three of them, but was bayoneted by the fourth, the steel plunging deep into his chest. His face still extraordinary in its immobility, he seized the bayonet, pulled it out of his own flesh, cut down the man and, with another superhuman leap, cleared the wall and vanished into the darkness.

The Russian soldiers were "left absolutely dumbfounded" by this spectacle, but they thought no more of it. What, after all, was the escape of one man when the rest of the murids had been killed, Ghazi Muhammad among them? Surely now, they must have thought, these ignorant mountaineers would reconcile themselves to the enlightened rule of the tsars. Little did the Russians suspect that the man who escaped—his name was Shamil—would wage unremitting warfare on them for the next quarter century and become one of the legendary guerrilla commanders of the century.[49]

✦ ✦ ✦

JUST LIKE THE English settlers of North America, the Russians started off on the periphery of a continent—in their case, Asia—and over the course of centuries advanced toward the Pacific Ocean as well as points north and south. Both nationalities, whose advance eventually collided in Alaska, justified their conquests with sweeping doctrines: the Americans claimed to be pursuing "manifest destiny," the Russians to be championing Orthodox Christianity.

From our perspective, the most telling similarity was in the adversaries they encountered. Both bumped up against some relatively advanced states: the United States would fight Britain, Mexico, and Spain; the Russians clashed with Poland, Sweden, Persia, Turkey, and China. But most of the opposition in both America and Asia came from nonstate peoples. The "Wild Field," as the Russians called their steppe frontier, was even more unsettled and dangerous than the Wild West, because Asian nomads were more numerous than the American Indians. Russian attempts to regulate relations with Mongol and Turkic tribes proved as unsatisfactory as the interactions of their American counterparts with the Seminole and Sioux. In both cases the tribes were so decentralized that no headman could bind all of his warriors or enforce control over recognized international boundaries. That led both Washington and St. Petersburg to fight countless small wars against skilled if primitive guerrillas.

The Russians had relatively little trouble subduing Siberia from the 1550s to the 1600s and Central Asia from the 1860s to the 1880s, because the terrain in both places was relatively flat and accessible. In between came the conquest of the Caucasian isthmus wedged between the Black Sea and the Caspian. That was tougher going. The Caucuses had some of Europe's tallest mountains, and they were home to obstreperous tribesmen, mostly Muslims, who had raided their more settled neighbors for centuries. "Every man was a born rider, a keen swordsman, and a good shot,"[50] wrote the English author John F. Baddeley, who traveled in the region during the late nineteenth century. Another English traveler, Lesley Blanch, who arrived in the twentieth century, described their violent code of conduct: "Vengeance, vendetta, or *kanly*, was often pursued through three or four generations, decimating whole families, till there was no one left."[51] Constantly warring among themselves, these mountain peoples would unite to repel outsiders.

General Alexei Yermolov, a hero of the Napoleonic Wars, tried to impose order on this unruly region, much as the Americans were to do with the trans-Mississippi West, when he was appointed its administrator in 1816. He began by erecting the fort that grew into the city of Grozny ("Menacing"). To deal with Chechens who sniped at his construction crews, he left a cannon at a predetermined spot not far from the city walls. When the Chechens rushed out of hiding to claim the seemingly abandoned gun, they were mown down by grape and canister shot. This was indicative of Yermolov's brutal methods, which were decidedly *not* of the population-centric school. "I desire that the terror of my name should guard our frontiers more potently than chains or fortresses . . . ," he declared in a classic expression of the "scorched-earth" approach to counterinsurgency practiced by Assyria, Nazi Germany, and many other autocratic states over the ages. "Condescension in the eyes of the Asiatics is a sign of weakness, and out of pure humanity I am inexorably severe. One execution saves hundreds of thousands of Russians from destruction, and thousands of Mussulmans from treason."[52]

For a time Yermolov did manage to bring about a semblance of pacification. But in the end he generated more rebellion than he suppressed. Leo Tolstoy, who as a junior officer served in the Caucasus, wrote that the inhabitants' feelings toward the Russians became "stronger than hate": "it was such repulsion, disgust, and perplexity at the senseless cruelty of these creatures, that the desire to exterminate them—like the desire to exterminate rats, poisonous spiders, or wolves—was as natural an instinct as that of self-preservation."[53] That repulsion manifested itself in the *gazavat* that broke out in 1829 in Chechnya and Dagestan, which together had a population of about 200,000.[54]

Neither Ghazi Muhammad, the first imam, nor his successor, Hamzat Bek, had much luck in rallying the highlands tribes. Tribal elders did not accept their authority to impose a puritanical version of sharia law that banned dancing, music, and tobacco. In 1834 Hamzat Bek was assassinated by tribal rivals.[55] Shamil, who had escaped the Russian assault on Gimri two years earlier, became the third and last imam. He had a good deal more success in fomenting a broad-based, long-lasting insurgency against the "infidels"—one that would continue to inspire Chechen rebels against Russian rule well into the twenty-first century.

✦ ✦ ✦

MUCH LIKE TOUSSAINT Louverture, another dispossessed freedom fighter of aristocratic lineage, Shamil was born to a nobleman in Gimri around 1796. He was a childhood friend of the slightly older Ghazi Muhammad, who helped him learn Arabic and instructed him in Islam. A skilled horseman, sword fighter, and gymnast, Shamil cut an impressive figure, standing six feet three inches and appearing taller still because of his heavy lambskin cap, the *papakh*. His flowing beard was dyed orange with henna, and his face was, in Tolstoy's telling, "as immovable as though hewn out of stone." His force of personality was such that one of his followers said that "flames darted form his eyes and flowers fell from his lips."[56] The escape from Gimri gave him a superhuman aura—an impression only heightened in 1839 when he escaped another Russian assault on another *aoul* by sending a raft loaded with straw dummies floating down a river while he and a few followers went in the opposite direction.[57]

To keep a desperate resistance going against overwhelming odds required the ability not only to inspire hope but also to instill fear. Shamil was a master of both. He traveled everywhere with his own personal executioner, chopping off heads and hands for violating the dictates of Allah and his humble servant, the Commander of the Faithful in the Caucasus.[58] He did not hesitate to slaughter entire *aouls* that did not heed his demands.

When a group of Chechens, hard-pressed by the Russians, sought permission to surrender, they were so afraid of his wrath that they conveyed their request through Shamil's mother, thinking this would make him more amenable. Upon hearing what she had to say, Shamil announced that he would seek divine guidance to formulate an answer. He spent the next three days and nights in a mosque, fasting and praying. He emerged with blood-shot eyes to announce, "It is the will of Allah that whoever first transmitted to me the shameful intentions of the Chechen people should receive one hundred severe blows, and that person is my own mother!" To the astonished gasps of the crowd, his murids seized the old lady and began beating her with a plaited strap. She fainted after the fifth blow. Shamil announced that he would take upon himself the rest of the punishment, and ordered his men to beat him with heavy whips, vowing to kill anyone who hesitated. He absorbed the ninety-five blows "without betraying the least sign of suffering." Or so legend had it.[59]

This street theater—or more accurately the tales told about it, which no doubt improved in the telling—helped animate Shamil's followers to maintain a fierce resistance. Indeed modern-day Chechen rebels such as the late Shamil Basayev, alleged architect of the 2005 Beslan school siege that killed over 350 people, continue to be inspired by the original Shamil's penchant for theatrical violence even if they have never been able to match his military success. He mobilized over ten thousand murids to conquer much of Chechnya and Dagestan and inflicted thousands of casualties on Russian pursuers. But just as extreme ferocity can backfire for a counterinsurgent, the same is true for an insurgent. Over time, his ruthlessness cost Shamil popular support—as it did for more recent Chechen rebels. Tribal chieftains who did not want to cede authority to this religious firebrand turned for support to the Russians. So did many ordinary villagers who balked at his demands for annual tax payments amounting to 12 percent of their harvest.[60] Even some of Shamil's top lieutenants defected, notably Hadji Murad, who went over to the infidels in 1851. He tried to return to the murids the following year but was killed by Russian troops—a tragic story that formed the basis of Tolstoy's novella *Hadji Murad*.

The Crimean War further damaged Shamil's cause by flooding the Caucasus with fresh Russian troops, raising the total from 30,000 to 200,000, to deal with the threat of an Ottoman invasion.[61] The British,

French, and Turks—Russia's enemies—talked of aiding the murids but did little. A British envoy who visited the region in 1855 was appalled that Shamil and his followers were trying to create "a new Empire in the Caucasus, based upon the principles of Mahomedan fanaticism and domination."[62]

In Iraq between 2007 and 2008 the success of the American "surge" was made possible by waning support for Al Qaeda in Iraq and an influx of American troops, but it still took the arrival of a new general with a fresh concept of counterinsurgency to deliver the coup de grâce to a faltering insurgency. Much the same thing happened in Chechnya and Dagestan in the 1850s. The Russian precursor of David Petraeus was Prince Alexander Bariatinsky. He took over as viceroy of the Caucasus in 1856, following the accession of his childhood friend as Tsar Alexander II. In contrast to the reactionary predecessor, Nicholas I, the new tsar was a modernizer and a liberal. He encouraged Bariatinsky to try a more conciliatory approach. Whereas Shamil traveled with his executioner, Bariatinsky traveled with his treasurer, doling out bribes to tribal leaders. Those elders also received more autonomy within the imperial system and protection from the fanatical murids. "I restored the power of the khans as a force inimical to theocratic principle," Bariatinsky explained.[63] In addition, he encouraged Muslim clerics to denounce Shamil as an apostate and to preach a doctrine of nonviolence. To address local grievances, he issued orders to allow women and children to escape from besieged *aouls* instead of simply killing everyone as in the past. He even sponsored greater educational opportunities for women. "I believe it is important," Bariatinsky wrote, "to win the greatest possible devotion of the territory to the government, and to administer each nationality with affection and complete respect for its cherished customs and traditions."[64]

Like all great counterinsurgents, even the most liberal, Bariatinsky did not limit himself to such "hearts and minds" appeals. Building on the work of his predecessor Mikhail Vorontsov, he undertook large-scale clear-cutting of forests to flush out the murids, and he built bridges to reach their mountain aeries. He also issued his soldiers rifled weapons, which were considerably more effective than the flintlocks employed in the past. Rather than undertake futile punitive expeditions, he launched a systematic reduction of all rebel strongholds in Dagestan.

The final push began in 1858 with three armies converging on the murids' fortresses. Shamil's aeries fell one after another until finally he was left with just 400 followers in the *aoul* of Gunib facing an army of 40,000. Seeing the hopelessness of the situation, Shamil surrendered on August 25, 1859. He pledged allegiance to the tsar and urged his followers to lay down their arms. Thus ended three decades of murid wars.[65]

✦ ✦ ✦

THE CIVILIZATIONAL STRIFE pitting Muslim raiders against countries full of unbelievers may not be new, but it has changed shape over the centuries. Shamil's willingness to give up was characteristic of other nineteenth-century Muslim resistance leaders such as Samory Touré in West Africa and Abd el-Kader in Algeria—and quite different from most of their twenty-first-century successors. Few nineteenth-century rebels was as fanatical as modern-day jihadists. Many showed greater regard for innocent life, even the life of Christians and Jews, than is the case with Hezbollah or Al Qaeda. Abd el-Kader won widespread approbation, including a letter of thanks from Shamil, for interceding during his exile in Damascus to protect Christians from Muslim rioters in 1860. It is hard to imagine a leader of Al Qaeda showing similar regard for "crusaders." In turn, it is hard to imagine Al Qaeda captives being treated as well as Shamil or Abd el-Kader were. Far from being sent to a detention facility such as Guantánamo, the former was given a country house in Russia and an allowance by the tsar, while the latter, after leading resistance against French rule in Algeria for fifteen years (1832–47), was provided a generous French pension and a comfortable exile.[66]

One thing that has not changed over the years is the steep cost of these wars. The British traveler and historian John Baddeley summed up the Caucasus after the end of their "pacification": "whole families exterminated, whole villages destroyed, whole communities decimated."[67] Even among the victors, the toll was high. According to a modern history, "From the annexation of eastern Georgia in 1801 until the end of the Circassian campaign in 1864, as many as twenty-four thousand Russian soldiers and eight hundred officers were killed in the Caucasus, plus perhaps three times that number wounded and captured."[68]

In other words, the pacification of the Caucasus was twenty-one times more costly than the pacification of the trans-Mississippi West. No wonder that Russian authors such as Tolstoy and Lermontov, who served in the Caucasus, produced a rich literature chronicling the Russian achievement in epic if ambivalent tones that in sheer artistic achievement put to shame the numerous novels and movies of the American West.[69]

Rudyard Kipling aside, the British did not produce a comparable literature of empire. But the raw materials were certainly there. It is hard, for example, to imagine a more moving or tragic event than the famous retreat from Kabul in 1842, which, like the wars in the Caucasus, occurred at a time—prior to the last quarter of the nineteenth century—when Europeans did not yet have an insuperable technological advantage over the peoples of Asia. Westerners may have possessed superior warships and artillery, but they did not yet have machine guns and repeating rifles, let alone radios, armored cars, and aircraft. Their opponents were often armed with rifles and muskets just as good as, if not better than, their own—and they fought on their home ground, which was often inhospitable to European attempts to bring massed firepower to bear. Even more brutally than Custer's Last Stand, the First Afghan War showed how under such conditions the arrogance and carelessness of Westerners could lead them to disaster.

24.

DARK DEFILES

The First Anglo-Afghan War, 1838–1842

THEY BEGAN MARCHING at 9 a.m. on January 6, 1842. The snow outside Kabul was already "ankle deep." From the start the stench of defeat wafted like a foul aroma over the 4,500 Anglo-Indian troops and 12,000 camp followers, including many women and children. There was no order to the march, and camp followers, pack animals (including a large number of camels), and baggage were hopelessly mixed up together. "Dreary indeed was the scene over which, with drooping spirits and dismal forebodings, we had to bend our unwilling steps," wrote Lieutenant Vincent Eyre.

While still in Kabul the British had been penned into their cantonment, their provisions running out, because of incessant attack from angry hordes of Afghans. They decided they had no choice but to march back to India. The Afghan leaders promised to let them go. But it soon became clear they had no intention of honoring their commitments. As the rear guard left Kabul around dusk on January 6, Afghans set fire to the cantonment. "The conflagration illuminated the surrounding country for several miles, presenting a spectacle of fearful sublimity," Eyre wrote. Meanwhile other Afghans were sniping at the column with their long-range jezail rifle, "under which many fell." Because of these attacks and sheer disorganization, the column advanced at a crawl and lost most of its baggage. Having covered just six miles, the refugees halted at 4 p.m. to make camp. There were hardly any tents or provisions. Tired soldiers and civilians alike sank down into the snow, and many died on the spot. Others froze overnight; their frostbitten legs "looked like charred logs of wood."

The next day offered no relief. Lady Florentia Sale, a brigadier's wife, noted in her diary, "The force was perfectly disorganized, nearly every man paralyzed with cold, so as to be scarcely able to hold his musket or move. Many frozen corpses lay on the ground. . . . The ground was strewn with boxes of ammunition, plate, and property of various kinds. . . . The enemy soon assembled in great numbers. Had they made a dash at us, we could have offered no resistance, and all would have been massacred."

Make a dash? That was not the tribal way. Why risk a frontal battle with a still-potent force when it was possible to let the elements do their work and pick off the stragglers one by one? The Afghans, like all raiders everywhere, could detect weakness from miles away. They knew they could take their time in picking apart the *feringees* (foreigners). The foreigners, for their part, must have occasionally wondered, as they desperately struggled for survival, how they had gotten into this mess in the first place.[70]

◆ ◆ ◆

BRITISH INTEREST IN Afghanistan was sparked by the worrisome proximity of Russia's advance in the Caucasus and Central Asia. In 1838 Lord Auckland, the governor-general of India, feared that Dost Muhammad Khan, the king of Afghanistan, was getting too friendly with the Russians. So he dispatched an expeditionary force to depose the Dost and replace him with Shah Shuja ul-Mulkh, a British client who had been living in exile in India since losing the Afghan throne three decades earlier.

Despite the manifest imperfections in their own society revealed in works such as *Oliver Twist* (published in 1838), British officials were confident that they were representatives of a superior race with a particular genius for government, and they viewed it as their right to chastise or even replace rulers in distant lands "who," as Kipling was later to write, "lack the lights that guide us."[71] At almost the same time that the British were invading Afghanistan, they were becoming ensnared in another war on the other side of Asia—the First Opium War (1839–42), fought to open up the Chinese market to British exports, including opium. That conflict was to have a happier ending from the British perspective than the war in Afghanistan. But that was hardly apparent at first, for the invasion of Afghanistan began smoothly—as smoothly as would the Russian invasion nearly a century and a half later and the American invasion two decades after that.

The grandly named Army of the Indus included 15,100 British and Indian soldiers (known as sepoys) and 6,000 mercenaries in Shah Shuja's employ. They were accompanied by a staggering 38,000 camp followers (servants, storekeepers, prostitutes, and the like) and 30,000 camels to haul a vast array of baggage, including linens, wines, cigars, and other "comforts which remote countries and uncivilized people cannot supply." Setting off in late 1838, this unwieldy expedition had little trouble as it marched to "Candahar" and from there to "Cabool," thus confirming British expectations that their armies would have little to fear from supposedly inferior adversaries in the "Orient." Dost Muhammad abdicated on August 2, 1839, and the British entered the capital shortly thereafter. The Dost would harass the British for the next year before giving up and being sent to exile in India. The only ominous development was the lack of enthusiasm for the country's new sovereign. A British officer noted that Afghans viewed Shah Shuja's arrival with "the most mortifying indifference."

Most of the British troops were soon sent back to India. The rest remained "to hedge in the throne with a quickset of British bayonets." The danger seemed so minimal that the married officers sent for their families and settled down to the serious business of life—cricket, fishing, hunting, ice skating. But all the while resentment was building among the Afghans who did not appreciate the *feringees* who romanced their women, traduced their mores, and imposed an unpopular king on them.[72]

Out of their own ignorance the British inadvertently provided the spark that set this powder keg on fire. Rulers in Kabul had traditionally paid generous "tributes" to the Pashtun tribes to keep traffic flowing through the passes of the Hindu Kush. In October 1841, however, William Macnaghten, the senior British diplomat, decided as a cost-saving measure to slash in half the annual subsidy paid to the Ghilzai tribal confederation. At the same time, also in the interest of parsimony, he decided to send another British brigade back to India. The Ghilzais instantly rose up and closed the Khyber Pass, thereby cutting off Afghanistan from India.

Major General Sir Robert Sale, whose 2,000-strong brigade was being sent home, found himself having to live up to his nickname "Fighting Bob" by fighting for every inch of ground against "ambuscades and plunderers."[73] Sale's brigade reached the relative safety of Jalalabad in eastern Afghanistan only on November 15, 1841, after suffering more than 300 casualties.[74] The wounded included Sale himself; a jezail bullet had struck his ankle. Once inside Jalalabad, his brigade was surrounded by "a fanatical and infuriated people" (to use Sale's own words). Sale was unable to leave or help the rest of the British forces in the country, even as he received "melancholy intelligence" of "the basest treachery" transpiring in the capital.[75]

Back in Kabul, on November 2, 1841, a mob gathered in front of the residency occupied by Sir Alexander Burnes, the second-ranking British diplomat and a well-known explorer. He tried to reason with the enraged Afghans, then to bribe them. Neither worked. He and his brother were cut to pieces along with their entire retinue.[76] There were still 4,500 Anglo-Indian troops on the outskirts of the city, and prompt action on their part might have quelled the disturbance. But their commander was anything but energetic. Sir William Elphinstone had seen no action since Waterloo. He looked it too. Fifty-nine years old, he was crippled by gout and exceedingly feeble. Lady Sale complained that "Elphinstone vacillates on every point."[77] Because he was "paralyzed by this sudden outbreak,"[78] it spread with disturbing rapidity.

The day after Burnes was murdered, the British commissariat was besieged and a relief force repelled by "concealed marksmen."[79] In the following days, as the troops became "grievously indignant at the imbecility of their leaders,"[80] the siege of the British cantonment grew ever tighter. By the end of November, as the rolls of sick and wounded were growing and provisions were running out, the British declared a willingness to pay handsomely for the privilege of a "safe retreat out of the country."[81] In one of their parlays on December 23, the Dost's son, Muhammad Akbar Khan, tried to seize William Macnaghten, the chief British diplomat. Macnaghten resisted and was shot down with a ceremonial pistol that he had once presented to his host. Soon the rest of the British force would suffer a similar fate.

All the problems encountered by the Kabul garrison at the beginning of their march—bitter cold, lack of supplies, enemy attacks, disorganization—grew worse over the next few days. By January 9, 1842, more than half the force was "frost-bitten or wounded." That day Akbar Khan offered to take into protective custody the married officers and their wives—a proposal that was eagerly accepted. General Elphinstone and a number of other officers also wound up as captives after venturing out to negotiate with Akbar Khan. In all more than a hundred Britons, including Lady Sale and her married daughter, became hostages. Their capture caused a frenzy in Britain because it tapped into primordial fears of the fate that "civilized" women could expect to suffer at the hands of "savages"; as the historian Linda Colley reminds us, tales of "white slavery" and the harem were never far from European minds in this period when "captivity narratives" of Europeans held by non-Europeans (especially in North Africa, India, and North America) were a popular form of literature.[82] But in fact the captives were the lucky ones. Most of them survived. There was no salvation for the "monstrous, unmanageable, jumbling mass," to cite Lieutenant Eyre's words, that they left behind.

Their end came in the "dark precipitous defile[s]" of the Hindu Kush. Afghan riflemen were arrayed all along the heights. From there, a British officer wrote, they "poured down an incessant fire on our column." Three thousand were said to have died in the Khurd–Kabul Pass alone. Another "fearful . . . slaughter" ensued in the Jugdulluk Pass. The tribesmen had barricaded the only exit and made "busy with their cruel knives and their unerring jezails."

The only Briton to survive the entire march was an assistant surgeon. Wounded and mounted on a dying pony, Dr. William Brydon reached Jalalabad on the afternoon of January 13, 1842—a scene memorialized in a famous Victorian painting, *The Remnants of an Army*. A few Indian soldiers and camp followers would arrive later, and 105 British prisoners would be rescued eventually. But most of the rest of the force that had left Kabul seven days earlier—16,000 people (including more than 700 Europeans)—had been wiped out. This "stupendous act of fatuity," as it was dubbed by a nineteenth-century writer, was the greatest single setback suffered by any army fighting guerrillas in the nineteenth century.[83]

✦ ✦ ✦

THIS CATASTROPHE DID much to engender Afghanistan's reputation as the "graveyard of empires." Yet Afghanistan is far from unconquerable. It was overrun by invaders from Alexander the Great in the fourth century BC to Genghis Khan in the thirteenth century AD and Babur (founder of the Mogul Empire) in the sixteenth century.

In 1842 the British, who still held Kandahar and Jalalabad, set out to retrieve their position by sending the so-called Army of Retribution, eventually numbering fourteen thousand men, marching through the Khyber Pass to erase "the most unmitigated discredit to the British name throughout Asia."[84] Its commander, Major General Sir George Pollock, figured out the importance of placing pickets on the hills along his line of march to prevent them from being used by enemy snipers.[85] On September 13, 1842, the British decisively defeated Akbar Khan's forces. Two days later they reoccupied Kabul. The Afghans holding Lady Sale and the other British hostages released their prisoners unharmed. At least a dozen of them—"seized," as one of them put it, "with a scribbling mania"—subsequently published accounts of their captivity, none more famous than Lady Sale's best seller, *A Journal of the Disasters in Afghanistan*.[86] Thus ended a "hostage crisis" that, Linda Colley argues, captured British attention every bit as much as the Iran Hostage Crisis was to transfix Americans in 1979–80—and for much the same reason: both crises revealed the unexpected vulnerability of a great power and occasioned fears, in both cases premature, about its imminent decline.[87] There was an important difference, however: the American public was to be denied the catharsis of retribution that the British now undertook in Afghanistan.

To impress on the Afghans that "their atrocious conduct . . . has not been suffered to pass with impunity,"[88] Pollock ordered Kabul's Great Bazaar to be dynamited. Meanwhile the "infuriated" British troops and camp followers, "incensed to madness,"[89] rampaged through the city streets, burning houses, looting shops, murdering people. Less than a month after his arrival, having demonstrated to his own satisfaction the "invincibility" of "British arms,"[90] Pollock marched back to India. Putting the best face on Britain's lack of ability to administer Afghanistan, the governor-general of India proclaimed that he would "leave it to the Afghans themselves to create a Government amidst the anarchy, which is the consequence of their crimes."[91]

By this time Shah Shuja had been assassinated, allowing Dost Muhammad to reclaim his throne. Following his death in 1863, his son, Sher Ali, sparked a virtual repeat of the 1838 crisis by receiving a Russian envoy but refusing to receive a British representative. In 1878 another British army marched into Afghanistan, this one armed with Martini-Henry breech-loading rifles and eventually two Gatling guns, thus giving it far more firepower than its predecessors had possessed. Sher Ali abdicated, and his son and successor signed a treaty ceding to Britain control of Afghanistan's foreign policy. A British "resident" arrived to oversee these arrangements in 1879, but, like his predecessor in 1841, he was murdered by an Afghan mob. So yet another British army, this one under the diminutive, red-faced lieutenant general Frederick Roberts (popularly known as "Bobs"), occupied Kabul and toppled yet another Afghan monarch before marching out once again in 1880 to avoid a costly occupation. Even this victorious campaign cost the British nearly ten thousand fatalities, mostly from disease. They also suffered another notable defeat, this time at the Battle of Maiwand outside Kandahar, where nearly a thousand soldiers out of a force of approximately twenty-five hundred men were killed by a much larger Afghan contingent that was equipped with modern artillery.[92]

Afghanistan maintained nominal independence but became a virtual British protectorate with the Raj in control of its foreign policy. So it remained until 1919. That year another uprising, a monthlong affair known as the Third Afghan War,[93] was easily quelled but prompted the British to let the Afghans go entirely their own way. For the preceding half century, however, the British had managed to achieve their essential objective of keeping Russian influence out of Afghanistan. Like the Romans after Beth-horon, they had shown an impressive ability to bounce back from disaster. That type of resiliency is essential to any nation involved in counterinsurgency warfare, which is inevitably prolonged and grueling.

The British had shown another important attribute for this type of conflict: the willingness to settle for minimalist rather than maximalist goals. Too often counterinsurgents facing a growing nationalist revolt—whether the Ottomans in Greece or the British themselves in the American Revolution—

lost everything by not being willing to compromise. The Ottomans might have maintained some degree of sovereignty over Greece, just as the British might have done with their North American colonies, if they had been willing to grant more local autonomy early on; later, as losses piled up and the war became emotional on both sides, such compromises became harder to contemplate. In Afghanistan, by contrast, the British won just enough control to minimize any danger of Russian meddling, without assuming so much authority that they would spark another major uprising. This was similar in an informal way to the legal arrangements emerging at the same time to turn settler colonies such as New Zealand and Canada into self-governing states that retained an association with the British Empire. Few other imperialists—not even the British themselves on other occasions—showed such prudence and pragmatism in the face of nationalist demands. And, as the retreat from Kabul in 1842 demonstrated, the price of imperial hubris could be steep.

25.

NORTHWEST FRONTIER

Britain and the Pashtuns, 1897–1947

MORE TROUBLESOME TO the British than the Afghans would be the Pashtun tribesmen living on the Raj's side of the Durand Line, which was drawn in 1896 to demarcate the border between Afghanistan and India. Britain took responsibility for this region after annexing the Punjab in 1849, but over the course of the next century it could never entirely subdue its fiercely independent and famously quarrelsome tribesmen. In a description published in 1815 and still applicable today, the British colonial official Monstuart Elphinstone, a cousin of the doomed General Elphinstone, wrote of the Pashtuns, "Their vices are revenge, envy, avarice, rapacity, and obstinacy; on the other hand, they are fond of liberty, faithful to their friends, kind to their dependents, hospitable, brave, hardy, frugal, laborious and prudent."[94] The similarities with the tribes of the Caucasus are not coincidental: one group of Muslim mountaineers is apt to resemble another.

The British made a distinction between the peoples of the lowlands, who could be controlled, and those of the hills, who could not. The former were incorporated into the Northwest Frontier Province, the latter remained in "tribal areas"—a division that still persists in Pakistan. The tribal "agencies," somewhat similar to American Indian reservations, were governed by jirgas (councils of elders) administering their traditional honor code, the *Pashtunwali*. Ordinary law enforcement, to the extent that it existed, was undertaken by the tribal police, the *Khassadars*. If the tribes raided settled areas, they were liable to face a punitive expedition from locally raised militias such as the Chitral Scouts and Khyber Rifles, which were commanded by British officers on loan from the Indian Army and performed much the same role as the tribal *auxilia* that had secured the frontiers of the Roman Empire. If the scouts got into trouble, they could send messenger pigeons to summon help from the Indian Army and later from the Royal Air Force.[95] Only in the direst emergencies were British regulars called in. Political officers worked hard to avoid such contingencies, like their Roman forerunners, by a combination of suasion and subsidies—much to the consternation of warriors on both sides itching for action.

One of the most effective political officers was Colonel Sir Robert Warburton, who became known as the "king of the Khyber." Like George Crook, he showed considerable sympathy for the people he was sent to administer and occasionally to fight. In his case, however, there was a direct family connection that was entirely lacking in the U.S. Army: despite centuries of warfare against, and interaction with, American Indians, not a single prominent army officer of the nineteenth century could claim to be descended from his foes. (William Tecumseh Sherman's father admired the famous Indian chief, which accounted for his son's middle name, but there was no familial connection.) Warburton, on the other hand, was the offspring of a marriage between a British officer and an Afghan woman, said to be one of Dost Muhammad's nieces, during the First Afghan War. He was born in an Afghan fort while his father was a hostage of Akbar Khan. Although educated in England, he became fluent in all the local languages after he first arrived as a colonial administrator in Peshawar in 1870.

He would stay in the region for nearly thirty years, the last eighteen as the political officer for the Khyber, negotiating with tribesmen who were (and are) suspicious of all outsiders. "It took me years to get through this thick crust of mistrust, but what was the after-result?" he wrote in his memoirs. "For upwards of fifteen years I went unarmed amongst these people. My camp, wherever it happened to be pitched, was always guarded and protected by them. The deadliest enemies of the Khyber Range, with a long record of blood-feuds, dropped those feuds for the time being when in my camp."[96]

Warburton retired in May 1897. Within months the frontier was aflame with a great uprising that he and many others were convinced could have been averted if he had still been on the job. The call to jihad was spread by religious leaders such as Sadhullah of Swat, whom the British called the "mad mullah." (To the British it was obvious that anyone who opposed them must be mad.) Numerous forts were attacked and the Khyber Pass closed. But fortunately for the British, the Pashtun tribes were just as decentralized as the American Indians and did not coordinate their attacks, making their revolt easier to quell.

One of the expeditions sent to "thoroughly chastise the tribesmen" was the Malakand Field Force, named after the Malakand Pass, the entrance to the Swat Valley. It was commanded by the wonderfully named Major General Sir Bindon Blood and accompanied by Winston Churchill, a young cavalry officer moonlighting as a newspaper correspondent. In his first book Churchill recounted the difficulties encountered by the troops in dealing with "a roadless, broken, and undeveloped country; an absence of any strategic points; [and] a well-armed enemy with great mobility and modern rifles, who adopts guerilla tactics." He found "that the troops can march anywhere, and do anything, except catch the enemy; and that all their movements must be attended with loss."

The solution hit upon by the British was the same as that employed by the Americans against the Indians and by the Russians against the Chechens. Churchill recounted how in the Tirah Valley the troops "destroyed all the villages in the center of the valley, some twelve to fourteen in number, and blew up with dynamite upwards of thirty towers and forts. The whole valley was filled with the smoke, which curled upwards in dense and numerous columns, and hung like a cloud over the scene of destruction."

When British troops did manage to catch tribesmen in the open, they wreaked devastation with their Lee-Metford rifles and exploding bullets. "No quarter was asked or given," Churchill wrote, "and every tribesman caught, was speared or cut down at once. Their bodies lay thickly strewn about the fields. . . . It was a terrible lesson, and one which the inhabitants of Swat and Bajaur will never forget."[97]

It was also a lesson that Churchill did not forget; his willingness to wage total war in World War II, including the bombing of German and

Japanese cities, which led to the deaths of hundreds of thousands of civilians, could be traced, at least in small part, to his exposure to this hard way of imperial warfare, far removed from the rules of chivalry that were supposed to govern European combat. His description of flames and destruction in the Swat Valley even anticipated future accounts of the bombing of Hamburg or Tokyo. But just as Anglo-American bombing did not break German or Japanese morale, so too the British reprisals on the Northwest Frontier did not have their intended effect. The "cruel misery" inflicted by British troops reaped what no less a personage than Field Marshal Lord Roberts described as "a rich harvest of hatred and revenge" and led to future uprisings.[98]

As late as the 1930s, the Indian Army officer and future novelist John Masters was describing the difficulties of dealing with the Pashtuns' "pin-pricking hit-and-run tactics" notwithstanding the considerable advances in British armaments since the days of the Malakand Field Force. "We had light automatic guns, howitzers, armored cars, tanks, and aircraft. The Pathan had none of these things . . . ," Masters wrote in his finely wrought memoir, *Bugles and a Tiger*. "And when he stayed and defended something, whether a gun or a village, we trapped him and pulverized him. When he flitted and sniped, rushed and ran away, we felt as if we were using a crowbar to swat wasps."

The ruthlessness on both sides had not diminished over the years. The Pashtuns "would usually castrate and behead" captives, Masters wrote, while the British "took few prisoners at any time, and very few indeed if there was no Political Agent about."[99] These were the wars of which Kipling wrote, "When you're wounded and left on Afghanistan's plains, / And the women come to cut up what remains, / Jest roll up your rifle and blow out your brains / An' go to your Gawd like a soldier."[100] On the Northwest Frontier, as on most other imperial battlefields, local fighters had no knowledge of the "laws of war" invented in the West, and Westerners had no intention of applying those laws to "savages."

Britain's wars against the Pashtuns lasted a century, until Indian independence in 1947 when the government of Pakistan took over the unenviable task of dealing with these "fierce men,"[101] to borrow Masters's evocative phrase. It is sometimes said that insurgents can win by not losing. But a stalemate of this sort favors the government. The British remained in control of India and reduced the Pashtuns to a minor nuisance that could be dealt with by a modest number of British volunteers overseeing armed forces composed primarily of Indians. Knowledgeable officials like Warburton, who won the tribesmen's trust, helped keep the problem manageable.

Only in recent years, with advances in technology that allowed this isolated frontier region to become the hub of a worldwide terrorist network, has the threat from the Pashtuns turned more serious, making a containment strategy inadequate in the view of most, if not all, Western policymakers. This led the United States and its allies, including Britain, into an ambitious effort after September 11, 2001, to use a combination of drone strikes and Special Operations raids in Pakistan and conventional military operations in Afghanistan to defeat such foes as Al Qaeda and the Taliban. As NATO troops patrolled from Maiwand district in southern Afghanistan to the passes of the Hindu Kush in the east, both sites of past British battles, the echoes of history were as unsubtle as an exploding IED.

26.

MISSION CIVILISATRICE

Lyautey in Morocco, 1912–1925

THE SPREAD OF Western imperialism was indisputably enhanced and accelerated by the strength of Western arms, but a small number of Europeans could hardly have controlled vast numbers of Africans and Asians with nothing but raw force. India, with a population of 250 million people, was garrisoned by just 68,000 British troops in 1899. Another 51,000 troops were stationed in the rest of the empire, which included 41 million people in Africa alone.[102] Like the ancient Romans, nineteenth-century Europeans combined a harsh response to native revolts with benign measures designed to win acquiescence to their rule. The great theoretician of these policies, which came eventually to be called the "hearts and minds," or "population-centric," school of counterinsurgency, was the French marshal Louis Hubert Gonzalve Lyautey.

Born in 1854 to an aristocratic family, Lyautey had his life forever altered by an accident that occurred when he was just eighteen months old: he fell out of a second-floor window in his native Nancy. Having narrowly escaped death, he spent the next two years confined to a bed. He could not walk normally until he was twelve, leaving him plenty of time to read and to dream. This sickly childhood produced the same result as it did for his contemporary Theodore Roosevelt, making Lyautey an intellectual as well as an adventurer eager to prove his manhood. Florid, creative, theatrical, egotistical, high-strung, impatient, decisive, idealistic: Lyautey was a poor fit for the rule-bound world of the late nineteenth-century French army, whose reactionary cast of mind was vividly revealed during the Dreyfus Affair. He hated his time at Saint Cyr, the French military academy, and afterward preferred to socialize with writers such as Marcel Proust rather than with his fellow officers. He got his comeuppance in 1894—the same year that another misfit, the Jewish captain Alfred Dreyfus, was convicted of treason on the basis of false charges of selling secrets to Germany—when he was dispatched to what was viewed as a hardship post in French Indochina.

France was then in a race with other European powers, notably Britain and Germany, to gobble up the remaining bits of Africa, Oceania, and Asia that did not yet have a Western flag fluttering overhead. The fever of acquisitiveness was reaching its height in all these regions, raising tensions that would help lead to the tragic events of August 1914. But imperial service was still frowned upon in the continental armies, as has usually been the case with counterguerrilla warfare, because it was seen as a distraction from "real" soldiering against fellow Europeans. As in Germany (and to a lesser extent in Britain, whose Indian Army was a world unto itself), there was a sharp distinction in France between the metropolitan and the colonial armies. The former was made up of draftees and led by officers who tended to be aristocratic, devoutly Catholic, unimaginative, and rigid. The latter, by contrast, was filled with volunteers from home and from other countries (most famously in the Foreign Legion) and led by officers who often came from middle-class backgrounds. As a French journalist noted years later, "Colonial officers were a hard-drinking profane, convivial group: they had little in common with the aristocratic officer corps stationed in France itself."[103] These colonial soldiers were widely seen by their domestic counterparts as duds and dolts when in fact they had to display greater flexibility, initiative, and inventiveness than was characteristic of the world of the parade ground, where the only attribute a soldier was expected to display was unquestioning obedience to orders. Few if any officers made the leap from one army to the other more successfully than Lyautey.

The historian Douglas Porch claims that part of the reason for his exile was that Lyautey was homosexual, but offers no evidence for this claim, which has also been made, with equally scant evidence, about other famous contemporaries such as Field Marshal Lord Kitchener and the novelist Henry James. It was true that Lyautey did not get married until he was fifty-five (to a younger widow), and it is possible he had homosexual proclivities but, as with Kitchener and James, there is no evidence he acted on them.[104] In any case his sexual tastes are hardly pertinent in explaining why he had fallen into disfavor with his superiors. He was a maverick and a troublemaker who had dared to criticize the army in a popular magazine for failing in its duty to educate and uplift conscripts.[105] He even became known as the "socialist captain."[106]

The posting to Indochina as a middle-aged major proved to be the pivotal event in Lyautey's life. There he met Colonel Joseph Gallieni, a more experienced colonial officer (a "magnificent specimen of a complete man," in Lyautey's awed description)[107] who shared his love for literature and his distaste for the "mummified existence" of the "routine-ridden" metropolitan army.[108] Upon meeting the new arrival, Gallieni told him to literally throw out all the regulations he had brought with him and instead learn his "job on the spot."[109] Lyautey would become Gallieni's "apostle" in promulgating the influential doctrines of "peaceful penetration" and "indirect rule"[110]—both far removed from the sort of direct assaults that would lead so many French soldiers to slaughter in the trench warfare of 1914–18.

Much like George Crook in the American Southwest, Gallieni employed light, mobile columns to trap Chinese bandits known as the "Black Flags," who terrorized northern Indochina. Along with these offensive operations, he established a series of military posts whose commanders combined civil and military powers in an attempt to win over the local population. He even distributed more than ten thousand rifles so that villagers could defend themselves.[111] Gallieni placed as much emphasis on economic development as on military operations. As Lyautey explained in a letter home, his mentor built "roads, telegraphs, markets . . . so that with pacification a great band of civilization advances like a spot of oil" (*tâche d'huile*). Thus was born a famous phrase still used in military circles to this day.

In an influential article published in 1900 while he was working with Gallieni to pacify Madagascar, Lyautey laid out his mentor's "method" for a wider audience. "Military occupation," he wrote, "consists less of military operations than of an organization on the march." That organization must consist of officers who "destroy only in the last resort" and instead focus on building markets, schools, and other projects designed to win the "submission of the inhabitants." This task, he contended, was far more difficult than ordinary war fighting of the kind practiced by his rivals in the metropolitan army. "Do you think," he asked, "that it does not need more authority, more sangfroid, more judgment, more firmness of character, to maintain in submission, without firing a single shot, a hostile and excitable population than to subdue it through gunfire once it has arisen?" There was no rule book for "pacific occupation." It could be achieved only by sending "the right man for the right place," a phrase that he wrote in English, by which he meant a man equally competent in military operations and civil administration, a man who understood local conditions, spoke the local languages, and sympathized with the local inhabitants. A man like Gallieni. Or himself.[112]

This is essentially the doctrine of "population-centric" counterinsurgency that in the twenty-first century the United States and its allies tried to implement in Iraq and Afghanistan—as distinguished from "enemy-centric" strategies that focus on killing guerrillas. Provincial Reconstruction Teams were the direct descendants of Lyautey's *l'equipe* (team) drawn from the military *service des affaires indigènes* and the civilian *contrôleurs civils*.[113] There is good cause for this continuity: pacification, Lyautey style, is much more congenial to liberal democracies than are the harsher policies implemented by earlier French generals in Haiti or the Vendée. Indeed Douglas Porch argues that Lyautey's doctrine was little more than "a public-relations exercise" designed to assure apathetic French voters that their country's *mission civilisatrice* could be advanced on the cheap.[114] That is unfair. There is no evidence that Lyautey was cynical about his deeply held ideas. It is, however, true that reality was messier than the pretty word pictures he drew. The Lyautey approach worked best where local elites were willing to cooperate. That was the case in Indochina, where the chief challenge to French authority came from Chinese bandits who were as alien to the Vietnamese as the French were—and more disruptive. "Indirect rule" was a harder sell in Morocco, a country of 5.4 million Arabs and Berbers.[115]

✦ ✦ ✦

After Indochina, Lyautey moved with Gallieni to Madagascar, another French colony. In 1903, as a newly promoted brigadier general, he was sent to administer a troublesome district in Algeria on the border with then-independent Morocco. From there he slowly expanded the "oil spot" of French control deeper south into the Sahara Desert and westward into Morocco itself. The sultan of Morocco became weaker and weaker until in 1912 Paris proclaimed a protectorate over his country. Lyautey was chosen as the first resident general, a post he would hold for the next thirteen years, interrupted only by a brief, unhappy stint as France's minister of war in 1917. (A colonial soldier par excellence, he was utterly out of place in the mass, industrial warfare waged in Europe.)

Described by one historian as a "slim man of above average height, with a fine forehead, dark brows over large pale blue eyes, and a striking sensual mouth hidden by the big moustache of those days,"[116] Lyautey reveled in his role as a Middle Eastern potentate. He wore a purple burnoose, rode on a saddle covered with tiger skin, and stayed in a silk-lined tent while he traveled the *bled* (countryside) to parley with "native notables." He made no effort to disguise his "passion for power."[117]

He found, however, that the "protectorate" was unpopular and the sultan uncooperative. Lyautey forced Sultan Abd el-Hafid to abdicate in 1912, giving the throne to his more pliable brother, Moulay Youssef. The new sultan was little more than a figurehead. All of the important ministries were in French hands, with Lyautey himself acting in effect as prime minister. French rule was only marginally more "indirect" than in next-door Algeria, which had been annexed outright.

As per his writings, Lyautey did place considerable effort on building ports, courts, hospitals, waterworks, schools, railroads, roads, power lines, and other infrastructure that Morocco lacked. These projects not only created an "immense . . . improvement in the welfare of its people," in the judgment of a British newspaper correspondent,[118] but also kept young men employed who might otherwise have spent their time sniping at the French. "A workshop is worth a battalion," Lyautey said.[119] However, he also had to expend a good deal of effort to put down opposition from recalcitrant tribesmen—and his methods were far from gentle.

Colonel Charles Mangin, a swashbuckling soldier reminiscent of Custer (but with better luck), was particularly brutal, if effective, in suppressing a holy war led by a self-proclaimed sultan named Ahmed el-Hiba. With 5,000 soldiers, 1,500 mules, and 2,000 camels, Mangin caught up with el-Hiba's *harka* (army) on the plain of Sidi Bou Othman outside Marrakech on September 6, 1912. El-Hiba had at least 10,000 men, but like the Mahdists (followers of a self-proclaimed Muslim messiah) fighting British troops in the Sudan fourteen years before, they made the mistake of mounting a frontal attack on a European army across open ground. Armed with 75-millimeter cannons, machine guns, and magazine rifles, Mangin slaughtered the Moroccans. At least 2,000 of el-Hiba's men died, while Mangin lost just 2. The outcome was reminiscent of a correspondent's description of Kitchener's victory at the Battle of Omdurman in 1898, which marked the end of the Mahdist uprising in the Sudan: "It was not a battle, but an execution."[120]

Mangin believed, probably rightly, that no diplomatic blandishments would have persuaded el-Hiba and his followers to support French rule. For the protectorate to prevail, they had to be smashed by force. But Lyautey's development projects, his concern for local sensitivities (he prowled the streets of Fez and Rabat, wrote a biographer, "questioning merchants and passers-by regarding their needs and wishes"),[121] his leniency in dealing with defeated rebels, and his outreach to religious leaders (*marabouts*) and tribal elders (*caïds*)—all this was more than window dressing. His efforts at outreach helped persuade most Moroccans to discontinue further resistance.

So effective were these policies that when the Great War broke out in 1914 Lyautey was able to send almost all of his 60,000 troops home, eventually to be replaced by older reservists unfit for duty on the Western Front.[122] Despite German efforts to stir up trouble, Morocco remained quiet, and Moroccan troops fought valiantly for France in both world wars.

The end of Lyautey's tenure would be marred by an Islamic revolt launched in 1921 by Abd el-Krim in the Rif Mountains of northern Morocco. Although the Rif was ruled by Spain, the insurrection spilled over into the French zone and embarrassed Lyautey when he was already old and sick. A left-wing government in Paris lost confidence in his leadership and sent Marshal Philippe Pétain, a hero of the Great War, to deal with the Rif. Abd el-Krim was defeated in 1926 by a massive Franco-Spanish force of more than half a million men.[123] In the early 1930s the last major unpacified part of the country—the Atlas

Mountains—was brought under control. Morocco remained relatively peaceful until 1956, when the French ended their protectorate in the face of growing opposition to concentrate all their efforts in Algeria.

The same pattern was visible in Egypt, Nigeria, and other countries where Europeans attempted "indirect rule," a term coined by the British proconsul Frederick Lugard: it was not always indirect, but it was generally successful. Admittedly that may be more of a testament to the weakness of local resistance than to the brilliance of European administrators. But there is no doubt that Lyautey and Gallieni had elucidated timeless precepts of great value—as long as they are not carried too far.

"Civil action" has to be part of any successful counterinsurgency. That does not mean, however, that it can be a substitute for military action. What Hubert Lyautey and countless other soldiers found was that counterinsurgency warfare requires a complex mixture of political and military action whose exact contours have to be determined by the "right man" on the spot. Perhaps Lyautey's most valuable contribution was to stress the need for "flexibility, elasticity, adaptation to time, place, and circumstance" rather than trying to impose a standard schoolhouse solution on complex and variegated situations. To get the kind of officers he wanted, Lyautey encouraged his subordinates to seek advanced degrees—a novel trend in a force that, like most modern militaries, was generally contemptuous of intellectuals. "He who is only a soldier is a bad soldier," Lyautey said. A good soldier must be a "complete man" with "an open mind on everything."[124]

Lyautey himself was a model soldier-administrator. But the kind of colonialism he practiced so successfully, which depended on a small number of European soldiers and envoys overawing much larger numbers of "natives," could not last much longer. That was evident from the difficulties encountered by Lyautey's English counterparts on the other side of Africa, where a colonial revolt was presenting the biggest challenge the British Empire had faced since the American Revolution. Like the American revolutionaries, the Boers were of European ancestry, but the methods they employed and the success they enjoyed would inspire non-European counterparts around the world—not to mention Irish revolutionaries located closer to the heart of the British Empire.

27.

COMMANDOS

Britain's Near-Defeat in South Africa, 1899–1902

"The first tidings of unsuccess were received in England with calmness. . . . That was the British way of doing things." So wrote Leo Amery, a future cabinet minister who was then a correspondent for the *Times*. (No other identification was thought necessary for Britain's—and the world's—leading newspaper.) "But gradually, as fuller news of the campaign . . . began to reach home . . . a feeling of uneasiness began to spring up."

That was putting it with typical English understatement. In fact something like panic gripped Britain during the cold and foggy "Black Week" at the end of 1899 as the public digested the "grave news" from South Africa. Headlines spoke of a "Severe Reverse" and "Our Heavy Losses." Three times that week British forces had attacked the Boers, and three times they had been repulsed—at Stormberg on Sunday, December 10, at Magersfontein on Monday, December 11, and, worst of all, at Colenso on Friday, December 15. Those "three stinging blows" had cost the British three thousand men killed and wounded and twelve field guns lost. Attempts to relieve the besieged towns of Kimberley, Ladysmith, and Mafeking had to be abandoned.

Casualties were much lower than they had been in Afghanistan in 1842, but more of those who perished were of British ancestry. It was widely believed that the conjunction of these three defeats made this week "the most disastrous for British arms in this century." "The nation was," in Amery's words, "more deeply stirred, more profoundly alarmed, than perhaps at any period since the eve of Trafalgar."

"Few who were in England at the time will forget the gloom of that black week in December," confirmed a barrister. Using virtually identical language, a university student wrote that "a deep gloom settled upon London, emptying of their frequenters the theatres, music halls, supper restaurants, and other haunts of pleasure seekers." For her part, Queen Victoria, who usually had an unerring sense of her subjects' sentiments, wrote that she was "terribly anxious" and "deeply grieved and troubled" about the "sad events" that had befallen "the Queen's dear brave soldiers."

What made the situation even more galling to the proud and self-righteous Britons was the undisguised schadenfreude—"the delight and foolish exultation," the writer Arthur Conan Doyle called it—displayed by so many other countries. Sherlock Holmes's creator could understand if the French were happy, "since our history has largely been a contest with that Power." But what about "the insensate railing of Germany, a country whose ally we have been for centuries"? It was the same in Austria, another country that would have been "swept from by the map by Napoleon" had it not been for British help. Conan Doyle harrumphed, "Never again, I trust, will a British guinea be spent or a British soldier or sailor shed his blood for such allies."

He was positively thunderstruck that "even our kinsmen of America" could revel in these reverses to the mother country. But it was true. Not a few Americans shared the sentiments of the expatriate artist James McNeill Whistler, who expressed "unbounded admiration" for the "pluck" of the Boers and their "beautiful war." Whistler constantly made "witty and amusing" comments at the expense of the "Islanders," such as the supposed tale of a lecturer who informed his audience that the "cream of the British army had gone to South Africa," only to have some unknown heckler yell out, "Whipped cream."[125]

✦ ✦ ✦

THERE WAS MORE than a bit of truth in this jape. The British had sent out storied regiments like the Black Watch. Now they were reeling in defeat—

whipped indeed—and their commanders had been revealed as rank incompetents. Britain's army had been expressly designed in the Victorian era for waging "small wars," yet it had utterly failed to quell the uprising among a few South African farmers, and now it faced a big war for which it was manifestly ill prepared. This was certainly the last thing anyone in the world, except perhaps a few Boers confident in the Lord's favor, had anticipated when war had broken out on October 11, 1899.

On paper the contest seemed absurdly one-sided. It pitted two republics of Afrikaans-speakers—the Orange Free State and the Transvaal—against the entire British Empire, which spanned the globe and controlled the neighboring Cape Colony and Natal. (All territories that are today part of South Africa.) Britain, with a population of 38 million and the world's most industrialized economy,[126] against the Boers ("farmers"), with just 219,000 people and a largely agrarian economy. The British expected a quick victory; they would not have precipitated the conflict otherwise. But the Boers possessed hidden strengths that would allow them to inflict embarrassing setbacks on "the khakis," as they called British troops.

While gold and diamond discoveries had made the Transvaal an attractive takeover target for the British, these riches also allowed the Boers to arm themselves with the most advanced weapons of the fin de siècle. Their Mauser magazine rifles and Krupp and Creusot artillery were superior to the equivalent weapons in the British arsenal. As for the men who wielded those weapons, they were mostly tough, hardy frontiersmen who had been riding and shooting since childhood. Although they were of European origin, primarily Dutch, the Boers' egalitarian and amateurish military system was in some ways quite similar to that of the Sioux, Chechens, Pashtuns, and other irregulars who fought Western armies in the nineteenth century. As one burgher noted, "Our system of warfare . . . resembles that of the Red Indians."[127] Aside from a small artillery corps, the Boers lacked a professional military. They had no uniforms, no drill sergeants, no general staff. They were defended by a militia made up of almost every adult male loosely organized into "commandos," ranging in size from a few hundred to a few thousand. When called up for service, the burghers showed up wearing their Sunday-best clothes, riding their own horses, and answering to their own elected officers. Boers fought when and where they liked and disregarded orders that displeased them. "With the Boers," wrote one young burgher, "each man is practically his own commander."[128]

All of these qualities made it tough to marshal the Boers for conventional military action. Their leaders tried to do just that in the opening months of the war, and they succeeded in fielding an army of almost fifty thousand men, which managed, as we have seen, to inflict a series of setbacks on the British army.[129] But their lucky streak could not continue indefinitely, and it did not. In the wake of Black Week, more troops were sent to South Africa along with a new commander to replace the discredited Sir Redvers Buller. The new chief was the elderly field marshal Lord Roberts, "a lithe, grey terrier of a man," in the words of the historian Thomas Pakenham.[130] His was "a name to conjure with," the *Times* wrote, "ever since his wonderful campaign amidst the mountains and snows of Afghanistan reminded the world what British soldiers could do if properly led."[131] Of course those campaigns from the Second Afghan War had occurred twenty years earlier. The Victoria Cross he had won for bravery during the Indian Mutiny was even more dated—thirty-five years old. Since coming home in 1893 after forty-one years in India, Roberts had been put out to pasture as commander of Her Majesty's forces in Ireland. But despite his advanced age and lack of recent combat experience, "Bobs" (or, as Kipling called him, "*Our* Bobs")[132] soon rewarded the public's enduring faith in him.

By the spring of 1900, the British force had swelled from 20,000 men to 250,000, and everywhere the Boer armies were in retreat. Bloemfontein, the capital of the Orange Free State, fell on March 13, followed by Johannesburg on May 31, and Pretoria, the capital of the Transvaal, on June 5. If the British had been facing a less determined opponent, the war might have been over. But the Boers were only beginning to fight, and the prickly independence that had proved such a detriment when conducting conventional military operations would become their greatest asset during the guerrilla operations that would last for the next two years.

✦ ✦ ✦

BY THE SUMMER of 1900, the least fit, wily, and motivated Boers had been killed or captured or had deserted. Those who remained numbered only about thirty thousand men, but they were exceptionally able fighters with first-rate leaders such as Louis Botha, Jacobus Hercules "Koos" de la Rey, and Judge James Barry Hertzog.[133] The most formidable of the lot was Christiaan Rudolf de Wet, whose name became, in a biographer's words, "a byword for supreme skill in mobile and guerrilla fighting." A forty-five-year-old farmer, he had no formal military education but had fought as a young man against Basuto tribesmen and against the British during a short, victorious conflict in 1880–81, gaining the same sort of on-the-job training as Francis Marion, Thomas Sumter, and other American irregulars who went from fighting Indians to fighting the British. In 1899 he had enlisted as a simple militiaman along with three of his sixteen children. By early the following year he had been elevated to commandant-general of the Free State's forces.

De Wet did not look or act much like a senior general in the Western sense. A British prisoner described him as "an undistinguished-looking man with a black pointed beard." One of his own men said he was a "sorry sight": "His manners were uncouth, and his dress careless to a degree." Then there was "his tactlessness, abrupt speech, and his habit of thrusting his tongue against his palate at every syllable." He also had an explosive temper. De Wet invariably carried a *sjambok* (leather whip), and he did not hesitate to apply it to those who displeased him, whether "Kaffirs" (a derogatory term for blacks—De Wet was an inveterate racist) or his own men. On one occasion, when a group of Boers did not appear when they were supposed to, De Wet raged, "I wish the British would catch and castrate every one of them, so that they may be old women in reality."

Despite (or perhaps because of) his irascibility, De Wet had a natural genius for guerrilla warfare. He insisted that his men give up their ponderous wagon trains—a decision hard to enforce because Boers were as attached to their covered wagons as the pioneers of the American West. But he was convinced that this war "demanded rapidity of action more than anything else. We had to be quick at fighting, quick at reconnoitering, quick (if it became necessary) at flying!" He "aimed at"—and achieved—all these goals.[134]

His first big success occurred at daybreak on March 31, 1900, when he struck the British garrison at Sanna's Post, site of the Bloemfontein waterworks. De Wet managed to stealthily assemble 2,000 men to attack a roughly equivalent number of Britons. On his signal, one part of his force began shelling the outpost. The British commander decided to retreat to Bloemfontein—and fell right into De Wet's trap. "Hands up!" screamed De Wet's men, and "a forest of hands rose in the air." De Wet wound up killing or wounding 350 British soldiers and capturing 480 more along with seven field guns and seventeen wagons. Best of all, he made a clean getaway, even though 30,000 "khakis" were within twenty miles.[135]

De Wet would continue to be a thorn in the lion's side with his marauding, which disrupted communications lines (railways were a favorite target) and mauled careless British columns. Virtually the only task at which he failed was his attempt to invade the Cape Colony in hopes of raising a rebellion among its 250,000 Afrikaners. Another commando, under Jan Christiaan Smuts, was more successful—at least in penetrating the Cape Colony. Neither Smuts nor anyone else managed to rouse the Cape's Afrikaner majority, the only thing that could have seriously shaken the British grip on the area.

✦ ✦ ✦

IF ANYONE COULD have succeeded at this task, it should have been the urbane, English-speaking Smuts, who had been born in the Cape as a British subject and had established his first law practice there after a dazzling career at Cambridge. Originally a fan of the empire builder Cecil Rhodes, he had become disenchanted by Rhodes's plots to undermine Boer independence, and in 1898 he moved to the Transvaal to join the cabinet as state attorney at age twenty-eight. After the fall of Pretoria, there was no more need for lawyers, so he became a commando leader instead, rallying his men with talk of George Washington and Valley Forge while finding personal inspiration in a Greek-language copy of Xenophon's *Anabasis*—an account of an epic march by Greek hoplites—which he carried in his saddlebag.

On the night of September 3, 1901, he crossed the Orange River, named after the Dutch royal house, which flowed westward across the veld and defined the boundary between the Orange Free State and the British-held Cape Colony. He had with him 250 handpicked men, including Deneys

Reitz, the eighteen-year-old son of a former Free State president. Within days the commando was trapped in the Stormberg Mountains of the eastern Cape, among peaks of 5,000 to 8,000 feet where less than two years earlier the British had suffered one of their Black Week reverses. Now British soldiers were visible, wrote Reitz, "in every valley and on every road . . . to bar our progress." They marched for forty hours straight, "all but finished for lack of sleep and rest," while trying to break through the cordon. They had no luck until one night a hunchbacked sympathizer appeared to show them an escape route down a sheer escarpment. The entire commando went down in the dark. "At times," recounted Reitz, "whole batches of men and horses came glissading past, knocking against all in their course, but luckily the surface was free of rock, and covered with a thick matting of grass which served to break the impact, and after a terrible scramble we got down without serious damage."

More troublesome than the British were the elements and their own lack of supplies. "By day we were wet and cold, and the nights were evil dreams," Reitz wrote. His wardrobe was falling apart: "a ragged coat and worn trousers full of holes, with no shirt or underwear of any kind. On my naked feet were dilapidated rawhide sandals, patched and repatched during eight months of wear, and I had only one frayed blanket to sleep under at night." He took to wearing a grain bag with holes cut out for his head and arms, but on a particularly cold night his grain bag "froze solid." Food was as hard to come by as clothes. Commandos survived on mealies (corn) and *biltong* (meat jerky). During their trek through Cape Colony, Reitz was eternally grateful to a farm woman who provided "the first slice of bread and butter and the first sip of coffee [he] had tasted for a year." Not all that they found to eat was equally nutritious: On October 1, Smuts wrote, he and some of his men "came across some wild trees bearing sweet and delicious looking fruit, but in reality a deadly poison." Smuts remained, he wrote, "lying in the jaws of death until the next morning."

Smuts's men managed to temporarily relieve their supply woes when they pounced on an isolated British military camp. "We had ridden into action that morning at our last gasp, and we emerged refitted from head to heel," Reitz remembered. "We all had fresh horses, fresh rifles, clothing saddlery, boots and more ammunition than we could carry away." This was only one of numerous occasions when the Smuts column managed to surprise and maul isolated British detachments, attacking them, as Smuts wrote about an October 3 battle in the Zuurberg Mountains near Stormberg, "with terrible loss" and forcing "a retreat that was terrible to see." Yet the British kept coming, in far greater numbers, forcing Smuts to flee.

Eventually, after a 2,000-mile trek, the marauders made their way in early 1902 to the rural, isolated northwestern Cape, on the edge of the continent, where they established a stronghold that British troops would never penetrate. From here they raided British-held towns, hoping against hope that they would last long enough to see the day when, as Smuts put it, "Right triumphs over might."[136]

Leaving aside whether the Boers, who were already notorious for their inhumanity to black Africans, truly had "right" on their side, it was a vain hope. The daring feats of Smuts and other commando leaders may have inspired the Boers and alarmed the British, but they did little to change the course of the war. In response, British commanders instituted a series of increasingly harsh but successful measures aimed primarily at the civilian population. The Boers may have been of European ancestry, which meant that they would not be treated by British troops with the same degree of inhumanity as "colored" adversaries, but neither were they "Englishmen"—so they would not get the same kind of consideration granted to American rebels more than a century earlier.

✦ ✦ ✦

BEGINNING IN EARLY 1900 Lord Roberts imported a common Northwest Frontier tactic by ordering Boer farms burned and livestock slaughtered if British troops had been fired on from the premises or if acts of sabotage had occurred nearby. His successor, the icy and impatient Lord Kitchener, expanded the practice after taking over in November 1900. An engineer by training, "K of K"—Kitchener of Khartoum—had acquired a reputation for machinelike efficiency during his conquest of the Sudan from 1896 to 1898. His "cold blue eye[s]," "firm jaw," "cruel mouth," and "heavy moustaches" were to become legendary.[137] Described by a fellow viceroy as "a molten mass of devouring energy and burning ambition,"[138] Kitchener was known for getting results, no matter the cost. In South Africa he added to that reputation by sanctioning the systematic destruction of the economic base on which Boer resistance depended, much as the Americans had done to the American Indians and as other British columns were then doing to the Pashtuns. Before the war was over, thirty thousand farms would be torched and 3.6 million sheep slaughtered.[139] "Farm burning goes merrily on," wrote one British officer, "and our course through the country is marked as in prehistoric ages, by pillars of smoke by day and fire by night. We usually burn from six to a dozen farms a day. . . . I do not gather that any special reason or cause is alleged or proved against the farms burnt. . . . We burn the lot without inquiry."[140]

Boer commandos engaged in some farm burning of their own, albeit on a much smaller scale. They torched farms belonging to *hensoppers* (hands-uppers), the Boers who went over to the British—akin to the Loyalists in the American Revolution who were similarly persecuted by "patriots." To provide a place for the families of *hensoppers*, the British set up refugee camps, or "government laagers." Soon they were being used not only to house those who wanted to be there but also those who didn't. Boer women and children whose male relatives were on commando were imprisoned in what became known as "concentration camps."

Although the term was new—first employed by John Ellis, a Liberal member of Parliament, in 1901[141]—the concept was not. Indian reservations in North America were essentially concentration camps. So were the *reconcentrado* camps that the Spanish general Valeriano Weyler had set up in Cuba in 1896–97. Half a million Cubans were incarcerated and over 100,000 died from starvation or disease. Weyler, who blithely explained that "one does not make war with bonbons," became known as "the Butcher."[142]

If Kitchener was aware of this dire precedent, he gave no sign of caring. His soldiers rounded up over 150,000 Boer women and children, along with their black servants and farm hands. No adequate provision was made to house that many people. Food, milk, clean water, bedding, medicines, bathroom facilities, soap—all were lacking. Flies and filth were everywhere. "When the 8, 10, or 12 persons who occupied a bell tent were all packed into it . . . there was no room to move, and the atmosphere was indescribable, even with duly lifted flaps," noted Emily Hobhouse, a strong-willed English pacifist who toured the camps in early 1901 on behalf of the South African

Women and Children's Distress Fund. When she complained to camp officers, they told her, "Soap is a luxury." Before long epidemics—measles, dysentery, diphtheria, typhoid—raced through the camps, killing at least 25,000 people.

This was the product not of deliberate policy but rather of neglect. The Germans, in their African campaigns against the Herero and Maji-Maji revolts, practiced genocide;[143] the British did not. Kitchener—who was said by a subordinate to lack "any personal feel for his troops,"[144] much less for the enemy's women or children—simply never bothered to visit a single camp.

The process of correcting his oversight was set in motion after Miss Hobhouse, "that bloody woman" to Kitchener, began publicizing her findings in June 1901. Liberal Party leaders such as David Lloyd George and Henry Campbell-Bannerman rushed forward to denounce these "methods of barbarism." By early 1902, conditions in the camps had improved and their death rate had fallen below that of many British cities, but by then Britain had suffered a black eye in world opinion.[145]

While embarrassing, the negative publicity was not enough to imperil the war effort. The opposition Liberals were outspoken in denouncing concentration camps, but they were split on the fundamental question of the war, while the ruling Tories were positively jingoistic. In 1900 Lord Salisbury's Conservative government called a "khaki election" to take advantage of British victories and won a substantial majority by labeling the opposition as "pro-Boer." ("To vote for a Liberal is a vote to the Boer," proclaimed one poster.)[146] The Boers hoped that a majority of the British public would turn against the war, but that did not happen. Nor were the Boers rescued by outside intervention. Many countries, especially Germany and the Netherlands, were sympathetic to their plight, but none was willing to fight on their behalf. Only two thousand foreign volunteers joined the Boers.[147] That left the British free to muster overwhelming resources to hammer the *bittereinders* (bitter-enders) into submission.

✦ ✦ ✦

THE BOERS, LIKE many other skilled guerrillas, were masters of mobility. Often their pursuers were left to grasp at thin air. The obvious answer was to limit their ability to travel freely. This is an objective that all security forces engaged in counterinsurgency must pursue. The methods employed vary widely, from the issuing of internal passports (the favored method of Russia's tsars and commissars alike) to the slaughtering of pony herds (as American soldiers often did in the Indian Wars). More recently American troops in Iraq and Afghanistan relied on biometric databases.

The British approach in South Africa was characterized, in the first place, by the erection of blockhouses, which spread like tumbleweed across the veld. Eight thousand were built in all, initially out of masonry and concrete and then, because they were faster to construct, from corrugated iron. Each was manned by ten or fewer very bored soldiers ("there was absolutely nothing to do," a subaltern griped) and located less than a mile from its neighbors. Some were even built on ox wagons so as to be portable. The gaps between blockhouses were filled by a relatively recent invention—barbed wire.[148] Meanwhile fearsome armored trains, bristling with Maxim guns, artillery, and searchlights, steamed across the veld like battleships on the ocean.[149] Thousands of troops were then dispatched on giant "beating" expeditions, as if on a grouse hunt, to "bag" Boers pinioned between the blockhouses and rail lines.

De Wet, the Boers' foremost guerrilla leader, was not impressed. He called the blockhouses "the policy of the blockhead." Whenever "it became necessary for us to fight our way through," he wrote, "we generally succeeded in doing so." All it took was a pair of wire cutters and the cover of darkness to slip past bored and inattentive sentinels. He was equally unimpressed by the farm burnings and concentration camps, which, he claimed, only hardened Boer determination.

But De Wet had to concede that other British stratagems were more effective: "night attacks were the most difficult of the enemy's tactics with which we had had to deal." He also paid grudging tribute to the British recruitment of blacks and "hands-uppers," including De Wet's own brother, Piet, who enlisted in the national scouts. "These deserters were our undoing . . . ," De Wet wrote. "[I]f there had been no national scouts and no Kaffirs, in all human probability matters would have taken another turn."[150]

The blacks and the Boer defectors were important because they provided the British with what any counterinsurgent most needs: timely intelligence about the enemy's location. When the war began, British military intelligence capabilities were anemic. During the conflict the Field Intelligence Department expanded from 280 men to more than 2,400,[151] and it came to include officers of outstanding ability such as Colonel Aubrey Woolls-Sampson.

A hot-tempered Cape Colony native of English ancestry who was a former gold miner, Woolls-Sampson had developed, according to his brother, "fanatical" hatred for the Boers. This is hardly surprising, for during the first Boer War (1880–81), which the Boers won, he had suffered three bullet wounds in one battle—including a shot through the jugular, which he barely survived. Later, in 1896, he was imprisoned by the Boers for his membership in a conspiracy of *Uitlanders* (foreigners) who were working with Cecil Rhodes to annex the Transvaal. He emerged from prison unbowed the following year. Even before the second Boer War broke out, he began to raise a new regiment, the Imperial Light Horse, to fight the Boers, who were masters of light cavalry tactics, on their own terms. While leading the Light Horse, he was wounded again, nearly losing his leg this time, and in his weakened condition he had to endure the four-month siege of Ladysmith. Throughout it all he remained, a former commander wrote, "mad to get at the enemy."

Not well suited to be a regimental commander (he was "too much inflamed with patriotism" to worry about mundane matters such as logistics or billeting), he now found his métier as an intelligence officer. Like T. E. Lawrence, his younger and more famous contemporary, whom he resembled in some ways, Woolls-Sampson was considered a bit of an oddball by his peers. He refused to socialize with fellow officers. Instead he spent his time talking with his "boys"—a group of Africans he recruited and paid out of his own purse to track Boer commandos after dark. The blacks, who shared his hatred of Boers (and, unlike the British, risked death if caught), provided invaluable intelligence that repeatedly allowed British columns to fall on Boer encampments at dawn.[152]

The pursuit of Geronimo two decades earlier through the Sierra Madre had shown the utility of small groups of soldiers, unencumbered by supply trains, who could match the mobility of fleet guerrillas. Many decades later that lesson would be validated by the experience of the Long-Range Reconnaissance Patrols in South Vietnam. So, too, in the Boer War the most successful British leaders—not only Woolls-Sampson but also Colonel Lord Rawlinson, Colonel Harry Scobell, and Lieutenant Colonel George Elliot Benson—fought much as "Brother Boer" did, leading small groups of mounted men on long treks across the veld without the hindrance of cumbersome supply trains. They "bagged" far more prisoners than did larger, more ponderous units.

✦ ✦ ✦

BY MAY 1902 the Boers had had enough. Much as they protested Kitchener's "relentless policy of attrition," they had to admit its effectiveness. Deneys Reitz wrote that "universal ruin . . . had overtaken the country. Every homestead was burned, all crops and live-stock destroyed, and there was nothing left but to bow to the inevitable." More than twenty thousand Boer fighters remained in the field, but they all told "the same disastrous tale . . . of starvation, lack of ammunition, horses, and clothing, of how the great block-house systems was strangling their efforts to carry on the war."[153]

Even so, the Boers did not agree to unconditional surrender. In return for giving up their independence, they won a pledge that there would be no retribution for their resistance except for Cape and Natal Afrikaners who were viewed as traitors by the British. Far from punishing the Boers, the British promised to help them rebuild and to introduce "as soon as circumstances permit, representative institutions leading up to self-government."[154] This anticipated the practices of future British counterinsurgents in Malaya, Northern Ireland, and other conflicts who found, as the Romans had done, that it is essential to offer political and social benefits to solidify battlefield gains and prevent future revolts.

The years immediately after the South African war saw an ambitious program of reconstruction overseen by the British high commissioner, Sir Alfred Milner, a warmonger turned peacemaker who set up schools, built railway and telephone lines, and imported seeds and livestock to reconcile the Boers to their involuntary membership in the British Empire.[155] In 1906 the Liberals won a large majority in Parliament and immediately began devolving power to South African whites. Because English emigration never took off, the Boers remained a majority. Before long they ruled not only the old Orange Free State and Transvaal but also Cape Colony and Natal, which together formed the Union of South Africa in 1910. The British, who had once complained about Boer mistreatment of blacks and coloreds, looked the other way as nonwhites were consigned to second-class status. So successful was the process of reconciliation that, notwithstanding a revolt by De Wet and a few other hard-liners in 1914, South Africa fought alongside Britain in World War I and World War II. Jan Smuts would go on to lead British troops as a field marshal and become a member of the Imperial War Cabinet.

Notwithstanding abuses on both sides, many participants later remembered the Boer War as "the last of the gentlemen's wars"[156]—and not without reason, especially when seen from the vantage point of the next great war, which would be fought with machine guns and mustard gas. In South Africa each side could count on the other to provide medical treatment to the wounded, neither side engaged in torture to elicit information, and captured soldiers were generally well treated. Thirty thousand Boer detainees were sent to well-run camps in places like Bermuda, Ceylon, and India, while the Boers, at least during the guerrilla phase, tended to release British prisoners unharmed. Kitchener even had two Australian officers, Harry "Breaker" Morant and Peter Handcock, shot after they were found guilty of killing prisoners. Although 7,000 Boer soldiers and 22,000 of their British counterparts died—in addition to at least 25,000 noncombatants who perished in the concentration camps—the butcher's bill was still lower than in what the military strategist J. F. C. Fuller, who as a young subaltern fought in South Africa, was to call the "massed proletarian conflicts" of the future.[157] Certainly it would be hard to imagine in future conflicts the kind of polite, even at times "very friendly conversation," which occurred at numerous meetings and in even more regular exchange of correspondence between British and Boer commanders to discuss the treatment of noncombatants, the provision of medical services, and other issues relating to the "rules and customs of war."[158]

28.

HIGH NOON FOR EMPIRE

Why Imperialism Carried the Seeds of Its Own Destruction

THE BOER WAR affirmed that the advantage in guerrilla conflicts still lay with European imperialists—but their enemies were closing the gap fast. The same message was sent by an eerily similar war fought at virtually the same time by the United States.

As a result of the Spanish-American War in 1898, the United States annexed the Philippines. Many Filipinos had no desire to be ruled from Washington. In 1899 they began a violent resistance that came to be known as the Philippine Insurrection. Like the Boers, the Filipinos fought initially in conventional formations and suffered heavy losses before reverting to guerrilla warfare. U.S. troops, like their British counterparts, engaged in human-rights abuses, including the use not only of concentration camps known as "protected zones" but also of the "water cure," a form of torture later known as waterboarding, which they had learned from the Spanish. Those abuses caused an outcry at home, as they were doing simultaneously in Britain during the Boer War, from the likes of Mark Twain and Andrew Carnegie. But the election of 1900 in the United States, as in the UK, delivered a resounding victory for the "prowar" candidate—Theodore Roosevelt. He brought the conflict to a successful conclusion in 1902 following the capture of the *insurrecto* leader Emilio Aguinaldo in a daring raid led by Brigadier General Frederick Funston. The successful campaign to hunt down the guerrillas and their leaders, overseen by General Arthur MacArthur (father of Douglas MacArthur), was accompanied, as in Morocco, by a benevolent campaign of reconstruction, including the opening of schools, hospitals, courts, and other institutions, all overseen by the civilian governor and future president, William Howard Taft. The proclamation of peace was followed, as in South Africa, by the expeditious devolution of self-government so as to reconcile the Filipinos to American sovereignty.

The Filipinos should have had more success than the Boers—there were far more of them (seven million), and they lived amid mountains and jungles, terrain that was far harder for troops to penetrate than the prairies of South Africa. And yet they managed to inflict far fewer casualties on the American forces: 4,234 American soldiers died, mostly from disease. In turn, Filipinos suffered far more heavily: 16,000 fighters killed in battle, another 200,000 civilians dead mostly of disease. The Boers were somewhat more successful in part because of their superior weaponry and greater skill in utilizing it: every Boer had a rifle, whereas many *insurrectos* had nothing more than a knife. But the Boers' main advantage was their superior nationalist sentiment. The Afrikaners thought of themselves as a single people and greatly cherished their independence, whereas Filipinos, like Native Americans, were split among numerous ethnic groups. Moreover, unlike Boers or American Indians, Filipinos had no experience of freedom. As a result they had trouble coming together to oppose American occupation.[159]

Although the insurgents were defeated in both the Boer War and the Philippine War, the two conflicts markedly decreased enthusiasm for imperialism. Casualties were higher than in previous "small wars," and they fell not just among a handful of professional soldiers but among wartime volunteers whose loss was more keenly felt on Main Street and High Street. As Leo Amery wrote in *The Times History of the War in South Africa*, the losses inflicted by the Boers were "a shock to a generation accustomed to the cheap glories of savage warfare."[160]

Military men who might have been contemptuous of "native" resistance in the past were acquiring newfound respect for the fighting prowess of guerrillas. That was evident in *Small Wars: Their Principles & Practice*, a popular British handbook that went through three editions between 1896 and 1906, and that would later inspire the U.S. Marine Corps' *Small Wars*

Manual, published in 1940. Its author—widely recognized as the foremost authority on the subject until T. E. Lawrence—was Colonel (later Major General) Charles Edward Callwell, an intelligence officer who had commanded mobile columns against the Boers. He wrote that "guerilla warfare is a form of operations above all things to be avoided. The whole spirit of the art of conducting small wars is to strive for the attainment of decisive methods, the very essence of partisan warfare from the point of the enemy being to avoid definite engagements."

Callwell offered mainly tactical advice, stressing the importance of "constantly harassing the enemy and . . . giving the hostile detachments no rest," subdividing "the whole area of operations . . . into sections, each of which has its own military force," "clearing the country of the supplies which may be useful to the enemy," and "utilizing the troops available as far as possible for mobile columns" that "should be as small as possible consistent with safety." He also stressed that no other kind of warfare placed as much emphasis on "self-reliant subordinate officers" or on "a well organized and well served intelligence department." While he wrote that regular troops had "to resort to punitive measures directed against the possessions of their antagonists," he also warned, "The enemy must be chastised up to a certain point but not driven to desperation," and that "wholesale destruction of the property of the enemy may sometimes do more harm than good."[161]

This was about as far as Callwell got in acknowledging the political aspect of counterinsurgency, which his British successors would view as paramount. Nor did he make any reference to press coverage, which would loom so large in later insurgencies. Politics and what would now be called information operations were not entirely absent even in the nineteenth century; witness the efforts of Bariatinsky in the Caucuses and of Lyautey in Morocco to court local notables. But such factors were not nearly as important as they would become. At the high noon of European empire, small numbers of Western soldiers armed with Maxim guns and repeating rifles generally could rely on "bold initiative" and "resolute action"[162] to crush enemies ranging from Pashtuns to American Indians without having to worry overmuch about placating native grievances—or courting a skeptical press corps.

It helped, too, that most of these conflicts occurred on the periphery of empire against enemies that were considered "uncivilized" and therefore, under the European code of conduct, could be fought with unrestrained ferocity. The very success of the imperial armies meant, however, that future battles would take place within imperial boundaries and that, as one historian notes, they would be "considered civil unrest rather than war."[163] Accordingly troops in the future would find their actions circumscribed by civil law and public opinion in ways they had not been in the nineteenth century.

Imperialism carried the seeds of its own destruction in other ways. By setting up schools and newspapers that promulgated Western doctrines such as nationalism and Marxism, Western administrators inadvertently spurred widespread resistance to their own rule starting in the 1920s. It was not only ideas that Westerners spread but weapons. By manufacturing and distributing all over the world countless weapons, from TNT to the AK-47, Europeans would ensure that in the twentieth century resisters to their rule would be far better armed than their predecessors had been.

Even at the turn of the twentieth century, the heyday of empire, astute observers could see that European dominance could not last indefinitely. The exact contour of events was impossible to predict a half century in advance, but as early as 1897 the eerily prophetic Rudyard Kipling was warning the complacent British public ("drunk with . . . power" after having won "dominion over palm and pine") that before long "all our pomp of yesterday" could be "one with Nineveh and Tyre"—"Lest we forget—lest we forget!"[164] Nineveh and Tyre were, of course, cities in ancient Sumeria that were ravaged by nomadic guerrillas. Kipling almost certainly did not have the threat of guerrillas in mind; he was simply referring to the inevitable decline and fall of all great civilizations. But, seen from the perspective of the postcolonial era, his poetical sally hit home with more accuracy than he could have realized.

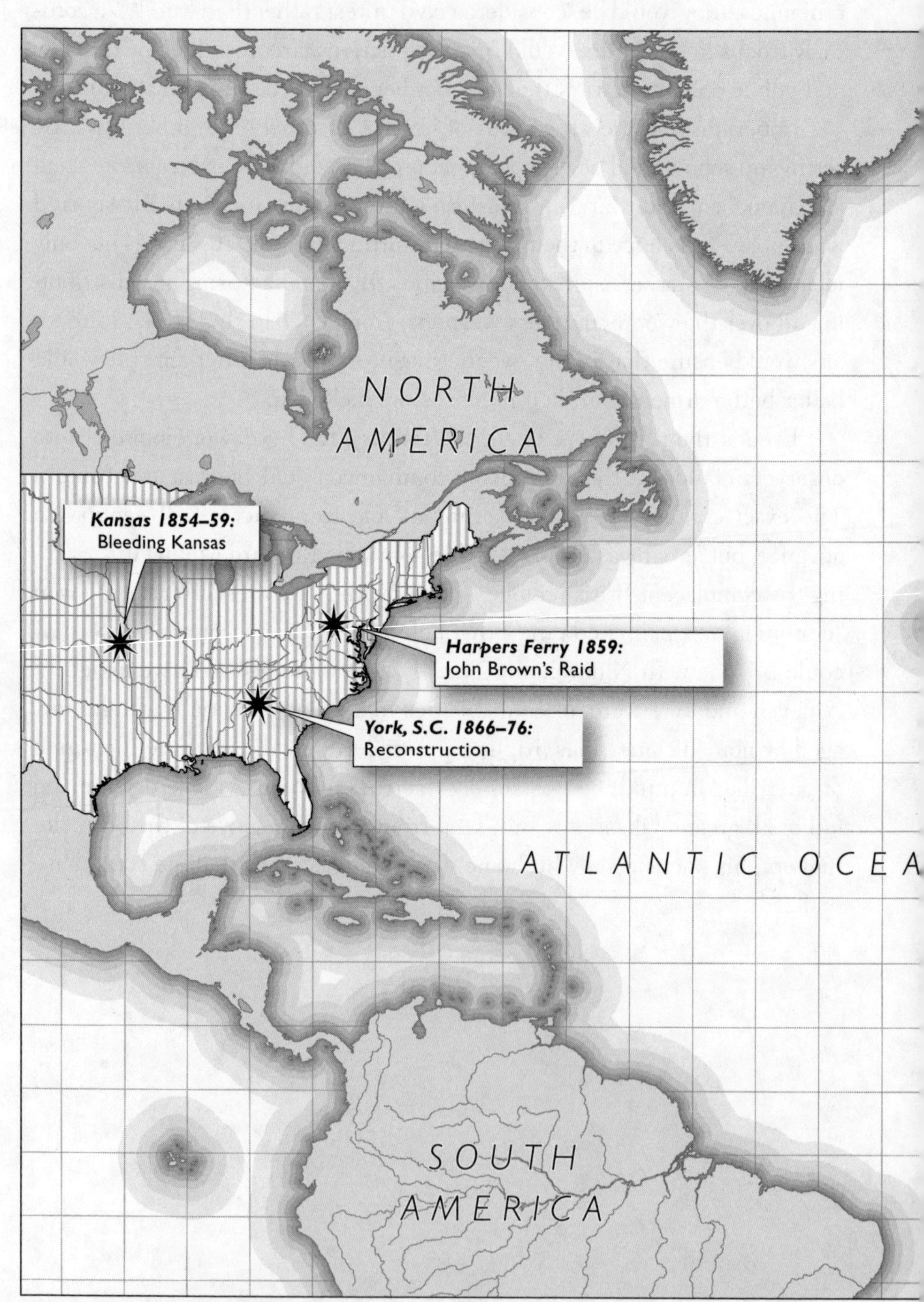
NORTH AMERICA
Kansas 1854–59:
Bleeding Kansas
Harpers Ferry 1859:
John Brown's Raid
York, S.C. 1866–76:
Reconstruction
ATLANTIC OCEA
SOUTH AMERICA

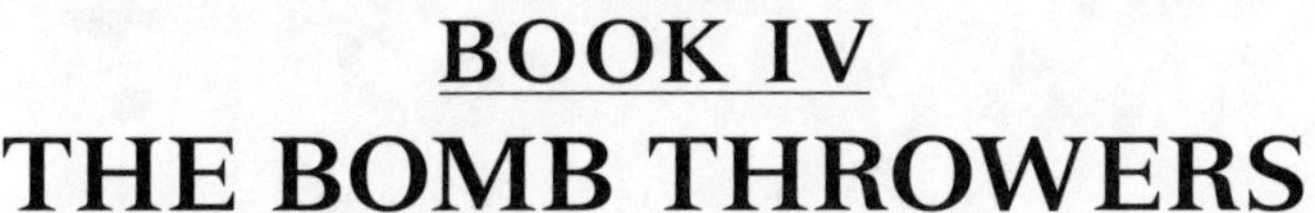

BOOK IV
THE BOMB THROWERS
The First Age of International Terrorism

EUROPE

Dublin 1916:
Easter Rebellion
Ireland 1919–21:
War of Independence

Moscow/St. Petersburg 1879–81:
People's Will
Russia 1902–17:
Socialists

France/Italy/Spain c. 1880–c. 1939:
Anarchists

Mediterranean Sea

Iran, Syria AD 1090–1256:
Assassins

AFRICA

29.

SUICIDE KNIFERS

The Assassins, AD 1090–1256

SO FAR TERRORISTS have been largely absent from this narrative. Partially this is a matter of terminology. Both European settlers in North America and their Indian enemies attacked civilians in order to instill terror, but since neither represented a nonstate group (the Europeans answered to a colonial government, the Indians to their own tribes and confederations), they were not "terrorists," any more than were the leaders of France as they were slaying en masse to extinguish uprisings in Haiti, Spain, and the Vendée. Terrorism, as defined here, must be carried out by substate groups. Moreover, while all of the guerrilla groups described so far killed some civilians—quite a lot of civilians in many cases—that was not their primary emphasis. They focused most of their attacks on military forces, and they were intent on physically defeating their enemies, not simply on scoring propaganda points. Thus all of these groups fall outside the definition of *terrorist* (see the Prologue)—a restrictive definition, admittedly, but one that makes sense lest, as too often happens, this term is employed so indiscriminately that it becomes devoid of all meaning.

The relative absence of terrorists up to this point, however, is due less to semantics than to the inescapable fact that prior to the nineteenth century there were very few terrorist groups. There has been, of course, no shortage of assassins throughout history, but few have been organized into groups that pursued political or religious aims primarily through a campaign of terror. Julius Caesar may be said to have been the victim of an act of terrorism, but his killers were hardly professional terrorists and their goal was not to spread terror. They were simply intent on ridding Rome of a ruler they did not like. Other cases of regicide (Charles I of England, Louis XVI of France, Nicholas II of Russia) have been a byproduct of a wider revolution, not of terrorism per se. Still other assassinations—Lee Harvey Oswald killing John F. Kennedy or Sirhan Sirhan killing Robert F. Kennedy—were the work of deranged individuals who may have been intent on sending a political message but who were not acting on behalf of any broader movement as far as we know.

The most successful premodern group to systematically employ terror was found, appropriately enough considering that region's centrality to modern terrorism, in the Middle East. They were popularly known as the Assassins. More properly they were the Nizari Ismailis, a Shiite sect of the eleventh century AD that was persecuted by the rest of the Muslim world. To carve out space to practice and proselytize their religion, their first great leader, Hasan-i Sabbah, took to assassinating his foes.

A "revolutionary of genius," he established in AD 1090 his stronghold in a fortress known as Alamut in the Elburz Mountains of northern Persia. From this remote location, reachable only by a single narrow track, he dispatched his *da'is* (missionaries) to win converts to the Ismaili cause. But Hasan-i Sabbah was not satisfied using nonviolent means to extend his sect. He also dispatched fedayeen (self-sacrificers) armed with daggers to slay Muslim notables—clerics, judges, teachers, administrators, soldiers—who opposed his heresies. In their eagerness to attain a spot in paradise, the fedayeen usually made little attempt to escape, thus becoming in effect suicide knifers. The term "assassin" was a corruption of "hashish-eater"—a label that was applied to the fedayeen by their enemies who assumed (erroneously) that only powerful drugs could induce these men to sacrifice their own lives in order to eliminate their enemies. In fact the fedayeen seem to have been motivated by nothing more than religious zeal; taking intoxicants would have made it hard for them to be as patient and clever as they were in carrying out plots that often required considerable dissimulation and playacting.

During the course of Hasan-i Sabbah's thirty-year reign, his fedayeen claimed only fifty victims, all men of some standing. But, while minuscule by the scale of most "reigns of terror," whether of the Mongols or of the French Revolution, this was sufficient to terrorize his enemies. From then on, according to an Arab chronicler, "No commander or officer dared to leave his house unprotected; they wore armor under clothes."

During all the years that Hasan-i Sabbah directed this campaign of terror he never set foot outside his Alamut stronghold, in fact rarely even left his room. He was, like many subsequent terrorist leaders, an intellectual, and he spent countless hours deep in study in his impressive library. He was a particularly devoted student of geometry, astronomy, and arithmetic. A Byzantine envoy who met him came away impressed: "His natural dignity, his distinguished manners, his smile, which is always courteous and pleasant but never familiar or casual, the grace of his attitudes, the striking firmness of his movements, all combine to produce an undeniable superiority."

But this civilized exterior concealed a deep strain of religious fanaticism. Early on he sent his wife and daughters away so as not to distract him; he spent the rest of his life apart from them. When he caught one of his sons drinking wine, he ordered his execution. Another son he executed for killing a man without permission, only to later discover that the charge was false. Hasan-i Sabbah's willingness to sacrifice his own children may have cast his humanity into doubt, but it helped to inspire his followers. Making use of such dedication, he succeeded in creating a state within a state—a series of Ismaili bastions scattered around the Persian countryside that the ruling Turkish Seljuks were too weak to wipe out.

Hasan-i Sabbah died, apparently of natural causes, in 1124. His successors were not his equals. The pace of assassinations slackened as the Ismaili movement in Persia lost energy and became consumed by internal quarrels. In time the movement's western outpost in Syria would become more dynamic. Here, too, the Ismailis managed to establish a network of fortresses defended by suicide knifers. The Syrian Assassins were led initially by Rashid al-Din Sinan, a native of what is today Iraq who became known to the Crusaders as "the Old Man of the Mountain." Sinan tried unsuccessfully to kill Saladin, the great Muslim hero who would lead an army of holy warriors to recapture Jerusalem from the Crusaders in 1187. He had more success in dispatching Conrad of Montferrat, king of the Crusader Kingdom of Jerusalem.

In 1192, while in Tyre, Conrad was approached by two young Christian monks he had befriended over the past six months. They spoke his Frankish language perfectly and were obviously men of learning. After a minute of polite conversation, they produced daggers from their robes and "fell upon him like two mangy wolves," in the words of an Arab chronicle. The wounded king stumbled into a church, where he was finished off by one of the assassins. Before his own death, the killer confessed that he had been sent by Sinan. The cause of this assassination remains obscure. But its impact on European minds was spectacular. A German priest was to write to a French king contemplating a further Crusade that the Assassins "are to be cursed and fled. They sell themselves, are thirsty for human blood, kill the innocent for a price, and care nothing for either life or salvation."

In the thirteenth century the Assassins finally confronted enemies who could not be deterred by the threat of assassination. Their Persian strongholds were overrun by the Mongols, who massacred large numbers of Ismailis along with everyone else. The Syrian redoubts fell at roughly the same time to the slave soldiers known as Mamluks, who would establish a dynasty ruling Egypt and Syria. Millions of Ismailis still exist today led by the Aga Khan, but they have not been a political force to be reckoned with since the calamitous events of the thirteenth century. Nor have they undertaken acts of terrorism since then.

Their reign of terror, which lasted two centuries, was enough to establish their reputation as one of the most successful terrorist groups in history. Thanks largely to the dark genius of Hasan-i Sabbah, they developed a highly effective organization, combining a covert hierarchy with a compelling ideology and rigorous methods of indoctrination that inspired his followers to sacrifice their lives for the cause. Those remain the essential ingredients for terrorist success down to the present day. But the Assassins also differed in crucial respects from most of their successors. As Bernard Lewis notes, "Unlike their modern equivalents, [the Assassins] attacked only the great and the powerful, and never harmed ordinary people going about the avocations."[1]

✦ ✦ ✦

THE SEARCH FOR the antecedents of terrorism can also take in the Sicarii, the "dagger-men" who roamed first-century Judaea killing Roman collaborators, as well as Guy Fawkes and the twelve other Catholic conspirators who tried but failed to blow up the British Parliament in the Gunpowder Plot of 1605.[2] The former helped precipitate the doomed Jewish Revolt against Rome, while the latter, if successful, might have wiped out Britain's entire ruling class in one shattering blow. Their activities show that Muslims have no monopoly on the use of terror. But the trail soon runs cold. Most other nonstate groups that habitually employed violence, such as the Thuggee cult, which waylaid travelers in India, were primarily interested not in scoring political or theological points but in accumulating lucre.[3]

✦ ✦ ✦

UNLIKE GUERRILLA WARFARE, the most ancient form of warfare, terrorism is strikingly modern. It has been made possible by the spread of four phenomena: destructive and portable weaponry, the mass media, literacy, and secular ideologies.

Dynamite was to prove the terrorists' weapon of choice, and it was not invented until 1866. Another popular terrorist weapon—the breach-loading pistol—came into widespread use around the same time. Certainly other weapons could have been, and sometimes were, utilized by terrorists, but barrels of gunpowder were not nearly as effective for blowing up your enemies as sticks of dynamite that were twenty times more powerful.[4] Nor were knives as deadly as pistols.

The spread of the mass media during the second half of the nineteenth century gave terrorists the ability to have a disproportionate political impact with a few acts of violence, something that was much harder to achieve in the days when news spread primarily by word of mouth. Mass-circulation newspapers and magazines that were produced by Linotype machines, got their news via the telegraph, featured photographs, and were sold cheaply to the working classes were first established in this period. It is no coincidence that modern terrorism was born at the same time.

A related development—the spread of schools and universities—helped create a growing number of educated people from whom terrorists could draw recruits and whom they could try to influence even in countries such as Russia that remained autocracies. Universities became petri dishes of extremist ideologies all over the world, both reactionary and radical. These included anarchism, nationalism, fascism, socialism, and communism. The spread of all of these seductive ideologies attracted adherents who were willing to use violence to advance their beliefs—including many who never attended a university or hardly even opened a book but were nevertheless influenced by speeches, discussions, articles, or pamphlets promulgating radical doctrines.

It is generally assumed that terrorism seldom "works," meaning that it seldom achieves its objectives. That is a valid if simplistic conclusion to draw about modern terrorism, whose annals are littered with failed groups, from the Basque ETA to the German Baader-Meinhof Gang. The nineteenth century provides further evidence of terrorist futility in the campaigns of the anarchists who failed to destroy existing states and replace them with idealized communal institutions. But there are also numerous examples of terrorists significantly influencing the course of history—sometimes even in the direction they sought. Relatively successful terrorist groups of the nineteenth and early twentieth centuries range from the Ku Klux Klan to the Irish Republican Army and the German and Japanese militarists of the interwar period. Even the Russian revolutionaries, although they did not bring down the Romanov regime with their campaign of assassinations and "expropriations," undermined it so much that they contributed to its eventual overthrow.

Why, then, did some terrorists succeed where others failed? To answer that question requires an examination of key terrorist campaigns from just before the U.S. Civil War to just after World War I—the first great age of international terrorism.[5] Some of the most prominent and influential terrorist groups of the era were the abolitionists and segregationists in the United States, Nihilists and socialists in Russia, anarchists across Europe and North America, and nationalists in Ireland. They did not all achieve their aims, but all changed history for better or worse. Even the anarchists, the most ineffectual of the bunch, would leave their mark by inadvertently giving rise to heightened international police cooperation symbolized by the formation of Interpol. For all of their notoriety, however, their influence was modest by comparison with that of the fanatic—or, depending on your perspective, the idealist—who helped spark the bloodiest conflict in U.S. history. His arrival on the political stage was announced with an act of violence that was shocking by the tamer standards of antebellum America if not those of the twenty-first century, when we have become accustomed to far worse atrocities.

30.

JOHN BROWN'S BODY

The Terrorist Who Helped Start the Civil War, 1856–1859

ELEVEN P.M., SATURDAY, May 24, 1856. The prairie was hauntingly dark, and a damp wind was blowing through the small farming settlement of Pottawatomie in the Kansas Territory. Suddenly the still of the night was broken by a knock on the door. Inside the cabin were James and Mahala Doyle and their five children—poor, illiterate farmers who had recently moved from Tennessee. They were, like most white Southerners, in favor of slavery even though they did not own any slaves themselves. A voice asked for directions to a neighbor's house. Roused from sleep, James opened the door and was shoved back by armed men bristling with revolvers and knives who told him they were members of an army even though they were not wearing uniforms. At their head, recalled the Doyles' youngest son, was an "old man" with a dark complexion and a "slim face." He told James Doyle that he and his sons—all members of the proslavery Law and Order Party—must surrender. They were now his prisoners.

Mahala Doyle pleaded tearfully to spare sixteen-year-old John, who had not been involved in any political activities. The old man relented. Then he marched into the darkness with James and twenty-two-year-old Drury and twenty-year-old William. Soon Mahala heard pistol shots, moans "as if a person was dying," and a "wild whoop." "My husband and two boys, my sons, did not come back anymore," she later said.

The next morning John wandered out in search of his father and brothers and found them a few hundred yards from the house. Drury's "fingers were cut off," he recalled, "and his arms were cut off; his head was cut open, there was a hole in his breast. William's head was cut open, and a hole was in his jaw, as though it was made by a knife, and a hole was also in his side. My father was shot in the forehead and stabbed in the breast."

Later that night two more proslavery men were pulled out of their homes and suffered a similar fate—cut apart with two-edged swords and shot for good measure. News of the murders soon spread panic among proslavery forces in Kansas. "WAR! WAR!" screamed the headline of the proslavery *Border Times*, which proceeded to exaggerate the number of victims: "Eight Pro-Slavery Men Murdered by the Abolitionists in Franklin County, K.T. *LET SLIP THE DOGS OF WAR!*"

As he rode back to camp, John Brown—the old man with the slim face—must have breathed a sigh of righteous satisfaction. He had smitten five of the devil's party and put the fear of a vindictive God into the rest. He had struck a blow for "the cause of Freedom." "Confidence seemed to be greatly restored amongst Free State men in consequence," he wrote a few weeks later. He would have been even more satisfied had he known that his reign of terror would help bring about a war that would destroy the hated slave power forever.[6]

✦ ✦ ✦

MENTION THE SUBJECT of irregular warfare in the American Civil War, and the first names that come to mind are John Singleton Mosby and William Clarke Quantrill, Confederate guerrillas of very different stripe. The model of a Southern cavalier, Mosby was a commissioned officer who led a relatively disciplined partisan unit, Mosby's Rangers, that harassed Union forces in Virginia. The disreputable Quantrill, by contrast, had scant legal authority as he led a gang of psychopathic "bushwhackers" in Missouri and its environs. They preyed not only on Union soldiers but also on Union sympathizers, their most infamous attack being the 1863 raid on Lawrence, Kansas, which demolished this abolitionist stronghold and killed at least 150 people. Quantrill is better remembered today, if only because his gang included desperados such as Jesse James who went on to become celebrated outlaws after the war. Yet for all the notoriety of these bushwhackers, their strategic impact was negligible. At most they diverted some Union troops from other tasks and delayed the South's surrender slightly. The Confederacy might have fared better if it had put more emphasis on such guerrilla operations, but it never did so, because this ran counter to the planter class's chivalrous notions of warfare and its desire to maintain the social order. Far more significant from the standpoint of irregular operations were the prelude and aftermath of the Civil War, which featured notably effective instances of terrorism carried out by abolitionists (before the war) and by segregationists (after).

The war was prefigured by violence in Kansas Territory, which in the 1850s became a battleground between antislavery Jayhawkers and proslavery Border Ruffians. The former were determined to take Kansas into the Union as a free state, the latter as a slave state. Both sides knew that the outcome could swing the delicate balance of power in Congress. Thus was born "Bloody Kansas"—a name now firmly entrenched in the historical lexicon but one that conveys an exaggerated image. One scholar estimates that just 157 violent deaths occurred in Kansas between 1854 and 1861 and only 56 of them were definitely political in nature.[7] That hardly seems like a huge toll compared with other irregular conflicts (in post-2003 Iraq more people were often killed in a single attack), but it loomed large at the time because the fighting inflamed passions on both sides of the Mason-Dixon Line, convincing Southerners and Northerners alike that their differences could be settled only at gunpoint. By the time Kansas was finally admitted into the Union as a free state, at the end of January 1861, full-blown war was merely months away. John Brown did as much as anyone to trigger the conflict.

He arrived in Kansas in 1855 along with one of his sons and a son-in-law, their wagon full of provisions and concealed weapons. Three of his sons were already there—a small part of the twenty children he had fathered with two different wives. Gaunt, grizzled, and stooped but still vigorous, he had behind him a lifetime of failure. He had tried his hand at surveying, farming, tanning, horse breeding, cattle trading, lumber dealing, and wool distributing, and he had wound up broke and bankrupt. He simply had no head for business. What he did have were deeply held Congregationalist beliefs and a fierce devotion to African-American rights. He had first become aware of the slaves' plight when he was just twelve years old and along with his father stayed at a home where a young slave of the same age lived. Brown recalled that the master of the house had made a "great pet" of him, "while the negro boy (who was fully if not more than his equal) was badly clothed, poorly fed; & lodged in cold weather: & beaten before his eyes with iron shovels or any other thing that came first to hand."[8] He would call slavery "the sum of all villainies"[9] and dedicate his life to its eradication.

Initially his work was peaceful. He helped slaves to escape via the Underground Railroad and ran an experimental community in upstate New York where whites and blacks could live as "brothers and equals."[10] But gradually he came to believe that force would have to be used to lead blacks out of bondage. Brown became "wild and frenzied" after proslavery militants rampaged through the antislavery town of Lawrence on May 21, 1856. The next day a proslavery congressman, Preston S. Brooks of South Carolina, viciously beat an antislavery senator, Charles Sumner of Massachusetts, with a metal-tipped cane on the very floor of the U.S. Senate. Brown "said it became necessary to make an example, and so strike terror, and put an end to that sort of thing"—"to show these barbarians that we, too, have rights."[11] On May 24 he and seven followers, including four of his sons and a son-in-law, set out for the proslavery settlement at Pottawatomie Creek, where they committed the five murders that quickly became a nationwide sensation.

A week later Brown rounded up twenty-six impoverished, bedraggled volunteers ("we had come to wearing ideas, suspicion, and memories of what had once been coats, pants, and hats," one of his men wrote) and led them against a camp of proslavery militiamen. Four of the militiamen were killed, and the other twenty-four surrendered in the grandly named Battle of Black Jack.[12] The Border Ruffians got their revenge in August 1856 when they razed the Free State settlement at Osawatomie, killing one of John Brown's sons and four other defenders. Brown and the rest of his small band were badly outnumbered and forced to retreat. Nevertheless "Old Brown of Osawatomie" became even more celebrated for his willingness to fight in accordance with the instructions he gave his men: "Take more care to end life well than to live long."[13]

Most abolitionists were pacifists. They did not condone murder and considered the Pottawatomie killings "terribly damaging" to their cause. Even a member of John Brown's gang thought "the transaction was terrible." But he changed his mind when he saw the disproportionate impact of the murders: "The pro-slavery men were *dreadfully terrified* and large numbers of them soon left the territory."[14] This and subsequent killings did not decide the outcome in Kansas, but they did make the balance of terror less one-sided than before. The repercussions of these acts spread far beyond Kansas's borders by giving rise to the erroneous impression in the South that John Brown, "the notorious assassin,"[15] was representative of Northern sentiment and that extreme methods were necessary to safeguard their "peculiar institution." Brown was in fact highly atypical, but he managed to find growing numbers of supporters in the North who were impressed by his actions and his forceful defense of them. (As Brown himself noted, he had an "unusual 'gift of utterance.' ")[16]

His preeminent backers, a wealthy and influential group known as the Secret Six, included Samuel Gridley Howe, an idealistic Boston physician who had earlier served with the Greek rebels.[17] They provided him with the financial wherewithal to carry out an audacious plot he had been hatching for two decades. Brown had been reading "all the books upon insurrectionary warfare he could lay his hands upon." He was deeply impressed by the "Spanish chieftains" who had resisted Roman rule as well as by "Schamyl, the Circassian chief" and by Toussaint Louverture in "Hayti." Inspired by their example, he came to believe that if he invaded the South with twenty-five to fifty men he could rouse a slave insurrection. The rebels could then establish a stronghold in the Blue Ridge mountains of Virginia ("admirably adapted to carrying on a guerilla warfare") and from there strike plantations on the plains. An English soldier of fortune who was a veteran of Garibaldi's campaigns tried to dissuade him, telling him that no "preparatory notice" had been given to slaves to make them respond positively to an invitation to rebel. But Brown, with his "iron will and unbending purpose," had too much confidence in African-Americans—and his self-assigned role as their Moses—to give up.[18]

Brown decided to launch his insurgency by seizing the federal armory at Harpers Ferry in what is now West Virginia to provide arms for soon-to-be-freed slaves. Pretending to be a gold prospector, he rented a nearby house, where his men gathered with weapons and supplies. The arsenal fell to his twenty-two raiders, including five blacks, on Sunday night, October 16, 1859. Brown and his men seized thirty-five hostages from among the armory workers and nearby farmers, including a distant descendant of George Washington. But, as warned, no slaves rallied to their cause. Instead the armory was surrounded, in the words of a contemporary journalist, by "a bristling cordon of men with every variety of arms, costume, accouterment, and of all ages and conditions." On a "drizzly" Monday night the ragtag militiamen gave way to ninety U.S. Marines rushed from Washington in crisp, bright-blue uniforms under the command of an army colonel named Robert E. Lee.

Brown made no attempt to break out. He craved a heroic if hopeless last stand. He and his men barricaded themselves with their hostages in a stone fire-engine house and prepared for the inevitable end. On Tuesday morning, October 18, Lee's aide, Lieutenant J. E. B. Stuart, appeared to demand that Brown surrender. He refused. A dozen marines then splintered the front door with a ladder that they used as a battering ram. They stormed inside "like tigers." "A storming assault is not a play-day sport," wrote Marine First Lieutenant Israel Green, who led the attack. "They bayoneted one man skulking under the [fire] engine, and pinned another up against the rear wall, both being instantly killed." Green himself used his saber to strike Brown twice "with all my strength." In just three minutes the hostage crisis was over.

Ten of the raiders had been killed, including two of John Brown's sons. Brown himself had been badly wounded; he escaped death only because Green struck him with a flimsy ceremonial sword rather than his usual sturdy blade. He was "a gory spectacle," with "a severe bayonet wound in his side, and his face and hair were clotted with blood." Even in that condition, however, he calmly and fluently answered questions for three hours from an assembled crowd of reporters and politicians.

Brown survived long enough to be proudly hanged on December 2, 1859 (he professed to be "quite cheerful" about the outcome), but not before he had turned his "mockery of a trial" into a national forum for his views—a strategy employed since then by countless political prisoners who have taken advantage of the mass media to communicate their message far beyond the courtroom. His stirring courtroom oration, delivered by a man with a long beard that made him look like a biblical prophet, won him countless admirers in the North. He concluded with a flourish: "Now, if it is deemed necessary that I should forfeit my life for the furtherance of the ends of justice, and mingle my blood further with the blood of my children and with the blood of millions in this slave country whose rights are disregarded by wicked, cruel, and unjust enactments, I say, let it be done."[19] *Let it be done.* Even those who were not yet abolitionists began to think that only a good cause could have inspired such stoical self-sacrifice.

John Brown was not much of a guerrilla. He never had enough men to pose the slightest military threat to the South. But he was a first-rate terrorist whose exploits and utterances received front-page publicity—as intended. His legend only grew after his death. The philosopher Henry David Thoreau compared him to Jesus,[20] and Union soldiers on the march sang "John Brown's Body," a ditty that inspired Julia Ward Howe, Samuel Gridley Howe's wife, to compose "The Battle Hymn of the Republic." The African-American leader Frederick Douglass summed up his impact: "If John Brown did not end the war that ended slavery, he did at least begin the war that ended slavery."[21] If so, that would make this zealous Puritan one of the more consequential terrorists in history—almost as important as the Bosnian students who ignited World War I.

Unfortunately for the African-American cause, segregationists would soon show they were even more adept at terrorism than their opponents.

31.

THE DESTRUCTION OF RECONSTRUCTION

Ku Kluxers and the War against Civil Rights, 1866–1876

Elias Hill was awakened after midnight on May 5, 1871. Lying in his tiny cabin in rural York County, South Carolina, he could hear the dogs barking and the men moving rapidly in the dark. They came first to his brother's house next door, where they whipped his brother's wife. "Where's Elias?" they kept demanding. When she told him, they barged into Hill's house. "Here he is! Here he is!" one of the men shouted triumphantly. They threw off his bedclothes and dragged him into the yard.

He could not resist because Elias Hill, now fifty years old, had been crippled since the age of seven. A dreadful disease, possibly muscular dystrophy, had shriveled his legs. They were no bigger than the size of a man's wrist. His arms, too, were withered and his jaw was strangely deformed. Overcoming his physical limitations, Hill had emerged as an unlikely leader in the "colored community." His father had purchased freedom for himself, his wife, and their son thirty years before, and Elias had learned to read from some white children. As he grew into adulthood, he had become a schoolteacher and a well-respected Baptist preacher who made a little extra money by writing letters on behalf of illiterate freedmen. He was also the local president of the Union League, a fraternal organization closely aligned with the Republican Party.

The Republicans advocated enforcing the newly enacted Thirteenth,

Fourteenth, and Fifteenth Amendments granting civil rights to former slaves, something that was intolerable to the former slave owners who could not imagine a "superior race" (themselves) granting any opportunities to an "inferior race."[22] The South may have lost the Civil War, but that did not mean that whites were prepared to cede power to blacks or their allies, who were vilified as "carpetbaggers" if they came from the North and "scalawags" if from the South.

Most whites were terrified of the horrors that supposedly would be visited upon them if those they had oppressed for so long were to take power. (The Haitian Revolution, with its savage violence, was an oft-cited example.)[23] White sentiment was summed up by one South Carolina newspaper that urged its readers, in a characteristically hysterical register, to fight against

> the hell-born policy which has trampled the fairest and noblest States of our great sisterhood beneath the unholy hoofs of African savages and shoulder-strapped brigands [U.S. Army officers]—the policy which has given up millions of our free-born, high-souled brethren and sisters—to the rule of gibbering, louse-eating, devil-worshipping, barbarians, from the jungles of Dahomey [west Africa], and peripatetic buccaneers from Cape Cod, Memphremagog [Vermont], Hell, and Boston.[24]

The Ku Klux Klan stood ready to fight the "hell-born policy" of racial equality. Founded in Pulaski, Tennessee, in 1866 by a half dozen Confederate veterans for "diversion and amusement," it originally resembled a college fraternity complete with "meaningless and mysterious" initiation rituals and secret signs. (The name derived from the Greek word for circle or band, *kuklos*.) But before long it had become a full-fledged terrorist organization that spread like a kudzu vine across an unrepentant South. A grand wizard was in nominal command: the former Confederate general Nathan Bedford Forrest. But the "Invisible Empire" operated with little or no central direction. As the historian Steven Hahn notes, "the Klan was less a formal organization than a rubric embracing a variety of secret vigilante and paramilitary outfits showing the marks of their local settings." KKK "dens" (i.e., terrorist cells) sprang up spontaneously, as did similar organizations such as the Knights of the White Camellia, the Pale Faces, and the White Brotherhood.

"Ku Klux" became a generic label for paramilitary organizations whose goal was to expel Republicans from office and to replace them with Democrats who would institute white-supremacist policies. The KKK was, in effect, the military arm of the Democratic Party, just as the Irish Republican Army would be the military arm of Sinn Féin. In many communities virtually all of the white men enrolled in the Klan, just as, before the Civil War, they had enrolled in militia companies and patrols designed to prevent slave uprisings. Total membership in the Klan and similar groups across the eleven states of the Confederacy was said to number half a million men. Because the bulk of its membership was made up of Confederate veterans, Hahn argues, it "may be regarded as a guerilla movement bent on continuing the struggle or avenging the consequences of the official surrender."[25] But unlike true guerrilla groups, the Klan did not target soldiers—only civilians like Elias Hill.

Their objectives and neuroses were apparent in the questioning of Hill, which was conducted by six masked "ghouls," as rank-and-file Klansmen were designated. Although the popular image has the Klan exclusively wearing white sheets, their disguises were more diverse. Hill recalled, "Some had a kind of check disguise on their heads. One had black oil-cloth over his head, and something like gloves covering his hands and wrists." They spoke in an "outlandish and unnatural tone" to disguise their voices and to inspire "awe and terror" in the supposedly "ignorant and superstitious . . . darkies" by pretending to be ghosts and goblins—a masquerade that would not have fooled a child, much less an educated preacher like Elias Hill.

The first question they asked Hill was "Who burned our houses?" Blacks were widely suspected of committing arson as a form of protest because they were too afraid to openly confront white supremacists.

"I told them it was not me," Hill recalled. "I could not burn houses; it was unreasonable to ask me."

The masked men did not like that answer. They hit him with their fists and extracted a phony confession. Next they wanted to know if Hill had told "the black men to ravish all the white women."

He said no and they struck him again. They asked him if he was president of the Union League—a particular bugbear for the Klan because it sought to organize freedmen. He admitted it. More blows.

"Didn't you preach against the Ku-Klux?" they demanded. In response to his denials, a strap was attached to his neck and he was dragged around the yard. Then a horsewhip was produced and he was hit eight times on the hip bone—"almost the only place he could hit my body," he later testified, "my legs were so short."

Finally, after more than an hour of torture in the chill night air, they left. But not before they had issued a series of demands. They wanted him to stop preaching. To stop subscribing to a Republican newspaper from Charleston. And to place an advertisement in the local newspaper renouncing "republicanism" and promising never to vote. If he did all those things, he could live. If not, he would be killed the following week.

That very same night in the very same small South Carolina community, the Klan paid a visit to a number of other black households. As Hill later told Congress, "They went and whipped J. P. Hill's wife the same night they were at my house . . . Julia, Miles Barron's wife: Rumor says they committed a rape on her . . . Samuel Simrell's house was burned down that night."[26]

At least they survived. Many did not. Jim Williams had grown up a slave in York County before escaping and enlisting in the Union Army. After the war he returned to become captain of a black militia company. On March 7, 1871—two months before the assault on Elias Hill—a group of forty or fifty masked men came to his house at 2 a.m. He was hiding under the floorboards, but the Klansmen, led by Dr. J. Rufus Bratton, a local physician, discovered his hiding place. They dragged him outside, tied a rope around a tree limb, and hung him. Not even elected officials were safe. Both state Senator Solomon Washington Dill, a white Republican, and state Senator Benjamin Franklin Randolph, a black Republican, were gunned down. So was a white poll manager who had the temerity to make whites wait in line to vote just like the Negroes.[27]

✦ ✦ ✦

SOUTHERN GOVERNMENTS, EVEN when under Republican control, were virtually helpless to fight the "Invisible Empire." White lawmen could not be counted upon to combat the Klan, nor white juries to convict them. Black militiamen were effective in some places, for instance Arkansas and Texas, but on the whole they were poorly trained and not well armed; as the historian Eric Foner noted, "blacks with military experience were far outnumbered in a region where virtually every white male had been trained to bear arms."[28] Moreover, in most places white Republican officeholders were afraid to employ black militia for fear of alienating moderate whites and harming their own chances of winning reelection. "Even in Republican areas . . . ," Foner wrote, "the law was paralyzed."[29]

That left the job of enforcing Reconstruction to an army of occupation that was pathetically inadequate to the task. The number of federal troops stationed in the South dropped from 87,000 in 1866 to 20,000 in 1867 and 6,000 in 1876. The Freedmen's Bureau in the War Department was supposed to help former slaves, but at its peak it had just 900 agents scattered across the South.[30] In short, there were far too few federal representatives to enforce upon 9.4 million Southerners (5.5 million of them white) the social revolution known as Radical Reconstruction, which was launched in 1867 after white Southerners had made plain their determination to resist granting ex-slaves any social or political rights.[31]

✦ ✦ ✦

No army officer tried harder than Major Lewis M. Merrill to realize the ideals of Reconstruction and to expose "the villainies" perpetrated by the Klan, but his experience showed just how futile the struggle was. He arrived in South Carolina in March 1871 with three companies from the Seventh Cavalry—troops temporarily diverted from fighting Indians to fighting the Ku Klux Klan. Even with this influx, there were fewer than 1,000 soldiers in a state of 705,606 people (including 289,667 whites).

A West Point graduate, Merrill was described as having "the head, face and spectacles of a German professor, and the frame of an athlete." An officer of "unusual talent," he had fought Border Ruffians in "Bleeding Kansas" in the 1850s and bushwhackers in Missouri in the 1860s, so he knew how to conduct a counterinsurgency. Although not a lawyer himself, he came from a family of lawyers and had previously served as a judge advocate general, so he knew how to utilize the law to achieve his objectives. He was, in the words of U.S. Attorney General Amos T. Akerman, "resolute, collected, bold, and prudent, with a good legal head, very discriminating between truth and falsehood; very indignant at wrong, and yet master of his indignation." In short, "just the man for the work."

Fuegian tribesmen in South America. Tribal warriors were the original guerrillas. (New York Public Library)

Ancient Mesopotamian sovereign, possibly Sargon of Akkad, ruler of the world's first empire (ca. 2334–2279 BC) and the first of countless kings who had to battle nomadic guerrillas. (The Image Works)

There was no "Eastern Way of War" that emphasized guerrilla tactics. These terra-cotta warriors buried in a tomb in 210 BC make clear that ancient Chinese armies were as conventional as their Greek or Roman counterparts. (The Image Works)

Roman siege of Jerusalem, AD 70. The legions dealt ruthlessly with rebellions, but there was more to Roman counterinsurgency than "they create a desert and call it peace." (The Image Works)

The Huns were ferocious raiders—essentially guerrillas—whose invasion of western Europe starting around AD 370 helped bring down the Roman Empire. (Mary Evans Picture Library)

To make good his claim on the throne of Scotland in 1306, Robert the Bruce employed guerrilla tactics against the English. (The Image Works)

Battle of Concord, 1775. The redcoats were outraged that "Yankey scoundrels . . . would never engage us properly," choosing instead to fire from behind trees and stone walls. (Granger Collection)

Francis Marion, "the Swamp Fox"—the most storied leader of irregulars during the American Revolution. (Granger Collection)

The American War of Independence was ultimately decided in the House of Commons (above). British voters tired of the war forced a change of government in 1782, showing the growing importance of public opinion. (Granger Collection)

"The Maid of Zaragoza" firing a cannon at French troops, 1808. The uprising by the Spanish people dashed Napoleon's hopes for a quick conquest. (Granger Collection)

The Peninsular War turned into a bloody struggle pitting *guerrilleros* (the first use of that word) against French occupiers and their collaborators. This drawing depicts a rebel killing a French soldier. (The Image Works)

The French were willing to use genocidal violence to squelch the Haitian Revolution (1791–1804). (New York Public Library)

That Haiti won its independence anyway was due in no small measure to Toussaint Louverture, "the Black Spartacus." (New York Public Library)

At the Battle of Navarino in 1827 (above), a combined English-French-Russian fleet sank a Turkish-Egyptian fleet. The first "humanitarian intervention" made Greek independence inevitable. (The Image Works)

Giuseppe Garibaldi, champion of Italian unification. The beau ideal of the irregular warrior, he was one of the first guerrillas to become an international celebrity and sex symbol. (The Image Works)

Jamestown massacre, 1622. In a surprise attack, Powhatan Indians wiped out more than one-fourth of the colonists—347 out of 1,240. Atrocities on both sides would characterize the Indian Wars for nearly 300 years. (Granger Collection)

Seventh U.S. Cavalry attacking a Cheyenne village on the Washita River in modern-day Oklahoma, 1868. Lieutenant Colonel Custer managed to retreat before being overwhelmed by larger numbers—this time. (Granger Collection)

General George H. Crook, one of the U.S. Army's most effective and humane Indian fighters. He was so unassuming that "he might have been taken for a Montana miner." (New York Public Library)

The Remnants of an Army, by Elizabeth Butler. This Victorian painting shows Dr. William Brydon, the sole European survivor of a 16,000-strong Anglo-Indian expedition to arrive in Jalalabad in 1842. (Art Resource)

With their jezail muskets, Pashtun warriors would bedevil British troops on both sides of the India–Afghanistan border from the 1840s to the 1940s. (New York Public Library)

(*Left*) Shamil led Muslim mountaineers in Chechnya and Dagestan against Russian rule, 1834–59. He had his own mother whipped for suggesting surrender. (New York Public Library)

(*Right*) Marshal Hubert Lyautey, ruler of Morocco, 1912–25. A soldier with literary flair, he invented the influential "oil spot" theory of pacification. (Bridgeman)

General Christiaan de Wet, the brilliant but irascible Boer guerrilla leader, with his staff. The Boers were as hard to catch on their ponies as American Indians. (The Image Works)

British soldiers gained a reputation for brutality during the Boer War, 1802–1902, which gave rise to the term "concentration camp." (Granger Collection)

John Brown was a terrible guerrilla leader whose attack on Harpers Ferry was a disaster. But he was a great terrorist who helped spark the war that led to the end of slavery. (Granger Collection)

Major Lewis Merrill was a dogged investigator, but he could not convict the Klansmen he identified in York County, South Carolina. (U.S. Army Military History Institute)

With a campaign of intimidation aimed at freed slaves and their Republican champions (as seen above in "Visit of the Ku-Klux," by Frank Bellew in *Harper's Weekly*, February 24, 1872), white supremacists destroyed the promise of Reconstruction. (New York Public Library)

Émile Henry's bomb explodes in the Café Terminus in Paris, 1894. Anarchists, one of the first transnational terrorist groups, killed political leaders and ordinary "bourgeois" alike. (The Image Works)

Michael Collins, mastermind of the Irish Republican cause in the War of Independence, 1919–21. He was said to be "full of fascination and charm—but also of dangerous fire." (The Image Works)

Russian Nihilists condemned to be deported to Siberia. Despite the tsarist state's reputation for heavy-handed rule, its police force was so small and weak that leftist terrorists were able to wreak havoc. (The Image Works)

The assassination of Archduke Franz Ferdinand in Sarajevo, 1914—the most consequential terrorist act in history because it sparked World War I. (The Image Works)

T. E. Lawrence, pictured in his "Lawrence of Arabia" regalia, advised and led Arab irregulars for only two years (1916–18), but he became one of the most influential practitioners and theorists of guerrilla warfare. (The Image Works)

Orde Wingate, a distant relative, was the closest World War II counterpart to Lawrence. An eccentric who gave interviews in the nude while brushing his private parts, he fought in Palestine, Abyssinia, and Burma. (AP)

Wingate's Chindits crossing a river in Burma, 1943. They paid a fearful price on their "deep penetration" missions while pioneering aerial resupply coordinated by radio. (Imperial War Museum)

Mao Zedong on the Long March, 1934–35. His propaganda genius turned a catastrophic defeat into a triumph of the spirit for the embattled Reds. (The Image Works)

Vo Nguyen Giap (*left*) and Ho Chi Minh in 1945, at the start of their long war against the French, Americans, and South Vietnamese. No one else applied the Maoist revolutionary model so successfully. (AP)

He set up headquarters in Rose's Hotel in Yorkville, the York County seat (population: 1,500), and set out about collecting intelligence amid what a visitor from New York called "a general air of dirty dreariness." When he first arrived, he was "kindly and courteously received . . . by the principal citizens of the town," as befitting the usual Southern custom. He was under the impression that he would have to deal with nothing more than "sporadic instances of mob violence." But before long he "became convinced that the Ku-Klux organization was not only a very large one and exceedingly well organized but a very dangerous one." "I never conceived of such a state of social disorganization being possible in any civilized community as exists in this county now . . . ," he later told Congress. "There appears to me to be a diseased state of public sentiment in regard to the administration of justice."

Employing informers ("pukers" in local parlance), Merrill eventually gathered evidence on eleven murders and six hundred cases of "whipping, beating, and personal violence, excluding numerous minor cases of threats, intimidation, abuse, and small personal violence, as knocking down with a pistol or gun." But although he could investigate, he could not prosecute. Because of "dishonest or intimidated juries and perjured testimony," he knew that "the local civil authorities were powerless to cope with the strength of the Ku-Klux conspiracy, even if willing to make the attempt, and I have been compelled to believe that the desire to make the attempt was entirely wanting." Such reluctance was hardly surprising given that "the conspiracy may be stated to have practically included the whole white community."

Alarmed by the evidence gathered by Major Merrill and other investigators, Congress in April 1871 passed the Ku Klux Klan Act. It created a new federal crime—"deprivation of any rights, privileges, and immunities secured by the Constitution"—and authorized the president to suspend the writ of habeas corpus to enforce it. Six months later, President Ulysses S. Grant lifted habeas corpus protections in nine South Carolina counties, including York—the first and last time this provision was invoked. Within two days Merrill's cavalrymen had arrested eighty-two suspects for crimes of "revolting wickedness." Hundreds more surrendered voluntarily, overflowing the Yorkville jail. Merrill said the Klansmen were "bewildered and demoralized" and "recognized . . . that the game was up."

In fact, the game was just beginning. There was no provision in the KKK Act for military tribunals, so the suspects were remanded to federal court in

32.

PROPAGANDA BY THE DEED

Anarchists, ca. 1880–ca. 1939

THE PALE, SLIGHTLY built young man in his "shabby black pants, vest, boots, and a white shirt with a black tie"—the typical uniform of a down-at-the-heels intellectual—would have attracted little attention as he wandered through the frigid night air of fin de siècle Paris. Unless, that is, someone had looked more closely at his overcoat and wondered what could have made that bulge in his coat pocket.

From his modest rented room in Belleville, a working-class district within sight of the newly completed Eiffel Tower, he walked down the elegant Avenue de l'Opéra. He stopped by a couple of fashionable boîtes—the Restaurant Bignon and the Café de la Paix—but they were too empty for his purposes. At 8 p.m. he reached the Hotel Terminus, next to a bustling railroad station. There were a substantial number of patrons in its café and more arriving, so he took a table, ordered a beer, and lit a cigar. By 9 p.m. more than 350 people were drinking aperitifs, smoking, and conversing, as if in a scene from *La Bohème*, while an "indifferent orchestra" played in the background.

But then any resemblance to the Puccini opera stopped. The man in black calmly opened the door, took the package out of his pocket, lit it with his cigar, and tossed it inside just as he was stepping onto the sidewalk. The homemade bomb weighed just four pounds. It was nothing more than a metal lunch pail filled with dynamite and buckshot along with a mercury fulminate fuse. Simple, but destructive. The explosion on February 12, 1894, shattered marble tables and metal chairs, "blew to atoms the windows and mirrors," and left holes in both the floor and the ceiling. Twenty people were injured, five badly. One of them would later die. It was hardly the sort of decadent scene that we have come to identify with the Belle Époque.

As smoke and screams emanated from the café, the bomber tried to get away. But he had been observed by a waiter who screamed, "Stop him!" A small crowd of passersby joined the chase in the gloaming darkness. As he ran, the bomber pulled out a pistol and fired several shots at his pursuers before a policeman finally grabbed him. The bomber tried to shoot him too, but after a short struggle he was arrested. Even when he was in custody, he continued to resist, screaming, "Pigs! I would kill you all!"

At first he gave his name as Leon Breton, then as Leon Martin. Within days it emerged that his real name was Émile Henry and this was not his first act of terrorism. More than two years earlier, on November 8, 1892, he had left a bomb outside the Paris offices of a mining company that had just broken a strike by its employees. The police had discovered the device and carried it back to their station house, where it detonated, killing five officers. At his trial Henry expressed only one regret—that he had not killed more people. He had hoped at least fifteen would die in the Café Terminus.

His brazenness was no surprise to the crowd of spectators because the twenty-one-year-old was already a dedicated anarchist—someone who believed that the state would have to be destroyed to bring about a nirvana where private property ceased to exist and people lived in perfect liberty and harmony. The only surprise was that he was not himself an impoverished worker or, as a London magazine put it, "of the loafer and low criminal type"—the stereotypes that polite society liked to project onto the anarchists. He was, the prosecutor noted, "a perfect little petty bourgeois." His father was a published author; an uncle was a marquis. Henry had been a brilliant student who had gone to work for another uncle who was a civil engineer. But he abandoned thoughts of a career to pursue his anarchist beliefs—inspired, no doubt, by the example of his father, who had been a leading member of the Commune, which took over Paris for seventy-two days in 1871. In one bloody week in May 1871, the communards had been routed, with 20,000 killed and 40,000 arrested.[36] Henry's father was forced into exile in Spain. That created an enduring grievance for anarchists such as Henry and his older brother, Fortuné, both of whom became associated with anarchist groups in the French capital.

They were also embittered by the terrible poverty that they saw around them, with the proletariat living in miserable slums while wealthy Parisians cavorted in opulent restaurants and music halls. As Émile Henry was to explain at his trial, "The factory owner amassing a huge fortune on the back of the labor of his workers. . . . The deputy, the minister whose hands were forever outstretched for bribes. . . . Everything I could see turned my stomach and my mind fastened upon criticism of social organization. . . . I turned into an enemy of a society which I held to be criminal."

Thus was Henry motivated to become a pioneer in urban terrorism, a phenomenon distinct from, even if it had some overlap with, the sort of rural terrorism practiced by the Ku Klux Klan or John Brown. By striking in the midst of heavily populated urban areas such as Paris, where their actions would instantly be sensationalized in the emerging mass-circulation newspapers and magazines, Henry and other anarchists showed how even a tiny terrorist organization (in his case, a band of one) could have a disproportionate impact on popular opinion.[37]

✦ ✦ ✦

IN FORMULATING HIS critique of society, which, he admitted, "has been voiced too often to need rehearsing by me," Henry had been influenced by three philosophers above all—the anarchist trinity.

First came the Frenchman Pierre-Joseph Proudhon (1809–65), a gifted sloganeer who claimed "property is theft" and "god is evil." Then there was Mikhail Bakunin (1814–76), a lumbering Russian nobleman with an unruly beard who spent a decade in tsarist prisons and ended his days in Swiss exile. He was Karl Marx's bitter rival in the International Working Men's Association (the First International) at a time when communism and anarchism were jostling for influence in revolutionary circles. With the Russian Nihilist Sergei Nechaev, Bakunin cooperated on a famous pamphlet, *Principles of Revolution*, which stated, "We recognize no other activity but the work of extermination, but we admit that the forms in which the activity will show itself will be extremely varied—poison, the knife, the rope, etc. In this struggle, revolution sanctifies everything alike." They also worked together on *Catechism of a Revolutionary*, which claimed, "Everything is moral that contributes to the triumph of the revolution; everything that hinders it is immoral and criminal." Although Bakunin subsequently broke with Nechaev, who became notorious for murdering a young fellow revolutionary in Russia (an incident that inspired Dostoevsky's novel *Demons*), he never repudiated his endorsement of violence.

The third great apostle of anarchism, Peter Kropotkin (1842–1921), was less given to inflammatory and even bloodthirsty pronouncements. A Russian prince who had turned against the old regime, he spent time in prison before escaping and settling, as had Marx, in England. Eventually he tried to dissociate himself from the doctrine of "propaganda by the deed"—the euphemism for terrorism coined by the Frenchman Paul Brousse in 1877[38]—but he refused to reject violence as Mahatma Gandhi or Martin Luther King Jr. would later do. "Personally I hate these explosions, but I cannot stand as a judge to condemn those who are driven to despair," Kropotkin said in a statement echoed by countless terrorist apologists through the ages.[39]

Most adherents of Proudhon, Bakunin, and Kropotkin were not violent, but some were. The police identified more than five thousand anarchists in France; one thousand were considered dangerous.[40] Anarchists were also concentrated in Italy, Russia, and Spain. Immigrants from those countries promulgated their doctrines as far away as North and South America. In the late nineteenth century, the world was transformed by "globalization," with the spread of railroads, steamships, and the telegraph, and, just as they would do a hundred years later with the Internet, airlines, satellite television, and cell phones, terrorists took advantage of this phenomenon.

Then, as now, London provided a safe haven for radicals, including for a time Émile Henry. Here exiles could print their books and pamphlets for distribution back home. They could even meet in their own clubhouse, the Autonomie Club off Tottenham Court Road. Scotland Yard, and in particular its Special Branch, which had been created in 1883 in response to Irish Fenian bombings, kept a wary eye on the foreign radicals but did not usually interfere unless they plotted against British targets. That was rare but not unheard of. In 1894, just three days after Henry's attack in Paris, a French tailor named Martial Bourdin tried to blow up the Royal Observatory in Greenwich but through "clumsy bungling" blew himself up instead, an incident that inspired Joseph Conrad's *The Secret Agent*.[41]

Outside of Britain the anarchists were more successful. President Sadi Carnot of France, Prime Minister Antonio Cánovas del Castillo of Spain, Empress Elizabeth of Austria-Hungary, President William McKinley of the United States, and King Umberto I of Italy were all slain by self-professed anarchists between 1894 and 1901. Other monarchs, including Kaiser Wilhelm I of Germany and the shah of Persia, narrowly escaped the same fate. Never before had any terrorist group killed so many heads of state, nor has any since then.[42]

Such killings posed, as King Umberto noted, a "professional risk" for rulers.[43] More shocking were indiscriminate attacks like Émile Henry's that were directed at ordinary people whose only crime was to be "bourgeois." Three months before Henry's attack on the Café Terminus, a Spanish anarchist, Santiago Salvador, had flung two bombs from a balcony into a crowded Barcelona theater during a performance of *William Tell*, Rossini's opera, which, ironically, tells the story of an earlier rebel against established authority. Twenty-two people were killed and five others wounded.[44] Many years later, in 1920, a horse-drawn wagon filled with explosives was blown up on Wall Street in New York. Thirty-eight people were killed and hundreds wounded, making this the deadliest terrorist attack on American soil until the 1995 Oklahoma City bombing. The perpetrators were never caught, but the leading suspect was the Italian anarchist Mario Buda, creating a climate of fear about Italian-Americans and other immigrants that intensified as the decade progressed.[45]

Many of these bloodlettings were justified as reprisals for punishments meted out for earlier attacks; the desire for revenge has always been the most powerful of terrorist motivations. In the twentieth century numerous radicals would claim they had been embittered by the case of Nicola Sacco and Bartolomeo Vanzetti, two Italian-American anarchists executed in Massachusetts in 1927 after a much criticized trial found them guilty of killing two men during an armed robbery. Émile Henry, for his part, said he was avenging August Vaillant, who had been executed for throwing a bomb into the French Chamber of Deputies that had injured a number of people but killed no one. (The president of the chamber had memorably proclaimed, "The session continues.")[46] Henry's arrest, in turn, led his friend, the Belgian anarchist Philibert Pauwels, to plant small bombs into two shabby Paris hotels, one of which killed an elderly landlady. Pauwels then tried to blow up the elegant Church of the Madeleine but killed only himself when his bomb exploded prematurely.[47]

✦ ✦ ✦

NEWS OF ANARCHIST outrages, hyped by the yellow press of the day, led to panic among the respectable classes. Between 1892 and 1894 Paris was the scene of eleven bombings, which killed nine people. As a result, wrote a newspaper correspondent, "the Parisians of 1894 . . . lived in daily dread of some fresh eruption. . . . If a trifling mishap occurred to a tramcar, through an electric wire getting out of order, people imagined that an explosive had been deposited on the line."[48] (Anyone who was in New York after 9/11 will recognize the reaction.) Anarchist beliefs were attributed to many ordinary criminals who, for their part, were happy to claim political motives for their acts. In 1887 a French burglar who had stabbed to death a policeman trying to arrest him defended himself by saying, "The policeman arrested me in the name of the law; I hit him in the name of liberty."[49]

There was widespread speculation that a nefarious Black International (black was the anarchists' color) was scheming to bring down Western civilization. Bakunin furthered this impression by inventing grand if nonexistent organizations with names such as the World Revolutionary Alliance. His fanatical friend Sergei Nechaev was designated its "accredited representative" No. 2771, falsely implying there were 2,770 others.[50]

It was true that anarchists sometimes crossed national borders to carry out their deeds—something that was easy to do because, as one anarchist noted, "Europe at that time knew no passports, and frontiers hardly existed."[51] The Austrian empress Elizabeth, for instance, was stabbed to death by an Italian anarchist in Switzerland. King Umberto was killed by an Italian-American anarchist living in New Jersey. But anarchists never had a unified command structure in any individual nation much less across all nations.

They did not even have joint training camps. Those were innovations that would await a subsequent wave of terrorism in the 1970s.

The very concept of an *anarchist organization* was an oxymoron. Anarchists were fierce individualists who resisted the kind of regimentation that Marxist leaders imposed on their parties, which helps to explain why anarchists were less successful. As Émile Henry noted, anarchism was not a "dogma, an unassailable, incontrovertible doctrine revered by its adepts the way Muslims venerate the Koran."[52] Although anarchists held occasional conventions (for example, a London congress in 1881 that endorsed "propaganda by the deed"), whatever cohesion they had—and it was not much—came from informal meetings and from newspapers such as *L'Endehors*, a Parisian weekly that was briefly edited by Henry. Most anarchist terrorists heeded the German exile Johann Most's advice in his jaunty how-to pamphlet, *The Science of Revolutionary Warfare* (1885), one of the first terrorist manuals ever produced: "If you want to carry out a revolutionary act, don't talk to others about it first—go ahead and do it!"[53]

For all their disunity, anarchists appeared to be so formidable that numerous governments responded with repressive measures in waging what the *New York Times* described in 1881—the year that both President James Garfield and Tsar Alexander II were assassinated—as "The War on Terrorism."[54] The most severe penalties were applied, as might be expected, in illiberal states such as Russia and Austria. But even in democratic France laws were passed to crack down on "evil-doers" who distributed anarchist propaganda or defended its doctrines. In the United States, Congress passed a law barring from the country any alien "who disbelieves in or who is opposed to all organized government." A more severe crackdown, known as the "Palmer Raids" after Woodrow Wilson's attorney general, A. Mitchell Palmer, occurred during the Red scare of 1919–20 when numerous radicals, including Emma Goldman and Alexander Berkman, were deported or imprisoned. Theodore Roosevelt reflected the supercharged atmosphere of the times when he said in 1908 that "when compared with the suppression of anarchy, every other question sinks into insignificance."[55]

Those today who believe that the world's response to 9/11 is entirely novel should realize that the anarchist menace of a century earlier prompted growing attempts at international police cooperation such as the anti-anarchist conferences in Rome (1898) and St. Petersburg (1904). The Russian secret police established a sizable operation in Paris with the French government's consent, and Italy deployed detectives to keep track of Italian anarchists around the world. Such steps laid the foundation for the creation in 1923 of Interpol, the International Criminal Police Commission. Anarchist groups were riddled with informers and provocateurs who kept the police forces of many countries well informed of their plots—and sometimes invented fresh plots simply to collect greater rewards for uncovering them.[56]

As usual, technology was a two-edged sword: the same cameras that made it possible for the mass media to publish pictures of terrorist attacks, thus furthering the perpetrators' aims, also made it possible for the police to photograph and identify suspects. This era saw the beginning of "mug shots," fingerprints, and forensic laboratories, all of which made the terrorists' jobs harder.[57]

✦ ✦ ✦

ANARCHISTS WERE CONVINCED that attempts to repress them would spur a public backlash. At his trial, just before he went to the guillotine, Émile Henry declared, "Hanged in Chicago, decapitated in Germany, garroted in Xerez [Spain], shot in Barcelona, guillotined in Montbrison and in Paris, our dead are many. But you have not been able to destroy anarchy. Its roots go deep; it sprouts from the bosom of a poisonous society which is falling apart. . . . It is everywhere . . . and it will end by defeating you and killing you."[58]

Henry was wrong. Anarchists did not defeat anyone. By the late 1930s their movement had been all but extinguished. In the more democratic states, better policing allowed terrorists to be arrested while more liberal labor laws made it possible for workers to peacefully redress their grievances through unions. In the Soviet Union, Fascist Italy, and Nazi Germany, anarchists were repressed with brute force. The biggest challenge was posed by Nestor Makhno's fifteen thousand anarchist guerrillas in Ukraine during the Russian Civil War, but they were finally "liquidated" by the Red Army in 1921.[59] In Spain anarchists were targeted both by Franco's Fascists and by their Marxists "comrades" during the 1936–39 civil war—as brilliantly and bitterly recounted by George Orwell in *Homage to Catalonia*. Everywhere anarchists were pushed into irrelevance by Moscow's successful drive to establish communism as the dominant doctrine of the left.

That the anarchists did not accomplish more was hardly surprising, since they were, in the words of a recent book, "demanding the impossible." They were in some ways the opposite of the Ku Klux Klan, which pursued a broad-based campaign of terror to achieve limited objectives. Anarchists, by contrast, committed isolated acts of violence over many years and in many different countries in pursuit of utopian goals. By one estimate, between 1880 and 1914 these "wild beasts without nationality," as an Austrian official dubbed them, struck in sixteen nations, killing 160 people and wounding at least 500. Ninety-three more people would die in anarchist attacks after World War I, not counting the Russian and Spanish civil wars.[60] Nowhere did they achieve much momentum.

Socialists suffered from many deficiencies of their own, but in the land of the tsars, at least, they would achieve a critical mass of terror that would contribute to the ultimate collapse of the old regime.

33.

HUNTING THE TSAR

The Nihilists on the Trail of Alexander II, 1879–1881

THE TSAR WAS sentenced to death on August 26, 1879. The verdict was delivered, incongruously enough, in a pleasant pine grove in a suburb of St. Petersburg where the wealthy had their dachas (summer houses). Here, amid the dry pine needles, assembled the executive committee of the People's Will (*Narodnaya Volya*)—twenty-five men and women who had dedicated their lives to bringing about a revolution in Russia.

They were all under thirty, all intellectuals, mainly of the middle class or the lower levels of the nobility. Most had attended university—still an anomaly in a society in which illiteracy was widespread. In their wealth and education, similar to the leaders of the American Revolution and the Ku Klux Klan but to few other contemporary rebels, they anticipated twentieth-century insurgent leaders such as Fidel Castro, Che Guevara, and Yasser Arafat. They were known as Nihilists, a term popularized by Ivan Turgenev in his 1862 novel, *Fathers and Sons,* but their agenda was more accurately described as "populist-socialist." Unlike the anarchists, who wanted to destroy the state, they wanted to seize control of it. Previously they had belonged to a group called Land and Freedom, but they had split off because some members of Land and Freedom had objected to the use of violence. The executive committee had no such compunctions.

Vera Figner was one of its members, a twenty-seven-year-old from a family of "prosperous noblemen," "a vivacious, merry, frolicsome girl," a onetime debutante who had abandoned a budding medical career and a husband to devote herself to the cause of the peasants of whom she knew little. (One historian has written, accurately if acerbically, that the Nihilists were "peasant-lovers in the sense in which some people are animal-lovers.") She believed, they all believed, that "so much inflammatory material had accumulated among the people that a small spark would easily flare up into a flame, and the latter into a gigantic conflagration."

And what better spark than the assassination of the Emperor and Autocrat of All the Russias? Alexander II had begun his reign as a reformer; he had freed the serfs in 1861. But in the ensuing years he had turned more conservative, refusing to grant a constitution or an elected parliament. This deflated the high expectations raised by his early years and sparked a violent backlash. In 1878 Nihilists killed General Nikolai Mezentsov, chief of the Third Section, the tsarist secret police. The following year it was the turn of Prince Dimitry Kropotkin, a provincial governor and cousin of the famous anarchist. Yet another terrorist shot and wounded the governor of St. Petersburg, a crime for which she was acquitted by a sympathetic jury. These were not isolated incidents of political murder like the killings of Julius Caesar or Abraham Lincoln but rather a concerted campaign of terrorism designed to bring down an entire state. Targeting the tsar himself was the pinnacle of the campaign.

The People's Will hoped to blow up the tsar's train as he was returning from a Crimean holiday in November 1879. Vera Figner journeyed to Odessa with a load of dynamite. Dressing up as an "upperclass doll" (her own words), she made an application to procure a job on the railroad for a man who was supposedly her janitor, actually a fellow conspirator. He got the job, but the tsar decided to take another route home so the effort was wasted. Another terrorist, pretending to be a merchant setting up a tannery, buried dynamite on a section of tracks. The tsar traveled over this route on November 18, but the explosives did not explode; the wires had not been connected correctly.

A third ambush still awaited in a suburb of Moscow where two Nihilists pretending to be a married couple rented a house five hundred feet from the tracks and tunneled their way toward the rail line through "cold wet mud." By November 19, when the tsar's train was to pass by, they were ready. Their intelligence indicated that the tsar's party would use three trains with Alexander himself in the fourth coach of the second train. They duly blew that coach to smithereens only to discover that Alexander had decided at the last minute to travel in the first train. The tsar did not even know about the blast until a courtier told him that "the fourth car of the retinue train has been turned into marmalade. There was nothing in it but fruit from the Crimea."

The tsar in the end was not safe even at home. Stepan Khalturin, a radical carpenter, had gotten a job in the tsar's Winter Palace, an immense affair of 1,050 rooms, 1,886 doors, and 1,945 windows that was in constant need of repair. He proved to be such a reliable and hardworking handyman that a police corporal approached him as a potential son-in-law. All the while Khalturin was slowly smuggling small bits of dynamite provided by the People's Will into his room in the cellar, two floors beneath the dining room. On the afternoon of February 5, 1880, Khalturin connected the wires and left the building. Fifteen minutes later, a thunderous explosion rocked the palace. Eleven people were killed and fifty-six injured, but the tsar was not among them. The dining room had been only slightly damaged and the tsar was not yet inside. Most of the casualties had occurred among his bodyguards who occupied a first-floor room between the cellar and the dining room.

Yet another attempt failed in August 1880 when one of the People's Will members overslept and failed to reach the bridge over which the tsar was traveling in time to set off a bomb. But the terrorists did not give up.

In December 1880 two of their operatives pretending to be "Mr. and Mrs. Kobozev" set up a "cheese shop" in St. Petersburg that was actually a front for a tunneling operation to install a mine under a street where the tsar was known to travel every Sunday to inspect his troops. As a backup, four assassins armed with handheld bombs were to be deployed on the street itself. The tunneling began in late January 1881 and was complete by the end of February.

Even as the conspiracy unfolded, the secret police were closing in. The People's Will had been able to continue operating with the aid of a mole who was working as a clerk in the police's Third Section. But following a reorganization in 1880 that moved the secret police, the Okhrana, to a new police department, the terrorists' luck began to change. By the end of February 1881 many members of the executive committee had been arrested, including their de facto leader Alexander Mikhailov and his successor, Andrei Zhelyabov. Both had been intimately involved in the tsar hunt, and both were now in solitary confinement in the forbidding Peter and Paul Fortress.

On Saturday, February 28, 1881, the day after Zhelyabov's arrest, a "sanitary inspector"—actually a police general—appeared at the cheese shop. He wanted to know what was in one of the barrels. "Mr. Kobozev" said it was cheese. If the general opened it he would have found dirt from the excavations but he could not be bothered, leading at least one historian to wonder whether the police were deliberately turning a blind eye to the murder of a tsar who was too liberal for their tastes.

That very night the remaining members of the executive committee met at Vera Figner's apartment to decide whether to abort the plot. They decided to proceed under the leadership of Sophia Perovskaya, Zhelyabov's aristocratic girlfriend, a beautiful blonde with blue eyes, "a delicate little nose," and a "charming mouth, which showed, when she smiled, two rows of very fine white teeth." Notwithstanding her "sweet and affectionate disposition," she was, in the words of a fellow Nihilist, "one of the most dreaded members of the Terrorist party." With her in the lead, the attack was scheduled for the next day, Sunday, March 1.

At 1 p.m. on a "dark, dreary" Sunday afternoon the sixty-three-year-old tsar set off for the troop inspection, resplendent in "a red cap, a red-lined overcoat with beaver's collar, and gold epaulets." Six Cossacks rode on horseback alongside his carriage and two sleighs full of policemen traveled behind him over the snow-covered cobblestone streets. By 2:15 p.m., after visiting a cousin, he was ready to return to the Winter Palace. The route he took did not carry him past the cheese shop, so it was now up to the bomb throwers. When Perovskaya gave the signal—blowing her nose into a silk handkerchief—three assassins deployed along the Catherine Canal Embankment. (One had lost his nerve at the last minute.)

As the tsar's carriage raced along, it was approached by a young blond man holding a small package. He swung his arm and there was a "deafening blast." Several people were killed or wounded but the tsar was unharmed. He got out of the carriage to inspect the damage, ignoring the coachman's pleas to keep going. As the tsar walked around, surrounded by his Cossacks, another young man approached and threw something at his feet.

Alexander and all those around him toppled over like bowling pins. Twenty people had been hit, including the assassin, Ignat Hryniewicki, who died a few hours later. "Through the snow, debris, and blood," recalled an officer, "you could see fragments of clothing, epaulets, sabers, and bloody chunks of human flesh."

The tsar, his legs shattered, died at the Winter Palace shortly thereafter. The seventh assassination attempt was the last.[61]

34.

"AN UNCONTROLLABLE EXPLOSION"

Socialist Revolutionaries in Russia, 1902–1917

UPON HEARING THE news, Vera Figner wept tears of joy and relief that the tyrant was dead. Soon she would be weeping tears of a different kind. For the death of the tsar did not lead to the death of tsarism. It simply led to the coronation of his reactionary son, Alexander III. On April 3, 1881, five of the terrorists, including Sofia Perovskaya, were hanged. Three others were condemned to life terms in prison. Figner wound up spending twenty years in solitary confinement. The People's Will was decimated. By 1883 its remnants were led by Sergei Degaev, a double agent working for the secret police who eventually killed his police handler and fled to America.[62]

Even after its collapse, the People's Will would serve as an inspiration to future revolutionaries. Lenin, for one, urged his acolytes to emulate its "party discipline and conspiratorial practices," and his older brother, Alexander Ulyanov, would join a successor organization—the Terrorist Faction of the People's Will. He was executed in 1887 for plotting to assassinate Alexander III, an event that helped radicalize the young Lenin.[63] Thereafter terrorism briefly disappeared from the Russian scene until reappearing bigger than ever at the turn of the century.

Its reemergence should be no surprise given that the essential conditions that created opposition to the tsarist regime remained unchanged.

The economy was in the throes of industrialization, creating an urban proletariat that lived in execrable conditions and a fledgling middle class that did not have power commensurate with its growing wealth. Education was also spreading: the number of university students increased thirteenfold between 1860 and 1914, the number of periodicals more than tripled between 1860 and 1900, and the literacy rate rose from 21 percent to 40 percent between 1897 and 1914.[64] But while society was modernizing and becoming politically aware, the regime remained frozen in an autocratic past where there was no way to affect peaceful change. That was a recipe for trouble. As the liberal former prime minister Count Sergei Witte wrote in 1911, "At the beginning of the 20th century it is impossible to pursue with impunity a medieval course of policy. . . . At the first weakening of the Government's power and prestige, [revolution] bursts out with the violence of an uncontrollable explosion."[65]

At the forefront of the explosion was the Socialist Revolutionary (SR) Party and its Combat Organization, which was dedicated to terror. It announced its existence in 1902 when one of its members walked into the office of the interior minister and killed him with two shots at point-blank range. His successor was murdered by another SR terrorist in 1904 who tossed a bomb into his carriage. The following year, 1905, it was the turn of Grand Duke Sergei Aleksandrovich, the tsar's uncle and governor-general of Moscow. He was obliterated by another hand-thrown bomb—a fate narrowly avoided by *his* successor, who in 1906 received only minor injuries in a blast that killed an aide.

The SRs, who called bomb throwing a "holy act," anticipated many of the practices of twenty-first-century terrorism. They were imaginative enough to talk about using a newly invented airplane to bomb the Winter Palace and ruthless enough to employ suicide bombers. In 1906, three members of an ultra-radical SR offshoot, the Maximalists, tried to kill the newly appointed prime minister, Pyotr Stolypin, a conservative reformer who was so notorious for hanging revolutionaries that the noose became known as "Stolypin's necktie." When the terrorists were denied entry to Stolypin's summer house, they shouted "Long live freedom!" and blew themselves up in his anteroom with suitcase bombs. Stolypin escaped, but twenty-seven others were killed and seventy injured, including two of his children.

Stolypin would be killed in another SR attack, in 1911 (the eighteenth attempt on his life), while attending the opera in Kiev with Tsar Nicholas II. The assassin, Dmitri Bogrov, was a police informer who had been uncovered by his comrades and forced to kill the prime minister as an act of atonement. Audaciously enough, he duped the secret police into providing him a ticket to the opera (Rimsky-Korsakov's *Tale of Tsar Saltan*) by promising to point out two other SR terrorists who were supposedly planning to assassinate Stolypin.[66]

The SRs' major competitors on the left, the Social Democrats, ostensibly eschewed terrorism in favor of fomenting a revolt of the proletariat. Leon Trotsky summed up their creed: "A single isolated hero cannot replace the masses."[67] But in practice both Social Democrat factions, the Bolsheviks and Mensheviks, sometimes practiced terror too, albeit to a lesser extent than the SRs. Lenin, the Bolshevik leader in exile, endorsed terrorism amid the turmoil of 1905 when the tsarist regime teetered on the brink of collapse. With workers' strikes spreading and workers' councils (or soviets) springing up, he urged his followers to "take every opportunity for active work, without delaying their attacks until the time of the general uprising."[68]

That invitation was eagerly welcomed by one of Lenin's most devoted disciples. Josef Djugashvili, later known as Stalin, was a pockmarked former seminarian from Georgia who commanded Bolshevik Battle Squads that waged a campaign of terror across the Caucasus. Throughout 1905 his "cutthroats" fought pitched battles against the Cossacks and the Black Hundreds vigilantes. By 1906 the tsar had regained control with a harsh campaign of repression, and Stalin had to go underground again. From hiding he cooperated with the Mensheviks to assassinate General Fyodor Griyazanov, the leader of the counterrevolution in the Caucasus.

Thereafter Stalin turned his attention to "expropriations," as political bank robberies were known. There was an epidemic of bank stickups in Russia, with almost two thousand recorded between 1905 and 1906—so many that confidence in the entire banking system was shaken. Stalin became a veritable Jesse James, leading his Technical Group, or "Outfit," to take down stagecoaches, trains, even steamships. Their most spectacular heist occurred on June 12, 1907, in one of the main squares of Tiflis, as the capital of Georgia was then known. Sixty brigands hijacked a heavily guarded shipment of cash. Throwing bombs and firing pistols, they mowed down Cossacks and police along with many innocent bystanders, and got away with at least 250,000 rubles ($3.4 million) that would go to fund Lenin's operations. Stalin also engaged in a protection racket, extorting industrialists in return for a pledge not to kill them or blow up their facilities. As with other acts of "social banditry," it was not always clear where political motives left off and pure avarice picked up. Although Stalin apparently did not pocket the proceeds, other revolutionaries certainly did.[69]

In addition to the socialists, Russian anarchists such as the Black Banner group were also active in carrying out assassinations and expropriations. Like Émile Henry, they sometimes tossed bombs into cafés simply to kill "bourgeois" patrons as part of a policy of "motiveless terror."[70] Also getting into the act were revolutionary parties that claimed to represent disaffected minorities within the Russian Empire; the Armenian Dashnak and the Polish Socialist Party were particularly active.

The sheer number of attacks was staggering. It has been estimated that during the last two decades of the old regime (1897–1917) seventeen thousand people throughout the Russian Empire were killed or wounded by terrorists, with the bulk of the attacks occurring between 1905 and 1910.[71] "So many governors were killed by the revolutionaries," wrote the tsar's brother-in-law, "that an appointment to the post of governor acquired the meaning of a death sentence."[72]

✦ ✦ ✦

HOW WAS THIS much violence possible in what was supposedly Europe's strictest police state? The tsar deployed not only the secret police, the Okhrana, but also a uniformed Corps of Gendarmes devoted to political repression. They were given virtually unlimited powers to censor publications, open mail, and detain individuals. One catchall law made it a crime punishable by a minimum of sixteen months' imprisonment to compose "written documents containing unpermitted judgments with regard to the ordinances and actions of the Government."

Draconian as these rules sounded, their application was tempered by what Count Witte described as the "lethargy, incompetence, and timidity prevalent among executive and administrative officers." In 1895 the Okhrana had only 161 full-time employees and the Gendarmes fewer than 10,000, most of whom did apolitical policing, to watch over 136 million people spread over eleven time zones. Russia had over "one hundred times fewer policemen" per capita than France, leaving the Romanov empire "significantly underpoliced" in one historian's judgment. Between 1867 and 1894, only 158 books were banned; Marx's *Das Kapital* was not one of them. During those same years 44 people were executed for political crimes, all of them assassins or would-be assassins. There was a big jump in executions during the 1905 Revolution: 3,000 to 5,000 people were killed in 1905–06. But that was still less than one-fourth the number slain in the Paris Commune. A greater number of revolutionaries was confined in prisons, yet most of them were better treated than common criminals because they were, after all, "gentlemen." For many radicals, prisons became schools of socialism where they could gain a "solid revolutionary education."

Another common punishment was exile in Siberia, but in 1880 there were only 1,200 political exiles, a figure that had increased to 4,113 by 1901. More were exiled following the 1905 Revolution (nearly 8,000 in 1906), but being sent to Siberia in the tsarist era had nothing in common with the hellish gulags that the Bolsheviks would later operate. Exiles lived in reasonable comfort in Siberian villages; they even received a stipend from the government, which could be supplemented by contributions from home. While in Siberian exile, Lenin brought out his mother and mother-in-law to take care of him and finished writing a weighty economic treatise. Escape was easy because police surveillance was so lax. The American traveler George Kennan (not to be confused with his distant relative and namesake, the future architect of "containment") reported in 1891 that Siberia "literally swarms with . . . escaped exiles" and that "thousands" leave "the very next day after their arrival." Stalin, for one, arrived in the Siberian village of Novaya Uda at the end of November 1903 and left at the beginning of January 1904, having served just one month of a three-year sentence.[73]

The most effective, if also most morally fraught, Okhrana tactic was the infiltration of terrorist groups. This backfired in the Degaev and Bogrov cases when informers committed shocking assassinations. But it was more effective in the case of the SR Combat Organization, which was taken over in 1907 by Evno Azef, who had been a well-paid Okhrana agent for the past fifteen years. The disclosure of his double life in 1908 discredited and demoralized the SRs. It would take them years to recover.[74]

In general police measures were strong enough to alienate a substantial portion of the population—but not strong enough to suppress the revolutionaries. As important as any coercive measure in restoring a measure of calm was Tsar Nicholas II's willingness to concede some liberal demands in October 1905 by granting a constitution and creating a parliament, the Duma. A Bolshevik organizer bemoaned "the corroding influence of the seeming freedom, of which we had a few breaths after the revolution of 1905."[75] This limited liberalization, combined with mass arrests and executions, ended terrorism as a serious threat by the eve of World War I. But the damage had been done.

Anna Geifman, the foremost student of the Russian terrorists, concludes that they "hastened the downfall of the tsarist regime." "To a large extent," she finds, "the revolutionaries succeeded in breaking the spine of Russian bureaucracy, wounding it both physically and in spirit, and in this way contributed to its general paralysis during the final crisis of the imperial regime in March of 1917."[76] But it is doubtful that the wounds would have been fateful without the trauma of defeat in World War I. Terrorism was at most one contributing factor among many to the collapse of the tsarist government.

When the tsar finally fell he was replaced, after a brief liberal interregnum, by a Bolshevik dictatorship whose leaders were steeped in the culture and tactics of the revolutionary underground. Stalin applied the methods he had learned as a young brigand in the Caucasus on a much greater scale to terrorize the entire Soviet Union. And, knowing from personal experience "the toothless way the tsarist regime [had] struggled with its 'gravediggers,' "[77] he made sure to create a more pervasive police state that could not be undermined by a few bomb throwers. Thus the antitsarist terrorists left a deep imprint on the history of Russia—and the world—even if they did not immediately succeed in their goal of overthrowing the state.

In few other countries were terrorists as effective. Ireland was one of the exceptions.

35.

SHINNERS AND PEELERS

The Irish War of Independence, 1919–1921

THEY SPENT FIVE days, five endless days, at the ambush site amid the shamrock-green fields. An informant had told them that a load of gelignite (an explosive more powerful than dynamite) was going to be conveyed to the Soloheadbeg Quarry in southern Ireland on January 16, 1919. They wanted the gelignite for themselves, but even more they wanted to make a statement—"not merely to capture the gelignite but also to shoot down the escort." So wrote Dan Breen, one of the nine masked marauders lying in wait in county Tipperary. A twenty-four-year-old railway lineman with, to quote a "wanted" poster, a "sulky bulldog appearance," he had been raised "only a stone's throw from the quarry" and "knew every inch of the ground."

Like most of his countrymen, he came from a poor farming family that "barely existed above the hair-line of poverty." "Potatoes and milk were our staple diet," he recalled. "On special occasion we had a meal of salted pork but the luxury of fresh meat was altogether beyond our reach." He had been forced to leave school at fourteen and had taken a job on the railroad. He also took on a covert role as one of two thousand members of the Irish Republican Brotherhood, a secret society better known as the Fenians, which had been fighting British rule since 1858. With the aid of Irish-American sympathizers, the Fenians had assassinated the chief secretary of Ireland and his undersecretary in Dublin's Phoenix Park (1882) and inadvertently killed twelve Londoners while trying to blast one of their members out of prison (1867). Those isolated acts of terrorism had been as ineffectual as the anarchist attacks of the same period. The British occupation of Ireland, already more than seven hundred years old, remained unshaken.[78]

In the early twentieth century, new republican groups sprang up: in 1902 a political party called Sinn Féin ("We Ourselves"), followed in 1913 by a military force called the Irish Volunteers that would become the Irish Republican Army. To the British, all of the republicans were dubbed "Shinners" (Sinn Féin is pronounced *shin fane*).

On Monday, April 24, 1916, during Easter week, fifteen hundred Shinners tried to seize power in Dublin by brute force. A similar effort by the Bolsheviks in Russia in November 1917 would face little opposition and lead to the overthrow of an already shaky provisional government during the "ten days that shook the world." British rule was not so easily shaken. Within five days the Shinners had been routed out of their stronghold in the ornate General Post Office by British troops (many of them Irishmen) backed by artillery. More than four hundred people were killed. Subsequently sixteen leaders of the Easter Rising were executed, creating fresh martyrs for the independence movement. There was no shortage of other grievances for the republicans to exploit going back to the Middle Ages.

"Sickened to death by British duplicity, cant and humbug . . . I decided to join the Irish Republican Brotherhood," Dan Breen later wrote. Subsequently he also joined the Irish Volunteers and became quartermaster of the South Tipperary Brigade. His neighborhood pal Sean Treacy, who by 1918 had served two terms in British jails, was its vice commandant. From 1913 to 1919, they drilled as best they could, trying to learn how to become soldiers from British military manuals, including C. E. Callwell's *Small Wars*. Their armaments were negligible—"a .45 revolver here and there, a few old, broken-down rifles," recalled one republican. " 'Twasn't worth a farthing." All the while they were frustrated by "the local Sinn Feiners, many of whom were not in favor of any stronger weapons than resolutions." So in January 1919, Breen, Treacy, and a few other Volunteers decided to take matters into their own hands. Without any authorization from above, they set out to fire the shots that would "begin another phase in the long fight for the freedom of our country."

On January 21, after five days of waiting, their scout finally dashed toward their hiding hole shouting, "They're coming, they're coming!" Two workers were guiding a horse-drawn cart loaded with a hundred pounds of gelignite. Accompanying them were two constables in the dark green uniform of the Royal Irish Constabulary, rifles slung over their shoulders. Both were local men, Irish Catholics like Breen and Treacy, one of them a widower with four children. The republicans viewed the "Peelers" (slang for policemen) as instruments of political repression—"deserters, spies and hirelings," in Breen's sneering words—but most of their work was apolitical crime fighting. These two constables, James McDonnell and Patrick O'Connell, were well liked by the locals and known to their attackers.

"Nearer and nearer they came," Breen wrote. "In the clear air we heard the sound of the horse's hooves and the rumbling of a heavy cart. Our nerves were highly strung." Breen said that after the ambushers shouted "Hands up!" the constables "raised their rifles" and made clear they "would die rather than surrender." Relatives of the two constables later claimed that they were not given a chance to surrender—an interpretation that Breen did nothing to dispel when years later he said, "You've got to kill and can't leave anyone alive afterward." The two constables were shot down in a hail of gunfire. Their killers then rode off with the explosives. Breen was only sorry there had not been more policemen escorting the gelignite. "If there had to be dead Peelers at all, six would have created a better impression than a mere two."[79]

That very day, a hundred miles to the north, the first Irish parliament, the Dáil Eireann, convened in a very different setting. It met in Mansion House, the stately residence of the lord mayor of Dublin, in the Round Room "with the statues standing in niches about the walls; the deep-cushioned chairs and sofas, gathered in a pleasant informal cluster in the center, deep sofas into which the deputies sank and from which, with the greatest difficulty, they rose to speak." All of the representatives were members of Sinn Féin who had been elected to the British Parliament in December but had refused to take their seats in Westminster. It was an important occasion even if only twenty-six of seventy-six legislators attended. The leader of the republican movement, Eamon de Valera, was imprisoned in England. Another leading republican, Michael Collins, was away preparing the plot that would bust de Valera out of captivity (employing, believe it or not, a duplicate key secreted in a cake). The proceedings were halting and sometimes comical because the English-speaking parliamentarians insisted on using a language—Gaelic—that some of them barely knew.

For all that, the Dáil which met on January 21, 1919, reached some momentous decisions. Its members issued a declaration of independence and an appeal to the "Free Nations of the World" then meeting at the Paris Peace Conference to recognize "Ireland's national status" and end "seven centuries of foreign oppression." They also named a government with de Valera as president and Collins as home minister (soon to be finance minister). It would take nineteen months before that government won international recognition, but its proclamation, however symbolic, was an important step in lending political legitimacy to the Irish War of Independence, whose first shots had been fired by a fateful coincidence in Tipperary that very day.[80]

✦ ✦ ✦

THE ASSOCIATED PRESS report on the Soloheadbeg shooting proclaimed, "New Era of Terrorism Begun!"[81] But Irish terrorism was nothing new. That Britain could not suppress this outbreak as easily as it had suppressed all others in the past was due in no small part to the genius of one man: Michael Collins. His title—minister of finance—did not hint at his real importance. Although he worked assiduously and successfully to raise hundreds of thousands of pounds for the revolution via a bond drive, his more important titles were director of intelligence of the Irish Republican Army and president of the Irish Republican Brotherhood. Even that did not convey his full significance. He was, in the words of an IRA officer, "virtually Commander-in-Chief in fact, if not in name."

Twenty-nine years old in 1919, Collins was already a veteran revolutionary who had spent time in a prison camp in Wales after taking part in the Easter Rising. He had grown up in county Cork, the youngest of eight children born to a prosperous if elderly farmer who died when Collins was still a boy. He was influenced not only by the traditional heroes of the Irish independence struggle, the "Bold Fenian Men," but also by De Wet and the other Boers who had given the British a black eye. (Years later he wrote to De Wet to thank him for having been his "earliest inspiration.") He was convinced, he later recalled, that "Irish Independence would never be attained by constitutional means," and that "when you're up against a bully you've got to kick him in the guts." To do just that, he was sworn into the Irish Republican Brotherhood in 1909 and then into the Irish Volunteers in 1914 while living in London, where he worked first for the British civil service and then for two financial firms.

"Mick" was tall, broad-shouldered, athletic, square-jawed, with "a mind quick as lightning," boundless energy, and undeniable charisma—"hearty, boisterous, or quiet by turn," in the words of an IRA officer. He was fond of whiskey, cigarettes, swearing, and female company. A woman who knew him thought he was a "real playboy"—an Irish Garibaldi, if you will, but without the Italian's air of sanctimony. Collins's friends described him as "full of fun" and a keen practical joker, but he also had a foul temper and a domineering temperament. He could be "harsh and sneering" with those who did not meet his high standards. It was in a British internment camp, later dubbed by a British intelligence officer "the nursery of the I.R.A.," that he first showed the gift for leadership that led fellow inmates to dub him "the Big Fellow." After his release in December 1916, having served six months, he assumed a leadership role in all three major nationalist organizations—the Irish Republican Brotherhood, the Irish Volunteers, and Sinn Féin—an unusual hat trick that put him at the center of the action.

Half accountant, half swashbuckler, Collins was capable of doing meticulous paperwork while also taking enormous personal risks. Throughout the war he seldom left Dublin (population: 230,000), even though he had a heavy price on his head. He worked from various homes and storefronts and frequently changed where he slept. He routinely put in seventeen- or eighteen-hour workdays before repairing to a pub or hotel to blow off steam. Sometimes he would pop up at an IRA safehouse without warning to swap a few jokes and ask, "Well, lads, how are ye getting on?" His visits bucked up morale among his men, who, one of them recalled, "loved and honored him."

He traveled without bodyguards or a disguise, cycling through the streets on an "ancient bicycle whose chain," one of his men wrote, "rattled like a mediaeval ghost's." He was stopped multiple times, but in his neat gray suit, which made him look like a stockbroker not a revolutionary, he always managed to bluff his way through—or else to threaten the police so convincingly that they did not feel like risking their lives to capture him. On more than one occasion he escaped out of a building through a skylight or a back door while British troops were rushing in through the front. One of his chief pursuers wrote that "he combined the characteristics of a Robin Hood with those of an elusive Pimpernel."

Part of the secret of Collins's success was his penchant for secrecy. He said, "Never let one side of your mind know what the other is doing." His best-kept secret was all the agents he cultivated inside the British administration. No fewer than four members of the Dublin Metropolitan Police's detective bureau, G Division, secretly reported to "the Big Fellow." So did at least a dozen uniformed constables. Other spies, working as secretaries in Dublin Castle or clerks in the post office, passed along important British correspondence and ciphers. In April 1919 one of his moles even gave him a midnight tour of G's headquarters, where he was able to spend five hours reading their most sensitive files. He then sent his men to warn the "G-men" to stop harassing the IRA—or else.

Those who ignored the warnings were targeted for "extermination" by Collins's personal hit team, known originally as the "Twelve Apostles" (it began with a dozen members) and then, when it grew, as "the Squad." While most IRA men were part-time volunteers, the Squad consisted of full-time, paid gunmen. Armed with powerful Webley .455-caliber revolvers, at least six Squad members were always on standby at their headquarters, first a house, then a cabinetmaking shop. They would play cards or tinker with lumber to pass the time while awaiting the call for "extreme action."

By the spring of 1920, twelve Dublin policemen who were, in the words of a Squad member, "making themselves frightfully obnoxious" had been shot, eight of them fatally. The dead included the head of G Division. A similar fate awaited the few, inept spies whom the British tried to infiltrate into the IRA's ranks. Collins justified these assassinations by saying, "We had no jails and we therefore had to kill all spies, informers, and double-crossers."[82]

After it became clear that the "G-men" had been "decimated,"[83] the British brought in their own intelligence specialists—a group of retired army officers known as the "hush-hush men" who often operated undercover. Collins decided to wipe them out at a stroke. "I found out these fellows . . . were going to put a lot of us on the spot," he later explained, "so I got in first." The operation, slated for Sunday morning, November 21, 1920, was assigned to the IRA's Dublin Brigade working closely with the Squad. The night before, Dick McKee, the brigade commander, was snatched in a British raid along with his deputy. But Collins, displaying nerves of steel, decided to proceed anyway—just as the Nihilists had proceeded with their plot against Alexander II despite the capture of their leaders.

Dozens of gunmen, including the future prime minister Sean Lémass, assembled at their assigned rendezvous points in Dublin shortly before 9 a.m. on November 21, a "calm, fine, grey winter's day." They were to hit twenty targets at eight hotels and rooming houses, with some of the men reserved as a covering force in case of trouble.

At 9 a.m. the Squad member Vincent Byrne led one contingent of ten operatives to a house at 28 Upper Mount Street where two British officers—Lieutenant Bennett and Lieutenant Ames—were staying. The door was opened by a "servant girl," who told them where the officers' bedrooms were located and how to get in by a back door. Byrne and another gunman dashed into one bedroom and ordered the officer they had caught to put up his hands. He asked what was going to happen to him. Byrne replied, "Ah nothing," then ordered him to march to another bedroom where the other officer was being held. Byrne later recounted, "He was standing up in the bed, facing the wall. I ordered mine to do likewise. When the two of them were together, I said to myself: 'The Lord have mercy on your souls!' I then opened fire with my Peter [a nickname for the Mauser C96 pistol]. They both fell dead." As Byrne left the house he passed the servant girl. She was crying.

In all, fourteen men were killed that morning, five wounded. Most were shot, like the two lieutenants at Upper Mount Street, after surrendering, some in front of their "terrified and hysterical" wives or girlfriends. Not all of them were intelligence operatives. Some were regular officers. The victims also included two police officers who stumbled across one of the assassination squads. "It has been a day of black murder," a British official wrote in his diary that night.

The reaction was immediate and violent. That afternoon a Gaelic football match was scheduled at Dublin's Croke Park. A substantial force of "Auxies" and "Black and Tans" showed up to "surround the ground" and search the crowd. The Auxiliary Division was made up of fifteen hundred former British army officers who had been recruited as a counterterrorism unit to complement the Royal Irish Constabulary. The "Black and Tans" were seven thousand British recruits sent to fill the constabulary's depleted ranks, the supply of Irish recruits having dried up. Because of a shortage of uniforms, many wore a mixture of the constabulary's dark-green, almost black, apparel and the army's khaki—hence their nickname, which they shared with a pack of hunting dogs. Both Auxies and Tans became notorious for their brutality, and never more so than on this Sunday afternoon when they opened fire on the crowd at Croke Park, killing twelve civilians and wounding sixty. The police claimed they had been shot at first, although even one Auxiliary officer conceded, "I did not see any need for any firing." The IRA believed it was simply revenge for that morning's assassinations.

Similar controversy shrouded the deaths of the Dublin Brigade commander Dick McKee, his deputy Peadar Clancy, and a man who had been captured with them. That Sunday the three detainees were killed by Auxies at Dublin Castle. The British claimed they had been trying to escape; the IRA believed, as a Squad member put it, that they had been "shot in cold blood . . . contrary to all the laws of God and man."[84]

✦ ✦ ✦

ALL THE FACTS of "Bloody Sunday" will never be known for certain, but its impact was clear. Like the Tet Offensive in 1968, it established as hollow official claims of progress (Prime Minister David Lloyd George had boasted just twelve days earlier of having "murder by the throat")[85] and encouraged the government to look for a negotiated solution. The war would continue for eight more months until the proclamation of a truce in July 1921, but increasingly the British forces were like a blinded fighter flailing and failing to hit a more nimble and elusive adversary.

For security's sake, many officials and officers had to move into Dublin Castle, where, wrote the army commander, Sir Nevil Macready, they were "reduced to a state of nerves that it was pitiable to behold." Something similar happened in the countryside where smaller constabulary outposts were closed and the police were "concentrated and immobilized" in large, fortified barracks. "Before Bloody Sunday," recalled a soldier stationed in Dublin, "we had occasionally gone into the town for an evening meal," but now "we had to give up doing so." An Auxie wrote that he felt "hunted" ("a horrible feeling") every time he left Dublin Castle. Even General Macready never ventured out without an automatic pistol, safety catch off, handy in his pocket or, when driving, in his lap. Instilling fear into the authorities—which meant that they were cut off from the populace and liable to lash out in counterproductive ways that would cost them further support—must be a key objective for any insurgent group; the IRA had managed to achieve that goal by 1920.[86]

Bill Munro, an Auxiliary in county Cork, a "hotbed of rebellion,"[87] later recalled the difficulty of operating with inadequate intelligence against the IRA's Flying Columns—full-time guerrilla fighters who operated in 35-man units. The Auxies would set off in their Crossley trucks or Rolls-Royce armored cars to chase down rumors of "an ambush being prepared at such and such a place," only to find that either the rumors were false or that by the time they arrived the IRA men "had melted away as they were warned long before we could get near." In some cases they stumbled upon recently vacated meeting sites, but "we had not the knowledge of the country off the road, as had our opponents, and it was impossible to follow up the participants in these meetings."[88]

Even the roads were hazardous: the IRA planted mines, destroyed bridges, and dug trenches to impede army movements. Ambushes were a regular occurrence, and often they were skillfully executed. For instance, on June 17, 1921, near the town of Banteer in county Cork, an IRA column used mines to blow up three of four vehicles in an Auxiliary convoy, and then opened "a heavy and concentrated fire" on the men inside "from a position of great natural strength." "These mines," wrote the British convoy commander, who was practically blown out of his vehicle, "were timed and fired with the utmost precision."[89]

In frustration, following IRA "outrages," British troops or police would rampage through towns, burning homes and businesses, shattering shop windows, beating and killing. "Towns showed jagged stumps of broken teeth where fire had spread," wrote an IRA officer; "raiding parties smashed property and looted."[90] This clumsy retaliation, an attempt at "out-terrorizing the terrorists,"[91] only engendered greater support for the IRA among a population that had been largely apathetic at the start of the struggle. A British intelligence estimate concluded that "from the beginning of 1921 . . . the bulk of the population was in a state of open rebellion or was in sympathy with such a rebellion."[92] In many areas the Shinners even ran a shadow government, complete with its own police force and courts, that was more effective in dispensing justice than the crown. In effect, even before the formal end of British rule, the IRA had already managed to reverse more than seven centuries of English "ascendancy."[93]

✦ ✦ ✦

THE BRITISH DEPLOYED 50,000 troops and 14,000 constables to fight 5,000 active Volunteers. It was not enough. British generals estimated that pacifying this nation of fewer than three million people would have required dispatching tens of thousands more personnel, possibly hundreds of thousands more, for an extended period.[94] That was more than a country "tired to death of war" could bear.[95]

The Liberal prime minister, David Lloyd George, was willing to place several counties under martial law, thereby allowing the trial of suspects in military courts.[96] He was even willing to turn a blind eye to Black and Tan rampages and the forcible interrogation and occasional killing of suspects "while trying to escape." "This kind of thing," Lloyd George said, referring to the IRA's attacks on police officers, "can only be met by reprisals."[97] But there were sharp limits on how far he was willing to go. As a onetime critic of Kitchener's policies in the Boer War, he was not willing to bomb Irish villages, execute captured terrorists en masse, or round up tens of thousands of civilians in concentration camps. He was not, in short, willing to treat Ireland as the British treated Iraq, where in 1920 a much larger revolt was ruthlessly suppressed at a cost of almost 9,000 lives.[98] Or like India, where in 1919 British troops killed more than 370 unarmed demonstrators in Amritsar.

Political limitations imposed in London frustrated many soldiers who griped, in the words of Field Marshal Sir Henry Wilson, chief of the Imperial General Staff and a rabid Unionist, that "the Sinn Feins" are "at war with our men whilst our men are at peace with the Sinn Feins."[99] "If this country was Mesopotamia or Egypt," General Macready, the British army commander in Ireland, wrote back wistfully, "I should have the greatest pleasure in the world in putting on the most extreme type of Martial Law, and have done with the thing, once and for all."[100]

But Lloyd George and other cabinet members knew that what War Minister Winston Churchill described as "iron repression"—a policy of "murder and counter-murder, terror and counter-terror"[101]—would not be accepted by the British public. Having just waged a war to liberate Belgium, the British were not willing to fight indefinitely to subjugate the small state next door—not when its people had expressed their preference for independence. Even Churchill, while defending "the integrity of the British Empire," denouncing the IRA's "murder conspiracy," and refusing to condemn Black and Tan rampages, nevertheless ruled out "the kind of methods the Prussians adopted in Belgium"—or, one is tempted to add, that the British themselves sometimes adopted in Asia and Africa.[102]

The one part of Ireland that the British government was determined to defend was the northern counties, where there was a substantial Protestant population. This was one of the sticking points of negotiations that began after a truce took effect on July 11, 1921. Eventually an Irish negotiating team that included Michael Collins took the best deal it could get. Under a treaty signed on December 6, 1921, the twenty-six southern counties would become the Irish Free State, a self-governing dominion of the British Empire like Canada, while the six counties of Northern Ireland would remain part of the United Kingdom. Bad as the exclusion of Northern Ireland was, to many republicans even more galling was a provision that Dáil members would have to swear to be "faithful to H.M. King George V." A narrow majority of the Dáil endorsed the treaty, but half the IRA would not recognize the result and took up arms.

As commander of the Free State Army, Collins led the fight against his former comrades in spite of his own "anguish."[103] He was killed in an ambush by the antitreaty IRA on August 22, 1922, while he was motoring with a small security detail through his native county Cork. The Big Fellow, who had eluded so many British manhunts, was not yet thirty-two when he fell at the hands of his own countrymen and former mates. Just a few weeks before, he had turned down his fiancée's entreaties to be more careful: "I can't help it and if I were to do anything else it wouldn't be me," he wrote her, "and I really couldn't stand it."[104] When they heard of his death, a thousand antitreaty republicans in a Free State prison spontaneously kneeled to recite the rosary in tribute to a man who had been their leader before he became their enemy.[105]

Notwithstanding Collins's demise, the civil war ended in May 1923 with a resounding victory for the protreaty forces. They won because they had greater resources, including weapons provided by the British, because public opinion was on their side (in the 1923 elections only 27.4 percent of the voters supported antitreaty candidates)[106]—and because they were willing to be harsher than the British had been. As one historian notes, "Altogether, in just over six months the new Free State Government executed seventy-seven Republicans by shooting, more than three times the number executed by the British Government in the two and a half years of the 'Anglo-Irish war.' "[107] This confirms the lesson of the Vendée: namely, that a homegrown regime with popular sentiment on its side can afford to be harsher in dealing with insurgents than a foreign military force trying to stay where it is not wanted—especially if that force answers to an elected government that is sensitive to the vagaries of both global and local public opinion.

To this day Northern Ireland remains part of the United Kingdom, despite decades of terrorism by IRA die-hards. The more recent IRA campaign failed in no small part because the British in later years regained the intelligence edge they had lost in 1919–21, when, in the depths of despair, a senior British intelligence officer had lamented that "no Englishman can fully grasp the psychology of the Irish rebel character."[108] It was a different story in the 1980s. In those days, when the Provisional IRA tried to launch a Tet-style offensive employing weaponry supplied by Libyan leader Muammar Qaddafi, high-ranking informants tipped off the Royal Ulster Constabulary's Special Branch. "The British knew the IRA was coming," wrote Irish journalist Ed Moloney, "and they were ready."[109]

This disparity in outcomes between the IRA war of the 1920s and the one in the 1970s–1990s serves to underscore the overriding value in any insurgency of acquiring good intelligence, for both insurgents and counterinsurgents. It is even more important than in conventional conflicts, where sheer firepower can be employed to destroy large enemy formations even if the details of their movements and capabilities remain unknown. In a war against an "invisible army," by contrast, accurate intelligence is needed to bring the enemy into the open—something that the British did not possess in the Irish War of Independence, any more than the federal army had in its post–Civil War conflict against the Ku Klux Klan, but that the police forces of various countries gradually acquired in their struggle against the anarchists.

✦ ✦ ✦

EVEN IF THE "Tan War" did not secure independence for the entire island, it was a remarkable achievement—the first successful revolt by a British colony since the American War of Independence. The cost: 4,000 killed or wounded, including 950 British soldiers and police.[110] As always happens, noted one Black and Tan, "the real sufferer in this fratricidal war was the non-combatant," civilians being targeted by both sides.[111]

There was hardly a single battle in the conventional sense. Broadly speaking, IRA operations in the countryside were in the guerrilla mode, targeting police barracks and police patrols, while in the cities they operated more as terrorists, killing off-duty policemen or civil servants. The terrorist orientation was especially strong on the British mainland, where the IRA carried out a handful of operations. The most spectacular were the burning of seventeen Liverpool warehouses in November 1920 and the assassination in June 1922, long after a peace treaty had been signed, of Sir Henry Wilson, who had just stepped down as chief of the Imperial General Staff. Other terrorist operations—such as the attempted assassination in December 1919 of the British viceroy, Lord French—failed. Michael Collins entertained even more ambitious plans such as truck bombing the House of Commons, kidnapping its members, and shooting members of the cabinet but never tried to implement them.[112] This was a wise decision given how badly attacks on the British mainland by a future generation of IRA terrorists would backfire. In 1979 the Provisional IRA murdered Lord Mountbatten, the last viceroy of India, and five years later attempted to assassinate Prime Minister Margaret Thatcher and the entire British cabinet by bombing the hotel where they were staying in Brighton. Those actions only redoubled Thatcher's determination to defeat the IRA. Michael Collins had been astute enough to avoid such excesses. His reasonableness and restraint were his strengths. Unlike most other terrorist or guerrilla leaders, he knew when to stop fighting even if he had not yet achieved all of his aims.

His experience shows that the most successful terrorist campaigns are waged for causes, usually nationalist, which have widespread acceptance among the population and are supported by political parties and regular or irregular military forces—just as the most successful guerrillas are supported by conventional military forces. By contrast a small number of terrorists acting on their own to implement a radical agenda has scant chance of success—as demonstrated not only by the anarchists but also by many subsequent terrorists such as the Red Army Faction and the Weathermen.

Terrorists do better, moreover, if they fight a democratic nation with a free press whose coverage will help to magnify their attacks while restraining the official response. There is not much terrorism in totalitarian states, because the secret police can ruthlessly snuff it out. The British government, on the other hand, could not even censor the press absent a declaration of war, which was lacking in Ireland. "We had a very bad Press," complained one Auxie—a problem he blamed, naturally, not on his colleagues' misconduct but on "floods of flabby sentimentalism by the Liberal Press." But even the normally nationalistic *Times* of London was harshly critical of "lynch law," writing in 1920 that "an Army already perilously undisciplined, and a police force avowedly beyond control have defiled, by heinous acts, the reputation of England."

Like many subsequent counterinsurgents, British soldiers in Ireland were "rankled most deeply" by their government's "disinclination or inability" to counter what they saw as distorted reporting that exaggerated their misdeeds while minimizing those of the enemy. General Macready raged against the "blackguard Press" and at the "perfectly futile" way that "Press Propaganda" was run by the "frocks" at Dublin Castle, the seat of British administration. His protests made no difference. Losing the "battle of the narrative" made it impossible for the British forces to prevail against a paltry number of combatants.[113]

36.

THE TERRORIST MIND

Sinners or Saints?

WE HAVE SURVEYED a wide variety of terror groups, ranging chronologically from the Assassins of the Middle Ages to the IRA of the early twentieth century and in size from the Ku Klux Klan with its hundreds of thousands of members to John Brown and his band of twenty-one—coincidentally about the same size as the executive committee of the People's Will. Some have been successful (the Assassins, KKK, and IRA); others, notably the anarchists, not so much. The Russian revolutionaries ultimately prevailed but their terrorism hardly overthrew the tsar by itself. At most it helped to undermine a regime whose collapse was brought about by military defeat in 1917.

Nevertheless the example of the Russian terrorists proved influential as far away as Bengal, where there were outbursts of anti-British terrorism from 1906 to 1917 and again from 1930 to 1934.[114] The Russian extremists also had many imitators in the Balkans, which after Russia itself emerged as the main theater of terrorist operations.

The longest-lived of the Balkan groups was the Internal Macedonian Revolutionary Organization (IMRO). Formed in 1893 to seek Macedonian independence or autonomy, it fought for nearly half a century, first against the Ottoman Empire, then against Yugoslavia and Greece. It assassinated the king of Yugoslavia, the prime minister of Bulgaria, and the foreign minister of France—without, however, achieving its goals.[115] Equally frustrated was the Armenian Revolutionary Federation (the Dashnak Party), which took on both the Russian and the Ottoman empires in the hope of carving out an independent Armenian state. Its members staged the spectacular seizure of the Ottoman Central Bank in Istanbul in 1896 but only succeeded in triggering pogroms in the capital that killed thousands of Armenians, prefiguring the genocidal violence inflicted on Armenians between 1915 and 1923.[116] Armenia did not achieve independence until 1991 and then not because of terrorism but simply because of the breakup of the Soviet Union.

The Serbian Black Hand group was, as we shall see, more successful in achieving a union of the South Slavs in a Yugoslav state but only very indirectly and in ways that it did not intend through its tenuous relationship with the Young Bosnians who assassinated Archduke Franz Ferdinand in 1914, thereby triggering a war that ultimately brought down the Austro-Hungarian Empire. Meanwhile, the Ustaša, a terrorist group with Italian sponsorship, managed to achieve its goal—an independent Croatian state—only because of a German invasion of Yugoslavia in 1941. As soon as the German armies rolled out, Croatia was swallowed up by Yugoslavia again, where it would remain for the next four decades.

The terrorists of yesteryear pioneered most of the techniques employed by present-day extremists, from car bombings to suicide bombings. There were even a few instances of mass hostage taking, notably John Brown's seizure of Harpers Ferry, which prefigured the airline hijackings and embassy takeovers of the 1970s.

✦ ✦ ✦

MOST OF THE academic literature stresses that there is no such thing as a "terrorist mentality" or a "typical terrorist." Walter Laqueur writes, "That their members have been young is the only feature common to all terrorist movements."[117] But that has not stopped analysts, participants, and, above all, artists from trying to depict the terrorist mindset. The "golden age" of terrorism produced striking portraits of its practitioners, both pro and con.

The most rapturous case in favor of terrorism was made by Sergei

Kravchinski (a.k.a. Stepniak), a Russian Nihilist who killed the chief of the tsar's secret police in 1878 and then fled to Switzerland and England. He published a memoir, *Underground Russia*, in which he attributed superhuman attributes to "the Terrorist," a label that, unlike later practitioners, he embraced: "He is noble, terrible, irresistibly fascinating, for he combines in himself the two sublimities of human grandeur: the martyr and the hero. . . . He has no other object than to overthrow this abhorred despotism, and to give to his country, what all civilized nations possess, political liberty."[118]

Contrast this idealized portrait with the villainous depictions drawn by two conservative novelists—Fyodor Dostoevsky and Joseph Conrad. Dostoevsky's *Demons* (1872) features a Nihilist known as Pyotr Stepanovich Verkhovensky, based on Sergei Nachaev. He is a "monster," "a crook," "a vile human louse" who murders one of his own followers and goads another to commit suicide. His goal, he tells a fellow revolutionary, is "getting everything destroyed: both the state and its morality. We alone will remain, having destined ourselves beforehand to assume power: we shall rally the smart ones to ourselves, and ride on the backs of the fools."[119]

In *The Secret Agent* (1907), Conrad offers an equally unflattering portrayal of "The Professor," an anarchist who stalks the streets of London with a bomb in his pocket, ready to blow "to pieces" everything within sixty yards should a policeman try to arrest him. The Professor dreams of a world "where the weak would be taken in hand for utter extermination. . . . Exterminate, exterminate! That is the only way of progress. . . . First the blind, then the deaf and the dumb, then the halt and the lame—and so on."[120]

Which of these depictions is the more accurate—the terrorist as saint or as sinner? Both are, of course, caricatures; actual human beings are seldom as virtuous or as vile. But Conrad and Dostoevsky were probably closer to the mark than Stepniak was.

Terrorists are outcasts who are hunted by the authorities. They are far more likely to wind up dead or in a dungeon than to succeed in achieving their goals. It stands to reason that most who are drawn to such a life would have an ideological compulsion verging on fanaticism. This is less true of large, nationalist organizations such as the KKK or IRA, which draw in a diverse membership and, for better or worse, enjoy broad societal sanction.

Their members often have a mental makeup similar to soldiers'—which many Ku Kluxers had been and which many Shinners would become. Truly marginal enterprises like the anarchist movement or the wilder fringes of the Russian revolutionary underground had fewer participants, and a larger proportion of them were criminal or cracked.

These were men like Simon Ter-Petrossian (a.k.a. Kamo), Stalin's chief henchman during his reign of terror in the Caucasus. He was finally caught in Germany and to prevent his extradition to Russia, writes Stalin's biographer Simon Sebag Montefiore,

> Kamo started to act like a madman in a way that only someone who had truly cracked could. . . . He pulled the hairs out of his head; tried to hang himself but was cut down; slit his wrists but was resuscitated. . . . The doctors were still skeptical and decided to put him through a series of torments that would have broken anyone else. He was burned by a red-hot iron and needles were driven under his nails, but he withstood it all.[121]

Or there was François-Claudius Koenigstein, alias Ravachol, a French anarchist who killed an elderly hermit to steal his money and broke into a recently deceased countess's grave in search of more loot before setting off several bombs around Paris in 1892. His name would become a byword for senseless political violence.[122]

No doubt disreputable characters can be found in all human enterprises. Security forces fighting terrorism have included quite a few sadists who have happily tortured and executed prisoners. In the Irish War of Independence, Captain Jocelyn Hardy acquired a gruesome reputation. He was an Auxiliary known as "Hoppy" Hardy because he had lost a leg on the Western Front and walked with a limp. One IRA officer recalled that during his interrogation Hardy beat him to a bloody pulp, nearly strangled him, held a red-hot poker in front of his eyes, and then placed a pistol next to his head and threatened to execute him.

But while relatively liberal armed forces like the British army may countenance some brutality, they will court-martial or dismiss the worst offenders—as happened with hundreds of Auxies and Tans in Ireland.

("Hoppy" Hardy was tried for murder but acquitted in a "verdict that," writes one historian, "seemed seriously at variance with the disclosed facts." He also escaped assassination by Mick Collins's Squad, which made a "very special effort" to "eliminate" him.)[123] By contrast, most terrorist organizations have been willing to make excuses for the Ravachols and Kamos, to justify any misdeed in the name of the larger struggle.

It is hazardous to generalize about terrorists or any other diverse group, but striking is the extent to which the extremists of a century ago conform to the observations made by observers of modern terrorism. The economist Alan Krueger, for instance, concludes that "terrorists tend to be drawn from well-educated, middle-class or high-income families." So if poverty does not cause terrorism what does? He points to "the suppression of civil liberties and political rights," explaining, "When nonviolent means of protest are curtailed, malcontents appear to be more likely to turn to terrorist tactics."[124] That certainly accounts for the prevalence of terrorism in tsarist Russia and even in colonial Ireland. Although Great Britain was a democracy, the Irish people, historically subjugated by the "Protestant Ascendancy," had sharply curtailed choices at the ballot box—they could not vote for independence. Krueger's findings suggest that in any war against terrorism—or, for that matter, against any insurgency—political reform can sometimes be the most important weapon. Indeed progressive welfare and labor legislation helped to quell terrorism in democracies such as France and the United States, while its absence fueled further revolt in Russia.

The observations of the psychiatrist Jerrold Post also ring true. Although he writes that "terrorists do not show any striking psychopathology," he does posit that many "individuals are drawn to the path of terrorism in order to commit acts of violence." He believes that for many "the cause" is only an excuse to pursue a lifestyle that allows a frustrated, unsuccessful youth to become a glamorous celebrity—a terrorist who is "engaged in a life-and-death struggle with the establishment, his picture on the 'most wanted' posters," who in certain circles "is lionized as a hero," and thereby acquires "a role and position not easily relinquished."[125] Those generalizations, made about late twentieth-century terrorists, apply equally well to their nineteenth-century forebears—and even to the Assassins of the Middle Ages.

But, and this must be kept in mind, there are always exceptions, often prominent ones. Michael Collins was no fanatic or outcast. He was a shrewd, popular, supremely sane leader who was admired even by his foes, notwithstanding his ruthless streak. (Lloyd George said he was "full of fascination and charm—but also of dangerous fire.")[126] In many ways he bore a greater resemblance to the most skilled and respected generals of history than to those "wild beasts," the disreputable anarchist or socialist terrorists of his day whose actions often bespoke a psychological compulsion rather than a well-developed strategy. If there has ever been a heroic and likable terrorist, the Big Fellow was it.

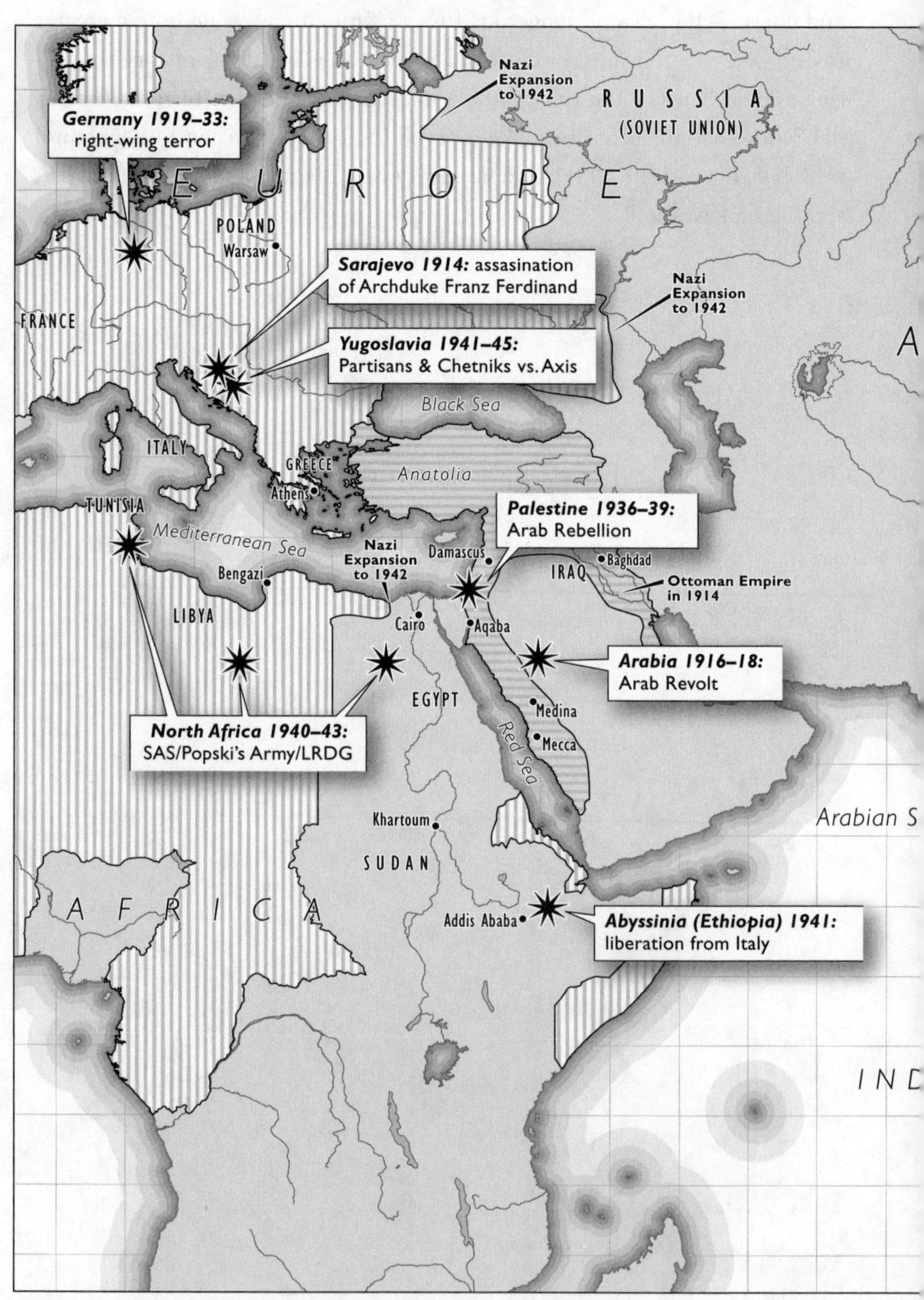

Nazi Expansion to 1942
RUSSIA
(SOVIET UNION)
Germany 1919–33: right-wing terror
EUROPE
POLAND
Warsaw
Sarajevo 1914: assasination of Archduke Franz Ferdinand
Nazi Expansion to 1942
FRANCE
Yugoslavia 1941–45: Partisans & Chetniks vs. Axis
Black Sea
ITALY
GREECE
Anatolia
Athens
TUNISIA
Palestine 1936–39: Arab Rebellion
Mediterranean Sea
Nazi Expansion to 1942
Damascus
Baghdad
Bengazi
IRAQ
Ottoman Empire in 1914
LIBYA
Cairo
Aqaba
Arabia 1916–18: Arab Revolt
EGYPT
Medina
Red Sea
Mecca
North Africa 1940–43: SAS/Popski's Army/LRDG
Khartoum
SUDAN
AFRICA
Addis Ababa
Abyssinia (Ethiopia) 1941: liberation from Italy

BOOK V
THE SIDESHOWS
Guerrillas and Commandos in the World Wars

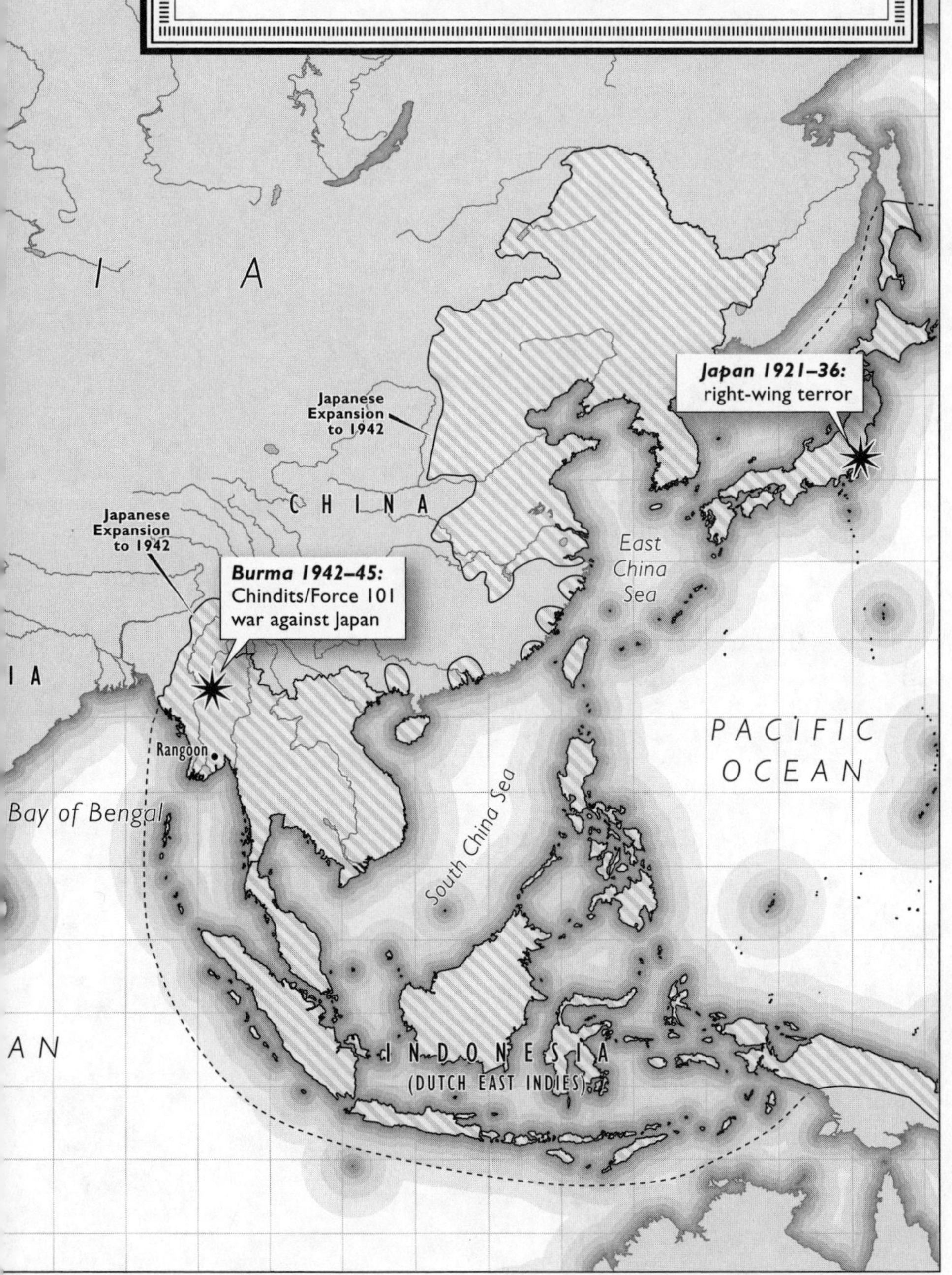

37.

THE THIRTY YEARS' WAR

Blood Brothers and Brownshirts, 1914–1945

It was the most consequential wrong turn in history. Archduke Franz Ferdinand was on a brief visit to observe army maneuvers in the Austro-Hungarian province of Bosnia-Herzegovina. The heir to the Habsburg throne was supposed to spend only a few hours in Sarajevo on Sunday, June 28, 1914—just long enough to view some troops, meet some notables, open a museum, inspect a carpet factory. But from the start the day had not gone according to plan. The archduke and his wife, Sophie, had been sitting in the back of an open-top touring car on the drive into town from the train station when, just after 10 a.m., a Bosnian printer named Nedeljko Cabrinovic tossed a bomb at them. The nineteen-year-old "Nedjo" had been so excited he had forgotten to count to ten after priming his crude hand grenade. The bomb bounced harmlessly off the royal automobile and injured two officers in a trailing car along with some spectators.

Nedjo tried and failed to end his life with a cyanide capsule. He was taken to a police station, where he was interrogated, but he refused to reveal that five other would-be assassins were still stalking Franz Ferdinand. Out of an excess of courage or a deficit of common sense, the archduke proceeded with his next stop at the town hall, where he was greeted by local dignitaries and gave a short speech. Afterward he decided to stop by the hospital to visit one of the officers who had been injured in the earlier bombing. His staff thought it would be safer to take the broad Appel Quay rather than the original route, publicized in advance, through the narrow, winding streets of the city center. But because of a miscommunication the lead vehicle in the six-car motorcade turned down Franz Josef Street as originally planned, followed by the luxurious *Graef und Stift* convertible flying an imperial emblem and carrying Franz Ferdinand and Sophie. When he realized what had happened, the royal chauffeur stopped the car in order to turn around.

By a colossal stroke of ill fortune, the archduke's car paused in the brilliant summer sunshine in front of Moritz Schiller's Jewish delicatessen and general store. Standing in front was none other than Nedjo's good friend Gavrilo Princip, another Bosnian radical armed with a bomb and a Browning pistol. The teenage terrorist, who was just shy of his twentieth birthday, must have been dumbfounded at the good fortune that had put his quarry only a few feet from him. He could hardly miss the archduke in his resplendent blue general's uniform and green peacock-feather hat or his wife next to him in her white silk dress and wide-brimmed hat piled high with ostrich feathers. "Gavro" drew his revolver and fired twice. Both the archduke and the duchess were dead by lunchtime.

In many respects the death of Franz Ferdinand resembled that of Tsar Alexander II, another assassination carried out by a group of young Slavic fanatics. But the consequences were much more serious and long-lasting. For the Austrian government chose to blame the Serbian government for the attack.

In reality the links to Belgrade were tenuous at best. Nedjo and Gavro were members of Young Bosnia, a small group of radicals whose goal was to create Yugoslavia, a state that would unite the South Slavs: the Bosnians, Croats, Serbs, and other nationalities. They had been provided with arms (four revolvers, six bombs) and smuggled into Bosnia by Serbian officers who were close to Colonel Dragutin Dimitrijevic, a.k.a. Apis. He was not only chief of intelligence for the Serbian General Staff but also head of a secret society called Union or Death, popularly known as the Black Hand, which was intent on driving Austria out of Bosnia-Herzegovina to create a Greater Serbia. Apis later testified that he had never thought the conspirators would succeed and had even tried to recall them at the last moment. Certainly there was no evidence that anyone in a senior position in Serbia's government had authorized the plot. But that did not stop Vienna from making intolerable demands on Belgrade. Germany backed its ally Austria, while Russia came to the aid of Serbia.

Thus one daring act of terrorism lit the fuse that ignited the deadliest war the world had yet seen. That the war probably would have broken out anyway over some other pretext does not diminish the enormity of this act or lessen its consequences.[1]

✦ ✦ ✦

THE FIRST WORLD WAR raged from 1914 to 1918. It was followed by an unstable armistice and then the eruption of open conflict in China in 1931 and in Poland in 1939. Those two conflicts merged to produce the Second World War. That war, too, had its roots in terrorism: specifically the terrorist campaigns waged by German and Japanese militarists in the 1920s and 1930s to seize power from more moderate regimes.

The fragile Weimar Republic, born in 1919 out of Germany's defeat, faced and survived an initial burst of left-wing and right-wing violence whose victims included Foreign Minister Walter Rathenau, assassinated by a rightist fanatic in 1922. The initial turmoil faded after Adolf Hitler's Beer Hall Putsch was foiled in 1923. Thereafter the Nazis sought power through political organizing backed by the thuggish SA (*Sturmabteilung*, or "Storm Battalion"). Popularly known as the Brownshirts—a name that, like the Blackshirts (Mussolini's paramilitaries), would have caused the liberal Giuseppe Garibaldi and his Redshirts to spin in their graves—the SA intimidated, beat, and killed political opponents and Jews. The Communists also engaged in street violence, employing a strong-arm squad called the Red Front Fighters' League, but they were no match for the Brownshirts, who numbered half a million men by the time Hitler became chancellor on January 30, 1933.

Much of Hitler's appeal was that he was the man who could restore "order"—which, of course, his own party had done as much as anyone to undermine. The arsonist was offering to turn fireman. The analogy is particularly apt given that Hitler was able to consolidate his rule thanks to the burning of the Reichstag on February 27, 1933, by Marinus van der Lubbe, a lone Dutch anarchist who had once been a Communist. Hitler used this isolated act of terrorism as an excuse to crack heads among the opposition and destroy the last vestiges of constitutionalism. From then on terrorism in Nazi Germany was to be a state monopoly.[2]

Japan's experiment with parliamentary democracy, which began in earnest in the 1920s, was expiring at the same time. Its death was even more directly tied to a campaign of terrorism, this one waged by fanatical military officers and ultra-nationalist agitators organized in groups such as the Blood Brotherhood, whose slogan was "One Member, One Death." Their victims included Prime Minister Kei Hara, killed in 1921, Prime Minister Hamagushi Osachi (1930), and, in 1932, a particularly busy year, Prime Minister Tsuyoshi Inukai, former finance minister Junnosuke Inoue, and the Mitsui corporation's director-general, Baron Dan Takuma. The conspirators behind the 1932 attacks had also contemplated assassinating the comedian Charlie Chaplin during his visit to Japan because they thought this "would cause a war with America."

Since 1924 Japan's government had been run by whichever political party had won a majority in the parliament. After the 1932 "incidents," as they were decorously known, military influence became predominant. But the radicals still were not satisfied: they intimidated and assassinated officers who were deemed too moderate, such as the elderly retired Admiral Makoto Saito, a former prime minister and lord privy seal. He was murdered along with the finance minister and the head of military education in 1936 during an aborted coup by junior army officers. The prime minster, Admiral Keisuke Okada, narrowly survived the 1936 revolt; he hid in a closet when his house was invaded by rebellious troops who murdered his brother-in-law by mistake. Getting the message, he resigned immediately afterward. None of his successors was any more successful in resisting the desires of the imperialist extremists.

Terrorism worked in Japan because the terrorists represented a significant and influential constituency, including a large portion of the armed forces. Even then terrorism was only partly responsible for bringing the militarists to power. Failed terrorist groups such as the anarchists, by contrast, had few supporters and those came from the fringes of society.[3]

✦ ✦ ✦

THE POLITICAL TURMOIL in Germany and Japan was part of a broader struggle that rent the world apart in the first half of the twentieth century. In essence it was a battle between totalitarianism and liberalism, although totalitarians of left and right were often at each other's throats. This clash of ideologies produced not only the two world wars but also lesser conflicts, including the civil wars in China, Mexico, Russia, and Spain. The whole 1914–45 period could be called "a second Thirty Years' War"—a term coined by the German expatriate scholar Sigmund Neumann in 1946.[4] (From our present-day perspective we might see a Seventy-Five Years' War lasting until the fall of the Berlin Wall in 1989.)

Most of the fighting during those years, even in civil wars, pitted conventional armed forces against one another and hence is of little concern from our perspective. But smaller-scale guerrilla warfare and terrorism did not disappear amid the clash of gargantuan fleets, armies, and air forces. Indeed this period produced some of the twentieth century's most notable practitioners of low-intensity conflict and some of the most influential doctrines for its prosecution. We will focus in particular on the influence of T. E. Lawrence, Orde Wingate, and Josip Broz Tito. Their efforts were very much "sideshows" that affected the ultimate outcome of the big wars only at the margins. But these sideshows left a lasting legacy. They made "special operations forces" (i.e., guerrillas in the service of the state) a prominent part of all modern militaries. They showed the limitations of even the most draconian counterinsurgency policies in quelling uprisings that enjoyed outside support. And, even more significant, they made inevitable the independence of Europe's Asian and African colonies by mobilizing and arming significant numbers of the "natives." The conclusion of this modern Thirty Years' War, which left the great powers of Europe wheezing and gasping, set the scene for decades' more fighting in wars of decolonization that would send the popular reputation of guerrillas soaring to new heights.

Our examination of this turbulent epoch begins with a slight, sensitive archaeologist from Oxford who improbably enough became one of the most storied irregular warriors in history.

38.

THE EVOLUTION OF AN ARCHAEOLOGIST

"Lawrence of Arabia," 1916–1935

THE RIDE FROM Palestine took eight days over a "rough track . . . through a harsh no-man's land where water was scarce and brackish when found, and nothing grew except the thorny scrub growths of the desert." Finally on April 9, 1918, the Egyptian Camel Corps, a hundred soldiers strong, reached Aqaba, a town on the Red Sea that had recently been liberated from the Turks by an Arab offensive.

The corps' commanding officer, Lieutenant Colonel Frederick W. Peake, found a "sleepy little port," described by another soldier as "a few mud huts and a broken down castle," whose normal population of four hundred had been swelled by a vast influx of military personnel. In the port were ships unloading stores. West of town several aircraft were parked on a newly cleared airfield. All along the shore were tents, a mixture of the white canvas favored by the British army, the "ornate oriental tents" of the Arab officers under Emir Feisal, and the "black goat-hair *beyts* of the assembled Bedouin."

These unlikely allies—Christians from northern Europe and Muslims from the deserts of Arabia—had been brought together by a shared interest in fighting the Ottoman Empire, an ally of Germany that was the imperial overlord of the Middle East. For the Arab Revolt to succeed it would need to overcome not only that enemy but also the mutual suspicions among these disparate fighters. "We hate the Arabs," admitted one British soldier, and the feeling was richly reciprocated.

Peake got a first taste of the "maddest campaign ever run" when a noncommissioned officer announced a party of Arabs to see him. At the head of the delegation was a blue-eyed man, only five feet five inches tall but muscular and lean, "dressed in extremely good and expensive Bedouin clothes." His feet were bare, the Arab custom being to take off one's sandals when entering a tent. Strapped to his belt was a beautiful gold dagger. In his hand was "the usual almond-wood cane that every Bedouin camel rider uses." His face was partly covered by his kaffiyeh. Peake imagined that this "regal-looking person . . . must be the Emir Feisal himself." He rushed over to greet him with "the usual flowery Arabic words of welcome and greetings." He was in for another shock when this "Arab," evidently bemused by the spectacle, cut him short in "perfect" English: "Well, Peake, so you have arrived at last. We have been waiting some time for you and your braves, and there is plenty of work for you up country."

Only then did Peake realize that he was speaking to Lieutenant Colonel T. E. Lawrence, a liaison officer and adviser to Feisal. But even that realization would not have meant much to him, for Lawrence was not yet famous. The mystique of "Lawrence of Arabia"—an appellation coined by a Chicago newspaperman—was to be a postwar phenomenon. In 1918 Lawrence was just another officer operating in great secrecy behind enemy lines to disrupt Turkish operations in the Holy Land. But the raw materials of his legend were already in place.[5]

✦ ✦ ✦

LAWRENCE WAS A misfit from the start because of what his Victorian and Edwardian contemporaries would have called his "illegitimate" birth. His father, Thomas Chapman, was a wealthy Anglo-Irish aristocrat who had abandoned his dour wife and their four daughters to run away with their much younger governess, Sarah Lawrence, who herself had been born to an unwed mother. Chapman never formally divorced his wife, so he and Sarah, "Mr. and Mrs. Lawrence," lived a cloistered existence as they raised four boys, including Thomas Edward, who was born in 1888. Ned, as he was known to his family (later simply "T.E." to his friends), became aware of this family secret as a child and feared ostracism and social ruin if it were revealed. Thus he grew up feeling an outsider to English society even as he earned a first in history from Oxford.

His alienation was heightened by his complete lack of interest in sports such as cricket or football. Nor did he partake in the rarefied British university social life so luxuriously depicted, in its 1920s incarnation, in Evelyn Waugh's *Brideshead Revisited*. He preferred solitary pursuits such as photography, bicycling, and collecting archaeological relics. Often he would stay up all night reading obscure books in Latin, Greek, or French. He trained himself to endure great privation, on one occasion going forty-five hours without food or sleep "to test his powers of endurance." That he was able to pass such tests was a testament not only to his extraordinary willpower but also to his physical fitness. As a teenager he would bicycle a hundred miles a day while touring France.

In 1909, in the summer before his senior year, Lawrence visited the Middle East for the first time to research his thesis on Crusader castles. He returned after graduation in 1910 and stayed nearly continuously until 1914 working at an archaeological site in Syria. Here he improved his Arabic and learned how to manage Arab workers.[6]

When war broke out in August 1914, he joined the Geographical Section of the General Staff in London, first as a civilian, then as a freshly commissioned second lieutenant. By the end of the year he was in Cairo working in military intelligence. He remained a staff officer—what he wryly called a "bottle-washer and office boy pencil-sharpener and pen wiper"[7]—until 1916, when the Arab Revolt broke out. Lawrence was a supporter of Arab aspirations to have their own nation stretching from the Persian Gulf to the Mediterranean, and he was feeling bored and restless with office work. A feeling of guilt crept in after two of his brothers were killed on the Western Front in 1915 and he was still safe in Cairo. So in October 1916 he applied for ten days' leave to accompany a British diplomat on a mission to assess the situation in the Hejaz, the western coastal region of Arabia where the revolt originated.

What they found was that the Arabs had been successful in driving the Turks out of the holy city of Mecca and, with the help of the Royal Navy, in seizing several Red Sea ports, including Jeddah, where they now landed.

But more than fifteen thousand Turkish troops were still deployed around Medina.[8] The rebellion was "standing still," Lawrence noted, "which, with an irregular war, was the prelude to disaster." He believed the problem was a lack of the right kind of leadership—the kind needed to "set the desert on fire."[9] The titular head of the revolt was Sharif Hussein, emir of Mecca, who aspired to be "King of the Arabs," but he was too old to take an active part in military operations. Lawrence was unimpressed by his sons Abdullah, Ali, and Zeid. He pinned his hopes on another son, Feisal, whose forces were operating far from the sea in an area seldom visited by Europeans.

To meet Feisal, Lawrence set out on a camel accompanied by a couple of guides, the first of many such journeys he would undertake over the next two years. It was also the first time during the war that he donned Arab clothes so "that I might present a proper silhouette in the dark upon my camel."[10] Lawrence found that the "long monotony of camel pacing" tired his "unaccustomed muscles" and "the pestilent beating of the Arabian sun" blistered his skin and made his eyes ache.[11] (Sunglasses were not yet commonly available.)[12] All he had to eat en route—typical of the fare he would consume during the revolt—was unleavened bread dough cooked over a fire, "moistened with liquid butter," and "scooped up like damp sawdust in pressed pellets with the fingers."[13]

Lawrence was exhausted by the time he reached Feisal on October 23, 1916, but he was elated to find that he "was the man I had come to Arabia to seek—the leader who would bring the Arab Revolt to fully glory."[14] The shy, "supercerebral"[15] twenty-eight-year-old English archaeologist forged a lasting friendship with the "hot-tempered, proud and impatient" thirty-one-year-old descendant of the Prophet whom he judged to be "far more imposing personally than any of his brothers": "A popular idol, and ambitious; full of dreams and the capacity to realize them."[16] So firm was their personal bond that Feisal persuaded the British authorities to send Lawrence back after a short sojourn in Cairo to act as his adviser. He would stay for the rest of the war.

✦ ✦ ✦

LAWRENCE'S CHALLENGE WAS to utilize up to fifty thousand Bedouin tribesmen effectively.[17] They were a "tough looking crowd" who went "about bristling with cartridge-belts, and fire off their rifles when they can." "As for their physical condition," Lawrence wrote, "I doubt whether men were ever harder."[18] But like all nomadic raiders going back to the days of Akkad, they had no discipline or cohesion. "One company of Turks firmly entrenched in open country could have defied the entire army of them; and a pitched battle, with its casualties, would have ended the war by sheer horror," Lawrence wrote.[19]

Other British officers had made similar observations and had concluded that the Arabs were useless as a fighting force. Many wanted to send British regulars to push the Turks out of Arabia. This Lawrence adamantly opposed, because he thought that the Arabs would be demoralized by the presence of large numbers of Christian troops. More than his fellow advisers, he understood the Arabs and identified with them. He was in favor of sending British weapons and British advisers, but he wanted the bulk of the fighting to be left to the Bedouin utilizing their age-old methods. "Arabs were artists in sniping," he noted; "their real sphere is guerrilla warfare."[20] "In mass," he explained, "they were not formidable, since they had no corporate spirit, nor discipline, nor mutual confidence. The smaller the unit the better its performance. A thousand were a mob, ineffective against a company of trained Turks: but three or four Arabs in their hills would stop a dozen Turks."[21]

He determined to eschew a "war of contact" in favor of a "war of detachment" focusing on the chief Ottoman vulnerability—the Hejaz railway running from Anatolia down the Arabian Peninsula, which was used to keep Turkish forces in the region supplied. The Arabs, Lawrence vowed, would be "a thing intangible, invulnerable, without front or back, drifting about like a gas," and they would be as hard to defeat as "eating soup with a knife."[22]

Lawrence took an active hand in raids against the railway, notwithstanding his lack of formal military training. "In military theory," he noted, he was "tolerably read." At Oxford he had studied authors such as Clausewitz and Jomini, but his "interest had been abstract, concerned with the theory and philosophy of warfare."[23] Now in Arabia he had to learn small-unit tactics on the fly, or rather on the camel ride.

✦ ✦ ✦

One of his lessons began at 7:50 a.m. on Monday, March 26, 1917, when he rode with thirty men from a desert camp to attack a railway station outside Medina. After a halt at midmorning at an oasis that "proved almost luxuriant with its thorn trees and grass," they mounted again and rode for another couple of hours before camping for the night. At 5:35 a.m. the next day they were on the move again. On the afternoon of Wednesday, March 28, they finally reached their target—the railway station at Abu el Naam.

To scout out the enemy, they "lay like lizards in the long grass" atop the "glistening, yellow, sunburned" hills that ringed the station. The Turkish garrison, they saw, consisted of "390 infantry, and twenty-five goats." On Thursday, March 29, they received Arab reinforcements—"300 men, two machine-guns, one mountain-gun, and one mountain howitzer." Lawrence judged the Arabs, though now almost as numerous as the Turks, incapable of capturing the fortified station. Instead he decided to destroy the rail and telegraph lines.

He set off just before midnight with a small party to lay a mine on the tracks. Then Lawrence had to shimmy up a telegraph pole himself because the Bedouin "proved unable to climb." He was so weak from a recent bout of dysentery and malaria that he lost his grip and fell sixteen feet to the ground, suffering "cuts and bruises." He slept for an hour, then arrived back at camp at daybreak, rubbing "sand out of red rimmed aching eyes," just in time to see the Arab artillery open fire on the station. "One lucky shell caught the front wagon of the train in the siding, and it took fire furiously," he recorded. "This alarmed the locomotive, which uncoupled and went off southward. We watched her hungrily as she approached our mine, and when she was on it there came a soft cloud of dust and a report and she stood still."

The train was derailed but managed to limp away, "going at foot pace, clanking horribly." Lawrence had hoped to fire a machine gun at the locomotive, but the unreliable Arab machine gunners had left their assigned ambush point to join in a more general attack on the railway station that was soon called off. Lawrence summed up the results: "We had taken thirty prisoners, a mare, two camels, and some more sheep; and had killed and wounded seventy of the garrison, at a cost to ourselves of one man slightly hurt."

It was not much of a battle in the conventional sense. The most Lawrence would say of it was that "we did not wholly fail."[24] But the cumulative effect of such actions was greater than their individual parts. For each raid forced the Turks to further concentrate their forces in a few entrenched garrisons, ceding the countryside to the Arabs. Before long it "dawned" on Lawrence "that we had won the Hejaz war": "Out of every thousand square miles of Hejaz nine hundred and ninety-nine were now free."[25] True, the Turks still held Medina, but so what? The Turkish garrison was trapped, and it was cheaper to keep it there than in a prisoner-of-war camp in Egypt. Lawrence counseled Feisal to make no further attempts to capture Medina but rather shift his focus to the Levant, where he could link up with a British army that was thrusting into Palestine from Egypt.

✦ ✦ ✦

THE KEY TO moving north would be the capture of Aqaba, the last Turkish-held port on the Red Sea and the port closest to the Suez Canal. From there Feisal's forces could be supplied as they moved into Syria. A more conventional officer would have planned an amphibious assault, but Lawrence rejected this approach because, while British troops "could take the beach," they would be "as unfavorably placed as on a Gallipoli beach," for they would be "under observation and gun-fire from the coastal hills: and these granite hills, thousands of feet high, were impracticable for heavy troops."[26] Lawrence decided that Aqaba "would be best taken by Arab irregulars descending from the interior without naval help." This would require a "long and difficult" trek to surprise the Turkish garrison from the rear—"an extreme example of a turning movement, since it involved a desert journey of six hundred miles to capture a trench within gunfire of our ships."[27]

Lawrence did not bother consulting his superiors before he set off from the port of Wejh on May 9, 1917; he was, a fellow officer said, "a law unto himself."[28] He was accompanied by fewer than fifty Arabs. They brought with them the essential tools of their trade: four hundred pounds of gold that would be used to buy the allegiance of tribesmen and six camels loaded with explosives that would be used to destroy railroad tracks and bridges. Two months later, on July 6, Lawrence rode with two thousand Arabs into Aqaba "through a driving sand storm."[29] Another British adviser later commented that "Lawrence could certainly not have done what he did without the gold, but no one else could have done it with ten times the amount." He was so successful because he had "established himself by sheer force of personality as a born leader and shown himself to be a greater dare-devil than any of his followers," able to "shoot straighter, ride harder, and eat and drink less."[30]

In the course of his exploits Lawrence was constantly getting sick or wounded. By the end of the Aqaba expedition he was "burned crimson and very haggard" and weighed less than a hundred pounds.[31] But even with a 20,000-pound bounty on his head, he was "absolutely without fear."[32] Sometimes he positively courted death, writing in June 1917, "I've decided to go off alone to Damascus, hoping to get killed on the way." Later, in an early edition of his memoirs, he wrote that "a bodily wound would have been a grateful vent for my internal perplexities."[33]

He was under great strain ("nerves going, and temper wearing thin")[34] not only from the demands of combat but also because he felt himself torn between two masters. The Arabs wanted independence, but Lawrence knew that Britain and France had concluded a secret treaty, the 1916 Sykes-Picot Agreement, to divide much of the Middle East between them. "We are calling them to fight for us on a lie," Lawrence complained, "and I can't stand it."[35]

Adding to his anguish was an incident that occurred on the night of November 20–21, 1917. While on a solitary reconnaissance of Daraa, Syria, in his usual white Arabic robes, Lawrence was captured by Turkish troops and hauled before Hajim Bey, the local Turkish commander. An "ardent pederast," the bey took a "fancy" to his captive who pretended to be a fair-skinned Circassian—one of the natives of the Caucasus forced by the tsar's armies to relocate to the Middle East. When Lawrence resisted his advances, he recalled, the bey called over his men to beat him savagely and to "play unspeakably" with him, meaning, probably, to rape him. Afterwards Lawrence was "too torn and bloody" for the bey's bed (his place was taken by a "crestfallen" corporal), so he was dumped in a makeshift prison. Less hurt than he appeared, he was able to run away, but he would never escape the trauma of what had transpired, especially because he later admitted to feeling a frisson of forbidden excitement during his ordeal—"a delicious warmth, probably sexual, was swelling through me." For the rest of his life he would express shame that "the citadel of my integrity had been irrevocably lost." He would subsequently find himself repelled by physical contact and unable to develop intimate ties with anyone.[36]

For the time being Lawrence kept quiet about his ordeal and went back to fighting the Turks. He did take care, however, to travel with more than two dozen Arab bodyguards—"a fine tough-looking band," in the words of one British soldier, any one of whom "would have given his life for Lawrence."[37]

By the end of 1917 the Anglo-Egyptian army under General Sir Edmund Allenby was breaking through Turkish defenses. Jerusalem fell on December 9. The next eleven months would be spent in driving the Turks out of the rest of the Levant, with the Arabs operating as a partisan adjunct on the right flank of the Allied advance. The campaign culminated on October 1, 1918, when the Allies entered Damascus down streets "aflame with joy and enthusiasm."[38]

The Arabs under Lawrence's guidance contributed to this victory by disrupting Turkish communications and tying down Turkish troops, making it impossible for Ottoman commanders to concentrate all of their 100,000 men in Palestine and Syria against Allenby's 69,000. By the end the Bedouin irregulars were supplemented by British armored cars and aircraft as well as by 8,000 Arab regulars, mostly former Ottoman soldiers, but it was still primarily an unconventional fight—and a vicious one.[39] The Arabs, enraged by Turkish atrocities, slaughtered Turkish prisoners on several occasions, and Lawrence was unwilling or unable to stop them.[40]

✦ ✦ ✦

AFTER THE WAR Lawrence attended the Paris Peace Conference as an adviser to both the Arab and the British delegations. He caused a sensation by wearing an Arab headdress along with a colonel's uniform. One American attendee described him as "the most interesting Briton alive . . . a Shelley-like person, and yet too virile to be a poet."[41]

Lawrence came away deeply disillusioned after the French took Syria and Lebanon while the British helped themselves to Palestine, Iraq, and Transjordan. He went on, however, to play an important role as an adviser to Winston Churchill at the Colonial Office in 1921 in remaking the map of the Middle East. In his dealings with Churchill, and in his memoir, *Seven Pillars of Wisdom*, which he was then in the process of revising, he exaggerated the role played by his friend Feisal during the war, while glossing over the weakness of the Arabs and the extent of the British aid they received. He wanted to convey the impression that Britain owed the Arabs and especially the Hashemites a major debt that had to be repaid.[42] Partly as a result of his machinations, Feisal was crowned the first king of Iraq, a new state cobbled together from three Ottoman provinces. His brother Abdullah was installed in Transjordan, yet another new state. Their father, Hussein, was left to rule the Hejaz until 1924 when he was defeated by Ibn Saud, founder of Saudi Arabia. Lawrence, who did not believe that the agendas of Arab nationalists and Zionists were incompatible, even used his influence with Feisal to persuade him to give up his family's claims to Palestine, which, under the terms of a League of Nations resolution approved in 1922, became a "mandate" governed by Britain with the intention of turning it into a "Jewish National Home."[43]

Feisal's grandson would be overthrown and killed in Baghdad in 1958, but the state of Iraq still exists and the Hashemites still rule Jordan. Palestine, of course, was to be divided into Israel, the West Bank, and the Gaza Strip. Thus Lawrence may be said to have played an important role in creating the modern Middle East. Indeed, near the end of his life, he would cite his role in crafting the postwar settlement, "which still stands in every particular—if only other peace treaties did!" as being more important than what he "did in Arabia during the war."[44] The results of that settlement turned out, however, to be far more problematic than Lawrence had foreseen. As the historian David Fromkin pointed out in his magisterial history *A Peace to End All Peace*, by 1922, shortly after Lawrence had finished his work at the Colonial Office, "the Middle East had started along a road that was to lead to the endless wars (between Israel and her neighbors, among others, and between rival militias in Lebanon) and to the always-escalating acts of terrorism (hijacking, assassination, and random massacre) that have been a characteristic feature of international life in the 1970s and 1980s."[45] And in the 1990s and 2000s and 2010s.

✦ ✦ ✦

ONCE HIS WORK at the Colonial Office was done, Lawrence sought to hide "out-of-sight,"[46] but he found this increasingly hard to accomplish because of an enterprising showman named Lowell Thomas. A former Chicago newspaperman, Thomas had spent a few days with Lawrence in Aqaba in 1918. Out of this thin material he created a popular book and lecture, accompanied by a slideshow, on "Lawrence of Arabia." His subject found Thomas's presentation to be "silly and inaccurate," but it played to packed houses from New York to London, month after month. Four million people were said to have viewed the show around the world,[47] lured by a romantic tale of derring-do that offered a welcome respite from the aftermath of the mass slaughter of the trenches. To escape the public klieg light, "the Uncrowned King of Arabia," as he was dubbed by Thomas,[48] enlisted under an alias as a lowly airman in the Royal Air Force to serve, in his own words, as a "*cog of the machine*."[49] Later he legally changed his name to T. E. Shaw. "Damn the Press," he fulminated, decrying intrusions into his privacy.[50]

In truth T.E.'s attitude to fame was ambivalent. While professing a passion for anonymity, he struck up high-profile friendships with literary giants such as George Bernard Shaw and Thomas Hardy, published a memoir, and sat for numerous portraits by leading artists. When his charade was discovered by the press in 1925, he had to leave the RAF temporarily and join the Royal Tank Corps, but, thanks to his friendship with the RAF chief of staff, he was allowed to rejoin the air force—"the nearest modern equivalent to going into a monastery in the Middle Ages," he explained to a friend, the poet Robert Graves.[51] Here he felt a sense of comradeship in the ranks with his fellow mechanist-"monks." He had only just left the RAF and settled in a small cottage in Dorset when he died in a motorcycle accident in 1935 while hurtling at top speed down a country lane as he loved to do. Winston Churchill called his death at age forty-seven the greatest blow the British Empire had suffered in years. He told reporters, "In Lawrence we have lost one of the greatest beings of our time."[52]

Not until much later did one of the more sordid details of his last years emerge. Between 1923 and 1935 he had found some perverse satisfaction in occasionally hiring a younger soldier to whip him—apparently as penance for his ordeal at Daraa. This is what psychiatrists call a "flagellation disorder." Lawrence's friends and family had no idea about this private behavior;

the beatings became public only when the soldier who administered them sold his story to a newspaper in 1968. Contrary to the widespread assumption, however, there is no evidence that Lawrence was a practicing homosexual; he consistently professed his own "sexlessness" and in all likelihood never entered into a sexual relationship with anyone, man or woman.[53]

✦ ✦ ✦

Opinion about this "strange character," who admitted that "madness was very near" for him, has been sharply divided over the years.[54] Some have derided him, with scant evidence, as an "unfortunate charlatan" who "lied compulsively,"[55] while boosters have compared him, rather preposterously, to Napoleon, Marlborough, and other "great captains" of history.[56] Lawrence never claimed such importance for his own work in a "side show of a side show." "My role was a minor one," he wrote with excessive modesty.[57]

A more balanced judgment was rendered by Franz von Papen, a future German chancellor and ambassador to Istanbul who as a junior officer served as an adviser to the Ottoman army. "The British can indeed count themselves fortunate to have had the services of a man with such understanding and affection for the Islamic world," Papen wrote. "From the military point of view his activities were probably not of great importance, but politically and economically they were of priceless value."[58] (By "economically" Papen was presumably referring to the access to oil that Britain secured.)

Lawrence's most lasting influence was as a glamorous practitioner of guerrilla warfare who was to inspire numerous imitators. A writer of the first chop, as well as a "witty and enlightening" conversationalist with an "impish sense of humor,"[59] he left copious guidance for latter-day Lawrences. What he called "my beastly book,"[60] *Seven Pillars of Wisdom*, which was not widely published until after his death, was rightly acclaimed as a great work of literature. The condensed version, *Revolt in the Desert*, became a best seller in his lifetime. Just as influential, for soldiers if not for the general public, were two of his articles.

"The Evolution of a Revolt," published by the *Army Quarterly* in 1920, was Lawrence's attempt to use his own experiences to expatiate on the subject of irregular warfare. It would form the basis of an entry called "Science of Guerrilla Warfare" compiled by a friend, the military strategist Basil Liddell-Hart, and published under the initials T.E.LA. in the *Encyclopaedia Britannica* in 1929. In it Lawrence coined numerous aphorisms that are still widely quoted: "The printing press is the greatest weapon in the armory of the modern commander"; "Irregular war is far more intellectual than a bayonet charge"; "Rebellions can be made by 2 per cent active in a striking force, and 98 per cent passively sympathetic." His conclusion was a direct challenge to the conventional military mindset: "In fifty words: granted mobility, security (in the form of denying targets to the enemy), time, and doctrine (the idea to convert every subject to friendliness), victory will rest with the insurgents, for the algebraical factors are in the end decisive, and against them perfection of means and spirit struggle quite in vain."[61]

Those words have formed a rallying cry for guerrillas and their acolytes ever since, but Lawrence's claim is less far-reaching than it appears on a quick read. Note all of the caveats: success is certain *only* if guerrillas have "mobility," "security," "time," and "doctrine." Few insurgencies have ever been vouchsafed all of those advantages. How many insurgents are able, after all, to call on the aid of the Royal Air Force, Army, and Navy? As one of Lawrence's fellow advisers to the Arabs noted, "Seldom has a force had greater liberty of action or greater security."[62] Lacking these advantages, most guerrillas fail to achieve their goals. Even the Arab Revolt was hardly an unalloyed success, insofar as the insurgents were not strong enough to prevent their European allies from grabbing most of the Ottoman possessions for themselves.

Reservations must also be kept in mind when reading Lawrence's other enduring essay, "Twenty-Seven Articles," written on August 20, 1917, a month after the capture of Aqaba. In it Lawrence offered some of his secrets for being an effective adviser. His shrewd advice included the following:

> Never give orders to anyone at all, and reserve your directions or advice for the C.O. [commanding officer], however great the temptation (for efficiency's sake) of dealing with his underlings. . . . Formal visits to give advice are not so good as the constant dropping of ideas in casual talk. . . . The less apparent your interference the more your influence.

> . . . Do not try to do too much with your own hands. Better the Arabs do it tolerably than you do it perfectly. It is their war, and you are to help them, not to win it for them.[63]

All of these aphorisms have been cited ever since by Western soldiers engaged in advisory work. The suggestion to "not . . . do too much" was especially popular with American and British soldiers in Iraq from 2003 to 2007 when it encouraged a destructive hands-off policy that allowed the fighting to spiral out of control. Only when General David Petraeus decided to do more to secure the populace did the tide start to turn. Those who might be tempted to quote Lawrence dogmatically—something that would have horrified him—should keep in mind his admonition that the "Twenty-Seven Articles" "are meant to apply only to Bedu: townspeople or Syrians require totally different treatment." He might have added, but did not, because it was self-evident, that his advice was meant for insurgents, not (as in Iraq) counterinsurgents.

Lawrence's most important achievement was not in crafting a template of guerrilla warfare or even military advising that could be transposed to any situation. Rather, by his own example he showed how hard any soldier fighting an irregular war must work to understand and adapt himself to local conditions. He made empathy into a powerful weapon of war, striving to understand the actions of both enemies and allies. "I risked myself among them a hundred times, to *learn*," he wrote of the Turks. He later attributed his success to "hard study and brain-work and concentration." His example, he declared, was at odds with the "fundamental, crippling, incuriousness" of so many of his fellow officers who were "too much body and too little head."[64]

Lawrence was a rare combination of body and head, "active and reflective." In some respects he resembled Marshal Lyautey, another misfit who approached the subject from the other side as a fighter against guerrillas but reached, as we have seen, similar conclusions about the need for "adaptation" and "elasticity."

39.

THE REGULAR IRREGULARS

The Birth of the Special Forces in World War II

GIVEN THE WELL-PUBLICIZED success enjoyed during World War I by Lawrence and, to a lesser extent, by Paul von Lettow-Vorbeck, a German officer who used hit-and-run tactics against the British in East Africa, it should be no surprise that the next world war would see an exponential increase in irregular operations. The advance of German armies across Europe was preceded by the Brandenburg commandos who spoke multiple languages and often operated in enemy uniforms. They had been set up on the initiative of Captain Theodore von Hippel, who had served under Lettow-Vorbeck and had also studied Lawrence's campaigns.[65] In May 1940 Brandenburgers disguised as Dutch troops seized a key bridge across the Meuse into the Netherlands and swooped down in gliders on Belgium's Eben Emael fortress. Later, in 1943, the SS major Otto Skorzeny employed gliders in a famous raid to spring Mussolini from his mountaintop prison in Italy. (Gliders in the 1940s served the role now played by helicopters.) The Italians, for their part, developed a highly capable maritime commando unit, the Decima MAS—forerunner of today's SEALs.

But it was the Allies who fielded the preponderance of the irregular forces used in World War II. They knew that it would take years to mass the giant armies needed to defeat the Axis. In the meantime, it was better to mount pinprick raids than do nothing at all. Or so figured Winston Churchill, who had seen firsthand as a junior officer in South Africa the impact of Boer commandos. When he took over as prime minister in May 1940 just as France was falling, he immediately established both the Army Commandos to "develop a reign of terror down the enemy coasts" and a civilian organization, the Special Operations Executive (SOE), to undertake "subversion and sabotage" in occupied lands—or, in his evocative phrase, to "set Europe ablaze." As an indication of how urgent the situation was, the formation of the commandos was approved three days after being proposed, and their first raid on the French coast took place fifteen days later.[66] Before long, numerous other British units were set up for operations behind enemy lines. The war in North Africa spawned the Long-Range Desert Group, the Special Air Service (SAS), and Popski's Private Army, all of which used trucks and jeeps to transverse trackless seas of sand, hitting the Germans and Italians where they least expected it. Not to be outdone, the Royal Marines, Royal Air Force, and Royal Navy formed commando-style detachments of their own.

All of these special operators made critical use of modern inventions such as the airplane and radio. But they were also inspired by the timeless lessons of history. SOE's first leaders, the army officers J. C. F. Holland and Colin Gubbins, had fought against the IRA. In addition, Holland had served with the Arab irregulars in World War I and had studied Boer tactics. Now they were determined to employ the same sorts of "ungentlemanly" tactics that T. E. Lawrence, Michael Collins, and Christiaan de Wet had mastered.[67]

The very name "commando," which became a generic term for all special operations units, was inspired by the Boers. Yet not all commando operations constituted guerrilla warfare per se, or as it is known today, "unconventional warfare." Many were examples of what in the modern military lexicon would be called "direct action"—short-duration raids launched against the enemy from bases on friendly soil. Guerrilla operations, by contrast, typically involve fighters who either lack fixed bases or base themselves in enemy-controlled territory. In either case they spend longer on the ground than the typical commando or Brandenburg team. The SOE was more of a guerrilla force, infiltrating its operatives into Axis-occupied lands to work with indigenous resistance movements. The differences blurred, however, when both SOE and SAS parachuted operatives into France in 1944 to disrupt German lines of communication.

✦ ✦ ✦

When the United States finally entered the war in December 1941, it followed the British lead by setting up the Office of Special Services (OSS) under General "Wild Bill" Donovan, whose mandate ran from intelligence gathering to propaganda. It particularly took to sabotage operations, carrying out advice contained in illustrated training documents with puckish titles such as "Arson: An Instruction Manual." The OSS also developed a line of secret weapons such as "Hedy," "a panic creator which simulates the sound of a falling bomb and subsequent explosion," and "Aunt Jemima," a flourlike substance with "greater explosive force than TNT."[68]

The U.S. Army, for its part, created in 1942 an analogue to the commandos—the Rangers. They were named in tribute to Robert Rogers, subject of the hit 1940 film *Northwest Passage*. Like the commandos, the Rangers often found themselves acting as the spearhead for conventional offensives, the most famous example being their scaling of the 100-foot cliffs at Pointe du Hoc on D-Day. The U.S. Marines set up similar Raider battalions, while Allied nations, including Australia, Belgium, Canada, and France, created their own special-warfare organizations to work with the British and Americans. The Soviet Union, too, embraced irregular operations by organizing large numbers of Partisans and *Spetsnaz* commandos, who would strike behind German lines.

✦ ✦ ✦

There had been "special operations" before—an appellation that can apply to any particularly risky and unconventional attack mounted by a small military force—going all the way back to the days of the Trojan Horse.[69] The first attempts to institutionalize the concept, to specially train and equip soldiers for hit-and-run raids, were undertaken in the eighteenth century with light infantry and rangers. But for the most part soldiers who took part in irregular operations before the 1940s had to improvise after being overrun: think of Francis Marion in the American Revolution or numerous Spanish soldiers in the Peninsular War. Their experiences were mirrored in World War II by soldiers ranging from Russians in their homeland to Americans in the Philippines who chose to fight as guerrillas rather than accept defeat. But the war also saw the most ambitious attempt yet to train and equip specialized forces for such missions.

That innovation did not sit well with the majority of regular soldiers, who saw no need for "elite" units. Those who volunteered for such assignments, and generally only volunteers were taken, tended to be, in the words of the British army captain W. E. D. Allen, either "the young and the keen" or the "stale and the restless": "The efficient soldier, good at his job, generally ignored the notices."[70] A disproportionate number of the volunteers were upper-class adventurers. Allen himself was a graduate of Eton and a former member of Parliament. The ranks of British special operators also included the actor David Niven; Lord Lovat, a Scottish peer and future cabinet minister; the novelist Evelyn Waugh; and the prime minister's son, Randolph Churchill. President Roosevelt's son James also served in special operations with Carlson's Raiders of the U.S. Marine Corps. The OSS got so many recruits from Wall Street and the Ivy League that wags joked its initials stood for "Oh So Social," while the SAS was stocked with Oxford and Cambridge graduates.

Part of this may have been snobbery on the part of higher-ups wearing the old school tie, but it was also a recognition that normal soldiers, no matter how competent, do not necessarily make good irregulars. Devil-may-care aristocrats might be better suited. At the other end of the social spectrum, the criminal underworld came in handy when recruiting for forgers and safecrackers.[71] Brigadier Dudley Clarke, who as a lieutenant colonel founded the British Commandos in 1940, wrote, "We looked for a dash of the Elizabethan pirate, the Chicago gangster, and the Frontier tribesman, allied to a professional efficiency and standard of discipline of the best Regular soldier. The Commando was to need something beyond the mass discipline which held the ranks steady when men stood side by side; his had to be a personal and an independent kind which would carry him through to the objective no matter what might happen to those upon his right and left." This meant, he concluded, that the "men would have to learn for once to discard the ingrained 'team-spirit' " of regular military formations.[72]

40.

WINGATE'S WARS

A "Wayward Genius" in Palestine, Abyssinia, and Burma, 1936–1944

FEW TOOK UP this admonition as eagerly or excessively as Clarke's fellow army officer Orde Charles Wingate, who would win renown for his irregular operations in Palestine, Abyssinia, and Burma, becoming the closest World War II equivalent to his distant relative T. E. Lawrence. His pioneering efforts to add guerrilla tactics to the arsenals of conventional armies often met with disdain and disbelief from more conventionally minded officers. Wingate did not care. "Popularity," he believed, "is a sign of weakness." Considered by his peers to be either a "military genius or a mountebank" (opinions differed),[73] he had been locked in an unceasing war against his superiors from his earliest days.

Even as a young cadet at the Royal Military Academy, Woolwich, he "had the power," recalled his best friend, "to create violent antagonisms against himself by his attitude towards authority."[74] Later, as a junior officer, Wingate was known to begin meetings with generals by placing his alarm clock on the table. After it went off, he would leave, announcing, "Well gentlemen, you have talked for one hour and achieved absolutely nothing. I can't spend any more time with you!"[75]

Wingate's first rebellion was against the stifling religious atmosphere in which he was raised. His father was a retired Indian Army colonel with a devotion to a fundamentalist Protestant sect called the Plymouth Brethren.

He and his wife brought up their seven children, including "Ordey" (his family nickname), in what one of his brothers called a "temple of gloom," with prayer mandatory, frivolity forbidden, and "fears of eternal damnation" ever present.[76] By the time he arrived at Woolwich, to train as an artillery officer, he had left the Plymouth Brethren, but he never lost his religious outlook. For the rest of his life he would be deeply influenced by the Bible, on which he had been "suckled" and which a friend said "was his guide in all his ways."[77] Another legacy of his childhood was that he developed a violent aversion to being regimented. At Woolwich he was in constant trouble, and he formed a low opinion of the "military apes" who tried to discipline him.[78]

After graduation he learned Arabic, and in 1928 he joined the British-run Sudan Defense Force as an officer overseeing local enlisted men. Here he battled elusive gangs of slave traders and poachers within Sudan, learning the hit-and-run tactics he would employ throughout his career.[79] He also developed many of his unconventional habits, such as wearing scruffy clothing ("his socks were very smelly and all in holes," a subordinate later noticed),[80] subjecting himself to great danger and discomfort, and receiving visitors in the nude. (He would become notorious for briefing reporters in his hotel room while "brushing his lower anatomy with his hairbrush.")[81] Other Wingate trademarks: a pith helmet, which he wore in the manner of a nineteenth-century explorer; an alarm clock, which he carried (he claimed "wrist watches are no damned good");[82] raw onions, which he munched like apples because of their supposedly salubrious properties; and a beard, which he grew from time to time in contravention of the King's Regulations, which permitted only a mustache.

While returning home on a steamship from the Sudan in 1933, he met an Englishwoman, Ivy Paterson, and her sixteen-year-old daughter, Lorna. Ivy noted Wingate's "medium height" (he was five feet six inches tall), the "forward thrust" of his head, and his "beautiful hands." But his most impressive feature was his eyes: "Rather deep set, and of a periwinkle blue, they were the eyes of a prophet and a visionary. . . . [I]n their fire and intensity, one was aware of the unusual force of his personality." That impression was reinforced when she heard Wingate hold forth in what another listener described as a "sandpaper voice" ("like the grating of stone against stone") on almost every "subject under the sun"—including his love of Beethoven and his dislike of "the wireless," as radio was then known. "He spoke brilliantly. But he could also be very quiet and silent for long periods."[83]

Ivy's daughter, Lorna, was instantly smitten. Orde was thirty-one years old and already engaged, but he, too, fell in love with this winsome schoolgirl. They married two years later shortly after her graduation from high school. His former fiancée was devastated but remained so devoted to Orde that she never married, because she felt no other man could match him. This was evidence of the strong devotion that Wingate could instill to counterbalance the antipathy he so often engendered.[84]

✦ ✦ ✦

IN 1936 CAPTAIN Wingate was dispatched to Palestine, then under British rule, to serve as an intelligence officer in the British force striving to put down an Arab rebellion. Notwithstanding his Arabist background, he became enamored of Zionism—so much so that even dedicated Zionists described him as a "fanatic." Wingate admired the Jews for making the desert "blossom like the rose," and he felt that they would be more valuable allies for Britain than the Arabs. This was not a view shared by the rest of the colonial administration, which, Wingate found, was "to a man, anti-Jew and pro-Arab." "Everyone's against the Jews," he said, characteristically, "so I'm for them."

At the moment the Jews were facing what would be the biggest Palestinian uprising until the First Intifada in the 1980s. Like the Second Intifada, this revolt was marked by urban terrorism, with bombings and shootings targeting both British authorities and Jewish civilians. By rushing in twenty thousand troops and taking punitive measures such as blowing up suspects' houses, the British managed to regain control of the cities. This forced the rebels to focus on attacks in the countryside against isolated Jewish settlements and police posts as well as against moderate Arabs.

At first the Jews responded with *havlaga* (restraint), but as the violence continued they began fighting back. Wingate was at the forefront of the counterattack. He found that "on the approach of darkness, the virtual control of the country passes to the gangsters." In 1938 he persuaded British and Zionist leaders to let him organize Special Night Squads to take back the night. They would be made up of British soldiers and Jewish "supernumeraries" who would venture stealthily out of fortified kibbutzim to "bodily assault" Palestinian gangs "with bayonet and bomb" and "thereby put an end to the terrorism."

Eventually the Night Squads numbered forty Britons and a hundred Jews who usually operated in squads of ten men. Their practice was to march at night and attack at dawn. Wearing khaki shorts and rubber-soled boots, veterans recalled, they would spend long hours walking single file over "dry, very stony ground, which was generally hilly, often steeply so," deliberately avoiding "the beaten path" and taking "a zig-zag or snakelike course." "Complete silence is the rule in all cases," Wingate instructed. "Members of Squads should try to cut down their smoking with subsequent coughing." Their goal was to obtain "complete surprise," and they often succeeded. Their unexpected appearance induced "panic" among the Palestinian rebels whom Wingate dismissed as "feeble," "ignorant and primitive."

In these raids Wingate displayed a flair for navigation in the dark, an "iron constitution," and an utter disregard for danger. During one battle he was shot five times in a "friendly fire" accident but, although "white as a sheet" and "covered in blood," he continued "giving orders in English and Hebrew quite calmly."

He instructed the Night Squads to treat Arab civilians, "as opposed to the terrorist, with courtesy and respect," but on one occasion he himself led a rampage through an Arab village to avenge the murder of a Jewish friend. Wingate later claimed that his squads killed at least 140 rebels and wounded 300 more, compiling a record unmatched by any British unit of similar size.

By the time Wingate left Palestine in 1939, he had earned the first of his three Distinguished Service Orders, Britain's second-highest decoration, and the lasting gratitude of Palestinian Jews, who called him simply *Hayedid* (the Friend). Veterans of his Night Squads, including Moshe Dayan and Yigael Yadin, would become leading generals in Israel's army, which they infused with his disregard of protocol, his insistence on fast-moving offensive operations led by officers from the front, and his emphasis on preempting terrorist attacks. "A dominating personality, he infected us all with his fanaticism and faith," Dayan later wrote.

In his own army Wingate was looked upon as a cantankerous wild man.

He was accused of having "forfeited our general reputation for fair fighting" and seen as a potential "security risk" who "puts the interests of the Jews before those of his own country." (Wingate shared confidential documents with Zionist leaders.) The British commander in Palestine, General Robert Haining, thought he "played for his own ends and likings instead of playing for the side," and dismissed his service as "nugatory and embarrassing."

But even his detractors had to admit that he had a gift for unconventional warfare that was reminiscent of his distant kinsman T. E. Lawrence, who was of equally diminutive stature. The Zionist leader Chaim Weizmann, who knew both men, said that Wingate's "intenseness," "whimsicality," and "originality" all reminded him of T.E.: "I thought of Lawrence more than once when Wingate sat opposite me, arguing fiercely, and boring me through with his eyes." The pro-Zionist Wingate bridled at the comparison with his pro-Arab relative, whose reputation he thought was exaggerated by "a great amount of romantic dust." But the comparisons only grew stronger after Wingate's involvement in the reconquest of Abyssinia, as Ethiopia was then called.[85]

✦ ✦ ✦

IN AN ACT of unprovoked aggression that alarmed much of the Western world, Benito Mussolini had invaded Abyssinia in 1935. Britain had given refuge to Emperor Haile Selassie but had provided no real help until Italy declared war on Britain in June 1940. Thereupon the emperor was whisked to Khartoum, capital of the Sudan, and the task of returning him to power was entrusted to the Special Operations Executive. Detailed for this assignment was Orde Wingate. He would have preferred to lead an army of Jewish soldiers to fight with the Allies in North Africa. As a consolation he applied his "ruthless energy" to the cause of Haile Selassie, a Coptic Christian who styled himself as the Lion of Judah and claimed descent from King Solomon and the Queen of Sheba. An acting lieutenant colonel on loan to SOE, Wingate was to lead a band of irregulars that he called Gideon Force after the ancient Israelite fighters.

On January 20, 1941, Wingate crossed from western Sudan into Abyssinia with the emperor, 1,600 Sudanese and Abyssinian fighters, 70 Britons, and 20,000 camels. Two conventional columns with a total of 60,000 troops, mainly Indians and Africans, marched at roughly the same time, one from northern Sudan, the other from Kenya to the south. As Gideon Force advanced, it left a trail of dying camels; the warm-weather dromedaries turned out to be ill-suited for Abyssinia's chilly highlands. But while the number of camels shrank, the ranks of fighters grew as tribesmen were recruited to the "patriot" cause. These guerrillas, in turn, were directed by SOE "operational centers," consisting of one British officer and four NCOs. The campaign, Wingate later noted, could not "have succeeded without the patriot support."

The Italian army of occupation numbered 300,000 men. Thirty-five thousand of them were deployed against Gideon Force, and they had armored vehicles, artillery, and air support—all of which Wingate lacked. He did not even have a proper logistics service, having to rely on "captured Italian rations or local produce." Making maximal use of his puny numbers, Wingate staged numerous assaults on Italian forts, usually at night, telling his men to move fast and "goading everyone to superhuman effort." By the time the Italians had assembled for a counterattack, the attackers were gone.

Wingate also skillfully employed bluff. He entered one newly liberated Italian fort to find the telephone ringing. An officer at another fort was calling to ask where the British were. Wingate instructed an Italian-speaking American war correspondent to "tell them that a British division ten thousand strong is on its way up the road" and "advising them to clear off." This the panicked Italians did posthaste.

Addis Ababa, already abandoned by the Italian army, was taken by South African troops on April 5, 1941, after a slog through what a contemporary magazine described as "misty rain and quagmires of red mud." A month later Wingate had the privilege of leading Haile Selassie into the capital. The emperor eschewed a white horse procured for the occasion, preferring the comfort of a car, so Wingate himself rode at the head of the victory parade. "I hope when we meet my subjects they will know which of us is Emperor," Haile Selassie commented wryly. The unofficial "emperor" had not won the campaign single-handedly, but he had played an important role; his tiny force had captured more than 15,000 enemy troops and killed 1,500 more.

Wingate thought his Abyssinian campaign could be a model for other occupied lands, "wherever there is a patriot population" that could be roused "by men of integrity and personality." He believed that employing a "corps d'elite" on a long-range "penetration" mission to galvanize local forces, as he had done, would be far more effective than what he wrongly denigrated as Lawrence's "wasteful and ineffectual" approach of providing "war materiel and cash" to local leaders. He claimed, "Given a population favorable to penetration, a thousand resolute and well-armed men can paralyze, for an indefinite period, the operations of a hundred thousand."

But despite what the official British military history rightly labeled a "remarkable achievement," Wingate was peremptorily sent back to Cairo and reduced to his regular rank of major because, as usual, he had offended his superior officers with his "rude and dictatorial and insistent" ways. One senior general was heard to grumble, "The curse of this war is Lawrence in the last," although in fact T.E. had shown far more tact in his dealings with General Allenby and his staff than Wingate ever displayed with anyone.[86]

✦ ✦ ✦

WINGATE HAD LONG battled depression. "I'm not happy," he said, with typical modesty, "but I don't think any great man ever is."[87] During the Abyssinian campaign he had also contracted cerebral malaria. Despondent at the lack of another assignment, he plunged a rusty knife into his throat while alone in a Cairo hotel room. An alert officer next door heard him fall and rushed him to the hospital, saving his life. Supposedly one of his colleagues from Abyssinia, exasperated by Wingate's incessant abuse, visited him at the hospital to demand, "You bloody fool, why didn't you use a revolver?"[88]

Attempted suicide might have ended Wingate's career, but he was fortunate that General Sir Archibald Wavell, who had previously made use of his services in Palestine and Abyssinia, still had faith in him. Wavell had been appointed commander in India, and he summoned Wingate to see what he could do to make life uncomfortable for the Japanese armies sweeping through Burma.

✦ ✦ ✦

Wingate arrived in India in March 1942, a few weeks after the fall of Rangoon. The Japanese were firmly in control, and there was no hope of a conventional counteroffensive in the short term. Nor was there a serious prospect of utilizing indigenous forces as he had done in Palestine and Abyssinia. Some hill tribes remained loyal to the British (Wingate would employ them as guides and guerrillas), but the majority of Burmese had no desire to fight for their former colonial masters. Wingate nevertheless believed the Japanese would be vulnerable to attack by "long range penetration" troops such as Gideon Force. "In the back area are his unprotected kidneys, his midriff, his throat, and other vulnerable points," he wrote. "The targets for troops of deep penetration may be regarded therefore as the more vital and tender points of the enemy's anatomy." The key to such action was "to maintain forces by air and direct them by wireless," both common practices today but novel ideas at the time.

To implement his ideas, Wingate was elevated to brigadier and given command of the Seventy-Seventh Indian Infantry Brigade, the foundation of what later became known as the Chindits (a corruption of "chinthe," a lion-like creature that guards Burmese temples). Although they would be sent on a mission far more arduous than an ordinary military operation, the Chindits were hardly picked troops. The largest elements were a British battalion made up mostly of married men in their thirties who had been performing garrison duty and a Gurkha battalion of peach-fuzzed young recruits. As Wingate noted, they "never dreamt they would serve as shock troops." After subjecting these "ordinary" men to a tough training regimen designed to teach them "to imitate Tarzan," Wingate divided them into seven columns of roughly four hundred men each, with fifteen horses and one hundred mules for transport. Each column was accompanied by a two-man Royal Air Force team equipped with powerful radios to coordinate air support, thus anticipating the military practices of later decades.

Originally their expedition, known as Longcloth, was supposed to coincide with a larger offensive into northern Burma, but Wavell decided to let the Chindits proceed on their own after the offensive was called off. All concerned knew they were running the risk that the full fury of the Japanese army could descend on this lone brigade.

On February 13, 1943, "Wingate's Circus," as the three thousand Chindits called themselves, began crossing the Chindwin, the "strangely beautiful" river separating Burma from India, using inflatable boats and rafts. Two of the columns ran into heavy resistance and turned back, but the rest kept advancing, blowing up bridges and railroads and ambushing Japanese patrols. The air drops worked well aside from the occasional "death by flying fruit," as some of the men referred to "injuries caused by dropped supplies." The RAF even dropped spare kilts, false teeth, and monocles as needed. More than two thousand Chindits then crossed the "swiftly flowing," mile-wide Irrawaddy River. They were now at least two hundred miles inside Burma, and enemy attacks, the intense heat, and various tropical diseases were taking their toll. As one of Wingate's aides noted, "malaria, scrub typhus, dysentery, and even cholera are endemic."

Wingate decided to turn back on March 26, 1943. The Chindits were now nearly surrounded by three crack Japanese divisions, so he told his men to break up into smaller parties and find their own way home. (He claimed that this "dispersal" had been inspired by Robert the Bruce's tactics.) This was when the expedition turned truly "horrid." Small groups of Chindits, generally twenty to forty strong, had to traverse hundreds of miles of "incredibly thick" jungle and "fiendishly steep and rocky" hills and then cross two major rivers with the enemy on their heels. Rations had been "grossly inadequate" to begin with; they were designed to sustain paratroopers for only a few days in the field. Now, as supply drops grew less frequent, the "food problem" became "acute." "Everyone was weak from lack of food," wrote Major Bernard Fergusson, a column commander who was tormented by "visions of chocolate *éclairs* and birthday cakes," "and morale depends more on food than on anything else."

Of the 3,000 Chindits, only 2,182 "emaciated" survivors returned, the last on June 6, 1943, their "stomachs caved inward," ribs sticking out, muscles transformed into "stringy tendons." Most would be judged unfit for future service. Some had marched fifteen hundred miles carrying, initially at least, more than seventy pounds of equipment.

Fergusson later conceded that the first Chindit expedition had few "tangible" achievements: "We blew up bits of a railway, which did not take long to repair; we gathered some useful intelligence; we distracted the Japanese from some minor operations, and possibly from some bigger ones; we killed a few hundred of an enemy which numbers eighty millions; we proved that it was feasible to maintain a force by supply dropping alone."

The biggest impact of Operation Longcloth was not apparent until Japanese generals were interrogated after the war: They said that the difficulty of defending against Wingate's raid led them to mount an offensive against India in 1944 in order to prevent future incursions. That attack failed and left them too weak to prevent the British recapture of Burma the following year. Against this indirect impact must be weighed the expedition's staggering cost.

General William Slim, commander of the Fourteenth Army, which ultimately retook Burma, judged the raid an "expensive failure" on purely military grounds but a public-relations triumph: "Skillfully handled, the press of the Allied world took up the tale, and everywhere the story ran that we had beaten the Japanese at their own game." This psychological fillip was important to soldiers and civilians alike at a time when Japan still reigned supreme in Asia.[89]

✦ ✦ ✦

AMONG THOSE IMPRESSED by the Chindits' achievement was Winston Churchill, who began to wonder whether Wingate "was another Lawrence of Arabia."[90] He took Wingate, by then a national hero, to his meeting in August 1943 with President Roosevelt and the Combined Chiefs of Staff in Quebec. Though only a junior general, Wingate so impressed the senior brass that they agreed to vastly expand his long-range penetration force and to provide him with his own air force. Thus was born No. 1 Air Commando, which would consist of almost four hundred transport aircraft, gliders, light aircraft, fighters, and bombers, all provided by the U.S. Army Air Forces. Their motto was "anyplace, anytime, anywhere," and they would prove as good as their word, not only dropping supplies and providing fire support as "flying artillery" but also evacuating casualties.

Armed with high-level authorization, Wingate returned to India, only to run into unremitting hostility from the British headquarters in New Delhi. Part of this was due to the natural skepticism of conventional officers who resisted "a new approach to war." But Wingate did not help his own cause. One staff officer recalled that when challenged he "replied with a long-winded diatribe accusing almost everyone of stupidity, ignorance, obstruction, and much else besides." This officer concluded that Wingate was "a thoroughly nasty bit of work." Wingate was typically unrepentant. "It is because I am what I am, objectionable though it appears to my critics, that I win battles," he shot back.[91]

Wingate was too weak to fight back effectively at first because on the way to India he had contracted typhus after foolishly drinking the water from a flower vase during a refueling stop. (He was thirsty and the canteen was closed.) But as he recovered his strength he got the upper hand against the "marsupial minds" at headquarters. He was promoted to major general and given command of a Special Force of some twenty thousand men, or two divisions' worth. The first expedition had been mounted with one brigade. Now he had six.

A new feature of the second Chindit expedition would be the establishment of fortified strongholds in enemy territory. Wingate defined the stronghold as "an orbit round which columns of the Brigade circulate," "a defended airstrip," "a magazine for stores," and, more colorfully, as "a machan overlooking a kid tied up to entice the Japanese tiger." In other words the strongholds were designed to goad the Japanese into costly and futile attacks. In the process, however, the Chindits would sacrifice the guerrilla's advantages of speed and mobility.

Operation Thursday, the second Chindit expedition, began with one brigade marching overland at the end of February 1944. The bulk of the force was to begin its fly-in on Sunday, March 5. At 4:30 p.m. that day, just half an hour before the first C-47 cargo aircraft was to lift off from an airstrip in India, an American reconnaissance flight revealed teak logs blocking one of the landing sites in the jungle, code-named Piccadilly. Had the landing been blown? Or had the trees been placed there in the course of normal logging operations? It was later revealed to be the latter, but there were more than a few anxious moments for the cluster of senior commanders huddled on the airstrip. Finally the decision was made to proceed, diverting the flights that would have gone to Piccadilly to another landing zone, Broadway, located 150 miles inside Burma.

The first C-47 roared off at 6:12 p.m. on March 5, followed by more aircraft at thirty-second intervals. Each airplane towed two gliders full of men jammed in with their supplies. Not all of the gliders made it over the seven-thousand-foot mountains. Ten of them crashed in India; six others got lost and came down in the wrong part of occupied Burma. For the thirty-seven gliders that reached Broadway, the trouble was only beginning.

Near the landing zone, the tow ropes were released and there was a "sudden tremendous silence" as the gliders headed for the dark ground. The men had no seat belts as they braced for impact. Reconnaissance flights had not revealed the presence of two deep ditches that were used by elephants to drag timber to the river. Some of the first gliders had their undercarriages ripped off and lay blocking the makeshift airstrip. The gliders just behind them had to maneuver sharply to avoid the wreckage. Many did not make it and created more obstructions. Attempts to clear the wreckage and help the wounded were complicated by the arrival of more gliders, which emerged from the darkness with the force of bombs. "At times the rending, tearing, crunching sound of wings and fuselages being torn apart was quite deafening," recalled "Mad Mike" Calvert, commander of the first brigade to be inserted, "then all would be quiet for a moment until the cries of the wounded men arose up from the wrecks. Their pitiful calls for help pierced into my shocked mind as I worked with the others to clear up the mess."

Calvert had been given a choice of signals to send: "Pork Sausage" if the landings were successful; "Soya Link" (a widely hated pork substitute) if not. At 2:30 a.m. on Monday, March 6, he sent out "Soya Link," thereby stopping all further flights. In India the faraway commanders figured the "Japs" had ambushed the leading parties. But in fact the Japanese were nowhere to be seen; they were befuddled by the errant gliders landing for hundreds of miles around. At Broadway, 30 Chindits had been killed and 20 wounded but more than 350 had landed unharmed. With the aid of a bulldozer that somehow emerged unscathed from the wreckage of a glider, they worked to clear and improve the airstrip. At 6:30 a.m. Calvert was able to send out "Pork Sausage." That night C-47s began landing at Broadway bringing in reinforcements. Another stronghold, Chowringhee, named after Calcutta's main street, was established not far away.

By March 13, 1944, eight days after the first landing, more than 9,000 men and 1,350 animals, mostly mules whose vocal cords had been cut to prevent them from braying, had arrived in Burma along with 250 tons of stores and batteries of field guns and antiaircraft guns. Wingate announced, "All our Columns are inside the enemy's guts. . . . This is a moment to live in history."

He would not live to see the rest of the history unfold. On March 24, while shuttling between bases in India, his B-25 bomber plunged into a hillside for reasons that remain mysterious. The man who had pioneered the concept of "long-range penetration operations" was just forty-one years old—even younger than T. E. Lawrence when he died.

One of his brigade commanders, Joe Lentaigne, took over the Chindits, but he was no "wayward genius," as one of his men described Wingate; no one was. The Chindits were soon subordinated to the acerbic American general "Vinegar Joe" Stilwell, who made no secret of his disdain for all "Limeys." He proceeded to decimate the Chindits in a lengthy campaign during the monsoon season, which turned roads into knee-deep mud and made it difficult to provide air support, by throwing them repeatedly against well-entrenched Japanese troops.

By the end of June 1944, while on the other side of the planet fresh Allied troops were beginning the liberation of France, the 77th Brigade, 3,000 strong initially, had only 300 fit men left, and they were, one of them noted, "yellow, bedraggled, bearded scarecrows." In the 111th Brigade even fewer were still able to fight—only 119 men. The brigade commanders demanded to be pulled out, noting that Wingate had not envisioned leaving them behind enemy lines for more than three months. Stilwell, stubborn to the end, resisted. Not until August 27, 1944, were the last Chindits flown out—almost six months after the initial landings.

The Chindits had lost 3,628 killed, wounded, and missing, or 18 percent of the force, and 90 percent of those casualties had occurred while under Stilwell's command.[92] They would fight no more. In 1945 they were disbanded. A similar fate was suffered by Merrill's Marauders, an American long-range penetration brigade trained by Wingate that was also "destroyed" in Burma under Stilwell's brutal directives.[93] Survivors of both units would curse Vinegar Joe for decades to come.

Controversy still shrouds the Chindits' operations. Did they substantially weaken the Japanese hold on Burma, as some historians argue, or only shave a "few months," as the official history has it, from the time when northern Burma would have been liberated anyway by regular Indian Army troops?[94] Contemporaries could not agree, and neither can historians. The only certainty is the courage and resilience the Chindits displayed while being pushed to the edge of human endurance and beyond.

✦ ✦ ✦

WINGATE'S ABILITY TO inspire strong feelings, for and against, did not end with his death. Churchill paid tribute to him as "a man of genius who might well have become also a man of destiny." This was an opinion shared by most of his men. One Chindit wrote, "When you first met him you thought he was a maniac—after a week you would have died for him."[95] Yet not all of his subordinates were in "awe of him." A Gurkha officer said, "We did not like him. . . . We were terrified of him."[96] Another officer recalled debating with his colleagues, "Is he mad?"[97] The strain of antipathy was much stronger among the staff officers over whom Wingate rode roughshod. One of them penned an acidulous assessment of him in the official British war history; it suggested that "the moment of his death" may have been "propitious for him."[98] This was the first and probably last time that any official history celebrated the death of a senior officer.

Jack Masters, a Chindit officer who became a well-known novelist, rendered perhaps the most evenhanded verdict when he wrote sixteen years after his commander's death:

> Wingate was sometimes right and sometimes wrong. It really does not matter. What does matter is that he possessed one of the most unusual personalities of recent history. He had a driving will of tremendous power. His character was a blend of mysticism, anger, love, passion, and dark hatred, of overpowering confidence and deepest depression. He could make all kinds of men believe in him, and he could make all kinds of men distrust him.[99]

The same might be said about most other successful guerrilla leaders; it is not a business that rewards those who are too amiable and agreeable.

41.

RESISTANCE AND COLLABORATION

Yugoslavia, 1941–1945, and the Limits of Scorched-Earth Counterinsurgency

THE END OF the Chindits and Marauders did not mean the end of irregular warfare in Burma. In 1943 the OSS infiltrated a unit code-named Detachment 101 to train Kachin tribesmen to fight the Japanese. By 1945 the OSS had over ten thousand guerrillas under arms, while the SOE had succeeded in winning over to the Allied cause the Burma National Army, commanded by Aung San, father of the future Nobel Peace Prize recipient Aung San Suu Kyi, who had initially been in the Japanese camp. By now both the SOE and the OSS, which had been plagued in the war's early years by all the mistakes that characterize a hastily improvised start-up, had gained from experience a much more professional approach to training and tradecraft. They showed what they had learned in Burma, making it, in the judgment of one historian, among "the most successful irregular military operations of the war."[100]

The experience of Burma was a microcosm of the rise and fall of the Greater East Asia Co-Prosperity Sphere. While more-liberal European empires lasted centuries before they expired, the sun rose and set much more quickly on the more-brutish Japanese empire acquired in imitation of the European example. This was due, of course, mainly to the strength of the opposition arrayed against it by the Allies. But the heavy-handed methods employed by the soldiers of the Rising Sun did not help. Unlike the Nazis in

Europe or the Middle East, the Japanese initially had some success harnessing nationalist sentiment with their slogan "Asia for the Asians." They attracted collaborators such as Aung San, Sukarno in the Dutch East Indies (Indonesia), and Subhas Chandra Bose in India. But the "stupid and swinish conduct" of Japanese soldiers, who in China pursued a "three alls" strategy ("kill all, burn all, destroy all"), had alienated most of their subjects by war's end. A 1947 CIA report about Indochina noted, "Japanese terrorism . . . roused the whole people to a general anti-imperialistic feeling."[101] That held true across Asia. There were significant resistance movements in Burma, China, Malaya, and the Philippines. In the Philippines alone there were around 225,000 guerrillas. By the time of MacArthur's landing in 1944, the guerrillas claimed to control 800 of the country's 1,000 municipalities. The guerrillas would not have prevailed without the help of Allied armies, but they did help to make life more difficult for the occupiers.[102]

The record of guerrilla resistance in Western Europe was less impressive. The continent smoldered but never saw an anti-Nazi blaze. The SOE pulled off occasional coups such as sending two Czech agents to assassinate the SS lieutenant general Reinhard Heydrich, the "blond beast," outside Prague in 1942. But the price was fearful. In retaliation for Heydrich's death, the Nazis eradicated two entire villages, Lidice and Lezaky, killing over five thousand people. Such overreaction sowed the seeds of hatred that would come back to haunt the Nazis in the future, but, as a historian of the SOE notes, "In the short run, terror worked, as it usually does."[103]

At least it did in Western and Central Europe where the topography was hardly favorable for guerrilla operations. To avoid bringing an awful fate upon their innocent neighbors, most European resistance movements adopted the refrain of the clandestine Norwegian Milorg (Military Organization): "Lie low, go slow."[104] Accommodation with the Nazis was made easier in the west by the fact that the Nazis did not have the same kind of pathological antipathy for the Belgians or French that they had for Jews and Slavs, whom they labeled *Untermenschen* ("sub-humans"). The Danes, Dutch, and Norwegians were even considered to be fellow Aryans, although that did not save them from invasion. In the Nazi orders for retaliation against partisan attacks, a German soldier's life was worth the lives of "only" five Danes compared with a hundred Poles.[105] Because German occupation in the west was so much milder than in the east, it aroused less opposition.

It was a different story in Eastern Europe. There is always a temptation for any counterinsurgent force, especially one sent by an illiberal state, to resort to the most sanguinary methods imaginable to eradicate resistance from armed civilians. Whatever their short-term impact, such blunderbuss tactics usually fail in the end by arousing more opposition than they eliminate. That was a lesson learned by the Akkadians in ancient Mesopotamia and the French in 1790s Haiti. Such methods are even more counterproductive, as the Japanese, Italians, and Germans were to discover, if the victimized populace can find outside allies to help it fight back.

To their own detriment, the Nazis disregarded the lessons of the more liberal British Empire, which Hitler claimed to admire. The Führer did not seem to notice that the British, in spite of their own dogma of racial superiority, made many accommodations with local rulers and local customs and always held out the hope, however faint, that at some point in the future the empire's subjects would be allowed to rule themselves. There could be no such hope for those enslaved within the Nazi ambit. "What made the Nazis' approach not only unusual but completely counter-productive as a philosophy of rule," notes the historian Mark Mazower, "was their insistence on defining nationalism in such completely narrow terms that it precluded most of the peoples they conquered from ever becoming citizens."[106] In so doing, Hitler disregarded the lessons not only of the British but also of the Romans, who extended citizenship across their domains.

Hard as it may be to believe in retrospect, there was nothing inevitable about the violent loathing that Nazi rule aroused. When the German armies rolled into the Soviet Union, many people, and not only minority nationalities, were ready to welcome them as liberators from Stalinist oppression. At least 650,000 Soviet citizens wound up wearing Wehrmacht uniforms, including many prisoners of war who volunteered to fight under Andrei Vlasov and other captured Red Army generals.[107] There were also numerous volunteers for Waffen SS units from the Baltic states, Ukraine, Hungary, and other parts of Eastern Europe—nearly half a million men in all.[108] But Hitler's draconian decrees and indiscriminate violence alienated most Eastern Europeans and helped give rise to a large and effective partisan movement in the Soviet Union that numbered more than 180,000 fighters and received substantial assistance from the Soviet military and intelligence apparatus.[109]

Like the British army in the American Revolution, the Napoleonic army in the Peninsular War, the federal army in the post–Civil War South, or, for that matter, the Japanese army in China, the Nazis compounded their woes in the East by not deploying enough troops to police rear areas effectively, thereby violating the imperative to achieve a sufficient ratio of counterinsurgents to civilians. The proper ratio is a matter of debate, with estimates ranging from one counterinsurgent per 357 civilians in a relatively peaceful situation to one counterinsurgent per 40 civilians in a more contested environment, but there is little doubt that in the central part of the Soviet Union the counterinsurgent forces were badly understrength: there were an average of just 2 German soldiers per three square miles.[110] After a partisan attack, German units might roll through a village and slaughter everyone in sight, but then they would move on, allowing the partisans to come back. Thus the Germans aroused much hatred but exercised little control: the worst of all worlds. As the power of the occupiers waned, guerrilla attacks increased in keeping with the plan outlined by one Polish resistance fighter in 1939, who had counseled that the underground should reveal itself only when Germany was on the verge of defeat "or at least when one leg buckles. Then we should be able to cut through veins and tendons in the other leg and bring down the German colossus."[111]

In France the German hold began to buckle following the Allied invasion on June 6, 1944. The French Resistance, the maquis, which had been relatively quiescent until then, chose that moment to step up its activities. Cooperation between the Allied armies and the Resistance was facilitated by Jedburgh teams parachuted into France ahead of D-day, each one composed of an SOE or OSS officer, a Free French officer, and a radio operator. General Dwight Eisenhower later claimed, "probably overgenerously" in the estimation of the historian Julian Jackson, that the work of the Resistance had been worth fifteen divisions to him.[112] After Mussolini's overthrow in 1943, Italian guerrillas also proved a valuable adjunct to Allied armies advancing up the peninsula; the guerrillas themselves strung up *Il Duce* and his mistress.

Irregulars who were not able to work with conventional forces did not fare as well. Following the 1943 Warsaw Ghetto uprising, the Nazis razed the entire ghetto. Following the 1944 Warsaw Uprising, they razed the rest of the city. Members of the Polish Home Army, which was behind the 1944 revolt, had mistakenly believed that the Red Army, which was within sight of Warsaw, would come to their aid. Stalin, however, cynically chose to hold back his troops while the Polish patriots, who might have resisted the imposition of Communist rule, were slaughtered. A similar fate was suffered by Naples in 1943 following a four-day uprising against the Nazis, proving once again what the Paris Commune and the Jewish Revolt had already demonstrated: that cities are death traps for large-scale rebellions.

✦ ✦ ✦

Outside the Soviet Union, guerrillas had the biggest impact in the Balkans. This should be no surprise because its rugged terrain, full of mountains and forests, had been home for centuries to irregular fighters who had battled Ottoman domination. Yugoslavia and its southern neighbors, Albania and Greece, all developed highly effective resistance movements that together tied down as many as 24 German divisions out of more than 270, and 31 more Italian divisions, along with Bulgarian, Hungarian, and locally recruited Axis forces—more than a million troops in all.[113]

Arguably the most illustrious resistance leader of the entire war, Josip Broz Tito, emerged out of this Balkan cauldron. An indifferently educated manual laborer with blue eyes, a handsome visage, and a taste for fancy clothes, he had been a labor organizer and operative of the Russian-run Communist International (Comintern) who had spent years in a Yugoslav prison for his subversive work. His original name was Josip Broz; "Tito" was a pseudonym that would cause the Allies much confusion in the early days of World War II—so little did the West know of him at first that some suspected it might not denote an individual at all but a Serbo-Croatian acronym for Secret International Terrorist Organization.

Tito was secretary-general of the Communist Party of Yugoslavia when the Germans invaded in 1941, his predecessor having been eliminated in a Stalinist purge. The Communists were as ill prepared as the rest of Yugoslavia to resist the Wehrmacht onslaught. But drawing on his World War I experience as a decorated sergeant major in the Austro-Hungarian army who had led a platoon that regularly penetrated Russian lines at night—the kind of foray that today would be dubbed "special operations"—Tito managed to organize his own resistance force, the Partisans, with scant outside support. He then outmaneuvered the other major guerrilla army in Yugoslavia, the royalist Chetniks, led by Dragoljub "Draža" Mihailović, a scholarly, long-bearded army colonel with a "mild manner," an always-present pipe, and "gentle eyes that peered sadly from behind thick lenses."[114] A professional officer, he had the full backing of the Yugoslav government-in-exile and of its patrons in London. But Mihailović was also a political naïf and a Serbian chauvinist who had little appeal to Yugoslavia's other nationalities.

Half Croatian, half Slovenian, and all politician, Tito was, by contrast, able to bridge his country's deep sectarian differences and organize a truly national force that survived seven major offensives of "merciless annihilation," in the words of an SOE adviser to the Partisans, mounted by the Germans between the fall of 1941 and the summer of 1944. In this war "with no front and no quarter" (to quote again from the SOE operative and Oxford don William Deakin), Tito's headquarters was on the verge of being overrun on several occasions, but each time he managed to escape, sometimes with only seconds to spare. Having started with just 12,000 party members, Tito by the fall of 1943 commanded a force of over 300,000 fighters. And unlike the Chetniks, who were sometimes drawn into collaboration with the Germans and Italians, the Partisans had no compunctions about relentlessly attacking the occupation forces, notwithstanding the harsh reprisals inevitably suffered by nearby villagers. They knew that German atrocities would only drive more people into their camp—literally so because of the German habit of razing villages near the site of Partisan attacks, forcing villagers to take refuge with the guerrillas.

Acutely conscious of the need to wage political as well as kinetic warfare, Tito took care, noted an OSS operative, "to indoctrinate every group in the liberated areas, even the children," who had to sing ditties such as "Tito Is My Mother and My Father." Every major Partisan unit also had its own printing press to produce Communist propaganda, leading another OSS liaison officer to conclude that "the teaching of Communism has now become as much a part of their activities as fighting." Much like Mao Zedong, Tito showed himself much more attuned to the demands of modern insurgency than the more narrowly military Mihailović or Chiang Kai-shek.

The turning point of the war came in 1944 when the British and American governments, despite their anticommunist leanings, decided to shift their support from the ineffectual Chetniks to the better-organized Partisans. Thereafter Tito's men received copious supplies from the air—more, in fact, than either the French or the Italian resistance received. Tito even relocated his headquarters in 1944 to the Adriatic island of Vis, where, like some James Bond villain in his island lair, he spent the rest of the war under the protection of Anglo-American air and sea power. The Soviet contribution, by contrast, was negligible until the Red Army entered Yugoslavia in September 1944. Their troops were instrumental in the liberation of Belgrade but then moved on, leaving the final battles in Yugoslavia to be won by Tito's forces, which by now had become a regular army.

"Yugoslavia," notes Mark Mazower, "was the only place in Europe where a partisan movement seized control." Tito did not relinquish that control until his death in 1980. He dealt harshly not only with his wartime rivals (Mihailović was captured and executed in 1946) but with all other contenders for power. Only his iron will kept alive the artificial nation of Yugoslavia, which was to expire in a blood-drenched cataclysm a decade after his demise.

Still, for all of Tito's undoubted cunning, ruthlessness, and fortitude, if the Nazi high command had been free to concentrate its resources in Yugoslavia for a prolonged period of time, the Partisans in all likelihood would have been crushed. (The Arab Revolt in World War I would have suffered the same fate if the Ottomans had not been fighting General Allenby's regulars at the same time.) As it was, the liberation struggle took a fearful toll on Yugoslavia: 1 million to 1.5 million people killed out of a prewar population of 16 million.[115] Such are the wages of insurgency, successful or not.

Elsewhere, outside the Balkans, most resistance movements had little more than nuisance value. Admiration for these freedom fighters should not obscure the reality that their role in helping Allied armies was hardly decisive or indispensable.

42.

ASSESSING THE "SUPERSOLDIERS"

Did Commandos Make a Difference?

WHAT OF THE "supersoldiers," the Western commandos who often operated in conjunction with local resistance fighters and garnered so much attention both from contemporaries and from posterity? What was their impact?

Their dramatic contributions cannot be denied. Heroic World War II special operations have provided rich inspiration for a long line of books, movies, and television shows, ranging from Alistair MacLean's *The Guns of Navarone* (1957) and ABC's *The Rat Patrol* (1966–68) to Hampton Sides's *Ghost Soldiers* (2001) and Quentin Tarantino's *Inglorious Basterds* (2009). One would have to have a heart of stone not to chortle over escapades such as that carried out by two young SOE officers wearing German uniforms who in 1944 kidnapped a German general on Crete and drove him in his own staff car through twenty-two checkpoints to a hideout and an eventual transfer by sea to Cairo.[116] But was this mission worthwhile? The loss of one general did nothing to shake the German hold on Crete. The loss of the brilliant field marshal Erwin Rommel might have been more significant, but an attempt by British commandos to kidnap or kill him in North Africa in 1941 was a "total failure" that resulted in the loss of thirty valuable men.[117]

Similar questions of cost-effectiveness could be raised about many other equally daring exploits. As could questions of morality. Operations in occupied territories inevitably subjected the local people to savage retaliation by the Germans or Japanese. They also implicated Britain and America in actions that were denounced by their enemies as "terrorism"—with considerable justification. Was it worth it?

Field Marshal Slim, one of the most respected commanders of World War II, wrote that "special units and formations . . . did not give militarily a worth-while return for the resources in men, material, and time that they absorbed." He thought they were positively deleterious because they skimmed off the best men from ordinary units, thereby lowering "the quality of the rest of the Army." Slim famously concluded, "Armies do not win wars by means of a few bodies of super-soldiers but by the average quality of their standard units."[118] Another British soldier groused about "anti-social irresponsible individualists" who contributed "nothing to Allied victory" and "who sought a more personal satisfaction from the war than of standing their chance, like proper soldiers, of being bayoneted in a slit trench or burnt alive in a tank."[119]

Similar thinking was prevalent in the senior ranks of all the Allied armies at war's end. Stalin naturally rushed to disband partisan formations that were not fully under his control and therefore could pose a threat to his regime. The Red Army and NKVD secret police were to spend several years after World War II suppressing nationalist guerrillas in Ukraine, the Baltic Republics, Poland, and other parts of the Soviet empire. In Britain, of all the special formations created during the war, only the Special Air Service, Special Boat Service, and Royal Marine Commandos survived and that only after an interregnum. (SAS was deactivated in 1945, reactivated in 1947.) The U.S. Marines, with their strong sense of egalitarianism, had disbanded their Raiders even before the war's end and would not field discrete special operations forces for another sixty years. The U.S. Army likewise did away with its Rangers. They were briefly revived during the Korean War, then disbanded again, until being reactivated again for good in 1969 to fight in Vietnam. The OSS also was dissolved after the war but had a faster rebirth as the CIA in 1947. The "unconventional warfare," that is, guerrilla warfare, mission—which before World War II had been performed by a combination of militia and regular soldiers on an improvised, ad hoc basis, and during the war had been carried out primarily by the OSS—was divided in the postwar era between the CIA and the Army Special Forces, which were established in 1952.

The post-1945 record thus reveals initial skepticism about the utility of special forces followed by their begrudging acceptance and eventually an enthusiastic embrace in the post-9/11 era. This ambivalence is not hard to explain. While the limited use of such operatives in World War I, most notably T. E. Lawrence, had been almost exclusively positive, the record in World War II was more extensive and more mixed. Missions behind enemy lines gathered valuable intelligence and kept enemy troops tied down on internal security duties. But raids also suffered heavy losses and left civilians vulnerable to retaliation. Even when successful, such pinpricks seldom had much of an impact on the course of the campaign. When asked after the war about the impact of the French Resistance on the German war machine, Armaments Minister Albert Speer scoffed: "What French resistance?"[120]

There were some sabotage operations that really hampered the Germans. In 1942 Greek partisans with the aid of the SOE blew up a portion of the Athens–Salonika railway that carried supplies to Rommel's Afrika Korps, hampering its retreat after the Battle of El Alamein. In 1943 an SOE team disguised as students on a skiing holiday blew up a Norwegian heavy-water plant that was needed for Germany's atomic-bomb program. In 1944 SOE agents in France replaced the normal axle oil in a train used to transport German tanks with an abrasive grease that gums up the works. This helped delay for seventeen days the arrival of a Waffen SS armored division in Normandy at the start of the Allied invasion. All those operations, and a few others, had genuine strategic significance. But such examples are rare.[121]

Against these successes must be weighed the more numerous failures, such as the infamous commando raid on the French port of Dieppe in 1942 or, on a lesser scale, the SAS attacks the same year on the Libyan port of Benghazi. In his rollicking memoir, Fitzroy Maclean, an aristocratic British diplomat turned soldier, described how he and a few other SAS operatives, including Randolph Churchill, were successfully escorted eight hundred miles across the desert to Benghazi in a specially modified Ford station wagon by the Long-Range Desert Group, only to find that, apparently having gotten advance warning, the Italian garrison was on its guard. They had no choice but to sneak out of town. On the way home, their vehicle overturned and Maclean woke up from a morphine haze to find himself with a "fractured collar bone, a broken arm and what seemed to be a fractured skull." After recovering, he participated in another, even bigger raid on Benghazi that likewise caused scant damage to the Axis but inflicted considerable casualties on the SAS and its supporting forces. Maclean was lucky to escape what another participant called "a complete fiasco." On a subsequent mission, David Stirling, founder of SAS, was captured by the Germans and spent the rest of the war a prisoner.[122] To its credit, the SAS did manage to destroy nearly four hundred German and Italian aircraft on the ground.[123] This was a serious but hardly mortal blow to the Afrika Korps, which could not possibly have been defeated save by the employment of conventional force.

Part of the problem in the war's early days was that training and doctrine, coordination and planning for special operations were still in their infancy. Early operations were often amateurish. But even the more professional forces at war's end still had a high rate of misfires. The Alamo Scouts, a small American outfit engaged in reconnaissance missions behind Japanese lines in the Pacific, was unique in having no fatalities.[124] Most special-warfare units suffered heavily. Britain's commandos, for example, saw nearly 10 percent of their men die in action—a far higher rate than in the regular army.[125] Civilians in the areas where irregulars operated paid a particularly stiff price. Ray Hunt, an American guerrilla leader in the Philippines, concluded that his efforts were of "great value to the American army in the latter stages of the war," but he nevertheless wrote that "the Filipino people would have been better off" had there been no uprising because so many of them "were killed, maimed, despoiled, and brutalized."[126] Hunt knew, of course, that the Filipinos would have been liberated eventually by the U.S. Army even if not a single guerrilla had taken up arms.

Perhaps the most important impact of behind-the-lines operations was psychological. Special operations were a bonanza for propagandists who portrayed every mission as a triumph against overwhelming odds—whatever the facts. (Fitzroy Maclean wrote after one of SAS's forays into Benghazi, "We were gratified to find ourselves and our operation described in the popular press in such glowing terms as to be scarcely recognizable.")[127] The fighting spirit of the Western publics was thus boosted in dark times as was the pride of occupied peoples who were led to believe they had aided in their own liberation.

From the Western perspective the latter consequence was to prove a mixed blessing. Proxy armies are always difficult for their sponsors to control—often impossible. By arming and aiding indigenous resistance movements (SOE alone distributed a million Sten submachine guns around the world),[128] Allied operatives were in many cases putting guns into the hands of people who would soon turn on them. The resulting "wars of national liberation" are the subject of the next section.

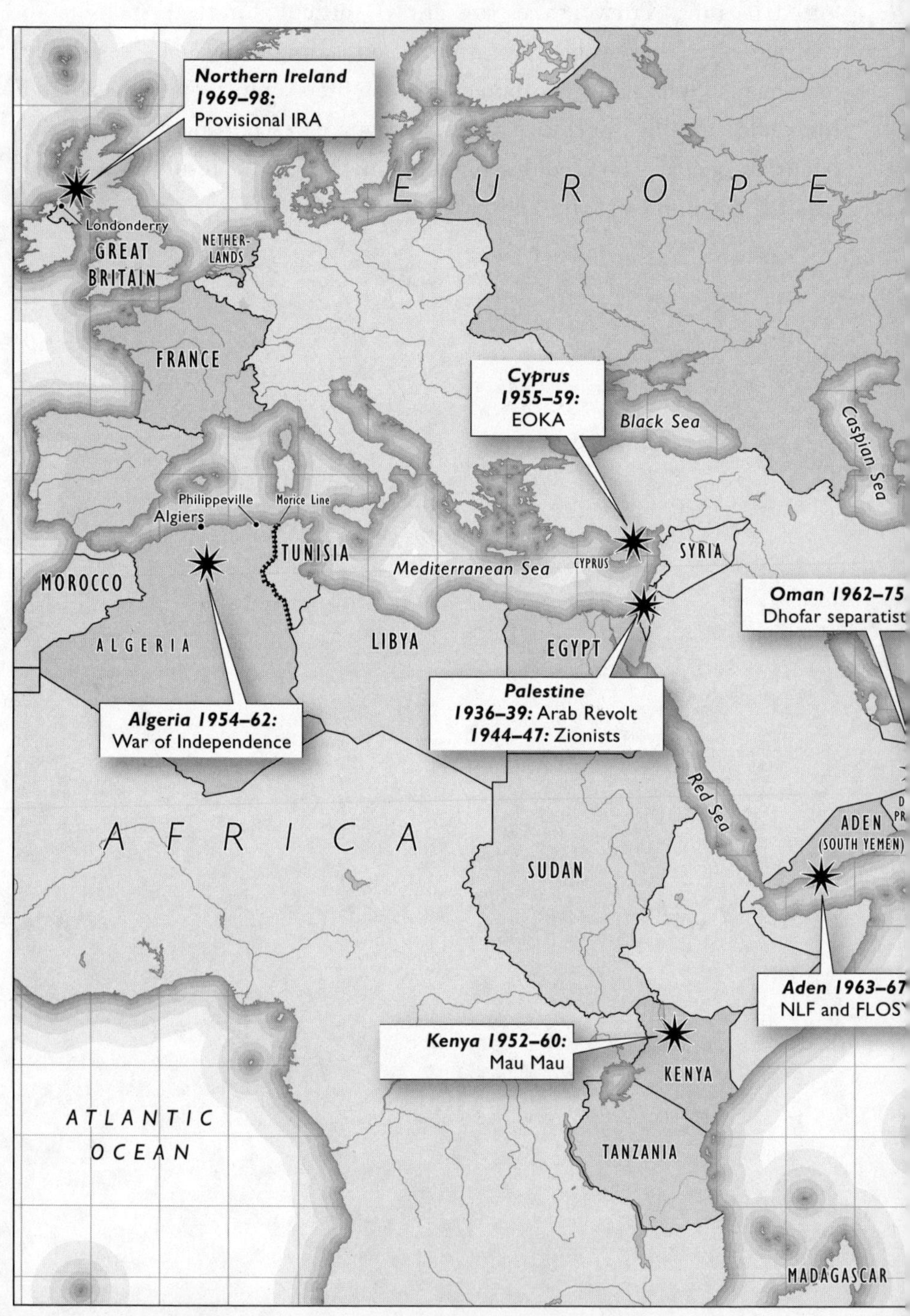
Northern Ireland
1969–98:
Provisional IRA
Londonderry
GREAT
BRITAIN
NETHER-
LANDS
E U R O P E
FRANCE
Cyprus
1955–59:
EOKA
Black Sea
Caspian Sea
Philippeville
Morice Line
Algiers
TUNISIA
Mediterranean Sea
CYPRUS
SYRIA
MOROCCO
ALGERIA
LIBYA
EGYPT
Oman 1962–75
Dhofar separatist
Palestine
1936–39: Arab Revolt
1944–47: Zionists
Algeria 1954–62:
War of Independence
Red Sea
ADEN
(SOUTH YEMEN)
A F R I C A
SUDAN
Aden 1963–67
NLF and FLOSY
Kenya 1952–60:
Mau Mau
KENYA
ATLANTIC
OCEAN
TANZANIA
MADAGASCAR

BOOK VI
THE END OF EMPIRE
The Wars of "National Liberation"

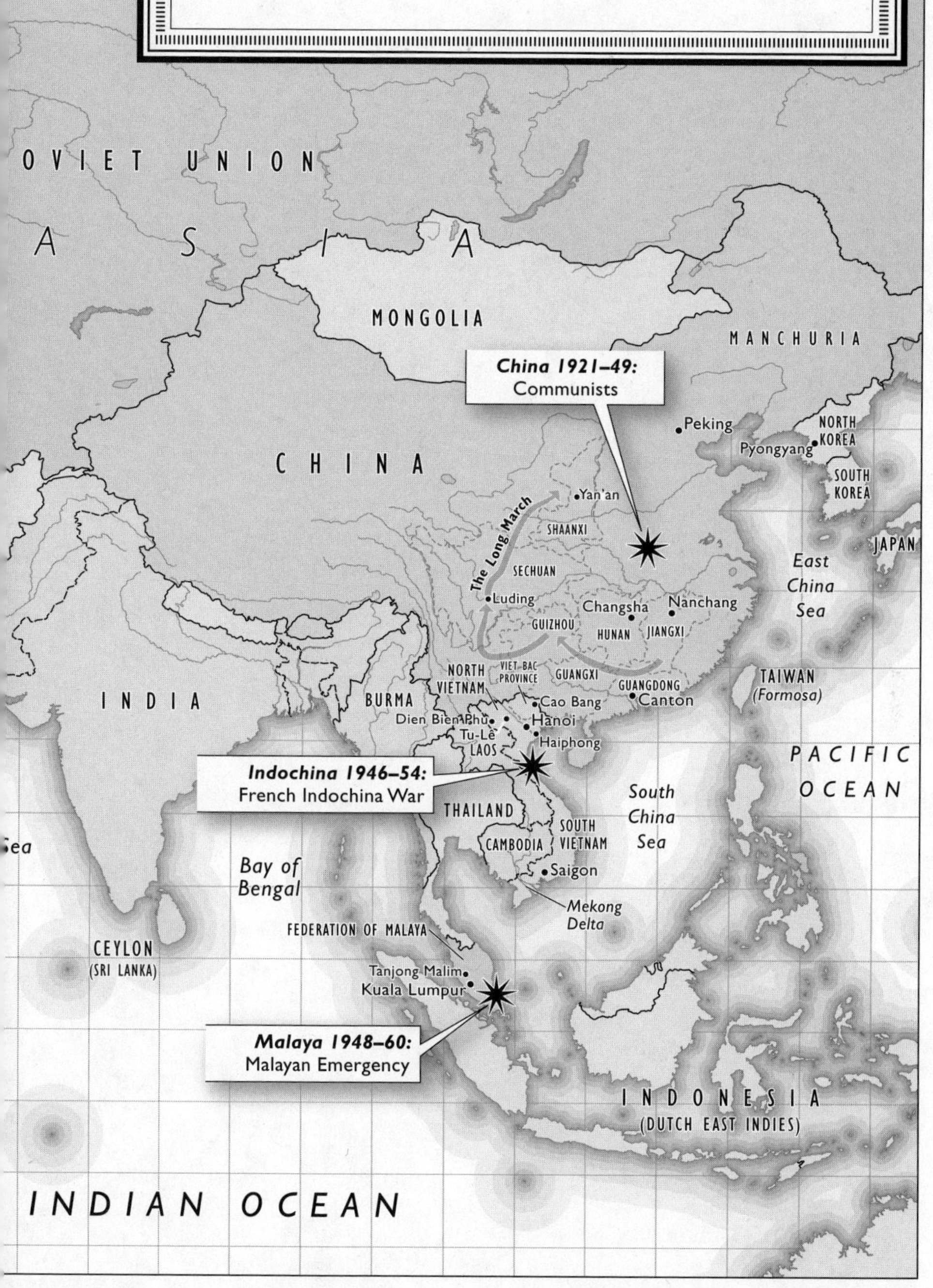

43.

THE WORLD AFTER THE WAR

The Slipping European Grip

German bombs and rockets had ceased to fall on Liverpool and London, but for the people of Britain life did not improve markedly after the end of World War II. "People are suddenly realizing," a *New Yorker* correspondent wrote soon after Japan's surrender, "that in the enormous economic blitz that has just begun, their problems may be as serious as the blitz they so recently scraped through." Some 750,000 houses had been destroyed or damaged, public debt was at record levels, the pound devalued, unemployment rising. Britain had to rely on a loan from the United States as a lifeline, even as the new Labour government was launching a dramatic expansion of costly government programs in health care, schooling, unemployment insurance, and old-age pensions.

Rationing remained in effect, covering everything from meat, eggs, and butter to clothes, soap, and gasoline. As one housewife noted, "Queues were everywhere, for wedge-heeled shoes, pork-pies, fish, bread & cakes, tomatoes—& emergency ration-cards at the food office." Even in the House of Commons dining room, the only meat on offer was whale or seal steak. The situation deteriorated even more in the harsh winter of 1947–48. Coal, gas, and electricity were all in short supply. Everyone seemed to be shivering and complaining, as the college student Kingsley Amis put it, "CHRIST ITS [*sic*] BLEEDING COLD."

The inclement weather heightened the sense of ruin and decay that Christopher Isherwood, the expatriate writer, found upon his return to London for the first time after the war. He noted that plaster was "peeling from even the most fashionable squares and crescents," that "hardly a building was freshly painted," and that "once stylish restaurants" had been "reduced to drabness and even squalor." He wondered, "Were there to be no fruits of victory?"[1]

The situation was profoundly worse in France, which at the end of 1944 was just emerging from the trauma of occupation and the death of more than 600,000 of its citizens. More than 10,000 women who were accused of having consorted with German soldiers had their heads shaved; many were beaten, even forced to run the streets naked with swastikas painted on their bodies.

Malnutrition was a serious problem, with the average height of children falling "dramatically." There was panic buying in bakeries, as customers who took too many baguettes were being attacked by those who had to do without. Even wine, the most Gallic of beverages, was hard to get. And that was not the only humiliating shortfall. In the new government proclaimed by Charles de Gaulle, notes a recent history, "writing paper was in such short supply that they had to use up the remaining batches of Vichy letterhead, striking out 'État Français' at the top and typing in 'République Française' underneath."[2]

✦ ✦ ✦

IT IS VITAL to underscore how weak the two biggest colonial powers were by 1945 in order to understand why decolonization swept the world in the next few years and why anti-Western guerrillas and terrorists appeared to be ascendant. This part of the book will examine Mao Zedong's triumph in China, Ho Chi Minh's victory in Indochina against the French, the FLN's defeat of the French in Algeria, and (the lone success for the counterinsurgents) Britain's suppression of a communist revolt in Malaya. But focusing on individual wars can easily give the sense that armed rebels defeated their old colonial masters. It would be more accurate to say that the empires were beaten from within. Nationalist uprisings contributed to the end of the imperial age, but seldom were they the decisive factor.

Even if Britain and France had been determined to hold on to all their overseas possessions after 1945, they would have been hard-pressed to do so. Both were essentially bankrupt. Neither country could comfortably fight a prolonged counterinsurgency. Especially not in the face of hostility from the rising superpowers that had usurped their place on the world stage. The Soviets, and later the Chinese, were always ready to provide arms, training, and financing to "national liberation" movements of a Marxist bent. The United States, for its part, despite its support for rebuilding Western Europe, had little sympathy with attempts to prolong European rule overseas. As the editors of *Life* magazine "bluntly" informed "the People of England" in 1942: "we are not fighting . . . to hold the British Empire together."[3] Indeed the United States pressed Britain to end its rule from India to Palestine. Later, as the Cold War heated up, Washington would modify its stance; it showed a willingness, for example, to bankroll the French war in Indochina. But in general the Americans viewed the continuation of colonial rule as a gift to communist subversives.

In 1948–49 the Truman administration threatened an end to Marshall Plan funding for the Netherlands if it did not end its efforts to put down a nationalist revolt in Indonesia.[4] Seven years later, in a more high-profile confrontation, the Eisenhower administration threatened to let the pound collapse unless Britain, and its allies, France and Israel, ended their military operation to seize the Suez Canal and overthrow Egypt's strongman, Gamal Abdel Nasser. Threatened with financial ruin, Britain and France had no choice but to give in, thus demonstrating the pathetic depth of their postwar weakness.

Even before then the British elite had already largely given up the imperial ghost. The theories of racial superiority that had once underpinned white rule over Asians and Africans had been discredited in different ways by the Nazis and Japanese. A British officer wrote in 1945 that, walking in Calcutta, he felt "rather like a Nazi officer must have felt walking along a Paris boulevard."[5]

Nationalism had been percolating for decades in what became known as the Third World, thanks to the proliferation of European ideas. The desire for independence had been held in uneasy check by fear of the consequences, but the fall of Singapore in 1942, when 85,000 British troops surrendered to a Japanese force one-third their size, shattered once and for all any illusions about European invincibility.[6] By war's end, colonial elites were no longer willing to accept European rule—and in most cases Europeans were not willing to impose it at gunpoint.

In 1946 a British government publication declared, "British 'Imperialism' is dead."[7] To be sure, even Clement Atlee's Labour government, which held power from 1945 to 1951, had no intention of dissolving the empire overnight. Initially Atlee hoped for a slow, stately process "to guide the colonial territories to responsible self-government within the Commonwealth."[8] But it soon became clear that procrastination would not be possible. Despite the opposition leader Winston Churchill's impassioned warnings that "premature, hurried scuttle" carried "the taint and smear of shame,"[9] independence was rushed for India, Palestine, and other colonies, leading to bloody civil wars. As one Labour minister acknowledged in 1948, "If you are in a place where you are not wanted, and where you have not got the force, or perhaps the will, to squash those who do not want you, the only thing to do is to come out."[10]

Come out Britain did beginning in 1947 with the transfer of power in India, continuing in 1948 with Burma, Ceylon (Sri Lanka), and Palestine, resuming in 1956 with Sudan, followed the next year by the Gold Coast (Ghana) and Malaya. The rest of the African colonies were given their freedom a few years later. By 1967, the year that Prime Minister Harold Wilson announced the abandonment of commitments "East of Suez," almost all of the empire was gone. Notwithstanding a few rearguard actions such as the Falkland Islands War in 1982, the age of imperialism was effectively over.

Most of the process was relatively peaceful. Jawaharlal Nehru and Mahatma Gandhi showed in India how civil disobedience, strikes, and protests—"a sort of non-violent warfare," Orwell called it—could shame a liberal empire into withdrawal. (These were methods, Orwell noted, that "could not be applied in a country where opponents of the regime disappear in the middle of the night and are never heard of again.") Their example of "shaking empires by sheer spiritual power"[11] (Orwell again) was emulated by

Kwame Nkrumah in Ghana, Julius Nyerere in Tanzania, Jomo Kenyatta in Kenya, and other independence leaders in Africa. All of them were helped by the United Nations' newfound ability to marshal international opinion against imperialism.

Where the British did face violent opposition, it did not take much to persuade them to leave. In 1947 the British cabinet decided to abandon Palestine after three years of attacks by Jewish terrorists, most belonging to the right-wing Irgun and Lehi (a.k.a. "the Stern Gang"), had killed 338 Britons—fewer than had died during one day of the retreat from Kabul in 1842. This was one of the more successful terrorist campaigns ever waged; Churchill called it a "hell-disaster." But as important as bombs, such as the one that blew up the British headquarters in the King David Hotel in 1946 (an Irgun operation that killed 91 people), was the force of moral suasion exemplified by the *Exodus* affair. In 1947 the Royal Navy intercepted a ship called *Exodus from Europe—1947* packed full of Jewish refugees trying to reach the Holy Land. In the process of taking over the vessel, Royal Marines killed and wounded a number of the passengers. The British then sailed the ship to Germany, where the passengers were off-loaded in "the land of their annihilation." As the Israeli historian Benny Morris notes, this was a "major propaganda coup": "Nothing could have done more to promote the Zionist cause."[12]

Britain generally fought only to hold on to a few bases such as Cyprus and Aden deemed to be of strategic significance—or, as in Malaya and Kenya, to prevent a takeover by Communists or other extremists. When they did choose to fight, the British often did so skillfully and successfully; their counterinsurgency record is better than that of the French during the same period, and some of their campaigns, notably that in Malaya, are still studied by military strategists. But Britain was as successful as it was in large part because it was careful to pick its spots and not get mired in hopeless struggles to perpetuate unpopular rule in the dawning age of national self-determination. Belgium likewise gave up its only colony, Congo, without a fight in 1960.

The French remained more truculent, perhaps in reaction to their all-too-accommodating behavior before the war. They saw a need to hold on to their empire in order to resurrect lost glory and erase the humiliation of defeat. In 1945–46 they slaughtered thousands of Algerians and Vietnamese, and hundreds of Syrians, to reestablish their rule. In 1947–48 they killed at least 11,200 people to quash a revolt in Madagascar.[13] But, like the British, the French were willing to grant independence to most of their African colonies with no bloodshed. (Even Madagascar became an independent member of the French Community, the Francophone version of the British Commonwealth, in 1960.) And, as we shall see, their will to prosecute the wars in Indochina and Algeria was severely limited.

So too with the Dutch, who abandoned Indonesia after an unpopular "police action" in 1947–48.

The Portuguese, under their fascist dictator Antonio Salazar, held out the longest. They did not abandon their Africa colonies, Guinea-Bissau, Angola, and Mozambique, until 1974–75 following a coup d'état in Lisbon. Significantly, the end of the Portuguese Empire, as with the Russian Empire nearly two decades later, was brought about on the home front—not on a distant battlefield.

✦ ✦ ✦

NONE OF THIS is meant to trivialize the accomplishments of nationalist rebels; only to place them in the proper perspective. That sort of perspective was lacking in the immediate post–World War II era when the myth of guerrilla invincibility was born. By the mid-1970s, following the American defeat in Vietnam, it was easy for an informed observer to believe that it was virtually impossible for a conventional army to defeat an unconventional foe. Nothing could be further from the truth; as our survey should have already shown, the odds remain stacked against those who adopt guerrilla or terrorist tactics. For guerrillas to triumph they usually require outside assistance along with a major lack of acumen or will on the part of the government under siege. All of these factors were present in China, whose civil war would serve as a template for postwar insurgencies.

Its inclusion in a section entitled "The End of Empire" may seem strange since the Chinese Communists triumphed over a homegrown regime, not one imposed from abroad. But the revolutionary struggle in China had long been fueled by opposition to imperialism, first Western, then Japanese.

Part of the Communists' winning strategy was to paint their enemies as the "running dogs" and "lackeys" of the "imperialists" and to depict themselves as the true champions of Chinese independence. Moreover, Mao Zedong's triumph would serve as inspiration for countless imitators across the Third World intent on overthrowing regimes ruled by Westerners or friendly to them. It is impossible to understand what came later—what happened in the 1950s and 1960s, the great age of communist and nationalist insurgency—without understanding how the "Reds" came to power in the world's most populous nation in the 1940s.

44.

THE RISE OF THE RED EMPEROR

Mao Zedong's Long March to Power, 1921–1949

THE STORY BEGINS in Shanghai. This is where the Chinese Communist Party was born—an appropriate birthplace because communism was a Western import and Shanghai was, and still is, the most Western of mainland Chinese cities. In the 1920s much of the metropolis was ruled by "foreign devils": Britons and Americans in the International Settlement, the French in their Concession next door, and the Japanese with an informal concession of their own. They had made Shanghai what it was—the "Paris of the East" or the "Whore of the Orient," take your pick—a modern, bustling metropolis of palatial hotels and department stores, exclusive clubs, sleazy opium dens, louche cabarets and anything-goes brothels, broad boulevards jammed with cars and carts, rickshaws and electric trams. It was a major center of commerce, journalism, and the arts and a draw for hucksters, merchants, bankers, prostitutes, gangsters, intellectuals, missionaries, and refugees from across China and, indeed, the world.[14]

This Westernized city depended on countless Chinese laborers who lived in slums where disease was rampant and opportunities for advancement minimal. And even their existence was luxurious compared with that of the peasants, the vast majority of the Chinese population, who led lives that had changed little for millennia, toiling the jade green earth, always a flood or drought away from starvation. The average income of China's 460 million people was just $12 a year, and 10 percent of the population owned more than 50 percent of the land. In retrospect historians can discern considerable evidence of positive evolution during this period, with rising standards of living, a vibrant intellectual scene, and the first stirrings of parliamentary democracy and the rule of law. But that was not how it looked at the time. Mao Zedong aptly summarized the contemporary consensus when he said that China was "semi-colonial and semi-feudal."[15]

Its humiliating backwardness had already sparked two unsuccessful uprisings that had undermined the imperial system: the Taiping Rebellion from 1850 to 1864 and the Boxer Rebellion in 1900. The Manchu dynasty was finally toppled by a military mutiny in 1911. Yet no durable government emerged after the last emperor's abdication. China was divided among regional warlords, many of them corrupt and predatory. A rising young generation hungered for an alternative, a regime that would make life better for all and restore the Celestial Empire's long-lost greatness.

It was in these conditions that in July 1921 thirteen delegates gathered in a girls' school, closed for the summer, on Rue Bourgeat in Shanghai's French Concession. They were joined by two European representatives of the Comintern, the Russian-run Communist International, which was responsible for convening the meeting. The First Congress of the Chinese Communist Party ended ingloriously a few days later when the delegates had to flee just ahead of a police raid. At the time the entire party had just fifty-seven members.

Although he was present at the First Congress, twenty-seven-year-old Mao Zedong was not one of its leaders. The first secretary-general was a prominent university professor from Peking. Mao, by contrast, was, in the words of a fellow attendee, "a pale-faced . . . youth" who "had not yet shaken off his rough Hunanese ways"; "in his long gown of native cloth [he] looked rather like a Taoist priest out of some village."[16]

Far from trying to hide his country bumpkin origins, Mao reveled in them, using his "rough" habits to shock his more cosmopolitan colleagues. Years later, when he was already on the cusp of power, a visitor "saw him absent-mindedly turn down the belt of his trousers and search for some guests"—lice. Like many peasants, he never learned to brush his teeth, preferring to rinse out his mouth with tea, and refused to visit a dentist. By the time he was China's "chairman," after a lifetime of chain smoking, his teeth were "covered with a heavy greenish film"; later they would turn black and fall out. He also refused to bathe, preferring to be rubbed down with a hot, wet towel. Likewise he resisted Western flush toilets; he would travel everywhere with a "squat-style privy." And he never lost his affinity for the oily, spicy cuisine of his native Hunan, which was to make him portly in middle age. He often joked that a "love of pepper" was necessary for any true revolutionary.[17]

It goes without saying, however, that Mao was no ordinary peasant. For a start, his family was more wealthy than most; his father would have qualified as one of the "rich peasants" he would later "liquidate." Perhaps it is no coincidence that Mao loathed his father. Born in 1893, he was, like many other guerrilla leaders, a rebel from childhood on, arguing with his "harsh and severe"[18] father in public, running away from home, even threatening to commit suicide if he didn't get his way. He firmly resisted his father's imprecations to prepare for a life on the farm. He was the "family scholar," always reading, always dreaming. His favorite books were tales of bandits and peasant rebels—the Chinese version of Robin Hood.[19] He also studied Chinese imperial history. Later in life, one of Mao's intimates was to write that he "identified with China's emperors" and "that his greatest admiration was reserved for the most ruthless and cruel."[20] No doubt he was drawn to strong leaders because the China of his youth conspicuously lacked them; from the ages of eighteen (1911) to thirty-five (1928) he lived in a country where warlords held sway and disorder reigned, even if it also saw rapid economic and intellectual progress, with the founding of great universities and the rudiments of parliamentary government.

Much as he hated his father, Mao benefited from his generosity in funding his education. He attended expensive schools at an age when most of his contemporaries were working the fields. Mao became politically aware while studying in Changsha, capital of Hunan Province. He was attracted to "liberalism, democratic reformism, and utopian socialism," and bemoaned the "ignorance and darkness" of his country. In 1911 he and his friends cut off their pigtails in defiance of the tottering Manchu dynasty. In an early indication of his dictatorial personality, this eighteen-year-old radical also "assaulted" friends and "forcibly removed their queues."

That year Mao joined a revolutionary army as a private but did not see battle. His arrogance was already becoming evident: as a student, Mao thought he was too good to fetch his own water from a well as the other soldiers did. He was not attracted to a military career and left after six months. He spent the next five years in a teacher training school. Upon graduation in 1918, he briefly followed one of his teachers to Peking, where he got a job as an assistant in the library of Peking University—the closest he ever got to a higher education. Here Mao met many of China's leading intellectuals, "but to most of them," he later recalled, "I didn't exist as a human being" because "my office was so low." He would amply repay such disdain decades later when he would consign millions of intellectuals to death, imprisonment, and hard labor.

Returning to Changsha in 1919, he became more active in politics. He founded a radical student newspaper and also a radical bookstore that turned a profit, showing his talents for propaganda and organization. Both skills—so essential for modern insurgency—would come in handy once he joined the nascent Communist Party as secretary of the Hunan branch, where his first job was organizing labor unions.[21]

✦ ✦ ✦

THE COMMUNIST PARTY was so weak in those days that its Russian sponsors forced it into a marriage of convenience with the Kuomintang, the Nationalist Party founded in 1912 by Sun Yat-sen, which claimed more than 100,000 members.[22] Following Sun's death in 1925, leadership was assumed by his brother-in-law, an idealistic young army officer of socialist leanings and Methodist faith who had studied in both Japan and Russia. His name was Chiang Kai-shek, and he had much in common with Mao. A biographer's description of Chiang—"Although often introverted, he could be a bully, self-righteous, and arrogant"[23]—applies equally well to Mao.

Chiang's initial power base was the Whampoa Military Academy, near Canton, where his political commissar was Zhou Enlai, already a dedicated Communist, later Mao's right-hand man. Mao, too, served the Kuomintang between 1923 and 1927; at one time, he was head of its Propaganda Department. The Communists eagerly cooperated with Chiang when he set out on his Northern Expedition in 1926 to defeat the warlords and unify the country—a task in which he was only partially successful.

Both Communists and Nationalists were prepared, however, to betray the other when the time was right. Chiang struck first. On April 12, 1927, his men, acting in cooperation with secret-society hoodlums, started killing and jailing Communists in Shanghai. Thus began China's protracted civil war, which was to last, on and off, for twenty-two years. The Communists were caught unprepared and suffered heavy losses. A pivotal role in their counter-offensive was played by Zhu De, a former warlord general with a "pock-marked complexion and bull-dog figure"[24] who was Kuomintang security chief in Nanchang, capital of Jiangxi Province. Zhu was among the renegade officers who led 20,000 troops in an uprising against the Nationalists on August 1, 1927. The revolt was quelled quickly, but it was to mark the birth of the People's Liberation Army. Some of the defeated troops under Zhu wound up joining a guerrilla force being organized by Mao Zedong in rural Jiangxi.[25]

By this time, Mao had already shown considerable interest in employing China's numerous peasants, rather than its tiny proletariat, as the instigators of revolution. "All imperialists, warlords, corrupt officials, and bad gentry will meet their doom at the hands of the peasants," Mao wrote in early 1927, predicting the country folk would rise "with the fury of a hurricane."[26] He did not know exactly how long it would take ("Marxists are not fortune-tellers"),[27] but he knew that a peasant revolution could not be carried out as quickly as an urban uprising like the one that had brought the Bolsheviks to power in Russia. The task of organizing a peasant army was essential to the process because, in Mao's view, "political power grows out of the barrel of a gun."[28] This ran contrary to Marxist orthodoxy, which favored political organizing among urban workers, and Mao was for many years in disfavor with the Russian-dominated party apparatus. He was even expelled from the Politburo at one point for "rightism."[29]

His doubters found vindication when Mao's Workers and Peasants Revolutionary Army, organized from among Kuomintang defectors, peasants, and miners, failed miserably in its September 1927 assault on Changsha, known as the Autumn Harvest uprising. Mao himself was captured and barely escaped. Much as Osama bin Laden would do in the fall of 2001 when he eluded an American manhunt by escaping across the Hindu Kush into Pakistan, he retreated with the battered remnants of his force into the inaccessible Jinggang Mountains on the Hunan–Jiangxi border. Here he supplemented his army by recruiting local bandits who hid out in the pine and bamboo forests among the "wolves, boars, even leopards and tigers."[30] In January 1929, under attack by the Kuomintang, they were forced to move to a new base on the Jiangxi–Fujian border. There were a few other Red bases scattered around China, but this became the biggest—the Central Soviet Area. Leadership was shared by Mao and Zhu De, who was older and had the military experience Mao lacked.

Working together so closely that many peasants assumed they were one man—"Zhu Mao"[31]—they began to formulate the guerrilla-warfare strategy that eventually, thanks to his cult of personality, would become associated with Mao alone. The heart of their approach was summarized in a sixteen-character formula that echoed Sun Tzu: "the enemy advances, we withdraw; the enemy camps, we harass; the enemy tires, we attack; the enemy retreats, we pursue." In carrying out these classic guerrilla-warfare precepts, the Communists were always conscious of the need to win peasant support. In Mao's famous formulation, "The people are like water and the army is like fish." So as not to "dry up the water" as "undisciplined armies" did, Red soldiers were instructed to "replace all doors when you leave a house" (doors were often detached and used as beds), "be courteous and polite," "pay for all articles," and "establish latrines a safe distance from people's houses."[32] Mao always stressed the need to "keep the closest possible relations with the common people."[33]

To broaden their appeal, the Communists embarked on a massive land redistribution campaign, taking property from the "evil gentry," "lawless landlords," and "rich peasants" and giving it to the poor.[34] Although he would be seen by credulous foreign sympathizers as someone carrying out a "moderate program of agrarian reform"—*not* "Communism as it is understood anywhere else in the world"[35]—Mao had not the "slightest compunction" about demanding, in his own words, the "massacre" of "the landlords and despotic gentry as well as their running dogs."[36] Like Stalin, he also lashed out ruthlessly against enemies, real or imagined, within the party in a prelude to the terrifying purges that would sweep China in the 1950s and 1960s.

Anyone who questioned Mao's strategy was accused of membership in a

Nationalist conspiracy called the AB (Anti-Bolshevik) League. Mao formed "committees for eliminating counter-revolutionaries" and told them to use "the most merciless torture" to ferret out supposed AB members. "Leniency toward the enemy is a crime against the revolution," he proclaimed in words that echoed the fervor of French revolutionaries of the 1790s. One accused party official recalled how his interrogators "burned my body with incense sticks" and then broke his two thumbs; they were "just barely hanging together by the skin." By such methods were phony confessions extracted that were used to round up more "traitors." One security man explained the technique: "You force him to confess, then he confesses, you believe him and you kill him; or, he does not confess and you kill him."

Thousands of cadres and soldiers perished in this internal bloodletting in 1930–31, which sparked a Red Army mutiny. The Nationalists, who, it should be noted, committed numerous massacres of their own, later claimed that 186,000 people had been killed altogether in the Jiangxi Soviet. Even if this figure was exaggerated, the reality was bad enough. Mao was not troubled in the least. He was, a confidant later wrote, "devoid of human feeling, incapable of love, friendship or warmth." The only thing that mattered to him, another colleague said, was "the moving of people through the motions of carrying out his own grand designs." All he would say about those who perished in the process was that "lives have to be sacrificed in the cause of the revolution."[37]

✦ ✦ ✦

CHIANG'S NATIONALISTS MOUNTED four unsuccessful "encirclement" campaigns against the Jiangxi Soviet with hundreds of thousands of troops. The Mao-Zhu strategy of "luring the enemy in deep" worked repeatedly. The Red Army would allow the better-armed Kuomintang forces to become overextended before counterattacking with devastating results. Yet Chiang did not give up. He mustered more than half a million troops for his fifth and final encirclement campaign beginning in August 1933.

This time the Nationalists adopted a new strategy at the urging of their German military advisers. Instead of blundering deep into Red territory, they advanced slowly, building thousands of blockhouses ("turtle-shells") connected by new roads, telephone, and telegraph lines.[38] This tactic, which had been employed by the British in the Boer War, strangled the Soviet base, reducing its defenders to starvation. Counterattacks against the well-entrenched Kuomintang troops were futile. The Communists were also hurt by a popular backlash against the terror they had inflicted on Jiangxi. This was one of the "methodological and technical errors" that caused the Politburo to strip Mao temporarily of most of his party posts.[39]

✦ ✦ ✦

IN OCTOBER 1934 the senior Communist leadership—which did not include Mao, who was out of favor and suffering from malaria—decided to leave Jiangxi and find a new base that could be better defended and supplied. The result was the storied Long March. Leaving behind a doomed rear guard of 10,000 to 15,000 soldiers to wage guerrilla war behind enemy lines, 86,000 Red Army troops and Communist cadres set out from Jiangxi, in southeast China, lugging their documents, printing presses, treasury, radios, even an X-ray machine. Four thousand miles and twelve months later, in October 1935, 4,000 bedraggled survivors, along with a few thousand more recruited en route, arrived in northwestern China's Shaanxi Province, across the border from Soviet-controlled Mongolia, after a long, circuitous trek that took them first west, then north. Along the way they had abandoned most of their equipment and experienced unimaginable trials and hardships not only from enemy pursuit by Nationalist and warlord troops but, even more so, from numerous natural obstacles such as mountains and swamps.[40]

The Long March has become so encrusted in legend that it is difficult to figure out what actually happened. Communist historiography has depicted "an army of heroes" happily risking death out of love for Marx and Mao.[41] The recent debunkers Jung Chang and Jon Halliday, authors of a best-selling Mao biography, on the other hand, have gone so far as to claim that the most storied battle of the march, at Luding Bridge, was a "complete invention" and that the march succeeded only because Chiang Kai-shek wanted it to. (Letting the Communists go was supposedly the price he had to pay to get his son back from the Soviet Union.)[42]

The available evidence hardly proves this conspiracy theory; Chiang surely wanted to eradicate the Communists, who threatened his rule. In fact he massacred many of them even while his son was studying in the USSR. It was true, however, that the marchers' survival was due partly to the willingness of many of their pursuers—warlord armies loosely allied with the Kuomintang—to let them go. The warlords feared that if the Communists were defeated, Chiang would come after them next. The march could never have started if Zhou Enlai had not negotiated an accord with the warlord of neighboring Guangdong Province to let them go. "The Red Army," wrote the journalist and historian Harrison Salisbury, "walked through Guangdong and the adjacent territory almost like tourists on a stroll."[43]

There was a similar lack of fortitude among the defenders of the Luding Bridge, a narrow, swaying, three-hundred-foot span that crossed the swirling Dadu River in Sichuan Province. By the time the Communist vanguard arrived on May 29, 1935, the defenders had removed most of the planks laid over the nine heavy chains, "each big link as thick as a rice bowl," which formed the bridge's base thirty feet above the swirling water (not five hundred feet as later claimed by Zhu De). In Communist lore, twenty-two Red soldiers had to crawl a hundred yards along the chains stretched precariously over the "deafening . . . roar of the rushing torrent" while the defenders shot at them and set fire to the other planks. Eighteen of the attackers made it to the other side, and with Mausers and hand grenades cleared a path for the rest of the army to follow.

What this hagiography leaves out is that the defenders' guns were so old and their cartridges so moldy that most of their bullets couldn't reach across the river. This was no accident. One of Sichuan's warlords had made a deal to let "the Red Army through without much of a fight." Moreover, one witness claimed many years later that Communist casualties would have been higher if they had not forced local peasants, all of whom were killed, to lead the way across the bridge. The battle really happened, contra Chang-Halliday, but it was not as heroic as later claimed.[44]

Other parts of the Long March hardly fit Communist mythology. Conscription was supposed to be reserved for "feudal" armies; Mao always denied that his forces were "compulsorily impressing the people."[45] In reality families that refused to provide sons for the Red Army were denounced as "traitors and deserters," which meant the loss of land, food, even their lives. One Long March veteran recalled, "The Party secretary in our village forced everyone with a dick to sign up." Many of these unwilling enlistees picked the first opportunity to slip away. In the first forty-six days, from October 16 to December 1, 1934, the marchers lost two-thirds of their strength. Only one major battle occurred during that period: Chiang's aircraft and troops caught part of the column while it was crossing the Xiang River. But it is estimated that only 15,000 marchers died here. Most of the other 30,000 must have deserted.[46]

Beyond desertion and defeat, the marchers suffered from the elements and lack of supplies. The Long March traversed twenty-four rivers and eighteen mountain ranges. Particularly difficult were the Great Snowy Mountains in western China, with their 14,000-foot peaks, which the marchers reached on June 12, 1935. The thin mountain air was tough on the wounded and ill; many expired en route.

Just as bad were the grasslands, an enormous stretch of water-logged tundra at an elevation of over 9,000 feet in northern Sichuan Province, where the marchers arrived three months later, on August 22, 1935. The few inhabitants of the grasslands were Tibetans who were hostile to these Han Chinese intruders trying to appropriate their meager food supplies. Employing guerrilla tactics of their own, the Tibetans would pick off isolated parties of Reds, "like vultures on a corpse." (The Communists would exact a terrible revenge with their massacres of Tibetans in the 1950s and 1960s and an animosity that continues to the present.) The ground itself was so marshy that men or animals could disappear after taking a wrong step. The survivors were so hungry that they took to eating boiled animal hides, leather belts, even horses' reins. Many drank the "bitter, black" swamp water even though there was "no wood to purify it by boiling." Dysentery and typhus spread through the ranks. When the marchers finally emerged from the grasslands after a harrowing week, they found fields of unripened corn and eagerly consumed the crops. A few minutes later they collapsed, holding their stomachs, their bodies shaking, screaming in agony, because "their stomachs could not digest the sudden intake after starving for so long."[47]

The Reds were lucky that even four thousand of them reached Shaanxi Province in the northwest, where another Communist group had already established a redoubt. They were luckier still that Mao had the wit to turn a catastrophic defeat into a public-relations victory. Mao and his crack team of propagandists created the myth of the "Long March," a term coined, ironically, by Chiang Kai-shek,[48] as a triumph of the spirit—"a new world record for military marches" by "brave heroes" intent on "going north to resist Japan." Mao even had the gall to claim that the "Red Army has already become an invincible force."[49]

In reality Mao was totally preoccupied with fighting the Nationalists, not the Japanese,[50] and the Red Army was still weak in 1935. The Long March did not win China for the Communists. It did, however, win the Communist Party for Mao.

During the march, he painted his opponents, a clique of Moscow-trained cadres, as "opportunists," "flightists," and "deviationists" who had lost Jiangxi because of their "erroneous military leadership."[51] A shooting war almost broke out en route against the Fourth Front Army, a larger Communist formation commanded by one of Mao's rivals, which linked up with his First Front Army in June 1935. But in September 1935 Mao was able to escape with his followers and consolidate power in his own hands with the assistance of the handsome and malleable Zhou Enlai, who had previously outranked Mao in the party hierarchy.

In Shaanxi he staged another reign of terror (the Rectification Campaign) to impose the "correct Marxist-Leninist line," a.k.a. "Mao Zedong Thought," and root out "spies" and "subjectivists." In other words, to crush any possible opposition. Mao was well on his way to becoming the Red Emperor.[52]

✦ ✦ ✦

FROM THE DAYS of America's War of Independence to Ireland's, public opinion had been growing in importance as a factor in guerrilla warfare. Twentieth-century insurgents could not undertake apolitical raids, like the nomads of old, and expect to be successful. A smart guerrilla leader, or for that matter a smart counterinsurgent, now had to harness the press for his own ends. Mao Zedong grasped that lesson from an early age when, as a twenty-six-year-old agitator, he had founded a radical newspaper and bookstore. Now as the unquestioned leader of the Communist Party of China, he unleashed a potent new weapon in his propaganda war against the Nationalist regime: an adventurous young reporter from the American Midwest named Edgar Snow.

Snow had been living in China since 1928 and, although not a party member, he was known to be sympathetic to the Communists—a "reliable" if "bourgeois" writer who could be counted on to recount the Communists' story as they wanted it recounted.[53] So in 1936 Snow was smuggled by the party underground past the Kuomintang blockade into the Red northwest. He traveled with George Hatem, a Lebanese-American doctor who was a committed communist, carrying what his wife described as "his sleeping bag, his Camel cigarettes, his Gillette razor blades, and a can of Maxwell House coffee—his indispensable artifacts of Western civilization."[54] Four months later, after meeting virtually the entire Communist hierarchy, Snow returned to Peking with a sensational scoop—a book that would garner widespread attention not only in Britain and America, where it was first published in 1937, but in China itself, where it came out in translation.

Red Star over China, in fact, would do more than any volume other than Pearl Buck's *The Good Earth* to shape Western impressions of China. It gave most Westerners, and for that matter most Chinese, their first account of the Long March and of the men behind it. Mao, with whom Snow formed a lifelong friendship, was painted in heroic hues as "a gaunt, rather Lincolnesque figure . . . with a head of thick black hair grown very long . . . an intellectual face of great shrewdness . . . [and] a lively sense of humor." Snow actually thought Mao, who would become one of history's worst mass murderers, was "a moderating influence in the Communist movement where life and death were concerned."[55] Thanks in part to *Red Star*'s publication, fresh recruits were soon flocking from China's cities to the Communist headquarters in Yan'an in Shaanxi Province.

The newcomers included Lan Ping (Blue Apple), the stage name of a twenty-four-year-old actress from Shanghai, Jiang Qing, who was "much better looking and more chic" than most of the other women in Yan'an. Mao had already been married three times. The first had been arranged for him at age fourteen by his parents but rejected by him. The second was to the daughter of one of his professors; he abandoned her in Changsha when he went to the mountains, and she was executed by Nationalist troops in 1930. His third wife, He Zizhen, accompanied him on the Long March even though she was pregnant and had to leave their toddler behind. (He was never heard from again.) She was wounded en route and gave birth to another baby, who was left with a peasant family and died. Mao lost interest in her after the march, and she left for Russia to receive medical treatment. While she was gone, Mao divorced her and married the alluring Blue Apple. She would become the notorious Madame Mao, who helped instigate the Cultural Revolution in 1966 and tried to seize power after Mao's death in 1976. But she could not hold his attention for long.

As China's "chairman," he would live apart from her, enjoying sex with a rotating bevy of young women, sometimes several at a time, supplied for him by the party apparatus. The girls, apparently not dissuaded by his questionable hygiene, were proud to serve the Great Helmsman; even to contract venereal disease from him was regarded as an honor. As in other communist countries such as the Soviet Union, where Stalin and his cronies enjoyed the high life, so in China: the puritanism preached by the Communists did not apply at the top.[56] The Communists were also hypocritical in their condemnation of the drug trade. In Yan'an they supported themselves in part through opium production, much as the Taliban would later do.[57] But it was really in the sexual arena that Mao came into his own: his exploits made other womanizing guerrilla chieftains, such as Garibaldi and Tito, seem chaste by comparison.

✦ ✦ ✦

HIS DECADELONG SOJOURN in Yan'an (1937–47) gave Mao the leisure not only to womanize but also to philosophize. During this period he expounded his major theories of warfare and class struggle. The most famous product of this period was the essay *On Protracted War*, which he wrote in 1938 over nine days, working in a cave by candlelight with little sleep or food, so absorbed that he did not notice a fire burning a hole in his shoe "until his toes felt the pain."[58] A similar but not identical document, whose Chinese-language original has never been found, was translated as *On Guerrilla War-*

fare by the U.S. Marine officer Samuel B. Griffith II, who in 1942 was to set up a Marine Raider Battalion inspired by Mao's teachings.[59]

Mao's name is closely associated with "people's war," but he disavowed the "right tendency" of "guerrilla-ism"—the assumption that hit-and-run raids by lightly armed fighters could by themselves defeat a determined foe. In *On Protracted War,* he wrote that "the outcome of the war depends mainly on regular warfare" and "that guerrilla warfare cannot shoulder the main responsibility." "It does not follow, however," he added, "that the role of guerrilla warfare is unimportant."

He posited a three-stage model of insurgency. First, "the enemy's strategic offensive and our strategic defensive." Second, "the enemy's strategic consolidation and our preparation for the counter-offensive." Third, "our strategic counter-offensive and the enemy's strategic retreat." He explained that in the first stage "the form of fighting we should adopt is primarily mobile warfare, supplemented by guerrilla and positional warfare." In the second stage "our form of fighting will be primarily guerrilla warfare, supplemented by mobile warfare." In the third and culminating stage, "mobile warfare" will be the primary form of fighting while "positional warfare" rises in importance. Throughout the first two stages, Mao saw political considerations as paramount—"that is, the policy of establishing base areas; of systematically setting up political power; of deepening the agrarian revolution; of expanding the people's armed forces." He cautioned that without secure bases that had been cleansed of "class enemies" the guerrillas could not win: "History knows many peasant wars of the 'roving rebel' type, but none of them ever succeeded."

In this revolutionary struggle, Mao posited the need for forces of differing level of ability, starting with a militia known as the "township Red Guards, then the district Red Guards, then the county Red Guards, then the local Red Army troops, all the way up to regular Red Army troops." Only the highest-level forces could undertake maneuver warfare; lower-level Red Guards would have to limit themselves to guerrilla attacks or to providing intelligence and logistical help. "The principle for the Red Army is concentration, and that for the Red Guards dispersion." He added that in the third, decisive stage much of the fighting "will be undertaken by forces which were originally guerrillas but which will have progressed from guerrilla to mobile warfare."

While the most commonly cited influence on Mao's work was the ancient sage Sun Tzu, considerable elements were also anticipated by Giuseppe Mazzini, the nineteenth-century champion of Italian nationalism who inspired Garibaldi and many other revolutionaries. In his *Rules for the Conduct of Guerrilla Bands* (1832), Mazzini, like Mao, posited a multistage struggle beginning with hit-and-run raids and culminating in "the formation of a national army." Like Mao, Mazzini called for a far-flung struggle run from the center—not by a politburo, a term that did not yet exist, but by a "Centre of Action" that sounds suspiciously similar. And, like Mao, he demanded that guerrillas be scrupulous in their dealings with the people whose support they sought: "Every band should be a living program of the morality of the party. The most rigorous discipline is at once a duty and a necessity among them. . . . Respect for women, for property, for the rights of individuals, and for crops should be their motto." Even Mazzini's tactical instructions were proto-Maoist. "The band must be ready to assault when the enemy believe them to be retiring," he wrote, "and to retire when the enemy are prepared to resist their attack."[60]

These similarities, which have seldom if ever been noted before, underline the fact that Mao's essential theories were not original, although he developed them much more elaborately than Mazzini or any other predecessor. Mao's theories derived credibility from the fact that, like T. E. Lawrence but unlike Mazzini, he actually led a storied guerrilla force—he was not just a theorist but a practitioner. In subsequent years Mao was to have another advantage in disseminating his work: his unquestioned control of the government of the world's most populous state. This was a book-promotion tool denied to most other authors, who, however much they would have liked to, could not threaten potential readers with torture and imprisonment for not buying their books. Mao unapologetically and egotistically employed his absolute power to help make his "laws of revolutionary warfare," bound in Little Red Books, by far the most widely distributed and influential manuals for insurgency ever published. Even Al Qaeda, while rejecting Mao's atheism, would later cite his military maxims approvingly.

It has been said that "nearly all contemporary insurgency theory" stems from *On Protracted War.* Mao's writing was particularly important in putting the stress on politics rather than on simple hit-and-run tactics of the kind that primitive rebels had employed since the dawn of time. But few other revolutions would pass through all three stages prescribed by Mao; like most insurgent manuals, *On Protracted War* was more a description of what happened in one place than a formula replicable elsewhere. Even in China, the Reds would never have triumphed had it not been for the intentional assistance provided by their Russian "comrades" and the inadvertent assistance of the "dwarf bandits," as the Chinese rudely referred to the Japanese.

Indeed the ultimate Communist triumph in China would serve less to vindicate Mao's theories than to show the importance of outside assistance for an insurgency to succeed. No other factor has been as important in the outcome of low-intensity conflicts. Some insurgents, such as Toussaint Louverture in Haiti and Michael Collins in Ireland and later Fidel Castro in Cuba, prevailed without substantial external support, but they were the exception, not the norm. More common was the case of the American patriots, Spanish *guerrilleros*, Greek klephts, Cuban and Philippine *insurrectos*, Arab irregulars in World War I, Yugoslav Partisans, French maquis, and other rebels who received copious outside aid—as did the Chinese Communists.[61]

✦ ✦ ✦

IRONICALLY JAPAN DID as much as any power to aid the Communist takeover even though its leaders had no sympathy for communism. (Japan's own Communist Party, founded in 1922, was outlawed and had to operate underground until 1945.) Yet Japan's invasion of China, which began in 1931 with the occupation of Manchuria and accelerated in 1937 with the occupation of most of the major cities and the coastline, dealt a near-fatal blow to Mao's enemies in the Nationalist regime. To meet this threat Mao and Chiang, the chairman and the generalissimo, were forced to reach an uneasy truce. In Mao's case the pressure was applied by Stalin, who wanted a united front to confront the fascists; in Chiang's case by a patriotic warlord who kidnapped him and only released him after he agreed to a deal. In 1937, the year of the terrible "Rape of Nanking," most of the Red Army was renamed the Eighth Route Army and ostensibly subordinated to Kuomintang control.

The truce gave the Communists breathing space while Chiang diverted most of his forces to fight the Japanese. At least three million Chinese soldiers were killed battling the invaders between 1931 and 1945 along with eighteen million civilians. More than 90 percent of the military dead were Nationalists.[62] It was not that the Communists refused to fight altogether, but, with one costly exception that was said to have been undertaken without Mao's approval (the 1940 Hundred Regiments Offensive), they generally eschewed large-scale attacks on the better-equipped, -trained, and -disciplined Imperial Japanese Army. They preferred to build up Red areas in the countryside where the occupiers were thin on the ground while staging occasional raids on Japanese lines. Communist strength soared even as Nationalist armies were being decimated.

All the while Mao was cynically accusing Chiang of neglecting the "War of Resistance" and husbanding his troops for a resumption of the civil war. This was widely believed, especially in the West, and cost Chiang considerable support. Ironically Mao's charges were more nearly a description of his own strategy, which, as one historian notes, "put self-preservation and expansion above fighting the Japanese."[63]

The Communist Party emerged from the war stronger than ever. The People's Liberation Army, as the Red Army was renamed in 1947, had numbered just 40,000 men in 1937. Now it was nearly a million strong. It was still outnumbered by the Kuomintang, however, whose army had 3.5 million men and American-supplied tanks and airplanes.[64] Chiang's forces were moved with U.S. help to take charge of areas that had been under Japanese occupation. By 1946, when the civil war resumed, they controlled 80 percent of China's territory and almost all its major cities.[65] Even Yan'an, the Communist capital, fell in 1947. Mao and other senior leaders had to flee the Nationalist advance.

The one major area that remained outside Chiang's grasp was Manchuria, which had been invaded by the Soviet army. When the Russians left in 1946, they turned over copious stocks of captured weaponry to their Chinese comrades. More supplies arrived by train from the Soviet Union, helping to balance out the aid that Chiang received from the United States and speeding the Communists' transition to conventional operations complete with artillery and armored cars.

In 1946 Chiang sent half a million of his best troops to conquer Manchuria. Their armored blitzkrieg made impressive progress at first but stopped just short of the Communist capital, Harbin, due in part to a cease-fire forced on Chiang by the American envoy George Marshall, who hoped to create a coalition government between Nationalists and Communists.[66] In their initial offensive the Nationalists overextended their supply lines, creating an opening for a devastating Communist counterattack in 1947 under the brilliant generalship of Lin Biao, a graduate of Whampoa Military Academy and a veteran of both the Northern Expedition and the Long March. Elsewhere in China, Mao pursued a rural "people's war" strategy, slowly gathering his forces to encircle the Nationalist-held cities, which were undermined from within by Communist fifth columns. However, contrary to Mao's expectations, it was high-intensity conventional military operations that proved decisive, not the efforts of his guerrillas.

Kuomintang mismanagement and especially the devastation left by the Sino-Japanese war made the insurgents' job easier. Increasing unemployment, tax hikes, and runaway inflation all eroded Chiang's popularity. Unable to survive on their salaries, many KMT officials turned to bribes, which further eroded their popularity—a problem later familiar in South Vietnam, Iraq, and Afghanistan, where pervasive corruption did much to undermine American-led counterinsurgency campaigns. Chiang recognized the issues but seemed powerless to address them. He never enjoyed the kind of absolute control over his own forces that Mao did. Chiang was an autocrat, too, but a less vicious, less organized autocrat who could not instill lockstep conformity even on his own army. Chiang himself complained that his commanders failed to obey his orders or cooperate with one another. He admitted that his whole regime was "decrepit and degenerate."[67]

Although more open societies such as the Republic of China, in both its mainland and Taiwanese incarnations, or the post-1979 People's Republic of China have proven better able to generate economic growth, there is little question that absolute dictatorships such as Maoist China have often been more adept at the type of mobilization and synchronization needed to prevail in wartime, if only because anyone who did not follow orders could expect a harsh retribution. Chiang could instill no such discipline on his own side, with parlous consequences for the future of his regime.

Once the Nationalist armies had suffered defeat in Manchuria in 1947–48, the entire edifice of Kuomintang power crumbled with stupefying rapidity that caught even Mao by surprise.[68] Some Nationalist troops fought hard to the end, but many others surrendered or defected en masse. As the Red triumph became more likely, hordes of waverers joined their ranks. In 1949 the Communists marched into Peking, and Chiang fled to Taiwan.

The war was over. China's agony was only beginning. At least fifty million people would die over the next quarter century because of Mao's deranged policies—far more than had been killed by the Nationalists and Japanese combined.[69]

✦ ✦ ✦

DESPITE THE MALIGN consequences of Maoism, China's self-proclaimed Great Helmsman maintained a potent appeal as a source of inspiration and support for other revolutionaries, especially in Asia.

In North Korea, Kim Il-sung won Mao's and Stalin's reluctant support for a conventional offensive against South Korea in 1950 that backfired—as had earlier North Korean attempts to wage guerrilla warfare against the South. It would take direct Chinese intervention, including the dispatch of a million armed "volunteers," to save the Pyongyang regime.

The Vietnamese comrades were cannier or perhaps simply weaker. They resolved to use guerrilla-style tactics to weaken the French. But all the while they firmly expected that, in accordance with Mao's teaching, someday they would field regular armies to win their "people's war." That day was to arrive sooner than anyone could have expected.

45.

ADIEU AT DIEN BIEN PHU

The Indochina War, 1945–1954

NOVEMBER 20, 1953. *10:30 a.m.* The morning mist had just burned away to reveal the village of Muong Thanh in northwestern Vietnam near the Laos border. It was situated in a valley eleven miles long and five miles wide bisected by the Nam Yum River. All around could be seen "lush green mountains" rising to six thousand feet. On these slopes lived Meo tribesmen who harvested poppies to produce opium. On the valley floor were ethnic Thai, simple farmers living in "stilted, peak-roofed huts built of thick bamboo and thatched with woven leaf." They were going about their usual routine, harvesting rice with short sickles amid the "clucking of poultry and the grunting of little black pigs." For the Vietminh troop stationed there it was a day of field exercises. They were setting up their mortars and machine guns around a dirt airstrip when they noticed a flight of two-engine aircraft high above. Later a peasant recalled how the aircraft spread "clouds of white specks that looked like cotton seeds. But soon they opened up and we saw that soldiers were hanging from them."

Inside the American-made C-47s, the same cargo aircraft that had delivered the Chindits to the jungles of Burma nine years earlier, the jumpmasters were shouting, "Go! Go! Go!" Two battalions of crack French paratroopers were swiftly out the door. One of the battalions was dropped too far south. That left responsibility for securing the area around the village to the Sixth

Colonial Parachute Battalion. Its 621 men—mostly French but also including 200 Vietnamese—were led by Major Marcel Bigeard. He was only thirty-seven years old but already a legend—a modern-day cavalier whose lack of fear and love of combat were reminiscent of warriors as disparate as Shamil, George Armstrong Custer, and Orde Wingate. Everyone in Indochina, it seemed, "knew his high forehead, his fair crew-cut hair, his bird-of-prey profile, his touchy independence"—and his extraordinary combat record, which would one day earn him four-star rank without benefit of a Saint Cyr education or the war college.

Born in 1916 to a railway worker, he had left school at fourteen to work in a bank and joined the army in 1936 as an enlisted man. He was still a lowly warrant officer when he was captured on the Maginot Line in 1940. The following year, after two failed attempts, he escaped from a German prisoner-of-war camp, Stalag 12A, and made his way to French West Africa to join the Free French. In 1944, using the call sign Bruno, which would become his lifelong moniker, he parachuted back into France to work with the Resistance and help the invading Allied armies—work for which he won both the French Legion of Honor and the British Distinguished Service Order.

In 1945, by now a captain, he first came to Indochina. By 1953 he was on his third tour after too many close escapes to recall. The worst of all had come the preceding year. He and his *paras* had been dropped into the village of Tu-Lê in the northern highlands to stop a Vietminh offensive and allow the evacuation of French garrisons in the region. His battalion was soon encircled by an enemy division. They had to fight their way out, walking nonstop for days through the jungle while carrying their wounded. Entire companies were wiped out en route, but Bigeard and a small group of survivors somehow managed to elude an enemy that outnumbered them ten to one.

Such setbacks did not sate Bigeard's thirst for battle. The peacocky personification of paratrooper panache, he still entered battle without a personal weapon and always led *Bataillon Bigeard* from the front. "If it's possible, it's done," he said. And if it's impossible? That "will be done" too.

The landing near Muong Thanh was certainly possible, almost routine, except for the presence of more Vietminh troops than expected around the drop zone. The battalion's medical officer was killed by a fluke shot to the head as he was fluttering to earth. Many of the paratroopers were scattered, and most of their radio sets were shattered. But Bigeard improvised successfully. While bullets "whistled" by his head in the thick elephant grass, he gathered groups of paratroopers and mounted an assault on the Vietminh, who fought fiercely and successfully to shield the escape of their regimental staff. Eventually he was able to contact B-26 bombers circling overhead. With the help of their air strikes and another battalion of paratroops inserted in the afternoon, Bigeard was able to secure the battlefield by nightfall. The French had lost fifteen men, the Vietminh more than a hundred.

It was one of the few victories the French forces were ever to win in this valley, whose name they would soon curse: Dien Bien Phu.[70]

✦ ✦ ✦

BY 1953 THE French Far East Expeditionary Corps had been fighting for more than seven years to regain control of Indochina from the League for the Independence of Vietnam (*Viet Nam Doc Lap Dong Minh Hoi*, or Vietminh). Ostensibly a nationalist alliance, the Vietminh was in fact dominated by the Communists and their charismatic leader, Ho Chi Minh. Just as Mao's path to power was paved by the Japanese, so too was Ho's. The Japanese occupied Indochina in 1940. The French Vichy regime remained in existence until 1945, but colonial control had weakened enough by 1941 to allow Ho and some other comrades to sneak back into northern Vietnam from across the Chinese border. It was the first time in thirty years that he had lived in his homeland.

Nguyen Tat Thanh had been born in 1890 to a poor Confucian scholar in central Vietnam. Ho Chi Minh (He Who Enlightens) was simply the most enduring of the many aliases he adopted. Expelled from school for anti-French activities, he left the country in 1911 as a lowly cook's helper aboard a steamship. After sailing around the world, he settled in France and, while supporting himself with menial work, became involved in anticolonial agitation. In 1920 he was present at the founding of the French Communist Party. Three years later he moved to Moscow to work for the Comintern's Far Eastern Bureau as "their token colonial." He would spend the next two decades as a Comintern operative. In this capacity he helped organize the Indochinese Communist Party in Hong Kong in 1930—an act for which he paid with a year and a half in a British prison.

Although "an accomplished Stalinist," in the words of one of his biographers, Ho projected an image of "frankness . . . and humility," "goodness and simplicity" that would eventually make him a beloved figure known as *Bac Ho* (Uncle Ho). He never became a megalomaniacal hedonist like Mao. Even as Vietnam's supreme leader, he would live in a small cottage on the grounds of the presidential palace, which was too opulent for his taste, and when forced to stay in a luxury hotel he would sleep on the floor. (Today Mao's modest cottage is a popular tourist attraction, located next to the grandiose mausoleum where Ho's embalmed corpse is on display—something he would have hated.) That was still a considerable step up from the cold, damp cave in Pac Bo, where he lived on first returning to Vietnam in 1941. Ho appeared thin and insubstantial, even fragile—"a wisp of a man," in the words of one visitor—and he wore a wispy goatee that gave him the mien of a scholar, but he was impressively inured to hardship.

From Pac Bo, just a mile from the Chinese frontier, Ho and his small band of followers began to build guerrilla bases and organize what would eventually become the People's Army. In 1942 he walked back to China hoping to win more support. Instead he was imprisoned for eighteen months by the Nationalist regime. Once he was released, Ho made contact with the OSS, which agreed to send a small team to his headquarters to facilitate anti-Japanese operations. The Americans provided arms and training and, more importantly, treated Ho when he contracted malaria and dysentery. Quite possibly they saved the life of this future foe.

Later this wartime cooperation would give rise to a myth that Ho could have become an American ally if only the United States, in the grip of Cold War paranoia, had not spurned him. The OSS was particularly taken with him; one of its reports described Ho as a "convinced Democrat" who "firmly advocates American methods for the economic development of his country." In fact, like Mao, about whom similar hopes were expressed by the likes of Edgar Snow, he was a dedicated Communist while being an equally dedicated nationalist. He was simply making use of his American contacts to divide the "capitalist camp" while creating a one-party state aligned with the "socialist bloc." He actually quoted from the U.S. Declaration of Independence when, in his Mao-style jacket and rubber sandals, he announced the formation of the Democratic Republic of Vietnam amid a sea of red flags fluttering over the colonial grandeur of Hanoi on September 2, 1945, the capital having been left open by Japan's defeat.[71]

Elections were subsequently held, which led to the formation of a coalition government. But the Communists held all the key positions, with Ho himself as president and minister of foreign affairs. Before long non-Communist politicians were being killed and jailed by the secret police amid what a CIA report described as a "pervading sense of fear."[72]

Vietminh attempts to consolidate power suffered a major setback when Allied troops arrived to accept the Japanese surrender—Chinese in the north, British in the south. And not far behind were the French seeking to reestablish their empire. In 1945 British and French troops cleared the Vietminh out of Saigon. On November 23, 1946, after having demanded that all Vietminh vacate the old colonial port of Haiphong, the French commander ordered his warships, aircraft, and artillery to open fire on the city, inflicting thousands of civilian casualties. On December 19, the Vietminh staged an uprising in Hanoi, but the French were on their guard and managed to drive them out. Thus they secured control of Vietnam's major urban centers, but much of the countryside, where most of the 24 million people lived, remained outside their grasp.[73] The Vietminh leaders retreated to their impenetrable lairs in the far north—an area known as the Viet Bac where, in the mountainous jungle, they established training camps, barracks, schools, even crude arms factories.

Not until October 7, 1947, did the French launch a major offensive against the Viet Bac. Operation Lea began with an airdrop by 1,137 paratroopers straight onto the Vietminh headquarters followed by motorized pincer movements designed to trap the insurgents. Ho Chi Minh barely managed to escape. But the armored thrusts bogged down along the narrow, winding roads as the Vietminh felled trees, planted mines, dropped bridges, and dug trenches. Within a month the offensive was called off, and the French were forced to retreat with little to show for their efforts: a pattern that would be repeated many times in the following years.[74]

Ho Chi Minh had outlined his strategy to an American reporter in 1946. He realized that the French had more firepower but, he said, "We have a weapon every bit as powerful as the most modern cannon: nationalism!" He compared the coming conflict to a "war between a tiger and an elephant": "If the tiger ever stands still the elephant will crush him with his mighty tusks. But the tiger does not stand still. He lurks in the jungle by day and emerges by night. He will leap upon the back of the elephant, tearing huge chunks from his hide, and then he will leap back into the dark jungle. And slowly the elephant will bleed to death."[75]

It was an uncannily accurate forecast.

✦ ✦ ✦

Ho's elephant killer was Vo Nguyen Giap, who was destined to be remembered as a military strategist of the first rank. Although Giap, born in 1911, was two decades younger than Ho, the two men had much in common, which helps to explain why they hit it off after meeting in China in 1940. Unlike Mao or Tito, neither was a peasant; both came from the impoverished if respectable mandarin class. They were even expelled for anti-French activities from the same high school—also the alma mater of their future nemesis Ngo Dinh Diem. Ho was kicked out in 1908, Giap in 1927. But, unlike Ho, Giap stayed in Vietnam and managed to complete his education after serving a two-year prison term.

He earned a law degree in 1937, the same year he joined the Communist Party, then went to work as a history teacher while publishing anti-French newspapers. In 1940, in order to avoid arrest, he left for China. He left behind his wife and sister-in-law, fellow Communists who were captured by the French and tortured to death. The same fate awaited Giap's father in 1947. Ho's ex-wife also died in a French jail. This gave both men, although part of the French-speaking elite, intensely personal reasons for detesting colonial rule.

Ho was impressed by his young follower's intelligence and determination and directed him to take charge of military affairs despite his complete lack of formal training. "The only academy I ever attended was the bush," Giap later said. Like T. E. Lawrence, whose works he cited as his "fighting gospel," Giap was a self-taught soldier of genius. His first influence was Napoleon, whose campaigns he knew by heart. He was also familiar with the guerrilla wars waged by Vietnamese heroes of the distant past against Chinese and Mongol invaders. But perhaps his greatest influence was Mao Zedong, whose strategy, developed to defeat a domestic opponent, he copied slavishly and successfully to fight against first one foreign foe, then another. Although the Nationalist regime that Mao faced had more legitimacy and staying power than the French or Americans in Vietnam, Giap's adversaries could bring more resources and sheer military competence against him. Thus he faced a challenge at least as daunting as that which confronted Mao and his marshals during the Chinese civil war.[76]

Like Mao, Giap planned a three-stage struggle—first "localized guerrilla war," then "war of movement," finally "general uprising"[77]—that would be waged by a three-tier force: a regular army, supplemented by regional forces of full-time fighters and a much larger village militia that carried out occasional acts of sabotage but whose most important contribution was to provide intelligence and logistical support. Ho and Giap also borrowed from Maoist tactics when they sent their cadres to mobilize villages with instructions not to "behave arrogantly" and even to pitch in to help with the rice harvest.[78] Once they had won over a majority of the villagers, cadres would liquidate "collaborators" and "landlords." Their lands were then to be distributed to the poorest farmers, who in turn were subject to Vietminh taxation and conscription.

✦ ✦ ✦

THESE TACTICS PROVED highly effective except in villages populated by Roman Catholics, who composed 10 percent of the population, or by adherents of the indigenous Cao Dai and Hoa Hao religious sects. Some ethnic minorities living in the mountains, such as the Thais and Meo, also proved resistant to Vietminh organizing. Some fifteen thousand of these Montagnards joined irregular units organized by enterprising French intelligence officers such as Major Roger Trinquier, later an influential counterinsurgency theorist, to employ guerrilla tactics against the Vietminh. The French also made common cause with the Binh Xuyen gangsters who ran Saigon's underworld.[79]

But—and this was the fatal weakness of the French war effort—for most Vietnamese the colonial cause held no appeal. In 1949 France granted

Vietnam, Cambodia, and Laos nominal independence as "associated states" of the French Union, but French representatives continued to hold the levers of power. The French accepted considerable American aid: by 1954 more than 30,000 tons of matériel a month was arriving, including everything from bombers and bombs to helmets and flak vests.[80] But they consistently rebuffed American advice to offer full-fledged independence—the only thing that might have won the support of non-Communist Vietnamese.

French tactics did not help. "Rape, beating, burning, torturing, of entirely harmless peasants and villages were of common occurrence," wrote an English Foreign Legionnaire. His fellow soldiers, many of them Germans too young to have fought in World War II, often boasted "of the number of murders or rapes they had committed or the means of torture they had applied or the cash, jewels, or possessions they had stolen." Locally recruited auxiliaries, often thugs or Vietminh deserters who had "stiff prices on their heads," were even worse—they were "feared and hated by the local population on account of their thieving, blackmailing, racketeering propensities."[81]

The French reaction to attacks was particularly brutal. A former French paratrooper reported what happened in 1946 after a unit came under fire in the Mekong Delta, the major rice-producing area of the south: "Before we resumed our march the soldiers set fire to the hamlet. One match was all it took to set the straw roofs alight. The water buffalo left behind by the peasants were shot."[82] For the peasants the loss of "these draft animals," a Vietnamese writer notes, meant "losing their livelihood."[83]

In his book *Street without Joy,* the French-American writer Bernard B. Fall, a respected expert on Indochina, remembered being in a C-119 Flying Boxcar aircraft in 1953 that took some ground fire. On his intercom he could hear the following conversation between two fighter aircraft flying in escort as they swooped toward a village far below:

> "Can't see a darn thing. Do you see anything?"
>
> "Can't see anything either, but let's give it to them just for good measure."
>
> Another swoop by the two little birds and all of a sudden a big black billow behind them. It was napalm—jellied gasoline, one of the nicer

> horrors developed in World War II. It beats the conventional incendiaries by the fact that it sticks so much better to everything it touches.
>
> "Ah, see the bastards run now?"
>
> Now the village was burning furiously. The two fighters swooped down in turn and raked the area with machine guns. As we veered off, the black cloud just reached our height. Scratch one Lao village—and we don't even know whether the village was pro-Communist or not.[84]

If the village wasn't Communist before this unprovoked attack, it would have been after.

The Vietcong played rough too; captured French soldiers were "impaled on bamboo stakes with their testicles stuffed in their mouths."[85] But their violence was usually directed against those who actually opposed them, whereas the French were often indiscriminate in their wrath. "We thank the French," wrote a senior Communist Party strategist, "for having helped 'Viet Minh-ize the Vietnamese people' by their words and deeds."[86]

As a result the Vietminh had no problem finding informers "willing to pass on . . . the slightest piece of information"[87]—or fighters willing to act on that intelligence. But training and arming them was harder—until the Communist triumph in China. After 1949 the Vietminh had access to Chinese training camps, weapons, and advisers, including some of Mao's most capable generals. This hastened the Vietminh's transformation from a ragtag guerrilla force into an army armed with its own artillery if not aircraft or tanks—a transformation that Mao's own forces had made just a few years earlier with Russian help.[88]

✦ ✦ ✦

USING HIS NEW troops, Giap launched an offensive in the fall of 1950 against the French outposts scattered precariously near the Chinese border along Colonial Route 4. The French tried to evacuate their fort at Caobang, but both the retreating troops and a relieving force were annihilated, costing them more than 4,500 soldiers and enough equipment to outfit an entire Vietminh division.

With the area north of Hanoi entirely under his control, Giap became overconfident. He may have been one of the most successful insurgent commanders of the twentieth-century—the general who humbled both a great power and a superpower—but he was also prone to disastrous miscalculations. The most famous of these was the 1968 Tet Offensive, which, despite its military failure, became a political success. There was no such silver lining to Giap's decision in early 1951 to launch an offensive designed to end the war quickly. Its target was the Red River Delta, the economic and population hub of the north.

The job of stopping Giap fell to the imperious and demanding newly arrived French commander, General Jean de Lattre de Tassigny, who had once served under Lyautey in Morocco and was dubbed the "French MacArthur" by the American press.[89] Proclaiming, "We shall not yield another inch of territory,"[90] he rallied the demoralized Expeditionary Corps and repelled the Vietminh assault. Caught in the flat, open delta, the attackers were literally roasted alive by newly arrived shipments of American-provided napalm, which burns at 1,800 degrees Fahrenheit—the first of many uses in Vietnam of this hellacious chemical weapon that would be widely employed by U.S. forces in the 1960s. A Vietminh officer recalled, "Hell comes in the form of large, egg-shaped containers. . . . There is no way of holding out under this torrent of fire which flows in all directions and burns everything on its passage."[91]

By the time Giap called off his offensive in the summer of 1951, he had lost over 20,000 killed and wounded. The Vietminh now moved back to a guerrilla-focused strategy, as they were to do again after the Tet Offensive. The French were ill prepared to deal with this eventuality, if only because they were spread so thin.

In 1953 the Expeditionary Corps had 228,000 soldiers and auxiliaries of whom only 52,000 were French. The largest component was 70,000 Vietnamese followed by 48,000 North and West Africans and 19,000 Foreign Legionnaires, 60 percent of them Germans. (Contrary to legend, most were not former Nazis: official policy was to exclude former SS men.) The Vietnamese National Army under Emperor Bao Dai contributed another 160,000 soldiers and auxiliaries, but most were ill trained and unmotivated to fight for a colonial power. The French and Vietnamese forces still outnumbered the Vietminh, who had 250,000 regulars and regionals, along with 2 million local militia, but a large portion of French manpower was tied down in static posts. Some 82,000 soldiers manned the De Lattre Line of more than nine hundred forts enclosing the Red River Delta. That left precious few troops to go after insurgent strongholds or to prevent Communist cadres from extending their grip across the countryside.[92] By the French military's own estimates, in 1953 it controlled only 25 percent of Vietnam.[93] Even venturing a few miles outside Saigon wasn't safe after dark.[94]

Giap boasted, "Our guerrillas and government take over within gunshot of their strong-points."[95] He wasn't exaggerating. A *Newsweek* correspondent reported from the Red River Delta in early 1953 that French forts were attacked almost every night. In the morning the troops had to sweep the roads for mines, which accounted for 60 percent of their casualties. "The French rule by day and the Reds by night," the article noted, adding that the defenders could not locate elusive attackers who took refuge in tunnels "only to pop up again half an hour after the French have pulled out."[96]

Acutely conscious of their inability to keep the guerrillas out of the villages, a revolving cast of French commanders sought to lure the Vietminh into a conventional battle where heavier French firepower might prevail. This was the genesis of the fateful decision in 1953 to launch Operation Castor by establishing a base at Dien Bien Phu, 180 miles from Hanoi and reachable only by air. Lieutenant General Henri-Eugène Navarre, the senior French commander, hoped that this "aero-terrestrial" outpost, similar to those established by the Chindits, could be used to stop the Communists from infiltrating Laos and from capturing the opium crop, a lucrative source of financing for both sides.[97]

In Navarre's estimation, Giap would then have no choice but to attack this "hedgehog," leading the Viets to slaughter on the valley floor. What Navarre could not envisage was that the Vietminh would actually have the firepower advantage because they would be able to transport artillery through hundreds of miles of "impenetrable" jungle.[98] But that is what happened.

✦ ✦ ✦

As soon as he received intelligence in late November 1953 that the French were fortifying Dien Bien Phu, Giap began to marshal his forces. Eventually, on the slopes around Dien Bien Phu, he would assemble four of his six regular divisions, a total of 50,000 combat soldiers and 50,000 support personnel. Transporting their equipment and supplies was a heroic undertaking, with few parallels in modern military history, that necessitated the marshaling of hundreds of thousands of peasants. Roads had to be hacked out of the jungle to allow Russian-made Molotova trucks to move heavy equipment. But most of the supplies were hauled by what Giap described as "an endless, linked human chain," their loads resting on hand-pushed "pack bikes" or on shoulder-borne bamboo yokes.

Artillery pieces were disassembled and hauled over many nights up the mountains around Dien Bien Phu, where they were positioned in carefully camouflaged gun pits. One Vietminh soldier recalled, "To climb a slope, hundreds of men crept in front of the gun, tugging on long ropes, pulling it up inch by inch. . . . Whole nights were spent toiling by torchlight to move a gun 500 or 1,000 meters." When a gun was in danger of sliding into a ravine, one soldier threw his own body under the wheel. Through such heroic exertions, the Vietminh managed to surround Dien Bien Phu with 206 field guns and mortars, including 105-millimeter howitzers and 37-millimeter antiaircraft cannons.

The French were hardly idle during the Vietminh buildup. Although they had little idea of the size of the threat they would shortly face, they had been working frantically to fortify their own positions under the command of Colonel (soon Brigadier General) Christian de Castries, who was seldom without a flat red kepi on his head and a riding crop in his hand. A cavalryman and world high-jump champion, he had once said he wanted nothing more than "a horse to ride, an enemy to kill, and a woman in bed." Legend had it that he named various strongpoints located on the low hills around Dien Bien Phu after his current and former mistresses. More likely, if prosaically, he employed random women's names in alphabetical order.

Grouped closely around the airstrip and command bunkers were Dominique, Eliane, Huguette, and Claudine. Farther north were Beatrice, Anne-Marie, and Gabrielle. Each "center of resistance" was made up of smaller outposts (Eliane 1, 2, 3, 4) with interlocking fields of fire and protective belts of barbed wire and mines. More than three miles south was an airstrip protected by Isabelle—too far from the others to contribute much to their defense. The French troops, assisted by prisoners who were employed as forced laborers, did the best they could to dig trenches and construct bunkers, but there were not enough engineers or materials to go around, so not all of the entrenchments could withstand a heavy barrage.

The primary French firepower consisted of twenty-four 105-millimeter guns and four 155-millimeter howitzers, the latter capable of hurling a 95-pound shell more than ten miles. The Vietminh had nothing comparable to the 155s, but in total number of artillery tubes they outnumbered the French by two or three to one.

Occupying these defensive positions were 10,813 men, a figure that would grow to 15,090 after the siege started and reinforcements, many of them volunteers, were parachuted in. In combat they consumed 180 tons of supplies a day, which also had to be flown in—including wine and cheese. The French even airlifted in two Mobile Field Brothels, "an all-important institution," staffed by Vietnamese and African prostitutes. Giap, by contrast, lived a Spartan life in his forward command post twelve miles to the north, sleeping on a grass mat and subsisting on rice and a few chunks of meat or fish.

Almost alone among French officers, Bruno Bigeard, a physical fitness buff, shared Giap's abstemiousness. Visitors to his mess could expect "a thin slice of ham and one small, isolated boiled potato" washed down with "steaming tea" rather than the multicourse banquets accompanied by copious quantities of wine and brandy that were de rigueur in most French messes.

✦ ✦ ✦

INTERMITTENT FIGHTING HAD been going on ever since French forces had first arrived at Dien Bien Phu. Units that ventured outside the wire were mauled. Those on the inside took casualties from intermittent shelling. A thousand men, or 10 percent of the garrison, were killed or wounded during this preliminary skirmishing. The siege started in earnest on the afternoon of March 13, 1954. "Shells rained down on us without stopping like a hailstorm on a fall evening," recalled a Foreign Legion sergeant. "Bunker after bunker, trench after trench, collapsed, burying under them men and weapons."

The fire was especially intense around Beatrice, which was held by 437 legionnaires. In command was Lieutenant Colonel Jules Gaucher, a legend within the legion who had served in Indochina since 1940. Around 7:30 p.m. a shell penetrated his command bunker, smashing his arms and legs and tearing open his chest. He died soon thereafter. The same fate befell many of his officers. The defense was left in the hands of sergeants and junior officers as wave after wave of Viet attackers emerged from surreptitiously dug "approach" trenches. The vanguard employed Bangalore torpedoes to open holes through the barbed wire and minefields. Then came the rest of the Viets with a frenzied disregard for the defenders' firepower. One Viet squad leader became a legend for throwing his body in front of a bunker's slit to momentarily block the machine gun, allowing his comrades to advance. The legionnaires fought valiantly, but after midnight a captain radioed, "It's all over—the Viets are here. Fire upon my position. Out."

Within days the Vietminh artillery closed down the exposed airstrip. From then on reinforcements and supplies could arrive only by parachute, and even this was increasingly hazardous—forty-eight planes were shot down. The lack of a safe landing strip also meant that the wounded could not be evacuated. Mutilated men overflowed the aid stations, their misery increased by the heat, stench, dirt, rain, mud, even maggots. A doctor described their "slow, gentle groans like a song full of sadness." Outside lay a growing pile of amputated limbs—"shriveled legs, arms, and hands, grotesque feet, all mixed up as in some witches' cauldron."

A number of Vietnamese, Thai, and African troops became internal deserters, taking refuge along the banks of the Nam Yum River. But morale remained strong among the *paras* and legionnaires, the elite forces. Bigeard and his battalion, which had been dropped into Dien Bien Phu for a second time after the siege began, mounted a particularly heroic effort on April 10 to retake Eliane 1. Hobbled by a pulled leg muscle, Bigeard directed the operation from a dugout in Eliane 4 equipped with eight radio sets, which he worked like an orchestra conductor.

The attack began at 6 a.m. with a ten-minute barrage that dropped 1,800 shells on the enemy positions. As soon as the shelling ended, the *paras* moved up the hill in small teams, going as fast as possible, bypassing pockets of resistance that were to be mopped up by the next wave. A flamethrower finished off the last blockhouse "in a river of flame" that left "the smell of charred human flesh." By 2 p.m. the attackers were at the summit, having lost nearly half of their ranks killed or wounded—77 out of 160 men. "It was necessary to annihilate the Viets to the last man. Not one withdrew," Bigeard recalled. "What marvelous combatants, these men trained by Giap."

More "marvelous combatants," two thousand of them, attacked again within hours. Bigeard, in turn, committed his only reserves—a few hundred legionnaires and Vietnamese paratroopers. The former advanced singing a German marching song, the latter the "Marseillaise." By 2 a.m., after hours of hand-to-hand fighting in trenches "filled with rotting corpses," amid "an overpowering stench," "blinded by dust and deafened by artillery fire," the Vietminh had been forced to retreat, leaving behind at least four hundred dead. Eliane 1 would be held for the next twenty days against relentless, World War I–style attacks that chewed up company after company of defenders.

Bigeard's hard-earned triumph only postponed for a bit the garrison's slow strangulation. The strongholds with their feminine names fell one by one, as if each were a virginal maiden succumbing to the advances of a brutish paramour. Each advance allowed the Vietminh to edge their artillery closer to the main camp. By early May, with, in the words of the historian Martin Windrow, "one-legged French soldiers manning machine guns in the blockhouses, being fed ammunition by one-armed and one-eyed comrades," the end was in sight. The last French hope was that the U.S. Air Force would come to the rescue (there was even talk of using atomic bombs), but President Eisenhower refused. On May 7, 1954, with Giap's troops nearing his command bunker, Castries received permission to stop fighting. The last message from the main camp went out at 5:50 p.m.: "We're blowing everything up. Adieu."[99]

✦ ✦ ✦

FOLLOWING THIS FIFTY-FIVE-DAY siege a total of 10,261 defenders out of 15,090 were still alive to surrender. Many of them were in bad shape, weakened by weeks of reduced rations and nonstop exertion. More than half would not survive a hellish captivity during which they were forced to march five hundred miles, subjected to political indoctrination, and denied by Western standards adequate food and medical care—which, in fairness, were also denied to the Vietminh's own troops. In all the eight-year war cost French forces 92,000 men killed, while the Associated States lost another 27,000. The Vietminh suffered even more heavily, losing an estimated 25,000 regulars killed and wounded at Dien Bien Phu and perhaps 250,000 men during the entire war.

In theory the French could have continued fighting, having lost at Dien Bien Phu only 3 percent of the total strength of the French Union armies in Indochina. In the same way the British could have continued fighting in North America after the Battle of Yorktown in 1781 or in Northern Ireland notwithstanding Michael Collins's success in blinding their intelligence apparatus by 1921. But politically the continuation of these unpopular wars was impossible for parliamentary governments that depended for survival on the approval of the voters. Even before the fall of Dien Bien Phu, a May 1953 poll in France had shown that only 15 percent of those surveyed wanted to stay in Indochina.[100] Part of the reason for the war's unpopularity was its financial cost: it consumed fully a third of the entire French defense budget.[101] For an impoverished, war-weary nation, the loss of Dien Bien Phu represented the breaking point. It was a crippling psychological blow and one that resonated far beyond Southeast Asia. The worst defeat suffered by a modern Western empire in a colonial war—the equivalent of Custer's Last Stand fifty-seven times over—it confirmed the lesson of Singapore's fall by showing that "black," "brown," and "yellow" combatants were no longer inferior to the Caucasians who had dominated them on the assumption that they were a "superior race." The bluff and bluster that had underpinned European empires, which allowed them to be maintained on the cheap (the only way they would be tolerated by domestic public opinion), had now been exposed once and for all. The remaining colonial holdings, beginning with French Indochina, could not last much longer. The age of Western empire, which had begun in the fifteenth century, was nearly over.

Ho Chi Minh had foreseen the eventual defeat of his enemies in 1946 when he told a French diplomat, "You will kill ten of my men while we will kill one of yours. But you will be the ones to end up exhausted."[102] His prophecy had now come true. In a development reminiscent of the Whig takeover of Parliament after the Battle of Yorktown in 1781, a new French prime minister, Pierre Mendès-France, took office in June 1954 committed to leading a humiliated nation into a new era of peace. The following month an agreement was reached at Geneva under which Vietnam would be split, at least temporarily, along the seventeenth parallel with the Vietminh in control of the north and a new, noncommunist government under Ngo Dinh Diem in the south.

That the French lost despite having considerably more resources than the Vietminh should hardly be surprising. Their war effort, like that of the Americans who fought in Vietnam a decade later, violated nearly every precept of what became known as population-centric counterinsurgency doctrine by adopting a conventional, big-unit, firepower-intensive strategy that alienated the populace while failing to trap the Vietminh. Moreover they could not cut off the insurgency from outside support—perhaps the most reliable indicator of an uprising's prospects. Its importance was underlined by the fact that in 1948, following his break with Stalin, Tito closed Yugoslavia's territory to the Greek Communists. They were soon defeated. By contrast, Mao stepped up his support to the Vietminh the following year. They were soon victorious.

As part of the Geneva Accords, the Vietminh returned 3,900 prisoners taken at Dien Bien Phu. After only four months' captivity, they already resembled concentration camp survivors. But most remained defiant—determined, as Bigeard said, to "continue the struggle" and do better "next time."[103] That opportunity was to arrive sooner than they could have imagined in, of all places, Algeria, a part of France since 1830.

46.

"CONVINCE OR COERCE"

The Algerian War of Independence, 1954–1962

THE USE OF torture is older than civilization itself, but its form has changed over the centuries. The Middle Ages were the heyday of elaborate instruments for inflicting pain such as the rack, a wooden machine with rollers and ratchets that was used to pull legs and arms out of their sockets; the iron maiden, an iron cabinet in which the victim stood while a torturer stuck spikes or knives into his body; and the head crusher, a metal vise used to compress a cranium. The harnessing of electricity, and specifically the development of a device called the magneto, in the late nineteenth century created new opportunities for ruthless security services.

The magneto was a small generator capable of producing a high-voltage spark. In the early twentieth century a hand-cranked version was used to start cars, movie projectors, airplane propellers, and other devices. It was also useful for powering field telephones of the kind that became ubiquitous among the world's armies. By the 1930s the French investigative service, the Sûreté, and the Japanese secret police, the Kempeitai, were using alligator clips attached to field telephones to aid in the interrogation of suspects in Indochina and Korea, respectively. Each crank generated a shock; the faster the operator turned, the more voltage came out. By the mid-1950s this device, nicknamed the *gégène*, had migrated to Algeria, where among the French forces it won favor over more traditional methods of torture such as the local version of waterboarding—a practice that dated back to at least the fourteenth century—known as the *tuyau* (water pipe). Of course less elaborate methods of coercive interrogation, such as beating, food and water deprivation, and exposure to heat and cold, remained in widespread use as well. The advantage of the *gégène* was that it was quick, left no marks, and was not likely to kill the subject prematurely unless he happened to have a heart condition.[104]

Henri Alleg was to learn firsthand of the *gégène* and the other fiendish tools of the interrogator's trade after his arrest on June 12, 1957. A "very nervous" detective held him at gunpoint until the arrival of the soldiers from the Tenth Parachute Division who had taken responsibility for security in Algiers after the start of a terrorist campaign by the National Liberation Front (FLN). A Sten submachine gun jammed against his ribs, Alleg was driven to the local "clearing center," where he was hailed as a "prize catch." A French Jew as well as a Communist Party member, Alleg had been the editor of the *Alger Républicain*, a newspaper that had been banned for supporting the struggle against French rule.

"Ah! So you're the customer? Come with me!"

Alleg followed a paratrooper lieutenant into a small room. He was told to get undressed and then was tied with leather straps to a wooden plank. Another paratrooper asked, "Are you afraid? Do you want to talk?" They wanted to know who had hidden Alleg while he was on the run. He refused to say. "You're still playing at heroes, are you?" the paratrooper said. "It won't last long. In a quarter of an hour, you'll talk very nice."

A sergeant then appeared with electrical wires attached to a *gégène*. The "shiny steel clips" were attached to one of Alleg's ears and a finger. As soon as the power was turned on, Alleg recalled, "A flash of lightning exploded next to my ear and I felt my heart racing in my breast. I struggled, screaming, and stiffened myself until the straps cut into my flesh." But he still refused to talk. The electrical clips were then attached to his penis, making his whole body shake "with nervous shocks, getting ever stronger in intensity."

Next he was untied and dragged by his tie, which was knotted around his neck like a dog's leash, to another room where the *paras* pummeled him mercilessly—first with their fists, then with a piece of wood, all the while taunting him: "Listen you scum! You're finished! You're going to talk! . . . Everybody talks here!"

Alleg still didn't talk, so a new session of electrical torture was ordered, this time employing a larger magneto. "In my very agony I felt the difference in quality," he wrote. "Instead of the sharp and rapid spasms that seemed to tear my body in two, it was now a greater pain that took possession of all my muscles and tightened them in longer spasms."

Next up was the *tuyau*. He was carried on a plank into the kitchen, his head wrapped in a rag, and his mouth wedged open with a piece of wood, while his head was soaked in water from a rubber tube attached to a tap. "Water flowed everywhere: in my mouth, in my nose, all over my face. . . . I had the impression of drowning, and a terrible agony, that of death itself, took possession of me."

Yet even this did not break Alleg. The enraged *paras* beat him again until he lost consciousness. After wakening him up with "blows and kicks," they decided to "roast him." A paper torch was lit, Alleg recalled, and "I felt the flame on my penis and on my legs, the hairs crackling as they caught fire."

Finally, "trembling with cold and nervous exhaustion," he was thrown into a cell. He tried to lie down but could get no rest on a mattress stuffed with barbed wire. He wanted to go to the bathroom but was told to "piss on yourself." No food or water was provided.

So it went for day after day of torture that began after nightfall and sometimes lasted until dawn. From other parts of the building, Alleg "could hear shouts and cries, muffled by the gag, and curses and blows." He "soon knew that it was in no way an exceptional night, but the routine of the building."

Alleg turned out to be more fortunate than most of the other "customers." At the end of his torture, he did not "disappear" or get "killed while trying to escape"—the fate of thousands of other detainees. After a month Alleg was moved to a prison where he was able to write an account of his ordeal. The resulting book, *The Question*, quickly sold sixty thousand copies in France before being banned.[105]

Alleg's account, and that of a few soldiers who objected to the widespread use of torture, raised anguished cries among a French populace that only too recently had suffered similar treatment from the Gestapo. How could "civilized" soldiers resort to such barbarous practices, critics asked? All too easily. The Algerian War, like the Indochina War, had been marked by savagery on both sides from the start.

✦ ✦ ✦

THE REVOLT HAD begun on All Saints' Day, November 1, 1954, with seventy scattered attacks across the country. The rebels had few weapons and their tactics were amateurish. At one mine, where the rebels hoped to seize 1,500 pounds of dynamite, they were driven away by a single Muslim security guard.[106] So ineffectual were these early efforts that the FLN decided to turn from guerrilla-style attacks on French security forces to terrorist attacks on French residents and their Muslim "collaborators."

Algeria differed from Indochina in that it had a substantial European settler population—nearly a million *pieds noirs* (black feet) living among 8.5 million Muslims.[107] Ramdane Abane, the most intelligent of the FLN leaders, who might have become an Algerian Mao or Ho if he had not died in 1957 at the hands of fellow rebels, believed in making life intolerable for the *pieds noirs* and moderate Muslims. He wanted to goad the security forces into reprisals that would turn the apathetic Muslim population toward the FLN. His sinister dicta: "We need blood in the headlines to make the world aware," and "one corpse in a jacket is always worth more than twenty in uniform."[108]

At virtually the same time in Kenya, Mau Mau rebels were targeting a much smaller number of European settlers—29,000 in all, of whom only 32 were killed.[109] Yet even this small number of deaths provoked a heavy-handed response from the British. Indeed, as the historian David Anderson argues, all of Europe's settler colonies in Africa—not only Kenya and Algeria but also Angola, Mozambique, Zimbabwe, and South Africa—saw brutal violence in the days of decolonization.[110] Next to South Africa, which by the 1950s was no longer a colony, Algeria had the largest white population on the continent, and therefore the scale of violence there was especially high.

On August 20, 1955, there were frenzied attacks on Europeans living around the port of Philippeville. In a nearby mining town, where 130 Europeans lived among 2,000 Muslims, FLN *fellaghas* ("bandits") went from home to home during the noonday siesta, slaughtering everyone inside. French paratroopers who arrived shortly thereafter found a scene of horrors. "When I saw children chopped up into pieces, with their throats slit or crushed to death, the women who had been disemboweled or decapitated, I think I really forgot what having any pity meant," wrote Major Paul Aussaresses. "What was hardest to believe was that these people had been massacred and mutilated by their Algerian Muslim neighbors, who had been peacefully living with them until then."

The troops found rebels mixed with civilians in the streets and "fired indiscriminately on the whole lot of them." "For two hours our submachine guys never stopped firing . . . ," a *para* recalled. "The barrel of my P.M. [submachine gun] got so hot I couldn't touch it." Eventually orders were given to take prisoners. Hundreds of Arab men were rounded up. The next morning they were massacred by "the regiment's automatic rifles and machine guns." The French counted 1,273 dead Muslims—so many, a *para* said, "that they had to be buried with bulldozers." "I was totally indifferent," Aussaresses wrote. "We had to kill them and I did it. That was all."[111]

Thus was set the pattern of terrorism and reprisal. It is irrelevant to ask who was more to blame—the FLN or the French? Both sides kept the "vicious circle" going.[112]

To be sure, in the spirit of Lyautey, the French tried some civic-action programs to win the allegiance of the population. These included giving Muslims more voting rights and spending more on their schools and social services. Teams from the Section Administrative Spécialisée—successors of the Service des Affaires Indigènes employed a few decades earlier in Morocco—spread across the countryside to improve life for Muslims. But it was too little, too late. French leaders, even Socialists such as the interior minister, François Mitterrand, refused to countenance independence, which was what the populace really wanted. In their view Algeria was as much a part of France as Burgundy or Provence. That outlook was reinforced by the powerful *pied noir* lobby, which had an outsize influence in France's fractured parliament and feared that if the Muslim masses took over, its constituents would face a grim choice between "the suitcase or the coffin."

In past colonial conflicts, Western armies, composed of soldiers whose own families typically lived far from the battlefield, were often a force of moderation compared with local settlers. The regular U.S. Army, for instance, was more restrained in its use of force against Indians than local militias such as the Colorado volunteers who perpetrated the Sand Creek Massacre in 1864. That was not the case in Algeria, where the French Army was determined to do whatever it took to avenge the defeat it had recently suffered in Indochina. Old salts even referred to their new enemies as "Viets." The Catholic and conservative officer corps was convinced, on the basis of scant evidence, that the FLN, just like the Vietminh, was part of a global communist conspiracy whose defeat justified any excesses. Indeed the primary lesson that French theorists of *guerre révolutionnaire* (revolutionary war) took away from Indochina was, as Colonel Roger Trinquier was to write in his widely cited 1961 book, *Modern Warfare*, that "*modern warfare* requires the unconditional support of the populace. This support must be maintained at any price."

There were a few abortive attempts to organize pro-French indoctrination sessions to gain this support with public slogan shouting and song singing, *á la Viet*, but such theatrics were greeted, wrote David Galula, another influential counterinsurgency theorist who served in Algeria, with "snickers and skepticism" from French soldiers and "complete impassivity" from Muslim villagers.[113] Most officers decided they could more effectively sway the populace by simply out-terrorizing the FLN. Their slogan became "Convince or Coerce."[114]

✦ ✦ ✦

THAT ATTITUDE WAS to have fateful consequences when the battle shifted to Algiers, a whitewashed, sun-baked city of French-style grand boulevards, chic shops, and popular beaches. Of 900,000 inhabitants, two-thirds were European. On September 30, 1956, bombs went off in the Milk Bar and Cafeteria, two popular *pied noir* haunts. A third bomb was planted in the Air France terminal but failed to explode. Three people were killed and fifty injured, including women and children.

The bombs had been planted by three attractive young Muslim women who could pass for Europeans. They had been recruited by Yacef Saadi, the FLN operations chief in Algiers who supervised a network of 1,200 fighters and 4,500 auxiliaries. He, in turn, was assisted by Ali Amara, better known as Ali la Pointe, a former pimp who had been radicalized in prison. He contributed to the mayhem by assassinating the president of the Algerian Federation of Mayors. By the end of 1956, wrote one resident of Algiers, "urban terrorism [had] reached an unprecedented height," with thirty attacks during Christmas week alone.

Unable to stop the FLN attacks, the civil authorities called in the Tenth Parachute Division under Brigadier General Jacques Massu, a soldier of "dash and vigor" with a face that resembled "a well-worn chopping block." He was, as an American diplomat living in Algiers said, "a tough man for a tough job." He had just led his men in a militarily successful but politically frustrating assault on the Suez Canal—an operation that was stopped short of its objectives by American pressure. Now he commanded four understrength *para* regiments, 4,600 men in all, wearing their distinctive "leopard" camouflage and bright red or green berets instead of helmets. The only exception was the Third Colonial Parachute Regiment, which sported high-peaked "lizard" forage caps designed by its publicity-loving commander, Lieutenant Colonel Marcel Bigeard.

The preceding year, on June 16, 1956, while campaigning in the interior, the *bled*, Bigeard had been shot just above the heart. Evacuation by helicopter and airplane saved his life. A few months later, on September 5, 1956, while jogging alone and unarmed in a seaside town, Bigeard was shot twice more at point-blank range by three young Arabs. A *pied noir* who was driving by refused to take him to the hospital; he didn't want to soil his car seats with blood. Bigeard barely survived. Now back in fighting form, he was at the forefront of efforts to protect the ungrateful *pieds noirs* from their Arab enemies.

His regiment—"a war machine of formidable precision"—was given the most important assignment: the Casbah. Literally it meant "the citadel," a term used to describe what was, to Europeans, the forbidding and menacing native quarter. Here, along dark, narrow, winding lanes, lived 100,000 Muslims. In their midst lurked Yacef Saadi, Ali la Pointe, and their confederates. But how to root them out?

The *paras*' methods were depicted with considerable accuracy in *The Battle of Algiers*, a 1966 film produced by Yacef Saadi. Their challenges included a general strike called by the FLN for January 28, 1957. This was broken by the simple expedient of rounding up Muslims at gunpoint and trucking them to work. Storekeepers who closed their shops had their shutters ripped off by armored cars. The entire city was placed under a "state of siege" that made it look like an "armed camp." Mobile checkpoints were set up to search "anyone with a brown skin." Meanwhile the "leopards" cordoned off the Casbah with barbed wire. A curfew was imposed and orders given to fire on anyone caught outside. The bodies were left in the streets until the following morning to impress upon the inhabitants that they had met a force "even more extreme than the FLN."

To figure out the lay of the land in the Casbah, "a spidery hive of sand-colored buildings," the *paras* conducted a census and created a map showing who lived in which house. This was the responsibility of Colonel Roger Trinquier, the hard-bitten old Indochina hand. A preliminary list of targets was then drawn up with the aid of police files. "Gentlemen, your mission is to take back the night from the FLN in Algiers," Massu told his subordinates. In the early morning hours of January 8, 1957, the first strike teams fanned out into the Casbah, breaking down doors and dragging hundreds of suspects in for questioning. While each regiment had its own interrogation centers, the most promising subjects were turned over to Major Paul Aussaresses, a veteran of secret service work in the Indochina War and in World War II as part of the Jedburghs. He reported directly to Massu, who viewed torture as a "cruel necessity."

Aussaresses set up operations in the Villa des Tourelles, a two-story structure on the outskirts of town. Every night he and his men gave their "guests" the same kind of treatment that Henri Alleg was to receive in another prison, the difference being, as Aussaresses noted, "the mere fact that they were at the Villa des Tourelles meant they were considered so dangerous that they were not to get out of there alive." After they had been "broken," Aussaresses recalled, "most of the time my men traveled about twenty kilometers outside Algiers to some 'remote location' where the suspects were shot with submachine guns and then buried." Other units had their own way of disposing of detainees. Rumor had it that the Third Colonial Parachute Regiment threw suspects out of airplanes over the Mediterranean; the victims were called *crevettes* (shrimp) *Bigeard*. In all, during the Battle of Algiers, 24,000 Muslims were arrested and 4,000 disappeared "without trace." Taken together those figures amounted to a third of the Casbah's population.

In recent years the myth has become prevalent that torture doesn't work, that suspects simply tell their interrogators whatever they want to hear. If that were the case, the prevalence of harsh interrogation methods—used by both insurgents and counterinsurgents throughout history—would be inexplicable. In fact few detainees are able to hold out as Henri Alleg did. Torture may be morally reprehensible, but there is little doubt that, at least in Algeria, it was tactically effective. By forcing captured terrorists to identify their confederates and by encouraging other detainees to turn informant so as to avoid the *gégène*, the *paras* were able to dismantle the FLN structure inside Algiers within a matter of months. By October 1957, following the capture of Yacef Saadi and the death of Ali la Pointe, the Battle of Algiers was over.[115]

✦ ✦ ✦

THE FRENCH WERE winning the war not only in Algiers but also in the rest of the country. They had started the conflict with around 50,000 troops. By 1956 there were 400,000 troops—one for every 21 Muslims. Even without counting at least 120,000 Muslim *harkis* (auxiliaries) who served in militia units, this exceeded the ratio of 1 counterinsurgent per 50 civilians that is sometimes said to be the minimum to defeat an insurgency. Acting under unlimited "emergency" powers, the security forces detained over 50,000 Muslims and killed many more.[116]

With the FLN combat organization all but shattered inside Algeria, the group became desperate to infiltrate fighters from its safe haven in neighboring Tunisia. To prevent this from occurring, the French constructed a 200-mile barrier along the border manned by 80,000 troops. The Morice Line, named after the minister of defense, consisted of an electrified wire fence, minefields, searchlights, and electronic warning systems. It proved far more effective than a better-known fortification named for an earlier defense minister: André Maginot. As soon as an FLN breakthrough was detected, the *fellaghas* would be targeted by prepositioned 105-millimeter howitzers and hunted by troops in jeeps or helicopters. This was the first extensive use of helicopters in war. More than two hundred were deployed, giving the *paras* the ability to trap and wipe out enemy contingents. "Attempts to break through are virtually all doomed to failure," wrote a French journalist.[117]

Meanwhile double agents were recruited within the FLN; the man Yacef Saadi nominated to succeed him in Algiers had been turned by French intelligence. Such coups sowed suspicion in FLN ranks and led to self-defeating purges. Outside Algeria, the French disrupted the FLN arms pipeline. Ships were intercepted in the Mediterranean and arms dealers assassinated in Europe. Also targeted were top FLN leaders in exile. In 1956 an FLN delegation led by Ahmed Ben Bella was flying on a Moroccan DC-3 to Tunisia when the French high command radioed the pilot, a French reservist, and ordered him to put down in Algeria instead. The entire party was arrested on the ground—much to their surprise, since they had been told by the canny stewardess that they were landing in Tunis.[118]

This unrelenting pressure prevented the FLN from making the transition, as the Vietnamese and Chinese Communists had done in accordance with Maoist teaching, to conventional warfare. Whereas Giap was able to mobilize entire divisions armed with heavy artillery, the FLN seldom operated in units of greater than company strength equipped with light weapons. There was no Algerian Dien Bien Phu and no significant sector of "liberated territory" inside Algeria, although the rebels would continue to enjoy safe havens in Tunisia and Morocco, neighboring states where the French "protectorate" had ended in 1956. By 1959, with the number of FLN attacks rapidly falling, the French armed forces had all but won the war militarily.[119] Yet they were about to suffer a crushing political defeat.

✦ ✦ ✦

THE INSTRUMENT OF the French army's undoing was its own hero—Charles de Gaulle. Both the *pieds noirs* and the army were disgusted with the weak Fourth Republic, run by an ever-changing cast of politicians who, they feared, would sell out to the enemy. In May 1958 a civil insurrection broke out in Algiers leading to the formation of a committee of public safety composed of *pieds noirs* and army officers under the leadership of General Massu. His *paras* actually seized power in Corsica and threatened to descend on Paris unless de Gaulle was returned to power.

The military's wish was granted. But de Gaulle did not turn out to be the diehard advocate of *Algérie française* that they had expected. The pragmatic president realized that permanently pacifying Algeria against the wishes of most of its populace would be too costly to contemplate. The war was already eroding valuable diplomatic capital at a time when France was struggling to emerge from its wartime devastation to become once again an important independent player on the international scene. Algerian independence was growing more popular at the United Nations and even in the United States, where in 1957 Senator John F. Kennedy called for an end to French rule. The French government tried to sell the war effort by hiring Madison Avenue public-relations firms, but the FLN proved more adept at the propaganda war. Its worldly envoys succeeded in winning international recognition despite their fighters' lack of success on the ground—a feat that would inspire the African National Congress, the Palestine Liberation Organization, and other "national liberation" movements that were to substitute public-relations prowess for traditional measures of military effectiveness.[120] The war was also losing support at home. The French public was appalled by the actions taken in their name. The army, in turn, was becoming dangerously politicized by its identification with the *pied noir* cause.

Under those circumstances, de Gaulle calculated that getting out of Algeria would enhance France's *grandeur*—the lodestar of his life. In 1959, as *le général* later wrote in his inimitable style, "France, through me, announced her intentions to place Algeria's destiny in the hands of the Algerians."[121]

"Ultras" among the army and *pieds noirs* fought desperately to avert the inevitable. In 1960 enraged Europeans took to the barricades in Algiers, slaughtering gendarmes who stood in their way. The uprising lasted only a week because it was not actively supported by the army. The following year a coterie of generals, including two former commanders in Algeria, Generals Raoul Salan and Maurice Challe, attempted a coup of their own. They briefly took control of Algiers, but the uprising unraveled when de Gaulle appealed over their heads to their soldiers, imploring them in a radio address to stay loyal.

Although they had lost the "battle of the transistors," some of the putschists were determined to continue the struggle. They formed the Secret Army Organization (OAS) and waged a vicious terrorist campaign that included several unsuccessful attempts to assassinate de Gaulle—the inspiration for the novel and movie *The Day of the Jackal*. Other foiled plots on the mainland included attempts to blow up the Eiffel Tower and Jean-Paul Sartre's apartment. But the OAS's main focus was in Algeria, where, ironically, it copied many of the FLN's organizational trademarks.

The OAS citadel was Bab-el-Oued, a neighborhood of poor Europeans in Algiers next to the Casbah. The OAS strike arm was the Delta Commandos, several hundred merciless gunmen led by Roger Degueldre, a "harsh" and "hard" former Foreign Legion officer who had been wounded at Dien Bien Phu. "The Deltas were intoxicated, it has been said, with *Algérie française* propaganda and anisette," a French journalist wrote, and they had no compunctions about committing murder. By 1962 Algiers was averaging thirty to forty killings a day—far more than during the earlier battle against the FLN and comparable to Baghdad during the early years of the Iraq War. "They kill in cars, on motorbikes, with grenades, automatic weapons, and knives . . . ," wrote a leading Muslim novelist before he too was slain by the OAS. "Terror reigns in Algiers."

The French army was finally provoked into a full-scale assault on Bab-el-Oued employing 20,000 troops supported by tanks, artillery, and air strikes. At the same time, using informers and brutal interrogations of detainees, the authorities systematically tracked down OAS leaders. Degueldre was arrested on April 7, 1962, and executed two months later. General Salan was arrested the same month and sent to prison. By the end of 1962 the OAS was finished. In some ways it resembled the post–Civil War Ku Klux Klan, another white-supremacist terrorist group, but with a decisive difference: the KKK had the tacit support of the majority of the Southern population (59 percent white), whereas the OAS acted on behalf of a European minority outnumbered almost nine to one.[122]

By the time Algeria officially became independent on July 3, 1962, most Europeans had either left or were about to do so. The FLN exacted a vicious revenge on Muslims who had fought for the colonialists. At least 30,000 *harkis* were killed, often after being tortured along with their families. This was a reminder that just as in Kenya, where the Mau Mau killed far more Africans than Europeans (1,800 vs. 32),[123] the war in Algeria was also a civil war pitting pro- and anti-French Muslims against each other. The war as a whole was said to have cost French forces 17,456 dead, 64,985 wounded, and

1,000 missing. European civilians suffered 10,000 casualties. There is no good figure of Muslim war dead; estimates range from 300,000 to one million.[124] Notwithstanding the terrible cost of independence, the FLN's success would inspire countless liberation movements across Africa that within a few years would put an end to the last remaining bastions of European colonial control.

✦ ✦ ✦

It is hard to exaggerate the bitterness felt within the French army after this defeat. The soldiers' attitude was captured in two novels written by the ex-paratrooper Jean Lartéguy: *The Centurions* (1962) and *The Praetorians* (1963). Indochina was bad enough: "the French Army," one of Lartéguy's *paras* says, "has been beaten by a handful of little yellow dwarfs because of the stupidity and inertia of its leaders." Now in Algeria, "enough's enough, we can't afford any more defeats." Yet that is just what happened. "Colonel Raspeguy," modeled on Bigeard, thinks bitterly, "A victor smells good even if he stinks of blood and sweat; the vanquished can drench himself in eau-de-Cologne from Dior, he'll still leave a smell of shit behind him."

Soldiers naturally blamed far-off superiors for this smelly surrender; they "felt hatred and disgust welling up against the people back in Paris . . . the highly-placed officials, untrustworthy generals, and shady politicians."[125] What few would acknowledge was that their own tactics had contributed to this disastrous outcome. The use of torture was not new; it had been widespread in Indochina. What was new was the level of public scrutiny such practices received when employed in Algiers, the most European of Algerian cities, with a substantial foreign press corps. The army was not prepared to cope with the resulting backlash. Roger Trinquier had expressed a common view in the ranks when he said prior to the Battle of Algiers, "I care little for the opinions of Americans or the press."[126] He should have cared more.

The Algerian War was the most dramatic example since the Greek Revolution in the 1820s of how a guerrilla organization defeated on the battlefield could nevertheless prevail by winning "the battle of the narrative." (The IRA and the American revolutionaries also made good use of public opinion, but they had not been militarily defeated like the Algerians and

Greeks.) A similar outcome had barely been averted in the Boer War and the Philippine War. From now on Western soldiers would have to pay increasing attention to an aspect of warfare—information operations—that had not unduly troubled their predecessors who had fought colonial conflicts in centuries past. The growing glare of media scrutiny would necessitate a kinder, gentler style of counterinsurgency—one that would be exemplified by the British strategy in Malaya.

47.

A MAN AND A PLAN

Briggs, Templer, and the Malayan Emergency, 1948–1960

On a typically torrid tropical afternoon on February 7, 1952, a "pale, wiry, and intense"[127] man stepped off a Royal Air Force aircraft onto the tarmac of Kuala Lumpur's primitive airport. General Sir Gerald Templer was dressed in a debonair tropical suit, a large handkerchief protruding from his breast pocket. With his thin mustache and slicked-back hair, he bore more than a passing resemblance to the actor David Niven, a fellow Sandhurst graduate and World War II veteran. But although Niven had left Hollywood to compile a distinguished wartime record, his military achievements paled by comparison with those of the older man, who had also fought in World War I. Templer had seen action from the Somme to Dunkirk and Anzio. In the interwar years he had competed in the Olympics as a hurdler and won a competition as the British army's top bayonet fighter.

His career had almost ended, along with his life, in 1944 when he was a division commander in Italy. While driving in a jeep, Templer passed an army truck at the precise moment when it hit a landmine. It was later said that he had nearly been killed by a flying piano that had been in the back of the truck. He survived but his back was broken. "Only general ever wounded by a piano," he joked, although the culprit actually appears to have been one of the truck's wheels.

That terrible accident turned out to be a stroke of fortune in disguise, for it meant that Templer had to give up battlefield command. He wound up working first at SOE in London, then as director of civil affairs and military government in the British zone of occupation in Germany, where he became famous, or more rightly infamous, for sacking Konrad Adenauer, future chancellor of West Germany, as mayor of Cologne. (He thought Adenauer too old and indolent.) This was followed by a stint as director of military intelligence in London.

These experiences in subversion, intelligence, and civil administration—along with his interwar stint in Palestine fighting the Arab Revolt, which taught him "the mind and method of the guerrilla"—turned out to be better preparation than a normal army career for the assignment he had now been given. Templer had been appointed high commissioner and director of operations in Malaya, combining the highest civil and military offices, as Lyautey had done in Morocco. Those extraordinary powers had been granted him by Prime Minister Winston Churchill because of the dire situation in Malaya.[128]

As in other countries that had been occupied by Japan, Malaya had fielded a guerrilla army with covert Allied support, in this case from the SOE's Force 136. After the war the Communist-dominated Malayan People's Anti-Japanese Army was reborn as the Malayan Races Liberation Army. It turned to fighting the returning British, in many cases using the same jungle camps and the same weapons they had employed against the Japanese. In 1948, following the murder of three British planters, the government declared a state of emergency that suspended civil laws and gave the police and army wide-ranging powers of search, arrest, and detention. (Suspects could be detained for up to two years without trial.)[129]

In spite of increasing pressure, the guerrillas appeared to be gaining strength under the leadership of Chin Peng, the twenty-six-year-old son of a Chinese bicycle-shop owner who had taken over the MRLA after the preceding secretary general, an informer for both the Japanese and the British, had absconded with the party treasury in 1947. Chin Peng was a "quiet character with incisive brain and unusual ability,"[130] in the opinion of one SOE officer who had worked with him—the self-contained antithesis of such outgoing, larger-than-life guerrilla chiefs as Michael Collins or Giuseppe Garibaldi. He had learned guerrilla warfare from the British themselves, and for his wartime work he had been awarded an Order of the British Empire. Like most Asian communists, he had also made a careful study of Mao Zedong's works, although in practice he proved to be hardly Mao's equal as a strategist.

The Communist Terrorists, as the British liked to label them, soon numbered more than 5,000 fighters aided by a larger number of part-time helpers in the *Min Yuen* ("People's Organization"). The insurgents drew much of their strength from Malaya's 2 million Chinese residents; they had few backers among the rest of the population of 5.1 million, composed of 2.5 million Malays, 500,000 Indians, and 10,000 Europeans.[131] Much as the Communist insurgents in Vietnam would target French plantations as well as French security forces, so too Malaya's insurgents would emerge from the jungle to carry out a reign of terror not only against British security forces but also against the economic underpinning of the country—rubber plantations and tin mines, which were managed by Europeans and worked by Chinese and Indians. British planters got used to having their bungalows fired on every night. Trains were derailed, rubber trees slashed, factories set afire. This reign of terror was designed to drive the Europeans out of the country, leaving the insurgents a free hand. By 1952 the Communists had killed 3,000 people and tied down 30,000 Commonwealth troops and 60,000 police officers.[132]

Their greatest triumph came on October 5, 1951, when thirty-six guerrillas set up an ambush along a steep roadway sixty miles north of Kuala Lumpur. At 1:15 p.m., they spotted a Land Rover carrying half a dozen policemen followed by a Rolls-Royce limousine flying the Union Jack. The Communists let loose a volley of rifle and machine-gun fire that hit almost every occupant of the Land Rover and wounded the driver of the Rolls. The back door of the limousine opened and an Englishman got out. He was cut down within a few yards. Thus did the guerrillas unwittingly kill Sir Henry Gurney, the senior representative of Her Majesty's Government in Malaya.[133]

It would later become clear that this was the high-water mark of the insurgency and that it was already beginning to subside. But this was not at all obvious to Gerald Templer on his arrival four months later as he drove from the airport to King's House, the official residence of the high commissioner, in a car still scarred with the bullet holes from the ambush that had killed his predecessor. The mood in Kuala Lumpur was grim. "We were on the way to losing control of the country, and soon," wrote the British colonial secretary, Oliver Lyttelton, while a British adviser spoke of a "general feeling of hopelessness."[134] The loss of Malaya, they knew, would be not only an economic blow to Britain (Malaya was the world's biggest exporter of natural rubber) but also a psychological blow—it would be seen as a victory for international communism and a defeat for the Free World.

✦ ✦ ✦

FIELD MARSHAL BERNARD Law Montgomery, Templer's mentor and a fellow Ulsterman, had penned a pithy note to Lyttelton advising that victory in Malaya required two things: "We must have a plan. Secondly we must have a man. When we have a plan and a man, we shall succeed: not otherwise." ("I may, perhaps without undue conceit, say that this had occurred to me," Lyttelton noted drily.) After his first choice withdrew from consideration, Monty pushed Templer as the man who could "deliver the goods."[135] What he did not seem to realize was that the plan that Malaya needed was already in existence.

Its author was Lieutenant General Sir Harold Briggs, a career Indian Army officer who had distinguished himself in the Burma campaign during World War II—a source of jungle-fighting experience for the British that was to prove invaluable in Malaya, which was four-fifths jungle.[136] Briggs had been called out of retirement in 1950 to become director of operations coordinating military and police activity in Malaya. In that capacity he produced what became known as the Briggs Plan: the subsequent blueprint of victory. It included multiple steps, from hiring more Special Branch inspectors and better coordinating police-military operations to clearing roads in isolated areas and deporting captured insurgents to China. Its centerpiece was the resettlement of Chinese squatters, an updated version of the "reconcentration" policies that had been employed in conflicts as varied as the American Indian Wars, the Cuban and Filipino insurrections, and the Boer War—and that was also to be employed in the decade ahead in Kenya, Algeria, and South Vietnam.

Between 400,000 and 600,000 squatters (there was no accurate count)[137] lived in shanty towns on the edge of the jungle, scraping out a meager living with farming and other jobs. They did not enjoy title to their lands, and they were alienated from the mainstream of Malay society. This made them a prime breeding ground for the insurgency. The Briggs Plan began the process of building five hundred New Villages where, protected by armed guards, perimeter lighting, and barbed wire, the squatters could be separated from the guerrillas.[138] Security was to be provided in the first instance by 50,000 Chinese Home Guards.[139] Nobody could enter or leave a New Village without an identity card, and curfew was strictly enforced. Workers were searched leaving the village for work in the morning to ensure that they were not smuggling out any rice to feed the Communists. The Briggs Plan instituted draconian penalties for anyone helping the guerrillas, "making the death penalty mandatory for convicted bandit food agents and money collectors."[140]

The resettlement plan actually proved popular in the end because the Chinese were provided title to their lands, electricity, clean drinking water, schools, and clinics. This stood in stark contrast to ill-fated French attempts to implement a similar policy in Algeria. By 1959 over a million Muslim villagers had been moved into fortified "regroupment camps," which, like the British concentration camps in South Africa six decades earlier, lacked basic amenities, including food, sanitation facilities, and medicine, and therefore became breeding grounds of disease and discontentment.[141] The New Villages were better run, but their inhabitants were hardly there by choice—they were kept inside at gunpoint.

With his focus on resettlement, Briggs deemphasized the sort of fruitless "jungle bashing" on which the army had wasted valuable resources in the war's early years. Too many brigade commanders newly arrived from Europe and, in the words of one officer, "nostalgic for World War II"[142] would send their troops thrashing through the dense vegetation only to discover nothing but empty guerrilla camps. "You can't deal with a plague of mosquitoes by swatting each individual insect," Briggs said. "You find and disinfect their breeding grounds. Then the mosquitoes are finished."[143]

There would still be operations to rout guerrillas in their jungle redoubts undertaken primarily by units such as the Special Air Service, commanded by the Chindit veteran "Mad Mike" Calvert, which were specially trained for long-range penetration and assisted by Dyak headhunters imported from Borneo to serve as trackers. Briggs, however, switched the bulk of his resources to "breaking the popular support for the rising,"[144] the foundation of any successful counterinsurgency strategy. As Robert Thompson, a Malayan civil servant and another veteran of the Chindits, put it, "The chief emphasis . . . must be on 'clear-and-hold' operations as opposed to 'search-and-clear' operations (or sweeps)."[145]

This was to prove an immensely effective strategy, but Briggs left Malaya at the end of 1951 sick, bitter, and disillusioned after eighteen months' service. He had been frustrated that he had been limited to a coordinator's role with limited authority over the security forces and the civilian officials who worked with the native rulers of the nine states that made up the Federation of Malaya.

✦ ✦ ✦

TEMPLER WAS TO get the powers that Briggs lacked, and he was to make full use of them. He had a mischievous, fun-loving side, but normally it was well hidden. Mostly he came across as imperious, demanding, driven—not someone who suffered fools gladly. During the desperate fighting of the 1944 Battle of Anzio, where he was a division commander, he had been nicknamed the Scalded Cat. He brought the same "electrifying" impact to Malaya, where he was appalled by the indolent attitude of many bureaucrats and planters—"chairbound . . . dunderheads," one correspondent called them, while the colonial secretary acerbically noted that many were "varnished with port and pickled with gin."[146]

When called upon to deliver a speech at an exclusive Kuala Lumpur club, Templer berated his privileged listeners, telling them that Communists "seldom go to the races. They seldom go to dinner parties or cocktail parties. And they don't play golf!" He threatened to close down another club until it admitted "natives."[147]

Templer's "brusque" directives, criticisms, and questions, delivered in a "clipped harsh voice," offended some; he was not afraid to tell an official who had earned his ire that he was a "stinker" or "no bloody good." But most were impressed by his "dynamic and sometimes abrasive personality." One district officer came away from a meeting "feeling like an electric torch which has just been filled with new batteries."[148]

As he explained in a letter to the colonial secretary, Templer did his best to drive bureaucrats "out of their offices and make them talk about the Emergency with the people on the ground, in whose head ultimately lies the solution."[149] Taking his own advice, he made a habit of roaming the country in an armored car, giving scant advance notice of his arrival to military units or villages, so they could not tidy up things. When he saw things that needed correcting, as he frequently did, he issued memoranda typed in red with a deadline for action. These "red minutes" delivered by dispatch riders were an echo of Winston Churchill's wartime memos marked "Action this day"—and just as effective in galvanizing a hidebound bureaucracy.

Templer secured his place in counterinsurgency history with his emphasis on political, rather than kinetic, warfare. "The shooting side of the business is only 25% of the trouble," he often said, "and the other 75% lies in getting the people of this country behind us."[150] Even more famously, he declared, "The answer lies not in pouring more troops into the jungle, but in the hearts and minds of the people."[151] This phrase echoed, no doubt inadvertently, lines written in 1776 by the British general Sir Henry Clinton ("gain the hearts and subdue the minds of America") and by John Adams in 1818 ("The Revolution was in the minds and hearts of the people").[152] Not until Templer used it, however, did "hearts and minds" turn into a byword and later a cliché. (That "nauseating phrase," as Templer called it in 1968, was to become a particular favorite of Lyndon Johnson's.)[153]

It is an injunction that has often been misunderstood to mean focusing purely on social, political, and economic efforts to win over the populace. Like Hubert Lyautey, William Howard Taft, David Petraeus and other exemplars of the "population-centric" school of counterinsurgency, Templer did believe in civic action. He encouraged the army to renovate schools, open hospitals to civilians, and generally help the populace. More importantly, to counter Communist appeals, he repeatedly emphasized to Malayans that they would be granted independence "in due course."[154] And, following the ancient Roman example, he pushed to extend Malayan citizenship to more than a million Indians and Chinese, thus giving them a stake in their adopted country.

But winning "hearts and minds" also involved coercive measures such as resettling the squatters—a process begun by Briggs and completed by Templer—which would be unthinkable for twenty-first-century British or American counterinsurgents. Robert Thompson, the former Chindit who worked closely with Briggs and Templer, noted that warfare was not a popularity contest: "What the peasant wants to know is: Does the government mean to win the war? Because if not, he will have to support the insurgent." "The government," he added, "must show that it is not only determined, but prepared, to be ruthless."[155]

✦ ✦ ✦

TEMPLER SHOWED THE requisite ruthlessness. In April 1952, after a British party was ambushed and twelve men killed, he arrived to demand "with a savage anger" that the residents of the nearby village of Tanjong Malim name the attackers. When they refused, he imposed a twenty-two-hour curfew and cut the rice ration in half. Forms were then circulated to all households so they could inform on the guerrillas anonymously. This led to thirty-eight arrests and, thirteen days later, to the lifting of the restrictions. Yet Templer took no joy in such tough measures, which reeked of "collective punishment" and aroused Parliament's ire. Eventually he abolished them.[156]

He also cracked down on the sorts of abuses that had been common in the early days of the emergency when British troops, many of them raw, frightened conscripts, had burned whole villages in retaliation for attacks and indiscriminately locked up and abused suspects: 200,000 people were held for less than a month, 25,000 for more than a month. On one occasion in 1948 Tommies had even massacred 24 Chinese civilians.[157]

Templer realized that such blunderbuss tactics only drove more recruits into the Communist camp. He took a more measured approach in which small units would act on the basis of good intelligence. "My absolute top priority," he declared shortly after arriving, "is to get the intelligence machine right."[158] The federal police's Special Branch was given lead responsibility for this task and expanded from two officers to more than two hundred.[159] Its detectives scored notable successes by interrogating Surrendered Enemy Personnel and by intercepting Communist couriers—Chin Peng's chief method of communicating with his forces. Templer pressed troops to capture rather than kill insurgents "because of the information we can suck out of them."[160] Whereas in Indochina and Algeria torture was routine, here even high-level suspects were not tortured. Troops were warned, "Confessions must not . . . be obtained by any inducement, threat, or promise."[161]

Templer did not neglect the need for offensive action. He often told security personnel, "Get out and kill those bastards—communist terrorists."[162] To help accomplish this task, he sent troops to a Jungle Warfare School and issued a tactical handbook titled *The Conduct of Anti-Terrorist Operations in Malaya*, which for the first time introduced a common operational approach.

One of the most important weapons in his arsenal was psychological warfare, which was employed "to cause general demoralization" in Communist ranks.[163] British aircraft dropped millions of leaflets offering guerrillas a safe-conduct pass to surrender. Other aircraft flew low over the jungle to broadcast appeals to give up. These "voice aircraft" were especially effective (and spooky) when they named individual guerrillas down below. Rewards were offered for insurgents "dead or alive," but higher sums were available if alive.[164]

The biggest inducement for surrender was that the guerrillas could not sustain themselves in the jungle. In some New Villages all rice was cooked communally in well-guarded kitchens, and individual possession of the precious grain was prohibited. To keep themselves fed the Communists began planting gardens in the jungle. Whenever these were discovered, they were destroyed, either by herbicide-spraying aircraft or by troops who would uproot and burn the crops.[165] Ching Peng recalled, "Our situation became so desperate at one point that I even looked into the possibility of making the rubber seed edible." This didn't pan out: rubber seeds contain a poisonous toxin that cannot be removed.[166] Thus Templer, showing that he could act ruthlessly when he felt the need to do so, literally starved the Communists into submission, much as the U.S. Army had once done to the Indians. By the time they gave up, most insurgents were a sorry sight, with, in the words of a British brigadier, "shaggy hair, emaciated countenance, ragged khaki uniform, and eyes like those of a hunted rat."[167]

As more Communists came in (eventually 3,982 surrendered or were captured),[168] Templer decided to designate certain areas as "white," meaning pacified. This involved the lifting of emergency regulations, including the curfew and food controls, thus providing an inducement for areas that were still "black" to fall in behind the government. By the time that Templer left Malaya on May 31, 1954, roughly a third of the country was "white" and the back of the insurgency had been broken. Significantly Templer and his wife drove to the airport in an open touring car.

✦ ✦ ✦

TEMPLER WAS ON his way to promotion to field marshal and a new job as chief of the Imperial General Staff. The country he left behind, eventually to be renamed Malaysia, was on its way to independence in 1957 with a pro-Western government led by Tunku Abdul Rahman. A British officer summed up Templer's accomplishment by noting that during his two years "two-thirds of the guerrillas were wiped out, the terrorist incident rate fell from 500 a month to less than 100, and the casualty rate went from 200 to less than 40."[169] No other counterinsurgency campaign waged abroad by a Western power in the postwar era was as successful.

Warning against overconfidence and mindful of the difficulty of measuring success in a counterinsurgency, Templer said in 1953, "I'll shoot the bastard who says this Emergency is over."[170] No one did say so, at least not officially, until 1960, when there were no casualties inflicted by the insurgents. That year the state of emergency was lifted. A few hundred of Chin Peng's die-hard followers would hold out in the jungles of neighboring Thailand until the signing of a peace treaty in 1989, but they would never seriously threaten Malaysia's stability again.

✦ ✦ ✦

IN EXAMINING WHY the British were successful in Malaya while the French failed in nearby Indochina, it must be noted that the former was a peninsula bordering a friendly country, Thailand, whereas the latter had a long land border with the decidedly unfriendly People's Republic of China. Isolating the insurgents from outside support is a critical part of any counterinsurgency, and that was much easier to achieve in Malaya than in Indochina. Chin Peng did not receive any significant aid from China or Russia, and his fighters never had any heavy weapons. Even small-arms ammunition was in short supply.[171]

The British were also helped by the fact that the rebellion was always limited to the Chinese, who made up 40 percent of the population. If the Communists had shown more skill in appealing to the Malay majority, they would have been much harder to defeat. But the Malays, mostly conservative Muslim farmers, remained loyal to their hereditary sultans, who were allied with the British.

In addition the British war effort benefited from a stroke of serendipity: the outbreak of the Korean War in 1950 caused a worldwide rise in commodity prices, including that of the tin and rubber produced in Malaya. The resulting economic boom allowed lavish spending on social services and provided plenty of good-paying jobs, which helped dispel the lure of the guerrillas.

Finally the British benefited from the enlightened generalship of Harold Briggs and Gerald Templer, who used the appropriate degree of force while rejecting the tougher but ultimately self-defeating tactics employed by French commanders in Indochina and Algeria.

For all these reasons, the British war in Malaya was far less costly, and far more successful, than the French and American efforts in Vietnam. Over twelve years the emergency cost the lives of 3,283 civilians, 1,865 security personnel, and 6,698 Communists.[172]

48.

"A DISTINCTIVELY BRITISH APPROACH"?

Why the British Succeeded—at Least Sometimes

DEBATE HAS RAGED ever since the end of the Malayan Emergency about whether and to what extent its lessons can be applied in other "counterinsurgencies"—a term coined in 1960.[173] British veterans of Malaya such as Robert Thompson, Richard Clutterbuck, and Frank Kitson suggested that the combination of civil-action and punitive measures they had employed could be used to quell other uprisings. Skeptics pointed to the demographic and geographic advantages enjoyed by the counterinsurgents in Malaya that did not necessarily exist elsewhere.

But such natural advantages can be frittered away by foolish policy choices. Ireland is an island and hence even more cut off from the outside world than Malaya. It is also much closer to Britain, and yet the British were defeated there in 1921. Cuba is also an island, yet it too would be the scene of a successful insurgency just as the Malayan Emergency was winding down. Even in Malaya the government hardly appeared predestined to succeed in the early 1950s. Only the implementation of successful counterinsurgency policies under Briggs and Templer saved the British from defeat and gave Malaya the iconic status it continues to enjoy in military circles.

The strategy that worked in Malaya was premised on close civil-military cooperation, a search for a political settlement, and the avoidance of large-scale "search and destroy" missions in favor of "clear and hold" operations designed to control the population combined with targeted raids on insurgent lairs utilizing accurate intelligence and minimal firepower. These have come to be seen as the defining features of what the historian Thomas R. Mockaitis calls a "distinctly British approach to counterinsurgency."[174] The British had arrived at this strategy after a process of trial and error in the interwar period, having seen that heavy-handed repression, such as that perpetrated by the Black and Tans in Ireland, had backfired. What might have been acceptable practice in the nineteenth century was forbidden to a liberal democracy under the evolving standards of the twentieth century.

It is fair to note, as the historian David French has done in critiquing Mockaitis's work, that the British approach was hardly free of violence or even human-rights violations. British troops committed some abuses in all their wars and always relied on considerable coercion—"meaning," French writes, "measures that ranged from curfews and cordon and search operations at one end of the scale of violence, through collective fines and large-scale detention without trial, and culminated in forced population resettlement and the creation of free fire zones." Distorted British memories of their own history that exaggerated how nice British soldiers had been to the population, French suggests, led British forces astray in twenty-first-century Afghanistan and Iraq, where they were so intent on avoiding conflict that they were unable to pacify their areas of operations. His points are well-taken. Nevertheless, there was a qualitative difference between the British and the French approaches, to say nothing of the even greater differences between the British approach and that of illiberal counterinsurgents such as Nazi Germany or Nationalist China. As French concedes, "the British did not wage 'dirty' wars in the same systematic manner and on the scale as the French did in Algeria." "Most members of the [British] security forces, most of the time, did operate within the law," French concludes, albeit within a law constructed to give them considerable latitude to maintain security.[175]

The British approach was hardly unique (similar methods were employed, for instance, in Morocco and the Philippines), but it was effective. The British prevailed not only in Malaya but also, to one degree or another, in Kenya between 1952 and 1960 against the Mau Mau movement;[176] in Cyprus between 1955 and 1959 against EOKA, the National Organization of Cypriot Fighters, a terrorist group seeking *Enosis* (union) with Greece;[177] in Oman between 1962 and 1975 against separatists fighting for independence for the province of Dhofar;[178] and in Northern Ireland between 1969 and 1998 against the Provisional IRA seeking its own version of *Enosis*—unification with the Republic of Ireland.[179] When the British deviated from their minimal-force strategy, it usually came back to haunt them, the classic example being the second Bloody Sunday, when on January 30, 1972, the Parachute Regiment killed thirteen unarmed Catholic protesters in Londenderry, thereby making the "Troubles" in Northern Ireland much worse. The one exception was Kenya, where the British were more brutal than usual (they interned 70,000 suspects and killed at least 12,000) but got away with it because the Mau Mau rebels belonged to a minority tribe, the Kikuyu, and lacked "a clearly defined nationalist ideology" that could appeal to the African majority. Even the most prominent Kikuyu politician, Jomo Kenyatta, opposed the rebellion, although this did not stop the British from locking him up for eight years.

The British, needless to say, did not win everywhere. Their empire was, after all, on the way to dissolution. We have already noted their failure to suppress Jewish terrorism in Palestine after World War II. They were equally unsuccessful in Aden and its associated territories, which they left in 1967, allowing the Marxist National Liberation Front to take over what would become known as South Yemen. But it was hardly Arab terrorism that chased the British out; almost all of the violence in Aden occurred *after* the British decision to leave had been announced in 1966 as part of a general retrenchment "East of Suez." At most the insurgency slightly accelerated the timetable for withdrawal.[180]

In Cyprus, meanwhile, the British hardly won an unqualified victory, but neither did EOKA achieve its objective of *Enosis*. Like many insurgencies, this one petered out in an unsatisfying compromise, with Cyprus gaining its independence but no union with Greece and Britain retaining two military bases.

The Irish Troubles also ended with a negotiated settlement, the 1998 Good Friday Agreement, which set up a power-sharing arrangement between the Unionists and Sinn Féin, the IRA's political wing, but kept Northern Ireland within the United Kingdom. The fundamental reason why the IRA failed to achieve its ultimate objective is the same reason why the Malayan

Races Liberation Army, the Mau Mau, and the Dhofar separatists also failed: They were fighting on behalf of an aggrieved minority, while the majority was on the government's side. (Protestants made up 53 percent of Northern Ireland's population, Catholics 44 percent.)[181] It is much harder for a counterinsurgent to win when the bulk of the population is sympathetic to the insurgent cause—as in Algeria and Indochina.

The Algerian and Indochinese wars were much larger than any of Britain's conflicts. The French confronted enemy forces numbering in the tens of thousands and even hundreds of thousands, whereas most of the guerrilla or terrorist groups Britain faced numbered only in the hundreds. This produced a startling disparity in casualties, with French forces losing more than 17,000 dead in Algeria and 92,000 in Indochina while the British had fewer than 2,000 soldiers and police killed in Malaya, 62 in Kenya, 156 in Cyprus, 35 in Oman, 200 in Aden, and 729 in Northern Ireland. In the 1959 Emergency in Nyasaland, today's Malawi, the British lost not a single member of the security forces.[182] In large part, of course, the relatively low losses were due to the weakness of the opposition the British faced. It is nevertheless telling that they had more success with their minimal-force approach than the French did with maximal force.

In no small part this was because the British paid greater attention to the political side of the business. Prior to the twentieth century and stretching back to the days of ancient Mesopotamia, colonial powers usually had enough legitimacy to suppress revolts on their own with scant regard for the sensitivities of "the natives" except for a few elites who could be co-opted with generous financial incentives. The British recognized that with the spread of new ideologies (liberalism, nationalism, socialism) and new forms of communication (newspapers, radio, television), this was no longer the case. In the modern world for a regime to be considered legitimate it had to be homegrown and preferably democratic. As Lewis Clark, the American consul general in Algiers, wrote in 1955, "No people will accept permanently a secondary status in a political community of today."

The French were slow to come to this realization—they lived for too long in what Clark aptly called "a dream world."[183] The Vietminh and the NLF might never have grown as powerful as they did if the French had been more willing to make political concessions early on, namely, to promise an end to colonial rule as the British did in Malaya. The need to wage counterinsurgency warfare on the political as well as the military level is one of the enduring lessons of the decolonization era—and one of the stark contrasts with an earlier epoch of imperial "small wars."

The same principle applied to insurgents. Mao Zedong and, following him, Ho Chi Minh, emphasized the need for political action combined with military measures as opposed to the sort of apolitical raiding tactics that had been common since the days of prehistory. It is no coincidence that they will be remembered as two of the most successful insurgent leaders of the twentieth century. A similar lesson was learned by the Zionists and other groups struggling for their own nation-states. Their victories showed that, although counterinsurgents still held the advantage in the 1950s, the odds of success for any broad-based revolt, especially one that could tap into nationalist sentiment, had increased dramatically since the late nineteenth and early twentieth centuries, to say nothing of earlier times. In the American West, the Colt revolver was dubbed "the Equalizer" because it allowed even those who were physically weak to kill the strong. In the same way, in the post–World War II era, the growth in influence of public opinion, both foreign and domestic, was the great equalizer that increasingly allowed the militarily weak to best the strong. The potency of this one-two punch, political and military, would be demonstrated anew not only in the second Vietnam War but also in countries as far-flung as Cuba and Israel.

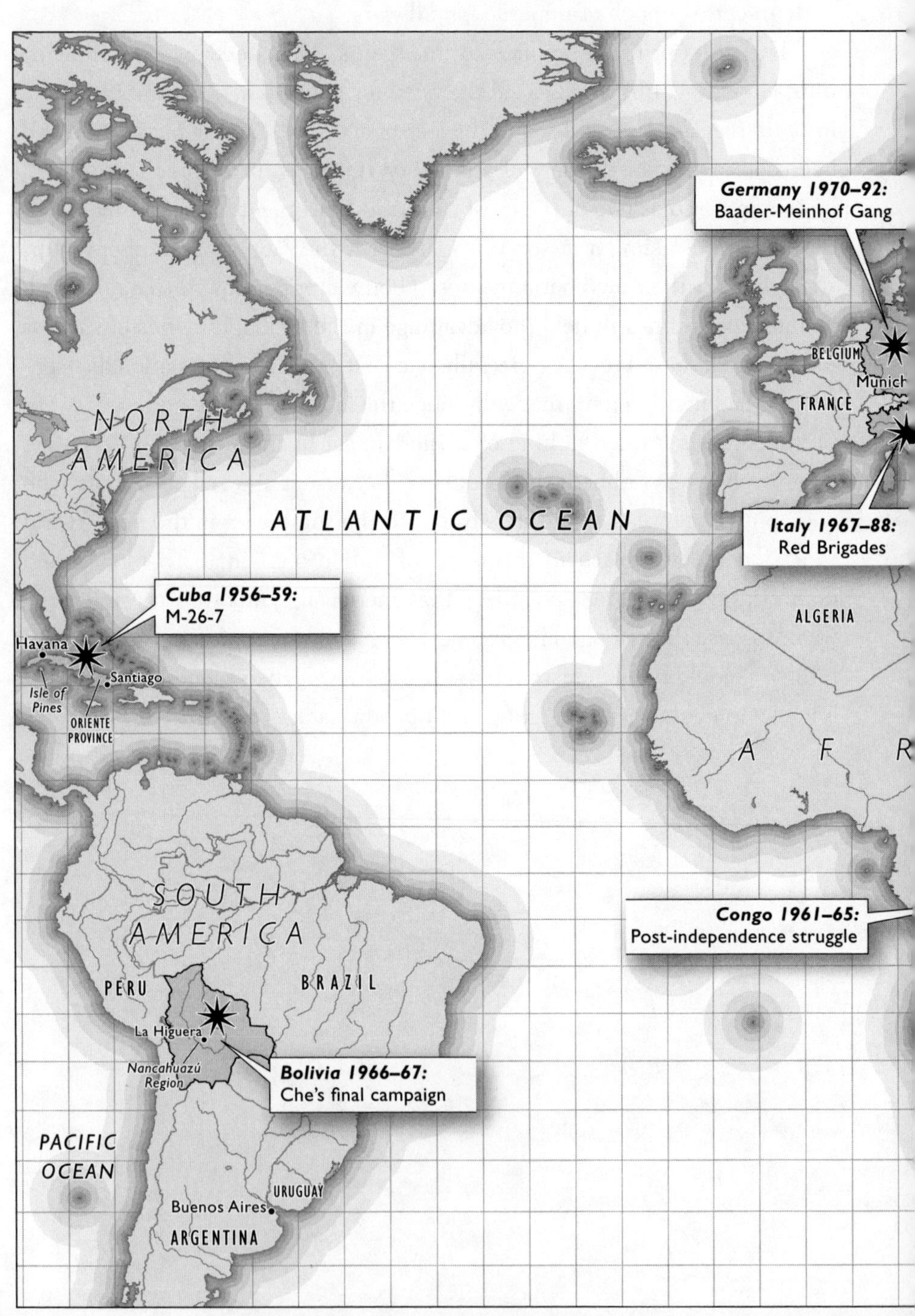
Germany 1970–92:
Baader-Meinhof Gang
BELGIUM
Munich
FRANCE
NORTH AMERICA
ATLANTIC OCEAN
Italy 1967–88:
Red Brigades
ALGERIA
Cuba 1956–59:
M-26-7
Havana
Santiago
Isle of Pines
ORIENTE PROVINCE
A F R
SOUTH AMERICA
Congo 1961–65:
Post-independence struggle
PERU
BRAZIL
La Higuera
Nancahuazú Region
Bolivia 1966–67:
Che's final campaign
PACIFIC OCEAN
URUGUAY
Buenos Aires
ARGENTINA

BOOK VII
RADICAL CHIC
The Romance of the Leftist Revolutionaries

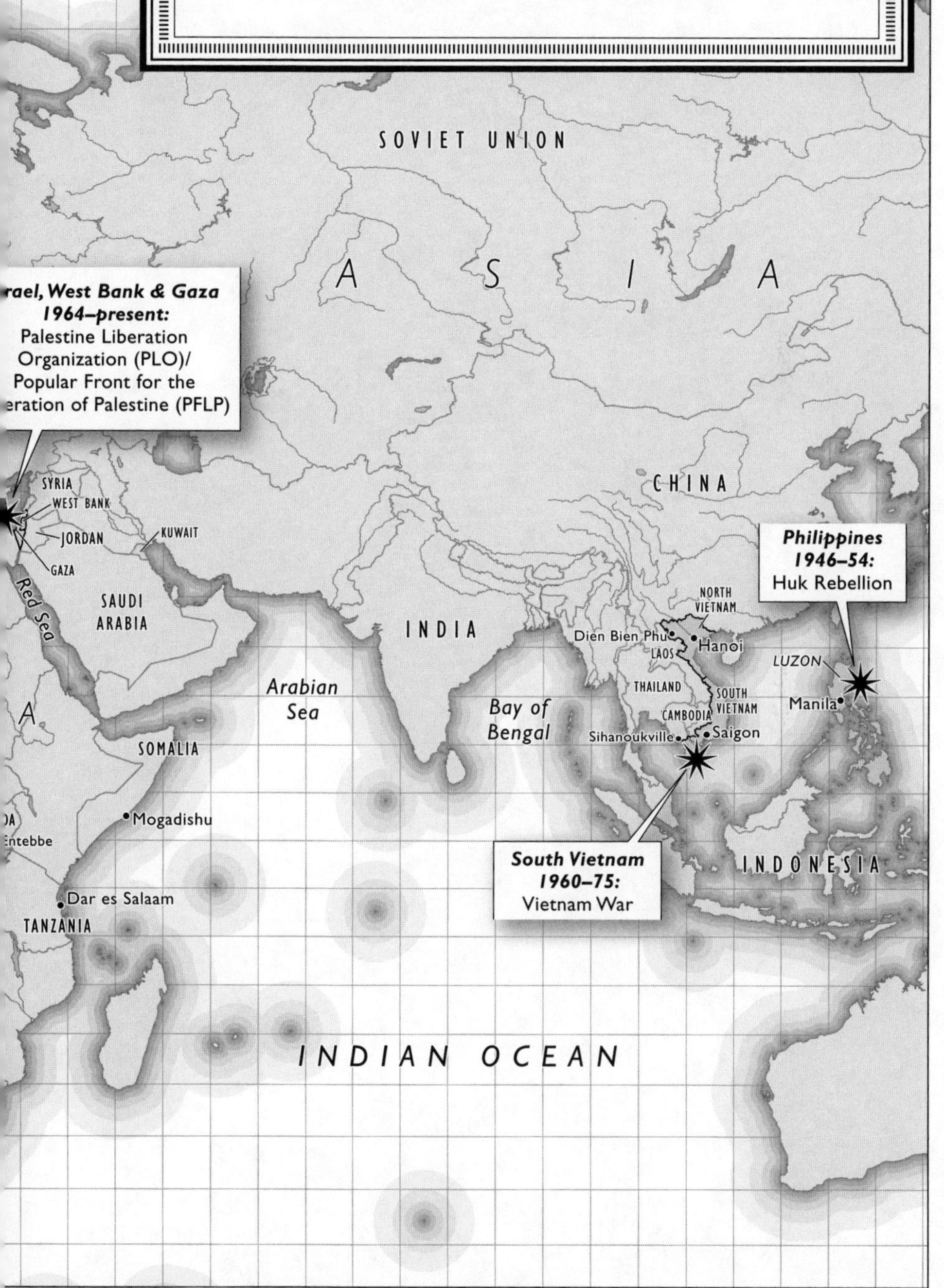

49.

TWO SIDES OF THE COIN

The Guerrilla Mystique in the 1960s–1970s

THE INCIDENCE OF guerrilla warfare and terrorism did not decline with the demise of the European empires. Quite the contrary. The years from 1959 to 1979—from Castro's takeover in Cuba to the Sandinistas' takeover in Nicaragua—were, if anything, the golden age of leftist insurgency. There remained a few colonial wars in Oman, Aden, Mozambique, Angola, and Guinea-Bissau, and a larger number of essentially ethnic wars in places like Congo, East Timor, and Nigeria's Biafra region that were fought to determine the nature of postcolonial states, but the primary propellant of conflict was socialist ideology, often mixed, as in the Basque ETA, the Kurdish PKK, the Popular Front for the Liberation of Palestine, the IRA, and even the American Black Panthers, with a strong dose of nationalist separatist sentiment. Radicals who styled themselves as the next Mao, Ho, Fidel, or Che took up AK-47s to wage either rural guerrilla warfare or urban terrorism—or in many instances both. This section will focus, first, on the Huk Rebellion in the Philippines and the U.S. war in Vietnam, then on Fidel Castro's path to power in Cuba and Che Guevara's attempts to export the Cuban revolution abroad, and, finally, on the rise of a new age of international terrorism in the 1970s led by Palestinian groups whose symbol and leader was Yasser Arafat. All of these conflicts save the Huk Rebellion garnered intensive international media coverage and brought guerrilla warfare and terrorism to the forefront of public attention, where they have remained ever since although not necessarily in the heroic hues of the 1960s–1970s.

Never before or since has the glamour and prestige of irregular warriors been higher. Tom Wolfe captured the moment in his famous essay "Radical Chic" (1970), which described in hilarious and excruciating detail a party thrown by the composer Leonard Bernstein in his swank New York apartment for a group of Black Panthers—one of myriad terrorist groups of the period whose fame far exceeded their ability to achieve their amorphous goals.[1]

American journalist Robert Taber was a good example of the sort of guerrilla groupie that Wolfe was mocking. Taber interviewed Fidel Castro during the Cuban revolution and later helped establish the pro-Castro Fair Play for Cuba Committee. He penned a widely read paean to guerrillas and terrorists, *The War of the Flea* (1965), analogizing them to an insect that "bites, hops, and bites again, nimbly avoiding the foot that would crush him." Taber believed that the fleas of the sixties were selfless idealists waging war on behalf of the "world's have-nots," "subjugated and exploited peoples everywhere," and that "to try to suppress popular resistance movements by force is futile."[2]

Yet some governments had considerable success in suppressing "resistance movements." The architects of the most successful counterinsurgency campaigns briefly became celebrities in their own right, consulted by presidents and prime ministers and profiled in popular magazines. Counterinsurgency was, as the Kennedy aide Arthur M. Schlesinger Jr. wrote in 1965, "faddish."[3] The 1960s saw the publication of influential manuals such as *Counterinsurgency Warfare: Theory and Practice* (1964), by the French officer David Galula, a veteran of the Algerian War of Independence and, as a military attaché, a witness to the civil wars in Greece and China. Even more widely read at the time was *Defeating Communist Insurgency: The Lessons of Malaya and Vietnam* (1966), by Sir Robert Thompson, a British veteran of the Chindits and the Malayan Emergency.

In spite of their differing origins, experts such as Galula and Thompson reached a remarkable degree of agreement that insurgencies could not be fought like conventional wars. The fundamental principles that set counterinsurgency apart were the use of "the minimum of fire" (Galula) and the priority given "to defeating the political subversion, not the guerrillas" (Thompson). Large-scale infantry or armor offensives, they argued, would prove counterproductive against an elusive foe. Truly defeating an insurgency would require creating a legitimate and responsive government and generating timely and accurate intelligence, as Templer had done in Malaya. Echoing Marshal Hubert Lyautey, the godfather of population-centric counterinsurgency theory, Galula wrote that a "soldier must be prepared to become a propagandist, a social worker, a civil engineer, a schoolteacher, a nurse, a boy scout."[4]

It was one thing to generate such hard-won lessons. Altogether more difficult was to get them accepted by military officers whose ideal remained an armored blitzkrieg and who had nothing but contempt for lightly armed, ragtag fighters who had never even been to a proper staff college. Even the British army, despite its long tradition of imperial policing, at first had tried to use conventional tactics in Malaya before recognizing their futility. The problem was even more acute in the U.S. armed forces. They too had a tradition of fighting guerrillas, ranging from American Indians to Philippine *insurrectos* and Haitian *cacos*. The U.S. Marine Corps had even produced a *Small Wars Manual* in 1935.[5] But those inglorious campaigns, never popular to begin with among professional soldiers, were seared out of the collective military mind in the cauldron of World War II. The U.S. armed forces emerged entirely focused on fighting a mirror-image foe—either the Red Army or a mini-me such as the North Korean army.

A handful of counterinsurgency experts tried to get the American military to use very different tactics to fight a very different foe. None was more innovative, more famous, or ultimately more frustrated than Edward Geary Lansdale, the "Quiet American."

50.

THE QUIET AMERICAN

Edward Lansdale and the Huk Rebellion, 1945–1954

THE SOBRIQUET WAS bestowed by the British novelist Graham Greene, who visited Saigon in the early 1950s and in 1955 published *The Quiet American*, a novel pitting a dissolute, world-weary British journalist, a Greene stand-in called Thomas Fowler, against a naïve young American named Alden Pyle who was widely believed, probably erroneously,[6] to have been inspired by Lansdale. Pyle is forever talking about creating a Third Force to save Vietnam from both the Communists and the French colonialists. Fowler thinks that Pyle is "too innocent to live." But his "ignorant and silly"[7] outlook has been vindicated by history. Seen from the vantage point of the twenty-first century, the Third Force—liberal democracy—has proved far more durable than either communism or colonialism. That was a lesson that Graham Greene, for all his literary genius, never grasped.

A more favorable portrait of Lansdale was penned by the lesser writers William Lederer, a U.S. Navy captain who actually knew Lansdale, and Eugene Burdick, a political science professor. Their best seller *The Ugly American* (1958) featured a motorcycle-riding, harmonica-playing Lansdale stand-in named Colonel Edwin B. Hillandale—or as he was better known to his staid embassy colleagues, "that crazy bastard." Hillandale "ate his meals in little Filipino restaurants, washing down huge quantities of adobo and pancit and rice with a brand of Filipino rum which cost two pesos a pint." He spent his weekends mingling with ordinary people in the provinces and generally "embraced everything Filipino."[8] To the authors he exemplified how American representatives in Southeast Asia should interact with the locals—but seldom did. It was an unassuming, self-effacing style that made the real-life Lansdale popular and influential from the moment he set foot in the Philippines.

He first arrived in the Philippines in 1945, pursuing, as always, an unconventional path. An ROTC cadet at UCLA, he had briefly joined the Army Reserves after leaving college without graduating in 1931. He then left the army to become a star of the San Francisco advertising industry. Among his achievements was helping a regional jeans maker, Levi Strauss, to roll out its products on the East Coast. After the attack on Pearl Harbor he went back into the army, working for military intelligence as well as the OSS and splitting his time between training new recruits and gathering intelligence. At war's end, by then a thirty-seven-year-old major working in military intelligence, he was assigned to Manila, where he immediately began immersing himself in Philippine culture.[9]

He was particularly interested in the Hukbalahap movement (originally an acronym for *Hukbong Bayan Laban sa Hapon*, or People's Anti-Japanese Army, later renamed the *Hukbong Mapagpalaya ng Bayan*, or People's Liberation Army), a Communist group that in 1946 began to fight the newly independent government of the Philippines. Leaving behind Manila's whirl of "slick" cocktail parties, Lansdale hopped into a jeep and drove into the rural areas, the boondocks, where he found, as he noted in his diary, that "fear starts as the sun sets each day." Here, amid nipa huts and carabao tracks, besieged by ants and mosquitoes, either "stinking hot" from the sun or "sopping wet" from torrential rains, he spent long hours talking with "folks on both sides of this squabble."[10]

In the process he developed sympathy for ordinary Huks, mostly "youngsters under twenty" who "believe in the rightness of what they're doing" and are driven to "armed complaint" by "a bad situation, needing reform." He even tried unsuccessfully to meet the Huk leader, Luis Taruc, whose secret headquarters was located close to the U.S. Air Force's Clark Air Base. Lansdale almost got shot in the attempt.

Often he was alone on these expeditions. Sometimes he was accompanied by a Filipino friend; a particular favorite was a "lovely, witty" young woman named Patrocinio (Pat) Kelly, who would one day become Lansdale's second wife.[11] His first wife, Helen, was not nearly as taken by the Philippines as he was, and they grew increasingly apart, but Lansdale would wait until her death decades later before remarrying.

Although the fictional Hillandale spoke fluent Tagalog, the actual Lansdale never learned any foreign language. This did not prevent him, however, from establishing an impressive rapport with Filipinos, Vietnamese, and other foreigners.[12] One of his subordinates later noted that "he had an amazing ability to communicate understanding through an interpreter."[13] It helped, of course, that most Filipinos spoke English, but he could use sign language and a few phrases to make himself understood even by primitive Negrito tribesmen who spoke only their own tongue. A colleague in Manila said, "He could make a friend of everybody except Satan." His secret? "He was a very good listener." A Filipino friend recalled, "He would *always* say things in such a nice, disarming, and charming way. He never ordered but only asked, 'What do you think about doing it this way?' or 'Don't you think this is how we should treat the problem?' "[14]

Lansdale's soft-spoken, modest manner offered a welcome contrast to the bombastic, hectoring approach adopted by too many other Westerners in the Third World. When someone did not open up immediately, he pulled out his secret weapon—a harmonica. Music could melt social barriers even with those who were at first suspicious of this uniformed American with his crew-cut hair and brush mustache, and Lansdale always said he learned a good deal about a country from its folk songs.

✦ ✦ ✦

THE MOST IMPORTANT friend Lansdale made in the Philippines was Ramón Magsaysay, who was just a congressman when the two met in 1950. By this time Lansdale had transferred from the army to the air force (he thought "there would be more elbow room for fresh ideas" in the new service)[15] and had gone to work for the newly established CIA—a covert relationship that would last from 1950 to 1956.[16] Lansdale established an immediate bond with the burly Magsaysay, who was the same age and had fought as a guerrilla against the Japanese before going into politics. Lansdale became Magsaysay's closest confidant, for a time even his roommate. The two men saw eye to eye on how to combat the Huks—and it wasn't the way that the Philippine security forces were going about it.

The army was attacking barrios with artillery and bombs and indiscriminately locking up and torturing suspects. "Democratic freedoms are completely smashed," wrote one guerrilla leader; "farmers and other citizens are attacked, arrested, shot, jailed and even killed."[17] This campaign was not as brutal as the Japanese or Nazi counterinsurgent campaigns of the Second World War, but it was just as counterproductive and even less effective, because it was overseen by a government that Lansdale described as "rotten with corruption"[18]—one fault that the imperial Japanese and Nazi governments, for all their evils, at least managed to avoid. The Huks, who numbered 10,000 to 15,000 active fighters and had at least 100,000 active sympathizers out of a population of 20 million,[19] only grew stronger under this ham-handed assault.

Magsaysay believed that the government had to win the trust of the people. So did Lansdale. He lobbied Washington to use its clout to get Magsasyay appointed secretary of national defense in 1950 to carry out this program. The new cabinet minister's motto was "All-Out Friendship or All-Out Force."[20] In essence this was the latest iteration of the population-centric counterinsurgency strategy that could be traced all the way back to the Roman Empire's combination of "bread and circuses" for compliant populations and crucifixion for captured rebels. The modern theory behind such an approach, which combined "attraction" and "chastisement," was laid out by Marshal Lyautey a half century earlier and would be further developed a decade later by Robert Thompson and David Galula. These strategies had already proven successful in the Philippines against an earlier generation of rebels who had resisted the imposition of American rule, and were now being implemented at virtually the same time in Malaya. The difference is that the fighting against the Huk Rebellion, unlike that in the Philippine Insurrection or the Malayan Emergency, was not being done by a foreign force; Filipinos themselves formed the whole of the security forces. That automatically gave them a certain level of legitimacy, one of the most important assets in any battle against guerrillas or terrorists. But it also placed greater importance on improving the abysmal performance of the indigenous army. In the Philippines the faults of the locals could not be masked by foreign fighting forces.

With Lansdale's advice, Magsaysay "practically had to reinvent the Armed Forces," noted a Filipino writer.[21] Troops "entering an inhabited area" were now told "to conduct themselves as though they were coming among friends," and they were issued candy and chewing gum to hand out to children, while being warned that "a soldier who steals a chicken from a farmer cannot claim to be the farmer's protector."[22] Magsaysay further burnished the army's image by assigning military lawyers to represent poor farmers in court cases against rich absentee landlords.

To make sure that soldiers were doing as they were told, Lansdale and Magsaysay would travel together to stage snap inspections in the field, much as Templer would do in Malaya. "No commander, even in the most isolated outpost, could go to bed at night sure that he would not be awakened before dawn by an irate Secretary of National Defense," wrote a Filipino officer who worked for Magsayay and an American officer who worked for Lansdale.[23] Magsaysay also encouraged the public to send him cheap telegrams informing him "about both the good and bad things they saw government troops doing."[24]

At the same time that soldiers were being turned into "goodwill ambassadors,"[25] they were also being trained to become better raiders. Magsaysay doubled the size of the armed forces to 51,000 troops[26] and sent well-equipped combat teams first into Manila, then into the boondocks to root out the hard-core rebels in their Luzon strongholds—"Huklandia." In simultaneous raids in 1950 much of the Huk Politburo was rounded up in the capital, causing Luis Taruc to lament, "Disaster followed disaster."[27]

Among the most effective units was Force X, whose men were disguised as Huks themselves—a technique also employed in Kenya by "pseudo-gangs" sent to ambush the Mau Mau and later in Rhodesia by the Selous Scouts fighting African insurgents.[28] Other "dirty tricks" practiced by Magsaysay, with Lansdale's guidance, included slipping the Huks booby-trapped ammunition.

As in Malaya, there was little use of artillery or airpower but extensive reliance on psychological warfare. As Templer was to do in Malaya, Lansdale and Magsaysay sent voice aircraft to overfly rebel areas and encourage surrenders by name while offering generous rewards for information that led to the capture or killing of Huks. Even the mother of the head Huk, Luis Taruc, was persuaded to make a broadcast calling for his surrender; he heard her voice "almost hourly" on the government radio.[29] Those who gave up could expect lenient treatment, including in some cases the provision of free land for homesteading.

The centerpiece of the "civic action" program was free and fair balloting. Magsaysay and Lansdale knew that the Huks had benefited from public disgust over rampant vote stealing in the 1949 presidential election. To prevent a recurrence, they employed the Philippine army to safeguard the 1951 congressional election and the 1953 presidential election. The winner of the latter contest was none other than Ramón Magsaysay, who had been ably supported once again by Lansdale. After his friend defeated the corrupt incumbent, Lansdale earned a new nickname: Colonel Landslide.

The American had used his advertising expertise and the CIA's covert funds to build up Magsaysay's public reputation. He even came up with a campaign slogan: "Magsaysay is my guy."[30] But fundamentally the honest, modest, and hardworking defense minister won not because of public-relations tricks but because he had become, as two veterans of the anti-Huk campaign noted, "the personification" of "dedicated, aggressive leadership."[31] The "peaceful, clean" elections delivered the coup de grâce to the Huks, who conceded that people no longer saw "the immediate need of armed struggle."[32]

"The Huks became," in Lansdale's words, "fish out of water."[33] Already isolated by geography from outside support (the waters around the Philippines were patrolled by the U.S. and Philippine navies), they were now cut off from internal support even in their central Luzon heartland. Luis Taruc had to seek refuge in mountains and swamps. In 1954, hunted and starving, he decided to follow the example of thousands of his followers and surrender.

Unfortunately the democratic reforms engineered by Magsaysay and Lansdale did not last, in part because Magsaysay did not live long enough to fully implement them—he died in an airplane crash in 1957. Thereafter Ferdinand Marcos usurped power and ruled as a dictator from 1966 to 1986, thereby providing an opening for both Communist and Muslim insurgents. After Marcos's overthrow, democracy returned to the Philippines, although the government continued to be plagued by pervasive inefficiency and corruption. Lansdale and Magsaysay had not brought paradise to the Philippines, but they had defeated a large-scale insurgency. Along with the contemporary defeat of insurgencies in Greece and Malaya, the Philippine experience offered a template of how Communist rebels, or any others for that matter, could be bested even at the postwar height of their appeal by preventing them from receiving outside assistance, bolstering the government's legitimacy and support, and improving the effectiveness and humanity of its security forces.

51.

CREATING SOUTH VIETNAM

Lansdale and Diem, 1954–1956

HAVING ENGINEERED THE defeat of the Huks, Lansdale found himself in demand in Washington as a counterinsurgency troubleshooter. His next assignment was to take him to Saigon, where his path would cross Graham Greene's. He arrived on June 1, 1954, less than a month after the fall of Dien Bien Phu, which signaled the end of French rule. Under the Geneva Accords a new government under the playboy-emperor Bao Dai was established in South Vietnam while the Communists took over the north. Bao Dai chose as his prime minister the veteran nationalist politician Ngo Dinh Diem, a fervent Catholic who had opposed both the French and the Communists. Few thought that Diem could last long. He was hard-pressed not only by the Communists but also by various sects with their own armies. These ranged from the Hoa Hao and Cao Dai religions, which were Buddhist off-shoots (the Cao Dai worshipped Jesus, Buddha, and Victor Hugo), to the outright gangsters of the Binh Xuyen who ran the Saigon underworld. Diem's formidable challenge was to build a new nation while under pressure from all sides—and without being able to count on the loyalty of his French-trained armed forces, whose chief of staff was plotting a coup against him.

Colonel Lansdale's job as head of the CIA's Saigon Military Mission was to help "Free Viet-Nam" survive.[34] Or as Secretary of State John Foster Dulles put it, "Do what you did in the Philippines."[35] To assist him he had a dozen operatives who shared, an American diplomat wrote, "a devotion to Lansdale and a commitment to hard, sometimes dangerous, work."[36] They were separate from the regular CIA station, operating out of a four-room bungalow on Rue Miche that doubled as Lansdale's living quarters. He always kept a good supply of hand grenades nearby in case of attack.

As in the Philippines, Lansdale spent long, wearying hours traveling around the country and cultivating its leaders. He was remarkably successful in spite of his inability to speak French or Vietnamese. Lansdale and Diem had to communicate through a translator but nevertheless "fell into the habit of meeting nearly every day" for hours at a time in the presidential palace over endless cigarettes and cups of tea. "Our association gradually developed into a friendship of considerable depth, trust, and candor," Lansdale wrote, although he later added that it wasn't "a blind friendship," because Diem "put other Vietnamese friends of mine in jail or exiled them."[37] The American operative tried to teach the South Vietnamese politician about the principles of the American Revolution and encouraged this "roly-poly figure dressed in a white sharkskin double-breasted suit"[38] to emulate George Washington's example and become the "papa" of his country.

In his unobtrusive way, Lansdale shared with his new friend his counterinsurgency philosophy, what some would later call "Lansdalism."[39] This was his own, uniquely American twist on the similar philosophies being espoused by Robert Thompson of Britain, David Galula of France, and other contemporary counterinsurgency strategists, although, unlike them, Lansdale would never publish a theoretical work laying out his teachings. (The only book he ever wrote was a memoir published in 1972.) The essence of "Lansdalism" was implementing the "basic political ideas" set out in the Declaration of Independence and Bill of Rights, which he believed "form an ideology of dynamic universality, as alive today as when conceived, and close to the hearts of men of good will throughout the world." He was convinced that "our ideology" was "far more appealing in Asia than anything the Communists can put forward." This sounded naïve to cynics like Graham Greene, but Lansdale was by no means a proponent of "fuzzy 'do-good-ism.' " Nor was he averse to tough military action—"a fighting man," he said, "must ever be ready for a fight." Like Galula and Thompson, however, he realized that it wasn't enough to kill guerrillas. To give the "Communists a memorable licking," it was necessary to practice "civic action" that would form "a bond of brotherhood between soldiers and civilians." "If you win the people over to your side," he told an audience of Green Berets, "the Communist guerrillas have no place to hide. With no place to hide, you can find them. Then, as military men, fix them . . . finish them!"[40]

✦ ✦ ✦

Under the Geneva Accords, Communist sympathizers were allowed to move to the north, while anti-Communists could go to the south. Overcoming resistance from his embassy superiors, Lansdale organized a massive effort using American military ships and aircraft to transfer refugees to the south. Knowing of the Vietnamese respect for soothsayers, he arranged for the publication of a popular almanac in which notable astrologers predicted good fortune for the south and a "dark future" for the north.[41] To discourage too many southerners from going north, he distributed a pamphlet allegedly from the Vietminh warning those who left to pack plenty of cold clothing because it would be useful when they went to join other "volunteers" in building railroads in China.[42] It was hardly all, or even mainly, Lansdale's doing, but nearly a million people went south while fewer than a hundred thousand moved north.

Lansdale's attempts to infiltrate anti-Communist guerrillas into the north, in an echo of the World War II operations of the SOE and OSS, proved less successful. His men succeeded in sabotaging the oil supply of Hanoi's buses, but that was the very limited extent of their success. Covert action was hard to pull off in an indigenous dictatorship. In World War II the Allies enjoyed limited success with sabotage operations in occupied lands where the Germans and Japanese were at an intelligence disadvantage. The Allies had no such success in the German and Japanese homelands, and neither did Lansdale in North Vietnam.[43]

He had better luck extending the reach of Saigon's government across South Vietnam in an example of what would now be called "nation building"—an important part of any successful counterinsurgency effort because, to blunt the appeal of a rebel force, it is necessary to establish governmental institutions that can safeguard the populace and respond to its concerns. Lansdale's instruments of civic action included a group of volunteer Filipino doctors and nurses whom he brought over, supported by both CIA and private donations, as part of a nongovernmental organization called Operation Brotherhood to offer free medical care to Vietnamese peasants.[44] He also encouraged Vietnamese bureaucrats to get out of the capital, shed their French suits for peasant-style black pajamas, and "foster self-rule, self-development, and self-defense" in the countryside.[45]

In many parts of the south, the only representatives of the new regime were soldiers. The Communists had warned that these "corrupt French puppets" would rape the people.[46] To counter such fears, Lansdale's operatives printed a code of conduct modeled on the one Mao Zedong had promulgated. Its theme: "Every soldier a civic action agent."[47] Lansdale knew that civilians' willingness to cooperate "sagged whenever military vehicles careered wildly through village roads, scattering inhabitants, chickens, and pigs in their path." So he made sure troops "were lectured on the courtesy of the road," and a "good driver contest was held, with prizes and medals for the most courteous driver in each unit."[48]

Once a province was pacified, Lansdale encouraged Diem to travel there to establish a personal connection with the people. When he did, the prime minister was often mobbed by "highly enthusiastic" crowds.[49] An indigenous leader such as Diem could generate far more popular support than even a relatively popular foreign counterinsurgent such as Gerald Templer, and his popularity was an invaluable, if short-lived, asset for his government.

✦ ✦ ✦

THIS WAS AN era when new states were emerging around the world. The United Nations had been formed by just 51 nations in 1945. By 1970, following a wave of decolonization, there were 127 members and counting.[50] The process of state formation was seldom smooth and easy. It certainly was not in South Vietnam, where Diem was having a hard time establishing control not only of the countryside but even of his own capital. The sects—the Hoa Hao, Cao Dai, and Binh Xuyen—had formed a "united front" with Emperor Bao Dai's support to overthrow him. Together, they had nearly 40,000 fighters, and they were concentrated around Saigon, while Diem's army, 150,000 strong, was of doubtful reliability and dispersed around the country.[51] On March 29, 1955, and then again on April 28, the Binh Xuyen briefly lobbed mortar rounds at the presidential palace. The rebels were covertly assisted by the French, who still maintained 94,000 troops in the south and who opposed Diem because he wanted to end their dominance. Junior French officers were even caught trying to kill Lansdale and other prominent *américains* who were helping Diem.[52] The French "hate our guts and want to see us fail where they failed also," Lansdale wrote.[53]

Lansdale urged Diem to confront the "united front" in order to solidify his own rule. He helped the president by funneling CIA funds to buy off some sect leaders.[54] The U.S. ambassador, retired general J. Lawton "Lightning Joe" Collins, had a different view. He had "grave doubts" about Diem and flew to Washington to persuade his old friend President Eisenhower to dump the prime minister.[55] Lansdale was not afraid to buck his boss on this issue—or any other. In their very first "country team" meeting, the ambassador ruled Lansdale out of order for questioning his priorities. Didn't Lansdale know that he was the president's personal representative? Lansdale replied, "I guess there's nobody here as the personal representative of the people of the United States. The American people would want us to discuss these priorities. So I hereby appoint myself as their representative—and we're walking out on you." And out he walked.[56]

Now, when he heard that Lightning Joe was trying to strike down Diem, whom he considered "a great patriot" and "probably the best of all the nationalists," Lansdale furiously typed a lengthy cable to Allen Dulles warning that "any successor government to Diem's acceptable to the French would be unable to carry out the reforms essential to deny Vietnam to the Communists."[57] A few years later he predicted that Diem's successors would be "highly selfish and mediocre people [who] would be squabbling for power among themselves as the Communists took over."[58] It was a prescient prediction in light of the "political and security vacuum"[59] that was to envelop South Vietnam after Diem was overthrown and killed in 1963 with American connivance. Diem's overthrow was later to be seen by CIA Director William Colby, among others, as "America's primary (and perhaps worst) error in Vietnam."[60]

In 1955 Diem survived in no small part because Lansdale helped persuade the Eisenhower administration to stand behind him. Before long Diem's army had routed the sects—an outcome predicted by Lansdale, who roamed Saigon to see for himself "the savagery of the street fighting,"[61] but doubted by desk-bound French and American officials who thought "it was impossible for Diem to win by force."[62]

Lansdale encouraged Diem to follow this military success by holding a national referendum to determine whether he or Bao Dai should be head of state. Despite Lansdale's warnings to keep the election fair, Diem's brother Ngo Dinh Nhu couldn't resist committing fraud to ensure that his brother won 98.2 percent of the vote. In spite of that "totally unbelievable" margin, there is little doubt that Diem was genuinely popular; one of Lansdale's team members believed he would have won 80 percent in a fair vote.[63]

By the time Lansdale left Saigon at the end of 1956, South Vietnam had defied the Cassandras to become a functioning state. Neil Sheehan was later to write with flattering exaggeration, "South Vietnam, it can truly be said, was the creation of Edward Lansdale."[64]

The question was whether his creation would be able to survive a growing Communist insurgency. By 1957 cadres were beginning a campaign of terror targeting the most honest and effective local officials, whom they denounced as the "spies, bandits and hirelings of the U.S. imperialists."[65] The insurgents were no longer called the Vietminh. Now they were known as the Vietcong (Vietnamese Communists).[66]

52.

THE OTHER WAR

The Limitations of Firepower in Vietnam, 1960–1973

LANSDALE WOULD BE able to affect the outcome of the second Vietnam War only indirectly from his new perch at the Pentagon's Office of Special Operations. His job was to help oversee the Department of Defense's intelligence programs. He was allowed to take only occasional trips back to Saigon despite Diem's desire to have him present full-time.[67] When it came to Vietnam, Lansdale recalled, "I was practically without voice."[68]

Lansdale, who had been promoted to brigadier general in 1960, was a victim of his own success. Following the publication of *The Quiet American* and *The Ugly American*, he had become the most famous military adviser since T. E. Lawrence—and just like Lawrence he earned both the wrath of resentful bureaucrats and the ear of senior officials.

The new president, John F. Kennedy, had read the works of Mao Zedong and Che Guevara and was intent on enhancing American capacity to fight what he called "subterranean war."[69] A few days after his inauguration Kennedy summoned Lansdale to the Oval Office and talked of making him ambassador to Saigon. That job offer was nixed by Secretary of State Dean Rusk, because Lansdale had acquired a reputation for being a "lone wolf"—not a "team player."[70] As the CIA's William Colby noted, "When an order appeared wrong, he simply ignored it and went on doing what he thought right (and frequently it was)." Lansdale's maverick ways, Colby wrote, "made him few friends among the more traditional bureaucrats and, more seriously, kept him from appointment to the kind of leadership positions where he might have been able to make major changes in American foreign policy."[71]

Thus he was an outsider while the Bay of Pigs operation was plotted. Lansdale thought it was "suicidal" to launch a D-day–style landing with fewer than fifteen hundred exiles; he favored starting with "a small guerrilla force . . . and gradually build[ing] up its bona fides." He subsequently became involved in efforts to overthrow Castro as chief of operations for an inter-agency operation code-named Mongoose. But he found his superiors, and in particular Attorney General Robert F. Kennedy, impatient with his hopes of creating a revolutionary organization within Cuba that would win "the warm, understanding, and sympathetic approval of the people." The administration "wanted fast action," meaning commando raids and plots to assassinate Castro. Among the "nutty schemes" that were considered, as one author aptly termed them, was a plan to airdrop toilet paper printed with pictures of Fidel Castro and Nikita Khrushchev to humiliate those Communist bosses. While few such proposals were actually implemented, their later exposure caused significant embarrassment to all concerned, including Lansdale, who would be hauled out of retirement to testify before the Senate's Church Committee in 1975. As with North Vietnam, so with Cuba: Lansdale's attempts to destabilize Communist dictatorships ended in ignominious failure.[72]

In spite of Kennedy's support for his efforts, Lansdale was also stymied in his attempts to get the U.S. armed forces to wholeheartedly embrace counterinsurgency warfare. In 1962 the president urged the armed forces to prepare for a "type of war, new in its intensity, ancient in its origins—war by guerrillas, subversives, insurgents, assassins, war by ambush instead of by combat."[73] To meet this challenge, he set up a Special Group, Counterinsurgency, whose members included his own brother. But the group was chaired by General Maxwell Taylor, a future chairman of the Joint Chiefs of Staff and ambassador to Vietnam whose own outlook was relentlessly conventional. He favored preparing for limited wars between regular armies.[74] Thus the armed forces paid the president lip service but nothing more. When JFK visited Fort Bragg, North Carolina, in 1961, the Army Special Forces proudly paraded in their new green berets, which the president had authorized them to wear over the opposition of the regular army, which despised any deviation from the norm. (The same color beret was worn by the British commandos with whom the first U.S. Army Rangers had trained in 1942.) Resplendent in their headgear, they staged a "real Cecil B. De Mille spectacular" for the president, one soldier recalled, which included a trooper in a "rocket contraption" flying across a lake and landing in front of the president.[75] The army, told to include guerrilla warfare in its curriculum, even instructed its typists "how to make typewriters explode" and its bakers "how to make apple pies with hand grenades in them."[76]

Such gimmicks may have been related, however tenuously, to *carrying out* a guerrilla war, but they had nothing to do with *countering* a guerrilla war, which was to be the army's main mission in the 1960s. As Lansdale noted, Kennedy's prodding produced "a lot of activity," but most of it lacked "the quality desired."[77] Senior officers thought that conventional training, doctrine, and organization would be sufficient for this task. Their outlook was summed up by General George Decker, army chief of staff from 1960 to 1962, who claimed, "Any good soldier can handle guerrillas."[78]

Similar sentiments had no doubt occurred to many other soldiers over the centuries before they were disabused of their illusions by rebels ranging from the ancient Maccabees to the nineteenth-century Spanish *guerrilleros* and the twentieth-century Irish Republicans. In fact, while guerrilla warfare on a tactical level utilizes many of the same skills as light infantry operations, the strategy of war among the people is entirely different from a clash between two uniformed forces on empty sand, soil, seas, or skies. Low-intensity conflict necessitates an emphasis on policing and controlling the population. The application of indiscriminate firepower can be counterproductive if it results in unnecessary civilian casualties and thereby drives more civilians into the rebels' arms. Thus a war against guerrillas typically requires a degree of restraint that is far from the norm in conventional conflicts.

✦ ✦ ✦

THAT WAS A lesson the U.S. armed forces were to learn at high cost in Vietnam—for neither the first nor the last time. The situation had deteriorated markedly since Lansdale's departure in large part because of North

Vietnam's decision in 1960 to form the National Liberation Front to wage war in the south. On a brief visit in 1961 Lansdale was shocked to find that the Communists had "been able to infiltrate the most productive area of South Vietnam and to gain control of nearly all of it."[79] He was even more dismayed to see "Vietnamese artillery firing on villages"—that was "something you don't do in a guerrilla war. . . . You never make war against your own people."[80]

Diem, for his part, was becoming more isolated in his presidential palace, "screened in," as Lansdale put it, "by his palace guard." Following Lansdale's departure Diem had no trusted interlocutor who could urge him to make democratic reforms. Instead he fell under the sway of his brother Ngo Dinh Nhu, "a truly Machiavellian character," in the words of a South Vietnamese official.[81] He propagated a crackpot, quasi-Marxist doctrine known as "personalism" and employed heavy-handed tactics to repress dissent, leading to a fatal confrontation with Buddhist monks.

"If the next American official to talk with President Diem," Lansdale wrote in 1961, "would have the good sense to see him as a human being who has been through a lot of hell for years—and not as an opponent to be beaten to his knees—we would start regaining our influence with him in a healthy way. . . . If we don't like the influence of Brother Nhu," he recommended, "then let's move someone of ours in close."[82] But no American representative after his own departure was able to establish that kind of rapport with the prickly president. Similar woes would plague future generations of American officials who had to deal with José Napoleón Duarte in El Salvador, Hamid Karzai in Afghanistan, and Nouri al-Maliki in Iraq. It is, indeed, a common issue in any counterinsurgency where an outside power is supporting but not controlling an ostensibly sovereign ally. It was not a problem that confronted the British in Malaya, the French in Algeria, or other imperialists fighting in their own colonies, but in those cases the lack of an independent indigenous government presented its own problems in winning popular support.

In South Vietnam the most promising counterinsurgency initiative enacted post-Lansdale was the Strategic Hamlets program set up at the urging of Sir Robert Thompson, the "suave" head of the British Advisory Mission[83] and, like Lansdale, one of the few prominent counterinsurgents with an air force background. (He had served as RAF liaison to the Chindits.) This population-resettlement and village-security plan was modeled on Malaya's New Villages and Israel's kibbutzim,[84] but under the misguided direction of Ngo Dinh Nhu the program expanded too fast. As Thompson noted, "It took over three years to establish 500 defended Chinese villages in Malaya. In under two years in Vietnam over 8,000 strategic hamlets were created, the majority of them in the first nine months of 1963."[85] That was far too many for the fledgling South Vietnamese armed forces to safeguard, allowing the enemy to infiltrate the new hamlets. After Diem's death in an American-backed coup, which came less than a month before Kennedy's own assassination, the program fell out of official favor, although efforts to safeguard hamlets continued.

With the Saigon government plunged into a period of uncertainty and the Vietcong growing in strength, the new president, Lyndon Johnson, faced a thankless choice: either employ more military might or risk letting an ally fall. In 1965, in response to ostensible North Vietnamese attacks on two U.S. destroyers on an intelligence-gathering mission in the Gulf of Tonkin, he launched Operation Rolling Thunder, a gradually escalating series of bombing raids on the north that would be punctuated by pauses meant to spur negotiations. The first American ground troops were dispatched to safeguard air bases, but soon they took on an active combat role. By the end of 1965 there were 184,000 American troops in the south, a figure that was to steadily increase until topping out at 540,000 in 1969.[86] North Vietnam responded by sending its own regulars south to fight alongside the Vietcong. That, in turn, led to a further deterioration of the security situation—not to mention the domestic situation in the United States, where the unpopularity of the war and the draft helped spark protests and riots on college campuses. By relying primarily on conscripts, the Johnson administration was ignoring lessons learned by, among others, the Roman, Chinese, British, and French empires, all of which had found that pacification operations far from home, seldom popular and invariably costly and long-lasting, were generally better left to professional soldiers who volunteered for this unglamorous duty rather than to unenthusiastic citizen-soldiers whose dispatch was certain to spark social unrest back home.

Nor was this the only lesson of guerrilla warfare past that went unlearned by the American forces. General William Childs Westmoreland, head of U.S. Military Assistance Command, Vietnam, was a courtly southerner who, if nothing else, looked the part of a general with his thick salt-and-pepper hair, bushy eyebrows, and granite features. A veteran of World War II and the Korean War, he was well schooled in conventional operations, but nothing in his background or education prepared him to face an enemy that did not stand and fight in the open like the Wehrmacht or the Korean People's Army. In 1964, when Westmoreland was first being considered for command in Vietnam, a brigadier general warned that "it would be a grave mistake to appoint him"—"He is spit and polish. . . . This is a counterinsurgency war, and he would have no idea how to deal with it."[87] That prediction turned out to be tragically on target.

On the basis of his limited experience, Westmoreland had a one-word solution to the insurgency: "Firepower."[88] U.S. aircraft would drop more bombs during the Vietnam War than during World War II, with most falling on South Vietnamese territory.[89] Predictably, however, the liberal employment of firepower, combined with the use of noisy aircraft, helicopters, trucks, and tanks, signaled every American attack well in advance and usually allowed the enemy to slip away. Communist troops occasionally would slug it out with American formations—for example, in the famous 1965 battle in the Ia Drang Valley that was the subject of the book and movie *We Were Soldiers Once . . . And Young.* But seldom would North Vietnamese or Vietcong units allow themselves to be trapped and annihilated. All that the massive expenditure of firepower achieved was to create lots of casualties and lots of refugees, thereby alienating the population of the south. "We really blew a lot of civilians away," a U.S. officer later admitted.[90]

Like Kitchener in the Boer War, Westmoreland was indifferent to civilian suffering—he measured the progress of the campaign by compiling highly suspect "body counts," and it was all too easy to count any dead peasant as a Vietcong fighter. Yet once American or South Vietnamese troops left an area, the Vietcong usually returned to reassert control. American forces were so busy chasing Communist formations around the sparsely populated highlands that they neglected to secure the country's sixteen million people, 90 percent of whom lived in the Mekong Delta and in the narrow coastal plain.[91]

Westmoreland hoped to cut off the insurgents by interdicting the Ho Chi Minh Trail, a network of roads running through North Vietnam, Laos, and Cambodia into South Vietnam. But he never succeeded, because the austere guerrillas did not require many truckloads of supplies to keep going. Moreover they had another supply line running straight from the Cambodian port of Sihanoukville. The Ho Chi Minh Trail was more important as an infiltration route for reinforcements (by 1966 over fifty thousand fighters a year were going south), but individuals hidden in the jungle were notoriously hard to hit from the air.[92]

There was, in fairness, more to the American war effort than conventional operations. There were also some promising counterinsurgency programs conducted in cooperation with the South Vietnamese. These included the Combined Action Program, which sent squads of marines to live in Vietnamese villages and protect them in cooperation with the Popular Forces militia; Civilian Irregular Defense Groups, which sent CIA and Special Forces personnel to mobilize ethnic minorities, the Montagnards, much as the French had done before them; Long-Range Reconnaissance Patrols, which sent small hunter-killer teams made up of American and South Vietnamese Special Forces to gather intelligence and ambush enemy forces; and the Phoenix Program, which sent American and South Vietnamese intelligence operatives to root out Vietcong cadres. These programs produced more enemy kills and fewer casualties among American forces and Vietnamese civilians than more-conventional operations. One Vietcong leader later said, "We never feared a division of troops, but the infiltration of a couple of guys into our ranks"—a feature of Phoenix—"created tremendous difficulties for us."[93]

But these programs were not quick enough or decisive enough for the U.S. military hierarchy, which was searching for what Lansdale derided as a "short-cut" or "magical formula."[94] Counterinsurgency came to be referred to as "the other war," and it was little more than a minor adjunct to the lumbering search-and-destroy missions that consumed 95 percent of American resources.[95] This was a major difference between the unsuccessful U.S. war effort in Vietnam and the more successful efforts of the British in Malaya and of the Filipinos in the Huk Rebellion. Those conflicts saw the employment of many counterinsurgency programs superficially similar to those utilized in South Vietnam, but they were the main effort—not a sideshow. In South Vietnam, mindlessly destructive "search and destroy" missions undid many of the gains won by more-focused counterinsurgency campaigns.

Notwithstanding steady increases in the forces at his disposal, Westmoreland never achieved his cherished objective—to reach a "crossover point" when he was killing more Communists than Hanoi could replace. Even as American commanders eagerly claimed credit for often exaggerated "body counts," the number of enemy fighters in the south steadily climbed. According to official American military estimates, there were 134,000 Communist regulars and guerrillas in the south at the end of 1965 and 280,000 by 1967. The CIA believed the actual figures were much higher—over 500,000 by 1968.[96]

Communist forces suffered staggering casualties—after the war, Hanoi admitted losing 1.1 million soldiers[97]—but it made little difference. North Vietnam was a dictatorship impervious to public opinion. The American public was more casualty conscious and began to turn against the war when it became apparent that little progress was being made in return for the sacrifice of so many American lives. Long before the final toll had reached 58,000 dead, millions of Americans had taken to the streets to protest the war's continuation, making it America's most divisive conflict since the Civil War. Hanoi deliberately played on public opinion in the United States, tailoring its propaganda to encourage antiwar activists, some of whom, most famously Jane Fonda in 1972, actually visited the north. The Hanoi line had it that the Vietcong were independent of the north and that Ho Chi Minh and other northern leaders were not really Communists.[98] These myths were believed by many in the West. The people of North Vietnam, by contrast, were cut off from anti-Communist appeals by government censorship.

Years later, after he had left Vietnam in ignominious defeat, Westmoreland and many of his military colleagues tried to shift the blame for their ill-chosen tactics to their political masters, especially President Lyndon Johnson and Secretary of Defense Robert McNamara. But while Johnson did micromanage the bombing of North Vietnam for fear of drawing into the war Hanoi's allies, China and the Soviet Union, he took a hands-off attitude toward operations in the south. "Within South Vietnam, the U.S. commander had very wide latitude in deciding how to fight the war," writes historian Lewis Sorley. "That was true for Westmoreland, and equally true for his eventual successor." "Westy," in short, had no one but himself to blame for his decision, eerily similar to that of earlier French commanders in Indochina, to fight a "war of attrition" that played directly to the Communists' strengths.[99]

✦ ✦ ✦

THE CONVENTIONAL—and futile—contour of the war effort was already well established by the time Lansdale arrived for his second tour of duty in South Vietnam in August 1965. His bureaucratic enemies had forced his retirement from the air force at the end of 1963, only a few months after his promotion to major general, but Vice President Hubert Humphrey remained a fan and thought Lansdale could still be useful. The CIA station chief in Saigon "damn near dropped his martini" when he heard that this "blunt and unorthodox" interloper had been appointed as a civilian to head the newly created Saigon Liaison Office, reporting directly to Ambassador Henry Cabot Lodge.[100]

Lansdale reassembled many of the old gang from the 1950s along with some newcomers—including the former Pentagon aide Daniel Ellsberg, who would achieve infamy in 1971 as the leaker of the Pentagon Papers, a classified history of the war. At his two-story villa on Cong Ly Street, Lansdale and his aides hosted a nonstop stream of Vietnamese visitors with whom they chatted over ginseng wine into the wee hours and sang folks songs.

By now Lansdale was a "living legend" who was expected by the press to perform "miracles."[101] But there was no native leader comparable in stature to Magsaysay or Diem for him to work with. Just as Lansdale had expected, Diem's downfall, which had been engineered by one of Lansdale's associates, the CIA officer Lucien Conein, had led to the rise of one uniformed dictator after another, each lacking legitimacy.

The biggest obstacle Lansdale encountered, however, was on the American side, in the "Pentagon East," the swollen and cumbersome U.S. bureaucracy in Saigon. When he had first arrived in South Vietnam in 1954, there were only 348 American servicemen in the entire country; by the end of his second tour, in 1968, the figure had grown to more than half a million.[102]

Lansdale, for his part, had only eleven team members.[103] He had no independent authority of his own, and his ability to exert any influence was limited by his own ineptitude at office politics, by his lack of high-level support in Washington, and by the bureaucracy's chronic suspicion of him. One official summed up their attitude: "We don't want Lawrences of Asia."[104]

The cause of such antipathy was not hard to discern. The Quiet American was in opposition to American policy as it had developed since the early 1960s. He did not want U.S. troops in South Vietnam, certainly not in such large numbers. "The military can suppress the Communist forces . . . ," he warned Ambassador Lodge, in an accurate summary of the lessons of thousands of years of guerrilla conflicts, "but cannot defeat them short of genocide." He favored political action at the "rice roots" level to develop a "viable democracy," guided by culturally savvy advisers rather than the kind of "heavy paternalism" he found among so many Americans in Vietnam who were in his view prolonging "the ills of colonialism."[105] He was aware of the need for military action but scathing in decrying the big-unit, firepower-intensive tactics of American and South Vietnamese forces. He warned in a 1964 *Foreign Affairs* article, "When the military opens fire at long range, whether by infantry weapons, artillery or air strikes, on a reported Viet Cong concentration in a hamlet or village full of civilians, the Vietnamese officers who give those orders and the American advisers who let them 'get away with it' are helping defeat the cause of freedom."[106]

When Lansdale tried to advance an alternative approach to pacification, he later admitted ruefully, his "ideas got clobbered time after time by the U.S. officials."[107] His prescience, and that of other experienced counterinsurgency hands, such as Robert Thompson, John Paul Vann, and Roger Hilsman, was widely recognized only after the Tet Offensive, which occurred a few months before he left Vietnam for good.

✦ ✦ ✦

ON THE NIGHT of January 30, 1968, General Vo Nguyen Giap, under pressure from hard-line Communist leaders, launched a surprise attack against Saigon and most of the other major cities of the south utilizing 84,000 fighters. Lansdale was awoken, along with many other residents of the capital, at 3 a.m. on January 31 by "some loud bangs nearby, followed by automatic weapons fire." Before long, firing had broken out "all over the place." A Vietcong suicide squad even managed to penetrate the heavily defended grounds of the U.S. embassy before being wiped out. Just like Giap's premature thrust into the Red River Delta in 1951, this attempt to strike a "decisive blow" was a costly defeat. An estimated 37,000 Communists were killed and 5,800 captured, while only 1,001 American and 2,082 South Vietnamese troops perished. The general uprising that Hanoi hoped to spark never materialized. Instead Vietcong brutality in Hue, where they executed 2,800 civilians during the three weeks that they controlled the city, caused a popular backlash in the south.[108]

But while unsuccessful militarily, the Tet Offensive reaped a valuable propaganda windfall for Hanoi by discrediting official proclamations that, as Westmoreland had claimed in November 1967, the war's "end" was in "view."[109] On the last day of March 1968, at 9 p.m., President Johnson took to the airwaves from the Oval Office, wearing a sober blue suit, a narrow red tie, and a grim expression on his heavily wrinkled face, to announce a partial bombing halt designed to "de-escalate the conflict." In a stunning surprise at the end of the forty-minute address, he added that, in order to concentrate all his energies on achieving "our hopes and the world's hopes for peace," he would not seek or accept "the nomination of my party for another term as your president." Thus the Vietnam War claimed its highest-profile victim: the Johnson presidency.[110] Nine days earlier the president had already relieved Westmoreland, kicking him upstairs to become army chief of staff. Westmoreland's request for even more troops was denied. This was a tacit admission that the war was not going well—something that the public already knew. Only 26 percent of those surveyed by Gallup shortly before his address approved of Johnson's handling of Vietnam.[111]

The next president, Richard M. Nixon, and his national security adviser, Henry Kissinger, had no choice but to launch a policy of "Vietnamization," which involved the gradual withdrawal of American combat troops while they searched for an "honorable" end to the conflict. Thanks to the mauling the Vietcong had received during the Tet Offensive, however, it was in no position to take immediate advantage of the American pullout. Westmoreland's deputy and successor, General Creighton "Abe" Abrams, kept the pressure on by putting more emphasis on providing "security for the people of South Vietnam's villages and hamlets" while gradually scaling back conventional operations. Abrams got rid of the "other war" mantra and replaced it with "one war."[112] He was greatly aided by the OSS and CIA veteran William Colby, who turned CORDS (Civil Operations and Revolutionary Development Support), a subordinate command charged with pacification, into an effective instrument of counterinsurgency. Security conditions in the south actually improved even as the number of American troops fell. By 1971 Colby and his daredevil subordinate, John Paul Vann, were able to motorbike across the Mekong Delta with no bodyguards—and no trouble.[113]

The following year Giap launched a conventional attack on the south—the third repetition of the same mistake he had made in 1951 and 1968. Trying to prematurely end an irregular conflict can be a costly blunder for either insurgents or counterinsurgents; in this type of war there are no shortcuts to victory. Giap was generally a study in patience; certainly he had more of a long-term outlook than either the French generals he had fought or their American successors. But he was prone to roll the dice on premature offensives that came to perdition—and that marred his reputation as one of the most successful guerrilla strategists of all time. Although there were few American ground troops left, the 1972 Easter Offensive was smashed by the South Vietnamese armed forces aided by American airpower. By January 1973, following the bombing of Hanoi and the mining of Haiphong harbor, the Hanoi government was ready to sign the Paris Peace Accords bringing the war to a halt—at least temporarily.

Despite Nixon's claims of having achieved "peace with honor," more than 150,000 Communist troops remained in the south, and they began violating the accords almost at once.[114] Even so South Vietnam might have survived if the United States had been willing to keep its troops in place, as it had done after the Korean War. But public opposition to the war and the Watergate scandal, which destroyed Nixon's popularity after a landslide reelection, made that impossible. American aid to the south was cut off entirely in 1974, even as China and the Soviet Union continued their support for the north. In 1975 a North Vietnamese invasion led to a quick collapse of the south. The end of the twenty-year war was brought about by regulars riding T-54 tanks, not by pajama-clad guerrillas, but it was the guerrillas who made possible the final Communist victory by wearing down the will of the American people to continue the struggle.

✦ ✦ ✦

HO CHI MINH, who died in 1969, did not live to see the end of the long struggle against "the imperialist and feudalist forces."[115] Long before his demise he had become an aging, ailing, avuncular figurehead while real power was exercised behind the scenes by the hard-line party leader Le Duan. More even than Vo Nguyen Giap, whom he derided as a "scared rabbit" for being afraid to confront the United States directly in 1965, Le Duan was the primary architect of one of the most humiliating drubbings ever suffered by a superpower.[116] The cost of his single-minded dedication to victory was staggering—much higher than any democratic politician could have tolerated. Hanoi estimated that the twenty-year war cost 3.6 million Vietnamese lives on both sides.[117]

Conventionally minded American soldiers such as Colonel Harry Summers later argued that the conflict had been lost because they had been forced to devote *too much* attention to "the guerrilla war in the south," while shortsighted politicians prevented them from addressing the "root of the trouble . . . at the source."[118] The war, it was claimed, could have been won only with a conventional invasion either of Laos to cut the Ho Chi Minh Trail or, better still, of North Vietnam itself to depose the Communist regime. This ignored the likelihood of intervention by China, which by 1967 had 170,000 troops in the north, should U.S. troops cross the seventeenth parallel.[119] It ignored, too, the lessons of the French Indochina War. The French had occupied the entire country and still had been defeated by determined guerrillas with supply lines stretching into China.

Fickle political leadership undoubtedly contributed to the worst military defeat in American history—but so did the obtuseness of a military establishment that tried to apply a conventional strategy to an unconventional conflict. The outcome might have been different if more attention had been paid to the advice of counterinsurgency experts such as Edward Lansdale, who had warned as early as 1964 "that the Communists have let loose a revolutionary idea in Viet Nam and that it will not die by being ignored, bombed, or smothered by us."[120] Lansdale did not believe the war was unwinnable if the right methods were applied. But that did not happen until after public support for the war effort had already collapsed in the United States.

Vietnam was far from the only place where guerrillas were triumphing over America's allies during the "Radical Chic" era. Another notable success for "people's war" was in some ways even more galling because it occurred right in the *Yanquis'* backyard, in a country that the United States had dominated ever since it sent its troops in 1898 to help Cuban *insurrectos* oust their Spanish overlords.

53.

M-26-7

Castro's Improbable Comeback, 1952–1959

"It wasn't a landing, it was a shipwreck." So said one of the eighty-two revolutionaries aboard the *Granma* when it finally reached Cuban soil before daybreak on December 2, 1956.

The voyage from Mexico, where these exiles had conducted their training, had been nightmarish. The thirty-eight-foot yacht, which they had bought for $20,000 from an American expatriate, was designed to handle a maximum of twenty-five passengers. Overloaded as it was, the *Granma* rode too low in the rough seas and rotten weather and steered clumsily. One passenger, Faustino Pérez, a future member of the Communist Party's Central Committee, recalled how "enormous waves—like bobbing mountains—toyed with the small but tenacious boat." Another passenger, a twenty-eight-year-old doctor named Ernesto "Che" Guevara, recalled how they made a "frantic search for antihistamines to combat seasickness, and could not find them." Before long, he wrote, "the whole boat assumed a ridiculous, tragic appearance: men clutching their stomachs, anguish written in their faces, some with their heads in buckets, others lying immobile on the deck in strange positions, their clothes covered in vomit. With the exception of two or three sailors, and four or five others, the rest of the 82 crew members were seasick."

When the *Granma* finally reached Oriente Province on the eastern coast of Cuba in the semidarkness of December 2, it grounded a hundred yards offshore. Most of the supplies and equipment had to be left on the boat while the men hopped into the water and waded ashore. "It was rough going . . . ," recalled Faustino Pérez. "After endless hours in the enormous swamp, struggling through mud, mangroves, and water, we finally began to touch solid ground. We lay down on the grass, exhausted, hungry, covered with mud, knowing that we were finally on Cuban soil."

Fidel Castro, the thirty-year-old lawyer who was the chief of this grandly named Rebel Army, had planned his landing in emulation of the landing of José Martí and other Cuban revolutionaries in 1895 to begin their war of liberation against Spain. It was designed to coincide with an uprising among urban revolutionaries in the nearby city of Santiago. But a longer than expected sea voyage had thrown the plan awry. By the time the *Granma* landed, there was nobody to greet them except the armed forces of dictator Fulgencio Batista. Within hours a coast guard vessel and army aircraft had arrived to bomb the mangrove swamps in which the *Granma* had gotten stuck. The rebels barely escaped. Fed and guided by local peasants who had no love lost for Batista's corrupt regime, Castro and his men marched east through the sugarcane fields, moving at night to avoid air attack. They were attempting to reach the Sierra Maestra, where, amid peaks averaging 4,500 feet, they reckoned they would be safe.

On the morning of December 5, "on the verge of collapse," in Che Guevara's words, after an exhausting all-night march, they pitched camp on a low hillside at Alegría de Pío. Unbeknownst to them, one of their peasant guides had informed the Rural Guard of their location, which was not hard to find anyway, because they had sustained themselves en route by eating sugarcane, leaving a trail of cane peelings behind them that did not require a bloodhound to follow. At 4 p.m. the rebels began to see aircraft in the sky, and then "within seconds" came a "hail of bullets"—"at least," Che later wrote, "that's how it seemed to us, this being our baptism of fire."

In the initial confusion Guevara and several other men were hit. "I felt a sharp blow in my chest and a wound in my neck; I thought for certain I was dead . . . ," he wrote. "I immediately began to think about the best way to die, since in that minute all seemed lost." Alone or in small groups, the inexperienced fighters scattered in panic, "flying like rabbits," leaving their equipment behind. Many were captured and executed. Others deserted. After the battle of Alegría de Pío fewer than two dozen fighters were left.

In his olive-green uniform and heavy horn-rim glasses, Fidel Castro spent the next five days hiding in the cane fields with two *compañeros*, listening apprehensively for the sounds of approaching soldiers. When he went to sleep Castro positioned the barrel of his rifle against his throat, vowing, "If I am found, I'll just squeeze the trigger and die."

His situation was every bit as desperate as that of Toussaint Louverture after the arrival of Victor Emmanuel Leclerc's expeditionary force in Haiti in 1802, of Mao Zedong after the failure of the 1927 Autumn Harvest uprising, or of Ho Chi Minh in his isolated Pac Bo stronghold after the occupation of Indochina by the Imperial Japanese Army. Yet even in this seemingly hopeless position Castro, like those other revolutionary icons, never lost faith. Trapped as he was, the loquacious young rebel could not refrain from talking—and dreaming. Speaking day and night in a "controlled whisper," he regaled his two companions with his future plans: how he was going to mobilize the peasants, carry out a social revolution, vanquish the *Yanquis*, and much else.

His two companions thought he was hallucinating. They were liable to be caught and killed any minute. Even if they escaped alive, how could a handful of ill-armed rebels overthrow an entrenched regime defended by forty thousand well-equipped soldiers? "Shit, he's gone crazy . . . ," one of Fidel's comrades told himself. "How can we beat Batista with these few people?"

The answer would come in the next twenty-five months.[121]

✦ ✦ ✦

TITO WAS A poor peasant. Mao a well-to-do peasant. Ho Chi Minh and Vo Nguyen Giap impoverished mandarins. Fidel Castro was downright rich. He was born in 1926 to a landowner who controlled over 25,000 acres in Oriente Province and lorded over his field hands with a silver-handled whip. Fidel's father, Angel, was a self-made man, an immigrant from Spain who had started out as a simple laborer and learned to read only as an adult. His lack of aristocratic lineage hindered Fidel socially when he attended an elite Jesuit high school in Havana; the other students looked down on him as "primitive" and "not cultured" even though he was captain of the basketball team. It did not help that he bathed infrequently and had "bad table manners." A resentful loner with a violent temper, Fidel was filled, a fellow student recalled, with "hatred against society people and moneyed people." He also clashed with his parents and teachers. "I'd started being a rebel . . . at like six or seven," he later said.

In this respect he was similar to the young Mao, Tito, and Stalin: all of these future Communist insurgents turned dictators had found themselves in conflict with their parents and society from a young age. All of them nursed a grudge against their supposed "superiors" and a political system that denied them the power that they saw as rightly theirs—and they were ready to use violence to seize what they wanted. Castro was different from Mao, Tito, and Stalin, if not from Giap, in having the benefit of a university education. Like a growing number of twentieth-century radicals and, for that matter, the nineteenth-century Russian Nihilists, he had become active politically while attending university—in his case the law school at Havana University, which he entered in 1945. Politics in Cuba was not a sport for milquetoasts; Castro usually carried a gun and was often involved in violent altercations with other students and the police. He neglected his studies, was twice accused of murder, and acquired a reputation as a swaggering "young political hoodlum." In those years "El Loco Fidel," as he was called by his schoolmates, had only one thing on his mind. A friend recalled, "Even if he was with a girl he kept talking about politics." Years later, once in power, he would become a prolific womanizer, like Mao and Tito, but, also like them, he would never lose his overriding interest in political machinations.

After graduating from law school in 1950, Castro opened a law practice yet did little legal work. Money was tight despite an allowance from his father that would continue until he was on the cusp of power. His beautiful blond wife, Mirta Díaz-Balart, a member of a pro-Batista family whom he had married in law school, often had no milk for their newborn son, "Fidelito." But the boy's father was too busy carousing with his political cronies to care. He was preparing to run as a candidate for the Chamber of Deputies in 1952 when the elections were suspended. Fulgencio Batista, a onetime army sergeant who had been president from 1933 to 1944, seized power for a second time. During his first stint in office he had been a progressive and popular leader who had won the backing of the labor unions and the Communist Party. However, upper-class Cubans had never much liked this mulatto from a lowly background who had once worked as a common laborer. Batista's brutality and corruption during his second stint in power ensured that he became increasingly unpopular with all classes. Castro immediately began plotting a revolution—as did many other radicals. If they could not seize power by the ballot box, they would do so by force.

The Castro of those years, at over six feet tall and pudgy, was already an imposing physical presence even if he did not yet sport his later trademarks—an unruly beard and an olive army uniform. In those days he favored dark suits, a thin mustache, and Brylcreem in his hair. Even as a tyro politico, however, he already displayed his talents as a "monologist," delivering the hours-long harangues that would be a lifelong hallmark. His manner, like that of Tito or Garibaldi, was said to be "rough and charming."

He was a leftist but not yet a member of the Communist Party. He would not join the party until he was already in a position, as Cuba's president, to give it orders; he never wanted to be bossed around by anyone. His initial political affiliation was with the *Ortodoxos*, a moderate opposition party that claimed to embody the ideals of José Martí, one of Castro's lifelong heroes. Castro's primary allegiance, however, was always to his own ambitions; he had a limitless need, a female friend noted, for "approval, applause, adoration." "He wants to be a god," she concluded.

Still ignorant of Marxism, which he would not embrace until years later, a self-confessed "political illiterate," Fidel did not read the works of Lenin, Mao Zedong, and other notable insurgents before embarking on his own insurgency. He was more influenced by Cuba's own independence struggle and by one of his favorite novels—Ernest Hemingway's *For Whom the Bell Tolls*, which recounts the adventures of a Republican guerrilla in the Spanish Civil War. "That book," he later said, "helped me conceive our own irregular war." Unlike Mao, he did not attach much importance to political organizing as a prelude to military action. He believed that a band of idealistic and dashing *guerrilleros* could spark an uprising on their own with a few bold attacks. This would later become known as the *foco* theory, but it seldom if ever worked—not even in Cuba.

✦ ✦ ✦

THE LONG AND tortuous journey that would take Castro to prison and exile before a return home to wage guerrilla warfare began in 1952. He spent much of the year traveling across Cuba in his beige Chevrolet, gathering followers with a promise to restore democracy. Before long he had twelve hundred recruits. For their first target he picked the forbidding Moncada army barracks in Santiago, surrounded by stout walls and guarded by more than four hundred soldiers. He hoped to seize weapons that could be used to equip his Rebel Army, but the attack, which occurred on July 26, 1953, was a fiasco. Most of Castro's force was captured or killed. Castro tried to escape with a few men to the mountains, but he was caught by the paramilitary Rural Guard. It was his good fortune that the lieutenant in charge was humane enough to disregard the take-no-prisoners edicts of his superiors.

In the best revolutionary tradition, Castro turned his trial into a forum for publicly promulgating his views. The judges allowed Castro, acting as his own lawyer, to lodge accusations of "assassination and torture" against the government. Castro wound up being sentenced to fifteen years in prison along with twenty-five companions, including his brother Raúl. But before he was done Castro had delivered a two-hour speech in his own defense that recalled John Brown's memorable oration after Harpers Ferry. There is no exact record of what he said, but in prison he reconstructed and no doubt embellished his remarks in a clandestinely published pamphlet: *History Will Absolve Me*. Its fiery conclusion: "I do not fear the fury of the miserable tyrant who snuffed out the life of seventy brothers of mine. Condemn me, it does not matter. *History will absolve me!*"

The notoriety he had acquired from the Moncada barracks attack, combined with the nobility of his defense, catapulted Castro to a leadership position among the anti-Batista forces. His time behind bars on the Isle of Pines, a tropical gulag, further burnished his revolutionary credentials, even though he was a privileged prisoner who was free to receive packages of books, food, and cigars. His prison reading began the ideological journey that culminated in his conversion to communism. While in prison he was also divorced by his wife, supposedly after she had mistakenly received a letter he had written to his mistress. He would have numerous flings in years to come (his bodyguards would procure bedmates) but, as one of his female friends noted, "His one true mistress was the revolution."

In 1955, under pressure from the prisoners' mothers, Batista extended an amnesty to Castro and his followers. This was part of a pattern with Batista, who was dictatorial enough to arouse widespread opposition but not dictatorial enough to suppress it. He had a perfect opportunity to kill his most dangerous foe or at least to lock him up for good—and he blinked. Castro would not make the same mistake when it was his turn to rule.[122]

✦ ✦ ✦

AFTER LEAVING THE Isle of Pines, Castro headed to voluntary exile in Mexico. Here he trained his forces, now known as the 26th of July Movement, or, in its Spanish initials, M-26-7. And here he met a new recruit, a physician known initially as El Argentino, who was destined to become the most romantic and celebrated guerrilla fighter since Garibaldi.

Like Castro but unlike Garibaldi, Che Guevara was no son of the working class. His family was not as rich as Castro's but it had a more aristocratic lineage; he was descended from one of Argentina's richest men. By the time Ernesto was born in 1928 most of the family fortune had been dissipated, but his parents still lived well—often beyond their means. They were Bohemian in lifestyle and liberal in outlook; his mother wore trousers and smoked cigarettes, which was considered daring in her day. Ernesto's father was a notorious ladies' man; eventually he and Ernesto's mother separated. Ernesto was closer to his mother than to his father. She nursed him through a childhood of asthmatic suffering—a disease that would make physical exertion agonizing for the rest of his days. Like Hubert Lyautey and Theodore Roosevelt, Guevara would drive himself to perform punishing feats to prove to himself and others that he was no longer the sickly boy he had once been. And like Lyautey and Roosevelt he grew up to be an intellectual as well as a man of action. His parents transmitted to him a love of both athletics and reading; he played rugby and golf and devoured Sartre and Freud, Lenin and Marx. From his parents, too, he inherited a disdain for societal conventions.

Guevara grew up rebellious and disobedient, fearless and stubborn. He liked to shock the bourgeois with his untidy appearance, boasting, for example, that he had not washed his shirt in half a year. Girls were drawn to this "easy-going" young man with, in the words of his first wife, a "commanding voice but a fragile appearance." He had "dark brown hair framing a pale face and fair features that emphasized his striking black eyes." Guevara would be only the latest in a long line of guerrilla chieftains, stretching back to Garibaldi and beyond, who proved irresistible to women—and they to him.

Guevara studied medicine at Buenos Aires University, but he had no intention of becoming a physician. His passions were travel and writing. His family had moved often when he was a child, and he kept moving as an adult, becoming for a time, if you will, a Latin Jack Kerouac. In 1950 he crisscrossed Argentina by himself on a motorized bicycle. Two years later he set off with a friend across South America on a motorcycle nicknamed *La Poderosa* (the Powerful One)—a seven-month journey chronicled in his *Motorcycle Diaries*. In 1953, after graduating from medical school, he embarked on yet another long transcontinental ramble with another friend.

Like Mao, who had been appalled by the conditions he encountered in 1917 while spending a summer with a fellow student as beggars on a walking tour of Hunan Province, Che saw much poverty, illiteracy, and untreated illness alongside vast wealth and privilege. He was, for instance, appalled by a meeting in 1952 with a Chilean copper miner who had been imprisoned for striking and whom he encountered, along with his wife, "frozen stiff in the desert night," without even "one single miserable blanket to cover themselves with." Just as Mao had blamed the inequities he saw not on the inherent difficulties of a transition from an agrarian to an industrial economy but rather on capitalism itself ("Money is the father and grandfather of the mean of spirit," young Mao was quoted as saying), so too Che focused his ire on capitalists—in his case, Latin American oligarchies and their *Yanqui* backers. He was particularly angered by the United Fruit Company plantations in Costa Rica. "I have sworn," he wrote home, "before a picture of the old and mourned comrade Stalin that I won't rest until I see these capitalist octopuses annihilated."

He was ineluctably drawn deeper into politics in Guatemala, where in 1954 he was a witness to the CIA-engineered coup that overthrew the leftist president, Jacobo Arbenz. Guevara "thoroughly enjoyed" himself and "licked" his "chops" during the fighting. "It's all been great fun here," he wrote, "with shooting, bombing, speeches and other touches that have broken the monotony." By the time he fled Guatemala in the fall of 1954, he was a dedicated Marxist and a budding war lover.

His next destination was Mexico City, long recovered from its days as a battleground in Mexico's own revolution (1910–20) and in the midst of a rapid expansion that would produce the ugly and crowded yet vibrant megalopolis that the novelist Carlos Fuentes would dub "the capital of underdevelopment." Since Mexico was ruled by the leftist Institutional Revolutionary Party (PRI), its leading city had become a draw for exiles such as Leon Trotsky, who was assassinated there in 1940, and literary rebels such as Jack Kerouac, who visited regularly in the 1940s–1950s, and William S. Burroughs, who lived there from 1949 to 1952.

While in Mexico City, Che recorded in his diary in July 1955, "I met Fidel Castro, the Cuban revolutionary." Guevara was impressed: "He is a young, intelligent guy, very sure of himself and extraordinarily audacious." He added, "I think we hit it off well." So well, in fact, that Guevara immediately signed up for M-26-7.

Not the least of the movement's attractions was that it offered an escape from what Guevara called a "disastrous conjugal situation." After she became pregnant, he had married a plump and homely older woman of Indian ancestry—Hilda Gadea—whom he had met in Guatemala. In spite of his love for his newborn daughter, he could not settle down to become a "boring family man." Now he didn't have to. During the campaign to come, he would acquire a younger and prettier girlfriend, a revolutionary activist named Aleida March, who would become his second wife. (Hilda, a good socialist to the end, claimed she amicably granted Che a divorce so that he could devote his full energy "to the struggle for the liberation of America.")

Initially Guevara was to serve only as a medical officer. But he excelled at military training and later at military operations. Despite his asthma, he drove himself so hard and so recklessly, much as Garibaldi and Wingate did, that eventually he became a senior officer, a *commandante*, notwithstanding the resentment some Cubans felt toward this foreigner. (His fastidious comrades were particularly appalled by Guevara's disdain for bathing.) The key to Guevara's rise was that, although more intellectual and more disciplined than Castro, he never challenged Fidel's primacy; there was room for only one Maximum Leader.[123]

✦ ✦ ✦

AFTER THE ONE-SIDED ambush at Alegría de Pío, in which most of Castro's men were caught or killed, Batista was convinced that M-26-7 was finished and withdrew most of his forces from the Sierra Maestra. That allowed the small number of survivors to recuperate and regroup with the help of friendly *guajiros* (peasants). Castro, like Mao, enjoined his men to treat the poor with respect. They always paid for their own food and lodging and often punished rebels who abused the population—a welcome contrast to Batista's army, which routinely stole from and abused the peasants. At the same time, Castro set up "people's trials" to punish "informers" and "exploiters"—categories elastic enough to include anyone who stood in his way. Like all successful insurgents, Castro knew how to mix love and fear, attraction and chastisement, to mobilize the populace.

Informers remained a problem. On January 30, 1957, a peasant led the Rural Guard to the guerrillas' camp, allowing Batista's aircraft to bomb and strafe them. Guevara personally executed the traitor; nobody else had the guts to do it.[124] Again, just as at Alegría de Pío, the rebels had to scatter in small groups. Again they barely escaped. And again they came back.

Their resurgence was made possible in no small part by a *New York Times* correspondent who arrived at their remote hideout on February 17, 1957. Castro was consciously copying José Martí, who had arranged an interview with the *New York Herald* shortly after landing in Oriente in 1895—and unconsciously copying Mao, who had made such shrewd use of Edgar Snow. His amanuensis was Herbert L. Matthews, an editorial writer who had a proclivity for identifying with those he covered, whether the Italian Fascists invading Abyssinia or the Republicans in the Spanish Civil War. Legend has it that Castro marched his men in circles to prevent the credulous correspondent from discovering how small and embattled the Rebel Army was. This is probably apocryphal. But it is true that he had an aide deliver a fictitious message from a nonexistent "second column," and that he boasted that his forces operated in "groups of ten to forty" when his entire army did not amount to forty men.

The credulous Matthews swallowed Castro's tall tales and regurgitated them on nothing less than the front page of the *New York Times*. He wrote that the "hero of Cuban youth" was "alive and fighting hard and successfully" for a "new deal for Cuba" that was "radical, democratic and therefore anti-communist." Batista had lifted censorship temporarily, so the stories were reprinted in Cuba, where they caused a sensation. Cubans had been told more than once that Castro had been killed. Now they learned that "Senor Castro," "a man of ideals, of courage, and of remarkable qualities of leadership," already had "mastery of the Sierra Maestra" and that "General Batista cannot possibly hope to suppress the Castro revolt." Matthews's claims were overblown, but they would become a self-fulfilling prophecy—the latest demonstration of the growing, and sometimes decisive, influence of "information operations" in modern guerrilla warfare.[125]

✦ ✦ ✦

A LITTLE-NOTICED ASPECT of the Matthews saga was the part played by the revolutionary underground in Cuba's cities. Matthews had been summoned from New York via Castro's contacts in Havana. Other urban radicals conducted Matthews to his rendezvous, slipping him past Batista's checkpoints and then back again in much the same way that urban Chinese Communists had done with Edgar Snow in 1936. Cuban revolutionaries would repeat the same service for other reporters such as Bob Taber of CBS, who would broadcast a glowing report on Castro in May 1957—*Rebels of the Sierra Maestra: The Story of Cuba's Jungle Fighters*.

This was only one of many services provided by an urban support structure that spread propaganda on Castro's behalf and funneled him recruits, money, medicine, arms, ammunition, food, and clothes. There were an estimated ten thousand revolutionaries in the *llanos* (plains), far more than in the *sierras* (mountains),[126] and prior to 1958 they were far more important. Few were Marxists. Many were rivals of Castro. These were men such as the charismatic student leader José Antonio Echevarría. After the publication of the Matthews articles, Echevarría led an ill-fated assault on the presidential palace in a desperate bid to upstage Castro. His death was a windfall for Castro by removing one of his chief competitors.

Other urban radicals carried on the fight, however. They organized strikes and mutinies and carried out numerous acts of sabotage and terrorism. These included setting fire to 400,000 gallons of jet fuel outside Havana, briefly occupying the national bank, and kidnapping an Argentine racing-car driver who was visiting Cuba. Even when unsuccessful, their activities diverted government attention away from the guerrillas in the Sierra Maestra and kept pressure on the dictator.

Castro's success would not have been possible if there had not been a broader turn against Batista among the Cuban population. Even wealthy businessmen contributed to his cause, some no doubt cynically buying insurance against political upheaval, others driven by genuine detestation of Batista and duped by Castro's promises of moderate reform. In March 1958 forty-six civic organizations representing 200,000 people called on Batista to resign.[127] But, for all the work of other regime opponents, it would be the *barbudos* (bearded ones) who would deliver the coup de grâce and their leader who would reap the rewards.

✦ ✦ ✦

A TURNING POINT came in the summer of 1958 when the guerrillas were able to repel a full-scale invasion of their "free territory" in the mountains. Batista assembled 10,000 soldiers, supported by aircraft and artillery. Castro had only 300 or so fighters. But geography was on his side. The army had to proceed along "steep and treacherous" trails that were impassable to horses, let alone jeeps. Castro's "cunningly camouflaged hut" could be reached only by a "shin-breaking clamber through nettled trees up an endless slope." That made it possible for a relatively small number of defenders to stop a much larger attacking force. After seventy-six days, having lost copious stockpiles of weapons and 1,500 dead, wounded, and captured, Batista had to call off the offensive.[128]

At the end of August 1958 Castro launched his own attack. Like Mao, he planned to encircle the cities from the countryside, but his forces were laughably small by comparison with Mao's, even accounting for the fact that Cuba is a much smaller country than China. Camilo Cienfuegos led one column of 82 men out of the mountains. Che Guevara led another column of 150 men. They were heading on foot for Havana, five hundred miles away. Castro himself marched out in September with a third column, 230 strong, to secure Santiago. If this had been a conventional war, these small bands would have had no chance of success. However, the Cuban army was demoralized and losing faith in Batista, who admitted that "panic was growing" as "military affairs went from bad to worse."[129]

On December 29, 1958, Guevara's column, now numbering 340 men, attacked the town of Santa Clara in central Cuba, a major transportation hub with a population of 150,000 and a garrison of 3,500 soldiers. Three bloody days of street fighting ensued that recalled the Redshirts' assault on Palermo in 1860. Like Garibaldi, Guevara prevailed with the help of civilians who barricaded the streets and threw projectiles at the army—in this case, Molotov cocktails. After Santa Clara's fall, nothing stood between the Rebel Army and Havana.[130]

By this time even the United States had all but abandoned Batista—there was no influential adviser like Edward Lansdale around to bolster him and push him to launch the sort of reforms that might have won him popular sympathy. Exasperated with this obdurate ally, the Eisenhower administration stopped arms shipments to him in March 1958, and the CIA, trying to cover its bets, provided covert funding to M-26-7.[131]

Batista had no choice but to flee the country on New Year's Eve, leaving behind, he wrote mournfully, "the suits, the dresses, the children's toys, the trophies won by the eldest at horse shows, the expensive gifts made to the children on their birthdays, pictures and works of art, jewels and ornaments of the First Lady, my personal possessions, acquired or presented to me from the 1930's on."[132] Asked upon his arrival in the Dominican Republic how he could have lost to such a small force, Batista told reporters "that the Army had not been prepared to counter the guerrilla tactics of the rebels."[133]

Rebel troops entered the capital on the night of January 1–2, 1959, amid general jubilation. The black-and-red flag of M-26-7, once forbidden, suddenly sprouted everywhere like flowers after a rainstorm. Cars raced through the streets, horns blaring, past joyous crowds who were certain that the new year signaled a new dawn for the beleaguered island.[134] That same day Castro marched into Santiago, where his movement had begun in 1953. This time he took the Moncada army barracks without a shot. All that remained was to consolidate power.

54.

FOCO OR LOCO?

Che's Quixotic Quest, 1965–1967

THE 26TH OF July Movement, which never had more than a few hundred fighters and that only at the end,[135] had scored one of the more improbable guerrilla victories ever by defeating an army of forty thousand and taking over a nation of six million people. Other victorious Communist movements, whether in China or Vietnam, were much larger by the time they won power. Even many unsuccessful insurgencies, from Greece to the Philippines, had many more fighters. In contravention of Maoist doctrine, Castro never managed to field much of a regular army. And, unlike Mao or Ho, his revolution triumphed without much outside help beyond donations from the Cuban diaspora. (Soviet support was still in the future.)

This was a tribute to Castro's genius for creating an aura of inevitability about his ascension by using a combination of small-scale attacks and large-scale publicity efforts. Ever since his imprisonment after the Moncada barracks attack, he had shown an uncanny talent for turning military setbacks into propaganda triumphs. Yet he would never have prevailed had it not been for Batista's debilitating weakness, which made even Chiang Kaishek appear to be strong by comparison. Batista presided over an unpopular regime rife with corruption. His army looked formidable on paper, but its commanders were chosen on the basis of personal loyalty, not merit, and most of its men were conscripts who had no desire to fight—which helps explain why fewer than three hundred of them died during the entire, two-year war.[136] Just as Batista's men were no match for Castro's, so too he was hopelessly outclassed in tactical maneuvering by the "cunning" rebel commander.[137] Castro was particularly adept at hiding his ideological views and forging an alliance of convenience with the non-Marxist opposition. He adamantly denied any "Communist infiltration" of M-26-7 or even "anti-Americanism."[138]

It did not take long for his façade of moderation to crumble. With his execution of hundreds of enemies, his refusal to hold elections, his confiscation of large landholdings and imposition of price controls, his alliance with the Soviet Union, his suppression of the independent press and political parties, and his imposition of a police state far more onerous than Batista's—by the early 1960s Castro had remade Cuba into a Communist state. This alienated many of his former comrades and alarmed the U.S. government, which mounted prodigious efforts, some of them overseen by Edward Lansdale, to overthrow him. In facing these threats to his rule, Castro could count on the staunch loyalty of his brother Raúl and Che Guevara, who had pushed him toward communism in the first place.

Guevara was such a hard-line Marxist that in coming years he would turn against the Soviet Union for being too soft and embrace Maoist China as his model. He was not a mass murderer on the scale of Mao, but he had no compunctions about shedding blood. He had once written, "I feel my nostrils dilate, savoring the acrid smell of gunpowder and blood, the enemy's death."[139] Castro took advantage of his bloodthirstiness by appointing Guevara in early 1959 to be commander of La Cabaña prison in a forbidding old stone fortress that had long guarded Havana's harbor, where he was to oversee the execution of hundreds of "counterrevolutionaries" after perfunctory trials. His dirty work done, he became a roving ambassador on behalf of the regime, minister of industry, and president of the national bank.

Guevara liked to joke that he had gotten the latter job at a meeting where Castro had asked whether there were any "communists" in the room. Guevara raised his hand, only to realize he had misheard; Castro had asked for an *economist*, not a communist.[140] Putting a self-admitted economic illiterate in charge of large sectors of the economy was not an inspired choice. With his fervor for enforced industrialization and expropriation of land, and his hostility to paying workers (he thought "Socialist Man" should labor for the good of society),[141] Guevara presided over a disastrous drop in sugar production and the pauperization of what had once been one of the richest countries in Latin America. Cuba was to become dependent on Soviet subsidies for decades to come.

Before long Che was bored with his work and ready for fresh challenges. He described himself as an "adventurer" and a "*condottiere* of the twentieth century."[142] Unlike Castro, who loved fine food and drink and playing the big shot, he was too abstemious to be interested in power or privileges. When his wife asked for the use of his official car to take one of their sick kids to the hospital, he told her to take the bus like everyone else; the gasoline belonged to "the people" and could not be used for personal reasons.[143] Guevara was an idealist or, if you prefer, a fanatic who worshipped "Saint Karl" and compared himself to early Christians "grappling with the Roman Empire in the form of North America." Like Garibaldi, he had little desire to be a ruler; he was a perpetual revolutionary. He was eager to strike fresh blows against "imperialism, colonialism, and neocolonialism"—to create, in his widely quoted phrase, "two, three, or many Vietnams."[144]

In 1960 he published *La guerra de guerrillas* (*Guerrilla Warfare*), a manual for other leftist crusaders. Much of it consisted of practical advice that might not have been out of place in a Boy Scout handbook—for instance, "carry no more than a extra pair of pants, eliminating extra underwear and other articles." Guevara's seminal contribution was his emphasis on the transformative abilities of guerrilla fighters—the *foco* (focus) of the revolution. "It is not necessary to wait until all conditions for making revolution exist," he claimed; "the insurrection can create them." His acolyte, the French intellectual Régis Debray, expanded this idea in his own manifesto, *Revolution in the Revolution?* "The setting up of military *focos*, not political '*focos*,'" he wrote, "is decisive for the future."[145]

The *foco* theory was romantic and inspirational but, as one expert notes, it was based on a "considerable distortion of the Cuban experience," which ignored the vital role played by the urban underground and by the general turn against Batista.[146] If *focoism* did not work in Cuba, its birthplace, what chance did it have elsewhere? It was a mirage that would ultimately lead its foremost champion to an unmarked grave.

✦ ✦ ✦

CHE DECIDED TO put his ideas to the test in the newly independent Congo, a turbulent state then seen as the frontline of the Cold War. After the overthrow and assassination in 1961 of the first post-independence leader, Patrice Lumumba, a variety of rebels were vying for power with Soviet and Chinese support against a weak regime backed by the West. The Congolese armed forces, commanded by General Joseph Mobutu, were pushing back the rebels with the help of a thousand South African mercenaries led by Colonel "Mad Mike" Hoare. Guevara set off with 130 Cuban soldiers to help the communist-backed rebels.

The Congolese rebels held only a sliver of "liberated" territory along the western shore of Lake Tanganyika, a vast inland sea lined with oil palms that had been "discovered," as far as Europeans were concerned, by the great explorers Sir Richard Francis Burton and John Speke in 1858. In the colonial era, the lake had separated the Belgian Congo from German East Africa; now it separated Congo from Burundi and Tanzania. What Che found there in the spring of 1965 appalled him. "The basic feature of the People's Liberation Army," he wrote in his diary, "was that it was a parasitic army: it did not work, did not train, did not fight, and demanded provisions and labor from the population, sometimes with extreme harshness."

Che tried hard to improve training and discipline but with little success because his newfound comrades lacked the dedication of Castro's band. The officers were either absent from the front, living in luxury in Dar es Salaam, or else they would spend "the day drinking until they got into the most incredible state." On those infrequent occasions when they led their men into battle, the officers "took the lead in running away." The ordinary fighters were just happy "to have a rifle and a uniform, sometimes even shoes and a certain authority in the area." They were utterly lacking in "revolutionary awareness." Indeed they lacked "any forward-looking perspective beyond the traditional horizon of their tribal territory." They placed far more faith in witchcraft than in Marxism-Leninism; they were convinced that medicine men could cast spells to make them invulnerable to enemy bullets. The men even refused to carry their own supplies, saying indignantly, "I'm not a truck," and later, "I'm not a Cuban." Guevara concluded that they were "lazy and undisciplined" and "without any spirit of combat or self-sacrifice"—"the poorest example of a fighter that I have ever come across."

Working with such unpromising material was dispiriting. It did not help that the Cubans were constantly coming down with malaria and other tropical diseases; Che noted that on one occasion, he "had the runs more than 30 times in 24 hours." Eventually even this inveterate optimist had to admit the situation was hopeless.

In November 1965, seven months after arriving, he and his men left the Congo for good. Within days the ruthless and ambitious Mobutu seized power and established a kleptocratic dictatorship over the country he renamed Zaire that would last for thirty-two years. He would finally be ousted in 1997 by Laurent Kabila, one of the rebel leaders Che had tried to help—and who turned out to be just as corrupt and abusive as his predecessor.[147]

✦ ✦ ✦

GUEVARA MADE NO attempt to put a positive gloss on his African experience. The very first words of his account, not published until long after his death, were: "This is the history of a failure." Yet not even this debacle could quench his revolutionary fires. He returned to Cuba only briefly in 1966—just long enough to prepare for another expedition. He chose Bolivia as his next target because of its central location in South America; he hoped to use it as a base to radiate revolution to neighboring countries, including his native Argentina.

The fact that Bolivia was poor, heavily Indian, rural, and mountainous made it, at first blush, an ideal *foco* site. Yet in most other ways it was far from promising. Bolivia already had had a revolution in 1952, which nationalized the largest mining companies and redistributed land to the peasants, turning them into a conservative force. General René Barrientos had seized power in 1964, but he was elected two years later with more than 60 percent of the vote. He was a populist who spoke Quechua, the Indian language, and took care to cultivate the peasants. He was also receiving substantial aid from the United States, which was alive to the dangers of Castroism spreading across Latin America.

Che arrived in Bolivia, disguised as a balding Uruguayan agricultural expert, in November 1966. He set up camp in the remote wilderness of southeastern Bolivia, the Nancahuazú region, and immediately began violating every precept laid out in his own guerrilla manual. "The guerrilla fighter is a social reformer," he had written, but in Bolivia he had no attractive program of social reform to offer. He had also written, "Where a government has come into power through some form of popular vote . . . the guerrilla outbreak cannot be promoted, since the possibilities of peaceful struggle have not yet been exhausted." In Bolivia the president's rule had been ratified at the polls.

"The guerrilla fighter needs to have a good knowledge of the surrounding countryside," Che had continued, but the Bolivian countryside was utterly alien to him and his men. He started with twenty-four fighters of whom only nine were Bolivians, and most of them came from the cities. "The guerrilla fighter needs full help from the people of the area," he had written, but not a single peasant joined his band. In April 1967 he was to admit in his diary, "The mobilization of peasants is nonexistent, except as informers." Nor did Guevara receive help from an urban underground. The Bolivian Communist Party had not asked him to come and did not think the time was right to launch armed struggle. Che was on his own.

Yet another precept that Guevara violated was the need for "absolute secrecy, a total absence of information in the enemy's hands." His movement's secrecy was shattered in March 1967 by two deserters who revealed the Cuban role, allowing President Barrientos to rally nationalist sentiment against the foreign invaders. Further details about Che's operations came from the interrogation of Régis Debray, who was captured in April 1967 after spending a few weeks with the rebels. Soon a team of seventeen Spanish-speaking Green Berets led by Major Ralph "Pappy" Shelton, a veteran of the Korean War and covert operations in Laos, arrived to train a Bolivian Ranger battalion to stop Che. CIA agents would provide intelligence for their operations.

The rebel band, which at its peak numbered fifty fighters divided into two columns, managed to ambush some of the security men, but the toll of pursuit began to wear on them. Temperatures were high, the jungle thick, "torrential" rainfall unceasing. As the situation worsened, so did Che's temper; he unleashed "murderous tongue-lashings" that reduced even veteran revolutionaries to tears. He was frequently sick, even debilitated, because he had lost his asthma medicine. The rebels were also short of food. The only way they could get fed was by holding peasants hostage. This practice naturally won them no friends and made it easy for the soldiers to get on their trail.

With the army "demonstrating more effectiveness in action," as Che had to admit, his small force suffered one setback after another. On August 31, 1967, he lost ten fighters in an army ambush. A month later another guerilla patrol was wiped out: three men killed, two deserted. By the end only seventeen fighters were left. On the morning of October 8, 1967, they were caught on the floor of a narrow canyon by a hundred Bolivian Rangers who had been alerted to their movements by a peasant. During a firefight that began in the early afternoon, Guevara was wounded in the leg and had his M2 carbine hit by a machine-gun bullet that rendered it useless. He tried to escape but, lame and unarmed, he did not get far.

As dusk fell Che hobbled with his captors to the nearby hamlet of La Higuera, where he was detained in a mud-walled schoolhouse. He was found there the next day by a Cuban-born CIA officer, Felix Rodriguez, an adviser to the Bolivian army who had flown in by helicopter. "His clothes [were] tattered and torn," Rodriguez later wrote, "his feet shod in rotting leather, his hair matted and filthy, his dream of a peasant uprising an utter failure." Rodriguez claimed that he tried to save Guevera's life but to no avail. Orders came down from the Bolivian High Command to "proceed with the elimination of Señor Guevara." A sergeant irate at having lost three buddies in combat volunteered to do the foul deed. Rodriguez had to concede that Che "died with courage." Legend has it that his last words were "I know you've come to kill me. Shoot, coward, you are only going to kill a man."[148]

To avoid creating a martyr's monument, his body (minus the hands, which were amputated to make a positive identification) was dumped into a mass grave that was covered by an airstrip. The fate of Che's corpse remained a mystery until 1997, when it was exhumed and flown to Cuba for a hero's burial.

✦ ✦ ✦

Reinforcements arriving at Dien Bien Phu, 1954. French commanders never imagined that Giap could assemble artillery to besiege their frontier fortress. (The Image Works)

Gerald Templer in Malaya, 1952. He became associated with winning "hearts and minds," even though he employed considerable coercion too. (The Image Works)

Marcel "Bruno" Bigeard, shown as a colonel in 1956, was a legendary French officer who fought the Germans, Vietnamese, and Algerians. Not even surrender at Dien Bien Phu could quench his thirst for battle. (Granger Collection)

French soldiers patrolling the Casbah, the "native" quarter of Algiers. They ripped out the insurgent infrastructure, but their brutal methods backfired. (Granger Collection)

Edward Lansdale (*left*), "the Quiet American," and Ramón Magsaysay. The two men worked together to defeat the Huk Rebellion in the Philippines (1946–54). (Hoover Institution)

President Johnson delegated the running of the ground war in South Vietnam to General William Westmoreland (*right*). Unfortunately, the World War II veteran didn't understand how to wage a counterinsurgency. (The Image Works)

U.S. troops slogging through a rice field, 1965. Large-scale "search and destroy" missions wasted American resources and failed to pin down the elusive Vietcong. (The Image Works)

Lansdale later worked with Ngo Dinh Diem to help create South Vietnam. (Image Works)

Black September operatives took the Israeli team hostage at the 1972 Munich Olympics—the most famous terrorist attack before 2001. This was indicative of Arafat's habit of operating through front groups. (The Image Works)

Fidel Castro (*left*) with Che Guevara, 1961. Despite their meager forces, they orchestrated a brilliant campaign to win power in Cuba. Afterward Che went from failure to failure. (The Image Works)

Yasser Arafat in 1969, already sporting his trademark uniform and kaffiyeh. He was a master at spinning military defeats into propaganda victories—a triumph of style over substance. (The Image Works)

Ahmad Shah Massoud (*right*) was one of the most skilled and moderate Afghan mujahideen commanders to fight the Red Army in the 1980s. (The Image Works)

Soviet troops leaving Afghanistan, 1988. Afghanistan is said to be "the graveyard of empires," but only the Soviet empire was destroyed there even in part. (The Image Works)

Remnants of the U.S. Marine barracks in Beirut, 1983. This deadly suicide bombing signaled the rise of a potent new threat from the Iranian-backed Hezbollah. (The Image Works)

Hezbollah militants in 2006 mourn Imad Mughniyeh, architect of the U.S. Marine barracks bombing and countless other terrorist operations. Fittingly, he was killed with one of his favorite weapons—a car bomb. (AP)

Osama bin Laden, a shy Saudi youth, became the most notorious terrorist in the world. He believed that "the media war" was 90 percent of the battle. (The Image Works)

General David Petraeus in Iraq, 2007. By resurrecting age-old principles of counterinsurgency, he managed to pull off an improbable come-from-behind campaign. (Author)

"Sons of Iraq" in Bayji, 2008. The rise of this Sunni militia, together with the surge in U.S. troops and a change in their tactics, helped reduce the power of Al Qaeda in Iraq and other terrorist groups. (Author)

Marine Lieutenant Colonel Daniel Schmitt meeting with elders in Marjah, Afghanistan, 2011. Such negotiations are an important part of any counterinsurgency campaign. (Author)

Well before then Che had passed into the realm of myth; the famous photograph Alberto Korda had taken of him in 1960 wearing a beret had become one of the most recognizable images on the planet.[149] His outsize fame is similar to that of another fanatical if heroic failure. Like Che, John Brown was a darling of progressive opinion in his day and a practitioner of *focoism avant la lettre*. His attempt to spark a slave revolt in Virginia was just as unsuccessful as Che's efforts to spark a communist revolt in Bolivia. Brown even had roughly the same number of followers at Harpers Ferry—twenty-two. The difference is that only a few years after Brown's hanging the scourge of slavery, which he had given his life to oppose, was eradicated, whereas the revolutionary forces that Che had championed went from failure to failure.

From the Colombian Revolutionary Armed Forces (FARC) and the Farabundo Martí National Liberation Front (FMLN) in El Salvador to the Tupamaros in Uruguay and the Montoneros in Argentina, Latin America in the 1960s and 1970s gave birth to a bewildering array of guerrilla and terrorist groups with similar names, similar proclivities for violence, and similar ideologies to justify their acts, notwithstanding bitter and self-defeating divisions between Trotskyites, Maoists, and pro-Moscow Communists. Most of these movements were inspired by "the glorious Cuban Revolution."[150] Some were based in rural areas in accord with Guevara's advice: "In the underdeveloped America the countryside is the basic area for armed fighting."[151] Others—particularly in more urbanized countries such as Argentina, Brazil, Chile, and Uruguay—were more influenced by the Brazilian Marxist Carlos Marighella's *Minimanual of the Urban Guerrilla* (1970), which substituted an urban *foco* for a rural one.

Marighella was head of National Liberation Action, a Brazilian terrorist group formed in 1967. It kidnapped several foreign diplomats, including the U.S. ambassador, hijacked a Brazilian airliner, and robbed numerous banks. But while Marighella focused on targets different from Guevara's, his views on the redemptive power of violence and the heroic qualities of the revolutionary were similar. "Today," he wrote, "to be 'violent' or a 'terrorist' is a quality that ennobles any honorable person, because it is an act worthy of a revolutionary engaged in armed struggle against the shameful military dictatorship and its atrocities."[152]

There was another resemblance: Marighella was just as unsuccessful as Guevara. In 1969 he was shot dead in an ambush by Brazilian police. His urban *foco* disappeared as rapidly as Che's rural *foco* in Bolivia.

The same fate was suffered by almost every rebel group in Latin America, rural or urban. The one exception was the Sandinista movement, which took over Nicaragua in 1979 from Anastasio Somoza, who was as weak, corrupt, and incompetent as Batista. But the Sandinistas were hardly an isolated *foco*. They had been organizing since 1961 and were part of a broad-based antiregime movement that came to include the Catholic Church, the chambers of commerce, and much of the upper class—something that happened nowhere else in Latin America outside of Cuba. And, just as in Cuba, the revolutionaries' triumph in Nicaragua was facilitated by a last-minute cutoff of U.S. aid to the old regime.[153]

✦ ✦ ✦

Even when ultimately unsuccessful, most of the Latin American revolutionary groups managed to inflict considerable carnage for substantial periods of time. Rural guerrilla movements, in particular, had the ability to stay alive for decades. But the social change they achieved was mostly negative by inadvertently spurring military takeovers. Latin military juntas unleashed the security forces, often complemented by paramilitary "death squads," to wreak carnage against the rebels and their suspected sympathizers—a category wide enough to encompass almost any leftist. As many as 30,000 people were said to have died in Argentina's "Dirty War" alone—the name given to the campaign by the junta in Buenos Aires against suspected leftists from 1976 to 1983.[154] The toll in Guatemala was even higher: a civil war that raged between 1960 and 1996 cost the lives of an estimated 200,000 people.[155]

Heavy-handed repression was counterproductive in Algeria and Indochina, where the counterinsurgents were foreigners who lacked popular support. Batista and Somoza showed how repression could backfire even when perpetrated by homegrown regimes. But by the early 1970s many Latin Americans, perhaps most, were genuinely alarmed about growing violence and chaos and the possibility of a communist takeover. This led to widespread if tacit support for the harsh steps taken by military regimes to restore law and order. Once the crisis passed, the public turned on the generals and demanded the restoration of civilian rule. By the turn of the millennium most Latin American insurgencies had been crushed and, not coincidentally, most Latin countries had become democratic.

The defeat of all these communist movements did not require direct American military intervention, except in the Dominican Republic and Grenada, but there was a considerable role for American military backing especially in El Salvador in the 1980s and Colombia in the 2000s. In both cases democratic governments, benefiting from much greater American support than Batista or Somoza had ever received, curbed the excesses of their own militaries and embraced the sort of population-centric counterinsurgency methods that had been used by Templer in Malaya and Magsaysay in the Philippines. El Salvador's FMLN gave up the armed struggle and became a political party in 1992. Colombia's FARC survived President Alvaro Uribe's 2002–10 offensive but as a much diminished force and one that appeared more interested in criminality than in revolution. For his success in beating back an insurgency that once seemed on the verge of power, Uribe deserves to be remembered along with Gerald Templer and Ramón Magsaysay as among the most effective counterinsurgents since World War II.[156] Though no American adviser of the stature of Edward Lansdale emerged from these conflicts, there were many "Quiet Professionals," as the Green Berets like to call themselves, who played an important behind-the-scenes role in bolstering indigenous counterinsurgency capacity.

Latin America was not, of course, the only region that experienced an epidemic of revolutionary violence in the 1960s and 1970s. This was a worldwide phenomenon that afflicted even the advanced liberal democracies of Western Europe and North America. Everywhere radicals inspired by the example of Mao, Ho, and Che—the one-name gurus of guerrilla-ism—mounted a violent assault on the "establishment." Many of them received direct support from Cuba, the Soviet Union, East Germany, and other communist or radical states. In the process they ushered in a second age of international terrorism that in sheer savagery easily eclipsed its forerunner, the anarchist epoch.

55.

THE CHILDREN OF '68—AND '48

The Raid on Entebbe and the Terrorism of the 1970s

At 12:20 p.m. on Sunday, June 27, 1976, Air France Flight 139 made a smooth departure from Athens airport, where it had stopped en route from Tel Aviv to Paris. The cabin crew was busy preparing lunch for the 246 passengers when a scream was heard from the first-class section. The flight engineer opened the cockpit door to investigate and found himself face to face with a young blond man waving a pistol and hand grenade. He had a Peruvian passport identifying him as Senor Garcia, but his real name was Wilfried Böse, and he belonged to an offshoot of the Red Army Faction—a German leftist group popularly known, after two of its founders, as the Baader-Meinhof Gang. Also on board was his girlfriend and fellow Revolutionary Cells member Brigitte Kuhlmann, who was sporting a ponytail and glasses. Waving a gun and hand grenade of her own, she took over the first-class cabin. At the same time, in the economy section, two Arabs stood and grabbed hand grenades they had smuggled aboard in tin candy boxes past the notoriously lax Greek airport security. Kuhlmann referred to them as "Comrade 39" and "Comrade 55." Fayez Abdul-Rahim Jaber and Jayel Naji al-Arjam were both senior members of the Popular Front for the Liberation of Palestine (PFLP)-Special Operations Command, one of numerous Palestinian splinter groups targeting Israeli interests.

The incongruous nature of this alliance—dispossessed Palestinians and "guilty white kids" from the West[157]—was made clear when Böse took to the intercom of the Airbus A300 to announce to the frightened passengers that they were under the control of the "Che Guevara Force and the Gaza Commando of the Popular Front for the Liberation of Palestine." The links between far-flung terrorist organizations became clear, too, when the hijackers issued a demand for the release of fifty-three terrorists detained by countries as disparate as Israel, France, West Germany, Switzerland, and Kenya. Among them was one of the Japanese Red Army operatives who in 1972 had gunned down twenty-six travelers in Israel's Lod Airport, today Ben Gurion Airport, at the behest of the PFLP. Those demands emanated from Entebbe airport in Uganda, where Flight 139 landed at 3:15 a.m. on Monday, June 28, after a refueling stop in Libya, and they received instantaneous coverage on television screens around the world.

Lenin had famously if perhaps apocryphally said, "The purpose of terrorism is to terrorize." The anarchists of the Belle Époque had shown how newspapers and magazines could be used for that purpose, but the spread of television allowed their late twentieth-century successors to vastly amplify their message. This "hostage crisis," like so many others in the 1970s–80s, received breathless coverage that, at least until its surprise dénouement, did much to achieve the hijackers' objective—to terrorize Israel and its supporters.

The terrified hostages did not know what to expect when the Ugandan army surrounded the airplane. Were they about to be rescued? It soon became clear, however, that Uganda's maniacal dictator, Idi Amin Dada, was working with the terrorists. Although Uganda had previously enjoyed good relations with Israel, Idi Amin, a Muslim, had embraced the Palestinian cause after seizing power in a military coup in 1971. He established close ties with Libya and Saudi Arabia, which provided him with financial aid that he could use to subsidize an economy badly battered by his decision to expel and expropriate the South Asians who had owned many of the country's most successful businesses. In 1972 Idi Amin had publicly proclaimed his belief that Hitler had been right when "he burned over six million Jews." The passengers therefore had much to fear as they were transferred to the airport's old terminal under the guns of the Ugandan soldiery. Here the four terrorists who had taken control of the airplane were joined by six compatriots. They were under the command of Dr. Wadia Haddad, who was operating from a temporary headquarters in Mogadishu, Somalia. A dentist by training, the well-educated Haddad had founded the Marxist-oriented PFLP in 1967 with George Habash, a fellow Palestinian medical student he had met in Beirut. Their specialty was spectacular terrorism; their favorite target, airliners.

Aerial piracy was as old as commercial air travel; the first recorded instance occurred in 1931 when a Pan Am airliner was hijacked in Peru by local revolutionaries who wanted to drop propaganda leaflets. The first airline bombing occurred just two years later when a United flight was blown up en route from Cleveland to Chicago, killing all seven on board.[158] But Habash and Haddad took airline attacks to new heights, making this the signature terrorist tactic of the 1970s, just as handheld bombs had been the signature weapon of the anarchist era and car bombs were to become the signature weapon of the 2000s. In 1968 PFLP operatives were the first to hijack an El Al aircraft; in February 1970 they blew up a Swissair jet in the air; and in September 1970, in a frenzy of attacks, they simultaneously seized four Western airliners. In response Israel dispatched commandos to blow up fourteen empty aircraft on the ground at Beirut airport in 1968 and, more importantly, introduced armed air marshals and other stringent and costly security measures on El Al. This forced the PFLP to set its sights on other nations' aircraft that were not as well protected. By 1976 even Habash had decided that attacks on non-Israeli and nonmilitary targets had gone too far. Haddad broke away to form his own ultra-radical faction, PFLP-Special Operations Group, which received considerable covert support from the KGB,[159] showing not for the first or last time the importance of outside backing for insurgents.

The PFLP-SOG members who had taken control of Flight 139 claimed that France and other countries were complicit in "Zionist crimes," but their animus was directed primarily against Israelis and Jews. On the evening of Tuesday, June 29, Böse announced that certain of the passengers were going to be moved to a separate room in the old terminal. As he began reading off the names from their passports, it became apparent that all those he named were Jewish. For the Jewish passengers, who included Holocaust survivors, the reading of the names in a German accent was chillingly reminiscent of

Auschwitz, where Dr. Josef Mengele had chosen who would die immediately and who would get to live a little longer. Over the next two days, 148 Gentiles were released and flown to France. Ninety-four Jews remained along with the 12 members of the Air France crew who courageously volunteered to stay behind.

The release of the Gentiles was, from the hijackers' perspective, a fatal mistake. As soon as they arrived in Paris, they were debriefed by Israeli operatives who learned vital details about the layout at Entebbe. Further information was provided by Israeli officers who had served in a military assistance mission to Uganda and by two Mossad agents who rented a small airplane and flew over the airport taking pictures. Their findings made possible the planning of a rescue operation.

Ever since the hijacking had started, Prime Minister Yitzhak Rabin, Defense Minister Shimon Peres, and fellow cabinet ministers had been debating whether to mount such an operation or whether to accede to the terrorists' demands as Israel had done many times before. The record of past rescue missions did not inspire much confidence. The most famous failure occurred at Munich airport in 1972 when a clumsy German attempt to free Israeli Olympic athletes had resulted in the death of all nine hostages and one policeman along with five of eight terrorists. Israeli security forces were better prepared for such difficult operations but often no more successful. In 1974 three Palestinian infiltrators from Lebanon had seized a school at Ma'alot in northern Israel. Army commandos rushed in but did not get to the terrorists fast enough, allowing them to kill twenty-one children and wound dozens more. The following year eight PLO operatives, who had landed by Zodiac boat on a beach, took over the Savoy Hotel in Tel Aviv. Again army commandos attacked. This time five hostages were freed but eight were killed along with three soldiers.

Both of these operations had been carried out by the army's elite Sayeret Matkal, known simply as "the Unit," which was modeled on the SAS. It had had more luck in 1972 when four Palestinians landed a hijacked Sabena Airlines flight at Lod Airport. Sixteen commandos disguised as airport technicians in white overalls, including Lieutenant Colonel Ehud Barak and Lieutenant Benjamin Netanyahu, both future prime ministers, managed to free the airplane with the loss of only one passenger. But hostage rescue was not the unit's specialty, and it had never conducted an operation so far from home. So few in the Unit believed that they would be given the order to fly to Entebbe. They did their best, however, to plan a successful operation.

Even as the attention of the world continued to be riveted on the plight of the hostages, who were growing worried they would never go home again, Israel's senior military and civilian leaders became increasingly confident that Operation Thunderball, as the operation was code-named, could be pulled off with acceptable losses. Rabin decided it was worth doing if even fifteen or twenty hostages and rescuers died. Better that than give in to blackmail.

At 2 p.m. on Saturday, July 3, 1976, four heavily laden C-130 cargo aircraft took off from the Sinai Peninsula bound for Entebbe, almost 2,500 miles away. Aboard was a 34-man assault team from the Unit that would free the hostages. There were also more than 130 other soldiers and four light armored vehicles to keep the Ugandan army at bay while the operation was going on.

A minute past midnight on July 3–4, 1976, the lead C-130 touched down at Entebbe. Within seconds the Unit's men, dressed in Ugandan army uniforms, were rolling down the dark tarmac in a black Mercedes and two Land Rovers outfitted with mock Ugandan license plates. They had to cover a mile from their aircraft to the old terminal and hoped that this ruse would make the sentries think that Idi Amin or some other big shot was in the limousine. But almost three hundred yards short of their destination they were stopped by two guards. One of them raised his rifle. Sayeret Matkal's commander, Lieutenant Colonel Jonathan "Yoni" Netanyahu, and another soldier in the Mercedes opened fire with silenced .22-caliber Beretta pistols. Their small-caliber ammunition did not stop the sentry, forcing another commando in a Land Rover to open fire with his unsilenced AK-47. The gunfire could have been disastrous by giving the terrorists time to kill their hostages. "I was seeing the entire element of surprise evaporate," wrote one of the Unit's officers. But luckily the hijackers were fooled by the Ugandan uniforms; they thought they were witnessing a coup attempt against Idi Amin—not a rescue attempt.

The Mercedes and Land Rovers screeched to a halt farther than planned from the terminal as "long bursts of fire shattered the night air." Running toward their objective, the Israelis were astonished to discover that one of the entrances they had planned to use was blocked. Their intelligence had been faulty. The whole assault was in danger of stalling until Netanyahu rushed to the front, urging his men forward. At the very moment a terrorist inside the terminal fired a shot that hit him. He fell, mortally wounded, but his men kept moving, obedient to his orders not to pause for casualties. They burst into the hall where the hostages were being kept and quickly cut down all seven terrorists on the premises, including the Germans, Wilfried Böse and Brigitte Kuhlmann. In the confusion three hostages were also killed, but the others were safe. Just four minutes had passed since the first C-130 had landed.

Meanwhile the backup Israeli force was securing the rest of the airport, despite constant if inaccurate fire from a determined defender in the control tower. The Israelis killed as many as fifty Ugandan soldiers and blew up seven MiG fighter aircraft on the ground to make pursuit impossible. By 1:40 a.m. the last C-130 had taken off, heading for refueling in Kenya before a return journey to Israel. Only one hostage was left behind—seventy-five-year-old Dora Bloch, who had been removed to a Kampala hospital and was murdered a few days later by Idi Amin's henchmen.

The hostages and their saviors were met by a rapturous Israeli public eager to erase the foul memories of military unpreparedness that had nearly led to catastrophe in the 1973 Yom Kippur War. Only the members of the Unit were not rejoicing; they were mourning their commander, Yoni Netanyahu, the only soldier who lost his life in Operation Thunderball. (Another soldier was crippled for life.) Yoni's memory would be carried on, burnished to superheroic proportions, by his family, including his younger brother, Benjamin, the future prime minister. The operation as a whole was celebrated not only in the news of the day but in books and films such as *Raid on Entebbe* (1977), in which Charles Bronson, Peter Finch, and other American actors played the Israeli principals.

For all the fame of the Entebbe operation, its aftermath was shrouded in considerable secrecy. Two years later, in 1978, Wadi Haddad died in an East German hospital from a mysterious ailment that attacked his immune system. Not until nearly three decades later would it be revealed that he had been poisoned by the Mossad, Israel's intelligence agency, which, knowing of his sweet tooth, had used a Palestinian agent to slip him doctored Belgian chocolates.[160]

✦ ✦ ✦

THE ENTEBBE HIJACKING was only one of many storied terrorist acts carried out in the 1970s by Palestinians and their sympathizers and collaborators among Western terrorist groups. There had been terrorist groups before, and even transnational terrorism was not new—it had been pioneered by the anarchists nearly a century earlier. But in the 1970s, the second great age of international terrorism, this trend reached new heights with terrorists attending each other's training camps in countries ranging from East Germany to Libya and even collaborating on attacks.

The Palestinians' motivations were obvious: they felt they had been robbed of their birthright and wanted back the land occupied by the state of Israel. What of their Western counterparts?

The Western terrorist organizations of the 1970s—Action Directe (France), the Baader-Meinhof Gang, the Red Brigades (Italy), the Communist Combatant Cells (Belgium), the Japanese Red Army, the Provisional IRA, the Basque ETA, the Greek Revolutionary Organization 17 November, the Quebec Liberation Front, the Black Panthers, the Weathermen, the Symbionese Liberation Army, and others—were, like many of their Latin American contemporaries and their Russian Nihilist predecessors, composed mostly of current or former college students. The most radical members of the sixties generation were not satisfied with peaceful demonstrations, building occupations, and draft-card burnings. Their rage against the "system"—and, truth be told, their love of adventure and rebellion for its own sake—led them to assaults on riot police, window breaking, and eventually, in a few cases, to bank robbery, murder, and hostage taking. They were aptly summed up by the East German spy chief Markus Wolf, whose service supported many of the European terrorist groups, as "spoiled, hysterical children of mainly upper-middle-class backgrounds."[161]

Influenced and encouraged by radical philosophers such as Herbert Marcuse, Régis Debray, and Frantz Fanon, who provided them with justifications for their acts, sixties radicals thought that they could emulate the Vietcong, M-26-7, or the Chinese Red Army without pondering the considerable differences between their own societies and Diem's South Vietnam, Batista's Cuba, or Chiang Kai-shek's China. Or, rather, they fell under the illusion that there was no real difference between such authoritarian regimes and the liberal democracies where they lived. They decided, in the face of all evidence to the contrary (the sixties was also the decade of the civil rights movement), that the only way to bring about change in corroding societies such as "Amerikkka" was through violent revolution.[162]

The Weathermen, an outgrowth of the Students for a Democratic Society, were the most restrained. In spite of their bloodcurdling promises to "tear up pig city" and "bring the war home," they largely desisted from murderous attacks after three Weatherman died in 1970 in the accidental explosion of a Greenwich Village town house where they were manufacturing pipe bombs. They would continue to set off bombs but typically would issue warnings to prevent injury. The worst blot on their record, and the coda to a rapidly fading era, was a 1981 armored car robbery that led to the death of two police officers and one security guard.[163]

The Symbionese Liberation Army was even shorter-lived but more violent. Its ideology was Maoist; its slogan, "Death to the Fascist Insect That Preys upon the Life of the People." Its membership consisted of ten white, middle-class Berkeley radicals led by an escaped African-American convict named Donald DeFreeze, who styled himself "general field marshal." The SLA became infamous for the 1974 kidnapping of the heiress Patty Hearst. After a few weeks of threats and indoctrination, she became their collaborator in bank robbery under the name "Tania," the nom de guerre of one of Che Guevara's followers. The group, which committed its first attack in 1973 (the murder of the black Oakland school superintendent), went out of business in 1975 following the arrest of Hearst and three of her captors-cum-comrades. In between, in 1974, DeFreeze and five other members had been slain in a two-hour shoot-out with police, shown on live television, in a house in South Central Los Angeles where they had stockpiled seventeen guns and 6,000 rounds of ammunition. Like John Brown, these radicals thought that they could spur a massive African-American rebellion with a spectacular act of violence and, like him, they were fatally disappointed.[164]

The West German Red Army Faction and its offshoots were larger, longer-lasting, and more destructive but no more successful. Their members killed more than thirty people and wounded more than ninety, including police officers, judges, prosecutors, businessmen, and American soldiers. In 1977 a dozen of its operatives even penetrated a U.S. military base in Germany in an unsuccessful attempt to steal nuclear munitions. Nor was the Entebbe operation their only foray into airline hijacking. In 1977 German radicals again cooperated with the PFLP to seize a Lufthansa Boeing 737, which they diverted to Mogadishu. Here a newly formed German counterterrorist unit, GSG-9, bettered Sayeret Matkal by storming the aircraft without any loss of life among the captives. (Three hijackers were killed and one wounded.) Back home the West German police mounted a massive manhunt that led to the incarceration of most of the Red Army Faction, which apparently never numbered more than thirty full-time operatives and a few hundred active sympathizers. Its early leaders, Ulrike Meinhof and Andreas Baader, killed themselves in prison in 1976–77. Thereafter the group showed an impressive ability to regenerate itself into second and third generations of militants with the aid of the East German secret police and various Palestinian groups and Arab states that provided access to training camps, financing, and weapons.

The sheer ability of this small band of militants to stay on the loose in a society as orderly and stable as West Germany—waging a "war of six against sixty million," in the only slightly exaggerated phrase of the Nobel laureate novelist Heinrich Böll—shows the difficulty of eradicating any determined insurgency, no matter how small. The Red Army Faction's failure to achieve any results, on the other hand, shows the difficulty of shaking a democratic government by force. The Baader-Meinhof Gang did not formally suspend operations until 1992, but long before then it had become an anachronism—another musty holdover from an era of tie-dyes and "be-ins."[165]

The same fate was suffered by the Italian Red Brigades (notorious for the kidnapping and murder of the former premier Aldo Moro in 1978), the Japanese Red Army, and similar groups. They all faded out around the time that the Berlin Wall fell, in no small part because of a decline in support from communist regimes. Their popular appeal was almost nil—less even than that of the anarchists, who could at least tap into the labor movement. Through their wanton cruelty the New Left terrorists, much like the anarchists, forfeited whatever public sympathy they might have generated.

Terrorist groups with a nationalist appeal, such as the ETA, IRA, and PKK, proved more enduring. They managed to achieve some political reforms even if they failed in their ultimate goal of secession. The most famous group of all was the Palestine Liberation Organization, which combined terrorism with shrewd diplomacy and savvy press operations. Under its longtime chairman, Yasser Arafat, the PLO proved to be a study in resiliency if not statesmanship.

56.

ARAFAT'S ODYSSEY

What Terrorism Did and Did Not Achieve for the Palestinians

Arafat, like Castro and countless other modern revolutionaries dating back to the Russian Nihilists, got his start in college politics. His full name was Muhammad Abdel-Rauf Arafat al-Qudwa al-Husseini; "Yasser" was a nickname that meant, ironically, "easygoing" or "carefree"—words that would never be used by anyone to describe this volatile, vain, and demanding character, who never expressed an interest in anything other than the Palestinian struggle. So devoted was he to the revolutionary cause that, he explained, he had no time to shave—he could not afford to lose 15 minutes a day, 450 minutes a month, "in the midst of guerrilla warfare." One of his few relaxations was watching cartoons—he claimed to like "Tom and Jerry" best because "the mouse outsmarts the cat." His monomania did not make him an easy person to like, but it did not set him apart from Che, Mao, or other successful revolutionaries—nor, for that matter, from many others who are successful in occupations ranging from business to sports.

Embarrassingly for a Palestinian patriot, Arafat's birthplace was probably Cairo, where his father, a merchant, had emigrated in 1927, two years before his birth, to pursue business interests. After his mother's death and his father's remarriage to a stepmother he hated, young Arafat was sent to live in Jerusalem with family members for a few years in the 1930s, but he soon returned to Cairo. In spite of his later claims of heroic battlefield exploits ("I fought in Jerusalem, in the south of Jerusalem and in Gaza," he told an interviewer in 1988), there is no evidence that he played any part in Israel's War of Independence in 1947–48, which led to the exodus of 700,000 Palestinian refugees. The following year he entered King Fuad University, later Cairo University, to study civil engineering. But as one of his friends recalled, in virtually the same words that were used about Castro (who entered the University of Havana in 1945), "His only activity was politics. Very seldom would he come to the School of Engineering."

His major achievement was to become president of the Palestine Students' Union—a feat he accomplished with the support of the Muslim Brotherhood. Arafat would never become an Islamist like the founders of Hamas but, unlike George Habash, Wadi Haddad, and many other Palestinian activists of the 1960s–1970s, he was not a radical leftist either. He was from the start a traditional Muslim with no ideological program beyond Palestinian statehood.

After graduation in 1956, Arafat moved to Kuwait—lured, like many other Palestinian professionals, by the oil-fueled economic boom. While working as a lowly road engineer for the Ministry of Public Works, he got together in a "discreet house" in 1959 with fewer than twenty other Palestinian exiles to create an anti-Israel group called Fatah (Conquest). Early support came from Syria and Algeria, which in 1964 allowed the nascent organization to establish its first training camps for a few hundred fighters.

Terrorism against Israeli settlers was hardly a new phenomenon; it had been a fact of life since the Arab Revolt of 1936–39. Following Israel's formation in 1948, which of course was partly the result of a terrorist campaign by Zionist groups against the British authorities, the Jewish state had faced a nonstop stream of infiltrations by Arab *fedayeen* (self-sacrificers). Between 1948 and 1956, these attackers killed more than two hundred Israeli civilians and many soldiers and helped precipitate the war against Egypt in 1956 and numerous smaller retaliatory raids. But these terrorist operations were undertaken by neighboring states such as Egypt and Syria, not by independent Palestinian groups. The Palestinians were too divided by clan loyalties and economic interests and insufficiently nationalistic to be a powerful force in their own right. Arab leaders were anxious to keep it that way: they wanted to use the Palestinian issue but not to give the Palestinians their own voice. Authoritarians to a man, the Arab heads of state did not want any Palestinian leader challenging their authority. Thus the Palestine Liberation Organization was created in 1964 under the auspices of Egypt's president, Gamal Abdel Nasser, whose domains included the Gaza Strip. (The West Bank was ruled by Jordan.) Its first leader was a nonentity totally dependent on Nasser's support. Arafat decided to launch his own campaign of terrorism in 1964, at a time when many thought Fatah was not yet ready, largely to steal a march on the PLO and its Egyptian patrons.

By this time he had already adopted his trademarks—a black and white kaffiyeh (head scarf), a face full of stubble, dark glasses, which he wore day and night, and, in spite of his lack of actual military service, an olive-green military uniform complete with a holstered Smith & Wesson revolver. These symbols became as important for him, and served much the same purpose, as Montgomery's beret or MacArthur's corncob pipe. They also helped distract from his unprepossessing appearance: "Only five feet four inches tall, with protruding eyes, a permanent three-day old stubble, and potbelly, Arafat was not," the journalist Thomas Friedman aptly noted, "what one would call a dashing figure."

Arafat's political astuteness more than made up for what he lacked in physical stature. From the start he made a habit of establishing shell organizations that would claim responsibility for attacks while providing him with plausible deniability. The first of these was called al-Asifa (the Storm). Under its banner, in the first days of 1965, Fatah operatives based in Syria launched their first attack on Israel—a failed attempt to sabotage the waterworks. Although most of the early operations were equally unsuccessful, each was heralded with a bombastic press release that claimed historic achievements. In the early days Arafat would tool around Beirut in his Volkswagen Beetle personally distributing his "boastful communiqués." Later he would develop a world-class propaganda machine to get his message out; in common with many other modern revolutionaries, he had internalized T. E. Lawrence's dictum that "the printing press is the greatest weapon in the armory of the modern commander." Arafat was abstemious when it came to cigarettes and alcohol, but he was addicted to publicity.

His early, amateurish attempts to organize a Mao-style insurgency in the

West Bank and Gaza Strip came to little. Shin Bet, the internal Israeli security service, was "relentless, fast, and ruthless." It was particularly adept at finding Palestinian informers through a combination of inducements (money, work or travel permits) and threats (prison, deportation). In late 1967 Arafat was fortunate to escape from a Ramallah safe house just ahead of a raid; the security men found his mattress still warm.

An Israeli officer was dismissive of Fatah: "We cannot dignify them with the name guerrilla or commando. . . . They are nowhere near Viet Cong standards." True, but irrelevant. No matter how much Arafat might deny it (he insisted the terrorist label was a "big lie" from the "Israeli military junta"), Fatah was a terrorist, not a guerrilla, organization, and its operations were designed to generate publicity and political support, not to militarily defeat, or even seriously harm, Israel. By that standard Arafat was succeeding. With the start of his attacks, wealthy Gulf Arabs began making substantial donations. The PLO was well on its way to becoming, in the words of one scholar, "by far the richest irredentist movement the world had ever seen."

Arafat was the only person who would know where the PLO's funds, eventually amounting to billions of dollars, were stashed. This became a powerful instrument of personal power that helped to explain his long-term survival. But while many of his associates were widely suspected of corruption, Arafat was not. Like Che Guevara, he seemed indifferent to material comforts—for most of his life he led a nomadic existence with few personal possessions other than his Rolex watch and his Smith & Wesson revolver. "There is," a journalist was to note in 1989, "no bric-a-brac in Arafat's life."

Arafat's early reputation was made by the battle of Karameh. This was a Palestinian refugee camp in Jordan that Fatah used as a base of operations. Israeli ground forces attacked it on March 21, 1968, in retaliation for a mine that had been planted on an Israeli road, blowing up a school bus. The Israelis encountered much heavier resistance than anticipated, losing 33 men. The defenders suffered more—the PLO lost 156 dead and 141 captured. It was hardly a victory in the conventional sense, and most of the fighting had been done by the Jordanian army, not the PLO. But Arafat showed a genius for spinning military dross into public-relations gold. He trumpeted Karameh as the first battle the Israelis had lost—and Arabs, eager for good news after the 1967 Six-Day War, believed him. Thousands of volunteers flocked to Fatah, and the Arab states substantially increased their support.

In 1968 Arafat appeared on his first cover of *Time*, which proclaimed that "everyone in the Arab world knows who he is." In 1969 he was elected chairman of the PLO, a position he would hold for the rest of his life. With his newfound wealth and power, he was able to expand his network of bases in Jordan into a state within a state. Palestinian gunmen swaggered around extorting "donations" at gunpoint and openly talked of overthrowing the "fascist regime in Jordan."

Nemesis was not long in coming.

The Popular Front for the Liberation of Palestine, which after Fatah was the PLO's second-biggest party and over which Arafat exercised little control, precipitated a crisis in September 1970 with its hijackings of Western aircraft, which were blown up in Jordan. Arafat expressed his disapproval of the PFLP's aerial piracy, but he made no attempt to stop it. This was too much for King Hussein, who had little respect for the double-dealing Arafat and feared that he was losing control of his own country. He ordered his army to expel the PLO. The Jordanian army, a professional force backed by armor, artillery, and aircraft, made short work of the cocky but "totally unprepared" and hopelessly outnumbered PLO fighters. At least two thousand of them were killed. Some of Arafat's men were so terrified of the ruthless Jordanians that they sought refuge in Israel. Arafat, for his part, relocated his operations to Lebanon. Openly challenging King Hussein was his first major miscalculation but far from the last.[166]

✦ ✦ ✦

To STAGE A comeback, in 1971 he organized a new front group called Black September. Its first victim was Jordan's prime minister, Wasfi Tal—"one of the butchers of the Palestinian people," according to PLO propaganda. He was gunned down in Cairo in 1971. In a grisly touch, one of his killers drank the dying man's blood from the floor. In 1973 Black September operatives invaded a party at the Saudi embassy in Khartoum and killed a Belgian diplomat along with the U.S. ambassador and his deputy—one of the few times that the PLO directly attacked the United States. Over the years Arafat made many enemies, but, in spite of his close links with the Soviet bloc, he was cautious enough to avoid a direct assault on a superpower. Black September's most notable operation was the seizure of the Israeli athletes at the 1972 Olympics, the most famous terrorist act prior to September 11, 2001. The photograph of a gunman standing on the Israeli team's balcony with a stocking mask over his head, looking like a pitiless visitor from another planet, became a defining image of the age.

Israel retaliated immediately by bombing PLO bases in Lebanon and Syria. At the same time Prime Minister Golda Meir secretly ordered Israel's intelligence agencies, as part of Operation Wrath of God, to hunt down and kill Black September and PFLP operatives wherever they could be found. The use of targeted killings by Israel was not new. As far back as 1956 Mossad agents had mailed a book bomb that had killed Lieutenant Colonel Mustafa Hafez, an Egyptian intelligence officer who directed fedayeen attacks from the Gaza Strip.[167] But the retaliation for Munich was especially ambitious and controversial.

It included a risky seaborne commando raid into the heart of Beirut in 1973: Operation Springtime of Youth. Several members of Sayeret Matkal, including its commander, Ehud Barak, dressed up as women to sneak past sentries and assassinate three top PLO leaders in their apartments, while paratroopers blew up the headquarters of a PFLP splinter group and other targets. Another high-profile success came six years later, in 1979, when Ali Hassan Salameh ("the Red Prince"), operations chief of Black September and a personal favorite of Arafat's, was killed in Beirut by a parked Volkswagen that exploded as he drove by.

Despite these achievements, Operation Wrath of God was hardly an unalloyed success. Black September's commander, Abu Daoud, was shot thirteen times in a Warsaw coffee shop in 1981 but survived. More embarrassing, in 1973 a Mossad team was captured in Norway after mistakenly killing a Moroccan waiter who had been mistaken for Salameh. This was the only documented case of mistaken identity, but many of those assassinated had only the most tenuous connection with the Munich massacre; they were picked because they were more easily accessible than senior PLO leaders. (Arafat was said to sleep in a different bed every night, and he was protected by a large force of bodyguards.) Nor were Israel's assassinations cost-free.

The PLO retaliated by kidnapping and killing Israelis abroad, including a failed attempt on the life of Golda Meir in 1973 and the successful takeover of the Israeli embassy in Bangkok in 1972.

Arafat disbanded Black September in 1973 and thereafter generally refrained from international terrorism while continuing terrorist operations in Israel and the occupied territories. It is hard to say whether Israel's targeted killings played a role in his decision. Certainly the Israeli habit of retaliation was a more effective deterrent than the tendency of European and Arab governments to release captured terrorists. Wasfi Tal's killers, for instance, were let go by an Egyptian court, while the three surviving Munich terrorists were released less than two months later by the German government after Black September hijacked a Lufthansa aircraft. (Bonn was rumored to have connived in the hijacking to get rid of its unwanted prisoners.) But it is doubtful that Israel's Wrath of God campaign alone led to Arafat's change of heart. Another major factor, surely, was warnings from Saudi Arabia and the United States of serious consequences if the PLO attacked their facilities or personnel again.

Probably Arafat calculated that he had reaped all the benefits possible from high-profile attacks such as the Munich massacre and that to continue them would undermine his political strategy. Nineteen seventy-four was a turning point in that regard. That year the PLO was recognized by the Arab League as the "sole legitimate representative" of the Palestinian people, and Arafat was allowed to address the United Nations General Assembly. Unlike some of the wild men drawn to the Palestinian cause—inveterate adventurers such as the Venezuelan Ilich Ramírez Sánchez ("Carlos the Jackal"), who stormed OPEC's Vienna headquarters in 1975 to hold the oil ministers hostage, or the Palestinian renegade Abu Nidal, whose men shot up the El Al counters at the Rome and Vienna airports in 1985—Arafat craved international legitimacy. He could be pragmatic in his use of terrorism, but he often miscalculated, and he did so again after establishing himself in Lebanon.[168]

✦ ✦ ✦

HERE, IN WHAT became known as Fatahland, he presided over a formidable network of businesses and quasi-governmental ministries, courts and schools, along with training facilities that hosted foreign terrorists such as the Baader-Meinhof Gang. He even set up his own semiregular Palestine Liberation Army, 15,000 strong. The presence of these armed Palestinians tilted the delicate balance of Lebanese politics and sparked a destructive civil war in 1975 that would last, on and off, until 1990. The fighting would claim more than 100,000 lives and leave large swaths of Beirut, once known as the Paris of the East, utterly devastated. The PLO found itself fighting alongside Muslim and Druze militia against Christian militiamen who received support from Israel. From its Lebanese lairs, the PLO also staged raids and missile strikes against Israel. These included the infamous "coastal road massacre" of 1978 when eleven Fatah operatives landed in rubber dinghies in Israel and hijacked a bus. In a shootout with Israeli security forces, 35 passengers were killed and 71 injured. Three days later the Israel Defense Forces (IDF) invaded southern Lebanon and established a "security zone" along the border policed by a Christian proxy force.

Yet PLO attacks continued, leading Israel in June 1982 to mount a full-blown invasion of Lebanon that culminated in a ten-week siege of Beirut, which led to widespread condemnation of the Jewish state. This was the point when Israel began to change in foreign perception from an admirable underdog, as it had been at the time of the Entebbe raid, to an abusive imperialist. That transformation, which would have serious repercussions for the Jewish state's international standing, accelerated after Israeli forces stood by while Christian Phalangist militiamen slaughtered Palestinian refugees in the Sabra and Shatila camps in September 1982. Before long Israel would come to feel trapped in Lebanon amid incessant guerrilla attacks on its forces from the newly formed "Party of God"—Hezbollah. Yet that was scant comfort for the PLO, whose military inadequacies had been exposed once again for all the world to see. In August 1982 Arafat had no choice but to agree to an American plan that led to the evacuation of the PLO headquarters to Tunisia, fifteen hundred miles away.

He declined, however, to follow the Libyan leader Muammar Qaddafi's helpful advice to commit suicide in protest. Arafat was above all a survivor who might advocate martyrdom for others but would never practice it himself. Although he had to dodge Israeli assassination attempts, he was not truly a front-line fighter like Christiaan de Wet, Michael Collins, or Che

Guevara. His role far away from the action, flitting by private aircraft from one high-level diplomatic engagement to another, made it easier for him to continue the struggle undaunted by the dangers and privations faced by his men. He refused even to admit defeat; the evacuation of Lebanon was portrayed as another glorious victory. "Another victory such as this," joked one of the PLO's moderates, "and the PLO will find itself in the Fiji islands."[169]

✦ ✦ ✦

"The Old Man," as Arafat had been known since he was a young man, was able to stage yet another resurgence through a serendipitous occurrence: in December 1987 Palestinian youths in the West Bank and Gaza Strip began clashing with Israeli occupation forces. The Intifada (uprising, or literally "shaking off") was not planned by the PLO, and it gained much of its power not from terrorism but from strikes, boycotts, and demonstrations. The activists abjured firearms in favor of stones, knives, and Molotov cocktails. It was not exactly Gandhi-style nonviolent resistance, but neither was it the deliberate slaughter of Israeli civilians—the PLO's previous pattern.

Israeli's security forces were perplexed about how to respond. "We were caught with our pants down," notes an official IDF historian. As soldiers of a liberal democracy, and one that was under unrelenting international scrutiny, they could not simply send tanks to crush unarmed demonstrators as the Chinese government was to do in 1989. Sometimes, especially at first, small Israeli units facing large mobs would resort to live ammunition. More often, especially as time went on, various alternatives were employed such as truncheons, tear gas, and rubber bullets. The security forces also beat, deported, and, above all, detained perceived troublemakers, some of whom were tortured during interrogation. Eighteen thousand Palestinians were arrested in the Intifada's first year alone. In addition, from 1987 to 1990, roughly six hundred Palestinians were killed by Israeli security forces compared with a hundred Israelis killed by Palestinians. This imbalance helped produce the impression of an Israeli Goliath pummeling a Palestinian David despite the relative restraint exercised by the Israelis. The Chinese army, which exercised no such restraint, killed some two thousand protesters in and around Tiananmen Square in 1989. But in modern times democratic

Western powers inevitably have been held to a higher standard than illiberal states such as Communist China—as Britain had discovered during the Irish War of Independence and France during the Algerian War and as the United States was to discover in Iraq and Afghanistan.

Like their American, British, and French counterparts, Israeli leaders failed to appreciate the importance of appearances. Much of the news media coverage showed young Palestinian rock throwers, their faces obscured by bandannas, pitted against heavily armed, menacing-looking Israeli soldiers and police. Although the PLO leadership did not start the demonstrations, it made sure to use its public-relations savvy to publicize them—a project that the international press corps, always happy to root for an underdog, was eager to cooperate in. "The battle of the narrative," which had been a relatively minor part of guerrilla warfare as recently as the early years of the twentieth century, had now become more important than actual combat in determining the course of events. The Israel Defense Forces had shown superlative skills in conventional combat; they were far less skilled in this new arena of warfare.

As a result of the Intifada, most Israelis turned against the occupation of the territories and for the first time became willing to recognize a Palestinian state. International sympathy for the Palestinians also increased. The Intifada was a public-relations victory approaching, but never quite reaching, those won in the nineteenth century by Greek rebels against the Ottoman Empire and by Cuban rebels against Spain or more recently by Algerian rebels against France.

Arafat, for his part, acquired a more accommodating mindset because of his disastrous decision to back Saddam Hussein's invasion of Kuwait in 1990, which cost the PLO much of its Persian Gulf money and caused a financial crisis. Thus the stage was set for the Oslo peace process. In 1993 Arafat and Israel's prime minister, Yitzhak Rabin, signed an accord that, in return for recognition of Israel, set up the Palestinian Authority, which would be given limited but growing authority over the West Bank and Gaza Strip.[170]

Yasser Arafat had nearly died in 1992 in an air crash in the Libyan desert. It was a miracle that he was alive not only physically but politically. A lifelong exile who had not set foot in the Palestinian territories for nearly thirty years, he was able to return in 1994 as co-winner of the Nobel Peace Prize and the internationally recognized leader of a quasi-state. One of the highlights of his long life was undoubtedly the rapturous reception he received from tens of thousands of cheering Palestinians in a Gaza City festooned with the red, green, black, and white Palestinian flag. He took as his headquarters a former Israeli compound in Ramallah in the West Bank, where he would receive a stream of visitors, ranging from heads of state to the author of this volume,[171] often meeting them in the early morning hours. (Arafat was an inveterate night owl.)

In 1990 the peripatetic sixty-two-year-old revolutionary even made a move in the direction of settling down by marrying in a secret ceremony a twenty-seven-year-old Palestinian Christian, Suha Tawil, who five years later gave birth to a daughter. The birth occurred, however, in Paris, where she spent much of her time. Her jet-setting caused much resentment among ordinary Palestinians mired in poverty. Their anger only grew when they saw that corruption was pervasive among the returned PLO cadres.

His own people were not the only ones disappointed with Arafat. Rabin had hoped that Arafat would do more to repress Palestinian militants than Israeli forces could do because he would not be restrained by courts, human-rights lobbies, or other "bleeding hearts."[172] It was not to be. Arafat sometimes captured terrorists and sometimes cooperated with them—whatever suited his purposes at the moment. The 1990s saw the first suicide-bomber attacks in Israel: more than thirty of them between 1993 and 2000.[173] Although these attacks were carried out by Hamas and Palestinian Islamic Jihad, not by the PLO, Arafat did little to stop them.

✦ ✦ ✦

In 2000, at Camp David, Prime Minister Ehud Barak offered Arafat a final-status agreement that would have ceded East Jerusalem, at least 90 percent of the West Bank, and virtually all of the Gaza Strip. Rather than sign a treaty that would have transformed him from a revered "freedom fighter" into the leader of a small and impoverished nation—and that might have exposed him to assassination by militants—Arafat unleashed, or at least did not try to stop, the Second Intifada. It began with apparently spontaneous riots in September 2000 after the Israeli opposition leader Ariel Sharon, already hated among Palestinians as the architect of the 1982 invasion of Lebanon and a champion of Jewish settlements in the West Bank and Gaza Strip, briefly visited the Temple Mount in Jerusalem, a site sacred to both Jews and Muslims. This new uprising quickly turned into a campaign of terrorism not of protest, as the First Intifada had been. Suicide bombers penetrated Israel's largest cities and inflicted more casualties than Israel had ever suffered from terrorism: 649 Israeli civilians died between 2000 and 2005. Arafat, as usual, tried to hide his involvement behind front organizations—the al-Aqsa Martyrs Brigade and the Tanzim, which cooperated with Hamas and Palestinian Islamic Jihad to carry out shootings and suicide bombings.

Once again, just as during the First Intifada, Israel's initial response was confused and restrained. "We were kind of clueless," admitted one senior Israeli intelligence officer. Having given up control of the West Bank's cities to the Palestinian Authority in the 1990s, Israelis had little desire to go back even though, in the words of the IDF's chief of staff, they had become "safe havens for terrorists." But in March 2002 Israel's patience snapped. That month 135 Israelis died in seventeen attacks including more than 30 slaughtered at a Passover Seder. "It was clear the situation could not continue as before," wrote an Israeli general.

Ariel Sharon, now the prime minister, ordered two controversial responses: one defensive, the other offensive. The defensive response was the erection of a costly barrier—in some places a wall, in other places a fence—to separate Israel and some of its settlements from Palestinian communities in the West Bank. This was complemented by an army offensive designed to retake control of the entire West Bank. Operation Defensive Shield, which began on March 29, 2002, went surprisingly smoothly. The only city that saw fierce combat was Jenin. But even that was not the massacre claimed by the Palestinians: the United Nations later determined that fighting in Jenin killed twenty-three Israeli soldiers and fifty-two Palestinians, fewer than half of them civilians. In all five hundred Palestinians, mostly militants, were killed in the initial operations and seven thousand arrested. Once again, just as in Jordan and Lebanon, Palestinian fighters proved unable to stand toe-to-toe with a professional army. In 2002 Arafat found himself trapped in his own Ramallah compound with Israeli D-9 armored bulldozers knocking down his very walls. By the time of his death in 2004, at age seventy-five, he was widely seen as discredited and decrepit—a resistance leader whose long struggle had culminated in disaster.

The First Intifada, unplanned by Arafat, had divided Israeli society. The Second Intifada, which was Arafat's handiwork, united it. This gave the Israel Defense Forces the backing they needed to score an impressive victory—comparable in its own way to the contemporary success of Colombian forces fighting FARC, of Sri Lankan forces fighting the Tamil Tigers, and of U.S. forces fighting various insurgents in Iraq in 2007–08. In 2002 there were fifty-three suicide attacks in Israel. In 2007 there was just one. And by 2009 there were none. What explains this turnabout, which flew in the face of the conventional wisdom, even among many in the Israeli security forces, that determined terrorists willing to lay down their own lives could not be stopped?

Three factors were particularly important. First, the IDF's success in sealing off the West Bank—an area smaller than the state of Delaware, with a population of two million Arabs. This prevented Palestinian forces from being resupplied. In 2002, for instance, Israel's navy intercepted a freighter, the *Karine A*, loaded with fifty tons of Iranian weapons intended for the Palestinians. This was a severe embarrassment for Arafat, who initially and unconvincingly denied that the weapons were bound for his forces. Within the West Bank, the erection of numerous roadblocks inhibited the movement of militants and civilians alike. Second, the IDF's ability to gather accurate intelligence, through both electronic means and human spies. This necessitated the reconstitution of capabilities that had been lost in the 1990s when much of the West Bank's population had been turned over to Palestinian control. Once they were able to operate on the ground, Israeli intelligence officers were once again able to recruit informers. Third, and most important of all, was the IDF's staying power. If the IDF had treated Operation Defensive Shield as a quick in-and-out operation, like so many previous raids into neighboring Arab states over the decades, or like the later operations against Hezbollah in 2006 and Hamas in 2008–09, it is doubtful that it would have achieved lasting success. "If we were removed from the West Bank, it would become like Gaza," argued a senior Israeli strategist in 2011. "You've got to keep mowing the grass all the time."

Because the IDF stayed on the ground, as the British did in Northern Ireland, it could continue gathering intelligence and acting on it within hours or sometimes minutes. This prevented Hamas, the al-Aksa Martyrs Brigade, and other terrorist groups from rebuilding their infrastructure. Many suicide bombers still tried to attack (thirty-six in 2009 alone), but few got through. As the terrorist threat waned, the IDF was able to dismantle some checkpoints, thereby improving life for the Palestinians. This was as far as the IDF would go toward trying to win the "hearts and minds" of a fundamentally—and understandably—hostile population. But even in 2011, more than a decade after the start of the Second Intifada, the IDF was still conducting nightly operations in the West Bank leading to the arrest of terrorist suspects. The creation of a truly sovereign Palestinian state—the object of Arafat's lifework—seemed as far away as ever.[174]

✦ ✦ ✦

LOOKING BACK OVER the long span of Arafat's armed struggle, from 1965 to 2004, it is hard to say whether terrorism "worked" or not. Certainly terrorist attacks put Arafat and the PLO on the map; neither the man nor the movement would have become world famous without them. By sparking an Israeli backlash the attacks also helped to radicalize a hitherto apathetic Palestinian population and gave rise to a national identity that had previously been lacking. But on at least three occasions—in Jordan in 1970, Lebanon in 1982, and the West Bank and Gaza Strip in 2000—Arafat's resort to terrorism produced major setbacks that delayed the attainment of statehood. It was a double-edged sword: Palestinians' association with terrorism brought their grievances international attention but also sullied their reputation and made Israel more intransigent.

Arafat apparently believed, at least in the beginning of his career, that through incessant attacks the Jews could be forced to cede sovereignty over Palestine as the French had been driven out of Algeria and the Americans out of South Vietnam. He had visited both Algeria and Vietnam, and came away deeply impressed by the FLN and the Vietcong. His onetime deputy Abu Iyad wrote, "The guerrilla war in Algeria, launched five years before the creation of Fatah, had a profound influence on us. . . . [It] symbolized the success we dreamed of."[175] This missed a crucial distinction. The French and Americans could abandon those distant conflicts without committing national suicide. From the Israeli standpoint, however, surrender was tantamount to another Holocaust. Israeli Jews would not leave their homes unless their armed forces were annihilated, and that was far beyond the modest military capabilities of the PLO. By one estimate between 1968 and 1985 its operations killed 650 Israelis or an average of 40 a year—hardly a fatal blow even to such a small nation.[176]

There is good cause to believe, as the liberal Israeli writer Gershom Gorenberg has argued, that the Palestinians would have made greater gains toward statehood if led by a Mahatma Gandhi or a Martin Luther King Jr. rather than by Arafat.[177] Liberal democracies such as Israel are more susceptible to appeals to their conscience than to brutal attacks that stir public outrage. It is significant that the biggest Palestinian gains came after the First Intifada, which was much less violent than the two decades of terrorist attacks that preceded it or the Second Intifada, which succeeded it. But Arafat rose to prominence by the gun, and he could never quite renounce it. He could not make the transition that a few other terrorist leaders, including the Israeli prime ministers Menachim Begin (onetime leader of Irgun) and Yitzhak Shamir (the "Stern Gang"), had made to being normal politicians. And his power, and that of other extremists, made it impossible for those Palestinians who advocated nonviolent resistance or compromise with Israel to come to the fore.

The biggest victims of Palestinian terrorism, in the final analysis, were the Palestinians themselves. More than 3,200 of them died in the Second Intifada alone—and without winning statehood.[178]

57.

LEFT OUT, OR REBELS WITHOUT A CAUSE

The End of the (Marxist) Affair in the 1980s

LIKE EVERYONE ELSE, guerrillas and terrorists are subject to popular moods and intellectual fads. From the late eighteenth century to the late nineteenth century, revolutionaries ranging from George Washington, Simón Bolívar, and Toussaint Louverture in the New World to, in Europe, Wolfe Tone, Francisco Espoz y Mina, and the two Giuseppes, Garibaldi and Mazzini, were inspired by liberal ideals that were then *au courant* among progressive thinkers. By the turn of the twentieth century the concepts of the Enlightenment had been superseded, at least in certain intellectual circles, by more extreme schemes for reorganizing society. It was in this milieu that anarchist terrorism flourished, anarchism then being a respectable ideology of the left. Anarchist terrorists were not much heard of after the 1920s, because by then anarchism had been displaced in the revolutionary vanguard by socialism.

A later generation of leftist terrorists and guerrillas emerged out of the anticolonial atmosphere of the 1940s and 1950s and enjoyed their moment in the sun in the 1960s and 1970s when progressive opinion glorified Third World movements of "national liberation" as idealistic battlers against the ogres of imperialism and "neoimperialism." This was the period when Ho Chi Minh, Che Guevara, Fidel Castro, and Yasser Arafat were on everyone's lips and on many a college dorm room wall. Even some of their adversaries, such as Edward Lansdale, Robert Thompson, and John Paul Vann, became well-known figures if not quite idols of youth. By the 1980s, as memories of colonialism faded, as the excesses of postcolonial rulers became more apparent, and as capitalism revived under the impetus of Ronald Reagan and Margaret Thatcher, leftist movements went into eclipse, and the guerrilla mystique faded like an old Volkswagen van that had been left out in the elements too long.

The liberation ideology of the postwar period was discredited not only by the economic failure of its patrons in the Soviet Union and the People's Republic of China, which had become evident by the 1970s, but also by the inhumanity of its proponents once in power. The most extreme illustrations could be found in the tens of millions of murders perpetrated by Stalin and Mao. From Idi Amin's Uganda to the Khmer Rouge's Cambodia, there were countless other examples of brutality on a lesser if still shocking scale that discredited the ideals that onetime insurgents had fought for. Even groups that never attained power, such as the Tupamaros, the Baader-Meinhof Gang, and the Popular Front for the Liberation of Palestine, cost themselves moderate support because of the indiscrimination with which they targeted civilians. To their own detriment, they ignored the lessons of more successful terrorist groups of the past, notably the IRA from 1919 to 1921 and the Irgun and Stern Gang from 1944 to 1947, which generally although not invariably focused their attacks to the occupation authorities. By contrast the terrorist groups of the 1970s specialized in high-profile operations, such as the hostage taking at the Munich Olympics and the hijacking at Entebbe, which targeted civilians in front of the world's television cameras. While successful in publicizing their grievances by means of this powerful new communications medium, they generated far more revulsion than support from viewers around the globe.

By the 1980s the bankruptcy of Marxism was apparent even to Marxist rulers. In the Soviet Union, Mikhail Gorbachev implemented perestroika and glasnost, but those reforms failed to stop the rot, and in 1991 the entire state collapsed. By then the Communist regimes of Eastern Europe had already been overthrown. China, after Mao's death in 1976, made a more gradual transition to capitalism (but not democracy) under the Long March veteran Deng Xiaoping. Vietnam was not far behind after Le Duan's death in

1986. The handful of states like Cuba and North Korea that remained unapologetically communist were economic basket cases. Few but the most purblind ideologues could imagine that the future was being born in these impoverished and oppressed lands or that it was worthwhile to launch an armed movement to emulate their wretched example.

The end of the old regimes in Moscow and Beijing also had a more direct impact on insurgent groups by cutting off a valuable source of subsidies, arms, and training. The Marxist terrorist groups of the 1970s had been unable to generate much of a support base of their own and expired along with the end of their foreign backers. Nationalist movements such as the PLO and IRA fared better, although they too were hobbled by a decline in outside support, demonstrating once again the importance of external aid for any insurgency. Some leftist guerrilla movements such as Colombia's FARC and India's Naxalites remained in existence, but they became increasingly marginalized. Even Nepal's Maoists finally gave up "people's war" in 2006 and signed a peace accord that forced them to compete for votes with other political parties. The Palestinian struggle continued, needless to say, but the Marxist PFLP was no longer at the forefront; it had ceased to be a major player long before George Habash's death in 2008.

Although leftist insurgency was on the wane, guerrilla warfare and terrorism were hardly disappearing. They were simply assuming different forms as new militants shot their way into the headlines motivated by the oldest grievances of all—race and religion.

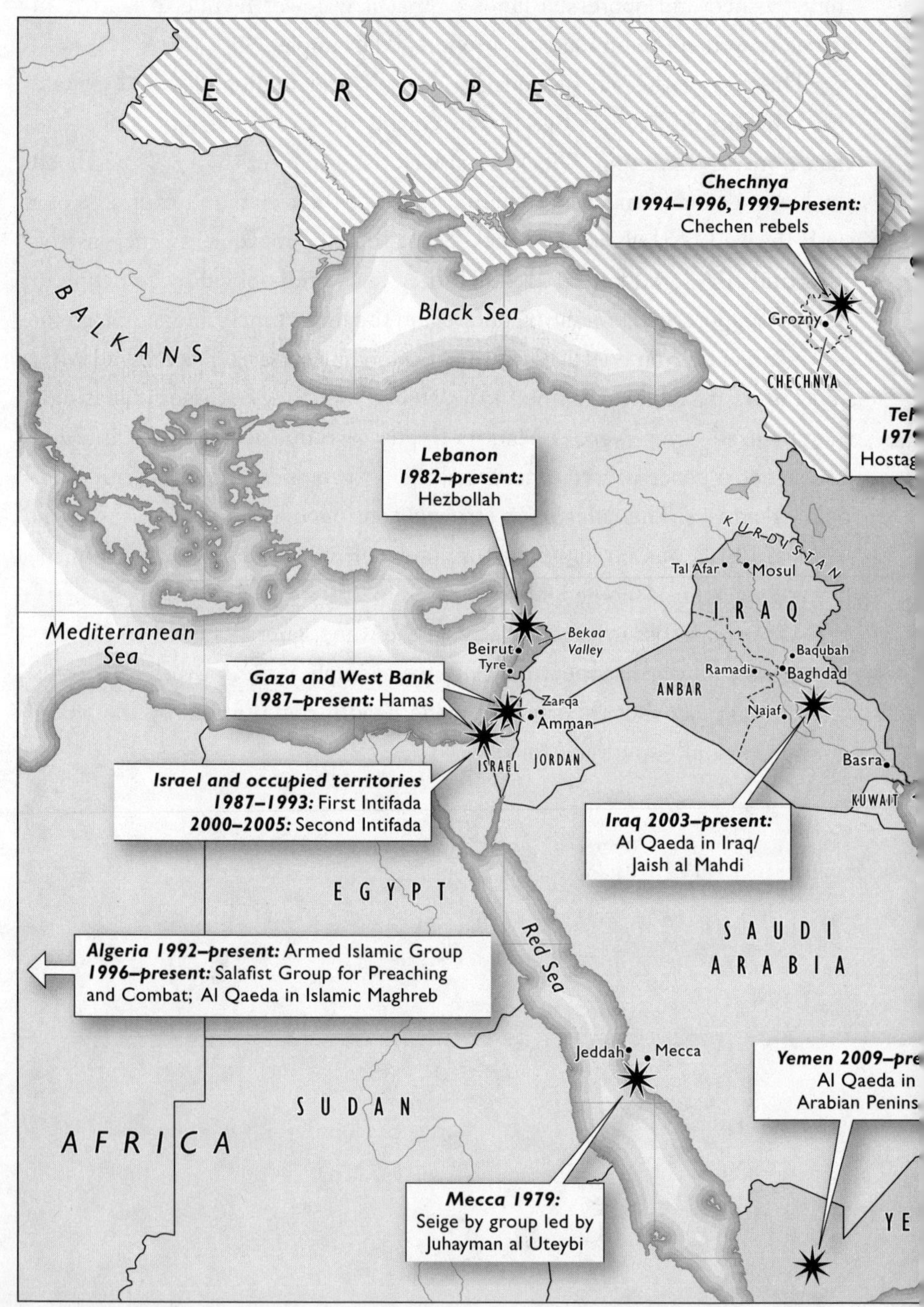

EUROPE
BALKANS
Black Sea
Mediterranean Sea
Chechnya
1994–1996, 1999–present:
Chechen rebels
Grozny
CHECHNYA
Lebanon
1982–present:
Hezbollah
KURDISTAN
Tal Afar
Mosul
IRAQ
Bekaa Valley
Beirut
Tyre
Gaza and West Bank
1987–present: Hamas
Zarqa
Amman
Baqubah
Ramadi
Baghdad
ANBAR
Najaf
Basra
KUWAIT
ISRAEL
JORDAN
Israel and occupied territories
1987–1993: First Intifada
2000–2005: Second Intifada
Iraq 2003–present:
Al Qaeda in Iraq/
Jaish al Mahdi
EGYPT
Red Sea
SAUDI ARABIA
Algeria 1992–present: Armed Islamic Group
1996–present: Salafist Group for Preaching and Combat; Al Qaeda in Islamic Maghreb
Jeddah
Mecca
SUDAN
AFRICA
Mecca 1979:
Seige by group led by
Juhayman al Uteybi

BOOK VIII
GOD'S KILLERS
The Rise of Radical Islam

58.

FIFTY DAYS THAT SHOOK THE WORLD

Tehran, Mecca, Islamabad, and Kabul, November 4–December 24, 1979

THE TRANSITION FROM politically motivated to religiously motivated insurgency—from leftist to Islamist extremism—was the product of decades, even centuries, of development. It could be traced back to the writings of the Egyptian agitator Sayyid Qutb in the 1950s–1960s; to the activities of Hassan al-Banna, who founded Egypt's Muslim Brotherhood in 1928; to the proselytizing of Muhammad bin Abd al-Wahhab, who in the eighteenth century created the puritanical movement that would one day become the official theology of Saudi Arabia; even to Ibn Taymiyya, the fourteenth-century theologian who laid the foundation for declaring fellow Muslims to be *takfir* (apostates) and thus subject to attack; and to the seventh-century Kharijites who believed that only the most fundamentalist Muslims were fit to rule.[1] But the epochal consequences of their ideas—which were to consign more-secular Muslim revolutionaries such as Yasser Arafat and his successor, Mahmoud Abbas, to growing irrelevance—did not seize the world's attention until the fateful fall of 1979.

The fifty days that shook the world began on November 4, 1979. That morning, amid a light rain, protesters began scaling the brick walls of the U.S. embassy compound on Takht-e-Jamshid Avenue in Tehran. Iranian police charged with protecting the embassy did nothing to stop them. The shah of shahs, Mohammad Reza Pahlavi, a stalwart American ally, had been driven out of office earlier that year. But the nature of the post-shah government remained far from settled. Islamist supporters of Ayatollah Ruhollah Khomeini who wanted to set up a theocratic dictatorship (*velayat-e faqih*, or "guardianship of the jurist") were jostling for influence with secular leftists and liberals. Many of the moderates were eager to continue their country's alliance with the United States; Prime Minister Mehdi Bazargan had just traveled to Algiers along with his foreign minister to meet with Zbigniew Brzezinski, the American national security adviser.

The embassy takeover had been organized by radical university students, including the future president Mahmoud Ahmadinejad, who wanted to strike a blow not only against the "Great Satan" but also against Mehdi Bazargan and other secularists. Thousands of students had been mobilized to overrun the embassy grounds and provided with placards, identification badges, bolt cutters, even strips of cloth to bind their captives. With Marine guards ordered to hold their fire, it did not take them long to overwhelm the skeletal embassy staff. As the blindfolded hostages were led out of the chancery building, a vast throng shouted ecstatically *God is Great!* and *Death to America!* Khomeini had not known in advance of the takeover, but seeing that popular sentiment was behind the students he embraced their cause in order to consolidate his power. Bazargan resigned in protest, thus removing a major obstacle to the Supreme Leader's accretion of absolute power.

President Jimmy Carter, good-natured to a fault, at first tried to be conciliatory and then ordered a hostage-rescue mission, which ended on April 25, 1980, in a fiery explosion at a rendezvous point in Iran code-named Desert One that killed eight American servicemen. The fifty-two hostages would not be freed until January 20, 1981, the very day that Carter left office and Ronald Reagan was inaugurated. Their 444-day, media-hyped ordeal would reveal America as a crippled giant, helpless to defend its own diplomats. Khomeini crowed, "Americans cannot do a damn thing." He was thus encouraged to make anti-Americanism, along with anti-Zionism, the centerpiece of his attempts to mobilize the Iranian people behind his leadership and to spread the Iranian revolution abroad.[2]

Iran was not the only American ally to feel the wrath of the Islamists that fall. Saudi Arabia was also targeted. Unlike the shah, a secular Westernizer, the Saudi royals were already Muslim fundamentalists—but not fundamentalist enough for the most extreme Salafists, who harked back to an early version of Islam practiced by their "pious predecessors." Hoping to spark a revolt that would overthrow the monarchy, hundreds of militants at daybreak on November 20, 1979, took over the Grand Mosque in Mecca—the holiest shrine in Islam—with rifles and automatic weapons they had smuggled inside coffins. Their leader was Juhayman al Uteybi, a bearded and volatile veteran of the Saudi National Guard who denounced the Saudi princes as "dissolute . . . drunkards" and castigated them for allowing "cinemas, clubs, and art shows" into the kingdom. Juhayman claimed that his brother-in-law, who also participated in the mosque takeover, was the Mahdi (messiah) who would usher in the Day of Judgment. Juhayman and his heavily armed followers bloodily repulsed initial attempts to retake the mosque. It would take two weeks and cost as many as a thousand lives for the Saudi security forces, with the help of French advisers, to end the uprising. Rebels who were not killed outright were tortured and executed.

In order to win the support of their religious establishment to fight in the holy of holies, the royals had to roll back the liberalization that had occurred in the 1960s–1970s. Women's pictures were banished from newspapers, theaters closed, goon squads from the Committee to Promote Virtue and Prevent Vice unleashed to crack down on any hints of sexuality in public. Even dog food was removed from supermarkets because dogs were considered unclean by pious Muslims. More menacingly, the Saudis increasingly resorted to what has been labeled "riyalpolitik" to safeguard their position. This meant increased spending to spread their harsh Wahhabi doctrine around the world: the very same doctrine that would one day inspire Osama bin Laden and his followers to turn on the Saudi monarchy and its backers in the West.[3]

The Saudis were so embarrassed at the seizure of the Mecca mosque that they tried, with some success, in the last pre-Internet decade, to black out all news about the incident, leading to wild speculation that the culprits were either Iranian agents or, alternatively, Jews and Americans. The latter theory spread like a raging wildfire through Pakistan.

On November 21, 1979, just one day after Juhayman had captured the Grand Mosque, mobs shouting "Death to American dogs!" converged on the U.S. embassy in Islamabad. As in Tehran a few weeks earlier, the demonstrators overran the compound with relatively little resistance. The Pakistani army and police were just as disinclined to intervene as their Iranian counterparts had been. President Mohammed Zia ul-Huq was moving his country in a more Islamist direction, and he had no desire to alienate the radicals by fighting them. The embassy personnel avoided disaster only because the Pakistani protesters were not as well organized or as determined as the Iranian students. Flinging Molotov cocktails, they burned the embassy's six buildings, but a hundred staff members took refuge in the secure-communications vault on the chancery's third floor. Although the vault's floor tiles cracked and buckled from the fires raging below, the Americans managed to hold out until nightfall when they emerged to find the mob gone. Only four embassy employees died—two Americans, two Pakistanis—along with two protesters. The outcome could have been worse, but the incident was bad enough: an ominous indicator of growing radicalization in the world's second-most populous Muslim state.[4]

Islamists were by no means the only significant insurgents of the turn of the millennium. The post–Cold War period had also seen the reemergence of ethnic and tribal conflict, principally in Africa and the Balkans. Those wars of race were characterized by at least as much savagery as the wars of religion, and their body count has been even greater. They were, however, of limited interest to the West and then primarily as a humanitarian matter. The jihadists, by contrast, were of great concern to the West whether they were seen as a strategic ally (the Afghan mujahideen) or a threat (Hezbollah, Al Qaeda, Al Qaeda in Iraq). This section will look at all of these groups, whose full trajectory is not yet clear but which have already shown an ability to humble superpowers—whether in the mountains and deserts of Afghanistan or in the rubble of the U. S. Marine barracks in Beirut and the World Trade Center in New York.

59.

RUSSIA'S VIETNAM

The Red Army vs. the Mujahideen, 1980–1989

Few could have imagined that jihadist insurgents would prove so powerful when the Soviet Union launched its textbook takedown of Afghanistan. The Soviet assault began on Christmas Eve 1979—exactly fifty days after the takeover of the American embassy in Tehran—with more than a division of paratroopers landing at Kabul airport and at the Bagram airbase thirty-five miles away. A day later, on December 25, a Motorized Rifle Division rumbled across the border from Soviet Turkestan and began racing south toward Kabul. Ostensibly these troops were only responding to pleas of assistance from a communist regime that had taken power in a coup the preceding year. The People's Democratic Party of Afghanistan, as the communists were known, had immediately begun to alienate the population by challenging age-old social customs and landownership patterns. Landlords and mullahs were arrested, women ordered to unveil. Even the color of the Afghan flag was changed from Islamic green to communist red. The government tried to repress the resulting unrest by sending aircraft to bomb civilian neighborhoods and soldiers to massacre entire villages. Such excesses only drew more recruits into a burgeoning holy war. By the end of 1979 more than half of the Afghan army had deserted and 80 percent of the country had fallen out of the central government's control.

The inner core of the Politburo in Moscow, led by the ailing eighty-year-old general secretary, Leonid Brezhnev, concluded that unless the USSR intervened, a "fraternal" regime would be toppled. They believed that the revolution was particularly imperiled by President Hafizullah Amin, a ruthless communist who had taken power just three months earlier by deposing and killing his predecessor. Amin, who had been educated at Columbia University, spoke English and expressed a desire for better relations with Washington. This led the KGB to suspect him, improbably enough, of being a CIA agent.

On December 27, 1979, KGB commandos wearing Afghan army uniforms and backed by the Red Army were ordered to assault the Tajbeg Palace, on the outskirts of Kabul, where Amin was holed up with 2,500 guards. Ironically, as the assault was about to start at 7:30 p.m., Amin was inside being treated for food poisoning (a KGB plot) by doctors from the Soviet embassy who had not been informed of the plan to eliminate their patient. When told that his palace was under attack, Amin asked an aide to contact the Soviets to save him, only to be told that the attackers *were* Soviets.

The KGB men were given a few shots of vodka and told "no one should be left alive" in the palace. The assault force encountered heavier than expected resistance from Amin's guards, who greeted them with heavy machine-gun fire and fought them from room to room. Dozens of KGB officers were killed and almost all of the rest wounded. But, firing automatic weapons and throwing grenades, the commandos finally gained control of the palace and killed Amin. One Russian recalled that "the rugs were soaked with blood" by the time they were done.

Elsewhere in Kabul, other Russian troops were occupying the government ministries, the radio and television stations, and other strategic points. They were aided by embedded Russian advisers who tricked Afghan soldiers into taking the ammunition out of their tanks and the batteries out of their trucks. It was a model takedown not only of the capital but of the entire country—faster and less costly than the American invasion of Iraq in 2003. Within a few weeks, eighty thousand Red Army troops were deployed across the country and a new president had been proclaimed: Babrak Karmal, a communist who had been a rival of Amin's.[5]

Western leaders were afraid that this was only the start of a Communist offensive toward the oil fields of the Persian Gulf. In fact Soviet leaders had no such plans. They were only trying to buttress a shaky ally, and they expected a quick in-and-out operation like that in Hungary in 1956 or Czechoslovakia in 1968. They had no idea that they had just launched a war that would last nine years, kill 26,000 Soviet soldiers,[6] help bring about the downfall of the Soviet empire, and give a considerable boost to the global forces of jihad.

Perhaps if Soviet leaders had studied the annals of guerrilla warfare more closely—to include the hardships endured by the "bourgeois" British forces in Afghanistan in 1839–42 and 1878–80—they might not have been so confident about the outcome. But even the most thorough survey of history would not have fully prepared them to confront an Afghan enemy far more dangerous than any the British had ever faced. Like their nineteenth-century predecessors, the rebels who were to fight Soviet invaders were inflamed by nationalist and religious zeal. But they were to enjoy advantages undreamed of by Akbar Khan or Sher Ali: namely, the provision of secure bases next door in Pakistan where they could receive arms and training. It would not take long for the Red Army to find out that in Afghanistan's vast and difficult terrain those advantages counted for more than all the modern weaponry at its disposal. It was in essence the same lesson learned by the American armed forces in Vietnam, and it would prove just as painful.

✦ ✦ ✦

THE RED ARMY'S education began in the Panjshir Valley, a narrow gash in the towering Hindu Kush mountains. Located forty miles north of Kabul, it is seventy miles long and runs in a northeasterly direction. The valley walls are sheer gray rock, the floor so narrow that at its widest point it is only a mile across. Travel in the 1980s was by a single dirt road, "no more than a stony path," which ran alongside the "blue-green," rapidly flowing Panjshir River. Here, before the coming of the Soviets, lived eighty thousand ethnic Tajiks, who scratched out a living raising chickens and goats, apricots and wheat. By 1980 the entire valley was under the control of Ahmad Shah Massoud, one of numerous mujahideen commanders who had taken up arms to resist the Soviet invasion.

Actually Massoud, like many of the "holy warriors," had begun fighting before the arrival of the Russians. Born in 1952 to an Afghan army officer, he had attended a French high school in Kabul followed by the Russian-built Kabul Polytechnic Institute, where he showed his mathematical ability. Like numerous other university students in the 1970s, Massoud became active in politics, but his politics were not of the secular leftist variety. Rather he became an adherent of the Muslim Youth, a militant movement inspired by the Egyptian Muslim Brotherhood. Their activities ran afoul of President Mohammad Daoud, a leftist who took power in 1973 from his cousin King Zahir Shah. (He, in turn, would be toppled by his communist allies five years later.) Massoud had to flee to Pakistan, where the government provided him and thousands of other fundamentalist Afghans with military training. After an aborted foray back into Afghanistan in 1975, he returned for good three years later to fight the new communist regime. He started, noted a journalist, with "fewer than 30 followers, 17 rifles of various makes, and $130 in cash." Within a few years he had created a force of 3,000 mujahideen. They would become the nucleus of the most formidable guerrilla movement the Soviets had ever faced.

This achievement was all the more remarkable considering that Massoud received considerably less outside assistance than other *muj* commanders who were based in Pakistan and were close to its Inter-Services Intelligence agency. Moreover in a country that revered age Massoud was not yet thirty at the time of the Soviet invasion. That he was able to thrive largely on his own was a tribute to his shrewdness and charisma. "He had an energy, an intensity, a dignity that was immediate and powerful and had an effect on everyone around," recalled the journalist Sebastian Junger. "When he was talking, I couldn't take my eyes off him. Something about him was just captivating."

Massoud was a devout Muslim who prayed five times a day, but he did not display the same dogmatism and extremism as the more hard-line *muj* commanders. He had "a kind of gentle fragility and a disarming sense of humor," a tolerance for others, and an interest in poetry and Sufi mysticism. He encouraged women to become educated and treated Soviet prisoners with "such compassion that Soviet soldiers preferred to surrender to him over anybody else"; one of them even became his bodyguard. (Other *muj* commanders, by contrast, were known for torturing captives.) He won the devotion of his men by displaying a complete lack of pretension and a genuine interest in their well-being. His fellow mujahideen remembered that "he washed his own clothes, even his socks," prepared his own food, and took his turn on guard detail at night. When he was given a new pair of shoes by a foreign visitor, he handed them to one of his men even though his own "toes were sticking out of one of his shoes."

The mujahideen were natural guerrillas like Shamil's Chechens or the Greek klephts—"ornery backwoodsmen" with a strong religious faith who had been fighting foreign interlopers (and one another) for centuries. Massoud was better educated than most, even if he had forgotten most of the French he had learned. He had read the classics of guerrilla warfare—Mao, Che, Giap—even books on the American Revolution, and he set out to apply what he had learned. Hawk-nosed and wispy-bearded, typically seen in a *pakol* (flat woolen hat) and safari jacket, his visage would soon became almost as famous as the men whose exploits he had studied. Within a few years he would be recognized, in the judgment of the travel writer Robert Kaplan, as "among the greatest guerrilla fighters of the twentieth century."

He not only used the Panjshir Valley as his base but, unlike other *muj*, also administered it as a "liberated zone" with its own schools, courts, mosques, prisons, a French-operated hospital, and a military training center. He was among the first of the *muj* to divide his forces into mobile groups of full-time fighters (*moutarik*) and a local militia of part-time helpers who would defend their villages (*sabet*). The *moutarik*, organized into companies of 120 men, wore olive uniforms and black army boots. They were armed with a motley assemblage of weapons either captured from the Red Army or bought in Pakistan, including AK-47 assault rifles, RPG-7 rocket-propelled grenades, DShK 12.7-millimeter machine guns, and even ZPU-2 antiaircraft guns. They posed a particular menace to the occupiers because the Panjshir Valley ends just a few miles from the Salang highway running from Kabul to the Soviet border. This was the main Soviet supply artery, and Massoud's men were constantly raiding it. At one point they even hijacked a black Volga sedan destined for Afghanistan's defense minister. Massoud's fighters disassembled it, hauled it to their valley, and put it back together for their commander to ride in.

✦ ✦ ✦

AS EARLY AS the spring of 1980, the Soviets launched their first offensive against the Panjshir—to little effect. By May 1982 they were preparing for their fifth assault with 8,000 Russian and 4,000 Afghan troops backed by a formidable array of airpower. Thanks to his excellent intelligence network, Massoud got wind of what was coming and staged a spoiling attack against the Soviet airbase at Bagram on April 25, 1982, damaging or destroying at least a dozen aircraft on the ground. This delayed the start of the weeklong bombing campaign that preceded the Soviet ground offensive. When the invasion finally came on May 17, the Soviets put their Afghan allies in the lead. Massoud let the Afghan soldiers proceed unharmed; many wound up defecting. But as soon as a Soviet armored column began entering the valley, his men dynamited the gorges to create a rockslide that blocked its advance. This held back the invaders but not for long. Not only did they break through the roadblock; they also sent forces into the northern end of the valley to catch Massoud in a pincer. At the same time six battalions, some 1,200 men, air-assaulted into the middle of the valley in Mi-6 and Mi-8 helicopters, while MiG-21 fighters and Su-25 ground-attack aircraft pulverized anything that moved.

"From dawn to dusk, they doggedly came," wrote Edward Girardet of the *Christian Science Monitor*, who witnessed the assault while embedded with Massoud's forces.

> First, one heard an ominous distant drone. Then, as the throbbing grew louder, tiny specks appeared on the horizon and swept across the jagged, snow-capped peaks of the Hindu Kush. Like hordes of wasps, the dull grey helicopter gunships came roaring over the towering ridges that ring this fertile valley. Soon the hollow thuds of rockets and bombs resounded like thunder as they pounded the guerrilla positions. . . . From one vantage point halfway up the Panjshir we could distinctly see the Soviet and Afghan government forces as they moved in dust-billowing columns of tanks, armored personnel carriers, and trucks along the single dirt road. . . . Through our binoculars, we could distinguish formal rows of BM-21 "Stalin organs," each capable of firing 40 rockets altogether car-

rying 4½ tons of explosives, and giant self-propelled howitzers pointing menacingly in our direction.

Massoud was caught off guard by this multipronged assault—but only temporarily. He was an "excellent chess player," and like all great chess players he learned to analyze a situation dispassionately. A British journalist who spent time with him found that he "never seemed to panic . . . he didn't seem to lose his cool." A fellow *muj* recalled that "he was always smiling" and "you would feel when you saw him smile . . . that we were winning." That upbeat attitude came in handy when the odds were stacked so heavily against him, as they were in 1982.

Along with most of the valley's residents, he and his men took refuge in the small side valleys adjacent to the Panjshir. Safe in caves and stone shelters that had been constructed "amid the nooks and crannies of towering bluffs," they could dash out at any time to strike the immobile army below. The Soviets could not reach their tormentors. They bombed and rocketed one guerrilla machine-gun position all afternoon until only one small tree was left standing. The next day the gun was firing again. "At first the Russians only set up tents on the valley floor," wrote Edward Girardet. "Later, when mujahideen firing became murderous, they were forced to dig trenches." By July the trenches were abandoned. The offensive had petered out, and the Soviets had to pull most of their forces out.

By the end of the war the Red Army had mounted nine major offensives, which cost it thousands of casualties, yet Massoud still controlled the Panjshir. His resilience in the face of repeated assaults by superior forces of undoubted skill and savagery was every bit as impressive as that of Toussaint Louverture in Haiti, Francisco Espoz y Mina in Spain, and Josip Broz Tito in Yugoslavia.[7]

✦ ✦ ✦

THE BATTLES OF the Panjshir were typical of the entire war. The Red Army conducted many big, blundering offensives but, as its own general staff later conceded, most "were wasted effort"—"more appropriate for the Northern European plain than the rugged mountains of Afghanistan."[8] Most of the country, from the towering peaks of the east to the barren deserts of the south, remained forever outside its grasp. The only exceptions were the major cities and the highways that connected them.

Frustrated by their inability to come to grips with the insurgents, whom they called *dukhi* (ghosts) or *dushman* (enemy), Soviet troops unleashed their anger on helpless civilians. In 1984 investigators from Helsinki Watch, precursor of Human Rights Watch, went to Pakistan to interview Afghan refugees, Soviet deserters, and Western visitors to Afghanistan. "From our interviews," they wrote, "it soon became clear that just about every conceivable human rights violation is occurring in Afghanistan, and on an enormous scale." Former prisoners testified about the interrogation methods of the Soviets and the KGB-trained Afghan secret police, the KhAD—"about electric shocks, nail pulling, lengthy periods of sleep deprivation, standing in cold water and other punishments." Horrific reprisals for attacks were also the norm. One Russian soldier recalled how in 1982 a captain and three soldiers got drunk on vodka and wandered into a village, where they were killed. The commander of a Red Army brigade, who happened to be the brother of the dead captain, then took his men into the village and slaughtered everyone in sight—approximately two hundred people.

Often their atrocities had no military purpose whatsoever. Russian soldiers were known to steal anything valuable and shoot anyone who resisted. Helicopter gunships even shot up moving vehicles so that soldiers could loot them. Such relentless attacks on the civilian population forced large numbers of Afghans to flee their homes, heading for Iran or Pakistan. Not even these pitiful columns of refugees, clutching their blankets and chickens, were safe. When caught in the open they were strafed and bombed by Soviet aircraft. Perhaps the biggest cause of civilian casualties was the mines that were scattered indiscriminately by the millions around the country. Many were "butterfly" mines dropped from the air that were designed to blend in with the countryside. They would usually maim rather than kill on the theory that a wounded person was more of a burden to the resistance than a dead one. There were also persistent, if unproved, reports of mines disguised as toys blowing the legs and arms off children that did much to mobilize world opinion against the Soviet invasion. Soviet troops even tore apart

Korans and bombed mosques or used them as bathrooms—the worst sacrilege imaginable in such a pious society.[9]

The invaders were not totally blind to the need for civil action to woo the populace as preached by generations of counterinsurgents from Lyautey to Lansdale. Between 1980 and 1989 Moscow sent $3 billion in nonmilitary aid to Afghanistan and dispatched thousands of advisers to assist the Afghan government.[10] But much of the spending went to the Sovietization of Afghan society—toward teaching Marxism-Leninism and Russian in the schools—which did nothing to win "hearts and minds" and in fact further alienated the devoutly Muslim population. Even occasional Soviet good works, such as building hospitals and power stations, were drowned in a sea of blood.

The invaders killed more than 1 million Afghans and forced 5 million more to flee the country. Another 2 million were internally displaced. Since Afghanistan's prewar population was 15 million to 17 million, its scale of suffering, with more than 6 percent of the population perishing, was comparable to Yugoslavia's in World War II.

Soviet leaders may not have cared from a humanitarian standpoint about all the hardship they inflicted but, like the Germans in Yugoslavia, they would have cause to regret the effect of their policies, which was to drive large numbers of men into the arms of the resistance. At least 150,000 fighters joined the mujahideen. The guerrillas thus outnumbered the Red Army, which never had more than 115,000 men in Afghanistan. The Soviets were aided by 30,000 Afghan government soldiers, mostly press-ganged conscripts of dubious reliability. There were also at least 15,000 Afghan secret policemen who worked closely with the KGB. They were more dedicated defenders of the regime, but they were too few in number to make up for the counterinsurgents' numerical disadvantage. (By contrast, facing a foe utilizing gentler methods, the Taliban in the post-2001 era were never able to mobilize more than 30,000 men to fight NATO forces, 140,000-strong at their peak, and 350,000 of their allies in the Afghan security forces.) For the Soviet-backed regime in Kabul, the counterinsurgency math—the proportion of security forces to population: in this case 1 to 100—was decidedly not in its favor.[11]

✦ ✦ ✦

NOR WAS THE composition of the occupation forces terribly advantageous. The United States had learned during the Vietnam War that sending large numbers of conscripts on such an inglorious, dangerous, and long-lasting mission, with little prospect of immediate gains to boost popular support, was a recipe for trouble: commanders would have to grapple with low morale among their own troops and opposition back home. The Soviet government was less susceptible to public opinion than its American counterpart, but it too would learn the folly of fighting a brutal counterinsurgency war with unmotivated conscripts.

Soviet soldiers were told that they were being sent to help a "fraternal ally" resist "U.S. imperialism and Peking hegemonism." It did not take long for them to see through this propaganda and to conclude, as one soldier put it, "Everyone around us was an enemy. . . . We didn't see any friendly Afghans anywhere—only enemies. Even the Afghan army was unfriendly." Soldiers knew that every time they ventured outside their well-protected bases they risked returning home on the "Black Tulip"—the transport aircraft that brought back zinc coffins. Even bases weren't totally safe: two soldiers who went to an outdoor latrine at Bagram were found with their heads impaled on sticks. After seeing a friend killed, one soldier said, "I was ready to destroy everything and everyone." Another soldier recalled how two soldiers from his company actually "fought between themselves for the right to shoot seven Afghans who were prisoners." After one of them shot six prisoners with "bullets in the back of the neck," the other soldier ran up shouting, "Let me shoot too! Let me!"

In a professional army, officers and NCOs are supposed to inspire and discipline soldiers and channel their aggression in a constructive direction. But in the Red Army the officers acquired a reputation as "jackals" who looked out primarily for their own comforts and allowed senior soldiers (the *dedy*, or grandfathers) to bully and beat the new men. Beset by what one soldier called "an all-encompassing moral corruption," they did little to restrain their frightened, unmotivated, trigger-happy men who acted in complete contravention of the teachings of Mao, Castro, Magsaysay, and other leaders, both insurgents and counterinsurgents, who had instructed their men to respect the populace in order to win its allegiance. All counterinsurgent forces commit some abuses: even the U.S. Army, which by the standards of most other armies has been relatively restrained, has been guilty of atrocities ranging from Wounded Knee to My Lai and Abu Ghraib. But the prevalence and scale of such human-rights violations in Afghanistan was much more troubling, and Red Army leaders did much less than their American counterparts to police their own ranks. Soviet soldiers were told, "Do whatever you want, but don't get caught." This became a license for rampant human-rights abuses, which inflicted not only great suffering on the Afghans but also considerable psychological trauma on the perpetrators—and that undermined their war aims.

Morale was not helped by the fact that the Red Army was unable to provide enough food, warm clothing, or heating oil to its troops even though the war was being fought next to its own territory. Some soldiers were reduced to eating rotten potatoes or cabbages. Almost 70 percent of them were hospitalized with serious illnesses, including typhus, malaria, hepatitis, and dysentery, often caught from drinking polluted water. Discipline was so lax that many soldiers sold arms and ammunition to the *muj* so that they could buy jeans or a cassette player to take home.

So dismal were the conditions that some soldiers shot themselves to get a quick ticket home. Others deserted. Many more took refuge in alcohol and drugs to escape the "sweet-and-sour smell of blood," which, one soldier said, "turned my stomach inside out with nausea." Troops got drunk on vodka, moonshine, aftershave lotion. Or they got high on marijuana, heroin, hashish, sometimes provided free by Afghan suppliers who were happy to corrupt their enemies. Said one soldier, "It's best to go into an operation stoned—you turn into an animal."[12]

✦ ✦ ✦

THE ECHOES OF the American experience in Vietnam—another unpopular counterinsurgency conflict fought, at least in its later stages, by disgruntled draftees—were not entirely coincidental. Just as the Soviet Union had extended aid to the Vietcong, so too the U.S. extended aid to the mujahideen to humble a rival superpower.

Washington had begun sending nonlethal assistance to the *muj*—radio equipment, medical supplies, cash—even before the Red Army's arrival. Immediately after the invasion, Jimmy Carter signed a presidential finding authorizing a covert program to supply the resistance with weapons. To keep the U.S. role secret, the CIA bought up Eastern bloc weapons from Egypt, Poland, China, and other sources, and shipped them to Pakistan. Saudi Arabia matched the American contributions dollar for dollar. Distribution was handled by Pakistan's Inter-Services Intelligence (ISI). It provided arms and training to the seven major resistance factions headquartered in the frontier town of Peshawar. From the border areas of Pakistan, which, in the words of an ISI brigadier, "had grown into a vast, sprawling administrative base for the jihad,"[13] the guns were smuggled into Afghanistan on trucks, horses, and mules or on the backs of the *muj* along what journalists called the "jihad trail." The Soviets went to great lengths to interdict this supply line but had no more luck than the Americans had had in disrupting the Ho Chi Minh Trail. There were simply too many mountain passes where columns of fighters could slip through. The *muj*, in one journalist's words, "could go long periods of time without food and water, and climb up and down mountains like goats."[14]

After September 11, 2001, some would argue that the United States had brought these attacks upon itself by arming the very men who now terrorized it. This was not literally true—there is no evidence that CIA or any other American government agency provided aid to Osama bin Laden. But it was true that in the 1980s American aid went to many hard-line Islamists who would one day become America's enemies. This was a byproduct of Washington's decision to turn over the disbursement of arms and money to Pakistan's president, Zia ul-Huq, who was turning increasingly Islamist.

His agents funneled most of the American-supplied weapons to the most extreme groups such as Gulbuddin Hekmatyar's Hizb-i-Islami (Party of Islam). A power-hungry former engineering student, Hekmatyar was widely hated by rival *muj* who thought, in the words of Robert Kaplan, that "his organization lacked fighting ability and squandered much of its resources attacking other guerrilla factions."[15] Unlike Ahmed Shah Massoud, he spent little time inside Afghanistan, preferring to politic in Peshawar. But he was ISI's fair-haired boy and a favorite of Saudi intelligence. Even the CIA was partial to him.[16] He was also close to Osama bin Laden, who had begun visiting Pakistan after the Soviet invasion.[17] The CIA provided some unilateral assistance to Massoud, as did British and French intelligence, but it was a pittance compared with the riches flowing to extremists such as Hekmatyar, who would one day battle American forces in Afghanistan.

This was a particular notable but hardly unique example of "blowback" from the distribution of aid to proxy forces—the European powers had experienced the same phenomenon after World War II when some of the resistance fighters they had equipped to fight the Japanese turned their guns on returning European imperialists.

✦ ✦ ✦

INITIALLY THE AMERICAN goal was simply to bleed the Soviets. But the Reagan administration shifted the objective from harassing the Soviets to defeating them. Aid increased from $30 million in 1980 to $630 million in 1987, which in effect meant more than $1.2 billion (roughly $3 billion in 2012 dollars) because of the Saudi add-on. In 1986 American officials turned up the pressure still further by dispatching Stinger antiaircraft missiles to the muj. The origins and impact of this decision have been widely misunderstood.

The book and movie *Charlie Wilson's War* fostered the impression that a hard-drinking, skirt-chasing Texas congressman was the primary mover behind the Stingers and other aid sent to the *muj*. Wilson was undoubtedly an influential supporter of the *muj* but only one of many. And, as even George Crile, author of *Charlie Wilson's War*, acknowledged, Wilson was not "directly involved" in the decision to send Stingers. His primary contribution had been to lobby in 1984 for the dispatch of antiaircraft cannons made by the Swiss firm Oerlikon. But since each one weighed 1,200 pounds and required twenty mules to transport, the Oerlikon was not a practical weapon to lug around Afghanistan. By contrast the Stinger weighed only 34 pounds and fired a missile that could lock onto an aircraft's infrared emissions.

The impetus for sending Stingers came not from Charlie Wilson but from two Defense Department officials—Undersecretary Fred Iklé and his aide Michael Pillsbury, a conservative former Hill staffer. They faced opposition from the Joint Chiefs of Staff, the State Department, and CIA, which feared the consequences of escalating the war by sending high-tech, made-in-America weapons. They succeeded, however, in winning over the State

Department official Morton Abramowitz, who in turn brought around Secretary of State George Shultz. Secretary of Defense Caspar Weinberger and CIA Director Bill Casey, two other skeptics, were also won over. In March 1986 President Reagan formally approved the dispatch of the Stingers.

Six months later, eight Mi-24 gunships were coming in for a landing at the Jalalabad airport at 3 p.m. on September 29, 1986. The Hind was the most feared Soviet weapon of the war, called *Shaitan Arba* (Satan's chariot) by the *muj*. It was equipped with an automatic Gatling gun, 80-millimeter rockets, and bombs and mines, and its heavy armor made it impervious to most machine-gun fire. But that day a band of mujahideen equipped with three Stingers managed to send three Hinds down in flames. The Russian General Staff later claimed that there was "no appreciable rise in the number of aircraft shot down after the introduction of the Stinger." Even if this was true, its presence on the battlefield forced Russian pilots to fly whenever possible above 12,500 feet—the Stinger's maximum range—thereby decreasing their combat effectiveness. The Russians' best weapon had been neutralized.[18]

While a blow to the occupiers, this was hardly the turning point of the war, as many believe. Even before the deployment of the Stingers, the new Soviet leader, Mikhail Gorbachev, had concluded that the war was unwinnable. On October 17, 1985, almost a year before the first Stinger was fired, he told the Politburo that he would seek a "withdrawal from Afghanistan in the shortest possible time."[19] The actual withdrawal would not be completed until 1989, and there would be much hard fighting ahead (including the biggest Soviet offensive of the entire war—Operation Magistral in 1987), but by 1986 the end was in sight.

✦ ✦ ✦

For the Russians, the nine-year ordeal finally ended on the "chilly winter morning" of February 15, 1989. At 11:55 a.m., Lieutenant General Boris Gromov, commander of the Fortieth Army, walked across the Friendship Bridge from Afghanistan to the Uzbek Soviet Socialist Republic, signaling the end of the Soviet combat role if not the end of the war itself.[20] Russia's withdrawal represented its first failure after centuries of colonial expansion and showed that even the most brutal counterinsurgency methods will not necessarily succeed if the occupiers lack legitimacy and if their adversaries operate on favorable terrain and receive outside assistance.

The KGB prevented public displays of dissatisfaction with the war at home; there were no antiwar marches as there had been in the United States during the 1960s. By the end of the 1980s, however, there was no way to camouflage this colossal failure, which undermined the already shaky legitimacy of Communist rule and further dispelled the aura of fear among its opponents. It is not entirely a coincidence that the Soviet Union lost control of Eastern Europe the very year it exited Afghanistan. Two years later the whole state collapsed. Afghanistan is said to be the "graveyard of empires," but, in point of fact, the Soviet empire was the first one to meet its end there, and even the Soviet collapse was mostly the result of factors that had nothing to do with the war. The British Empire, by contrast, had reached the peak of its Victorian glory following its defeat in Afghanistan in 1842.

✦ ✦ ✦

IRONICALLY THE AFGHAN regime, ruled since 1986 by a former secret police chief named Najibullah, outlived its Soviet sponsor. This was due in no small part to the chronic disunity of its foes. Najibullah was finally toppled in 1992, after Russian aid had ended, by an alliance of Ahmad Shah Massoud's Tajik guerrillas and Abdul Rashid Dostum's Uzbek militia. The new government was dominated by Massoud, its army commander, but he was not as adept at politics as at guerrilla warfare—no Tito he. He could not bring the disparate *muj* factions together; he could not even stop Hekmatyar from shelling Kabul in an attempt to seize power for himself. Chaos reigned across the country as warlords competed for influence and criminals ran wild.

These intolerable conditions led in 1994 to the rise of the Taliban, an ultra-fundamentalist group of Pashtun students riding Toyota pickup trucks who promised to restore order. Most of them were war orphans who had known no peace and had been educated in Saudi-funded *madrassas* in Pakistani refugee camps where nothing but jihadism was taught. Pakistan switched its support from Hekmatyar to the Taliban, and in 1996, following a ten-month siege, the Taliban entered Kabul as the new rulers of Afghanistan.

One of their first acts was to castrate, shoot, and publicly hang Najibullah. Massoud pulled back to the Panjshir, blowing up the gorges behind him to block pursuit. Along with his allies from the Northern Alliance, he held out against the full might of the Taliban and its new Arab allies from Al Qaeda for the next five years. He finally met his end on September 9, 2001, when he was blown up by two Al Qaeda suicide bombers disguised as TV journalists. Two days later came the attacks on the World Trade Center and the Pentagon, which alerted the entire world to the dangers posed by Massoud's foes.[21]

Actually there had been many warning signs before—not only in 1979 but in subsequent years. Lebanon, in particular, was full of terrible portends if only someone could have read the signs. This was the petri dish where in the 1980s a new style of warfare was developed that utilized suicide bombers to inflict mass casualties—a tactic that Osama bin Laden would later harness with such terrifying ruthlessness.

60.

THE A TEAM

The "Party of God" in Lebanon, 1982–2006

A HARBINGER OF the troubles to come hit with explosive force on Sunday, October 23, 1983. That morning, in Beirut, Colonel Tim Geraghty awoke as usual at dawn, slipped on his camouflage uniform and combat boots, splashed cold water on his face, and walked downstairs to his operations center. A youthful-looking veteran of the Vietnam War and service with the CIA, handsome and square-jawed, he was the commander of the Twenty-Fourth Marine Amphibious Unit. Its 1,800 marines were part of a multinational peacekeeping mission dispatched to the Lebanese capital the preceding year.

The marines had come originally in August 1982 to oversee the evacuation of PLO fighters after the Israeli invasion. They returned in September, following the murder of Lebanon's Christian president, Bashir Gemayel, and the subsequent massacre committed by Christian Phalangist militia in two Palestinian refugee camps, Sabra and Shatila. The marines' ambiguous mission was to "establish a presence" and somehow ameliorate the agonies of Lebanon's civil war, then in its seventh year. They were supposed to be strictly impartial, but, because the United States supplied and trained the Christian-dominated Lebanese armed forces, the marines were increasingly drawn into the civil war on their side. Shiite and Druze militiamen who were fighting the Lebanese army began targeting the marines too.

Throughout September 1983 the marines suffered casualties from sniper and artillery attacks on their headquarters at Beirut airport. A tenuous cease-fire had taken hold, however, on September 26. When he got up on October 23, Geraghty found the situation "relatively quiet." Only a small number of cooks, sentries, and other marines were awake at 6:22 a.m.—the moment when, Geraghty recalled, "shards of glass from blown-out windows, equipment, manuals, and papers flew across my office." His ears still ringing, he grabbed his helmet and a .45 pistol to find out "what the hell" was going on. As soon as he stepped outside, he found himself "engulfed in a dense, gray fog of ash," of the kind that would be familiar two decades later to survivors of 9/11. Looking north he could see little through the "acrid fog." Standing next to him was a major who looked south and gasped, "My God, the BLT building is gone." More than three hundred marines and sailors had been billeted in the headquarters of the Battalion Landing Team, the ground-combat component of Geraghty's force. Now the whole building had been reduced to rubble.

There had been a few suicide car bomb attacks in Lebanon during the preceding two years, including a costly attack on the U.S. embassy in Beirut the prior spring, but nothing on this scale. A yellow Mercedes Benz truck traveling at more than thirty-five miles per hour had plowed straight through a barbed wire and concertina fence into the main entrance of the battalion headquarters. Packed with the explosive PETN (pentaerythritol tetranitrate) augmented with compressed butane, the truck went up in a "bright orange-yellow flash" with the equivalent of 12,000 pounds of TNT—one of the biggest nonnuclear blasts on record. Across Beirut people could hear the "horrendous dull roar" and see a mushroom cloud rising over the airport. The four-story building, made of steel-reinforced concrete, was lifted clear off its foundations before collapsing on itself.

Geraghty found a "heinous scene" reminiscent of "those black-and-white newsreels of Europe during World War II": "Mangled, dismembered corpses were strewed throughout the area in a grotesque fashion. One Marine's body, still within his sleeping bag, was impaled on a tree limb." As rescue crews arrived, they could hear "mournful moans beneath the ruins." There were so many dead that the marines ran out of body bags and had to request an emergency resupply.

In all 241 marines and sailors had been killed—the corps' greatest single-day loss since the Battle of Iwo Jima in 1945. At almost the same time, another truck bomb hit a building housing French paratroopers two miles away, killing 58 of them. Both attacks were claimed by a shadowy group calling itself Islamic Jihad. This was an ultra-radical breakaway faction of the Shiite Amal movement that would soon become known as Hezbollah. Its initial acts showed that this new movement was willing and able to operate on a more ambitious scale than previous terrorist groups, from the Ku Klux Klan and the Socialist Revolutionary Combat Organization to the PLO and the Baader-Meinhof Gang, which had been limited by either a lack of resources or a lack of will from killing too many people. Most of these past groups had calculated that if they went beyond a certain point they would spark a self-defeating backlash. From the outset, Hezbollah displayed fewer such compunctions—although more than Al Qaeda and its offshoots subsequently were to evince.[22]

✦ ✦ ✦

THE BIRTHPLACE OF this effective and remorseless new organization was Lebanon's Bekaa Valley, where 1,500 members of Iran's Revolutionary Guard Corps had been dispatched with Syrian cooperation to train militants who would fight the Israeli invaders. The Iranians found many volunteers eager to fight the "Zionists" and "infidels" from among the Lebanese Shia, a disenfranchised group that had been increasingly organized and radicalized since the early 1970s. Among the most prominent volunteers were a pair of young Shiite clerics, thirty-four-year-old Subhi Tufeili and thirty-year-old Abbas Musawi, both educated in the seminaries of Najaf, Iraq, where Ayatollah Khomeini had lived in exile until 1978. They would become Hezbollah's first two secretaries-general.[23]

Even more important to the organization's early development was its de facto director of military operations, Imad Mughniyeh. A terrorist prodigy born in south Lebanon and raised in the slums of Beirut, he was only twenty years old in 1982 but had already served in the PLO's elite Force 17. After the Israel Defense Forces evicted the PLO from Lebanon, he joined Hezbollah. Over the following two decades, he would work closely with Iranian operatives to carry out virtually all of Hezbollah's high-profile attacks, from suicide bombings to hostage takings. One of his Israeli adversaries called him "one of the most creative and brilliant minds I have ever come across." Prior to Osama bin Laden's emergence, Mughniyeh was the world's most wanted terrorist, but unlike Bin Laden he shunned the media spotlight. He even underwent plastic surgery to disguise his appearance. Marines saw him in 1982–83 directing attacks on their positions, but they did not know his name; they called him "Castro" because of his bushy beard. Hezbollah disclaimed any knowledge of his existence until his death in 2008, when he was celebrated as one of its revered *shaheeds* (martyrs) and honored with his own museum.[24]

This was symptomatic of the secretiveness that surrounded the entire organization; it would not admit its existence until the release in 1985 of a manifesto denouncing the "aggression and humiliation" inflicted by "America and its allies and the Zionist entity."[25] Hezbollah preferred to make its mark with spectacular attacks, especially suicide attacks, rather than bombastic statements. The very first target struck by suicide bombers in Lebanon was the Iraqi embassy; a 1981 attack killed 27 people. (Iraq was then at war with Iran, whose proxies were behind the blast.) The next year it was Israel's turn: in November 1982, a Peugeot full of 1,300 pounds of explosives rammed the Israeli headquarters in Tyre, Lebanon's southernmost city, killing 75 Israelis and perhaps 27 Lebanese prisoners. This was the first suicide attack on an Israeli target but far from the last. Almost exactly a year later, another Israeli headquarters in Tyre was struck by an explosives-packed Chevrolet pickup, killing 28 Israelis and 35 prisoners. The U.S. embassy in Beirut was another repeat target. It was first hit in April 1983 by a GMC pickup truck, killing 63 people. The following year, in September 1984, an attack on the U.S. embassy annex in a Beirut suburb, this time by a Chevrolet van, killed 24 more.

Such attacks made Hezbollah synonymous with suicide bombing—a tactic that had not been used by Palestinian terrorists of the 1970s or even by the Afghan mujahideen. Although employed sporadically by some terrorists of the past such as the turn-of-the-century Russian socialists and the medieval Assassins, suicide attacks had been associated most prominently with the Japanese kamikazes. Their use in the waning days of World War II highlights the fact that this is the weapon of the weak—and the fanatical. That made it a natural tactic for Hezbollah since the Shiites have always been weak by comparison with the Sunnis, who comprise 90 percent of the Muslim world. The very foundation of the Shiite faith is veneration of a *shaheed*, Muhammad's grandson, Hussein, slain in AD 680 by a caliph who rejected his claim to be the rightful heir to the Prophet. In the 1980s Iran made ample use of suicidal volunteers, the Basij, to fight the better-equipped Iraqi army. Tens of thousands of boys, some as young as ten, were given plastic keys to heaven and sent to run through minefields in human-wave attacks.[26]

Hezbollah brought the same ethos of martyrdom to its operations, even though the Koran expressly forbids suicide and the killing of innocents. "Every man, young and old, loves to blow himself up to tear apart the bodies of the invading, occupying Jews," Hezbollah's leader, Hassan Nasrallah, declared in 1998. The willingness of its members to forfeit their own lives, Hezbollah proclaimed, could allow it to vanquish better-armed but supposedly softer foes such as the "fearful and cowardly" Israelis—a refrain that would be echoed in later years by many other Islamist groups. Unlike many of its successors, however, Hezbollah limited its suicide attacks to military targets.[27]

Suicide attacks were only one weapon in Hezbollah's arsenal and became progressively less important as the group developed other capabilities. Indeed, as of 2011, Hezbollah had not mounted a single suicide operation since 1999. It also flirted early on with airplane hijacking before abandoning this tactic too. Its most famous skyjacking was the seizure of TWA flight 847 in Beirut in June 1985 which led to the murder of an American sailor, whose body was dumped on the tarmac.

A third tactic, popular with Hezbollah during its infancy but since discarded, was hostage taking. It began with the seizure in 1982 of David Dodge, acting president of the American University in Beirut. He was released 366 days later after having been smuggled in a crate to Tehran. Almost a hundred other Western hostages were seized in Lebanon in the following decade. The longest-held was the reporter Terry Anderson, who spent almost seven years in captivity (1985–91). He was luckier than two other hostages—CIA Station Chief William Buckley and Marine Lieutenant Colonel William "Rich" Higgins, who was part of a United Nations peacekeeping mission. Both were tortured and murdered.

These attacks were not simply the result of cruelty or blood lust. They were part of a calculated strategy designed to drive Israel, the United States, and other Western influences out of Lebanon, leaving Iran and its allies predominant. That strategy worked. Less than four months after the attack on their headquarters in Beirut, Ronald Reagan "redeployed" the marines out of Lebanon. To Colonel Geraghty's disgust, the United States never mounted any retaliation, refusing to join in French and Israeli air strikes on Iranian and Hezbollah positions in the Bekaa Valley. The hostage taking that followed exposed "the greatest Satan of all"[28]—the United States—to further humiliation when Reagan's aides secretly contrived to sell arms to Iran in return for their release. Three hostages were let go but more were taken, and meanwhile the administration was almost brought down by the Iran-contra scandal. Iran and its proxies finally gave up on hostage taking in 1992 following the death of Ayatollah Khomeini and the advent of a slightly more moderate regime in Tehran.[29]

✦ ✦ ✦

HEZBOLLAH'S ATTACKS ON Israel ("a cancerous growth that needs to be eradicated")[30] were even more pervasive and just as effective. The Shia had at first welcomed the Israeli invasion of Lebanon as a reprieve from the PLO's oppressive rule, but the Israelis overstayed their welcome in an unsuccessful attempt to establish a friendly, Christian-led government in Beirut. Hezbollah undoubtedly would have been formed even if the invasion had never occurred, but Israel's presence accelerated the militarization of the Shia. Hezbollah's 1982 suicide bombing of the Israeli headquarters in Tyre was just the start of a guerrilla campaign to drive the invaders out.

Israeli security forces responded by setting up roadblocks, rounding up and harshly interrogating suspects, destroying villages, bombing Hezbollah hideouts. But, as Israeli commanders later acknowledged, their heavy-handed approach only alienated the population—much as the French had done in Algeria and Indochina.[31] For all their efforts, Israel's feuding intelligence agencies could not crack the insurgent cells that sniped at, and bombed, their troops. Suicide bombers sometimes rammed Israeli convoys, but the "Islamic resistance" also used sophisticated roadside bombs provided by Iran that stymied Israeli jammers. In 1985, amid disaffection at home and mounting casualties (650 dead, 3,000 wounded),[32] the Israel Defense Forces pulled back to a security zone in the south of Lebanon. It was the first military defeat in Israel's history but not the last at Hezbollah's hands.

Israel's retreat emboldened Hezbollah to pursue its ultimate aims—the "final obliteration" of the "Zionist entity" and the creation in Lebanon of an Islamic republic modeled on Iran.[33] In seeking to accomplish its grandiose objectives, Hezbollah was able to reach far outside Lebanon, thanks to the assistance of Iran's Revolutionary Guards and its intelligence organizations. In 1992 their operatives blew up the Israeli embassy in Buenos Aires, killing 29 people. In 1994, another bomb tore apart a Jewish community center in Buenos Aires, killing 85 people. Hezbollah and the Revolutionary Guards were also widely suspected in the 1996 bombing of the Khobar Towers complex in Saudi Arabia, which killed 19 American airmen.[34] In addition Hezbollah provided training and support to numerous other terrorist groups, ranging from Al Qaeda in the 1990s to Iraq's Jaish al Mahdi after 2003. Many subsequent terrorist attacks, such as Al Qaeda's truck bombing of two U.S. embassies in Africa in 1998 and various roadside bombings of U.S. troops in Iraq after 2003, were modeled on the methods Hezbollah had pioneered in Lebanon.[35]

In fighting back, Israel claimed a notable success in 1992 when one of its Apache gunships blew up a car in which Hezbollah's secretary-general, Abbas Musawi, was traveling along with his family. Sixteen years later, in 2008, the onetime terrorist prodigy Imad Mughniyeh met his end in Damascus—killed, appropriately, by his favorite weapon, a car bomb, in an attack attributed to Mossad. Sometimes terrorist organizations are crippled by the removal of their leaders; that was the fate of Peru's Shining Path after the capture of Abimael Guzmán in 1992 and, in the more distant past, of the Lusitanian rebels against Roman rule in Spain after the death of Viriathus in 139 BC. Hezbollah was already so well established, however, that it would not be slowed by the elimination of Musawi and Mughniyeh.

Musawi was immediately succeeded by his corpulent protégé, Hassan Nasrallah, a thirty-two-year-old cleric from the slums of East Beirut who was the son of a fruit and vegetable seller but wore the black turban signifying descent from the Prophet Muhammad. Like Musawi, he had studied in

Najaf, where he had imbibed Khomeini's teachings. He revealed himself to be at least as shrewd, ruthless, and charismatic as his predecessor. He was even gifted with a sense of humor, willing to laugh at his speech impediment and other foibles—something it would have been hard to imagine Osama bin Laden doing.

Nasrallah won the devotion of his followers when his oldest son died in a 1997 clash with Israeli commandos. The sons of most Middle Eastern leaders were dissolute playboys. That Hezbollah leaders—like an earlier, somewhat heretical, Shiite terrorist, Hasan-i Sabah, founder of the Assassins—were willing to sacrifice their own offspring significantly enhanced their credibility.[36]

Nasrallah moved Hezbollah away from being purely a terrorist organization. Like Mao, Ho, and Castro, he recognized the importance of political action. Unlike them, he was even willing to compete in more or less free elections, although Nasrallah continued to use considerable coercion to turn out the vote and to silence critics. Over the objections of some members, Hezbollah became a political party that, starting in 1992, competed in Lebanon's elections and appointed cabinet ministers. It also expanded its role as a provider of social services to Lebanon's poor Shia, running a vast network of schools, hospitals, construction companies, loan providers, and other businesses funded mainly by Iran, which provided Hezbollah with an estimated $100 million a year.[37] It had its own version of the Boy Scouts, the Mahdi Scouts, and a Martyrs' Association to help the widows and orphans of suicide bombers. It even sold souvenirs to tourists such as the bracelet and lighter adorned with Nasrallah's image that this author purchased in the Bekaa Valley in 2009. More importantly it set up its own website, four newspapers, five radio stations, and a satellite television station, Al Manar (The Lighthouse), to get its message out. Amazingly, this nonstate group did a more effective job of spreading its message than its Zionist adversaries, who had the full resources of the Israeli state behind them.[38]

Its foray into politics did not, however, mean that Hezbollah was eschewing military force. Far from it. Lebanese politicians, generals, and journalists who stood in its way—or in the way of its patrons in Damascus and Tehran—were liable to meet a nasty end. The organization was suspected, most notoriously, in the massive 2005 car bombing that killed former Prime Minister Rafiq Hariri, who was intent on forcing Syrian troops out of Lebanon. But most of Hezbollah's martial energies went into the struggle against Israel, which it used to justify its refusal to disarm in common with other militias following the end of Lebanon's civil war in 1989.

✦ ✦ ✦

THE 1990S SAW many bloody guerrilla struggles around the globe. Any list of the grim lowlights would have to include the former Yugoslavia, where Orthodox Serbs were battling Muslim Bosnians, Catholic Slovenians, and other ethnic groups; Kashmir, where Pakistan-backed Muslim insurgents were resisting rule by Hindu-majority India; Chechnya, where Orthodox Russian soldiers were trying to suppress resistance from Muslim Chechens; Nagorno-Karabakh, where Armenian Christians were seeking autonomy from Muslim Azerbaijan; Somalia, where various clans and parties were fighting for control after the breakdown of central authority; and Rwanda, where hard-line Hutus were slaughtering the Tutsi minority and moderate Hutus. For all of their diversity, each of these conflicts was rooted in differences of ethnicity that were seized upon by nationalist ideologues and that were exacerbated in most cases, Rwanda and Somalia excepted, by differences of religion. It was such conflicts that led the political scientist Samuel Huntington in 1993 to claim that the world was seeing a "clash of civilizations." His thesis was overstated—there were at least as many clashes *within* civilizations as between them—but it gained widespread currency because it seemed to account for the prevalence of conflict in the first decade after the end of the Cold War. Certainly Lebanon fit the mold. In the 1990s, this small Mediterranean state was still recovering from its own civil war, and it was relatively peaceful by comparison with countries such as Rwanda, where over 800,000 people would die, but it too saw a struggle rooted in ethnicity and religion.

Throughout that decade Hezbollah waged a guerrilla war in southern Lebanon against the IDF and its 2,500 proxies, primarily Christians, in the South Lebanese Army. Hezbollah had only a few thousand full-time fighters, but that was enough to harass the larger and better-equipped IDF. Its low-level attacks in the southern "security zone," often employing roadside bombs, killed an average of 17 Israeli soldiers a year along with 30 South Lebanese Army soldiers[39] and sparked a potent antiwar movement in Israel led by the mothers of slain soldiers. Hezbollah knew it did not have to kill that many people, because it could magnify its attacks through its powerful propaganda arm. It cleverly nurtured antiwar sentiment in Israel by broadcasting images of dead or wounded soldiers followed by the Hebrew-language tagline "Who's Next?"[40]

In May 2000, Prime Minister Ehud Barak finally withdrew Israeli troops from Lebanon after eighteen years. Nasrallah promptly claimed a "great historic victory . . . achieved by martyrdom and blood." The lesson that Hezbollah and others drew—including the Palestinians, who soon thereafter launched the Second Intifada—was that, in Nasrallah's words, even "with all its atomic weapons, Israel is weaker than cobwebs."[41] Far from admitting that its raison d'être—opposing Israeli occupation—had been removed, Hezbollah made fresh demands for Shebaa Farms, a small sliver of the Israeli-occupied Golan Heights that had previously belonged to Syria, not Lebanon.

Long-simmering tensions with Israel boiled over in 2006, resulting in Israel's biggest war since the 1982 invasion of Lebanon. On July 12, Hezbollah operatives infiltrated northern Israel and ambushed two IDF Humvees, killing three soldiers and kidnapping two more. Two hours later, Israeli troops went in pursuit, but Hezbollah knocked out a Merkava tank with a mine and killed five more soldiers. Israel's prime minister, Ehud Olmert, responded with aerial and artillery strikes targeting Hezbollah infrastructure in southern Lebanon and on the outskirts of Beirut. Over a hundred high-rise buildings in the capital's suburbs were demolished, but most were unoccupied because of Israeli warnings. To increase the pressure on Lebanon to bring Hezbollah to heel (something that its government was too weak to do), the Israeli navy blockaded the Lebanese coastline while the Israeli air force bombed the Beirut airport. During the next month Israeli aircraft would drop more than 12,000 bombs and missiles while Israeli ground and naval forces would fire more than 150,000 rockets and artillery shells. Yet even all this firepower could not prevent Hezbollah from firing an unceasing barrage of 122-millimeter Katyusha rockets into northern Israel. These short-range, unguided missiles could be set up in minutes almost anywhere, making them impossible to knock out from the air.

In frustration the Israeli cabinet authorized a limited ground incursion, eventually amounting to 15,000 troops, but the IDF found Hezbollah a tougher-than-expected foe—quite a change from the Palestinian rock throwers and ineffectual Arab conscripts it had gotten used to fighting. Before the conflict Hezbollah had constructed an elaborate system of bunkers, tunnels, and safe houses linked together by a private communications system and stocked with ample food, water, and ammunition. Once the battle started, its fighters were able to resupply themselves and to maneuver effectively under fire: always the crucial tests of any fighting force. With no front to defend, they were able to attack Israeli troops from unexpected directions, knocking out tanks and troop concentrations with missiles ranging from the older Sagger to the more modern Kornet. Hezbollah even fired a C-802 antiship missile, Chinese-designed and Iranian-supplied, which inflicted significant damage on an Israeli missile boat ten miles offshore.

Hezbollah's ability to wage such sophisticated warfare led some analysts to suggest that it was at the forefront of a new trend—"hybrid warfare," which combines conventional and unconventional tactics.[42] There is something to this analysis, although one may doubt how new "hybrid warfare" actually is. Most successful insurgents of the past, whether the American colonists or Chinese Communists, combined guerrilla and conventional tactics. Many others, such as the FLN, IRA, and Vietminh/Vietcong, combined terrorism with guerrilla warfare as Hezbollah did.[43] Where Hezbollah really excelled, however, was not in ground combat but in manipulation of the news media.

The turning point of the war was the July 30 Israeli air strike on suspected Hezbollah positions in the town of Qana. An apartment building was flattened, leading to the death of seventeen children and eleven adults. (Initial casualty estimates were much higher.) The resulting footage of mangled bodies being pulled out of the wreckage, which Hezbollah made sure received widespread distribution, increased pressure on Israel to halt its offensive, which was said to be "disproportionate." Israelis could complain with some justification that there was no similar level of media scrutiny of counterinsurgency campaigns waged by nondemocratic powers such as Russia against Chechen separatists, Peru against the Shining Path, or Algeria against Muslim fundamentalists. But there was not much Israel could do about the existence of this double standard—or about the fact that, as a small, isolated state dependent on American support, it was especially vulnerable to international pressure. This was a weapon against which Israel's Merkava tanks and F-16 fighters were powerless. Like the Greeks in the 1820s, the Cubans in the 1890s, the Algerians in the 1950s, and the Palestinians in the 1980s, Hezbollah had mastered jujitsu information operations, turning its enemy's strength into a disadvantage in the battle for global sympathy. The efficacy of such efforts was all the greater because of the spread of the Internet and satellite television.

On August 14, 2006, a cease-fire went into effect. Israeli troops pulled back to their own border and Hezbollah filtered back into southern Lebanon. Thirty-four days of war had resulted in the death of 119 Israeli soldiers and 42 Israeli civilians. A total of 1,100 Lebanese civilians were killed; estimates of Hezbollah fatalities ranged from 250 (its own figure) to 650 (the Israeli figure), in either case only a small portion of Hezbollah's total force of at least 15,000.[44]

✦ ✦ ✦

IN SOME WAYS Hezbollah emerged chastened from this conflict. In December 2008–January 2009, when Hamas, a Sunni movement inspired by Hezbollah's example, fought its own war against Israel in the Gaza Strip, Hezbollah prudently refrained from establishing a second front in the north, suggesting that it had no desire for a repeat of 2006. By most measures, however, Hezbollah emerged stronger from the second Lebanon war. By 2010, having rearmed with Syrian and Iranian help, Nasrallah claimed to have 40,000 missiles, compared with just 13,000 at the start of the 2006 campaign.[45] Hezbollah also spent hundreds of millions of dollars to rebuild war-damaged areas, thus strengthening its hold on the Shiite population. In 2011 Hezbollah and its allies toppled Lebanon's Sunni, pro-Western prime minister, Saad Hariri, and replaced him with a politician more to their liking.

Hezbollah's ascendance was symptomatic of Israel's inability over numerous campaigns since the 1960s to decisively defeat guerrilla foes, who could not be vanquished as swiftly or completely as regular Arab armies had been. In many ways Israel's problems were analogous to those of the United States in Vietnam, Iraq, and Afghanistan, France in Algeria and Indochina, and Britain in Cyprus and Aden. The difference, of course, was that Israel could not simply bring its forces home without worrying about the consequences of leaving unrepentant enemies only a few miles from its population centers.

To defend itself, Israel regularly launched punitive strikes that too often only strengthened the relationship between terrorist organizations and the civilians among whom they operated. Air strikes could damage movements such as Hezbollah or Hamas but could not prevent their regeneration. That would have required reoccupation, which Israel hesitated to do because it had no desire for another long and costly occupation of Arab territory; imperialism was no longer an acceptable option in the modern West of which Israel considers itself a part. Israel had some success in ending the terrorist threat from the West Bank, because it did undertake a partial reoccupation during the Second Intifada and because of the serendipitous emergence after Arafat's death in 2004 of a more moderate Palestinian Authority leadership under Mahmoud Abbas and Salam Fayyad. But no such regime appeared in Lebanon, where an increasingly radicalized Shiite community was on the ascent. Thus the best Israel could hope for was an uneasy truce that could be broken at any moment.

✦ ✦ ✦

DURING ITS FIRST quarter century of existence, Hezbollah had amply lived up to the description of a former American official who suggested in 2003, "Hezbollah may be the 'A-Team of Terrorists' and maybe al-Qaeda is actually the 'B' team."[46] Certainly Al Qaeda could not match Hezbollah's quasi-conventional military capabilities, its wholly owned radio and television networks, and its ability to dominate and administer a substantial geographic region. Nor could most other Islamist groups. The vast majority of Islamic insurgents, like the vast majority of non-Islamic insurgents, failed miserably. They were repressed with considerable bloodshed in Algeria, Egypt, Morocco, Syria, Saudi Arabia, and other Middle Eastern lands by unelected rulers who, unlike their Israeli or American counterparts, were largely impervious to public opinion. The war in Algeria was particularly ugly, leading to the death of at least 100,000 people in the 1990s.[47] Of course, as we have seen, even the most illiberal counterinsurgents could still lose if they aroused the ire of the entire population, as the Nazis did in Yugoslavia or the Soviets in Afghanistan. But the most extreme Islamist groups never came close to claiming majority support, and their proclivity for targeting civilians, many of them Muslims, cost them in the court of public opinion. Thus Arab dictators were able to maintain enough legitimacy to crush armed Islamist uprisings, if not the more broad-based popular insurrections that broke out during the 2011 "Arab Spring."

Islamists, predictably, fared no better in areas where Muslims were in the minority. From East Asia to Western Europe, from North America to South Asia, radicals plotted against the state with little success. Even Russia managed to defeat an insurgency in Chechnya, which declared independence in 1991. The Russians invaded in 1994 and pulled out in 1996, stymied by Chechen guerrillas who, like their nineteenth-century predecessors, resisted to the death. But the Russian army returned in 1999 to subdue the breakaway province using scorched-earth tactics. An estimated 100,000 Chechens were killed out of a prewar population of just a million—a death rate considerably greater than that suffered by Yugoslavia in World War II, if still less than that of Haiti during its War of Independence. Perhaps 20,000 Russian soldiers also perished.

Russia's success in Chechnya, along with Sri Lanka's success a few years later against the Tamil Tigers, showed that even in the twenty-first century a brutal approach could work as long as the counterinsurgents did not care about world opinion and were operating on their home soil, where they enjoyed a de facto level of legitimacy that Israel could never acquire in Lebanon or France in Algeria. Such a strategy could be stymied only if outside powers came to the rebels' aid—as occurred not only in Afghanistan in the 1980s but also in Bosnia in 1995, Kosovo in 1999, Iraqi Kurdistan in 1991, and Libya in 2011, but not in Chechnya or Sri Lanka.[48]

Failing to overthrow their own regimes, Islamic revolutionaries from all over the world had to seek refuge in the 1990s in a handful of sympathetic, virtually ungoverned places, notably Somalia, Sudan, Yemen, Pakistan's tribal territories, and Afghanistan. Out of such unpromising conditions arose a terrorist group that would soon eclipse Hezbollah in notoriety, if not in effectiveness.

61.

THE TERRORIST INTERNATIONALE

Osama bin Laden and Al Qaeda, 1988–2011

AL QUDS AL ARABI, an Arabic-language newspaper in London, published on February 23, 1998, a statement it had received by fax. It was headlined, "Declaration of the World Islamic Front for Jihad against the Jews and the Crusaders," and it was signed by five men—two Egyptians, including a physician named Ayman al-Zawahiri, one Pakistani, one Bangladeshi, and, above them all, a Saudi styled as "Shaykh Usamah Bin-Muhammad Bin-Ladin." In rich, almost poetic Arabic interspersed with quotations from the Koran and Muslim scholars, the authors laid out what would become a familiar litany of grievances against the "crusader-Zionist alliance," which, in the wake of the 1991 Gulf War, they held responsible for "occupying the lands of Islam in the holiest of places, the Arabian Peninsula, plundering its riches, dictating to its rulers, humiliating its people, terrorizing its neighbors, and turning its bases in the Peninsula into a spearhead through which to fight the neighboring Muslim peoples." Since the Americans had declared "war on God, his messenger, and Muslims." the authors declared, they were issuing a fatwa, a legal ruling, that "to kill the Americans and their allies—civilians and military—is an individual duty for every Muslim."[49]

Even then, Osama bin Laden was hardly unknown in the West. The CIA had already formed a unit to track him: Alec Station. He had already been mentioned sixteen times in the *New York Times*, beginning in 1994.[50]

No stranger to American television, he had even been interviewed by CNN the preceding year, and he would do an interview with ABC News that year. But he was invariably described as a bankroller rather than a practitioner of terrorism. His organization, Al Qaeda, which had been formed in 1988, was still obscure. In 1998 Bin Laden was living in Taliban-controlled Afghanistan. He was known to harbor a grudge against the United States, which he held responsible for expelling him from Saudi Arabia, but he was hardly seen as being in a position to do much about it. His declaration of war against the world's mightiest nation was judged so inconsequential that it was not covered in a single American newspaper or magazine. It was as if a wild-eyed street-corner preacher had declared his intention to fight city hall.

Just six months later the world would have cause to reassess its opinion of Bin Laden. On August 7, 1998, Al Qaeda suicide bombers detonated explosives-filled trucks in front of the U.S. embassies in Kenya and Tanzania, killing 213 people, including 12 Americans. The Clinton administration now took Bin Laden seriously enough that on August 20, American warships fired dozens of Tomahawk cruise missiles against Al Qaeda training camps in eastern Afghanistan as well as against a pharmaceutical factory in Sudan wrongly suspected of manufacturing chemical weapons for Al Qaeda. The missiles, however, killed few fighters. Bin Laden escaped unscathed with his stature enhanced. This only increased his contempt for the United States ("too cowardly and too fearful to meet the young people of Islam face to face") and confirmed to him the wisdom of the strategic choice he had made. In a fatwa released two years earlier, in 1996, he had written that, "due to the imbalance of power between our armed forces and the enemy forces," the most "suitable means of fighting" was to use "fast moving, light forces that work under complete secrecy"—"in other words to initiate a guerrilla warfare."[51]

Bin Laden was hardly novel in his determination to use asymmetric means to fight a more powerful foe: this was, as we have seen, an impulse as old as the state itself. Nor was his religious fanaticism rare among irregular warriors: the first terrorist groups, after all, were the Jewish Zealots and the Muslim Assassins. However, most guerrilla and terrorist groups in the past had confined their attacks to a single country or group of countries adjacent to one another and had generally modulated their violence to avoid a devastating backlash. Bin Laden had grander ambitions—he aimed at nothing less than "destroying" the United States as a prelude to toppling its allied states throughout the Middle East and ultimately making the "word of Allah . . . supreme" throughout the world.[52] By 1998 Bin Laden's organization had already been associated with attacks in Algeria, Bosnia, Ethiopia, Kenya, Somalia, and Tanzania, and it was just getting started. In years to come few corners of the world would be spared the predations of jihadists inspired, trained, funded, directed, or armed—sometimes all of the above—by Al Qaeda.

The trend toward transnational terrorism had already been evident among the anarchist groups of the late nineteenth century and the leftist groups of the 1970s, but Al Qaeda took this tendency to new heights thanks to its skill in utilizing common yet sophisticated technologies. The passenger aircraft made it easy to travel the world. The telephone, fax, satellite television, and eventually the cell phone and Internet made it easy to raise funds, spread propaganda, recruit and deploy followers. The computer made it easy to run a complex organization. And cheap, reliable, mass-produced weapons such as the AK-47, rocket-propelled grenade, and, above all, explosives made it easy to kill. Bin Laden may have advocated a return to a medieval brand of Islam, but he showed a genius for using sophisticated technology and management techniques to marshal the first truly global insurgency. And he brought to his side many similar men who, like him, had little religious training but were well versed in technical subjects and familiar with the ways of the modern world. Like drug traffickers, computer hackers, and other international criminals, they represented the dark side of globalization in the twenty-first century.

✦ ✦ ✦

OSAMA BIN LADEN'S rise to become the global face of terror—eclipsing earlier celebrities such as Carlos the Jackal, Abu Nidal, and even Yasser Arafat—was, to say the least, improbable. He was a shy child, soft-spoken and polite, forever in the shadow of his more dynamic and outgoing older brothers—and there were lots of them. Osama's father, Muhammad, was a one-eyed Yemeni immigrant who had come to Saudi Arabia with nothing and built the kingdom's largest construction company with the patronage of the royal family. He had no fewer than fifty-four children from twenty-two wives. Osama was the eighteenth son, born in 1957 to a simple Syrian girl. Muhammad divorced her two years later and conveniently married her off, as was his wont, to one of his executives. Osama grew up in awe of his father, whom he seldom saw. After the patriarch's death in an airplane crash in 1967, leadership of the clan fell to Osama's oldest brother, Salem, who was everything he was not—an irreligious, fun-loving, guitar-playing jokester who liked to spend time in Europe and America.

Osama grew up far removed from this jet-setter lifestyle. He lived in a staid middle-class household with his mother and stepfather in the Red Sea port of Jeddah. Even as a youngster Osama was religious but not to an outlandish degree by Saudi standards. He prayed five times a day but also watched television, loved to ride horses, and played soccer. As he grew older he became more puritanical, refusing to watch movies, listen to music, or take pictures: all activities he deemed "un-Islamic." Unlike many of his siblings who were educated abroad, Osama attended the private Al Thagr School in Jeddah, where he was an average student, followed by economics studies at Jeddah's King Abdul Aziz University, from which he never graduated. In college he was influenced by the radical writings of Sayyid Qutb, the Egyptian apostle of Islamism who had been executed by the secular regime of Gamal Abdel Nasser in 1966, and whose brother was on the faculty.

In 1974, at seventeen, Bin Laden married a fifteen-year-old Syrian cousin. In subsequent years he would, in emulation of his father and in accordance with the teachings of the Koran, take more wives, including two teachers with doctorates. (He told wife number one that he was acting altruistically so that he could "have many children for Islam.") In all he would produce at least twenty children. His family lived in a bizarre household where air conditioners and refrigerators were forbidden. The abstemious Bin Laden was happy to eat meager fare and wear drab clothes and expected his family to do likewise. They were forbidden American soft drinks, indeed all cold beverages, along with toys, sweets, and even prescription drugs, forcing his asthmatic children to sneak inhalers. Long hikes through the desert with little or no water were mandatory for the boys to toughen them up for the jihad. The girls were secluded at home with their mothers and not allowed to venture out without a male guardian. In this joyless household even jokes and laughter were forbidden; children caught laughing could expect a caning from the stern paterfamilias.

The major turning point in Bin Laden's life occurred in 1979 with the Soviet invasion of Afghanistan. His first wife recalled that her "husband's heart was burned to a crisp" by the suffering inflicted by the Red Army. He began to travel to Pakistan to provide funding and support to the mujahideen. At the time he was active in his family's construction business; like his father, he was known for getting his hands dirty alongside his men. But in the 1980s he began to carve out a separate identity in the anti-Soviet jihad.

In Pakistan he met Abdullah Azzam, an older Palestinian cleric who was one of the founders of the Muslim Brotherhood's Palestinian branch, Hamas. No doubt eager to gain access to the Saudi's fortune, Azzam became a mentor to Bin Laden. Together in 1985 they created the Services Office, the precursor to Al Qaeda, to help Arab volunteers fight the Soviets. The Services Office published a slick magazine, *Jihad*, and raised funds all over the world, including in the United States, thus creating the networks Al Qaeda would later utilize. There is no evidence that Bin Laden got any support from the U.S. government, but he did have connections with Saudi intelligence, which apparently used him to funnel aid to the *muj*.

Not content to be simply a fund-raiser or an armchair philosopher such as Prince Kropotkin, the anarchist sage, Bin Laden began to venture into Afghanistan. In 1986 he established a base for fifty or sixty Arab fighters near the village of Jaji in eastern Afghanistan. This became known as al Masada (the Lions' Den). The following year he participated in a weeklong battle, avidly covered by the Arabic press, in which the Arabs fought bravely before retreating. In 1989 he took to the field again to lead his Arab volunteers to capture Jalalabad from Najibullah's forces. This attack was a costly fiasco that demonstrated Bin Laden's limitations as a battlefield commander. But it did not dent his carefully nurtured reputation as a fearless warrior for the faith who had voluntarily abandoned the easy life of a wealthy Saudi. Like Arafat, Bin Laden knew how to turn battlefield defeats into propaganda victories.

As the decade progressed Azzam and Bin Laden drifted apart. Azzam opposed the idea of a separate Arab fighting force, and he admired Ahmad Shah Massoud; Bin Laden hated Massoud and was close to his fundamentalist enemies. Azzam was active in the founding of Al Qaeda al-Askariya ("the military base") in Bin Laden's Peshawar home in 1988; its goal was to keep "the flame of jihad" alive after the end of the Soviet war in Afghanistan. But in 1989 Azzam was blown up in Peshawar by unknown assailants.

By then Bin Laden had come under the influence of a new father figure—Ayman al-Zawahiri, a brilliant surgeon from a prominent Egyptian family who in 1973 had founded a group called Islamic Jihad. He had been imprisoned for three years following Anwar Sadat's assassination in 1981, which his group had helped to orchestrate. The torture he experienced behind bars further embittered and radicalized him. Whereas Azzam opposed killing civilians and wanted to concentrate on expelling foreign invaders from Muslim lands, Zawahiri sought to overthrow moderate Muslim regimes and to kill Muslim "apostates." Azzam's death, in which Zawahiri was widely suspected, removed a major moderating element from Bin Laden's life. So did the death of Salem, Osama's older brother and head of the Bin Laden family. He perished in an accident in Texas in 1988 while piloting his own ultralight airplane.

With Azzam and Salem out of the way, Bin Laden became for the first time a leader in his own right—not just the financier but the absolute boss of Al Qaeda. At six feet five, he towered literally and figuratively above his growing entourage. All Al Qaeda members had to swear personal loyalty to the Saudi. Even Zawahiri, who has been described as the real brains of the operation, showed him deference, if only because he was dependent on Bin Laden's financial largesse.

✦ ✦ ✦

By 1989 Bin Laden was back in Saudi Arabia, where he was feted by the government as a military hero. The following year he went from idol to outcast. He turned against the royal family after Saddam Hussein invaded Kuwait and the king rebuffed his offer to deploy his "Afghan Arabs" to defend the kingdom. Instead the Saudis turned to U.S. troops. The presence of so many "unbelievers" on holy soil was anathema to Bin Laden even though his family company received lucrative contracts to support the U.S. military. His growing public criticism of the royals forced him to relocate in 1992 to Sudan, which was ruled by an Islamist regime. Here he combined his jihadism with business, setting up paramilitary training camps along with companies to grow sunflowers, build roads, and make leather jackets, among other enterprises.

The first terrorist attack ever attributed to Al Qaeda occurred in, of all places, Italy in 1991 when one of Bin Laden's followers stabbed the exiled, seventy-seven-year-old king of Afghanistan but failed to kill him. Another Al Qaeda plot the following year was not much more successful—bombs were set off in two Aden hotels frequented by U.S. troops, but the only victims were a tourist and a hotel worker. Other schemes worked better. Bin Laden was later to brag of sending his men to help train and support Somali tribesmen who in 1993 ambushed a U.S. Special Operations force in Mogadishu, bringing down two Black Hawk helicopters and killing nineteen Americans. In 1995 Bin Laden's followers were linked to a car bomb that exploded in front of a Saudi National Guard office in Riyadh, killing seven people, including five Americans. There was also suspicion of Al Qaeda involvement in the 1996 bombing at the Khobar Towers complex in Saudi Arabia that killed nineteen Americans. (Bin Laden praised both attacks in his homeland but denied responsibility.) Egypt was another major target: in 1995 Islamists bombed the Egyptian embassy in Pakistan and tried to assassinate Egyptian President Hosni Mubarak while he was visiting Ethiopia.

As a result of these high-profile attacks, Bin Laden acquired such a notorious reputation that Saudi Arabia stripped him of his citizenship and Sudan expelled him in 1996. The only country that would accept him was Afghanistan, then being taken over by the Taliban. Al Qaeda did not require the same sort of state support that other terrorist groups, ranging from the PLO to Hezbollah, had received. Rather than seeking out strong states that could support it, Al Qaeda looked for weak states that could not resist its encroachments. By the late 1990s no state in the world was weaker than Afghanistan, which had been devastated by almost constant warfare since 1978.

✦ ✦ ✦

Here, in one of the world's most primitive places, Bin Laden had to rebuild his organization. The task was made all the more difficult because he had lost millions of dollars in Sudan and his own family had cut him off. Never as rich as publicly rumored, he had received roughly a million dollars a year from his family since 1970, but after 1993 or 1994 he was on his own. From then on he would have to raise funds from wealthy Gulf businessmen and Muslim charities. Sometimes he and his family did not have enough to eat (they would subsist on a diet of eggs, bread, and pomegranates "caked with sand"), but he would ensure that the jihad was funded.

The FBI later estimated that Al Qaeda raised $30 million a year prior to 9/11. While defending against terrorism is costly, carrying it out is not; the entire 9/11 operation was said to cost less than half a million dollars. Other operations were even cheaper—the estimated cost of the USS *Cole* attack in 2000 was $50,000; the 2004 Madrid bombings, only $10,000.

Most of Al Qaeda's funds went to support training camps in Afghanistan where thousands of jihadists came for instruction. Bin Laden provided his recruits with lodging, food, salaries, weapons, vehicles, training manuals. He even produced an *Encyclopedia of Jihad* with thousands of pages of advice on how to carry out effective attacks. To manage this growing enterprise—Jihad Inc.—Bin Laden appointed managers and set up computerized personnel and payroll systems reminiscent of any other start-up company. Journalist Peter Bergen has called Al Qaeda "the most bureaucratic terrorist organization in history."

Jihadists eager for induction into Al Qaeda camps had to fill out lengthy questionnaires, as if they were applying for college, asking them not only standard background questions ("Have you worked previously in a military field?" "What are your hobbies?") but also "How much of the Koran have you memorized?" The training curriculum, set up with the aid of an Egyptian-born former sergeant in the U.S. Army, covered a wide variety of weapons—from Soviet DShK machine guns to Israeli-made Uzi submachine guns. Recruits even learned to drive tanks. But, although some Al Qaeda fighters took part in quasi-conventional operations against the Northern Alliance in Afghanistan, most would fight in ways far removed from conventional tank battles.

Al Qaeda came to specialize in spectacular "martyrdom" operations such as the small-boat attack that killed seventeen sailors aboard the USS

Cole in Aden harbor in 2000. This, like the 1998 Africa embassy bombings and the 2001 attacks on the World Trade Center and the Pentagon, was an operation planned and executed by "Al Qaeda central." Many more attacks were carried out more or less independently by jihadist operatives inspired or trained but not directed by Bin Laden. This trend became especially pronounced after 9/11, when Al Qaeda leaders were put on the run, but even before then most graduates of its camps never joined Al Qaeda. That was a privilege accorded only to a few hundred carefully screened "brothers." Most of the jihadists who trained in the camps signed on with loosely affiliated organizations such as Jemaah Islamiyah in Indonesia, Harakat ul-Mujahideen in Kashmir, or the Armed Islamic Group in Algeria.

To foster a worldwide campaign, Bin Laden mounted an ambitious propaganda effort, even sitting down for interviews with ABC, CNN, and Al Jazeera. He would distribute video and audio messages through his in-house production arm, Al Sahab (the Clouds), while his followers set up thousands of jihadist websites. Bin Laden, who obsessively monitored the BBC even from remote hideouts, was convinced that "the media war" was one of the "strongest methods" of promoting jihadism—"its ratio may reach 90 percent of the total preparation for the battles." Few if any previous insurgents, save perhaps for Yasser Arafat, had put quite so much emphasis on the propaganda battle. This may be explained by the growing ubiquity of the Internet, cellular phones, and satellite television, whose potential Bin Laden intuitively grasped, and also by Al Qaeda's relative lack of conventional military capabilities, which meant that it had no choice but to emphasize the "information war" to fill the space between its relatively infrequent attacks.

Al Qaeda's foot soldiers tended to be middle-class but often felt alienated from their society. Some were Muslim immigrants, or children of immigrants, living in Europe. Others lived in stultifying dictatorships such as Saudi Arabia, Egypt, and Syria. Like most terrorists, they were motivated by what the researcher Louise Richardson calls the "Three R's"—revenge, renown, reaction. They were seeking *revenge* for the wrongs the West had supposedly inflicted on Muslims stretching back to the Crusades; *renown* for themselves in an attempt to give meaning to an otherwise insignificant existence; and to provoke a *reaction* from their adversaries.

Many believed that the best way to achieve all three goals would be to carry out a "martyrdom operation." There was keen competition within the ranks for the honor of becoming a *shaheed*. Al Qaeda leaders did not, however, voluntarily sacrifice themselves or their children. They believed that they had to remain alive to secure victory over God's enemies. To achieve this goal, influential jihadist thinkers, little known in the West, such as Abu Ubayd al-Qurashi, Yusuf al-Ayiri, and Abu Musab al-Suri, made a close study of military strategy and history. Their writings were sprinkled with references not only to Clausewitz and Sun Tzu but also to Mao, Giap, Guevara, Marighella, Taber, and other leftist proponents of irregular warfare. They were enthralled by the success of insurgents in expelling superpowers from Vietnam and Afghanistan, Lebanon and Somalia. This gave them an exaggerated regard for guerrilla and terrorist tactics, which over the years have failed far more than not.

Bin Laden became convinced that the United States was a "paper tiger," effeminate and cowardly, a foe that could be brought low with a few sharp blows. He decided to make the "far enemy"—the United States—the focus of Al Qaeda attacks, sure that once its power had been broken, "all the components of the existing Arab and Islamic regimes will fall as well," and then he would be able to establish a fundamentalist caliphate across the Middle East. This turned out to be a gross strategic miscalculation. Bin Laden exaggerated the extent to which the United States propped up "apostate" regimes in the Middle East; they were kept in power more by their secret police than by their alliances with the United States. Notwithstanding the failure of earlier Islamist uprisings, he would have been better advised to fight Arab regimes directly without provoking the United States. That approach worked for the Islamists who took over Iran, Afghanistan, and Sudan in violent upheavals and, via the electoral process, Turkey, Tunisia, and Egypt. But Bin Laden had bigger horizons and less awareness of his own limits. A combination of shrewdness and hubris led him to stage the most deadly terrorist attack of all time.[53]

✦ ✦ ✦

THE IDEA FOR the "planes operation" originated with Khalid Sheikh Mohammed, one of numerous terrorist entrepreneurs drawn by Bin

Laden's charisma and resources. He was an engineer of Pakistani origin who grew up in Kuwait and was educated in the United States. He had joined the Muslim Brotherhood at sixteen and became active in the struggle against the Soviets in Afghanistan. He would later fight in Bosnia in 1992. He was tangentially linked to the truck bombing of the World Trade Center in 1993, which was masterminded by his nephew Ramzi Yousef, who had trained in an Al Qaeda camp in Afghanistan. That attack killed six people but failed to topple the Twin Towers. In 1994, while they were living in Manila, he and Yousef talked about blowing up twelve American airliners over the Pacific. Two years later he wound up in Afghanistan where he presented Bin Laden with a plan to hijack ten American passenger aircraft, crash nine of them into prominent buildings, and land the tenth plane at an airport where, after having killed all of the adult male passengers, he would emerge to deliver an anti-American diatribe to the television cameras.

Like a good CEO, Bin Laden refined his subordinate's overly ambitious proposal into a more practical plot: one that incidentally would not allow Mohammed to usurp Bin Laden's self-appointed role as the face of global jihad. He then supplied money and men to carry out the scheme. So it was that on September 11, 2001, nineteen men hijacked four aircraft using box cutters—a particularly inventive touch that showed the meticulous surveillance and planning behind the operation. By then airplane hijackings had lost their shock value, but crashing the hijacked airliners into their targets, rather than landing, as at Entebbe, to open negotiations, was a savage twist that riveted the entire world in a way that no act of terrorism had done since the 1972 Munich Olympics.[54]

The immediate results of the operation exceeded even Bin Laden's expectations. He had envisaged at most the destruction of three or four floors, not of the entire Twin Towers. The death toll of nearly three thousand exceeded that inflicted in the last major enemy attack on American soil, at Pearl Harbor on December 7, 1941, which had been undertaken by a major nation-state not by a small nongovernmental organization. Bin Laden was particularly gleeful about the financial costs of the attack, estimated at $500 billion; the former economics major imagined that he could bankrupt the world's wealthiest country.[55]

Bin Laden was soon to learn that the United States was not as weak as he had imagined. Although he occasionally had said that he welcomed an invasion of Afghanistan as a way to bleed the United States in a "long guerrilla war . . . like we did against the Soviets,"[56] he had done little to prepare for what actually occurred. Within weeks of 9/11 a small number of CIA operatives and Special Forces arrived in Afghanistan with suitcases full of cash and high-tech communications equipment to galvanize the Northern Alliance. By early December the Taliban had fallen and Al Qaeda had been routed by Northern Alliance attacks backed by American airpower. Bin Laden and Zawahiri were able to escape into Pakistan thanks to the blunders of American military commanders and their bosses in Washington who did not send enough troops to trap them in the Tora Bora mountains outside Jalalabad in November–December 2001. Still, many of their colleagues were caught or killed. Many more would be hunted down in the years ahead, including eventually Bin Laden himself.

To say that the Bush administration had been caught off guard by the 9/11 attacks was an understatement. Still focused on great-power rivalries and rogue states such as Iran and Iraq, the president and his aides had discounted intelligence that suggested that the greatest danger to America was posed by a stateless terrorist network. In a sense, Bush and his advisers were victims of conventional historiography, which emphasized conventional conflicts among states while neglecting the ubiquitous and important role of guerrilla warfare in the unfolding of history.

After 9/11 Bush desperately played catch-up. As part of the "global war on terror," the president and Congress created new domestic-security agencies and knocked down many of the bureaucratic barriers that had prevented cooperation between law enforcement and intelligence. More controversially Bush authorized a number of steps that went well beyond the bounds of traditional law enforcement, including the use of "enhanced interrogation techniques" on high-value detainees such as Khalid Sheikh Mohammed, who was waterboarded 183 times after being arrested in Pakistan in 2003; the warrantless wiretapping of those who might have terrorist connections in the United States; the "rendition" of detainees back to their countries of origins even though some of those countries (e.g., Egypt, Algeria, and Jordan) were notorious for their use of torture; the indefinite detention without trial of eight hundred suspected terrorists at Guantánamo Bay and at CIA-operated "black sites"; the creation of military tribunals to try terrorist suspects; and the targeted assassination of Al Qaeda leaders with Predator drones in countries such as Pakistan and Yemen.[57]

Such measures were denounced by civil libertarians and, once the immediate post-9/11 fear had abated, many of them were curtailed through a combination of congressional and court action. But, for all the criticism of Bush's policies, his actions were actually restrained by comparison with steps taken by other countries, even democracies such as Britain, France, and Israel, when they had faced their own terrorist threats. They were restrained, too, by comparison with the curtailments of civil liberties by Abraham Lincoln in the Civil War, Woodrow Wilson in World War I, and Franklin D. Roosevelt in World War II. Even if one assumes that all "stress techniques" were torture, as many undoubtedly were, they were utilized on only twenty-eight detainees in carefully monitored circumstances to ensure no lasting physical harm. Compare that with the thousands tortured far more savagely by the French in Algeria and often killed afterward. Rightly or wrongly, the United States was held in the court of global opinion to a standard attained by few other states that had battled large-scale terrorism. The inarticulate Bush, unfortunately, did a poor job of explaining and defending American actions. For all its faults, however, the Bush administration also did serious damage to the jihadists. The Al Qaeda strategist Abu Musab al-Suri lamented in 2004, "The Americans have eliminated the majority of the armed jihadist movement's leadership, infrastructure, supporters and friends."[58]

Jihadists were able to stage further attacks after 9/11 on a smaller if still horrific scale. Some of the more prominent examples included the 2002 bombing of a Bali nightclub (202 dead), the 2004 bombing of the Madrid train system (191 dead), the 2005 bombing of the London subway system (52 dead), and the 2008 shootings in Mumbai (163 dead). But with some minor exceptions (the Madrid attack contributed to Spain's exit from Iraq), such attacks did nothing to advance the agenda of Al Qaeda and its associated groups. Quite the contrary. By slaughtering so many innocents—including so many Muslims—jihadists turned Muslim opinion against them and spurred a global crackdown against them. Even Saudi Arabia, which had hitherto been apathetic in the struggle against the Islamists, got tough following the 2003 bombings in Riyadh that killed 35 people. The United States was able to knit together an effective global coalition to counter Al Qaeda because it was seen as a threat to a growing number of countries. International cooperation foiled numerous plots, including an ambitious attempt to bring down seven airliners over the Atlantic in the summer of 2006 using liquid explosives. Many other schemes, such as the attempted shoe bombing of a flight from Paris to Miami in 2001 or the attempted car bombing of Times Square in 2010, were undone by sheer incompetence or bad luck.

Before 9/11 terrorists had generally refrained from inflicting massive civilian casualties because they realized that such attacks could backfire. As the terrorism analyst Brian Jenkins wrote in the 1970s, "Terrorism is theater, terrorists want a lot of people watching, not a lot of people dead."[59] Al Qaeda and other Islamist organizations violated that dictum and paid the price in lost support. The Chechen rebels offered a case in point: they forfeited all sympathy after their 2002 hostage taking in a Moscow theater, which left 169 dead, and their 2004 hostage taking at a school in Beslan, in North Ossetia, which left 331 dead, more than half of them children.

The same phenomenon—nihilistic violence turning counterproductive—was evident in Algeria and Egypt in the 1990s and in Iraq in the 2000s. In Algeria and Egypt, Islamist uprisings were suppressed by homegrown military regimes. In Iraq, however, the post-Saddam state was too weak to respond effectively. The job of battling insurgents was left to the "infidel" army of a foreign superpower that had done little to prepare for guerrilla warfare since its humiliating defeat in Vietnam.

62.

CARNAGE IN MESOPOTAMIA

Al Qaeda in Iraq since 2003

It began in August 2003—Iraq's descent into hell. On August 7 a truck bomb outside the Jordanian embassy in Baghdad killed nineteen people. On August 12 a suicide bomber drove a cement mixer loaded with explosives into the United Nations headquarters in Baghdad. Among the twenty-two dead was the UN's senior representative in Iraq, the popular Brazilian diplomat Sergio Vieira de Mello. Worst of all was the attack on August 29 in Najaf. A parked vehicle, most likely a Toyota Land Cruiser, exploded at around 2 p.m. just outside the Imam Ali mosque, the most sacred shrine in the entire Shiite faith. Noon prayers were just ending. Ayatollah Mohammed Baqir al-Hakim, one of the country's leading Shiite clerics, was leaving after his weekly sermon and thousands of the faithful were milling around. The blast left a three-foot-wide crater in the street, killing more than eighty people, including Hakim. According to a witness, "Pieces of flesh were found on the rooftop of the building opposite the mosque and smeared across the windows." Afterward a reporter found that "the air reeked of burned rubber, and streets were coated in oil, twisted metal, glass and debris."[60]

Such grotesque scenes would be repeated all too often in the years ahead. U.S. troops had little trouble toppling Saddam Hussein's decrepit regime in a few short weeks of fighting in the spring of 2003, which highlighted the American mastery of conventional combat operations. Unfortunately American commanders had been overly focused on the initial assault and were unprepared to restore order and rebuild governance. The resulting power vacuum allowed sundry Sunni and Shiite extremists to wreak havoc, slaughtering tens of thousands of Iraqis and thousands of foreign troops in one of the most destructive terrorist campaigns ever recorded. At the forefront was the group that was responsible for the August bombings and many more to come: Monotheism and Jihad, or, as it was eventually renamed, Al Qaeda in Iraq (AQI).

Its founder was Abu Musab al-Zarqawi, whose own father-in-law was said to have been the suicide bomber in Najaf. He would for a brief time emerge as the most famous jihadist in the world after Osama bin Laden and Ayman al-Zawahiri, but he differed greatly from those educated offspring of distinguished families. Born Ahmad Fadil al-Khalaylah in the grimy Jordanian industrial city of Zarqa, whose name he took, he was a tattooed high school dropout, a former video store clerk and petty criminal, uneducated and barely literate, a hard drinker and street brawler. He eventually found Allah and in 1989, at the age of twenty-three, made his way to Afghanistan, where he trained in an Al Qaeda camp. After returning to Jordan, where he served five years in jail for his subversive activities, he was back in Afghanistan by 1999. Soon he was leading his own jihadist group.

U.S. attacks in the fall of 2001 caused him to flee with his followers to Iran, which cynically provided him with aid and shelter notwithstanding his anti-Shiite sentiments. From there Zarqawi and his men infiltrated Iraq beginning with the Kurdish areas in the north that were, ironically, protected by American airpower. By the time the U.S. armed forces entered Iraq in the spring of 2003, in search of weapons of mass destruction that Saddam Hussein no longer possessed, Zarqawi was ready to "burn the earth under the feet of the invaders."[61]

More secular Sunni groups, led by former Baathists, concentrated on sniping at the occupying troops and blowing up their vehicles with improvised explosive devices—time-honored guerrilla techniques that would have been all too familiar to French forces in Indochina and British forces in Malaya a half century earlier. Zarqawi, by contrast, preferred sick, flamboyant gestures such as televised beheadings of hostages that took advantage of the newest communications technologies. On May 11, 2004, a jihadist website posted a video in which five masked men decapitated a Jewish-American businessman, Nicholas Berg, who was dressed in an orange jumpsuit similar to those worn by detainees at Guantánamo. The CIA believed that Zarqawi personally wielded the knife that cut off Berg's head. The way that this video was distributed online, taking advantage of newly available broadband Internet access, was typical of the sophistication with which AQI promulgated its propaganda. Just as nineteenth-century anarchists had taken advantage of the spread of newspapers and magazines, and the Vietcong and PLO had taken advantage of broadcast television, so these twenty-first-century insurgents showed how the latest technology could be harnessed to spread terror.

While focused primarily on Iraq, Zarqawi did not forget about his homeland. In 2005 his suicide bombers hit three American-owned hotels in Amman, killing sixty civilians, mainly Muslims, and thus sparking mass revulsion in Jordan. But his most destructive actions were suicide car bombings in Iraq. There were more suicide attacks in Iraq between 2003 and 2008 than in any other country in history. "By April 2008," writes Peter Bergen, "suicide attacks had killed more than ten thousand Iraqis."[62]

Although the political scientist Robert Pape claims that "suicide terrorism is mainly a response to foreign occupation,"[63] most of the suicide bombers in Iraq were not Iraqis and their targets were not foreign occupiers.[64] They came primarily from other Arab lands via Syria (Saudis composed the largest group), and they struck mainly at Shiite civilians and Iraqi security personnel. Clearly they were motivated by religious ideology, not nationalism, since most of them had never previously visited Iraq before immolating themselves on its soil.

It is perhaps pointless to look for rational motives behind such heinous crimes, given how rabidly Zarqawi hated Shiites. In a letter he had written that was intercepted by American authorities, he referred to Shiites as scorpions, snakes, rats, infidels, and "devils in the bodies of men." To the extent that his attacks on Shiites were animated by more than sheer animus, Zarqawi appeared determined to spark a Shiite backlash that would "awaken the inattentive Sunnis as they feel imminent danger."[65] AQI could then emerge as the Sunnis' defender. So far so good. The next step was not clear, however. How could the Sunnis, who accounted for no more than 25 percent of Iraq's population, prevail against the Shiite majority? Far more likely that the Sunnis would be annihilated.

The counterproductive nature of Zarqawi's attacks was clear even to his nominal superiors in Al Qaeda. In July 2005 Zawahiri sent him a letter of admonishment. "Many of your Muslim admirers among the common folks are wondering about your attacks on the Shia . . . ," he wrote. "My opinion is that this matter won't be acceptable to the Muslim populace however much you have tried to explain it, and aversion to this will continue."[66]

Zarqawi was free to ignore this good advice because his own organization operated independently of Al Qaeda central. By its peak in 2005–06, AQI was raising nearly $4.5 million a year, primarily from criminal rackets such as gasoline smuggling, car theft, and extortion.[67] The organization that Zarqawi built was strong enough to survive his own death; he was killed by a pair of bombs dropped by an F-16 on June 7, 2006, after having been tracked down to a safe house outside Baqubah by the U.S. Joint Special Operations Command.[68]

By then the disintegration of Iraq was well under way. AQI's February 22, 2006, bombing of the Golden Mosque in Samarra, a revered site for Shiites, sparked a fierce backlash. Shiite death squads responded with a campaign of ethnic cleansing to push Sunnis out of Baghdad. Every day dozens of Sunni bodies would be found around the capital, some with evidence of torture from power drills, others simply shot through the temple. The number of Iraqi civilians killed jumped from 5,746 in 2005 to 25,178 in 2006.[69]

An all-out civil war appeared to be starting with U.S. troops in the role of helpless bystanders. American commanders were focused not on stamping out the violence but on turning over control to Iraqi security forces. Unfortunately the Iraqi forces were badly trained and heavily infiltrated by Shiite militants. They fed rather than doused the flames of sectarian conflagration. Amid pervasive insecurity, ordinary Iraqis gravitated for protection to sectarian militias. By 2006 AQI had gained dominance of an area larger than New England in western and northern Iraq,[70] while the leading Shiite militia, the Jaish al Mahdi (Mahdist Army) led by Moqtada al Sadr, asserted its control in central and southern Iraq.

The seemingly hopeless situation began to reverse itself in September

2006 when tribal sheikhs around Ramadi launched a counterattack against AQI in cooperation with U.S. soldiers and marines. The tribes were offended that AQI had usurped their authority and their sources of revenue, primarily from smuggling. Because of its Salafist beliefs, AQI had even banned smoking—a favorite pastime across Iraq. Those who resisted its edicts were assassinated, sparking blood feuds with tribesmen. "The situation became unbearable," one sheikh recalled.[71] Similar sentiments had been expressed in nineteenth-century Chechnya by tribal elders offended by Shamil's edicts. This led them to cooperate in the 1850s with Russian occupiers seeking to quash his jihadist movement. Yet even the tribesmen opposed to Shamil never took up arms against him en masse as the Sunni tribesmen of Anbar Province now proceeded to do against AQI. Eventually more than 100,000 Sunnis would join the Sons of Iraq, as the anti–Al Qaeda militia came to be called.

There was nothing inevitable about this massive switch of allegiance. There had been disaffection among the tribes before, and it had always been repressed ruthlessly by AQI. This uprising too would likely have failed if U.S. troops had been on the way out in 2007 as the majority of the American public desired. But at the end of 2006, after more than three years of drift, President Bush made an unpopular decision to turn around a failing war effort. Over the opposition of the Joint Chiefs of Staff and most lawmakers, he decided to send 20,000 more troops to Iraq—a figure that would eventually grow to 30,000. At the same time he made a clean sweep of his Iraq team. Out went Secretary of Defense Donald Rumsfeld, General John Abizaid, the head of Central Command, and General George Casey, the senior officer in Iraq: all of the architects of the worst disaster in American military history since Vietnam. In an echo of Westmoreland's fate, Casey was elevated to become army chief of staff.

Until then, Bush had loyally acceded to the dogged desire of Rumsfeld, Abizaid, and Casey, all of whom he had picked personally, to minimize the American footprint in Iraq, because he did not want to repeat Lyndon Johnson's supposed mistake of micromanaging the Vietnam War.[72] This was a striking example of the importance of studying military history and of not relying on historical myths. In reality, as we have seen, Johnson only micromanaged the air strikes on North Vietnam; the ground war in the South he left to Westmoreland to run as he saw fit. The problem was that Westmoreland, like many of his successors in Iraq, approached an unconventional conflict with a relentlessly conventional—and Pollyannaish—mindset that seemed impervious to any evidence of failure.

As the situation on the ground in Iraq grew ever grimmer and as the American public turned against the war effort, Rumsfeld and the generals continued to issue blithe assurances, as McNamara and Westmoreland had once done, that progress was actually being made even if no one else could discern it. Eventually even Bush, who entered office with no national-security background, realized that he could no longer trust the chain of command in which he had naïvely reposed so much faith. With his own presidency hanging in the balance, the president turned for a new concept of operations to outside advisers such as the military historian Frederick Kagan and the retired general Jack Keane who urged the president to abandon the drawdown envisioned by Rumsfeld, Abizaid, and Casey and instead to send all the reinforcements he could find to Iraq.

To implement this "surge," the president called on a general with a professorial air and a mild manner that only partially masked a fierce will to win. If Osama bin Laden had become the leading insurgent of the early twenty-first century, David Howell Petraeus was about to become the leading counterinsurgent.

63.

COUNTERINSURGENCY REDISCOVERED

David Petraeus and the Surge, 2007–2008

BEFORE HE COULD conquer Iraq, Petraeus first had to conquer the U.S. Army, an institution famously resistant to intellectuals such as this Princeton Ph.D. His most effective weapons were his fitness and his toughness. Even into his fifties, he was known for engaging in push-up contests with soldiers half his age—and winning. Intensely competitive, he interviewed potential aides by taking them out for a run and gradually ramping up the pace to see if they could keep up.

In 1991, while still a lieutenant colonel, he was accidentally shot in the chest with an M-16 by one of his own soldiers during a training exercise. He barely survived after emergency surgery performed by Dr. Bill Frist, a future Senate majority leader. Yet in less than a week he was demanding a discharge from the hospital so he could get back to his battalion. To prove to the doctors that he was good to go, he took the intravenous tubes out of his arm and dropped to the hospital floor to do fifty push-ups. Nine years later, while skydiving in 2000, Brigadier General Petraeus's parachute collapsed seventy-five feet above the ground, and he landed so hard that he fractured his pelvis. He had to have a metal plate and screws inserted. But that did not keep him from returning to a punishing pace of work and workouts. Nor was he appreciably slowed in 2009 by a bout of prostate cancer that he kept secret and treated with radiation.

Petraeus had revealed that his slight frame—only five feet nine, 150 pounds—concealed impressive reservoirs of endurance. That enabled him to dispel doubts about whether he was too reserved and cerebral to lead men in combat, something he would not have a chance to do until 2003, when he was already a two-star general.

Unlike many officers of his generation, who hailed from clans with generations of military service, Petraeus was the first in his family to wear a uniform. He was born in 1952, an immigrant's son. His father was a Dutch merchant-marine captain who had come to the United States after the Nazis overran the Netherlands and had captained American merchant vessels in some of the toughest convoys of World War II. His mother was a part-time librarian who imbued him with a love of reading. He grew up in Cornwall-on-Hudson a few miles from West Point, and when the time came to apply to college he could not resist the challenge of gaining admittance to this exclusive institution. The fierce competitiveness that would mark his entire career was exhibited at West Point, where he was a "star man," meaning he was in the top 5 percent academically, as well as a cadet captain and a member of the ski and soccer teams. He even entered the premed program simply because it had the most demanding curriculum on campus. Shortly after graduation in 1974 he notched another accomplishment by marrying Holly Knowlton, the brainy daughter of the academy superintendent. Later he would become the only officer ever to finish first at both the Ranger School, a punishing nine-week endurance test, and the Army Command and General Staff College, a yearlong academic course for majors.

His insatiable hunger for accomplishment—his desire to win every contest, earn every ribbon, best every rival—along with his obvious intellect, which he made no effort to hide, irritated less driven and more low-key officers but was made somewhat more palatable by his disarming sense of humor, his seemingly low-key personality, and by his concern for the well-being of his fellow soldiers. At the Ranger School, for instance, he was credited with helping to push a buddy to complete the course. Later Petraeus would develop a reputation for nurturing junior officers. He was no Courtney Massengale, the self-centered, political general at the center of Anton Myrer's best-selling novel *Once an Eagle*, a military favorite since its publication in 1968. But neither was he the sort of back-slapping, tobacco-chewing good ol' boy (see: Franks, Tommy) who often rose to the top of the U.S. Army.

A different path was charted for him by one of his early mentors, General John Galvin, himself a soldier-scholar who would command NATO and in retirement become dean of the Fletcher School of Law and Diplomacy. Galvin pushed young Captain Petraeus, then his aide, to pursue graduate studies in a civilian institution. He chose Princeton's Woodrow Wilson School of Public Affairs and International Affairs, where from 1983 to 1985 he was exposed to viewpoints far outside the range normally heard in the army's ranks. That experience helped make him comfortable in the academic and media worlds that are so alien to most soldiers.

While teaching at West Point's Social Studies Department, Petraeus wrote his doctoral dissertation on the impact of the Vietnam War on the U.S. Army. It was a subject that had fascinated him since joining the army in the aftermath of that traumatic conflict. While on a training exercise in France in 1976, he had become an admirer of Marcel "Bruno" Bigeard, the legendary French paratrooper who had fought in World War II, Indochina, and Algeria; he later treasured an autographed photograph from Bigeard and corresponded with him until Bigeard's death in 2010. He also read books by Bernard Fall, Jean Larteguy, David Halberstam, David Galula, and other authors who wrote about the French and American experience in Indochina. Most army officers in the 1980s were eager to put Vietnam behind them and to do as little as possible to prepare for counterinsurgency because this was seen as such a thankless form of warfare. Not Petraeus. In his Ph.D. thesis he argued "that American involvement in low-intensity conflict is unavoidable" and that "the military should be prepared for it."

Petraeus's own experience with such conflicts prior to Iraq had been distinctly limited. In 1986 he spent a summer working for General Galvin, by then head of U.S. Southern Command, during which he visited El Salvador and other Latin American countries to learn about their counterinsurgency operations. In 1995 he spent three months working for the United Nations on nation building in Haiti. Then, in 2001–02, he spent ten months in Bosnia on peacekeeping duty. These were the sum of Petraeus's experiences not only with low-intensity conflict but with combat of any sort: he had missed out on the 1991 Gulf War, which for many of his peers had been a baptism of fire. While that conflict was raging, Petraeus, much to his frustration, had been in Washington as an aide to the army chief of staff, General Carl Vuono. Many of his peers looked down upon such assignments, far removed from the troops, and scoffed that Petraeus, like Colin Powell, was a "political general," not a muddy-boots soldier. There was some truth to this gibe, at least prior to 2003, but such assignments gave Petraeus valuable exposure to the policy-making process and civil-military interactions at the highest level. He would draw on those experiences, which most of his peers did not have, when he entered Iraq at the head of the 101st Airborne Division in the spring of 2003. Like those other military intellectuals, Hubert Lyautey and T. E. Lawrence, he would show that he could not only think originally but act effectively in the cauldron of combat.[73]

✦ ✦ ✦

FEW AMERICAN COMMANDERS were well prepared for the chaotic post-invasion phase of Operation Iraqi Freedom. Too many officers neglected nation-building and instead, like the Israelis in Lebanon or, two centuries earlier, the French in Spain, chased after elusive insurgents in heavy-handed combat operations that killed or incarcerated too many Iraqis and thus wound up alienating the population. They were abetted in this wrongheaded approach by senior civilians such as the secretary of defense, Donald Rumsfeld, who had capably run the Department of Defense in 1975–77 at the height of the Cold War but appeared out of his depth facing a very different sort of conflict. In 2003 he went so far as to deny that there was any "guerrilla war" in Iraq. Rumsfeld spoke contemptuously of the rebels as "pockets of dead enders" and seemed to think that the greatest threat Iraq faced was "creating a reliance or dependency" on American aid.[74]

Petraeus, by contrast, was acutely aware that a powerful insurgency was growing and that it could not be stopped by firepower alone. In his headquarters in Mosul, he displayed a sign that showed his appreciation of the basic tenets of population-centric counterinsurgency as elucidated by David Galula and Robert Thompson: "We are in a race to win over the people. What have you and your element done to contribute to that goal today?"[75] Without waiting for guidance from Baghdad—where Lieutenant General

Ricardo Sanchez, the senior military officer, and Ambassador L. Paul Bremer III, the senior civilian, were hopelessly out of their depth—Petraeus began nation building across northern Iraq. He did not neglect offensive action; the 101st scored a notable coup by locating and killing Saddam Hussein's sons, Uday and Qusay, on July 22, 2003. But he emphasized nonkinetic "lines of operation." He set up a representative government in northern Iraq, restarted telephone service, paved roads, created a police force, and even struck deals with Turkey and Syria to swap Iraqi oil for badly needed electricity.

Petraeus joked to a reporter that his role was a "combination of being the president and the Pope," and some Iraqis nicknamed him "King David."[76] His high-profile role grated on more conventional officers, who groused that this major general was getting outside his "lane," but Petraeus understood what they did not—that it was vital to establish a functioning government quickly, and that required someone to take ownership of Iraq's myriad problems. He also understood another truth of modern war—that it was vital to engage in the "battle of the narrative." As a result he was more open to the press than most of his peers were, yet he avoided the kind of indiscretions that later would prematurely end General Stanley McChrystal's command in Afghanistan. Petraeus managed to convey candor in interviews while always staying "on message." His expert manipulation of the news media did much to enhance not only his own career but also the missions he was charged with carrying out.

✦ ✦ ✦

In mid-April 2004, less than two months after returning home with the 101st, Petraeus came back to Iraq to assess the state of the Iraqi security forces. He found their performance to be poor. In June, by now a lieutenant general, he took charge of a new organization, Multi-National Security Transition Command–Iraq, charged with equipping and training the Iraqi forces—an effort he later described as "building the world's largest aircraft, while in flight, while it's being designed, and while it's being shot at."[77] He increased the number of soldiers and police from 95,000 to 192,000,[78] but his efforts could not keep up with the pace of the deteriorating security situation. Desertion, corruption, and militia infiltration were rampant. As violence levels continued to rise, the Iraqis proved unable to take over security responsibilities from coalition forces. There were many times when Petraeus, in the opinion of two reporters who followed him closely, "looked tired and dispirited" even as he tried hard to project an air of confidence and determination.[79]

In September 2005 he left Iraq to take command of the Combined Arms Center at Fort Leavenworth, Kansas, charged with overseeing the army's doctrine, training centers, and staff college. He later admitted, "Some suggested I was being sent out to pasture." But he turned this backwater into an unlikely forum to remake the entire war effort.

The army's doctrine for counterinsurgency, or, as it was known in the acronym-mad military, COIN, had not been revised for decades. Petraeus set out to create a new manual that drew not only on historical experience, especially in Algeria and Malaya, but also on the more recent experience of soldiers, including himself, in Iraq and Afghanistan. Petraeus chose an unconventional path for writing this manual of unconventional warfare—he enlisted not only brainy officers but also academics, journalists, aid workers, and others seldom if ever consulted by the military in the past. Petraeus explained that he sought their input because at Princeton he had benefited from his "out-of-my-intellectual-comfort-zone experience." It would not have escaped the attention of this media-savvy general that involving influential civilians would help promote the product of the "COINdinistas" led by his old West Point classmate Conrad Crane. The resulting U.S. Army–Marine Corps *Counterinsurgency Field Manual* was published in December 2006 and was immediately downloaded 1.5 million times. It was even reviewed in the *New York Times*, an honor accorded to no previous military manual.[80]

The manual essentially encapsulated the best practices of population-centric counterinsurgency, drawing on classics written by the likes of Charles Callwell, T. E. Lawrence, Robert Thompson, and, above all, David Galula. It began with the basics: "The primary objective of any COIN operation is to foster development of effective governance . . . by the balanced application of both military and nonmilitary means." The manual stressed the importance of "unity of effort" between civil and military actors, the primacy of "political factors," the need to "understand the environment," and to provide "security for the civilian populace." One of its most important pieces of advice was to "use the appropriate level of force": "An operation that kills five insurgents is counterproductive if collateral damage leads to the recruitment of fifty more insurgents."

In a similar vein the manual counseled that "some of the best weapons for counterinsurgents do not shoot," stressing the importance of information operations, political action, and economic development. The manual also warned, "Sometimes the more you protect your force, the less secure you may be." This was a direct criticism of the tendency of American units in Iraq to hunker down behind huge blast walls, cutting themselves off from contact with the population and making themselves easy prey for IED's every time they ventured outside. There was also an implicit criticism of the misconduct committed at Abu Ghraib prison. Soldiers were warned to "treat non-combatants and detainees humanely."[81]

Field Manual 3-24, as it was known in military circles, would become the most influential official publication on guerrilla warfare, at least in the English-speaking world, since C. E. Callwell's *Small Wars* (1896) and the Marine Corps' *Small Wars Manual* (1935). It was not, however, uncontroversial within the military. It would face pervasive criticism from active and retired soldiers that its authors had inappropriately attempted to apply a template of mid-twentieth-century wars against leftist-nationalist guerrillas onto twenty-first-century wars of religion and race that were not as susceptible to appeals for "hearts and minds." Critics did not, however, offer a compelling alternative of how the forces of a Western liberal democracy should conduct themselves in this type of warfare. Many of them seemed to be under the mistaken impression that scorched-earth tactics would be more effective—a myth that a study of counterinsurgencies from ancient Akkad in Mesopotamia to Nazi Germany in the Balkans and the Soviet Union in Afghanistan should have dispelled.

◆ ◆ ◆

WHEN HE WROTE the manual, Petraeus did not know for certain that he would get a chance to implement its precepts in Iraq; there had been hints of such a future assignment but nothing assured.[82] That rumored opportunity arrived faster than expected when General Casey was kicked upstairs to become army chief of staff. A newly promoted four-star, Petraeus arrived in Baghdad in February 2007 to find the situation worse than he had realized. Entire sections of the city had been transformed into a ghost town. Five extra U.S. brigades were coming as part of President Bush's "surge," but most experts, including Casey, doubted that those reinforcements would be sufficient to reverse the downward spiral. There would still be only 170,000 coalition soldiers in a country of 25 million. There were also more than 325,000 Iraqi security personnel, but their loyalty and competence remained suspect.

Petraeus was later to note, "Had we employed the forces as was the case previously, the results would have been the same."[83] But, acting in close concert with Lieutenant General Ray Odierno, a hulking, bald-headed artilleryman who was in charge of day-to-day operations, he implemented a new strategy straight out of the new field manual—and out of the annals of successful counterinsurgencies, from the Boer War to the Huk Rebellion. Rather than isolating troops on giant Forward Operating Bases, Petraeus and Odierno pushed them into smaller Joint Security Stations and Combat Outposts located in population centers. Soldiers would no longer "commute to work." Now they would live where they patrolled so that they could familiarize themselves with the neighborhood and gain the confidence of its residents. Foot patrols of the kind described in this book's Prologue were encouraged as an alternative to driving around in heavily armored vehicles. To help protect their "areas of operation," troops were told to erect giant concrete barriers that would impede car bombs and control access. Their mission was no longer transitioning to Iraqi control; they were there to win the war. Petraeus outlined his "big ideas" in the "Counterinsurgency Guidance" he issued to the command: "Secure and serve the population"; "Live among the people"; "Hold areas that have been secured"; "Pursue the enemy relentlessly."[84]

It is one thing to propagate a campaign plan; it is altogether more difficult to implement it across an organization of 170,000 people. Indeed there had been some isolated counterinsurgency successes in Iraq before. For example, Colonel H. R. McMaster's Third Armored Cavalry Regiment had in 2005–06 significantly decreased the level of violence in Tal Afar, a city in northern Iraq, utilizing tactics that anticipated Field Manual 3-24. Yet at the same time other commanders had pursued a very different and much more conventional approach. For all of General Casey's lip service to the concept of counterinsurgency, it had not been implemented across the country.

Petraeus was aware of the shortfall and addressed it much as the equally energetic and willful Templer had done in Malaya—albeit with some modern technological flourishes. Petraeus drove his ideas home in his morning PowerPoint conference with staff and subordinates known as the Battle Update and Assessment, in the nonstop emails he dispatched from two laptops that an aide always carried with him, and in twice-a-week "battlefield circulations" where he went to patrol with, and talk to, the troops. He made a point of sharing his email address widely and chatting with the lowliest soldiers under his command. He was a firm believer in flattening traditional hierarchies and giving his subordinates freedom to improvise. He was also an impressively hard worker, like most of the other officers in Iraq, routinely putting in seventeen-hour days, seven days a week.

More conventionally minded soldiers harrumphed that Petraeus was turning soldiers into social workers, but that criticism was far off the mark. The number of insurgents killed or locked up soared in 2007 (U.S. forces wound up detaining 27,000 Iraqis)[85] but without generating the popular backlash that had accompanied offensive action earlier in the war. The difference was that now troops living in Iraqi neighborhoods were able to gain tips from the populace that allowed them to pinpoint insurgents and avoid the sort of counterproductive roundups of young males that had occurred in years past.

Senior commanders had hesitated to send troops to bed down in population centers before because they feared that this would lead to a spike in casualties that would erode public support for the war back home. This fear was not entirely misplaced. Indeed the summer of 2007 saw some of the most violent months of the entire conflict, with more than 100 U.S. soldiers dying each month in April, May, and June. But then, like a fever breaking, losses began to fall, ebbing to a low of 25 killed in December. A year later, in December 2008, only 16 American soldiers died.[86] In all 4,484 American soldiers would die in Iraq by the end of 2011, but only 577 of those fatalities occurred after 2007. Just as significant was the rapid decline in civilian losses: from 23,333 slain in 2007 to 6,362 in 2008, 2,681 in 2009, 2,500 in 2010 and 1,600 in 2011. As of the end of 2011, the entire conflict would claim the lives of at least 70,000 Iraqi civilians and 15,000 Iraqi security personnel—and perhaps many more.[87]

Most of Petraeus's focus in 2007 was on breaking AQI's hold on Anbar

Province and the Baghdad "belts." He calculated that once the threat from AQI had been reduced, Shiites would no longer seek protection from Moqtada al Sadr's Mahdist Army. That gamble paid off in 2008 when Prime Minister Nouri al-Maliki sent Iraqi troops with substantial American backing to clear the Mahdists out of their strongholds in Basra and Sadr City. Iraq remained divided by deep sectarian and political divisions that threatened its future, but it had stepped back from the abyss. And the security situation continued to improve in 2009, 2010, and 2011 even as U.S. troops numbers fell, although there was no guarantee that the situation would remain stable after the last U.S. military personnel left at the end of December 2011.

Some skeptics claimed it was not the "surge" that had brought about a 90 percent reduction in violence but the decision by more than 100,000 Sunnis to switch sides after being paid to join the Sons of Iraq program. No question, their defection was vital to the outcome, but monetary inducements alone were not sufficient to explain their change of allegiance—any more than the gold that T. E. Lawrence disbursed could be used to explain his success in mobilizing Bedouin tribesmen for the Arab Revolt. Tribesmen, like most people, are interested above all in safeguarding their own interests. They would not accept payoffs unless they were confident that they would be alive to spend their newfound wealth. Only when the Anbar sheikhs were convinced, as one of them told the author Bing West, that the marines were "the strongest tribe" and would be staying in Iraq for the long haul (or so they thought) were they willing to join the American side. If U.S. forces had been drawing down, rather than ramping up, in 2007, it is doubtful that the Sunni Awakening would have occurred.

The emergence of the Sunni Awakening was not a repudiation but a confirmation of Petraeus's counterinsurgency doctrine: it showed how improvements in the security situation could snowball by inducing waverers and even enemies to come over to the government's side once they were convinced that this was the winning side. Yet, no matter how successful the surge was tactically, it could not by itself guarantee long-lasting stability. Successful security operations only create the potential for inclusive and effective governance that addresses minority grievances and binds the country together. That opportunity had been seized in countries such as South Africa in the 1900s, Malaya and the Philippines in the 1950s, El Salvador in the 1980s, Northern

Ireland in the 1990s, and Colombia in the 2000s. It was far from clear, however, that Prime Minister Maliki, a militant Shiite leader, would have the perspicacity of a Magsaysay or a Uribe. Indeed his sectarian and divisive agenda, no longer checked by a U.S. military presence after 2011, threatened to undo the gains that American troops and their Iraqi allies had fought so hard to achieve—and to alter the historical assessment of the surge's ultimate success or failure.[88]

✦ ✦ ✦

THE FACT THAT population-centric counterinsurgency had worked in Iraq, at least temporarily and tactically, was, on one level, not terribly surprising, given its success in other lands and other years. But several aspects of the Iraq experience were unusual. In the first place, few if any countries, with the possible exception of Colombia, had ever recovered after being so close to collapse. In Malaya, Templer had prevailed after early setbacks, but the level of violence there was much lower than in Iraq, and Malaya was a much smaller country. Moreover Templer did not have to worry about much foreign interference, whereas Syria and Iran provided substantial support to the Sunni and Shiite insurgents, respectively. Finally in Malaya, as in most guerrilla conflicts, the insurgents had been isolated in the hinterlands far from the capital, whereas in Iraq the major cities—Fallujah, Ramadi, Mosul, Baqubah, Baghdad—were the battlegrounds. This was a double-edged sword: the sheer number of attacks in Baghdad and other urban areas magnified the crisis but also made it possible to improve the situation quickly by flooding the cities with American troops.

Equally ambivalent in its impact was the decentralized nature of the Iraqi insurgency: while AQI and the Jaish al Mahdi became the dominant groups among the Sunnis and Shiite, respectively, there were many other "resistance" organizations as well—by one count, fifty-six in all.[89] Unlike Communist uprisings, this one had no central insurgent bureaucracy and no widely recognized leader like Ho Chi Minh or Fidel Castro. The lack of unity made it harder for the insurgents to prevail but also made it harder to stamp them out—"decapitating" strikes, such as the elimination of Zarqawi, could not defeat a diffuse uprising.

While urban insurgencies have traditionally failed, few insurgencies since the end of World War II had been defeated primarily by a foreign power. In most successful counterinsurgencies of recent decades, an indigenous government received substantial aid from abroad, even those where the bulk of the fighting was done by its own troops. This was not the case in Iraq, where American troops took the lead in 2007 despite the growing public opposition to the war in the United States. They were successful partly because they were not supporting a dictatorial regime, as the Russians had done in Afghanistan, but an elected government that, for all its faults, was broadly representative of the population. Like the British in Malaya, and unlike the French in Algeria and Indochina, the Americans made clear that they were not bent on an indefinite occupation by signing an agreement in 2008 calling for the withdrawal of U.S. forces by the end of 2011. It helped also that U.S. troops were seen as neutral arbiters in Iraq's sectarian landscape. They were trusted by most Iraqis more than their own security forces.

As a result of his success in Iraq, Petraeus was given the thankless task of undertaking another difficult counterinsurgency effort, this one in Afghanistan—a country that had suffered years of neglect while the Bush administration concentrated America's resources on Iraq. His task was made all the more difficult by rampant corruption in Afghanistan's own government, by the presence of Taliban sanctuaries in Pakistan, and by growing war weariness back home. Petraeus arrived at President Barack Obama's request in July 2010 and left a year later to become CIA director, having claimed some progress but no dramatic turnaround as in Iraq. The conflict against the Taliban, the Haqqani Network, and other insurgents had started before the war in Iraq, and it would last longer. The war in Afghanistan showed that the *Counterinsurgency Field Manual*, however sound in its distillation of the lessons of history, offered no magic formula for instantly defeating determined guerrillas. Even under the best of circumstances any struggle against an entrenched insurgency would be difficult and protracted. And Afghanistan was hardly the best place to implement the precepts of counterinsurgency, as invaders from Alexander the Great to the British and Russians had previously discovered.

64.

DOWN AND OUT?

The Failures and Successes of the Global Islamist Insurgency

THE EVISCERATION, AT least temporarily, of Al Qaeda in Iraq was only one of many setbacks suffered by the jihadists after 9/11. The most momentous of these was the death of Osama bin Laden on May 2, 2011, in a gutsy raid by U.S. Special Operations Forces on his compound in Pakistan that was ordered by President Obama over the objections of some of his advisers. Popular protests and insurrections proved to be far more potent instruments of change than terrorist operations. In 2011 uprisings shook regimes from Libya to Bahrain in ways that Al Qaeda never did. Far from toppling any Muslim governments, the Islamists managed to turn much of the *umma* against them. The Pew Global Attitudes Project recorded a sharp drop in those expressing "confidence" in Bin Laden between 2003 and 2010—in Pakistan from 46 percent to 18 percent, in Indonesia from 59 percent to 25 percent, in Jordan from 56 percent to 14 percent.[90]

Yet even a small minority is enough to sustain a terrorist group, and Al Qaeda had shown an impressive capacity to regenerate itself. Its affiliates continued to operate from the Middle East to Southeast Asia. There was a particularly close connection between Al Qaeda central and its "branded" franchises, Al Qaeda in the Arabian Peninsula (Saudi Arabia and Yemen) and Al Qaeda in the Islamic Maghreb (North Africa). Meanwhile other Islamist groups such as Lashkar-e-Taiba, the Tehrik-i-Taliban (Pakistani

Taliban), the Afghan Taliban, and the Haqqani Network—sympathetic to Al Qaeda but not formally affiliated with it—continued to show considerable strength in Afghanistan and Pakistan, while Hamas controlled the Gaza Strip, Hezbollah held sway in Lebanon, and the Shabab bid for power in Somalia. The turmoil that swept the Middle East during the Arab Spring of 2011 offered fresh opportunities for extreme Islamists, including some sympathetic to Al Qaeda, to take power. Based on their record as of 2012, Islamist groups were considerably more successful in seizing power than the anarchists but considerably less successful than the liberal nationalists of the nineteenth century or the communists of the twentieth century.

The best bet for Al Qaeda or any other terrorist group to have a big impact would be to acquire nuclear, chemical, or biological weapons, which Osama bin Laden had said was a "religious duty" for all Muslims.[91] Even without such apocalyptic weapons, terrorist groups have the capacity to drag nation-states into fresh wars as Al Qaeda did with the 9/11 attacks, which led to the American invasion of Afghanistan. Hezbollah and the PLO have also caused interstate conflicts by leading Israel to intervene in Lebanon, while Pakistan-based jihadist networks have almost sparked a war between India and Pakistan on several occasions with their attacks on Indian soil. The possibility of terrorists' setting off a war between nuclear-armed states is not all that far-fetched, considering that a terrorist act was the proximate cause of World War I.

To defend itself against such calamitous possibilities, America and its allies sought to erect a variety of defenses. Mostly it was a matter of improved security, police work, and intelligence gathering. The military played an important role, too, though seldom as central as in Iraq and Afghanistan—countries whose previous governments had been toppled by an American invasion. In states with a functioning or semi-functioning government the American role was limited to providing training, weapons, intelligence, and other assistance. Emblematic of this "low footprint" approach was the U.S. Joint Special Operations Task Force sent to the Philippines in 2002 to neutralize jihadist groups such as Abu Sayyaf. Comprising fewer than six hundred American personnel, it engaged in no direct combat. Rather it helped train and support the Philippine armed forces while carrying out civil-action projects such as building medical clinics and schools.[92]

Barack Obama came to office critical of many aspects of the Bush-era war on terror. However the practices he had most strongly criticized, such as the use of "stress techniques" in interrogations, already had been stopped in Bush's second term. Other policies, such as holding detainees indefinitely at Guantánamo and trying them via military tribunals, Obama had to accept because of congressional opposition to ending them. In still other areas—such as drone strikes in Pakistan—Obama actually authorized more attacks than his predecessor had done. He also showed more willingness than his predecessor to order potentially risky commando missions such as the one that killed Osama bin Laden. Many liberals were disappointed that Obama had not gone far enough in rolling back Bush policies; many conservatives were equally upset because they thought he had gone too far. But most Americans appeared satisfied with a robust counterterrorism approach that had won bipartisan support in Congress—and kept them safe in the decade after 9/11.

Yet there was no guarantee that this streak of counterterrorist success would continue. As the "planes operation" showed, defeats in a struggle against an "invisible army" could materialize with shocking suddenness and not just on a distant battlefront but on the home front itself. This was not a threat that Britain, France, Russia, and other Western powers that had battled Islamic insurgents in previous centuries had had to grapple with—Chechens did not attack Moscow in the nineteenth century, any more than Pashtuns attacked London or Moroccans Paris—but it was an inescapable reality of war in the globalized world of the twenty-first century.

EPILOGUE

Meeting in Marjah, October 23, 2011

LIKE DIPLOMATS WITH guns, the marines assembled around their hulking MRAP (Mine Resistant Ambush Protected) armored vehicles that might have wandered off the set of a *Star Wars* movie. Their tan boots crunched softly on the dried mud and gravel of their desert base, a modest collection of sand-colored tents covered with camouflage netting and outfitted with hastily assembled plywood furniture, all of it enclosed, almost like a medieval fortress, by rows of dirt-filled Hesco bastions and concrete Jersey barriers designed to stop suicide bombers and enemy rockets. All that was missing was a moat. Conditions were so primitive that there were no Port-a-Potties, much less latrines with running water; the men relieved themselves into plastic "piss tubes" stuck into the dirt. Towering above them were long, thin antennae thrusting upward as if to extend a metal hand through the ether itself to connect this remote outpost with its higher headquarters and with smaller elements in the field. As they listened to a short mission brief, the marines stood next to their armored vehicles in their camouflage fatigues, weighed down with M-4 rifles, spare magazines, body armor, radios, Camel-Baks, first-aid kits, and other assorted paraphernalia.

Suddenly out of a limpid blue sky a strange apparition with giant wings appeared amid a volley of deafening thwacks. Neither airplane nor helicopter but a combination of both, the V-22 Osprey landed at Camp Hanson with its tilt-rotors pointing upward to disgorge a handful of security experts sent from Kabul to assess this Area of Operations. Lieutenant Colonel Daniel A. Schmitt, the wiry and energetic commander of the 3-6 (Third Battalion, Sixth Marine Regiment), stepped forward to greet his visitors on this warm fall day, helmet in hand, and to usher them into the MRAPs for the drive ahead—thirty bone-rattling minutes over dirt roads fringed by orchards and farm fields, heading from the northern edge of settlement straight into the population center.

Sunday, October 23, 2011. The Marjah district of southern Afghanistan's Helmand Province.

Four and a half years after Captain David Brunais had led a squad of soldiers from the Eighty-Second Airborne Division onto the streets of Baghdad, another American officer was departing another American base in another country to engage in another of the time-tested rituals of counterinsurgency. Just as Brunais's patrol was designed to consolidate the gains his troopers had made through an assault into ungoverned terrain, so too with Schmitt's "Key Leader Engagement," the fancy term that the American military conferred on meetings with local notables.

American marines, the 3-6 among them, had first entered this area, long notorious as a Taliban safe haven and center of the flourishing drug trade, in February 2010. The high hopes of commanders, who had spoken overoptimistically of bringing "government in a box," were stymied initially by the low quality of Kabul's representatives and the fighting ability and tenacity of the local insurgents. There was no set-off-the-fireworks victory, no instant turnaround to be had in Marjah, but then there never is when battling an entrenched guerrilla group. Gradually, however, after hard fighting and serious losses on both sides, the marines were able to push the Taliban out of town. Once there had been two marine battalions in Marjah. Now there was only one reinforced battalion, and it was increasingly turning over control of the town itself to the Afghan army and police so that it could pursue the Taliban into the empty desert that lay outside the narrow agricultural belt, literally a "green zone," that stretched along the Helmand River Valley. Some of the Taliban remained in town, of course, but they found it prudent to hide their weapons, at least for the time being.

The situation was much safer than it had been back in May 2011 when the 3-6 battalion had arrived for its second deployment to Marjah. Yet Schmitt still took the precaution of having a marine with a hand-held metal detector sweep the path ahead, on the lookout for buried mines, after he and his visitors dismounted from the armored vehicles and were walking to an elder's gated and heavily guarded house. Capricious and deadly, IEDs had taken a fearsome toll on the marines in Helmand, killing many and leaving many others without arms or legs. Most of these infernal devices were so well concealed that they could be detected only with a metal detector or a set of well-trained eyeballs.

Once inside, marines and visitors alike engaged in a routine that had become second nature to American troops over the past decade who seemed eager to show by their actions that the age of the "ugly American" was long past. They took off their body armor, leaving it in heaps outside, and walked in to sit down on the floor along the periphery of a spacious salon. Sitting next to them on threadbare carpets were local potentates. At the head of the room, crouched on the floor next to Schmitt, was the owner of the house, Hajji Baz Gul, sporting a traditional flowing white *shalwar kameez*, a black vest and turban, and a substantial salt-and-pepper beard. ("Hajji" was an honorific denoting one who had made the pilgrimage to Mecca.)

Meetings with elders like him had been a part of the routine for counterinsurgents since the days of Alexander the Great, and indeed, aside from an expensive watch on his wrist, he did not look as if he would have been out of place in a sit-down with the Macedonian conqueror. Such conversations are designed to exchange information and to reach a modus vivendi between occupiers and occupied. They are not a substitute for the violence and coercion of warfare—killing and jailing insurgents—but they are an essential complement to it. Such diplomatic work took up much of the time of American commanders from the platoon level to the division and beyond, and it distinguishes counterinsurgency from conventional conflict, where the pure kinetic battle is all. Winning a counterinsurgency is a lot more complicated than simply pumping out a lot of lead and involves risks in addition to being shot or blown up—risks such as food poisoning and terminal boredom.

A manservant arrived to distribute with grimy black hands a lunch of rice, cucumbers and tomatoes, and scrawny, incinerated pieces of chicken, all washed down with cold cans of soda. As the assembled company of

Americans and Afghans ate with their own hands off plates set on the floor, another elder entered and sat down on the other side of Schmitt from where the first elder had crouched. Hajji Moto Khan was wearing a virtually identical outfit; the only difference was that his beard was perceptibly longer and whiter, which denoted higher standing in this patriarchal community. For the next hour, the Americans and Afghans engaged in a stilted, slow-motion conversation, punctuated by elaborate avowals of affection, through a marine translator. The elders were making a plea for greater infrastructure investment, while Schmitt was making a plea of his own for greater security cooperation.

Tension simmered not far beneath the surface of this ostensibly friendly interaction. Moto Khan had previously been a local leader of the Taliban. Another elder sitting in the back of the room had lost two sons fighting the marines. These men had no love lost for their camouflaged guests, but as wily survivors they could calculate their own-self interest—and much as their counterparts in Iraq's Anbar Province had done in 2007, they had decided to throw in their lot with "the strongest tribe," at least for the time being.

Thanks to their cooperation, Marjah, once the epicenter of violence in Afghanistan, had turned remarkably peaceful. After leaving the elder's house, the biggest obstacle that Schmitt encountered was flocks of stubborn sheep blocking the road. No snipers targeted his men, no IEDs went off to blow up his MRAPs. He was even able to lead his visitors on a walk through an open-air market, helmets off to reflect the greater sense of security. Once closed, the market was now bustling, with kids running around, stalls piled high with everything from vegetables to plastic flip-flops, and jingle trucks and motorcycles clogging the main street. Schmitt pointed proudly at this accomplishment, which was more significant in his mind than any number of insurgents caught or killed.

Despite this scene of apparent tranquility, a major question hung ominously in the air like the portent of a far-off storm: Would these gains endure once all the marines had gone? Much the same question had been asked by American soldiers in Iraq in 2007.[1]

Little, it seemed, had changed during the preceding four and a half years. Notwithstanding the considerable differences between Iraq and

Afghanistan, American forces were conducting counterinsurgency using roughly the same set of tactics, techniques, and procedures, and experiencing many of the same frustrations and joys. But then by some measures little had changed over the past five thousand years. Brunais and Schmitt were walking in the footsteps of counterinsurgents going back to Sargon of Akkad, while Al Qaeda in Iraq and the Taliban were spiritual descendants of the tribes from the Persian highlands that had bedeviled Akkad and other Mesopotamian states. Both sides had much to learn from the past about how to wage insurgency and counterinsurgency—how to overthrow governments and how to safeguard them.

Those lessons will remain of paramount importance long after the wars in Afghanistan and Iraq are concluded, for if there is one constant of history, it is the ubiquity and inevitability of guerrilla warfare. It is a form of combat that has been immanent in all cultures, at all times, whenever one side was too weak to face another in open battle. There is no reason to think that this method of warfare will be outdated anytime soon; rather, there is cause to fear that it could assume terrifying proportions in the future. Should some group of insurgents obtain weapons of mass destruction, especially nuclear weapons, a terrorist cell the size of an infantry squad could easily acquire more destructive capacity than an entire conventional army. That is sadly not the world of science fiction. If that were to occur, guerrilla warfare would take on an importance not countenanced in five thousand years of world history. Even if that technological leap does not manifest itself anytime soon, it seems reasonable to augur that guerrillas will continue to humble and humiliate the world's great powers, as they have done so successfully in the past, and that soldiers following in the footsteps of Brunais and Schmitt will inevitably find themselves thrown into the cauldron of irregular warfare.

To modify George Santayana's famous observation: "Only the dead are safe; only the dead have seen the end of guerrilla war."[2]

IMPLICATIONS

Twelve Articles, or The Lessons of Five Thousand Years

In 1917 T. E. Lawrence wrote an essay called "Twenty-Seven Articles" summing up many of the lessons he had learned as an insurgent. What follows might be called Twelve Articles. It sums up the lessons of Invisible Armies.

1. Guerrilla warfare has been ubiquitous and important throughout history. Tribal warfare, pitting one guerrilla force against another, is as old as mankind and still exists in modified form in some parts of the world. A new form of warfare, pitting guerrillas against "conventional" forces, is of only slightly more recent vintage—it arose in Mesopotamia five thousand years ago. Therefore labeling guerrilla warfare as "irregular" has it backwards: it is the norm; interstate war is the exception.

Much of the world's population lives in states whose current boundaries and forms of government were determined by insurgencies waged by or against their ancestors. Think of the United Kingdom, which was "united" by the success of the English in defeating Scottish and Irish insurgencies. That London rules much less territory than it did a century ago is in part the result of successful insurgencies by groups ranging from the IRA to the Zionists. Preceding all of them, of course, was the war waged by American colonists. The state they created reached its present borders only by waging three centuries of unremitting warfare against Indian irregulars.

These are just a few illustrative examples, which could be extended endlessly. It is hard to think of any state in the world that has avoided the ravages of guerrilla warfare—just as it is hard to think of any organized military force that did not have to spend, however unwillingly, a considerable portion of its time and resources fighting guerrillas.

2. Guerrilla warfare is not an "Eastern Way of War"; it is the universal war of the weak. Thanks largely to the success of Chinese and Vietnamese Communists in seizing power, there has been a tendency to portray guerrilla tactics as the outgrowth of Sun Tzu and other Chinese philosophers who were supposedly at odds with the kind of conventional tactics preached by Western sages such as Clausewitz. In reality, ancient Chinese and Indian armies were as massive and conventional in their orientation as the Roman legions. It was not the Chinese who had a cultural proclivity toward guerrilla warfare—it was their nomadic enemies in Inner Asia. For them, as for other tribesmen ranging from the Sioux to the Pashtuns, irregular warfare was a way of life. But even tribal peoples such as the Turks, Arabs, and Mongols, who enjoyed great success with guerrilla tactics during their rise to power, turned to conventional armies to safeguard their hard-won empires. Their experience suggests that few if any people have ever chosen guerrilla warfare voluntarily; it is the tactic of last resort for those too weak to create regular armies. Likewise, terrorism is the tactic of last resort for those too weak to create guerrilla forces.

3. Guerrilla warfare has been both underestimated and overestimated. Before 1945 the inherent value of guerrilla campaigns was generally underestimated. Because irregulars refuse to engage in face-to-face battle, they did not get the respect they deserve—notwithstanding their consistent ability to humble the world's greatest empires, from the days of the Barbarian assaults on Rome to Haiti's uprising against French rule in the 1790s. Since 1945, however, popular sentiment has swung too far in the other direction, enshrining guerrillas as superhuman figures who cannot be defeated by force. "Hence," as one expert noted in 1967, "the modern guerrilla was almost invested with the nimbus of invincibility."[1] This is largely because of the success enjoyed by a handful of guerrilla leaders such as Mao Zedong,

Ho Chi Minh, and Fidel Castro in the immediate postwar period that gave rise to the radical chic of the 1960s–1970s. But focusing on their exploits distracts from the ignominious end suffered by the great majority of insurgents, including Castro's celebrated protégé, Che Guevara. In reality guerrilla warfare is neither invincible nor unwinnable. The truth lies somewhere in between: although often able to fight for years and inflict great losses on their enemies, guerrillas have seldom achieved their objectives. Terrorists have been even less successful.

4. Insurgencies have been getting more successful since 1945 but still lose most of the time. According to a database compiled for this book (see the Appendix), out of 443 insurgencies since 1775, insurgents succeeded in 25.5 percent of the concluded wars while incumbents prevailed in 63.6 percent. (The other 10.8 percent were draws.) Since 1945 the win rate for insurgents has gone up to 40.3 percent. But counterinsurgents still won 50.8 percent of post-1945 wars. And those figures actually overstate insurgents' odds of success somewhat because many present-day rebel groups that are still in the field have scant chance of success. If ongoing uprisings are judged as failures, which they have been so far, the win rate for insurgents would go down to 21.9 percent in the post-1945 period, while the counterinsurgents' winning percentage would rise to 68.7 percent. Balanced against this is the fact that some terrorist or guerrilla groups that do not manage to attain their stated goals can still call attention to their struggle and win some concessions from the other side. The IRA and PLO are good examples.

5. The most important development in guerrilla warfare in the last two hundred years has been the rise of public opinion. What accounts for the fact that guerrillas have been getting more successful since 1945? Much of the explanation can be found, I believe, in the growing power of public opinion brought about by the spread of democracy, schools and colleges, communications technology, the mass media, and international organizations—all of which have sapped the will of states to engage in protracted counterinsurgencies, especially outside their own territory, and heightened the ability of insurgents to survive even after suffering military setbacks.

Before the rise of public opinion, most guerrillas were largely apolitical tribesmen who may have excelled at hit-and-run raiding but had no conception of political mobilization. They did little or nothing to woo undecided people or to undermine the will of the opposing populace, save by brute force. Sometimes, as in the case of the late Roman Empire, the targets of their inveterate attacks were weak enough that they finally succumbed. More often, however, the tribesmen were beaten back by settled civilizations that could muster more powerful armies. The strategic advantage in those days lay with the defenders, notwithstanding the attackers' immense tactical skills at fighting on horseback. As states got stronger from the seventeenth century on, the advantage titled further in their favor.

The balance of power began to shift toward insurgents because of the growth of public opinion, a term that first appeared in print, appropriately, in 1776. Notwithstanding their military setbacks in North America, the British might eventually have been able to restore control had not a parliamentary revolt in 1782 forced the downfall of Lord North's ministry and the rise of a Whig government dedicated to negotiating an end to the conflict. A few decades later the Greek rebels of the 1820s benefited from public opinion in the West, where philhellenes rallied their governments to oppose Ottoman abuses. A similar strategy would be pursued by many rebels of the future, from the Cubans opposing Spanish rule in the 1890s to the Algerians opposing French rule in the 1950s and Hezbollah opposing Israeli power since the 1980s. A spectacular vindication of this approach occurred during the Vietnam War, when the United States was defeated not because it had lost on the battlefield but because public opinion at home had turned against the war. The same thing almost happened in Iraq in 2007.

Public and press opposition is particularly potent when brought to bear against liberal states whose will to continue a war is dependent on popular support. But the growing power of public opinion affects even the calculations of illiberal regimes that find it harder to repress rebellion because of the spread of technologies such as Twitter and YouTube, of media outlets such as CNN and Al Jazeera, and of organizations such as the United Nations and Human Rights Watch. Today insurgency and counterinsurgency have to be waged not only on the ground but in cyberspace and on satellite television. These are realms where innovative Islamist groups such as Al Qaeda and Hezbollah have excelled and more hidebound conventional militaries have lagged.

6. Conventional tactics don't work against an unconventional threat. Regular soldiers often assume that they will have no difficulty besting ragtag fighters who lack the firepower or discipline of a professional fighting force. Their mindset was summed up by General George Decker, U.S. Army chief of staff from 1960 to 1962, who said, "Any good soldier can handle guerrillas." The Vietnam War and countless other conflicts have disproven this bromide. Big-unit, firepower-intensive operations snare few guerrillas and alienate many civilians. To defeat insurgents, soldiers must take a different approach that focuses not on chasing insurgents but on securing the population. This is the difference between "search and destroy" and "clear and hold." The latter approach is hardly pacifistic. It too requires the application of violence and coercion but in carefully calibrated and intelligently targeted doses. As an Israeli general told me, "Better to fight terror with an M-16 than an F-16."[2]

7. Few counterinsurgents have ever succeeded by inflicting mass terror—at least in foreign lands. When faced with elusive foes, armies too often have resorted to torturing suspects for information and inflicting bloody reprisals on civilians. Such strategies have worked on occasion, but just as often they have failed. The point is well illustrated by revolutionary and Napoleonic France's experience. The French revolutionaries killed indiscriminately and successfully to suppress the revolt in the Vendée, a region of France, in the 1790s. But French armies failed to pacify either Spain or Haiti in spite of their willingness to be just as brutal. Even in the ancient world, when there were no human-rights lobbies and no CNN, empires found that pacifying restive populations usually involved carrots as well as sticks. There were considerable benefits to the Pax Romana that won over subject populations; there was much more to Roman counterinsurgency than "they create a desert and call it peace."

The brute-force approach is most successful when the rebel movement is very weak or, better still, nonexistent and the counterinsurgents are trying to pacify their own territory, where they have at least some degree of legitimacy, considerable knowledge of the human and geographic terrain, and can bring overwhelming force to bear. Stalin's Great Terror in the 1930s and Mao's Cultural Revolution in the 1960s are cases in point. But in many other instances, like those of the Nazis in the Balkans and the Soviets in Afghanistan, even the willingness of counterinsurgents to inflict genocidal violence was not enough to prevail; their atrocities simply drove more people into the arms of rebels who had external backing. That is why the political scientist Stathis Kalyvas, a leading student of internal wars, has concluded that "indiscriminate violence seems to be counter-productive, with the exception of situations where there is a high imbalance of power."[3]

8. Population-centric counterinsurgency is often successful, but it's not as touchy-feely as commonly supposed. The fact that the U.S. and other liberal democratic states cannot be as brutal as dictatorial regimes, or, more precisely, choose not to be, does not mean they cannot succeed at counterinsurgency, as is sometimes claimed;[4] they simply have to practice a more humane style of counterinsurgency exemplified by Edward Lansdale and Gerald Templer. David Petraeus showed in Iraq in 2007–08 how successful population-centric counterinsurgency could be, at least in narrow security terms, even if the "surge" did not bring about a lasting political settlement. The same lesson was taught by President Alvaro Uribe who implemented a similar "democratic security" strategy in Colombia at the same time, and by the Israel Defense Forces during their successful operations to suppress the Second Intifada. Other notable successes for population-centric tactics occurred in Northern Ireland in the 1990s, El Salvador in the 1980s, and Malaya in the 1950s.

A more popular term for population-centric strategy is "winning hearts and minds," a deceptive phrase first coined by General Henry Clinton during the American Revolution and popularized by Gerald Templer in the 1950s. This term, by now a cliché, suggests that the counterinsurgents are trying to win a popularity contest. Some governments have tried this approach: between 2003 and 2007 the United States spent at least $29 billion in development aid in Iraq[5] in the hope that this would generate socioeconomic benefits that would cause the Iraqi people to reject the insurgents. This strategy failed because of a pervasive lack of security: if supporting the government entails a high risk of getting murdered, few will be enticed to do so because of the provision of better education or trash collection. In most conflicts, the majority of the population has sat on the fence until it was clear which side was likely to win, something that did not occur in Iraq until the surge took effect in 2007. Likewise during the American Revolution, successful British offensives caused Tories to become more active, whereas British retreats led more colonists to declare rebel sympathies. This underscores an important point made by Stathis Kalyvas: "Gaining control over an area brings collaboration, and losing control of an area brings much of that collaboration to an end."[6]

The only way to gain the necessary control is to garrison troops 24/7 among the civilians; periodic "sweep" or "cordon and search" operations, even when conducted by counterinsurgents as cruel as the Nazis, fail because civilians know the rebels will return the moment the soldiers leave and exact a terrible revenge on anyone who collaborated with them. The populace will embrace the government only if it is less dangerous to do so than to support the insurgency, which is why successful population-centric polices aim to control the people, not to win their love and gratitude. As John Paul Vann, the legendary American adviser in South Vietnam, said, "Security may be ten percent of the problem, or it may be ninety percent, but whichever it is, it's the first ten percent or the first ninety percent. Without security, nothing else we do will last."[7]

9. Establishing legitimacy is vital for any successful insurgency or counterinsurgency—and, in modern times, that is hard to achieve for a foreign group or government. It is, in fact, the second-most important requirement after physically securing the population. Before the twentieth century it was easy for unelected rulers, even foreigners, to obtain legitimacy: rule by emperor, kings, and chieftains was the norm throughout much of history. The spread of nationalism and democracy in the intervening years has made it difficult for unelected regimes, particularly if imposed from abroad, to gain popular allegiance. Thus, when fighting insurgents abroad, great powers today are forced to buttress the legitimacy of homegrown regimes rather than simply impose their own colonial officials at bayonet point, as their ancestors might have done. For the United States, this task was relatively easy to accomplish in states such as Colombia and the Philippines where the United States was supporting established, democratically elected governments. It was much more of a challenge in South Vietnam, Afghanistan, and Iraq where the Untied States was trying to create legitimate governments from scratch. For the Soviet Union in Afghanistan, backing a militantly atheistic regime in a devoutly Muslim land, this was a mission impossible.

Legitimacy is a problem for insurgents as well. Anarchism faded out as a revolutionary threat because it was never able to establish its credibility as a governing creed. Leftist insurgencies faded away after the collapse of the Soviet Union and the market reforms in China discredited Marxism-Leninism. Today jihadism, meaning violent extremism not mainstream Islamism, is imperiled by its lack of popular legitimacy even in the Muslim world. Hamas and Hezbollah have done better than other armed Islamist groups because they have provided social services to win over the people of Gaza and Lebanon.

The ideology that has proven most popular and hence most durable as a motivating force for guerrillas and terrorists is neither liberalism nor anarchism nor socialism nor Islamism but, rather, nationalism. Its appeal may be judged from the fact that even though most terrorist groups of the 1970s failed, those that had a nationalist appeal, such as the PLO and IRA, managed to win important concessions, whereas those that advocated radical social change, such as the Baader-Meinhof Gang and the Weathermen, disappeared without a trace after the death or imprisonment of their leaders.

10. Most insurgencies are long-lasting; attempts to win a quick victory backfire. According to the *Invisible Armies* database, the average insurgency since 1775 has lasted ten years. The figure is even longer for post-1945 insurgencies—fourteen years. Interestingly there is little correlation between the length of a conflict and the insurgents' chances of success. This flies in the face of the conventional wisdom summed up by the Vietnamese Communist strategist Truong Chinh in 1947: "To protract the war is the key to victory. . . . Time is on our side."[8] Protracting the conflict did favor the insurgents in Indochina, where their enemies were foreigners who would eventually tire of the conflict. But time is not usually on the insurgents' side when fighting a homegrown regime. In the *Invisible Armies* database, there is little difference in outcomes between insurgencies that last fewer than ten years and those that last more than twenty years—the incumbents won 64.3 percent of the former and 63.9 percent of the latter.

The fact that low-intensity conflict tends to be "long, arduous and protracted,"[9] in the words of Sir Robert Thompson, can be a source of frustration for both sides, but attempts to short-circuit the process to achieve a quick victory usually backfire. The United States tried to do just that in the early years of the Vietnam and Iraq wars by using its conventional might to hunt down insurgents in a push for what John Paul Vann rightly decried as "fast, superficial results."[10] It was only when the United States gave up hopes of quick victory, ironically, that it started to get results by implementing the tried-and-true tenets of population-centric counterinsurgency. In Vietnam, it was already too late, but in Iraq the patient provision of security came just in time.

A particularly seductive version of the "quick win" strategy is to try to eliminate the insurgency's leadership. Such strategies do sometimes work. The Romans managed to stamp out a revolt in Spain by inducing some of the rebels to kill their leader, Viriathus, in 139 BC. The Americans managed to hasten the end of the Philippine insurrection by capturing its leader, Emilio Aguinaldo, in a daring 1901 raid. But there are just as many examples where leaders were eliminated but the movement went on, sometimes stronger than ever—as both Hezbollah and Al Qaeda in Iraq did. High-level "decapitation" strategies work best when a movement is weak organizationally and focused around a cult of personality. Even then leadership targeting is most effective if integrated into a broader counterinsurgency effort designed to separate the insurgents from the population. If conducted in isolation, leadership raids are about as effective as mowing the lawn; the targeted organization can usually regenerate itself.

Insurgents can also stumble if they attempt a premature offensive to achieve victory, as General Giap did in 1951 and 1968. Both insurgents and counterinsurgents would be well advised to heed Field Marshal Templer's sagacious observation: "I have always said," he wrote from Malaya in 1953, "that the complete cure of it all will be a long slog."[11]

11. Guerrillas are most effective when able to operate with outside support—especially with conventional army units. From the guerrillas' standpoint, the most important advantage they can enjoy next to having a popular cause is having outside support. Best of all is to be able to operate in conjunction with conventional units, either their own or an ally's. This keeps a conventional army off balance. When it masses to fight main force units, it leaves its lines of communication vulnerable to guerrilla attacks. When it disperses to focus on the guerrillas, it leaves itself vulnerable to attack by the main force. In a few cases guerrilla leaders such as Mao Zedong and Ho Chi Minh have been able to build their own main force units. But such precedents are rare. More common is for rebels to work with foreign allies, the classic examples being American rebels cooperating with French forces against the British, Spanish *guerrilleros* cooperating with Wellington against Napoleon, and Arab rebels cooperating with Allenby and Lawrence against the Ottomans.

Even when they do not have main force units to work with, guerrillas greatly benefit from foreign funding, arms, training, and safe havens. No other factor correlates so closely with insurgent success—as demonstrated by examples as varied as the Vietcong and the Afghan mujahideen. One of the factors that greatly aided counterinsurgents in the ancient world was that insurgents were usually devoid of outside support. When insurgents do have substantial aid and it is cut off, the result can be catastrophic, as it was for the Greek Communist Party, which was cut off by Yugoslavia in 1948, and Angola's UNITA, which was cut off by South Africa and the United States in the 1990s.

We must not, however, exaggerate the impact of foreign support. It is possible to win with little or no outside backing, as Fidel Castro showed in Cuba and Michael Collins in Ireland. It is also possible to lose even if you have substantial foreign backing, as Al Qaeda in Iraq, the Popular Front for the Liberation of Palestine, and other groups have discovered. However, even if foreign sanctuaries cannot necessarily lead an insurgency to victory, they can keep it from being totally defeated: that has been the experience of Colombia's FARC, which was kept alive in large measure by support from Venezuela's Hugo Chávez after it suffered a long string of defeats starting in 2002.

12. Technology has been less important in guerrilla war than in conventional war—but that may be changing. All guerrilla and terrorist tactics, from suicide bombing to hostage taking and roadside ambushes, are designed to negate the firepower advantage of conventional forces. In this type of war, technology counts for less than in conventional conflict. Even the possession of nuclear bombs, the ultimate weapon, has not prevented the Soviet Union and the United States from suffering ignominious defeat at guerrilla hands. To the extent that technology has mattered in low-insurgency conflicts, it has often been the nonshooting kind. As T. E. Lawrence famously said, "The printing press is the greatest weapon in the armory of the modern commander." A present-day rebel might substitute "the Internet" for "the printing press," but the essential insight remains valid.

However, the role of weapons in this type of war could grow in the future if insurgents get their hands on chemical, biological, or especially nuclear weapons. A small terrorist cell the size of a platoon might then have more killing capacity than the entire army of a nonnuclear state like Brazil or Egypt. That is a sobering thought. It suggests that in the future low-intensity conflict could pose even greater problems for the world's leading powers than it has in the past. And, as we have seen, the problems of the past were substantial and varied.

APPENDIX

THE *INVISIBLE ARMIES* DATABASE

This database of insurgencies since 1775 is designed to supplement the historical narrative. It draws on existing databases, but it is designed to be more wide-ranging, more detailed, and more accurate than any previous compendium.

Outcomes are coded as 0 (an insurgent victory), 1 (a draw), 2 (a victory for the regulars), or 3 (ongoing). A coding of 2 is used even if the incumbent makes some political concessions and even if the insurgent group is not completely destroyed militarily. For example the British defeated the Provisional IRA in 1998 even though the Good Friday Accord gave the republicans representation in government. The IRA did not, however, achieve its goal of unification with Ireland. A 1 is coded when there is no clear-cut winner and the conflict ends in a negotiation in which both sides make significant concessions. For instance, EOKA was said to have gotten a draw rather than a victory in Cyprus because it forced the British out (save for two air bases) but did not unify Cyprus with Greece.

Many databases (see, e.g., Lyall and Wilson, "Rage") include only conflicts that pass a certain threshold, such as inflicting over 1,000 battle deaths. This excludes groups such as the Ku Klux Klan and the Baader-Meinhof Gang, and produces bias in favor of insurgents—just as a study of start-up companies would be biased in favor of entrepreneurs if it were limited to only those firms that achieved a certain revenue threshold or stock price. Most start-ups, like most insurgent groups, never get very far, and this fact needs to be recorded. Therefore this database attempts to include all significant insurgent movements since 1775. What does significant mean? That they caused some deaths and drew some attention from contemporaries and historians. Some of these groups may seem insignificant, but the same could have been said about the Chinese Communist Party when it was founded by thirteen delegates in Shanghai in 1921. Purely criminal enterprises such as the drug gangs of Mexico or the pirates of Somalia have been excluded.

There are two separate summaries of results: one that includes only resolved insurgencies and another that counts ongoing insurgencies as an incumbent victory. Most other databases exclude ongoing insurgencies altogether, but given that some guerrilla and terrorist groups have been struggling and failing for decades (e.g., FARC and the Kachin separatists), not counting them at all can give a skewed impression of insurgent prospects.

In a number of wars the insurgents prevailed only because of the intervention of outside forces. In conflicts such as the Greek War of Independence in the 1820s and the Cuban War of Independence in the 1890s, where the insurgents did much to spur that outside intervention, the outcome is scored as a 0. In other conflicts, such as most of the resistance fronts of World War II, the insurgents had little discernible impact on the intervention by outside powers, and therefore the outcome is recorded as a 1.

REGULARS	INSURGENTS	START	END	DURATION (days)	DURATION (years)	OUTCOME
UK	American Colonies	4/19/1775	9/3/1783	3059	8.381	0
USA	Cherokee Indians	5/1776	6/1794	6605	18.096	2
Dutch/Boers	Xhosa	12/1779	7/1781	578	1.584	1
USA	Northwest Indians	11/1785	8/3/1795	3562	9.759	2
Russia	Chechnya (Sheikh Mansur)	7/1785	6/1791	2161	5.921	2
UK	Australian Aborigines	5/29/1788	2/1869	29467	80.732	2
France	Haitians	8/21/1791	1/1/1804	4515	12.370	0
France	Catholics and Royalists in the Vendée	3/1793	1/1800	2497	6.841	2
Russia	Poles	4/17/1794	4/19/1794	2	0.005	2
USA	Whiskey Rebellion	7/1794	10/1794	92	0.252	2
UK	Irish	5/23/1798	9/8/1798	108	0.296	2
Russia	Georgia	9/1802	9/1841	14245	39.027	2
UK	Irish	7/23/1803	7/23/1803	1	0.003	2
UK	Kingdom of Kandy (Sri Lanka)	1/31/1803	10/30/1818	5751	15.756	2
Ottoman	Serbs	1/1804	10/3/1813	3563	9.762	2
UK	Irish in Australia	3/4/1804	3/4/1804	1	0.003	2
UK	Spanish Colonists (Invasion of Rio de la Plata)	6/1806	7/1807	395	1.082	0
France	Calabria (Italy)	3/1806	3/1811	1826	5.003	2
Haiti	General Petion (Civil War)	10/17/1806	10/8/1820	5105	13.986	0
Ottoman	Janissaries	1807	1808	ND	1.000	2
France	Spanish Guerrillas (Peninsular War)	5/2/1808	4/17/1814	2176	5.962	0
UK	Australia (Rum Rebellion)	1/26/1808	1/1/1810	706	1.934	2
Spain	Bolivia	7/16/1809	4/1/1825	5738	15.721	0
Spain	Ecuador	8/10/1809	5/22/1822	4668	12.789	0

REGULARS	INSURGENTS	START	END	DURATION (days)	DURATION (years)	OUTCOME
France/Bavaria	Tyrol (Austria)	4/1809	2/1810	306	0.838	2
Spain	Mexico	9/16/1810	9/27/1821	4029	11.038	0
Spain	Chile	9/18/1810	1/15/1826	5598	15.337	0
Spain	Argentina	5/18/1810	4/5/1818	2879	7.888	0
USA	Tecumseh/Shawnee Indians	10/1809	11/7/1811	767	2.101	2
Spain/Portugal	Uruguay	5/18/1811	7/1821	3697	10.129	0
Spain	Peru	6/1811	12/1824	4932	13.512	0
Spain	Venezuela	7/5/1811	10/1823	4471	12.249	0
France	Russian Partisans	6/1812	12/8/1812	190	0.521	0
USA	Creek Indians	7/1813	11/7/1814	494	1.353	2
Ottoman	Serbia	4/1815	11/1817	945	2.589	2
Russia	Caucasus (Shamil et al.)	c. 1817	c. 1864	ND	47.000	2
USA	Seminole (First War)	2/1817	5/28/1818	481	1.318	2
UK	Pindaris	11/6/1817	6/3/1818	210	0.575	2
France/Spain	Spanish Carlists	12/1/1821	4/6/1823	492	1.348	2
Ottoman	Greece	3/25/1821	4/25/1828	2588	7.090	0
Portugal	Avilez Rebellion/Brazil	9/1821	8/29/1825	1458	3.995	0
Netherlands	Padris (West Sumatra)	1821	1837	ND	16.000	2
UK	Burma	9/24/1823	2/24/1826	884	2.422	2
UK	Ashanti Kingdom (Ghana)	1/20/1824	8/7/1826	930	2.548	1
China	Kashgari Rebels	1825	1828	ND	3.000	2
Mexico	Yaqui & Mayo Tribes	10/25/1825	4/13/1827	535	1.466	2
Netherlands	Prince Diponegoro	7/23/1825	3/28/1830	1710	4.685	2
UK	Bharatpuris	12/1825	1/1826	32	0.088	2
Portugal	Pedro IV/Liberals	7/1/1829	7/5/1834	1831	5.016	2
Russia	Poles	11/29/1830	9/8/1831	283	[illegible]	[illegible]

Ottoman	Syria	10/1/1831	12/27/1832 [partly illegible]	[illegible]	[illegible]	[illegible]
USA	Blackhawk	5/14/1832	8/2/1832	80	0.219	2
Spain	Carlists	7/15/1834	7/15/1840	2193	6.008	2
Brazil	Republican Rebels	1/6/1835	5/1837	846	2.318	2
USA	Seminole	12/28/1835	8/14/1842	2421	6.633	2
UK	Quebec and Ontario	11/6/1837	11/1838	360	0.986	2
Texas	Cherokee	5/1838	3/1839	304	0.833	2
UK	Afghans	10/1/1838	10/12/1842	1472	4.033	0
Uruguay	Colorados and Blancos (Civil War)	3/1838	2/1852	5085	13.932	2
France	Abd al Kadr (Algeria)	11/1/1839	12/23/1847	2974	8.148	2
Ottoman	Bosnians	1841	1841	183	0.501	2
UK	Maoris	6/17/1843	5/1872	10546	28.893	2
UK	Sindhs	2/15/1843	8/1843	167	0.458	2
Haiti	Dominican Republic	2/27/1844	4/21/1849	1880	5.151	0
France	Morocco	8/6/1844	9/10/1844	36	0.099	2
UK	Sikhs	12/13/1845	3/9/1846	87	0.238	2
Habsburg Empire	Krakow	2/15/1846	3/3/1846	16	0.044	2
USA	Navajo	8/1846	1/14/1864	6375	17.466	2
UK	Xhosa	1846	1847	366	1.003	2
USA	Mexican guerrillas (Mexican-American War)	5/12/1846	2/2/1848	632	1.732	2
Spain	Carlists (Second War)	5/15/1847	5/1/1849	718	1.967	2
Mexico	Mayans in Yucatán (Caste War)	8/17/1848	3/4/1855	2390	6.548	2
Habsburg Empire	Hungary	9/9/1848	8/13/1849	338	0.926	2
Kingdom of the Two Sicilies	Sicilian Revolutionaries	1/12/1848	1/27/1848	15	0.041	2
Habsburg Empire	Italian Revolutionaries	3/13/1848	10/31/1848	232	0.636	2
Prussia	Greater Poland	3/1848	5/1848	61	0.167	2

REGULARS	INSURGENTS	START	END	DURATION (days)	DURATION (years)	OUTCOME
Ottoman	Wallachia	6/1848	9/1848	92	0.252	2
USA	California Indians	9/1850	7/22/1863	4707	12.896	2
UK	Xhosa	1850	1853	1097	3.005	2
China	Taiping Heavenly Kingdom	10/1/1850	7/31/1864	1674	4.586	2
UK	Burma	4/1852	1/1853	276.5	0.758	2
China	Nian Militia	11/1853	8/1868	5387	14.759	2
USA	Sioux	8/19/1854	9/3/1855	380	1.041	2
China	Hakka Clan	1855	1867	ND	12.000	2
UK	Santals (India)	1855	1856	366.5	1.004	2
USA	Yakima	10/6/1855	9/5/1858	1065	2.918	2
USA	Seminole	12/1855	3/1858	821	2.249	2
USA	Kansas (Pro- and Anti-Slavery Forces)	5/21/1856	9/15/1856	117	0.321	2
France	Algeria (Kabylia Region)	1856	1857	366.5	1.004	2
France	Toucouleur Empire	1857	1857	183	0.501	2
UK	Sepoy Mutineers (India)	5/10/1857	4/7/1859	697	1.910	2
USA	John Brown	10/16/1859	10/18/1859	2	0.005	2
China	Miao	10/25/1860	5/1/1872	4206	11.523	2
France	Indochina	8/31/1858	6/5/1862	1375	3.767	2
China	Hui/Chinese Muslims	10/25/1860	12/26/1872	4445	12.178	2
USA	Apache Tribe	12/4/1860	4/7/1864	1220	3.342	2
UK	Maoris	1860	1870	ND	10.000	2
Habsburg Empire	Kingdom of Piedmont-Sardinia	3/4/1860	3/23/1870	3672	10.060	0
USA	Confederate Bushwhackers	4/12/1861	4/9/1865	1458	3.995	2
USA	Sioux	8/17/1862	7/2/1868	2146	5.879	2
France	Mexico (Revolt against Maximilian)	4/16/1862	2/5/1867	1756	4.811	0
UK	Ashanti Kingdom (Ghana)	1863	1864	ND	1.000	1

Russia	Poland	1/22/1863	4/19/1864	[illegible]	[illegible]	[illegible]
Spain	Dominican Republic (Dominican Restoration War)	8/1863	3/1865	578	1.584	0
Russia	Poles	1/1863	5/1864	486	1.332	2
China	Sinkiang	7/1864	7/3/1871	2558	7.008	0
Russia	Central Asian Khanates	9/1864	8/1873	3256	8.921	2
UK	Bhutan	1/1865	11/11/1865	300	0.822	2
USA	KKK/White Supremacists (Reconstruction)	1866	1876	ND	10.000	0
Ottoman	Crete (First War)	5/29/1866	2/22/1867	270	0.740	2
USA	Sioux (Red Cloud's War)	12/21/1866	11/6/1868	686	1.879	1
UK	Ethiopian Empire	12/1867	4/13/1868	120	0.329	2
Spain	Cuba (Ten Years' War)	10/10/1868	2/10/1878	3410	9.342	2
UK	Red River Rebellion (Canada)	10/1869	8/24/1870	327	0.896	2
Prussia	Francs-Tireurs (Franco-Prussian War)	7/15/1870	5/10/1871	299	0.819	2
France	Algeria	3/1871	1/1872	307	0.841	2
France	Paris Commune	4/2/1871	5/29/1871	57	0.156	2
USA	Apache	4/1871	6/1873	792	2.170	2
Spain	Carlists	4/20/1872	2/20/1876	1402	3.841	2
USA	Modocs	11/30/1872	5/22/1873	173	0.474	2
France	Tonkin (Indochina)	1873	1885	4384	12.011	2
Netherlands	Aceh	1873	1913	ND	40.000	2
UK	Ashanti Kingdom (Ghana)	1/1873	2/1874	395.5	1.084	2
USA	Comanche, Kiowa, Southern Cheyenne, Arapaho Tribes	6/27/1874	5/8/1875	315	0.863	2
Ottoman	Herzegovina & Bulgaria	6/30/1876	3/1877	244	0.668	0
USA	Apache (Geronimo)	9/1876	9/1886	3652	10.005	2
USA	Sioux (Great Sioux War)	3/17/1876	11/25/1876	253	0.693	2

REGULARS	INSURGENTS	START	END	DURATION (days)	DURATION (years)	OUTCOME
Russia	Caucasian Imamate	1877	1878	ND	1.000	2
USA	Nez Perce	6/17/1877	10/5/1877	110	0.301	2
Japan	Satsuma	1/29/1877	9/24/1877	239	0.650	2
UK	Afghanistan	11/20/1878	9/2/1880	652	1.786	1
Habsburg Empire	Slav Nationalists	7/13/1878	9/10/1919	15033	41.186	0
USA	Cheyenne	9/13/1878	1/22/1879	131	0.359	2
Argentina	Patagonian Tribes (War of the Desert)	4/6/1879	7/8/1880	459	1.258	2
Russia	People's Will (Narodnaya Volya)	8/1879	2/1883	1280	3.507	2
UK	Zulu Kingdom	1/11/1879	7/4/1879	175	0.480	2
UK	Boers	12/30/1880	4/5/1881	97	0.266	0
France/Italy/Spain	Anarchists	c. 1880	c. 1939	ND	59.000	2
Britain/Cape Colony	Basotho (Gun War)	9/1880	5/1881	243.5	0.667	0
France	Tunisian Rebels	3/31/1881	4/4/1882	370	1.014	2
UK	Egypt (Arabi)	2/1/1881	9/13/1882	589	1.614	2
Britain	Mahdist Uprising (Sudan)	9/13/1882	12/30/1885	1204	3.299	0
France	Madagascar	6/1/1883	12/17/1885	930	2.548	1
France	Can Vuong (Vietnam)	7/1885	12/12/1888	1260	3.452	2
France	Wassoulou Empire (First Mandingo War)	1885	1886	366	1.003	2
Russia	Afghanistan	3/30/1885	4/1885	17.5	0.048	1
UK	Burma	1885	1886	366	1.003	2
Ottoman	Crete	1888	1889	ND	1.000	2
France	Kingdom of Dahomey (Benin)	1889	1892	1096.5	3.004	2
USA	Sioux (Pine Ridge Campaign/Wounded Knee)	12/29/1890	1/15/1891	17	0.047	2
France	Senegal	1890	1891	366	1.003	2
France	Kingdom of Siam	7/1893	10/1893	92	0.252	2
UK	Ndebele People (First Matabele War)	11/1/1893	1/23/1894	83	0.227	2

Yugoslavia	IMRO	11/1893	Aug-44	18505	50.699	2
Australia	Jandamarra's War	11/1894	4/1897	882	2.416	2
France	Madagascar	12/12/1894	10/1/1895	293	0.803	0
France	Wassoulou Empire (Second Mandingo War)	1894	1895	ND	1.000	0
Korea	Tonghak Rebels	2/1894	3/1895	393	1.077	2
Netherlands	Lombok (Bali)	1894	1894	183	0.500	2
UK	Ashanti Kingdom (Ghana)	1894	3/14/1905	ND	6.000	2
Spain	Cuba	2/24/1895	4/20/1898	1152	3.156	0
Italy	Ethiopia	12/7/1895	10/21/1896	320	0.877	0
Japan	Taiwanese Rebels	5/29/1895	10/21/1895	146	0.400	2
Brazil	Canudos Rebels	10/1/1896	10/5/1897	369	1.011	2
Spain	Philippines	5/30/1896	5/1/1898	701	1.921	0
Ottoman	Crete	2/1896	2/15/1897	367.5	1.007	0
UK	Ndebele People (Second Matabele War)	3/1896	10/1896	214	0.586	2
Ottoman	Druze Rebels	1896	1896	183.5	0.500	1
UK	Madhist Rebels (Sudan)	9/1896	11/4/1899	1145.5	3.138	2
UK	Pashtun Tribes (Northwest Frontier Campaign)	8/1897	4/1868	243.5	0.667	2
UK	Northern Nigeria	1897	1897	183	0.501	2
UK	Indian Muslims	8/1897	4/1898	243.5	0.667	2
UK	Temne and Mende Tribes (Sierra Leone) (Hut Tax War)	2/1898	5/1895	91.5	0.251	2
USA	Philippines	2/4/1899	7/4/1902	1246	3.414	2
Colombia	Liberal Party (Thousand Days War)	9/1/1899	6/15/1903	1383	3.789	2
UK	Boers	10/11/1899	5/31/1902	963	2.638	2
UK	Somaliland	9/1899	3/5/1905	1998	5.474	2
Foreign Powers in China	Boxer Rebellion (China)	6/17/1900	8/14/1900	59	0.162	2

REGULARS	INSURGENTS	START	END	DURATION (days)	DURATION (years)	OUTCOME
Bolivia	Acre Rebellion	8/6/1902	3/21/1903	227	0.622	0
Rashidi State	Saudi Rebels (Unification of Saudi Arabia)	Jan-02	9/23/1932	11209	30.710	0
Ottoman	Ilinden/VMRO Rebels	8/2/1903	11/2/1903	92	0.252	2
Germany	Herero (Namibia)	1/12/1904	11/16/1905	674.5	1.848	2
Russia	Socialists/Liberals (1905 Revolution)	1/22/1905	1/1/1906	344	0.942	2
Germany	Maji-Maji (Tanganyika)	Jul-05	Jun-06	335	0.920	2
Russia	Poles	6/21/1905	6/25/1905	4	0.011	2
UK	Zulu Kingdom	Mar-06	Jul-06	123	0.337	2
Spain	Morocco	Jul-09	Oct-09	92	0.252	2
Mexico	Revolutionaries	11/20/1910	5/21/1920	3470	9.507	0
France	Morocco	7/1/1911	3/30/1912	273	0.748	2
China	Republican Rebels	10/11/1911	12/31/1911	81	0.222	1
China	Tibetan Separatists	3/1/1912	4/1/1913	396	1.085	0
USA	Mexico (Occupation of Veracruz)	4/21/1914	11/23/1914	216	0.592	2
UK	Von Lettow-Vorbeck (East Africa)	11/2/1914	11/25/1918	1484	4.066	1
USA/Haiti	Cacos	7/3/1915	8/14/1934	6982	19.129	2
Ottoman	Arab Revolt	6/5/1916	10/30/1918	877	2.403	0
UK	Easter Rebellion	4/24/1916	5/1/1916	7	0.019	2
France	Morocco	1916	1917	366.5	1.004	2
USA	Dominican Republic	May-16	Sep-24	3045	8.342	1
Russia	White Army (Russian Civil War)	12/9/1917	3/18/1921	1195	3.274	2
China	Tibetans	1/7/1918	Aug-18	222	0.608	0
Russia	Caucasian Imamate	Aug-17	Sep-25	2953	8.090	2
Russia	Revolutionary Insurrectionary Army of Ukraine	1918	1921	ND	3.000	2
Germany	Workers Councils'	1/6/1919	May-19	115	0.315	2

UK	Afghanistan	5/19/1919	8/8/1919	85	0.233	1
UK	IRA (Irish War of Independence)	1/19/1919	12/6/1921	1052	2.882	0
United States	Anarchists	1919	1927	ND	8.000	2
France	Syria	1920	1920	183.5	0.503	1
Italy	The Senussi (Libya)	6/1/1920	7/1/1932	4414.5	12.095	2
UK	Iraq	Jun-20	1921	382.5	1.048	2
Russia	Turkestan (Ibrahim Bek)	11/10/1921	6/30/1931	3519	9.641	2
Spain/France	Rif Rebels	7/18/1921	5/27/1926	1774	4.860	2
Japan	Militarists/Ultra-Nationalist Secret Societies	c. 1921	c. 1937	ND	16.000	0
Ireland	Anti-Treaty IRA	Apr-22	May-23	395	1.082	2
Iraq/UK	Kurds	Jun-22	Jul-24	761	2.085	2
UK	IRA	1923	1969	ND	46.000	2
Germany	Nazis (Beer Hall Putsch)	11/8/1923	11/11/1923	3	0.008	2
Turkey	Sheikh Said's Rebels (Kurdish)	1924	1925	ND	1.000	2
France	Druze Rebels (Syria)	7/18/1925	6/1/1927	684	1.874	2
USA/Nicaragua	Nicaragua (Sandino)	Jul-27	Jan-33	2011	5.510	2
China	Communists	8/1/1927	7/7/1937	3628	9.940	1
Romania	Iron Guard	6/24/1927	9/4/1940	4821	13.208	0
Mexico	Cristero War	Oct-27	Apr-29	548	1.501	1
Yugoslavia	Croat Nationalists/Ustase	Jun-27	Apr-41	5053	13.844	0
UK	Saya San's Rebellion(Burma)	Dec-30	Jun-32	548.5	1.503	2
Japan	Chinese guerrillas	9/19/1931	8/14/1945	5078	13.912	1
Peru	Aprista Rebels	7/7/1932	7/17/1932	10	0.027	2
UK/India	Pashtun (NW Frontier Revolt)	1936	1939	ND	3.000	2
UK	Arab Revolt (Palestine)	4/20/1936	5/17/1939	1123	3.077	2
USSR	Finland	11/30/1939	3/12/1940	103	0.282	2
Germany	French Resistance	6/23/1940	8/29/1944	1528	4.186	1

REGULARS	INSURGENTS	START	END	DURATION (days)	DURATION (years)	OUTCOME
Soviet Union	Chechnya	1940	1944	4	0.011	2
Germany	Soviet Partisans	Jul-41	Jul-44	1096	3.003	0
Germany and Italy	Yugoslavia (Partisans/Chetniks)	May-41	Apr-45	1431	3.921	0
Japan	Philippine Resistance	4/9/1942	8/15/1945	1224	3.353	1
Italy/Germany	Albanian Resistance	Nov-41	Oct-44	1065	2.918	0
Japan	SOE/Malayans	2/15/1942	9/2/1945	1295	3.548	1
Germany	Greek Resistance	5/1/1941	Aug-44	1188	3.255	0
Japan (Burma)	Chindits/OSS/Burmese	2/18/1943	May-45	804	2.203	1
Germany	Warsaw Ghetto Uprising	4/19/1943	5/16/1943	27	0.074	2
Germany	Italian Resistance	9/8/1943	5/2/1945	602	1.649	1
Germany	Warsaw Uprising	8/1/1944	10/2/1944	62	0.170	2
UK	Palestine (Zionists)	2/1/1944	5/14/1948	1564	4.285	0
Greece	Communists	12/3/1944	10/16/1949	1778	4.871	2
Soviet Union	Forest Brothers (Baltic States)	Apr-05	1956	ND	12.000	2
Soviet Union	Ukraine (UPA)	1944	1953	ND	9.000	2
Colombia	Liberal &Communist Parties ("La Violencia")	9/15/1945	12/31/1966	4856	13.304	1
Netherlands	Indonesia	11/10/1945	10/15/1946	340	0.932	0
China (KMT)	PLA (Communists)	Aug-45	12/7/1949	1589	4.353	0
France	Vietminh (Indochina)	Dec-46	12/29/1954	2950	8.082	0
France	Madagascar	3/29/1947	12/1/1948	613	1.679	2
China	Taiwanese Insurgents	2/28/1947	3/21/1947	21	0.058	2
Burma	Kachin and Karen (KNU)	Aug-48	Ongoing			3
UK	MRLA (Malaya)	Feb-48	7/31/1960	4564	12.504	2
Philippines	Huks	9/1/1950	May-54	1338	3.666	2
China	Tibet	Oct-50	Aug-54	1400	3.836	2

France	Tunisia	Mar-52	Mar-56	1461	4.003	0
UK	Mau Mau (Kenya)	10/20/1952	1956	1351.5	3.703	2
UK	EOKA (Cyprus)	7/2/1952	8/13/1959	2598	7.118	1
Cuba	26th of July Movement (Castro)	7/26/1953	1/1/1959	1985	5.438	0
Indonesia	Darul Islam	9/20/1953	11/23/1953	64	0.175	2
Laos/USA	Pathet Lao	Apr-53	12/2/1975	8280	22.685	0
France	FLN (Algeria)	11/1/1954	7/1/1962	2799	7.668	0
France	Cameroon	1955	1960	1827.5	5.007	0
India	Naga	Oct-55	Nov-75	7336	20.099	2
United States	White Segregationists	1955	1968	ND	13.000	2
South Vietnam/USA	Vietcong/PAVN	10/26/1955	4/30/1975	7126	19.523	0
Soviet Union	Hungary	10/23/1956	11/30/1956	38	0.104	2
China	Tibet	3/1/1956	3/22/1959	1117	3.060	2
Indonesia	Leftists	12/15/1956	12/31/1960	1478	4.049	2
Spain	Morocco/Sahrawi Rebel (Ifni War)	Nov-57	Dec-57	30	0.082	2
Algeria/France	OAS	5/1/1958	Mar-63	1765	4.836	2
Spain	ETA	Jul-59	10/20/2011	19104	52.340	2
Rwanda/Belgium	Hutus	Nov-59	Sep-61	670	1.836	0
DRC	Katanga	7/11/1960	1/15/1963	918	2.515	2
Namibia	SWAPO	4/19/1960	3/21/1990	10928	29.940	0
Guatemala	EGP, ORPA, FAR, PGT, URNG	Nov-60	Dec-96	13179	36.107	2
South Africa	ANC, PAC, Azapo	12/16/1961	8/1/1990	10455	28.644	0
Venezuela	Revolutionary Left Movement, FALN	Apr-60	Dec-63	1339	3.668	2
Ethiopia	Eritrean Separatists	9/1/1961	5/24/1993	11588	31.748	0
Iraq	Kurds	9/16/1961	11/22/1963	798	2.186	2

REGULARS	INSURGENTS	START	END	DURATION (days)	DURATION (years)	OUTCOME
Nicaragua	Sandinistas	Jul-61	7/19/1979	6592	18.060	0
Portugal	Angola	2/3/1961	11/11/1975	5394	14.778	0
Algeria	CNDR/FFS(Kabylie)	Sep-63	Apr-65	550	1.507	2
Oman/UK	Dhofar	1962	1983	ND	21.000	2
Portugal	Guinea Bissau	Dec-62	Dec-74	4384	12.011	0
Portugal	Mozambique	Jun-62	6/25/1975	4772	13.074	0
Yemen	Yemeni Republicans (North Yemen Civil War)	11/15/1962	9/3/1969	2485	6.808	0
Canada	Front de Libération du Québec	Mar-63	Jan-71	2863	7.844	2
Uruguay	Tupamaros	7/31/1963	Jun-73	3593	9.844	2
Sudan	Anya Nya	10/1/1963	2/28/1972	3073	8.419	1
UK/Malaya	Borneo	Jan-63	Aug-66	1308	3.584	2
Colombia	FARC, ELN, EPL, M-19	1963	Ongoing			3
UK	FLOSY/NLF (Aden)	Dec-63	11/30/1967	1460	4.000	0
Kenya	NFDLM (Shifta War)	Dec-63	1/31/1968	1522	4.170	2
DRC	Eastern Congo (Orientale, Nord-Kivu, Sud-Kivu, Katanga)	9/1/1964	11/5/1967	1160	3.178	2
Rhodesia	ZANU-PF (Bush War)	Jul-64	Dec-79	5631	15.427	0
Peru	Revolutionary Left Movement	6/9/1965	10/23/1965	136	0.373	2
Thailand	Communist Party	Nov-65	Jan-83	6270	17.178	2
Israel	PLO	1965	Ongoing			3
Chad	FROLINAT	Nov-65	Aug-79	5041	13.811	0
Chile	MIR	1965	Ongoing			3
Dominican Republic	Constitutionalists	4/24/1965	6/3/1966	405	1.110	2
Iran	Mujaheedin e Khalq	1965	Ongoing			3
India	Mizo National Front	1966	Ongoing			3
Northern Ireland	Ulster Volunteer Force/Loyalist Volunteer	May-66	May-07	14975	41.027	1

Nigeria	Biafra	7/6/1967	1/12/1970	921	2.523	[illegible]
India	Naxalites	1967	Ongoing			3
Cambodia	Khmer Rouge	Jan-68	4/16/1975	2662	7.293	0
Brazil	ALN, VPR	Feb-68	Sep-71	1308	3.584	2
Philippines	MNLF	3/18/1968	9/2/1996	10395	28.479	2
Israel	PFLP-General Command	1968	Ongoing			3
USA	Weathermen	6/20/1969	Nov-77	3056	8.373	2
UK	Provisional IRA	Dec-69	Jul-97	10074	27.600	2
Philippines	Communist Party of the Philippines/New People's Army	1969	Ongoing			3
Japan	Japanese Red Army	8/29/1969	4/14/2000	11186	30.647	2
Germany	Red Army Faction (Baader-Meinhof)	6/5/1970	Mar-98	10131	27.756	2
Italy	Red Brigades	Aug-70	Dec-88	6697	18.348	2
Jordan	PLO	9/17/1970	9/24/1970	8	0.022	2
Pakistan	Bangladesh	3/26/1971	12/17/1971	266	0.729	0
Sri Lanka	JVP	4/5/1971	6/9/1971	65	0.178	2
Burundi	Hutu Rebels	4/29/1972	7/31/1972	93	0.255	2
Pakistan	Baluchi Seperatists	1973	Ongoing			3
Egypt	Gama'a al-Islamiyya	1973	Ongoing			3
USA	Symbionese Liberation Army	Mar-73	9/18/1975	931	2.551	2
Bangladesh	Bangladesh-Shanti Bahini	1/7/1973	12/2/1997	9095	24.918	1
Ethiopia	Anti-Derg Militias	Nov-74	May-91	6025	16.507	0
Israel/Jordan	Abu Nidal Organization	1974	Ongoing			3
Indonesia	Fretilin	9/11/1974	8/30/1999	9119	24.984	1
Angola	UNITA	8/9/1975	8/2/2002	9855	27.000	2
Lebanon	Sunni, Shia, and Christian militias (Civil War)	4/13/1975	10/13/1990	5662	15.512	1
Angola	Cabinda Province	1975	Ongoing			3

REGULARS	INSURGENTS	START	END	DURATION (days)	DURATION (years)	OUTCOME
Indonesia	East Timor	11/29/1975	8/30/1999	8675	23.767	0
Greece	Revolutionary Organization 17 November	12/23/1975	9/5/2002	9753	26.721	2
Morocco	Polisario	2/27/1976	Sep-91	5665	15.521	2
Indonesia	GAM (Aceh)	12/4/1976	Jan-05	10255	28.096	2
Argentina	FAR, ERP/MTP ("Dirty War")	3/25/1976	7/16/1982	2304	6.312	1
Mozambique	RENAMO	Dec-76	10/4/1992	5786	15.852	2
Syria	Muslim Brotherhood	Jul-76	2/28/1982	2068	5.666	2
DRC	FLNC	3/8/1977	5/31/1977	84	0.230	2
Philippines	MILF	1977	Ongoing			3
Turkey	Revolutionary People's Liberation Party	1978	Ongoing			3
Cambodia	FUNCINPEC, KPNLAF	Mar-79	May-93	5175	14.178	1
Iran	Kurdish Democratic Party Iran	1979	Ongoing			3
France	Action Directe	May-79	2/21/1987	2853	7.816	2
Iraq	Kurdish Peshmerga	10/1/1980	9/6/1988	2897	7.937	2
Nigeria	Maitatsine Sect (Kano)	Apr-80	Apr-85	1826	5.003	2
Peru	Shining Path, MRTA	1980	Ongoing			3
Soviet Union	Afghanistan	Jan-80	2/15/1989	3333	9.132	0
El Salvador	FMLN	10/10/1980	Jan-92	4100	11.233	2
Somalia	Anti-Barre Clans (SSDF, SNM, Isaaqs)	Jul-80	1/29/1991	3864	10.586	0
Nicaragua	Contras	Aug-81	Apr-90	3165	8.671	1
Uganda	NRA	Jan-81	1/19/1986	1844	5.052	0
Israel	Hezbollah (Southern Lebanon)	6/4/1982	5/25/2000	6565	17.986	0
Senegal	MFDC	Dec-82	Dec-04	8036	22.016	2
Portugal	Forças Populares 25 de Abril	12/6/1983	9/24/1984	293	0.803	2
Sri Lanka	Tamil Tigers	Jul-83	May-09	9436	25.852	2
Sudan	SPLM	[illegible]	[illegible]			

Turkey	PKK	1983	Ongoing			3
India	Sikhs	1984	Ongoing			3
Japan	Aum Shinrikyo	1984	Ongoing			3
South Yemen	Civil War	1/13/1986	1/24/1986	11	0.030	2
Uganda/DRC/Sudan	Lord's Resistance Army	1986	Ongoing			3
Uganda	ADF/NALU	1986	2000	ND	14.000	2
Uganda	UPA/UFM	1986	1993	ND	7.000	2
Israel	Hamas	1987	Ongoing			3
Israel	Palestinian Intifada	Dec-87	9/13/1993	2113	5.789	1
United States/Allies	Al Qaeda	1988	Ongoing			3
Burundi	Hutu Rebels	8/18/1988	8/22/1988	4	0.011	2
India	Kashmiri Separatists	1989	Ongoing			3
Papua New Guinea	Bougainville Revolutionary Army	Dec-88	Apr-98	3408	9.337	0
India	Lashkar e Taiba	1989	Ongoing			3
Pakistan/Kashmir	Harakat ul-Mujahidin	1989	Ongoing			3
Mali	Tuareg Insurgents	Jun-90	Jul-95	1856	5.085	1
USA	Panama (Operation Just Cause)	12/20/1989	12/24/1989	4	0.011	2
Afghanistan (Najibullah)	Mujahideen	2/19/1989	4/15/1992	1151	3.153	0
Liberia	NPFL	12/24/1989	11/22/1996	2525	6.918	1
Moldova	Dniestr Separatists	Sep-90	7/21/1992	689	1.888	0
Rwanda	RPF	10/1/90	7/18/94	1386	3.797	0
Israel	Kahane Chai	1990	Ongoing			3
Morocco	Moroccan Islamic Combatant Group	1990	Ongoing			3
Croatia	Republic of Serbian Krajina	Apr-90	Aug-95	1948	5.337	2
Djibouti	FRUD (Afar Insurgents)	Aug-91	5/12/2001	3572	9.786	1
Iraq	Shiiites and Kurds	3/1/1991	3/31/1991	30	0.082	2

REGULARS	INSURGENTS	START	END	DURATION (days)	DURATION (years)	OUTCOME
Uzbekistan	Islamist Movement of Uzbekistan	1991	Ongoing			3
Philippines	Abu Sayyaf	1991	Ongoing			3
Sierra Leone	RUF, AFRC	Mar-91	Jan-02	3959	10.847	2
Somalia	Various	1991	Ongoing			3
Yugoslavia	Slovenian Nationalists/Separatists	6/27/1991	7/5/1991	10	0.027	0
Nigeria	Niger Delta Rebels	1991	Ongoing			3
Lebanon	Asbat al-Ansar	1991	Ongoing			3
United States	Patriot Movement	Aug-92	May-01	3195	8.753	2
Algeria	MIA/FIS/AIS, GIA	Jan-92	Feb-02	3684	10.093	2
Azerbaijan	Nagorno-Karabakh	Feb-88	5/16/1994	2296	6.290	1
Bosnia	Republik Srpska (Serbs)	6/6/1992	12/31/1994	938	2.570	1
Georgia	Abkhaz Secessionists	8/14/1992	12/1/1993	474	1.299	0
Tajikistan	UTO	May-92	6/27/1997	1883	5.159	2
Bangladesh	Harakat ul-Jihad-i-Islami	1992	Ongoing			3
Burundi	Civil War	Oct-93	4/12/2005	4211	11.537	0
Indonesia	Jemaah Islamiyah	1993	Ongoing			3
Mexico	EZLN	1994	Ongoing			3
Afghanistan	Taliban	Aug-94	9/27/1996	788	2.159	0
Central African Republic	MLPC	1994	1997	ND	3.000	2
Afghanistan	Northern Alliance	Nov-96	Dec-01	1856	5.085	0
Chad	MDD, FNT, CSNDP, FARF	10/15/1991	May-98	2390	6.548	1
Russia	Chechnya	12/11/1994	8/31/1996	629	1.723	0
Rwanda	Interahamwe	7/18/1994	Ongoing			3
Yemen	South Yemen	2/21/1994	7/7/1994	136	0.373	1
Ireland	Continuity Irish Republican Army	1994	Ongoing			3

Mexico	Zapatista Army of National Liberation	1994	Ongoing			3
Libya	Libyan Islamic Fighting Group	1995	Ongoing			3
Serbia	KLA	Feb-96	6/10/1999	1225	3.356	0
Pakistan	Lashkar-e-Jhangvi	1996	Ongoing			3
Nepal	CPN	2/13/1996	4/26/2006	3725	10.205	1
DRC	Alliance of Democratic Forces for the Liberation of Congo-Zaire	Oct-96	May-97	212	0.581	0
China	Uighurs	1996	Ongoing			3
Congo	Cobra and Ninja Rebels	Jun-97	Dec-99	913	2.501	2
Colombia	United Self-Defense Forces of Columbia	Apr-97	4/12/2006	3298	9.036	2
Kenya/Tanzania	Al Qaeda in East Africa	1998	Ongoing			3
DRC	Eastern Congo Militias (Second Congo War & Aftermath)	1998	Ongoing			3
Guinea Bissau	Military Junta	6/7/1998	5/10/1999	337	0.923	0
Algeria	GSPC/Al Qaeda in the Islamic Maghreb	1998	Ongoing			3
Russia	Chechnya/North Caucasus	1999	Ongoing			3
Liberia	LURD, MODEL	4/25/1999	8/11/2003	1569	4.299	0
Pakistan	Jaish-e-Mohammed	2000	Ongoing			3
Israel	Palestinians (Second Intifada)	9/28/2000	2/8/2005	1594	4.367	2
Saudi Arabia/Yemen	Al Qaeda in Saudi Arabia & Islamic Jihad of Yemen/AQAP	2000	Ongoing			3
USA/Afghanistan	Taliban/Haqqani Network/Hizb-I Islami Gulbuddin	2001	Ongoing			3
USA/Iraq/ Western Europe	Ansar al-Islam	2001	Ongoing			3
Ivory Coast	Forces Nouvelles	2002	Ongoing			3
Pakistan	Tehrik-i-Taliban	2002	Ongoing			3

REGULARS	INSURGENTS	START	END	DURATION (days)	DURATION (years)	OUTCOME
Sudan/Chad	Darfuri Rebels	2003	Ongoing			3
Iraq	AQI/JAM/Kata'ib Hizballah/Baathist Nationalists	2003	Ongoing			3
Iran	PRMI/Jundallah (Baluch)	2003	Ongoing			3
Greece	Revolutionary Struggle	2003	Ongoing			3
Thailand	South Thailand rebels	2004	Ongoing			3
Yemen/KSA	Houthi Rebels	2004	Ongoing			3
Uzbekistan	Islamic Jihad Union	2004	Ongoing			3
Israel	Hezbollah (Second Lebanon War)	7/12/2006	8/14/2006	33	0.090	1
Mali	Tuareg Insurgents	5/2007	2/2009	642	1.759	1
Pakistan	Tehrik-e Taliban Pakistan	2007	Ongoing			3
Libya	Transitional National Council	2/15/2011	10/23/2011	250	0.685	0
Syria	Free Syrian Army	2011	Ongoing			3
Mali	Tuareg/Ansar-al-Dine	2012	Ongoing			3

SUMMARY OF DATABASE

RESOLVED INSURGENCIES				
Insurgent Victories	96 (25.20%)			
Draws/Compromises	42 (11.02%)			
Incumbent Victories	243 (63.78%)			
COUNTING 61 ONGOING CONFLICTS AS INCUMBENT VICTORIES				
Insurgent Victories	96 (21.72%)			
Draws/Compromises	42 (9.50%)			
Incumbent Victories	304 (68.78%)			
BY TIME PERIOD	INSURGENT VICTORIES	DRAWS	INCUMBENT VICTORIES	
Pre-1945	50 (20.49%)	21 (8.61%)	173 (70.90%)	
Post-1945 (resolved)	46 (39.60%)	21 (15.33%)	70 (51.09%)	
DURATION (RESOLVED) (YEARS)				
Average Duration Pre-1945	5.489			
Average Duration Post-1945	9.677			
Average Duration (Overall)	6.97			
BY LENGTH OF INSURGENCY	TOTAL RESOLVED	INCUMBENT VICTORIES	DRAWS	INSURGENT VICTORIES
Insurgencies <10 Years	293	196 (66.89%)	34 (11.60%)	63 (21.50%)
Insurgencies >20 Years	32	21 (65.63%)	3 (9.38%)	8 (25.00%)

ACKNOWLEDGMENTS

This is a Council on Foreign Relations book. During the six years that I worked on this volume, from 2006 to 2012, I had the inestimable good fortune to be the Jeane J. Kirkpatrick Senior Fellow in National Security Studies at the Council on Foreign Relations. It could not have been written otherwise. The Council's president, Richard Haass, and two directors of studies, James Lindsay and Gary Samore, were always supremely supportive of me and my work. I am deeply grateful to them, and to all my Council colleagues (especially Amy Baker, Janine Hill, and all the other members of the Studies Department; Irina Farkianos, vice president for national programs; and Patricia Dorff, the editorial director), as well as to the Council's distinguished roster of members, for creating such a congenial atmosphere for producing serious writing and analysis. I learned a lot, in particular, from the visiting military fellows who spend a year at the Council in between service on the front lines. The Council is a vibrant intellectual community that has made an important and enduring contribution to the development of American foreign policy since the 1920s, and I am honored to be a small part of it.[1]

One of the benefits of being at the Council is having a research associate, and I have benefited immensely from the first-rate young men and women who helped me while I was laboring on this book: Sarah Eskries-Winkler, Michael Scavelli, Rick Bennet, and Seth Myers. While I did all of my own research and writing, they helped by tracking down books, making logistical arrangements, preparing budgets, and performing a thousand other tasks. Rick and Seth played a particularly important role by helping to compile the *Invisible Armies* database.

I am also grateful for the financial, intellectual, and moral support of a number of generous individuals who have made my work at the Council possible. They include Roger Hertog and the Hertog Foundation; Robert Rosenkranz, Alexandra Munroe, Dana Wolfe, and the Rosenkranz Foundation; Heather Higgins and the Randolph Foundation; Marin Strmecki and Nadia Schadlow and the Smith Richardson Foundation; Dianne J. Sehler and the Bradley Foundation; and Steven Winch—along with some others who prefer to remain anonymous. Roger Hertog was particularly helpful in sharing his high-level contacts when I needed to make a research trip to Israel. In Israel, Daniel Polisar, the president of the Shalem Center, and his assistant, Jordana Barkats, went out of their way to arrange interviews with a who's who of the Israeli security establishment. Robert Rosenkranz and Alexandra Munro, for their part, were extraordinarily generous in allowing me to stay at their house in London while doing research in the British archives.

Several friends and colleagues took time to read all or part of this manuscript. Thanks to Barry Strauss, Robert Utley, Peter Mansoor, Arthur Waldron, Reuel Gerecht, Rufus Phillips, Rick Bennet, and especially to Mallory Factor, who made critical comments that I took to heart. I am also grateful to Steve Biddle and Jeff Friedman for their feedback on the database, and to two anonymous reviewers who offered a detailed critique of the manuscript at the Council's request.

During the past nine years (2003–12) I made more than a dozen trips to Afghanistan and Iraq to do "battlefield circulations" and talk with senior military and civilian officials. The information I gained not only contributed to the treatment of Iraq and Afghanistan in this book but also shaped my views about low-intensity conflict in general. I am grateful to the senior commanders who made these visits possible, especially Generals David Petraeus, Ray Odierno, Stanley McChrystal, and John Allen. Their subordinates were invariably accommodating and welcoming; I can remember many fascinating discussions of counterinsurgency tactics in war-zone chow halls and inside moving armored vehicles. In addition I am grateful to the Special Operations Forces that hosted me in the Philippines and in Colombia; to the American Jewish Committee for including me in two trips for American security analysts to Israel while that country was at war (against Hezbollah and Hamas); and to Lee Smith for arranging a fascinating visit to Lebanon.

I owe thanks to all the librarians and archivists at all the institutions I visited during the course of my research: they were unfailingly professional, helpful, and deeply informed. I owe a special debt to Miles Templer, Field Marshal Templer's son, for opening his home to me so that I could examine his father's papers. The librarians at the Council were also helpful in allowing me to borrow books from other institutions—and never complaining about my ridiculously long lists of requests.

My agents and friends, Glen Hartley and Lynn Chu, were a font of good advice and invaluable support—as always. It was a pleasure to work with Robert Weil and the entire team at W. W. Norton, especially his assistants, Phil Marino and William Menaker. Bob is an old-fashioned editor who still believes in meticulously marking up manuscripts with a pencil, and I benefited immensely from his discerning eye, both in the early days when I was struggling to find the right narrative approach and at the end of the process when I had to make revisions to an already completed manuscript. I have never worked with a better editor and doubt I ever will. David Lindroth drew the handsome maps. Seth Myers acquired the illustrations.

Finally I owe a considerable debt of gratitude to my loved ones—especially my children, to whom this work is dedicated—for putting up with my lengthy absences from home and general air of distraction while working on this book.

NOTES

EPIGRAPHS

1 Miot de Mélito, *Memoirs*, 557. The count was a courtier who served Joseph Bonaparte, Napoleon's brother and onetime king of Spain.

2 Trinquier, *Modern Warfare*, 74. Trinquier was a veteran of the French Indochina and Algerian wars.

PROLOGUE

1 *Guardian*, Oct. 23, 2010.

2 Brunais's patrol: Based on the author's personal observations.

3 According to the International Institute for Strategic Studies, there were 161 conflicts raging around the world in 2010, almost all of them internal wars involving low-intensity tactics. The same database lists 363 nonstate armed groups.

4 Weinstein, *Rebellion*, 5.

5 Histories of guerrilla warfare: See, e.g., Asprey, *Shadows*; Laqueur, *Guerrilla Warfare*; Ellis, *Barrel*; Polk, *Violent Politics*; Arnold, *Jungle*; O'Neil, *Insurgency.* Histories of terrorism: Burleigh, *Blood*; Carr, *Infernal Machine*; Carr, *Lessons*; Bowden, *Terror;* Laqueur, *Terrorism.*

6 Laqueur, *Terrorism*, 6. For definitions I also draw on Hoffman, *Terrorism*; Kalyvas, *Logic*; Chaliand, *Terrorism*; Cronin, *Ends*; Richardson, *Terrorists*; Bowden, *Terror*; O'Neill, *Insurgency.*

7 Burke, *Select Works*, 315.

8 Crossman, "Ethics."

9 Heer, *Extermination*, 112–13.

10 Osanka, *Guerrilla Warfare*, xvi.

BOOK I: BARBARIANS AT THE GATE

1 For an attempt to translate the events of the Jewish war into modern dates, see Levick, *Vespasian*, 40–42.

2 Roman army: Goldsworthy, *Roman Warfare*; Hackett, *Warfare*; Heather, *Fall*; Campbell, *Roman Army*.

3 Ambush: Josephus, *War*, in *Complete Works* ("continued": 2.19.6; "unexpected": 2.19.7; "covered," "fell," "contrivance": 2.19.8; "calamity": 2.20.1); Suetonius, *Twelve Caesars*, 284 (eagle); Gichon, "Campaign"; Goodman, *Rome*, 9–10.

4 End of revolt: Josephus, *War*, 2.19.8 ("flight"), 6.5.1 ("ground"), 6.8.5 ("blood"); Suetonius, *Twelve Caesars*; Tacitus, *Histories*; Cassius Dio, *Roman History*; Goodman, *Rome*; Price, *Under Siege*; Levick, *Vespasian*.

5 Hanson, *No Other*, 94.

6 Thucydides, *Peloponnesian*, 3.82–83.

7 Aetolions: Ibid., 3:94–98, 250–53.

8 Alexander in Central Asia: The best account is Holt, *Land of Bones* ("thick": 76). See also Arrian, *Campaigns*; Curtius, *History*; Diodorus, *Historical Library*; Plutarch, *Lives*; Green, *Alexander*; Fuller, *Generalship*; Stein, *Alexander's Track*; Worthington, *Alexander*.

9 Maccabees: Josephus, *Jewish Antiquities*, in *Complete Works*; 1 and 2 Maccabees; Hayes, *Jewish People*; Bright, *Israel*; Shanks, *Ancient Israel*; Hearn, *Maccabees*; Scolnic, *Brother's Blood*.

10 Diaspora revolt: Cassius Dio, *Roman History*, 68.32; Eusebius, *Ecclesiastical History*, 4.2; Bloom, *Revolts*. Bar Kokhba revolt: Cassius Dio, *Roman History*, 69.12–13; Yadin, *Bar-Kokhba*; Hayes, *Jewish People*, 211–15; Goodman, *Rome*, 464–69; Isaac, *Limits*, 84; Bloom, *Revolts*.

11 David: I Samuel 16–31; Josephus, *Jewish Antiquities*, 6.12–13; Bright, *History of Israel*, 193–95; Shanks, *Ancient Israel*, 85–98; McKenzie, *King David*, 70–110; Gabriel, *Military History*, 234–35.

12 LeBlanc, *Constant Battles*, 128–56; Gat, *War*, 157; O'Connell, *Of Arms*, 26–33.

13 Spalinger, *Ancient Egypt*, 36 (force size), 83–100; Hackett, *Warfare*, 29–32; Ferrill, *Origins*, 54–57.

14 Tatersall, *Beginnings*, 91.

15 Diamond, "Vengeance."

16 Edwards, *West Indies*, 1.527 ("dastardly").

17 Malone, *Skulking*, 24.

18 Keegan, *Warfare*, 9.

19 Underhill, *Newes*, 36.

20 Keeley, *War before*, 65.

21 Ibid., 195, 93.

22 Ferrill, *Origins*, 23–24; Keeley, *War before*, 37; Guilaine, *Origins*, 67–72.

23 Mann, *1491*, 43.

24 Sargon: Hamblin, *Warfare* (cup bearer: 73–74; "king of the world": 76; weapons: 98;

"bread and beer": 96; "mass slaughter": 79; "show mercy": 76, 99; "annihilated": 78; "all the lands": 80; "lawless": 103; "serpent": 103); Yadin, *Art*, 1.48 ("revolutionary"); Liverani, *Akkad*; Sasson, *Civilizations*, vol. 2; Frayne, *Royal Inscriptions*; Westenholz, *Legends* (wicker basket: 41; "ruin": 71; "lion": 99); Lewis, *Legend*; Meador, *Inanna*; Hallo, *Exaltation*; Snell, *Near East*; Bradford, *Arrow*.

25 Invasion of Mesopotamia: Hamblin, *Warfare* (wall: 110–11; "no cities": 155; "enemy": 120; "ruined": 121; "corpses," "goats": 122).

26 Xenophon, *Cyropaedia*, 1.1.5.2.

27 Herodotus, *Histories*, 1.201–16; Farrokh, *Shadows*, 48–49.

28 Scythians: Herodotus, *Histories*, 4.64–65 ("drinks," "arms"); Hildinger, *Warriors*, 5–14; Barfield, *Frontier*, 20–28; Grousset, *Empires*, 6–15; Sinor, *Cambridge History*, 97–110.

29 Herodotus, *Histories*, 4.120.

30 Ibid., 4.126–27.

31 Ferrill, *Origins*, 69; Saggs, *Assyria*, 262.

32 Herodotus, *Histories*, 1.95. See also Hackett, *Warfare*, 36–53; Saggs, *Assyria*; Holland, *Persian Fire*, 1–7; Bradford, *With Arrow*, 41–49.

33 Strauss, *Spartacus*; Shaw, *Spartacus*.

34 "Bleaching": Tacitus, *Histories*, 1.62. "Hiss": Florus, *Epitome*, 2.30.

35 Polybius, *Histories*, 10.15.4.

36 Price, *Under Siege*, 175.

37 Tacitus, *Agricola*, 81.

38 Death of Vetilius: Appian, *Wars*, 63.266. Platius's losses: 64.270. "Agile": 62.263. Death of Viriathus: 74.311–14; Richardson, *Romans in Spain*, 65.

39 "Marched": Josephus, *War*, 5.9.1. "Begged": 5.9.3.

40 Herod: Richardson, *Herod*; Perowne, *Herod*; Hanson, *Ancient Strategy*, 175–76.

41 Scheidel, *Economic History*, 45–49.

42 Goodman, *Rome*, 397.

43 Josephus, *War*, 2.12.1; Goodman, *Rome*, 386.

44 Josephus, *War*, 6.6.2.

45 Madden, *Empires*.

46 Tabachnick, *Enduring Empire*, 129.

47 Madden, *Empires*, 178.

48 Gibbon, *Decline*, 1.1.

49 Goldsworthy, *Rome Fell*, 16.

50 Gibbon, *Decline*, 1.170.

51 Mitchell, *Later Roman Empire*, xiv, notes that scholarship since the 1960s "has changed our perceptions of the later Roman Empire ineradicably, and to a large extent supplanted the paradigm of decline and fall, established by Gibbon." See also Heather, *Fall*, 141; Jones, *Later Roman Empire*, 1027. Goldsworthy, *Rome Fell*, 11–25, notes the historical pendulum swinging back to "decline and fall."

52 Goldsworthy, *Rome Fell*, 258.

53 "Guerrilla mode": Ellis, *Barrel*, 39.

54 Huns: Ammianus, *History*, 31.2.1–12 ("beasts," "very quick," "indomitable"); Jordanes, *Origins*, 36.188 ("treachery"); Priscus, "Court" ("haughty"); Schaff, *Select Library*, 6.130, 161 ("these brutes"); Thompson, *Huns*; Man, *Attila* (impalement: 128–29); Howarth, *Attila*; Matyszak, *Enemies*, 270–81; Hildinger, *Warriors*, 57–74; Kennedy, *Mongols* (stirrups: 28–30); Mitchell, *Later Roman Empire*, 197–202; Goldworthy, *Rome Fell*, 22 ("After 217"), 314–35.

55 Heather, *Fall*, 346.

56 Ibid., 446–47.

57 Goldsworthy, *Rome Fell*, 415.

58 Keegan, *Warfare*, 387.

59 Hanson, *Carnage*.

60 Keegan, *Warfare*, 221.

61 "Without fighting": Sawyer, *Seven Classics*, 161. "Deception": 158.

62 "Gongs": Ibid., 266. "Capturing": 265. Drummer, "climb": 267.

63 Chinese armies: Ibid., 10–11; Peers, *Soldiers*, 36; Graff, *Military History*, 29–31.

64 Graff, *Military History*, 13–14.

65 Debate: Cosmo, *Ancient China*, 210–15; Barfield, *Perilous Frontier*, 54.

66 Han: Lewis, *Chinese Empires* (market: 83); Loewe, *Everyday Life*; Chang, *Rise* (50 million: 1.177; 500,000: 1.85); Hardy, *Establishment* (120,000 mandarins: 101).

67 Sinor, *Cambridge History*, 1–18; Soucek, *Inner Asia*, xi–xii.

68 Graff, *Military History*, 57.

69 Sima, *Records*, 2.196.

70 Ibid., 129–30. "Girdles": 145.

71 Barfield, *Perilous Frontier*, 49; Kierman, *Chinese Ways*, 81; Chang, *Rise*, 1.158.

72 Cosmo, *Ancient China*, 203.

73 Sima, *Records*, 2.129.

74 Ambush: Sima, *Records*, 1.78–79, 2.138–39 ("gifts": 138); Barfield, *Frontier*, 35–36; Cosmo, *Ancient China*, 191–92; Sinor, *Cambridge History*, 121–22.

75 Sima, *Records*, 2.139; Barfield, *Frontier*, 45–48; Cosmo, *Ancient China*, 192–94; Lewis, *Chinese Empires*, 132–33; Graff, *Military History*, 64; Chang, *Rise*, 1.145; Sinor, *Cambridge History*, 122–25; Yu, *Trade*, 40–51.

76 Barfield, *Frontier*, 51; Yu, *Trade*, 36–37.

77 Sima, *Records*, 2.149.

78 Ibid., 194.

79 Cosmo, *Ancient China*, 213.

80 Chang, *Rise*, 1.129.

81 Wu: Chang, *Rise*, 1.89–96, 1.145 ("avenge"); Pan Ku, *History*, 2.27.

82 Sima, *Records*, 2.67, 247–51; Perdue, *Marches West*, 35; Cosmo, *Ancient China*, 232.

83 Cosmo, *Ancient China*, 203–4; Lewis, *Chinese Empires*, 139.

84 Chang, *Rise*, 1.86.

85 Lewis, *Chinese Empires*, 138.

86 Goldsworthy, *Roman Warfare*, 105–9; Hackett, *Warfare*, 165–67, 170–73; Holland, *Rubicon*, 161–62; Mackay, *Ancient Rome*, 98, 125–26.
87 "Hardship," "exhausted": Sima, *Records*, 2.64–65. "Hide currency": 2.69. Revenues: Barfield, *Frontier*, 57.
88 Chang, *Rise*, 1.2, 155, 224.
89 Barfield, *Frontier*, 58–63; Graff, *Military History*, 65.
90 Wright, "Equation Revisited," concludes "that an overall preponderance of the evidence does point to some strong connection between the two groups."
91 Perdue, *China Marches West*, 282–87; Lorge, *War*, 164–66; Barfield, *Frontier*, 293–94; Graff, *Military History*, 127–29.
92 Waldron, *Great Wall*.
93 May, *Mongol*, 21.
94 Graff, *Military History*, 67.
95 Kennedy, *Mongols*, 16–21.
96 Uyar, *Ottomans*; Crowley, *1453*.
97 Uyar, *Ottomans*, 5.
98 Parker, *Illustrated History*, 84–87; Prestwich, *Edward I*, 44.
99 "Burning": Barber, *Black Prince*, 50. "Revenue": 52.
100 John, *Chronicles*, 334.
101 Scott, *Robert*, 4.
102 Barrow, *Robert*, 88.
103 Murray, *Rob Roy*, 39.
104 Wallace: *Chronicle of Lanercost*, 175–76; John, *Chronicle*, 2.332; Bower, *History*, 194–95; Fisher, *Wallace*, 226–53; Mackay, *Wallace*, 245–68 ("half living": 265).
105 Bruce: Barbour, *The Bruce* ("valiant," "so good": 103; "endeavour": 160; "harry": 81; "such a blow": 107; "sweat": 109); John, *Chronicles* ("raw herbs," "hiss": 335); Bain, *Calendar*, 2.474 ("accomplices"), 2.483 ("traitor"), 2.495 (cages); Bower, *History* ("art": 199); Scott, *Robert* ("moor": 4); Barrow, *Robert* ("speed, surprise": 221); Barron, *Scottish War*, 260–94; McNamee, *Robert*, 112–36.
106 "Mishaps": John, *Chronicle*, 333.
107 Barbour, *The Bruce*, 171; Scott, *Robert*, 139; Sadler, *Border Fury*, 117–18.
108 *Chronicle of Lanercost*, 207.
109 Froissart, *Chronicles*, 47. See also *Chronicle of Lanercost*, 194–95; John, *Chronicles*, 341–42; Barrow, *Robert*, 305–19.
110 Scott, *Robert*, 193; McNamee, *Robert*, 217.
111 Campbell, *Black Death*, 49; Campbell, "Benchmarking."
112 Barbour, *The Bruce*, 318.
113 "Heroes": Hobsbawm, *Bandits*, 20. "Universal": 21.
114 Schiller, *Thirty Years' War*, 109.
115 "Undisciplined": Maurice, *Strategikon*, 96. "Deceit": 116. "Strategems," "greedy": 119.

BOOK II: LIBERTY OR DEATH: THE RISE OF THE LIBERAL REVOLUTIONARIES

1 Enlightenment warfare: Boot, *War Made New*, ch. 3; Childs, *Warfare* (400,000 soldiers: 89); Weigley, *Battles*, 46–58; Duffy, *Military*.

2 "Fire": Ewald, *Treatise*, 13. "Overrun": Zimmerman, *Popular History*, 1567.

3 Russell, "Redcoats," 631.

4 Duffy, *Military Experience*, 268.

5 Rogers: Rogers, *Journals*, 80 ("wood service"), 44 ("flames"), 9 (scalping), 139–44 (St. Francis raid), 82–86 (rules); Brumwell, *Devil* ("resolute," "dress": 101); Ross, *Run* ("few words": 2); Cuneo, *Rogers* ("deceiving": 60).

6 "Necessary": Grandmaison, *Petite guerre*, 6, 8. "New": Ewald, *Treatise*, 64.

7 Adams, "Too Dumb"; Spring, *With Zeal* ("inert": 254).

8 Anderson, *Crucible*, 288, estimates that 40–60 percent of military-age men in New England served in the French and Indian War.

9 Lexington and Concord: Peckham, *Sources* ("crush evils": 1.129); Percy, *Letters* ("scattered": 52; "incessant": 50; "inevitable": 54; "men who know": 53); "Intercepted Letters" ("above ten": 225; "savages": 225; "peasants": 224; "country people": 225; "properly": 226); Mackenzie, *Diary* ("enraged," "put to death": 1.20–21); Evelyn, *Memoir* ("scoundrels": 53; "cowards": 53; "incessant": 54); Gage, *Correspondence*, 1.396–99; Balderston, *Lost War*, 29–30; Hudson, *Lexington*, Appendix ("disperse": 528; "regulars are coming": 541); Stiles, *Literary Diary*, 1.551–52 ("colonist hussars"); Barker, *British in Boston*, 31–38; Revere, *Accounts* ("roar of musketry"); Heath, *Memoirs* ("corpulent": 1; "obtainable": 1); Emerson, *Diaries* ("disorder": 72); Lister, *Concord Fight*; Sutherland, *Late News*; Willard, *Letters*, 76–95. For secondary accounts see Fischer, *Revere's Ride*, 184–266 (1774 raid: 44–45; Gage's wife: 386–87; "Regulars are coming": 109; "Indian manner": 247); Smith, *West Cambridge*; Birnbaum, *Red Dawn*, 142–94; Galvin, *Minute Men*; Tourtellot, *Lexington*; Ferling, *Miracle*, 29–33; Middlekauff, *Glorious*, 270–81.

10 Emerson, "Concord Hymn": http://www.bartleby.com/102/43.html.

11 "Dirty": *WP*/RW: 1.336. "Stupidity": 1.372. "Proper": 1.90. "Broken": 6.396. Also see Ferling, *Miracle*, 75–78, 208; Kwasny, *Partisan War*, xi.

12 *AP*, 3.185.

13 Lee: *Lee Papers*, 2.383–89 ("European plan": 384; "impeding": 388). "Cultivated": Shy, *Numerous*, 127.

14 Kwasny, *Partisan War*, 330–31.

15 120,000 inhabitants: Mitnick, *New Jersey*, 15. British abuses: Mellick, *Old Farm*, 322–28; Stryker, *Documents*, 1.245–47; Fischer, *Crossing*, 172–81.

16 Muenchhausen, *Howe's Side*, 8.

17 "Rascal": Ibid., 7. "Chances": 16.

18 Spring, *With Zeal*, 14.

19 2,500 troops: *WP*/PR, 8.576. "Annoy": Fischer, *Crossing*, 349.

20 "Hornets": Stryker, *Documents*, 1.314. Casualties: Fischer, *Crossing*, 415–19, 536.

21 Clinton, *Rebellion*, 192.

22 Tarleton, *Campaigns*, 38–44; Wilson, *Southern Strategy*, 234; Gordon, *South Carolina*.

23 "Gentlest": Wickwire, *Cornwallis*, 175.

24 "Reconciliation": Clinton, *Rebellion*, 8. "Hearts": "Conversation with Lord Drumond," Feb. 7, 1776, HCP.

25 Mackenzie, *Diary*, 1.56.

26 Tarleton: Tarleton, *Campaigns*, 40 ("irregularities"), 101 ("campaigns"); Scotti, *Brutal Virtue*, 19 ("cool), 39 (over 500); Atlay, "Tarleton" ("middle height": 234–35); Bass, *Green Dragoon*, 11–22; Buchanan, *Courthouse*, 58–64; Conway, "To Subdue," 392 ("fire and sword"); Balderston, *Lost War*, 122 ("soup ladle"); Hoffman, *Uncivil*, 62 ("stripped").

27 Bass, *Gamecock*; Gregorie, *Sumter*.

28 Waring, *Fighting Elder*.

29 Marion: Lee, *Memoirs*, 174 ("small"), 584–85; James, *Sketch*, 21 ("his frame"); Moultrie, *Memoirs*, 223 ("active"); McCrady, *South Carolina*, 1.568–72; CSR; FMP; Rankin, *Marion*; Bass, *Swamp Fox*; Horry, *Life*; James, *Sketch*; Sims, *Life*.

30 Moultrie, *Memoirs*, 223.

31 Marion to Horatio Gates, Oct. 4, 1780, CSR.

32 "Scarcely": Tarleton, *Campaigns*, 205; Cornwallis, *Correspondence*, 1.71; Clinton. *Rebellion*, 476.

33 Marion to William Moultrie, July 28, 1781, in *Year Book 1898*, 380.

34 "Swamp Fox": James, *Sketch*, 32. For the Parson Weems version, published in 1824 in cooperation with one of Marion's officers (who complained that Weems had "carved and mutilated" his manuscript with "many erroneous statements"), see Horry, *Life*, 123. This was probably the inspiration for William Gilmore Simms to use "swamp fox" in his 1844 account: *Life*, 99.

35 Snow's Island: James, *Sketch* ("slept": 38); Bass, *Fox*, 104–5, 156–57.

36 "Shadow": *Greene Papers*, 7.17. "Strokes": 7.18. "Keep up": 6.520.

37 Ibid., 8.168.

38 Cornwallis, *Correspondence*, 1.80.

39 Ferling, *Miracle*, 574.

40 8,000 men lost: Ketchum, *Yorktown*, 246; Ferling, *Miracle*, 538. 34,000 troops left: Mackesy, *War*, 525. British population: Conway, *British Isles*, 28.

41 Fischer, *Revere's Ride*, 415.

42 Somerville, *Own Life*, 187. See also Conway, *British Isles*, 130–33; Bradley, *Popular Politics*, 59–89.

43 Great Britain, *Parliamentary Register*, 2.218.

44 Trevelyan, *Revolution*, 3.208; Billias, *Opponents*, 45.

45 Lutnick, *Revolution*, 59.

46 Davidson, *Propaganda*, 56–58; Stoll, *Samuel Adams*, 115–16; Puls, *Samuel Adams*, 127–29.

47 Fischer, *Revere's Ride*, 275.

48 Lutnick, *Revolution*, 75.
49 Berger, *Broadsides*, 165–67; Isaacson, *Benjamin Franklin*, 339–40.
50 Lutnick, *Revolution*, 25.
51 Balderston, *Lost War*, 33.
52 "Suicide": Lutnick, *Revolution*, 108. "Grave": 168. "Enough": 121. "Sick": Conway, *British Isles*, 129.
53 Casualties: Peckham, *Toll*, 132–33; Clodfelter, *Warfare*, 142. Population: http://www.census.gov/newsroom/releases/pdf/cb10-ff12.pdf.
54 Addington, *Patterns*, 15.
55 *Greene Papers*, 7.75.
56 Mansoor, *Hybrid*.
57 Confusion: Mackesy, *War*, 20–24, 33, 514; Fischer, *Washington's Crossing*, 66–78; Gordon, *South Carolina*, 58–59; Conway, "Subdue America," 406.
58 Addington, *Patterns*, 12–14; Mackesy, *War*, 29, 524–25. In addition, a maximum of 11,000 Loyalists served with the British forces at any one time. The rebels never had more than 35,000 men under arms.
59 Montanus, "Failed."
60 Vendée: Bell, *Total War* (250,000: 156); Secher, *Genocide* ("crushed": 110); Ross, *Banners*; Paret, *Internal War*.
61 Calabria: Finley, *Monstrous*; Davis, *Napoleon*; Colletta, *Naples*.
62 Eyck, *Loyal Rebels*; Broers, *Under Napoleon*.
63 Zaragoza: Rudorff, *Death* ("infernal": 141; "foaming": 170; "fury": 127; "madmen": 158); Brandt, *Legions* ("death lurked": 58); Jacob, *Travels*, 123 ("feminine"); Vaughan, *Narrative* ("well bred": 4; "to the knife": 23; "enraged populace": 26); Fraser, *Cursed War* ("hell opened": 167); Southey, *Peninsular War* ("raving," "knife": 2.25); Oman, *Peninsular War*, 1.140–62; Esdaile, *Peninsular War*; Bell, *Total War*; Gates, *Spanish Ulcer*.
64 Bourrienne, *Memoirs*, 3.123.
65 Esdaile, *Peninsular War*, 38–40; Tone, *Fatal Knot*, 49–50; Fraser, *Cursed War*, 56–71.
66 Napoleon, *Correspondence*, 1.341.
67 "Guerrilla": Esdaile, *Resistance*, 137–60.
68 Tone, *Fatal Knot*, 53.
69 "Heretics": Esdaile, *Fighting Napoleon*, 63. Antichrist: Rudorff, *Death*, 43.
70 Fraser, *Cursed War*, 132.
71 Blaze, *Captain Blaze*, 100.
72 Espoz y Mina: Espoz y Mina, *Breve extracto* (13,000 men: 35; customs, courts: 39-43); Tone, *Fatal Knot* ("Lancers": 208; "little king": 132; lemon seller: 134; killed 5,500: 140); Fraser, *Cursed War* ("slightly blond": 391); Southey, *Peninsular War*, vol. 5; Esdaile, *Fighting Napoleon*.
73 Troop levels: Sherer, *Military Memoirs*, 274; Tone, *Fatal Knot*, 3–4; Gates, *Spanish Ulcer*, appendix 2.
74 Suchet, *Memoirs*, 1.57.

75 Brandt, *Legions*, 165.

76 Disorganization: Fraser, *Cursed War*, 422–23; Connelly, *Gentle*, 148, 168–72, 188.

77 Rocca, *Memoirs*, 147–48.

78 Lieven, *Russia*, 218–19; Zamoyski, *Moscow*, 327–30. Notwithstanding the activities of a few famous partisan leaders such as Denis Davidov, Zamoyski writes (329) that "modern Russian historians are generally agreed that there is no guerrilla that could bear any comparison with the Spanish model, and that the contribution of the peasants was largely confined to opportunistic pillage and murder."

79 Wellington to Earl of Liverpool, May 28, 1812, *Dispatches*, 9.191.

80 Espoz y Mina, *Breve extracto*, 23.

81 Gates, *Total War*, 280. No exact casualty figure exists. Estimates that included wounded and prisoners range from 240,000 to 600,000. See Fraser, *Cursed War*, 417.

82 Suchet, *Memoirs*, 1.44.

83 Wellington, *Dispatches*, 11.349.

84 "Studied": Jomini, *Art of War*, 29. "Terrible": 26. "Scarcely": 27. "Chivalrous": 31.

85 "Fire": Clausewitz, *On War*, 777. "Artificial": 776. "Soul": 781. In addition to ch. 25 of *On War* ("Arming the Nation"), Clausewitz worked on a study about guerrilla warfare that was never published and does not survive. See Paret, *Internal War*, 34–35; Sumida, *Decoding*.

86 Jomini, *Art of War*, 31.

87 Start of revolt: Edwards, *Survey* ("screams": 68; nailed alive: 74; "field of carnage": 63; "terror": 70); Edwards, *History Civil*, 3.351 (*arretez*); Hopkirk, *Account* (infant emblem: 17; sawed in half: 18; "the torch": 18); Popkin, *Revolution* ("blameless": 56; "tatters," "utensils," "assassin": 77); Heinl, *Written* ("vengeance": 40; slave punishments: 23–24); Rainsford, *Account* ("indulgence": 88); Parham, *My Odyssey*, 27–45 ("unchained": 40); Geggus, *Studies*, 5 (sugar, coffee), ch. 6 (Bois Caiman ceremony); Stoddard, *French Revolution* ("wall of fire": 131); Dubois, *Avengers* (veterans: 109).

88 Louverture, *Revolution*, 1.

89 Louverture: Geggus, "Toussaint" ("contacts": 116); Rainsford, *Account*, 240–45; Bell, *Toussaint Louverture*, 57–83; Dubois, *Avengers*, 171–76 ("Black Spartacus": 172); Geggus, *Studies*, 16; Popkin, *Revolution*, 277 ("haughty").

90 Lacroix, *La révolution*, 214.

91 "Brigands": Howard, *Haitian Journal*, 79. "Ambuscades": 80. "Lolling": 43. Drowned: 49.

92 For the constitution's text see Louverture, *Revolution*, 45–61.

93 Louverture, *Memoir*, 324–25.

94 Bell, *Toussaint*, 293.

95 Rainsford, *Account*, 252–53.

96 Dubroca, *Life*, 62–63.

97 "Lash": Popkin, *Racial Revolution*, 277. "Splendor": 279.

98 Chazotte, *Black Rebellion*, 34.

99 "White and black": Fraser, *Pauline*, 67. Affair with Napoleon: 142–44.

100 Napoleon, *Correspondance*, 7.504.

101 Pachonski, *Caribbean Tragedy*, 137; Heinl, *Written*, 111.

102 Lacroix, *La révolution*, 320.

103 "Word of honor": Louverture, *Memoir*, 316. "Surrounded": 318. "Frightful": 326.

104 Leclerc, *Lettres*, 254.

105 Beard, *Toussaint*, 168.

106 "Inhuman": Popkin, *Revolution*, 297. "Tiger": 345. "Panic": Chazotte, *Black Rebellion*, 61.

107 Bourrienne, *Memoirs*, 2.91.

108 Pachonski, *Caribbean Tragedy*, 99; Dubois, *Avengers*, 289.

109 Leclerc, *Lettres*, 256.

110 Atrocities: Fick, *Making*, 220–22; Hassal, *Secret History*, 99 (burned alive); Pachonski, *Caribbean Tragedy*, 113–14 (dogs); Rainsford, *Account*, 327 ("putrefaction"); Léger, *Haiti*, 135–36; Ott, *Revolution*; Popkin, *Revolution*, 332 ("fat"); *Annual Register* (1803), 329 ("atrocious").

111 Dubois, *Avengers*, 277, 295; Auguste, *L'expedition*, 163–65.

112 Popkin, *Revolution*, 331.

113 *Annual Register* (1803), 333.

114 Bell, *Toussaint*, 252; Dubois, *Avengers*, 269.

115 Méneval, *Memoirs*, 1.194.

116 Slave revolts: Geggus, *Studies*, 55; Davis, *Inhuman Bondage*, ch. 11; Shaw, *Spartacus*, 12–13.

117 Price, *Maroon Societies*, 7. See also Zips, *Black Rebels*, ch. 4; Campbell, *Maroons*.

118 *Annual Register* (1803), 334.

119 Fick, *Haiti*, 15–19; Geggus, *Studies*, 5.

120 Dubois, *Avengers*, 172.

121 Casualties: Scheina, *Latin America's Wars*, 1.xiii–xiv ("six times"); Auguste, *L'expedition Leclerc*, 316; Girard, *Paradise Lost*, 49; Geggus, *Studies*, 20; Duffy, *Soldiers*, 328–29.

122 1798 revolt: Kee, *Green Flag* ("without mercy": 99; six weeks: 122; 50,000 killed: 123; military was Irish Catholic: 99); Gordon, *Rebellion* (salt in wounds: 253); Elliott, *Wolfe Tone*.

123 Slatta, *Bolivar's Quest*, 41.

124 "Intelligent, "cowards": *Letters*, 34. "Own way": 28.

125 Péta: "Adventures of a Foreigner—IV" (November 1826) ("regular fire," "dreadful cries," "torrent"); Brewer, *Greek War*, 148–53; St. Clair, *Greece*, 97–102; Gordon, *History*, 1.387–94; Finlay, *History*, 1.326–31; Howarth, *Adventure*, 93–96.

126 Fireship: Brewer, *Greek War*, 163–64; Gordon, *Greek Revolution*, 1.367–69; Finlay, *History*, 1.316–18; Howarth, *Adventure*, 44–45.

127 Chios: Argenti, *Massacres*; Brewer, *Greek War*, 164–66; Gordon, *Greek Revolution*, 1.367–69; Finlay, *History*, 1.311–14, 319–20.

128 Walsh, *Residence*, 1.385.

129 "Adventures of a Foreigner—I" (August 1826).

130 Trelawny, *Recollections*, 192.
131 Byron, "On This Day I Complete My Thirty-Sixth Year."
132 St. Clair, *Greece*, 66.
133 Green, *Sketches*, 207.
134 See, e.g., Wellington, *Despatches*, 3.113–16.
135 NA/ADM; Woodhouse, *Battle*; Codrington, *Memoirs*, vol. 2.
136 Letter from Codrington, Oct. 21, 1827, NA/ADM.
137 St. Clair, *Greece*, 274–75.
138 Bass, *Freedom's Battle*, 151.
139 "Rampant": Roosevelt, *Letters*, 93. "Humanity": 122–23.
140 Melena, *Recollections*, 230; Parris, *Lion*, 15.
141 Garibaldi, *Autobiography*, 1.19.
142 Mazzini, *Writings* ("method": 1.109; "merit": 1.374); Hibbert, *Garibaldi*, 15 ("dangerous"); Mack Smith, *Mazzini*; Bayly, *Mazzini*.
143 Macaroni: Ridley, *Garibaldi*, 46. "Destined": Hibbert, *Garibaldi*, 17.
144 Tortured: Garibaldi, *Autobiography*, 1.45–47; Ridley, *Garibaldi*, 67–69; Trevelyan, *Garibaldi's Defence*, 26. "Chivalrous": Riall, *Garibaldi*, 45.
145 Ridley, *Garibaldi*, 43, 118, 139, 187, 318.
146 Garibaldi, *Autobiography*, 2.23.
147 Ridley, *Garibaldi*, 178; Mack Smith, *Garibaldi*, 24.
148 Winnington-Ingram, *Hearts of Oak*, 93.
149 Anita: Garibaldi, *Autobiography*, 1.78–79 ("mine"); Ridley, *Garibaldi*, 85–94; Riall, *Garibaldi*, 43 ("two years"); Valerio, *Anita*; Hibbert, *Garibaldi*, 19–21; Parris, *Lion* ("wench": 55).
150 Riall, *Garibaldi*, 47–58; Scirocco, *Garibaldi*, 125–30; Parris, *Lion*, 64.
151 Garibaldi, *My Life*, 3.
152 Ibid., 9–14; Garibaldi, *Autobiography*, 1.258–88 ("holy": 261).
153 Rome and retreat: Garibaldi, *Autobiography*, 2.19–20 (wanted guerrilla war), 1.2–3 ("scum," "vice"), 2.22 ("entreaties"), 2.23 ("timidity"), 2.40 (bushes), 2.32 ("suffering"); Forbes, *Campaigns*, 334 ("Antichrist"); Ossoli, *Memoirs*, 2.64 (lions); Dandolo, *Volunteers*, 189–290; Mazzini, *Life*, 5.192–64; Trevelyan, *Garibaldi's Defence*; Ridley, *Garibaldi*, 308 ("hunger"); Riall, *Garibaldi*; Mack Smith, *Garibaldi*; Hibbert, *Garibaldi*, 45–121.
154 Melena, *General Garibaldi*, 229.
155 Vecchj, *Caprera*, 5.
156 Melena, *Public*, vii.
157 Hibbert, *Garibaldi*, 171–72; Ridley, *Garibaldi*, 426–28; Riall, *Garibaldi*, 180–82.
158 Melena, *Public*, 26.
159 Ibid., 14.
160 1859 campaign: Trevelyan, "War-Journals"; Parris, *Lion*, 152 ("disorganizing"); *Times* (London), July 26, 1859; Hibbert, *Garibaldi*, 146–62; Ridley, *Garibaldi*, 397–415.
161 Trevelyan, *Thousand*, 226–27; Ridley, *Garibaldi*, 436–41.
162 Thousand: Riall, *Garibaldi*, 183–84; Ridley, *Garibaldi*, 443–44; Mack Smith, *Garibaldi*, 91–92; Forbes, *Campaign*, 143 ("religion").

163 Calatafimi: Garibaldi, *Autobiography*, 2.165 ("hail"), 2.167 ("immeasurable"); Garibaldi, *My Life*, 95 ("decrepit"); Abba, *Diary* ("intoxicated": 33; "covered": 37; "miracle: 39; "traces": 41); Forbes, *Campaign*, 30–33; Mundy, *H.M.S. Hannibal*, 86–88; Hibbert, *Garibaldi*, 211–14.

164 Palermo: Garibaldi, *My Life*, 101 ("joined us"), 104 ("balcony"); Trevelyan, *Thousand*, 303 (population, troops); Abba, *Diary*; Trevelyan, "War-Journal" ("fallen"); Forbes, *Campaign* ("feints": 42; "carnage": 57; "rules": 93); Mario, *Red Shirt*; Mundy, *H.M.S. Hannibal*, 110–85; *Times* (London), June 18, 1860; Hibbert, *Garibaldi*, 219–37.

165 Forbes, *Campaign*, 233.

166 *New York Times*, Oct. 29, 1860.

167 Ridley, *Garibaldi*, 515, notes, "He had ruled 4,000,000 subjects in April 1859; in November 1860 he ruled 22,000,000, of whom 9,000,000 had been given to him by Garibaldi in the former Kingdom of Naples."

168 Forbes, *Campaigns*, 2.

169 Parris, *Garibaldi*, 277.

170 *Times* (London), April 12, 1864; *New York Times*, April 28, 1864; Parris, *Garibaldi*, 287; Hibbert, *Garibaldi*, 341.

171 Ridley, *Garibaldi*, 521–23; Parris, *Lion*, 269–70.

172 Trevelyan, *Thousand*, 6.

173 Lieber, *Instructions*, 26, 29; Hartigan, *Lieber's Code*; Grimsley, *Hard Hand*, 144–51; Fellman, *Inside War*, 82–84.

174 Franco-Prussian War: Hatley, "Inevitable" (16,000 men: 279; "element": 247; Châtillon-sur-Seine: 250–51); Howard, *Franco-Prussian War*, 249 ("pause"), 251 ("not soldiers"); Wawro, *Franco-Prussian*, 288–89, 309; Showalter, *German Unification*, 319; Ridley, *Garibaldi*; Garibaldi, *Autobiography* ("oppressed": 3.403); Horne, *Atrocities* ("harsh": 140–41); Hibbert, *Garibaldi*, 360 ("execrable"); Melena, *Public*, 285 ("left").

175 Mack Smith, *Garibaldi*, 179.

176 Hibbert, *Garibaldi*, xiii.

177 Bin Laden to Zawahiri, 2002. Harmony Database, CTC, AFGP-2002-600321.

178 Shelley, *Hellas*, 51.

179 Hassal, *Secret History*, 152.

180 "Misery": Riall, *Garibaldi*, 369. "Base": 371.

181 Bolívar, *Selected Writings*, 1.117.

182 Ibid., 2.761. San Martín also warned of "anarchy": Harrison, *Captain*, 175.

BOOK III: THE SPREADING OIL SPOT: THE WARS OF EMPIRE

1 In 1450, 1800: Lynn, *Acta*. In 1914: Headrick, *Tools*, 3.

2 Thornton, *Warfare*, 150.

3 Morris, *Washing*.

4 Boot, *War Made New*, 77–103.

5 Kopperman, *Braddock*; *WP*/CS, 1.336; Anderson, *Crucible* (casualty figures: 760, n. 17); Russell, "Redcoats"; Grenier, *Way*.

6 Jamestown: Smith, *Historie* ("beasts": 1.281; "barbarously": 1.280; "destroy them": 1.286); Kingsbury, *Records* ("skies fall": 3.550; "defacing": 3.551; "viperous": 3.553; wine: 4.98–99, 102, 220–22; "perpetual": 3.672); Price, *Love*, 200–21; Kupperman, *Jamestown*, 304–16; Rountree, *Powhatan*, 69–78 (Indian dress); Rountree, *Pocahontas's People*, 73–77; Neill, *Memoir*, 57 ("happy league"); Vaughan, "Expulsion"; Shea, *Virginia Militia*, 25–38; Horne, *Land*, 255–62; Steele, *Warpaths*, 46; Utley, *Indian Wars*, 8; Grenier, *First Way*, 23–24; Taylor, *American Colonies*, 129–37; Fausz, "Barbarous Massacre."

7 A paraphrase of Wilson, *Weep*, 47.

8 *WP*/CS, 2.233.

9 Champlain, *Works* ("frightened," "lost courage": 2.100); Fischer, *Champlain's Dream*, 265–70; Trigger, *Aataentsic*, 249–54; Steele, *Warpaths*, 64–65.

10 For the use of "Indians," rather than "Native Americans," see Mann, *1491*, appendix A.

11 Morgan, *Heroes*, 16 ("horror"), 17 ("cherished").

12 Mann, *1491*, 87.

13 Malone, *Skulking Way* (firearms: 42–45; Indian marksmanship: 52); Starkey, *Native American Warfare*, 20–25; Trigger, *Cambridge History*, vol. 1, pt. 2, pp. 5–21.

14 Rowlandson, *Narrative*, 68.

15 Parkman, *France*, 402.

16 Mann, *1491*, 94, notes that estimates of Indian population in the New World prior to 1492 range from 8 million to 112 million. He adds (132) that "the High Counters seem to be winning the argument, at least for now." For the case against the High Counters, see Henige, *Numbers*.

17 Snow, "European Contact."

18 Bradford, *Plymouth*, 327.

19 Wilson, *Weep*, 75.

20 King Philip's War: Cook, "Interracial Warfare" (casualty figures); Drake, *King Philip's War*; Lepore, *Name of War*; Schultz, *King Philip's War* (253 years: 2); Leach, *Flintlocks*.

21 Wilson, *Weep*, 21.

22 Saggs, *Assyria*, 263–68.

23 70,000 removed: Vandervort, *Indian Wars*, 122. "Brute": Rozema, *Voices*, Kindle location 2363.

24 Missall, *Seminole Wars*; Mahon, *Second Seminole War*; Sprague, *Florida War*.

25 Sand Creek: U.S. Congress, *Report* ("brains": 42); Greene, *Sand Creek*; Hoig, *Sand Creek*; Hatch, *Black Kettle*, 146–67.

26 Washita: Hardorff, *Washita* (buffalo trail: 107–8; "heap Injuns": 137; "close": 111; "moody": 153; "watch tick": 207; "village rang": 114; "eyelids": 208; "determined defense": 82; "gorgeous": 210; "superior": 88; ponies killed: 26–27, 144; mistress: 231; "nice": 171; casualties: 78–79); Custer, *Wild Life*, 206–33; Godfrey, "Reminiscences"

("Wilderness"); Brewster, "Battle" ("oppressive," "boys"); Barnitz, *Life* ("dispatch[ed]": 220; "surprising": 227); Spotts, *Campaigning*; Keim, *Troopers*, 145 ("mutilation"). For secondary sources, see Greene, *Washita*; Hoig, *Washita*; Epple, *Custer's Battle*; Hatch, *Black Kettle*; Utley, *Regulars* ("total war": 144); Brill, *Custer, Black Kettle*; Wert, *Custer* (mistress: 287–88); Utley, *Cavalier*, 64–78; Barnard, *Hoosier*.

27 The U.S. army and civilian figures are for 1848–90; the figure for Indians is for 1865–90. Vandervort, *Indian Wars*, xiv.

28 "Better": Hassrick, *Sioux*, 32. "Courting": 33. "Suffer": 34. Coup: 90–91.

29 270,000 Indians: Commissioner of Indian Affairs, *Report 1866*, 372. 100,000 hostiles: Utley, *Frontier Regulars*. 5.8 million Americans: Utley, *Indian Wars*, 161. 30,000 Sioux: U.S. Commissioner of Indian Affairs, *Report 1866*, 371.

30 Utley, *Indian Wars*, 193.

31 U.S. Secretary of the Interior, *Annual Report 1873*, 3–4.

32 Utley, *Regulars*, 15.

33 Ibid., 22.

34 Crook: Cozzens, *Eyewitnesses*, 5.213, 246; Bourke, *Border*, 110 ("lance"); AHEC/CKP, box 1 ("vices": Diary, Jan. 31, 1873–Feb. 15, 1873; cribbage: Diary, Aug. 13, 1885–Dec. 11, 1887; "pastime": A. H. Nickerson, "Major General George Crook and the Indians: A Sketch").

35 Aleshire, *Fox*, ix.

36 Cozzens, *Eyewitnesses*, 5.217.

37 Crook, "Apache Problem," 263–65 ("wildest," "physique," "pard," "trail").

38 Bourke, *Border*, 443.

39 Diary, Jan. 31, 1873–Feb. 15, 1873, AHEC/CKP, box 1.

40 Geronimo: AHEC/CKP; Aleshire, *Fox*; Crook, *Autobiography*; Miles, *Recollections*, 445–532, and *Serving*, 219–32; Bourke, *Border*; Bourke, *Apache Campaign*; Roberts, *They Moved* (266 mules, 327 men: 228; $2: 309); Aleshire, *Fox*; Utley, *Frontier Regulars*, 344–96; Vandervort, *Indian Wars*, 192–10; Geronimo, *Story*; Gatewood, *Memoir*; Thrapp, *Apacheria*; Cozzens, *Eyewitnesses*, vol. 1.

41 Alcohol, swearing: Utley, *Cavalier*, 108–9; Wert, *Custer*, 46; Barnett, *Touched*, 80.

42 "Genial": A. H. Nickerson, "Major General George Crook and the Indians: A Sketch," AHEC/CKP, box 1. "Pomp": Bourke, *Border*, 108.

43 Cozzens, *Eyewitness*, 4.251.

44 Little Bighorn: Utley, *Frontier Regulars*; Yenne, *Sitting Bull* and *Indian Wars*; Cozzens, *Eyewitnesses*, vol. 4; Michino, *Lakota Noon* (estimates of Indian strength: 3–12); Gray, *Custer's Last Campaign* and *Centennial Campaign*; Wert, *Custer*; Utley, *Cavalier*; Vandervort, *Indian Wars*; Hutton, *Custer Reader* and *Soldiers West*; Scott, *Perspectives*; Godfrey, *Account*; AHEC/CKP, box 1 ("lithe": A. H. Nickerson, "Major General George Crook and the Indians: A Sketch"); Utley, *Cavalier*, 65 ("Indians enough").

45 Utley, *Indian Wars*; St. Clair, *Narrative*; Trigger, *Cambridge History*, vol. 1, pt. 1.

46 Reasonable choice: Friedman, "Strategy Trap."

47 Miles: AHEC/NAM ("nature": Winfield S. Hancock to 2nd Corps Headquarters, June 24, 1863, box 1; "sleepless," "uncommon": Francis C. Barlow to Sen. Henry Wilson, Nov. 28, 1863, box 1; "pounding": Phil Sheridan to Adjutant General, Oct. 25, 1877, box 2); Finerty, *War-Path* ("no rest": 298); Remington, *John Ermine* ("light fires": 136); Miles, *Recollections* ("Esquimaux": 219; 60 below: 218); Cozzens, *Eyewitnesses*, vol. 4; Utley, *Frontier Regulars*; Greene: *Lakota*, *Yellowstone*, *Battles*, *Morning*; Robinson, *Good Year*; Andrist, *Long Death*; DeMontravel, *A Hero*; Wooster, *Nelson A. Miles*.

48 Vandervort, *Indian Wars*, 46.

49 Gimri: Baddeley, *Conquest* (snow: 276; "ferocious": 266–69; Germentchug: 27–274); Blanch, *Sabres* ("bare": 70; "wild beast": 73–74); al-Qarakhi, *Shining* (pulled out sword: 22); Gammer, *Resistance*, 58–59; Allen, *Caucasian Battlefields*, 47–48 ("Wahabi").

50 Baddeley, *Conquest*, xxxvi.

51 Blanch, *Sabres*, 1.

52 Yermolou: Baddeley, *Conquest* (abandoned gun: 107; "terror": 97); King, *Ghost of Freedom*, 45–50; Gammer, *Resistance*, 29–38, and *Lone Wolf*, 31–44; Blanch, *Sabres*, 22–26; Longworth, *Russia*, 199–200; Dunlop, *Chechnya*, 13–18.

53 Tolstoy, *Hadji Murat*, 63.

54 Gammer, *Resistance*, 22.

55 Origins of gazavat: Gammer, *Resistance*, 39–65; Gammer, *Lone Wolf*, 45–50; King, *Ghost*, 64–73; Zelkina, *Quest*, 121–68; Blanch, *Sabres*, 54–124; Baddeley, *Conquest*, 230–88; Dunlop, *Chechnya*, 23–24; Seton-Watson, *Russian Empire*, 291–92.

56 Shamil's appearance: Blanch, *Sabres*, 48 (height), 52 (henna), 129 ("flames darted"); Tolstoy, *Hadji Murad*, 67 ("hewn").

57 Second escape: Blanch, *Sabres*, 162–74; Baddeley, *Conquest*, 328–43; King, *Ghost*, 79–80; Gammer, *Resistance*, 96–109.

58 Baddeley, *Conquest*, 438.

59 Blanch, *Sabres*, 129–33; Baddeley, *Conquest* ("betraying": 378); Gammer, *Resistance*, 239–40.

60 Zelkina, *Quest*, 223.

61 Gammer, *Muslim Resistance*, 24; King, *Ghost*, 90.

62 J. A. Longworth to the Earl of Clarendon, July 20, 1855, NA/CIR.

63 Vernadsky, *Source Book*, 3.609.

64 Ibid.

65 War's end: Blanch, *Sabres*, 293–301, 390–410; Baddeley, *Russian Conquest*, 437–82; al-Qarakhi, *Shining*, 61–65; King, *Ghost*, 84–92; Gammer, *Resistance*, 277–79, and *Lone Wolf*, 63–64; Zelkina, *Quest*, 226–34; Barrett, "Remaking."

66 Abd el-Kader: Kiser, *Commander* (Shamil's thanks: 303); Churchill, *Abdel Kader*; Danziger, *Abd al-Qadir.*

67 Baddeley, *Conquest*, 480.

68 King, *Ghost*, 76.

69 See Lermontov's *A Hero of Our Time* and Tolstoy's *Hadji Murad*, *The Cossacks*, and "The Wood-Felling: A Junker's Tale," in *Sevastopol and Other Military Tales*, 154–205.
70 Start of march: Kaye, *History* ("ankle-deep": 2.329); "Brydon's Ride," in Sale, *Journal* ("charred": 161); Sale, *Journal* (frosty: 95; "disorganized": 102); Eyre, *Military Operations* (size of force: 196; "dreary": 195; "conflagration": 199; "fell": 199).
71 Kipling, "Hymn before Action" (1896).
72 Army of the Indus: Kaye, *History*, 1.379,388, 389 ("comforts"), 1.464 ("bayonets"); Waller, *Beyond*, 137–38; Havelock, *Narrative*, 1.23 ("mortifying"); Gleig, *Sale's Brigade*, 69–73 (cricket).
73 Gleig, *Sale's Brigade*, 100.
74 Kaye, *History*, 2.336–37.
75 Sale to T. H. Maddock, April 16, 1842, NA/RBJ ("fanatical," "melancholy").
76 Lunt, *Bokhara Burnes*; Burnes, *Cabool*.
77 Sale, *Journal*, 37.
78 Ibid., 20.
79 Kaye, *History*, 2.191.
80 Ibid., 196.
81 Ibid., 273.
82 Colley, *Captives*.
83 End of march: NA/AC; Kaye, *History* ("ankle-deep": 2.329; "incessant": 2.162; "dark": 2.384: "cruel": 2.385); "Brydon's Ride," in Sale, *Journal* ("charred": 161); Sale, *Journal* ("frost-bitten": 108); Eyre, *Military Operations*, 195–235 (size of force: 196; "faintest semblance": 201; "monstrous": 205; 3,000 died: 209; "slaughter": 208; 700 Europeans: 196); Marshman, *Memoirs*, 50 ("stupendous"); Gleig, *Sale's Brigade*; Stewart, *Crimson Snow*, 145–75; Macrory, *Retreat*, 197–238; Waller, *Beyond*, 236–55; Tanner, *Afghanistan*, 193 (hostages); Norris, *First Afghan War*, 378–81; Dupree, *Afghanistan*, 388–93.
84 Maj. Rawlinson to Maj.-Gen. Nott, Feb. 1, 1842, NA/AC, 75.
85 Low, *Pollock*, 255–58.
86 Colley, *Captives*, 354 ("scribbling").
87 Ibid., 363.
88 Pollock to Maj. Gen. Lumley, Oct. 13, 1842, NA/AC, 217.
89 Low, *Pollock*, 416.
90 Kaye, *History*, 3.376.
91 Proclamation by governor general, Oct. 1, 1842, NA/AC, 214.
92 Second Afghan War: Robson, *Road* (casualties: 299); Intelligence Branch, *Official Account*; Hanna, *Second Afghan War*; Roberts, *Forty-One Years*, vol. 2; Hensman, *Afghan War*.
93 Third Afghan War: Robson, *Crisis*.
94 Elphinstone, *Caubul*, 253.
95 Schofield, *Afghan Frontier*, 163.
96 Warburton, *Eighteen Years*, 343.
97 Malakand Field Force: Churchill, *Malakand Field Force*, 127 ("chastise"), 204 ("roadless," "march anywhere"), 168 ("destroyed"), 66 ("no quarter"); Churchill,

Young Winston's Wars; CAM/CHUR, 28/23; Blood, *Four Score;* Pioneer, *Risings*; Schofield, *Afghan Frontier*, 107–11; Swinson, *North-West Frontier*, 232–55.

98 Great Britain, *Hansard's*, 54.749, March 7, 1898.

99 "Pinpricking," "we had": Masters, *Bugles*, 194–95. "Castrate": 199. "Few": 197.

100 Kipling, *Complete Verse*, 414–16.

101 Masters, *Bugles*, 201.

102 Maurice, *History*, 1.91–92.

103 Henissart, *Wolves*, 29.

104 Porch, *Morocco*, 85–86. For a response, see Singer, *Force*, 200–201.

105 Lyautey, "Du rôle social."

106 Windrow, *Our Friends*, 170.

107 Lyautey, *Lettres*, 1.122.

108 Maurois, *Lyautey*, 47.

109 Ibid., 54.

110 Gann, *Proconsuls*, 90.

111 Indochina: Ibid., 80–108; Hoisington, *Lyautey*, 7; Gershovich, *Military Rule*, 30; Thompson, *Indo-China*, 74; Earle, *Makers*, 238–40; Windrow, *Our Friends*, 191–209.

112 Lyautey, "Du rôle colonial."

113 Porch, *Morocco*, xxii; Bidwell, *Morocco*, xi.

114 Porch, *Morocco*, 187. For a contrary view see Hoisington, *Lyautey*, 53, 206.

115 Morocco population: Park, *Historical Dictionary*, 98.

116 Windrow, *Our Friends*, 167.

117 Burnoose: Maurois, *Lyautey*, 115–17. "Notables": 158. "Passion": 50.

118 Harris, *Morocco*, 295.

119 Maurois, *Lyautey*, 196.

120 El-Hiba: Porch, *Morocco*, 266–67; Hoisington, *Lyautey*, 46; Gershovich, *Military Rule*, 96; Maxwell, *Lords*, 129–30; Bidwell, *Morocco*, 104; Windrow, *Our Friends*, 403. "Execution": Boot, *War Made New*, 148.

121 Maurois, *Lyautey*, 168–69.

122 Gershovich, *Military Rule*, 80.

123 Rif: Woolman, *Rebels* (half million: 196); Gershovich, *Military Rule*, 122–66; Pennell, *Country*.

124 Lyautey, *Lettres*, 2.129. Degrees, "bad": Earle, *Makers*, 258.

125 Black Week: Amery, *Times History*, 3.2 ("unsuccess," "stinging"), 3.3 ("stirred") ; Fitzgibbon, *Arts*, 2 ("deep gloom"); NA/SAD, vol. 1; Doyle, *Great Boer War*, 108–9 ("disastrous"); Pennell, *Whistler*, 253–54 ("whipped"); *Times*, *Guardian*, *Observer*; Victoria, *Letters*, 3.434 ("grieved"); *Daily Telegraph*, Dec. 11, 1899 ("grave news"), Dec. 16 ("reverse"); *Daily Mail*, Dec. 15 ("heavy losses"); Farwell, *Anglo-Boer War*, 139–47; Pakenham, *Boer*, 252–64.

126 Population: http://www.parliament.uk/commons/lib/research/rp99/rp99-111.pdf. Industrialized: Kennedy, *Rise and Fall*, 200.

127 Schikkerling, *Commando*, 207–8.

128 Reitz, *Commando*, 142.

129 Maurice, *History*, 1.1; Amery, *Times History*, 2.88.
130 Pakenham, *Boer*, 253.
131 *Times* (London), Dec. 18, 1899.
132 Kipling, "Bobs" (1892).
133 Maurice, *History*, 4.5; Pakenham, *Boer War*, 486.
134 De Wet: Pienaar, *With Steyn*, 97 ("sorry sight"), 103 ("castrate"); Wilson, *After Pretoria*, 1.49; De Wet, *Three Years*, 75 ("rapidity"); Rosenthal, *De Wet*, foreword ("byword"); Rosslyn, *Captured*, 256 ("undistinguished").
135 Sanna's Post: De Wet, *Three Years* ("hands up": 66); Rosenthal, *De Wet*, 74–78; Amery, *Times History*, 4.29–50; Pakenham, *Boer War* (30,000 men: 414); Farwell, *Anglo-Boer War*, 257–63.
136 Smuts raid: Reitz, *Commando*, 112 (George Washington), 215 ("every valley"), 218 ("finished"), 219 ("glissading"), 212 ("evil dreams"), 209 ("ragged"), 223 ("froze"), 210 ("first slice"), 230 ("refitted"); Smuts, *Smuts*, 63 (*Anabasis*), 61 (250 men); Smuts, *Papers*, 1.433 ("poison"), 1.434 ("terrible"), 1.437 ("right").
137 James, *Heels*, 12.
138 Mosley, *Glorious Fault*, 119.
139 Farwell, *Anglo-Boer War*, 353.
140 Phillipps, *With Rimington*, 201.
141 Great Britain, *Hansard's*, 90.180, March 1, 1901.
142 Reconcentrado: Tone, *War*, 193 (deaths), 164 ("bonbons"); Thomas, *Cuba*, 329–31.
143 Pakenham, *Scramble*; Hull, *Destruction*.
144 Hamilton, *Commander*, 67.
145 Concentration camps: Hobhouse, *Brunt*, 116 ("indescribable"), 118 ("luxury"), 153 ("barbarism"); Hall, *Bloody Woman*, 3 ("bloody"); Hamilton, *Commander*, 67 ("feel"); Martin, *Concentration Camps*, 31 (death figures); Judd, *Boer War*; Pakenham, *Boer War*, 549 (150,000).
146 Pakenham, *Boer War*, 492.
147 2,000 volunteers: Judd, *Boer War*, 247.
148 Blockhouses: NA/BLOCK; Fuller, *Last*, 107–48 ("nothing to do": 111); Wilson, *After Pretoria*, 2.546–50; Maurice, *History*, 4.568–76.
149 NA/AT.
150 "Blockhead": De Wet, *Three Years*, 260. "Succeeded": 261. "Night": 263. "Undoing: 18. "Probability": 224.
151 Andrew, *Secret Service*, 29; Pakenham, *Boer War*, 573.
152 Woolls-Sampson: Sampson, *Anti-Commando* ("fanatical": 99; "mad": 150; "enflamed": 134); Farwell, *Anglo-Boer War*, 356–57; Pakenham, *Boer War*, 573.
153 "Attrition": Reitz, *Commando*, 314. "Ruin," "disastrous": 322.
154 Maurice, *History*, 4.562.
155 Reconstruction: Amery, *Times History*, vol. 6; *Milner Papers*, 2.367–403; Thompson, *Forgotten Patriot*, 219–38.
156 Fuller, *Last*.

157 "Massed": Fuller, *Last,* 7. Fatalities: Amery, *Times History,* 7.25.
158 "Friendly": Lt. Gen. Bindon Blood, Aug. 27, 1901, NA/SAD, 1.159. "Rules": 1.160.
159 Philippines: Boot, *Savage Wars,* ch. 5.
160 Amery, *Times History,* 3.3.
161 Callwell, *Small Wars,* ch. 11.
162 Ibid., 24.
163 Mockaitis, *Counterinsurgency,* 18.
164 Kipling, *Complete Verses,* 327. See also Gilmour, *Recessional,* 119–24.

BOOK IV: THE BOMB THROWERS: THE FIRST AGE OF INTERNATIONAL TERRORISM

1 Assassins: Lewis, *Assassins* ("genius": 37; "dared to leave": 51; "cursed and fled": 1; "unlike": xi); Daftary, *Assassin Legends*; Bartlett, *Assassins* (50 victims: 68; "dignity": 97); Juvaini, *History*; Hodgson, *Secret Order.*
2 Fraser, *Faith*; Williamson, *Gunpowder Plot.*
3 Dash, *Thug.* For a comparison of Thugs, Sicarii, and Assassins, see Rapoport, "Fear."
4 Jensen, "Anarchist Terrorism."
5 Rapoport, "Fourth Wave."
6 Pottawatomie: BSC ("Freedom," "confidence": Brown to John Brown Jr., July 9,1858); U.S. House, *Special Committee,* 1193–206 ("come back": 1193; "old man": 1195; "cut off": 1195); Brown, *Truth,* 20–41; Oates, *To Purge,* 126–38 (damp wind: 134); Carton, *Patriotic Treason,* 187–93; Reynolds, *John Brown,* 138–78; Villard, *John Brown,* 148–88 ("WAR": 189).
7 Watts, "How Bloody," 123.
8 Ruchames, *Brown Reader,* 38.
9 Hinton, *John Brown,* 679.
10 Reynolds, *John Brown,* 152.
11 "Wild": Brown, *Truth,* 70. "Strike," "example": 68. "Barbarians": KSH/WJB, 281.
12 Black Jack: BSC; KSH/JBP; KSH/BBJ; KSH/WJB ("memories"); Oates, *To Purge,* 152–54; Carton, *Patriotic Treason,* 207–12; Reynolds, *John Brown,* 185–88.
13 Osawatomie: BSC; Brown to family, Sept. 7, 1856, KSH/JBP; Bridgman, *With Brown*; Reynolds, *John Brown,* 199–201 ("end": 200); Carton, *Patriotic Treason,* 216–20; Oates, *To Purge,* 169–71.
14 "Damaging": Brown, *Truth,* 70. "Terrified": 74.
15 Reynolds, *John Brown,* 175.
16 Brown to John Brown Jr., July 9, 1858, BSC.
17 Renehan, *Secret Six,* ch. 3.
18 "All the books": Hinton, *John Brown,* 182–83. "Admirably": 673. "Iron": *Life, Trial,* 14. "Preparatory": Reynolds, *John Brown,* 241.
19 Harpers Ferry: *Life, Trial* ("gory": 85; "mockery": 55; "forfeit": 95); BSC ("cheerful": Brown to Mary Ann Brown, Oct. 31, 1859); Boteler, "Recollections" ("drizzly");

Green, "Capture" (blue; "tigers"); Daingerfield, "John Brown"; Rosengarten, "Brown's Raid"; Chambers, "School-Girl"; Moore, "Eyewitness": Strother, "Invasion" ("variety"); Carton, *Patriotic Treason*; Reynolds, *John Brown*; Oates, *To Purge*.

20 Thoreau, *Writings*, 10.234.

21 Ruchames, *Brown Reader*, 331.

22 Fleming, *Documentary*, 1.455–56.

23 Rable, *No Peace*, 26; Zuczek, *Rebellion*, 160.

24 Zuczek, *Rebellion*, 127.

25 KKK origin: Lester, *Ku Klux Klan* ("diversion": 53; "mysterious": 56; 500,000 members: 30; "kulos": 55); Fleming, *Documentary*, vol. 2; Trelease, *White Terror*, xv–64; Hahn, *Nation*, 257 ("rubric"), 269 ("guerrilla"); Foner, *Reconstruction*, 342, 425; Franklin, *Slavery*, 248–51.

26 Elias Hill: Unless otherwise specified, all quotations are from U.S. Congress, *KKK Report*, 5.1406–15, 1477. See also Martinez, *Carpetbaggers*, 77–78; Lester, *Ku Klux Klan* ("terror": 73; "ignorant": 74; "darkies": 22) Budiansky, *Bloody Shirt*, 131–33; West, *York County*, 83–84; Trelease, *White Terror*, 371–72.

27 KKK murders: U.S. Congress, *KKK Report*, 5.1472, 5.1678–79, 5.1712–41 (Williams); Rubin, *Scalawags*, 46–47; Zuczek, *Rebellion*, 54; Martinez, *Carpetbaggers*, 1–6, 25; Trelease, *White Terror*, 116, 367; West, *York County*, 123–25 (Williams); Budiansky, *Bloody Shirt*, 122–23; Williamson, *After Slavery*, 260; Lamson, *Glorious Failure*, 83–84.

28 Foner, *Reconstruction*, 437.

29 Ibid., 434.

30 Sefton, *Army*, 261–62; Trelease, *White Terror*, xxxiv; Gillette, *Retreat*, 35. 900 agents: Foner, *Reconstruction*, 143.

31 *1870 Census* (online).

32 York: U.S. Congress, *KKK Report*, 5.1482 ("sporadic"), 5.1600 ("powerless"), 5.1602 (600 cases), 5.1465 ("beating, whipping"), 5.1603 ("white community," "wickedness"), 5.1602 ("game"), 5.1605 ("crushed"); *New York Tribune*, Nov. 13, 1871 ("German professor"; "dreariness"); Akerman to Merrill, Nov. 9, 1871, ATA ("villainies"); Letters Sent, vol. 1.10, NARA/RPY ("kindly"); "respectable": vol. 2.64, NARA/RPY; NARA/DOJ-SC, box 1, folder 5; NARA/DOJ-LS, reels 13–14; Casey to President, Aug. 7, 1862, NARA/LM, roll 38 ("talent"); Martinez, *Carpetbaggers*, 76–106, 133–233; Zuczek, *Rebellion*, 93–122 (sentences, convictions: 101, 122; Bratton: 120); Budiansky, *Bloody Shirt* ("just the man": 136); West, *York County*, 80–108, 126–30 (Bratton); Fleming, *Documentary History*, 2. 123–30 (KKK Act); Rable, *No Peace*, 156 ("no peace"); Trelease, *White Terror*, 362–80, 401–8.

33 Lester, *Ku Klux Klan*, 90.

34 For an overview of the historical evidence on the "deal" to remove troops, see Kousser, *Region*, 417–51.

35 3,000 killed: Budiansky, *Bloody Shirt*, 7. 650,000 to 850,000 killed: *New York Times*, April 2, 2012.

36 Horne, *Fall*.

37 Émile Henry: Merriman, *Club* ("black pants": 149; Eiffel Tower: 147; Café: 1–3, 149–55; "perfect little": 185; "kind of society": 16); *New York Times*, Feb. 13, 1894; Vizetelly, *Anarchists*, 157–62; Malato, "Anarchist Portraits"; *Review of Reviews* (Jan.–June 1894), 9.269 ("loafer"); Guerin, *No Gods* ("turned my stomach": 3.41); Lonergan, *Forty Years*, 172 ("indifferent"); Carr, *Anarchism*, 65–66; *Cyclopedic Review of Current History* (1894), 201 ("atoms"); Joll, *Anarchists*, 136–38; Rudorff, *Belle Epoque*, 165–67; Butterworth, *World*, 326–28.

38 Brousse, "La propagande." Bakunin had inspired the phrase in 1870: "We must spread our principles, not with words but with deeds, for this is the most popular, the most potent, and the most irresistible form of propaganda." Bakunin, *On Anarchism*, 195–96.

39 Anarchist philosophers: Marshall, *Demanding*; Butterworth, *World*; Joll, *Anarchists* ("despair": 153); Guerin, *No Gods*; Kropotkin, *Memoirs*; Bakunin, *On Anarchism*; Avrich, *Portraits*; Kedward, *Anarchists*.

40 Jensen, "Anarchist Terrorism," 120.

41 Vizetelly, *Anarchists*, 159–60; *Cyclopedic Review of Current History* (1894), 208–9; Oliver, *Movement* ("clumsy": 104); *New York Times*, Feb. 16, 1894.

42 Bowden, *Terror*, 134–61.

43 Joll, *Anarchists*, 130.

44 Bookchin, *Spanish Anarchists*, 102; Kedward, *Anarchists*, 41; *New York World*, Nov. 9, 1893.

45 Gage, *Day*; Davis, *Wagon*; Avrich, *Sacco*, 204–7.

46 Malato, "Anarchist Portraits"; Carr, *Anarchism*, 63–65; Merriman, *Club*, 137–46; Vizetelly, *Anarchists*, 145–54.

47 Vizetelly, *Anarchists*, 169; *Cyclopedic Review of Current History* (1894), 201; Merriman, *Club*, 174–78.

48 Vizetelly, *Anarchists*, 163–64.

49 Joll, *Anarchists*, 133; Weber, *France*, 117.

50 Avrich, *Portraits*, 41.

51 Serge, *Memoirs*, 17.

52 Guerin, *No Gods*, 3.43.

53 Most, *Revolutionary Warfare*, 60.

54 *New York Times*, April 2, 1881.

55 Butterworth, *World*, 373.

56 Police cooperation: Jensen, "Campaign"; Zuckerman, *Secret Police*; Deflem, "Wild Beasts"; Ruud, *Fontanka*, 79–100; Liang, *Police*, 151–82.

57 Carr, *Infernal*, 32.

58 Guerin, *No Gods*, 3.42; Butterworth, *World*, 327–28.

59 Avrich, *Portraits*, 111–24; Palij, *Makhno*; Joll, *Anarchists* (15,000: 187).

60 Jensen, "Campaign"; Deflem, "Wild Beasts."

61 Tsar hunt: Radzinsky, *Alexander II* (sentenced to death: 315; "cold wet mud": 318;

"marmalade": 322; blind eye: 400; "red cap": xv; "deafening": 413; "bloody chunks": 415); Figner, *Memoirs* (pine grove: 68; "populist socialist": 74; "prosperous": 12; "vivacious": 28; "spark": 47; "doll" 79; "struck dumb": 94); Stepniak, *Underground* ("charming": 126; "sweet," "dreaded": 127); Marshall, *Demanding*, 284 ("doomed man"); Hingley, *Nihilists* ("peasant-lovers": 74); Figes, *Natasha's Dance*, 9 (Winter Palace); Ulam, *Name* (Winter Palace casualties: 340–41; "uncompromising": 353); Lincoln, *Romanovs*, 442–47 ("dreary": 446); Seth, *Russian Terrorists*; Ruud, *Fontanka*, 46–51; Daly, *Under Siege*, 31–33; Footman, *Conspiracy*; Venturi, *Roots*, 633–720; Kennan, *Siberia*, 2.433–36 ("Nihilists"); Bergman, *Vera Zasulich*; Siljak, *Angel*.

62 Pipes, *Degaev*; Ulam, *Name*, 380–89; Land, *Enemies*, 207–10; Seth, *Russian Terrorists*, 158–63.

63 Pomper, *Brother*; Naimark, *Terrorists*, 130–53; Ulam, *Name*, 328 (emulate), 392–93.

64 Education: Figes, *Tragedy*, 93 (literacy), 108 (urban), 163 (university students); Brooks, *To Read*, 4 (literacy), 112 (periodicals).

65 Witte, *Memoirs*, 210.

66 SRs: Geifman, *Thou* (airplane: 17; suicide: 74); Geifman, *Death*, 101 (opera); Savinkov, *Memoirs*; Hildermeier, *Revolutionary* ("holy act": 54); Ascher, *Stolypin* (18th attempt: 2; suicide bombers: 138–39; assassination: 371–89); Lincoln, *Romanovs*, 650–68; Ruud, *Fontanka*, 173–200; Daly, *Watchful State*.

67 Trotsky, *Individual Terrorism*, 22.

68 Geifman, *Thou*, 91.

69 Stalin: Montefiore, *Young Stalin* (street battles: 128–50; Tiflis holdup: 3–16, 178–81); Deutscher, *Stalin*, 70–72, 84–90; Geifman, *Thou*, 21 (2,000 robberies); De Lon, "Stalin," 182 ("cut throats"), 183–86 (Tiflis robbery).

70 Avrich, *Russian Anarchists*; Geifman, *Thou*, 127–38.

71 Geifman, *Thou*, 21; Ruud, *Fontanka 16*, 278.

72 Alexander, *Once*, 224.

73 Russian repression: Pipes, *Old Regime*, 281-318 (44 executed: 315; exiles: 311); Deutscher, *Stalin*, 49 ("education"); Ruud, *Fontanka*; Daly, *Under Siege* (8,000 exiled: 181; 3,000–5,000 killed: 182), and *Watchful State* (100 times fewer, "underpoliced": 5; 200–300: 7); Lauchlan, *Hide-and-Seek* (161 employees: 85); Zuckerman, *Secret Police in Russian Society*; Figes, *Tragedy*, 139 (*Das Kapital*); Kennan, "Penal Code" ("unpermitted"); Kennan, *Siberia*, 2.461 ("swarms"); Witte, *Memoirs*, 257 ("lethargy"); Geifman, *Thou*; Montefiore, *Young Stalin*, 107–15; Deutscher, *Stalin*, 57–58.

74 Azef: Geifman, *Entangled*; Nikolaejewsky, *Aseff*; Geifman, *Thou*, 232–37; Savinkov, *Memoirs*, 312–51; Ascher, *Stolypin*, 270–71; Seth, *Russian Terrorists*, 177–292; Ruud, *Fontanka*, 125–51; Daly, *Watchful State*, 84–97.

75 Day, *Watchful State*, 72.

76 Geifman, *Thou*, 249.

77 Daly, *Watchful State*, xi.

78 Fenians: Short, *Dynamite War*; Golway, *Irish Rebel*; Kee, *Green Flag*, 299–351 (2,000 members: 504).

79 Ambush: Breen, *My Fight*, 7–35; Dan Breen interview: http://www.youtube.com/watch?v=SYiOUyhSvd0 ("got to kill"); NAI/DB; Hopkinson, *Irish War*, 115–16; Griffith, *Curious Journey*, 134 ("farthing"); O'Malley, *Wounds*, 97 (*Small Wars*).

80 Dáil: *Freeman*, Oct. 12, 1921 ("chairs"); NLI/PBP, 912/14 ("national status"); Kee, *Green Flag*, 630–31; Hopkinson, *Irish War*, 38–39, 207–9.

81 *New York World*, Jan. 22–23, 1919.

82 Collins: Hart, *Mick* (whiskey, cigarettes, swearing: 35; nickname: 105; "fun": 136; "lightning": 207; workdays: 244; 12 shot: 212–14; "playboy": 341); Coogan, *Michael Collins* (admired De Wet: 13; description: 20; Foy, *Intelligence War* ("never let": 40; moles: 44–51); NAI/MCC ("constitutional," "no jails": Interview with Gen. Crozier, 422/13); NLI/PBP, 916/4 (Collins to De Wet, Sept. 21, 1921: "inspiration"); Winter, *Tale* ("Robin Hood": 345); O'Malley, *Wounds*, 123 ("hearty"); Barry, *Guerilla Days*, 241 ("harsh," "virtually"); Neligan, *Spy*, 74 (appearance), 88 ("rattled"); Stapleton, "Michael Collins's Squad" ("extermination"); Kavanagh, "Intelligence Organisation"; NA/IBR, 88 ("nursery"); NAI/JB; NAI/VB ("getting on," "loved": 36; "extreme action": 32); NAI/BCB; NAI/PM ("obnoxious": 16); NAI/JL; NAI/PL; NAI/CD; NAI/WJS.

83 Neligan, *Spy*, 84.

84 Bloody Sunday: Maj. E. L. Mills, report, Nov. 22, 1920, NA/IRE ("any need"); Proceedings of Courts of Inquest, Nov. 23, 1920, Dec. 8, 1920, NA/IRE ("surround"); Andrews, *Dublin* ("winter's day": 162); IWM/RDJ; NAI/VB, 53–57 ("both fell dead"); NAI/PM; NAI/JL; NAI/WJS ("hysterical": 29); NAI/JJS; NAI/CD ("spot": Interview with Gen. Crozier, 422/13); Dalton, *Dublin Brigade*, 101–9; Woodcock, *Officer's Wife*, 20 ("hush-hush"), 61–69 ; Foy, *Intelligence War*, 140–77 (casualties: 173–74); Sturgis, *Last Days*, 76 ("black day"); Kee, *Green Flag*, 693–95 (size of Auxies and Tans: 671); Horgan, *Lemass*, 17–18; Macready, *Annals*, 2.507–10; Hart, *Mick*, 240–42; Neligan, *Spy*, 122–25; Sheehan, *British Voices*, 88–90; Hopkinson, *Irish War*, 46–47 (barracks), 89–91; Winter, *Tale*, 321–24; Stapleton, "Collins's Squad" ("laws of God"); Crozier, *Ireland*, 99–105, 116–17.

85 *New York Times*, Nov. 10, 1920.

86 "Pitiable": Macready, *Annals*, 2.470. Pistol in lap: 2.469. "Immobilized": Winter, *Tale*, 291. "Evening meal": Barton, *Spurs*, 206. "Hunted": Montmorency, *Sword*, 357.

87 Macready, *Annals*, 2.499.

88 Gleeson, *Bloody Sunday*, 55–78.

89 Lt. W. E. Crossley, "Report on ambush of 'L' Coy," June 17, 1921, NA/IRE.

90 O'Malley, *Wounds*, 240.

91 Callwell, *Wilson*, 2.264.

92 Hart, *British Intelligence*, 29.

93 Shadow government: Macready, *Annals*, 2.477–78; NLI/PBP, 913/3; Barry, *Guerilla Days*, 84; Duff, *Sword*, 70; Hopkinson, *Irish War*, 44.

94 Troop strength: Hart, *I.R.A.*, 113; Kee, *Green Flag*, 682, 719; Hopkinson, *Irish War*, 49; Collins, *Nationalism*, 176. Population: 1926 Census, www.cso.ie/census/census_1926_results/Volume1/C%201%201926%20V1.pdf.

95 Macready, *Annals*, 2.435.
96 NA/DRA.
97 Gilbert, *Churchill*, 4.461.
98 Corum, *Airpower*, 54–57; Omissi, *Air Power*, 18–38; Jacobsen, "By the Sword."
99 Wilson to Macready, June 7, 1920, IWM/NMC, vol. A.
100 Macready to Wilson, July 13, 1920, IWM/NMC, vol. A.
101 Churchill, *World Crisis*, 297.
102 "Integrity": Gilbert, *Churchill*, 4.470. "Conspiracy": 4.461. "Prussians": 4.455.
103 Collins to Kitty Kiernan, Aug. 4, 1922, NLI/KK.
104 Collins to Kitty Kiernan, Aug. 8, 1922, NLI/KK.
105 Barry, *Guerilla Days*, 243.
106 English, *Irish Freedom*, 328.
107 Kee, *Green Flag*, 744.
108 NA/IBR, 6.
109 Maloney, *Secret*, 23.
110 Hart, *Mick*, 199 (4,000); Hart, *I.R.A.*, 30, 66–67; Kee, *Green Flag*, 671, 699; Hopkinson, *Irish War*, 201. Collins, *Nationalism*, 170, gives a lower overall figure (751 killed, 1,200 wounded) but a higher figure for crown forces: 550 dead, 1,027 wounded.
111 Duff, *Sword*, 64.
112 NAI/CD, 13–14; O'Malley, *Wounds*, 319; Hart, *Mick*, 220–23; Dalton, *Dublin Brigade*, 67; Hopkinson, *Irish War*, 70.
113 Propaganda war: Macready, *Annals*, 2.471 ("rankled"), 2.553 ("inability"); IWM/NMC, vol. C ("futile": Macready to Wilson, March 10, 1921; "blackguard": Macready to Wilson, March 18, 1921); Kenneally, *Paper Wall*, 159 ("defiled"), 160 ("lynch"); Montmorency, *Sword* ("bad Press": 353; "flabby": 355).
114 Marks, *Shaped*, 17–37; Carr, *Infernal*, 35; Heehs, "Terrorism."
115 IMRO: Djordjevic, *Balkan*, 178–80, 220–21; Pettifer, *Macedonian*, 9–13; Gross, *Violence*, 54–57.
116 Balakian, *Burning Tigris*, 45, 103–10.
117 Laqueur, *Terrorism*, 120.
118 Stepniak, *Underground Russia*, 42–45.
119 "Monster": Dostoevsky, *Demons*, 306. "Crook": 420. "Louse": 560. "Destroyed": 607.
120 "Pieces": Conrad, *Secret Agent*, 56. "Exterminate": 249.
121 Montefiore, *Young Stalin*, 182–83.
122 Vizetelly, *Anarchists*, 111–27; Merriman, *Club*, 70–87; Butterworth, *World*, 300–302.
123 Hardy: O'Malley, *Wound*, 271–77; NAI/WJS, 49 ("special"); Kee, *Green Flag*, 691 ("variance").
124 "Drawn": Krueger, *What Makes*, 3. "Curtailed": 7.
125 Reich, *Origins*, 25–40.
126 Hart, *Mick*, 307; Dalton, *Brigade*, 11–12.

BOOK V: THE SIDESHOWS: GUERRILLAS AND COMMANDOS IN THE WORLD WARS

1 Franz Ferdinand: Smith, *Morning*; Dedijer, *Road*; Owings, *Sarajevo Trial*.
2 Nazis: Evans, *Coming*; Kershaw, *Hubris*; Shirer, *Rise*; Campbell, *SA* (500,000: 120).
3 Japanese militarists: McClain, *Japan* (Brotherhood: 415); Gordon, *Japan*, 161–90; Drea, *Imperial Army*, 163–90; Toland, *Rising Sun*, 3–34; Byas, *Assassination* (Chaplin: 28–29).
4 Neumann, *Future*, 6.
5 Aqaba: Jarvis, *Arab Command*, 28–30 (source of all quotes unless otherwise specified); IWM/FGP, box 4; "Literary Fringes," IWM/FTB ("huts"); Brown, *Letters*, 116 ("maddest"); Rolls, *Chariots*, 238 ("hate").
6 Early life: Wilson, *Lawrence* ("endurance": 44; bicycling: 40); Liddell Hart, *Lawrence*; Brown, *Letters*; Mack, *Prince*.
7 Brown, *Letters*, 69.
8 Bruce, *Crusade*, 58.
9 Lawrence, *Pillars*, 67.
10 Ibid., 77.
11 Ibid., 84.
12 Barr, *Desert*, 142.
13 Lawrence, *Pillars*, 86.
14 Ibid., 91.
15 Storss, *Memoirs*, 186.
16 Brown, *War*, 80.
17 Bruce, *Crusade*, 54.
18 Brown, *War*, 70.
19 Lawrence, *Pillars*, 104.
20 "Sniping": Ibid. "Sphere": Brown, *War*, 77.
21 Lawrence, *Pillars*, 136.
22 "Detachment": Ibid., 194. "Gas": 192. "Soup": 193.
23 Ibid., 188.
24 Abu el Naam: Ibid., 197–203; Brown, *War*, 111–16; Wilson, *Lawrence*, 388.
25 Lawrence, *Pillars*, 189.
26 Ibid., 168.
27 Ibid., 225.
28 Young, *Arab*, 162.
29 Lawrence, *Pillars*, 312.
30 Young, *Arab*, 157.
31 Lawrence, *Pillars*, 319.
32 "Fear": Young, *Arab*, 162. Bounty: Wilson, *Lawrence*, 460.
33 Brown, *Letters*, 111.

34 Ibid., 124.
35 Ibid., 111.
36 Rape: Lawrence, *Pillars*, 441–47 ("torn," "delicious": 445); Wilson, *Lawrence*, 459–61; Brown, *War*, 165–66; Brown, *Letters*, 165–67, 360; Mack, *Prince*, 226–42; Barr, *Desert*, 201–6.
37 "Rank and File," 1936, IWM/TWB.
38 Stirling, *Safety*, 94.
39 100,000 vs. 69,000: Bruce, *Crusade*, 208. 8,000 Arab regulars: 217.
40 Lawrence, *Pillars*, 370; Winterton, *Tumultuous*, 71; Wilson, *Lawrence*, 557–60; Woodward, *Hell*, 202–3; Bruce, *Crusade*, 77, 242; Barr, *Desert*, 293.
41 Shotwell, *Peace Conference*, 131.
42 Wilson, *Lawrence*, 630; Fromkin, *Peace*, 498.
43 Fromkin, *Peace*, 507.
44 *New York Times*, May 26, 1935.
45 Fromkin, *Peace*, 9–10.
46 Brown, *Letters*, 246.
47 Ibid., 343–44.
48 Thomas, *With Lawrence*, 3.
49 *New York Times*, May 26, 1935.
50 Lawrence to Robertson, Feb. 13, 1935, IWM/LTEL.
51 *New York Times*, May 26, 1935.
52 Ibid., May 20, 1935.
53 Sex life: Wilson, *Lawrence*, 703–5, 750–51; Mack, *Prince*, 415–41 ("disorder": 427); Lawrence, *To Liddell Hart*, 163 ("sexlessness"); Brown, *Letters*, xxvi–xxvii.
54 "Strange": Abdullah, *Memoirs*, 170. "Madness": Lawrence, *Pillars*, 32.
55 "Charlatan": Edmund Ironside to Wingate, June 8, 1939, OWA. "Lied": Leebaert, *To Dare*, 406. Leebaert claims, at 405, without offering any evidence, that *Seven Pillars* was "heavily fanciful." The most thorough biography of Lawrence, which Leebaert does not cite, finds it, to the contrary, "remarkably accurate on questions of fact" (Wilson, *Lawrence*, 12).
56 Liddell Hart, *Lawrence*, 382–84.
57 "Side show": Brown, *War*, 272. "Minor": Lawrence, *Pillars*, 23.
58 Papen, *Memoirs*, 80–81.
59 "Witty": Wavell, *Soldier*, 59. "Impish": 61.
60 Brown, *Letters*, 249.
61 Brown, *War*, 260–73.
62 Bray, *Sands*, 156.
63 Brown, *War*, 142–47.
64 "Incuriousness": Lawrence, *To Liddell Hart*, 75. "Active": 140.
65 Lucas, *Kommando*, 24.
66 Durnford-Slater, *Commando*, 14 ("terror"); Young, *Commando*, 8–13 (urgency).
67 Foot, *SOE*, x.

68 "Arson": Box 180, folder 4, NARA/OSS. "Hedy," "Jemima": "New Weapons for Sabotage," Oct. 13, 1943, box 200, folder 8, NARA/OSS.

69 See Leebaert, *To Dare,* for an overview of special operations that applies that label promiscuously and anachronistically to various units throughout history.

70 Allen, *Guerrilla War,* 9.

71 Foot, *SOE*, 69.

72 Clarke, *Assignments*, 219.

73 "Popularity": Mosley, *Gideon,* 146. "Mountebank": 6.

74 Tulloch, *Wingate*, 24.

75 IWM/ACP.

76 "Gloom": Bierman, *Fire,* 11. "Damnation": IWM/OWP, 97/20/2.

77 "Suckled": Mosley, *Gideon,* 10. "Guide": Yehuda Yaari, "Wingate as a I Knew Him," IWM/OWP, Chindit box 5.

78 Thesiger, *Life*, 320.

79 Anglim, "Formative Experiences."

80 Tulloch, *Wingate*, 74.

81 Dodds-Parker, *Ablaze*, 65. See also Mosley, *Gideon*, 115; Burchett, *Adventure*, 47.

82 Bierman, *Fire*, 155.

83 Meeting Wingate: Hay, *Genius*, 18–22. His height: Bierman, *Fire*, 16. "Sandpaper": James, *Chindit*, 88.

84 Bierman, *Fire*, 48, 389.

85 Palestine: OWA ("rose": Wingate to mother, Oct. 14, 1936; "anti-Jew," "soldiery": Wingate to "Cousin Rex," Jan. 1, 1937; "virtual control," "bodily," "feeble," "ignorant": "Appreciation . . . of the Possibilities of Night Movements," June 5, 1938; "zigzags": "Principles Governing the Employment of SNS," June 10, 1938; "silence," "surprise": "Organization and Training of SNS," Aug. 1938; "nugatory": "Remarks of General Officer Commanding," July 10, 1939; 140 killed: "Brief History of SNS," Oct. 13, 1938); IWM/ACP; King-Clark, *Blast* ("gangsters": 160; "iron": 162; "courtesy": 164; "stony": 171; "calmly": 189); Bierman, *Fire* ("for them": 63; 140 men: 99; rampage: 115; "dust": 131); Morris, *Victims*, 148–49; Dugdale, *Baffy*, 80 ("fanatic"); Oren, "Friend"; Mosley, *Gideon*, 40–78; Rooney, *Wingate*, 34–47; Sykes, *Wingate*, 135–205; Dayan, *My Life*, 46 ("path," "infected"); Bethel, *Triangle*, 37 ("forfeited"); Mockler, *Selassie's War*, 281 ("risk"); Mosley, *Gideon*, 78 ("risk); Weizmann, *Trial*, 398 ("intenseness"); Burchett, *Adventure*, 46 (Lawrence); Sykes, *Wingate*, 132–33 (Lawrence).

86 Abyssinia: IWM/OWP, box 7 (troop strength, casualties, "patriot population," "men of integrity": Wingate, "The Ethiopia Campaign," Aug. 1940–June 1941; "Italian rations", "patriot support," "corps d'elite," "paralyze": Wingate, "Appreciation of the Ethiopian Campaign," June 18, 1941); NA/AAD ("clear off": 11); IWM/MT; Dodds-Parker, *Ablaze*, 54–73; Thesiger, *Life*, 311–54 ("curse": 320; "when we meet": 330); Allen, *Guerrilla War* (camels: 38); Mosley, *Gideon* ("favorable": 115; camels: 117–21; killed and captured: 126–27; bluff: 133; "rude": 136); Foot, *SOE*, 251–64; Playfair, *Mediterranean* ("ruthless": 1.404; size of force, "remarkable": 1.427); Bierman, *Fire*

("goading": 202; "tell them": 206); Spencer, *Ethiopia*, 87–99; Mockler, *Selassie's War* ("favorable": 286); Rooney, *Wingate*, 48–75; Sykes, *Wingate*, 236–320; Shirreff, *Bare Feet*; Haile Sellasie, *My Life*, 2.141–67; *War Illustrated* (April 25, 1941) ("mud").

87 Thesiger, *Life*, 333.

88 Ibid., 353.

89 First Chindit expedition: IWM/OWP, Chindit box 1 ("maintain forces", "90%": Wingate, "Report to Commander, 4th Corps, on Operations of 77th Indian Infantry Brigade in Burma, February to May 1943"); Fergusson, *Chindwin* ("horrid": 146; "acute": 149; "weak": 173; "éclairs": 192; 70 pounds: 249; "not much": 241); Fergusson, *Trumpet*, 174 ("grossly"); Calvert, *Mad*, 112–32 (1,500 miles: 130; 1944 offensive: 131–32); Slim, *Defeat*, 162–63 ("failure", "press"); Tulloch, *Wingate* ("anatomy": 63; "maintain": 62; "endemic": 58; casualties: 89; 1944 offensive: 91–92); Stibbe, *Return* ("shock troops": 57; "beautiful": 61–62; "circus": 68; "thick," "steep": 82); Masters, *Mandalay*, 214 ("flying fruit"); Bierman, *Fire* (Robert the Bruce: 297; casualties: 307); Rooney, *Wingate*, 76–102; Thompson, *Enemy Lines*, 130–72; Lewin, *Chief*, 211–14; Allen, *Burma* ("shock troops", "ordinary": 149); Rolo, *Raiders* ("Tarzan": 33; "circus": 45; mile-wide: 107; "swiftly flowing": 111; spare kilts: 63; "emaciated": 175); Burchett, *Adventure*; Sykes, *Wingate*, 360–432; Chinery, *March*, 20–91; Kirby, *Against Japan*, 2.309–31; Thompson, *Hills*, 19–33; Hoe, *Re-Enter*.

90 Moran, *Diaries*, 113.

91 Wingate to Michael Calvert, Aug. 8, 1942, IWM/OWP, Chindit Box 1.

92 Second Chindit expedition: IWM/OWP ("machan," "orbit": Wingate, "The Stronghold"); HIA/ACW, box 80, file 5; IWM/LFMS; Masters, *Mandalay*, 177–291 ("threshold": 268; "111 Company": 282); Fergusson, *Green Earth*; Calvert, *Prisoners* ("silence": 27); Calvert, *Mad*, 132–83 ("brilliant": 139; "rending": 143; "shrouds": 155; "exhausted": 176; 300 men: 180); Slim, *Defeat*, 216–18, 258–81; Tulloch, *Wingate*, 114–255 (2:30: 202; "approach": 156; "war": 136; casualties: 253; 90 percent: 239); Towill, *Chronicle* (no seatbelts: 19; vocal cords: 73); Bierman, *Fire* ("any time": 346); Rooney, *Wingate*, 111–201; Thompson, *Enemy Lines* ("waste away": 234); Kirby, *Against Japan*, vol. 3 ("guts": 183; 3 months: 410; 3,628 lost: 415); Pownall, *Diaries*, 2.142 ("nasty"); Mosley, *Gideon*, 5 ("marsupial"); Allen, *Burma* (400 aircraft: 319); Sykes, *Wingate* ("guts": 522); Chinery, *March*, 110–239; Romanus, *Command Problems*, 220–23; James, *Chindit* ("wayward": 87); Stilwell, *Papers* ("Limeys": 276, 287, 306); Milner, *To Blazes*; Van Wagner, *Air Commando*; Baggaley, *Chindit Story*; Thompson, *Hills* ("stream by stream": 58; "scarecrows": 61); Allen, *Burma*, 348 ("villainously").

93 Ogburn, *Marauders*, 273. See also Romanus, *Command Problems*, 238–56.

94 Substantially: Rooney, *Wingate*, 199. "Few months": Kirby, *Against Japan*, 3.445.

95 "Genius": Rooney, *Wingate*, 207. "Maniac": 205.

96 "Awe": Thompson, *Enemy Lines*, 137. "Terrified": 138.

97 James, *Chindit*, 87.

98 Kirby, *Against Japan*, 3.223.

99 Masters, *Mandalay*, 160. Cited in Thompson, *Enemy Lines*, 256.

100 Burma: Smith, *OSS*, 264 ("successful"); Peers, *Burma Road* (10,000: 220); Cruickshank, *SOE*, 163–91; Hilsman, *American Guerrilla*; Dunlop, *Japanese Lines*.

101 Japanese empire: Mazower, *Empire*, 588–90; Lapham, *Raiders*, 213–18 ("stupid": 217); Hartford, *Sparks*, 108 ("there alls"); "The Viet Nam Government," July 29, 1947, NARA/CREST, CIA-RDP82-00457R000700750001-5 ("terrorism").

102 Philippines: Lapham, *Raiders* (800 towns: 209; 225,000: 226); Greenberg, *Hukbalahap*, 17 (15,000); Kerkvliet, *Huk*, 88; Hunt, *Behind*; Volckmann, *We Remained*.

103 Foot, *SOE*, 281.

104 Mazower, *Empire*, 478.

105 Bennett, *Swastika*, 101.

106 Hitler admired British: Mazower, *Empire*, 581. "Counter-productive": 7.

107 Ibid., 462.

108 Ibid., 456.

109 Slepyan, *Stalin's Guerrillas*, 51.

110 Two German soldiers: Cooper, *Nazi War*, 144. For an overview of COIN ratios see Goode, "Force."

111 Mazower, *Empire*, 472–73.

112 Jackson, *Dark Years*, 557.

113 Cancian, "Wehrmacht"; Kennedy, *Antiguerrilla*, 44, 49; "Yugoslavia," June 30, 1943, NARA/OSS, box 211, folder 8.

114 "Gentle": Vuckovich, *Tragedy*, 39.

115 Tito: Djilas, *Wartime*; Djilas, *Tito*; Dedijer, *Diaries*; Dedijer *Tito Speaks*; Maclean, *Approaches* (Tito's name: 280); Maclean, *Barricade*; Roberts, *Tito*; Deakin, *Embattled* ("no front": 14; "annihilation": 27); CAM/DEAK; West, *Tito*; Tomasevich, *Chetniks* and *Occupation*; Kurapovna, *Shadows*; Pavlowitch, *Disorder*; Vuckovich, *Tragedy*; Rootham, *Miss Fire*; NA/TITO; John G. Goodwin, "Final Report of Mulberry Team," March 1944–March 1945, NARA/OSS, box 88, folder 11; Robin S. Newell, "Report of Geisha Mission," May 19–Oct. 13, 1944, ibid. ("teaching"); Rex D. Deane, "Redwood Team Report," Jan. 31, 1945, NARA/OSS, box 58, folder 3; Lindsey, *Beacons* ("indoctrinate": 237); Jackson, *Dark Years*, 557 (more than Italians or French received); Mazower, *Empire*, 518 ("only place"); Berenbaum, *Victims*, 64 (over 1 million killed).

116 Moss, *Ill Met*.

117 Thompson, *Enemy Lines*, 52–55 ("failure": 55); Gordon, *Desert War*, 78–82.

118 Slim, *Defeat*, 546–47.

119 Verney, *Going*, 145.

120 Hawes, *Resistance*, 197.

121 Successful operations: Foot, *SOE*, 298–99, 323–24, 336–37; Foot, *Resistance*, 180, 281; Mackenzie, *History*, 452, 623, 654–55; Haukelid, *Skies*.

122 North Africa: Maclean, *Approaches*, 199–62 ("fractured": 226); Thompson, *Enemy Lines*, 94–98 ("fiasco": 96); Wynter, *Special Forces*, 142–46, 167–75; Mortimer, *Stirling's Men*, 47–48; Gordon, *Desert War*, 95–96, 126–28.

123 Thompson, *Enemy Lines*, 106.

124 Alexander, *Shadows*, 5.
125 Cohen, *Commando*, 56.
126 Hunt, *Japanese Lines*, 269.
127 Maclean, *Approaches*, 256.
128 Foot, *SOE*, 98.

BOOK VI: THE END OF EMPIRE: THE WARS OF "NATIONAL LIBERATION"

1 Britain: Kynaston, *Austerity*, 102 ("blitz"), 20 (750,000 houses), 71 ("queues"), 105 (whale), 196 (Amis), 191–92 (Isherwood).
2 France: Beevor, *Paris*, 264 (height), 77 (women shaved), 265 (bakeries), 101 (paper); Gildea, *France*, 65–100; Jackson, *Dark Years*, 570–99 (10,000: 581).
3 *Life*, Oct. 12, 1942.
4 McMahon, *Colonialism*; Westad, *Cold War*, 114.
5 Bayly, *Forgotten Wars*, 221.
6 Bayly, *Forgotten Armies*, 146.
7 Hyam, *Declining*, 94.
8 Ibid., 162.
9 Wolpert, *Shameful Flight*, 132.
10 Hyam, *Declining*, 109.
11 "Warfare": Orwell, *Essays*, 4.467. "Heard": 4.469. "Shaking": 4.463.
12 Zionists: Bethel, *Triangle*, 358 (338 killed, "hell"); Begin, *Revolt*; Bell, *Terror*; Morris, *1948*, 44 ("coup").
13 Gildea, *France*, 21; Grimal, *Decolonization*, 243, 357.
14 Shanghai: Bergère, *Shanghai*; Clifford, *Spoilt Children*; Sergeant, *Shanghai*; Dong, *Shanghai*.
15 Population, income, ownership: Guillermaz, *Communist Party*, 7. "Semi-colonial": Mao, *Military Writings*, 77. Positive: Dikotter, *Openness*; Waldron, *From War*.
16 Party Congress: Chang, *Rise* ("pale-faced": 1.140); Short, *Mao*, 117–22; Guillermaz, *Communist Party*, 57–60; Chang, *Mao*, 25–27; Saich, *Power*, 3–19; Kuo, *Analytical History*, 1.14–37, 341–50.
17 "Guests": Snow, *Red Star*, 96. "Greenish": Li, *Private Life*, 99. Bathe: 100. Privy: 133. Smoking: Ch'en, *Mao*, 211. "Pepper": Snow, *Red Star*, 93. Spence, *Mao*, 98, notes his "deliberate cultivation of a coarse manner."
18 Snow, *Red Star*, 131.
19 Wilson, *Long March*, 26.
20 Ch'en, *Mao*, 25.
21 Young Mao: Snow, *Red Star* ("scholar": 133; "forcibly": 140 ; "liberalism": 149; "exist": 151); Li, *Private Life*, 122 ("ruthless"); Spence, *Mao*, ("ignorance": 18; water: 15); Short, *Mao*; Siao-yu, *Mao and I*; Chang, *Mao*; Terrill, *Mao*; Schram, *Road*, vol. 1; Ch'en, *Mao*.
22 Short, *Mao*, 147.
23 Taylor, *Generalissimo*, 38.

24 Band, *Two Years*, 242.

25 Zhu De revolt: Gao, *Zhou*, 59–61; Smedley, *Great Road*, 199–25; Guillermaz, *Communist Party*, 150–56; Kuo, *Analytical History*, 1.281–85.

26 Saich, *Power*, 198.

27 Mao, *Military Writings*, 75.

28 Ibid., 274.

29 Snow, *Red Star*, 165.

30 Wilson, *Long March*, 41.

31 Terrill, *Mao*, 99; Smedley, *Great Road*, 176.

32 Mao-Zhu slogans: Mao, *Military Writings*, 72; Schram, *Road*, 5.499; Snow, *Red Star*, 173–74; Short, *Mao*, 222; Braun, *Agent*, 55; Mao, *Aspects*, 50 ("fish," "dry").

33 "Interview with Mao Zedong," Oct. 25, 1937, HIA/NW, box 22, file 591.

34 Saich, *Power*, 199.

35 Band, *Two Years*, 244. See also Forman, *Report*, 177: "the Chinese Communists are no more Communistic than we Americans are."

36 Schram, *Road*, 3.74.

37 Mao's methods: Short, *Mao* ("merciless": 269; "hanging": 273; "confess": 281); Li, *Private Life*, 120–21 ("devoid", "sacrificed"); Rittenberg, *Stayed Behind*, 450 ("designs"); Sun, *Long March* ("leniency": 53); Griffin, *Counter-Revolutionaries* (186,000 killed: 18); Saich, *Power*, 496, 530–35; Chang, *Mao*, 89–109; Guillermaz, *Communist Party*, 216–17; Benton, *Mountain Fires*, 71–72, 81–82; Saich, *Perspectives*, 79–116; Kuo, *Analytical History*, 2.331–44.

38 Hartford, *Sparks*, 187–88, offers differing estimates of the number of blockhouses.

39 Saich, *Power*, 533.

40 Number of marchers: Salisbury, *Long March*, 2; Wilson, *Long March*, 227; Chang, *Rise*, 2.445. Rearguard: Benton, *Mountain Fires*, 6–8. Mao claimed the Long March covered 25,000 *li* (7,700 miles), but according to Jocelyn, *Long March*, 326–27, it was only 12,000 *li* (3,750 miles), still a long trek.

41 Wilson, *Long March*, 233.

42 Chang, *Mao*, 153. Regarding the supposed "Reds-for-son swap," the authors concede (135), "It was not an offer that could be spelt out." For a critical examination of their claims, see Benton, *Monster*.

43 Salisbury, *Long March*, 63.

44 Luding Bridge: Braun, *Agent*, 119–20; Salisbury, *Long March*, 220–30; Sun, *Long March* ("through": 146); Snow, *Red Star*, 194–99; Wilson, *Long March* ("rice bowl," "roar": 168); Jocelyn, *Long March* (30 feet: 248; locals in lead: 250).

45 "Interview with Mao Zedong," Oct. 25, 1937, HIA/NW, box 22, file 591.

46 "Traitors": Sun, *Long March*, 21. "Dick": 29. 30,000: 79; Salisbury, *Long March*, 103.

47 Grasslands: Braun, *Agent* (24 rivers, 18 mountains: 146); Sun, *Long March* ("vultures": 167; "bloated": 171; leather: 172; "intake": 175); Snow, *Red Star*, 200–206; Wilson, *Long March*, 175–84, 204–21 ("sat down": 178; "bitter": 209; boiled hides: 216); Peng, *Memoirs*, 380–84; Jocelyn, *Long March*, 258–303.

48 Yang, *From Revolution*, 2.

49 "Record," "invincible": Schram, *Road*, 5.71. "Heroes": 5.92.

50 Braun, *Agent*, 101.

51 Saich, *Power*, 643–48, 1168.

52 Mao's ascent: Hsiung, *Bitter Victory*, 92–94; Guillermaz, *Communist Party*, 363–68; Chang, *Mao*, 240–49; Short, *Mao*, 379–96; Saich, *Perspectives*, 299–338; Saich, *Power* ("correct": 1164); Short, *Mao*, 379–96; Kuo, *Analytical History*, 4.396–423.

53 Thomas, *Season*, 136.

54 Ibid., 132.

55 "Lincolnesque": Snow, *Red Star*, 90. "Humor": 92. "Moderating": 95.

56 Mao's wives: Chang, *Mao*; Snow, *Red Star*, 459–61 ("slender": 460); Li, *Private Life*, 356–64 (young beauties); Snow, *Communists*, 250; Barrett, *Dixie Mission*, 83 ("chic"); Short, *Mao*.

57 Saich, *Perspectives*, 263–98; Kuo, *Analytical History*, 3.595–603.

58 Ch'en, *Mao*, 209.

59 Arthur Waldron and Edward O'Dowd, "Introduction to Second Edition," in Mao, *On Guerrilla*, 13–14.

60 "Formation," "Centre," "morality": Mazzini, *Writings*, 1.369. "Retiring": 1.375.

61 Mao's precepts: Mao, *Military Writings*, 278 ("guerrilla-ism"), 246 ("outcome"), 210–19 (three stages), 247 ("primary"), 66 ("base areas"), 168 ("roving"), 66 ("Red Guards"), 33 ("concentration"), 247 ("originally"), 78 ("laws"). For assessments, see Connable, *Insurgencies End*, 7 ("nearly"); Wilson, *Scales*, 117–43; Osanka, *Guerrilla Warfare*, 131–77; Graff, *Military History*, 229–49; Stout, *Perspectives*, 126 (Al Qaeda).

62 Casualties: Waldron, "Remembering." 90 percent KMT: Taylor, *Generalissimo*, 7.

63 Hsiung, *Bitter Victory*, 83.

64 Ibid., 79, 102; Guillermaz, *Communist Party*, 328.

65 Westad, *Decisive Encounters*, 69.

66 Levine, *Anvil*, 130; Chang, *Last Chance*, 52.

67 Eastman, *Seeds*, 203.

68 Westad, *Encounters*, 209.

69 Courtois, *Black Book*, 463–64.

70 Bigeard: Bigeard, *Gloire*; Bergot, *Bigeard*; Roy, *Dienbienphu*, 185 ("profile"); Fall, *Street* (Tu Le: 66–70); Singer, *Cultured*, 267–345 (10 to 1: 286); Roy, *Dienbienphu* ("possible": photo caption); Windrow, *Last Valley*, 120–21; Morgan, *Valley*, 192–94.

71 Ho: Duiker, *Ho Chi Minh*, 94 ("token"), 95 ("Stalinist"), 136 ("goodness"), 251 ("mat"), 302 (saved Ho), 573 (using Americans), 348 (Diem's brother), 361 ("shit"); Sainteny, *Ho Chi Minh* ("frankness": 66; sleep on floor: 77); Brocheux, *Ho Chi Minh*; Quinn-Judge, *Missing Years*; Ho, *On Revolution* and *Writings*; Patti, *Why*, 199 ("wisp"); "Who's Who of Members of Present Government," Nov. 7, 1945, NARA/OSS, box 200, folder 5 ("Democrat").

72 "The Viet Nam Government," July 29, 1947, NARA/CREST, CIA-RDP82-00457R000700750001-5.

73 Duiker, *Ho Chi Minh*, 402.

74 Lea: Ibid., 408–10; Currey, *Victory*, 138–40; Fall, *Street*, 28–31; Windrow, *Last Valley*, 95–96; Porch, *Secret Services*, 300–301; Elliott, *Willow*, 165–67.
75 Schoenbrun, *France*, 234–36; Duiker, *Ho Chi Minh*, 379.
76 Giap: Currey, *Victory* (bush: 147; "gospel": 154); Macdonald, *Giap*; *Time*, Feb. 9, 1967 ("bush").
77 Macdonald, *Giap*, 99–100.
78 Giap, *Unforgettable*, 46.
79 Vietminh adversaries: Trinquier, *Maquis*; Fall, *Street*, 267–79; Windrow, *Last Valley*, 218–19; Porch, *Secret Services*, 326–33; Macdonald, *Giap*, 111–12.
80 NARA/MAACV-OM, 1952–54.
81 "Rape": Ainley, *To Die*, 30. "Feared": 32–33. Germans: Porch, *Legion*, 531–32.
82 Scholl-Latour, *Ricefields*, 29.
83 Elliott, *Sacred Willow*, 195.
84 Fall, *Street*, 110–11.
85 Scholl-Latour, *Ricefields*, 32.
86 Truong Chin, *Writings*, 111.
87 Ainley, *To Die*, 106.
88 Zhai, *China* (generals: 63); Chen, "China."
89 *Time*, Sept. 24, 1951.
90 *New York Times*, Feb. 18, 1951.
91 Fall, *Street*, 39.
92 Troop strength: Window, *Last Valley*, 147 (Vietminh), 170 (French); Lawrence, *First Vietnam War*, 217, 221; Giap, *Dien Bien Phu*, 911; Fall, *Street*, 180 (80,000); Morgan, *Valley of Death*, 101 (82,000); Dalloz, *Indo-China*, 104; Porch, *Legion*, 531 (60 percent German).
93 Morgan, *Valley*, 70.
94 Bodard, *Quicksand*, 83.
95 Starobin, *Eyewitness*, 70.
96 *Newsweek*, April 23, 1953.
97 "Illicit Opium Traffic Southeast Asia," CIA memo, Dec. 13, 1948, NARA/CREST, CIA-RDP82-00457R002100350002-2.
98 Bodard, *Quicksand*, 23.
99 Dien Bien Phu: Bigeard, *Gloire* ("lush": 134; "whistled": 135; "not one": 174); Roy, *Dienbienphu* ("clucking": 37; "possible": photo caption); Fall, *Hell* ("cotton seeds": 10; "hailstorm": 137; firing slit: 140; 3 rounds: 102; "flame": 233); Simpson, *Tiger*, 89–100 ("stilted": 94; "thin slice": 99); Giap, *Dien Bien Phu* ("human chain": 84; 5:05 p.m.: 221; "mat": 383); Windrow, *Last Valley* ("administrative": 233; "whole nights": 293; artillery: 294–95, 708–11, 343–51; 180 tons: 417; Gaucher: 383: "all over": 385; 300 dead at Eliane: 504; "one-legged": 591; 3 percent: 629; 92,000 killed: 653); Currey, *Victory* (tons of rice: 191; "horse to ride": 185; mistresses: 187); Grauwin, *Doctor* (Gaucher: 83; "groans": 97; "shriveled": 252); Langlais, *Dien Bien Phu*; De Borchgrave, "Great Stand" (170 tons); Morgan, *Valley* (Giap's HQ: xv–xvii; 1,000

killed: xvi; "Verdun": 246; "rotting": 429; Eliane 1: 428); Fall, *Street*, 263 (48 planes), 300 (500-mile march); Porch, *Secret Services*, 318–57 (opium); Porch, *Foreign Legion*, 555–65; Macdonald, *Giap*; Dinh Van Ty, "Iron Horses"; Burchett, *North*, 47–59; Simpson, *Dien Bien Phu* (mistresses: 39); Macdonald, *Giap*, 124–61; Ainley, *To Die*, 59 ("all important); *Newsweek*, April 5, 1954 ("Verdun").

100 Morgan, *Valley*, 163.

101 "Probable Developments in Indochina Through Mid-1953," CIA memo, Aug. 23, 1952, NARA/CREST, CIA-RDP79R01012A00100004014-0.

102 Sainteny, *Ho Chi Minh*, 89.

103 Bigeard, *Gloire*, 210.

104 Magneto: Rejali, *Torture*, 141–62.

105 Alleg, *The Question*. Servan-Schreiber's *Lieutenant in Algeria* was another prominent antitorture memoir.

106 Horne, *Savage War*, 91.

107 Connelly, *Revolution*, 18.

108 "Headlines": Morgan, *My Battle*, 21. "Corpse": Horne, *Savage War*, 132.

109 29,000: Anderson, *Hanged*, 9. 32 killed: 4.

110 Ibid., 6.

111 Massacre: Aussaresses, *Casbah*, 45–55 ("pity," "indifferent"); Leuliette, *St. Michael*, 149–52 ("indiscriminately," "hot," "machine guns," "bulldozers").

112 Behr, *Problem*, 99, quoting Yacef Saadi.

113 "Support": Trinquier, *Modern Warfare*, 17. "Snickers": Galula, *Pacification*, 53–54.

114 Lazreg, *Torture*, 98.

115 Battle of Algiers: Aussaresses, *Casbah*, 85 ("extreme"), 85 ("take back"), 121 ("dangerous"), 122 ("remote"), 123 ("grunt"); Bigeard, *Gloire*, 274–86, 303–8; Trinquier, *Temps perdu*, 231–60, 270 ("precision"); Massu, *Bataille* (Jan. 8: 88; strike: 92; 4,600 men: 98; census: 140; "necessity": 168); Horne, *Savage War*; Morgan, *My Battle* (Bigeard shot: 118; "shrimp": 139; "baskets": 161); NARA/DS ("unprecedented": Lewis Clark, Jan. 3, 1957, box 3379, 751S.00/1-257; "tough": Ibid., Jan. 15, 1957; "siege": Ibid., Jan. 21, 1957; "brown skin": Merritt N. Cootes, March 1, 1957, 751S.00/3-157; "absence": Ibid., March 12); Kettle, *Algeria*, 106 ("enormous"), 398 ("without trace"); Connelly, *Revolution*, 131 (arrests, disappearances); Clark, *Turmoil* (146 casualties: 327), 387 ("dash"); Porch, *Secret Services*; Gale, *Englishman*, 133 ("spidery"); *Time*, May 26, 1958 ("chopping-block"); Lazreg, *Torture* ("crevettes": 53); Rejali, *Torture*, 481–92 (informants: 484); Singer, *Cultured*, 310–12 (Bigeard shot).

116 Troop strength: Kettle, *Algeria*, 485–86; O'Ballance, *Insurrection*, 141; Clark, *Turmoil*, 301–2, 307; Paret, *Revolutionary*, 41; Gortzak, "Indigenous Forces" (120,000); Galula, *Pacification*, 10–11, 13, 244. 1:50: U.S. Army, *Counterinsurgency*, 23; Connable, *Insurgencies End*, 129–31.

117 Morice Line: Horne, *Savage War*, 263–65; Roy, *Algeria*, 86 ("doomed"); O'Ballance, *Insurrection*, 117–20; Alexander, *Algerian War*, 12 (helicopters), 15 (80,000 troops).

118 Horne, *Savage War*, 159–61; Kettle, *Algeria*, 69; Morgan, *My Battle*, 26; Connelly, *Revolution*, 114–15; Porch, *Secret Services*, 369–74.

119 Connelly, *Revolution*, 292.
120 Public opinion: Connelly, *Revolution* (inspire ANC: 5); Evans, *Memory*; Wall, *France*; Ulloa, *Francis Jeanson*; Dine, *Images*.
121 De Gaulle, *Hope*, 75.
122 OAS: Henissart, *Wolves* ("harsh": 161; 30–40 killings: 319); Bocca, *Secret Army*; Horne, *Savage War*, 480–534; Feraoun, *Journal*, 313–14 ("terror"); Porch, *Secret Services*, 396–403.
123 Anderson, *Hanged*, 4.
124 Casualties: Horne, *Savage War*, 538; Kettle, *Algeria*, xiii–xiv.
125 "Dwarfs": Larteguy, *Centurions*, 51. "Enough": 304. "Hatred": 370. "Shady": 320. "Shit": *Praetorians*, 23. Modeled on Bigeard: Dine, *Images*, 29.
126 Trinquier, *Temps perdu*, 240.
127 Clutterbuck, *Long War*, 80.
128 Templer's background: TEMP (Adenauer: J. A. Barraclough to Templer, May 16, 1954); Cloake, *Templer*; "Battle of Malaya" ("mind").
129 Barber, *Running Dogs*, 70.
130 Chin Peng, *My Side*, 30.
131 Population: Lyttelton, "Cabinet Paper: Malaya," Dec. 21, 1951, TEMP; Stubbs, *Hearts*, 12; Barber, *Running Dogs*, 15, 17. 5,000 fighters: Chin Peng, *My Side*, 26.
132 3,000 killed: Barber, *Running Dogs*, 139. Police, army: Stockwell, *Malaya*, 327; Thompson, *Insurgency*, 48; Lyttelton, *Memoirs*, 358; Stubbs, *Hearts*, 159.
133 Gurney: Chin Peng, *My Side*, 287–88; Barber, *Running Dogs*, 130–31; Stubbs, *Hearts*, 133; Miller, *Menace*, 190–93; Stockwell, *Malaya*, 301–2; Mackay, *Domino*, 111–14.
134 "Losing": Cloake, *Templer*, 199. "Hopelessness": Ramakrishan, "Transmogrifying."
135 "Plan," "occurred": Lyttelton, *Memoirs*, 364. "Goods": Copy of Jan. 1, 1952, letter from Montgomery to Churchill, TEMP.
136 Coates, *Suppressing*, 143.
137 Harper, *Making*, 176.
138 Thompson, *Insurgency*, 140; Short, *Rats*, 391.
139 Stubbs, *Hearts*, 158.
140 Stockwell, *Malaya*, 220.
141 Horne, *Savage*, 338.
142 Clutterbuck, *Long War*, 51.
143 "Battle of Malaya."
144 Stockwell, *Malaya*, 237.
145 Thompson, *Insurgency*, 117.
146 "Scalded": Cloake, Templer, 127. "Electrifying": 213. "Chairbound": Miller, *Menace*, 163. "Varnished": Lyttelton to Templer, May 16, 1952, TEMP.
147 "Seldom go": Cloake, *Templer*, 263. Close down: 265.
148 "Clipped": Robinson, *Transformation*, 108. "Stinker": "Battle of Malaya." "Bloody": Raj, *War Years*, 127. "Dynamic," "brusque": Blake, *View*, 140. "Torch": Cloake, *Templer*, 213.
149 Templer to Lyttelton, Sept. 12, 1952, TEMP.
150 Templer to Lyttelton, Nov. 3, 1952, TEMP.

151 Barber, *Running Dogs*, front page.
152 Adams, *Works*, 10.266.
153 Stubbs, *Hearts*, 1.
154 Stockwell, *Malaya*, 372.
155 "Mean to win": Thompson, *Insurgency*, 146. "Ruthless": 144.
156 Tanjong Malim: Stockwell, *Malaya*, 424–25; Cloake, Templer, 222–23; "Battle of Malaya"; Barber, *Running Dogs* ("savage": 158); Ching Peng, *My Side*, 297; Clutterbuck, *Long War*, 81–82; Stubbs, *Hearts*, 165; Miller, *Menace*, 206–10; Mackay, *Domino*, 126–27.
157 Abuses: Short, *Rats*, 160–69; Stubbs, *Hearts*, 73–74; Chin Peng, *My Side*, 239–40; Stockwell, *Malaya*, 328 (detainees).
158 Templer to Lyttelton, Feb. 20, 1952, TEMP.
159 Templer to Lyttelton, Feb. 7, 1953, TEMP.
160 Templer to Lyttelton, Sept. 12, 1952, TEMP.
161 "Inducement": *Conduct of Operations*, 4.2.3.
162 Raj, *War Years*, 127.
163 *Conduct of Operations*, 3.12.1
164 Ramakrishan, *Propaganda*, 189–90.
165 Henniker, *Red Shadow*, 181.
166 Chin Peng, *My Side*, 270.
167 Henniker, *Red Shadow*, 210.
168 Barber, *Running Dogs*, 270.
169 Clutterbuck, *Long War*, 80.
170 Cloake, *Templer*, 261.
171 Coates, *Suppressing*, 50.
172 Casualties: Short, *Rats*, 507–8; Thompson, *Insurgency*, 27; Barber, *Running Dogs*, 270; Stewart, *Smashing Terrorism*, 339; Nagl, *Eat Soup*, 103.
173 In 1960: Andrew Birtle of the U.S. Army Center of Military History, email to author, Dec. 20, 2010. Nagl, *Eating Soup*, and Tilman, "Non-Lessons," offer differing views in the debate over Malaya's lessons.
174 Mockaitis, *Counterinsurgency*, ix.
175 "Measures": French, *British Way*, 248. "Dirty": 249. "Operate": 248.
176 Anderson, *Hanged* (statistics: 4–5, 9); Elkins, *Reckoning*; Branch, *Mau Mau* (casualties: 5; "ideology": xi). Elkins's book won a Pulitzer Prize but is marred by sensationalistic descriptions (e.g., calling British prisons a "gulag") and very high estimates of Kenyans killed and detained that are not supported by other sources.
177 Holland, *Revolt*; Grivas, *Memoirs*; Crawshsaw, *Revolt* (casualties: 349); Rosenbaum, "Success"; Byford-Jones, *Grivas* (casualties: 185).
178 Hughes, "Model Campaign"; Peterson, *Oman's Insurgencies*; Arkless, *Secret War*; Gardiner, *Service*.
179 Geraghty, *Irish War*; English, *Struggle* (casualties: 380); Saville, *Report*.
180 Aden: Walker, *Aden* (200 killed: 285); Hinchcliffe, *Without Glory*; Pieragostini, *South Arabia*.

181 http://www.statistics.gov.uk/cci/nugget.asp?id=980.

182 French, *British Way*, 57.

183 "Secondary": Lewis Clark to John W. Jones, April 22, 1955, NARA/DS, box 3333, 751S.00/1-155. "Dream": Clark to Secretary of State, Jan. 4, 1957, NARA/DS, box 3379,751S.00/1-257.

BOOK VII: RADICAL CHIC: THE ROMANCE OF THE LEFTIST REVOLUTIONARIES

1 Wolfe, *Radical Chic*.

2 "Bites": Taber, *Flea*, 49. "Have-nots": 173. "Futile": 176. For Taber's pro-Castro views see, Anderson, *Che*, 292, 389.

3 "Faddish": Schlesinger, *Days*, 342.

4 "Propagandist": Galula, *Counterinsurgency*, 62. "Fire": 95. "Subversion": Thompson, *Insurgency*, 55. For background see Cohen, *Galula*; Marlowe, *Galula*; and Thompson, *Hills*.

5 Boot, *Savage Wars*.

6 Greene denied any connection to Lansdale and had apparently finished his manuscript before Lansdale arrived in Saigon. See Sherry, *Greene*, 2.416–17; Nashel, *Lansdale's War*, 159.

7 Greene, *Quiet American*, 23.

8 Lederer, *Ugly American*, 110.

9 Early life: HIA/EGL, boxes 69–70; Currey, *Unquiet*.

10 "Fear": Lansdale diary, March 19, 1947, HIA/EGL, box 72, diaries 1946–48. "Stinking": Dec. 26, 1946. "Sopping": Oct. 30, 1946. "Squabble," "rightness": March 30, 1947. "Slick": April 11, 1947.

11 Lansdale to Ben, June 12, 1973, HIA/EGL, box 83, file 118.

12 LBJ/LOH, 24 ("I didn't speak [French] at all"); "Foreign Language Qualifications," Oct. 16, 1961, HIA/EGL, box 69, misc. file; Currey, *Unquiet*, 5.

13 Rufus Phillips, email to author, July 23, 2010.

14 Currey, *Unquiet*, 44–45.

15 Lansdale, *Midst*, 5.

16 "Connection with CIA," Lansdale memo, Dec. 15, 1985, HIA/EGL, box 70, biographical file/memo.

17 Kerkvliet, *Huk*, 195.

18 Lansdale, *Midst*, 25.

19 Greenberg, *Hukbalahap*, 57.

20 Valeriano, *Counter-Guerrilla*, 103.

21 Martinez, *Magsaysay*, 176.

22 "Friends," candy: Valeriano, *Counter-Guerrilla*, 206. "Chicken": 201.

23 Ibid., 207.

24 Lansdale, *Midst*, 48.

25 Valeriano, *Counter-Guerrilla*, 207.

26 Greenberg, *Hukbalahap*, 67, 110.
27 Taruc, *Tiger*, 91.
28 Kitson, *Gangs*; Cline, "Pseudo Operations."
29 Taruc, *Tiger*, 137.
30 Nashel, *Lansdale's War*, 32–33.
31 Valeriano, *Counter-Guerrilla*, 139.
32 Kerkvliet, *Huk*, 238.
33 Lansdale, *Midst*, 85.
34 "Preliminary Working Draft Prepared in State for Discussion at OCB Meeting of January 19, 1955," NARA/CREST, CIA-RDP80R01731R002900480007-6.
35 LBJ/LOH, 7.
36 Simpson, *Tiger*, 113.
37 "Depth": Lansdale, *Midst*, 159. "Blind": U.S. Department of Defense, *Pentagon Papers*, 11.7.
38 "Roly-poly": Lansdale, *Midst*, 158.
39 *Washington Post*, Aug. 25, 1965.
40 "Universality": Lansdale speech at Principia, April 9, 1965, HIA/EGL, box 73, file 1. "Fuzzy": Speech at Yale, Nov. 23, 1964. "Fight," "hide": Speech at Special Warfare School, Aug. 30, 1962. "Brotherhood," "licking": Speech at Air Force Academy, May 25, 1964.
41 Lansdale, *Midst*, 226.
42 Currey, *Unquiet*, 160.
43 Department of Defense, *Pentagon Papers*, 1.577–79; LBJ/LOH, I.28–29.
44 Rufus Phillips, email to author, Aug. 21, 2011.
45 Lansdale, *Midst*, 213.
46 Phillips, *Vietnam*, 67.
47 Ibid., 53.
48 Lansdale, *Midst*, 232–33.
49 "Monthly Report of TRIM Activities," May 1–31, 1955, NARA/MAAGV-OM, box 2, folder 30.
50 http://www.un.org/en/members/growth.shtml.
51 "Background—South Vietnam O/B," March 23, 1955, NARA/CREST, CIA-RDP79R00890A00030052-2.
52 Lansdale, *Midst*, 316–18; Phillips, *Vietnam*, 78.
53 Lansdale to family, May 2, 1955, HIA/EGL, box 83, file 188.
54 "The Crisis in Saigon," Memo to DCI, April 4, 1955, NARA/CREST, CIA-RDP7900904A000200020005-2; Nashel, *Landsdale's War*, 59–60; Currey, *Any Cost*, 224–25; Rufus Phillips, email to author, Aug. 21, 2011.
55 Collins to Dulles, April 27, 1954, NARA/DS, box 3333, 751G.00/4-155.
56 "Interview II," Sept. 15, 1981, HIA/EGL, box 79, file 285; Lansdale, *Midst*, 204; Phillips, *Vietnam*, 33.
57 "Patriot": Lansdale, *Midst*, 155. "Successor": Phillips, *Vietnam*, 64. See also U.S. Department of State, *Foreign Relations: Vietnam, 1955–1957*, 145, 301–30; U.S.

Department of Defense, *Pentagon Papers*, 1.229–35, 2.26; Anderson, *Trapped*, 111–15.

58 U.S. Department of Defense, *U.S.-Vietnam*, 11.2.

59 Phillips, *Vietnam*, 223.

60 Colby, *Lost Victory*, 366.

61 Lansdale, *Midst*, 301.

62 Paris Embassy to Dulles, April 4, 1955, NARA/DS, box 3333, 751G.00/4-155.

63 "Unbelievable": Simpson, *Tiger*, 151. 80 percent: Phillips, *Vietnam*, 327.

64 Sheehan, *Lie*, 138.

65 Terror: Duiker, *Road*, 196; Moyar, *Forsaken*, 79; Karnow, *Vietnam*, 254–55; Currey, *Victory* ("spies": 227); "Order of Battle," Oct. 1, 1963, AHEC/MACV.

66 Currey, *Victory*, 234, claims Lansdale concocted "Vietcong," but Lansdale's associate Rufus Phillips believes the claim is false: Phillips, email to author, Aug. 21, 2011.

67 U.S. Department of Defense, *Pentagon Papers*, 2.126; Phillips, *Vietnam*, 121.

68 Lansdale to Robert Komer, May 30, 1971, HIA/EGL, box 4, file 106.

69 "Subterranean": Schlesinger, *Days*, 340. Reading: Sorenson, *Kennedy*, 632; Hilsman, *Move*, 415.

70 U.S. Department of State, *Foreign Relations: Vietnam 1961*, 1.13–28 ("wolf," "player": 19); U.S. Department of Defense, *Pentagon Papers*, 2.440–43; Hilsman, *Move*, 419; Jones, *Death*, 23–24.

71 Currey, *Unquiet*, x.

72 Mongoose: U.S. Department of State, *Foreign Relations: Cuba, 1958–1960*, 1116 ("warm"); Bohning, *Obsession* ("nutty": 92; toilet paper: 102); NARA/CREST; Freedman, *Kennedy's Wars*, 153–61; Nashel, *Landsdale's War*, 72–76; Weiner, *Ashes*, 184–88 ("fast": 186); McClintock, *Statecraft*, 203–7; "Interview II," Sept. 15, 1981, HIA/EGL, box 79, file 285 ("suicidal," "bona fides").

73 http://www.jfklibrary.org/Historical+Resources/Archives/Reference+Desk/Speeches/.

74 Taylor, *Trumpet*.

75 Duncan, *New Legions*, 146.

76 Krepinevich, *Army*, 53.

77 Lansdale to McNamara, April 7, 1962, HIA/EGL, box 96, file 1.

78 Krepinevich, *Army*, 37; Blaufarb, *Era*, 80.

79 U.S. Defense Department, *U.S.-Vietnam*, 11.5.

80 "Interview II," Sept. 15, 1981, HIA/EGL, box 79, file 285.

81 Bui Diem, *Jaws*, 91.

82 U.S. Department of Defense, *U.S.-Vietnam*, 11.8; U.S. Department of Defense, *Pentagon Papers*, 2.26.

83 *Time*, Dec. 26, 1969.

84 H. A. F. Hohler to Foreign Secretary, Jan. 30, 1963, NA/BRIAM.

85 Thompson, *Insurgency*, 140.

86 Gibson, *Perfect War*, 95.

87 Sorley, *Westmoreland*, 67.
88 Krepinevich, *Army*, 197; Sorley, *Westmoreland*, 218.
89 Gibson, *Technowar*, 319; Sorley, *Better War*, 83; Clodfelter, *Statistics*, 225.
90 Krepinevich, *Army*, 205.
91 16 million: Smith, *Handbook*, 60. 90 percent: Krepinevich, *Army*, 167.
92 Duiker, *Ho*, 551.
93 Karnow, *Vietnam*, 617.
94 Lansdale, "Viet Nam."
95 Krepinevich, *Army*, 180.
96 U.S. Department of Defense, *Pentagon Papers*, 4.303, 4.403; "Order of Battle," Oct. 1, 1963, AHEC/MACV; Sorley, *Westmoreland*, 188 (CIA estimate).
97 *New York Times*, April 23, 1995.
98 Directive, April 28, 1971, DPC #2150901041, April 1971; Duiker, *Ho*, 552, 557.
99 "Latitude": Sorley, *Westmoreland*, 73. "Attrition": 90.
100 "Dropped": Phillips, *Vietnam*, 251. "Blunt": *New York Times*, Aug. 21, 1965.
101 "Miracles": *Washington Post*, Aug. 20, 1965. "Legend": Ibid., Feb. 25, 1966.
102 *Washington Post*, Sept. 29, 1968.
103 "Team Assignments," Oct. 8, 1965. HIA/EGL, box 96, file 6.
104 *Washington Post*, Aug., 20, 1965.
105 "Genocide": LBJ/POL. "Rice roots," "ills": LBJ/B1967.
106 Lansdale, "Viet Nam."
107 Lansdale to Leo Dowatch Jr., March 13, 1974, HIA/EGL, box 70, biographical file/memoranda.
108 Tet: Braestrup, *Big Story*; Oberdorfer, *Tet*; Westmoreland, *Reports*, 310–34 (casualties: 332); Duiker, *Road*, 288–97 ("decisive": 289); Davidson, *At War*, 473–529; Duiker, *Ho*, 557; Ang, *Other Side*, 113–40; Lansdale to "The Old Team," Feb. 10, 1968, HIA/EGL, box 73, file 2 ("bangs").
109 *Washington Post*, Nov. 22, 1967.
110 http://www.lbjlib.utexas.edu/johnson/archives.hom/speeches.hom/680331.asp.
111 *New York Times*, April 1, 1968.
112 Sorley, *Better War*, xiii.
113 Colby, *Lost Victory*, 303–6.
114 Peace treaty: Berman, *No Peace*; Karnow, *Vietnam*, 671 (150,000 men); Kissinger, *Ending*; Nguyen, *Palace File*; Kimball, *War Files*.
115 Duiker, *Ho*, 512.
116 Le Duan: Asselin, "Le Duan"; Currey, *Victory*, 229; Duiker, *Ho*, 548 ("rabbit"); Ang, *Other Side*.
117 *New York Times Magazine*, Aug. 10, 1997.
118 "Guerrilla": Summers, *Strategy*, 127. "Root": 173.
119 Duiker, *Ho*, 546; Zhai, *China* (170,000: 135).
120 Lansdale, "Viet Nam."
121 Landing: Franqui, *Diary* ("shipwreck": 124; "rough": 123); Guevara, *Reminiscences*

("tragic": 14; ("collapse": 17; "hail": 18; "lost": 19); Castro, *My Life*; Szulc, *Fidel* ("trigger", "controlled": 32; "slight": 29; "crazy": 34); Anderson, *Che*; Taibo, *Guevara*; Quirk, *Castro*; Thomas, *Cuba* ("rabbits": 899); Cesar Gomez interview, HIA/GAG, box 9, file 27; Perez, "Granma" ("bobbing").

122 Young Castro: Szulc, *Fidel* ("assassination": 289); Castro, *My Life* (25,000 acres: 29; "six": 41; *For Whom*: 209; Chevy: 108); Castro, *Struggle* ("absolve": 220–21); Castro, *Prison Letters*; Quirk, *Castro* (whip: 9; school/prison: 12; "hatred": 18; "gangster": 27); Geyer, *Prince* (no milk: 72; mistress letter: 130); Casuso, *Cuba* ("hoodlum": 115; "approval": 174; "mistress": 172); HMP; Thomas, *Cuba*; Emilio Caballero interview, HIA/GAG, Box 7, File 48 ("talking politics"); Rafael Díaz-Balart interview, HIA/GAG, box 8, file 29 ("monologist"); Waldo Díaz-Balart, HIA/GAG, box 8, file 30 ("primitive"); Armando Llorente interview, HIA/GAG, box 11, file 4 ("loco," "charming"); Ramon Mestre interview, HIA/GAG, box 11, file 29 (bathed); Jose Rasco interview, HIA/GAG, box 12, file 32 ("manners").

123 Young Guevara: Anderson, *Che* (Argentino: 184; richest men: 4; rugby shirt: 37; "twin evils": 52; "frozen stif": 76; "octopuses": 121; divorce: 382); Guevara, *Motorcycle Diaries* ("blanket": 77) and *On the Road* ("pirate": 63; "fun": 80; "hit it off": 99); Debray, *Praised Be*, 96 ("no interest"); Gadea, *My Life* ("black eyes": 24; Sartre and Freud: 60–61); Granado, *Traveling*; Taibo, *Guevara* ("Stalin": 31); Castañeda, *Compañero* (Kerouac: 46; "Stalin": 62; "disastrous," "boring": 95); Siao-yu, *Beggars*, 148 ("money").

124 Anderson, *Che*, 229; Taibo, *Guevara*, 112; Castañeda, *Campañero*, 102.

125 The Matthews articles appeared on Feb. 24–26, 1957. See HMP; Matthews, *Cuban Story*; DePalma, *Man* (marching in circles: 84); Felipe Pazos and Javiar Pazos interviews, HIA/GAG, box 12, files 14–15.

126 Wickham-Crowley, *Guerrillas*, 191.

127 Sweig, *Revolution*, 111.

128 Batista offensive: Szuc, *Fidel*, 445–49; *Washington Post*, Sept. 14, 1958 ("steep," "shin"); Castro, *Struggle*, 399–415; Batista, *Betrayed*, 80 ("panic"); Franqui, *Diary*, 316–86; Taibo, *Guevara*, 170–78; Quirk, *Castro*, 182–94; Thomas, *Cuba*, 996–1004; Castañeda, *Campañero*, 116.

129 Batista, *Betrayed*, 80.

130 Santa Clara: Guevara, *Reminiscences*, 267–69; Anderson, *Che*, 348–53; Franqui, *Diary*, 474–78; Taibo, *Guevara*, 237–49; Castañeda, *Campañero*, 133–38.

131 CIA: Weiner, *Ashes*, 155; Anderson, *Che*, 259–61; Szuc, *Fidel*, 427–29; Geyer, *Prince*, 183.

132 Batista, *Betrayed*, 135.

133 *New York Times*, Jan. 2, 1959.

134 Ibid.

135 Thomas, *Cuba*, 1042; Wright, *Era*, 16.

136 Castañeda, *Campañero*, 137; Thomas, *Cuba*, 1040.

137 Casuso, *Cuba*, 137.

138 "Infiltration": *Washington Post*, Sept. 15, 1958. See also *New York Times*, April 18, 1959; *U.S. News & World Report*, March 16, 1959.

139 Guevara, *Motorcycle Diaries*, 164.

140 Rene Monserrat interview, HIA/GAG, box 11, file 39.

141 Anderson, *Che*, 458.

142 Rojo, *My Friend*, 181–82; Anderson, *Che*, 599.

143 Anderson, *Che*, 538; Castañeda, *Campañero*, 236.

144 "Saint Karl": Guevara, *Road*, 114. "Roman Empire": Debray, *Praised Be*, 98. "Imperialism": Anderson, *Che*, 584. "Vietnams": Guevara, *Guerrilla Warfare*, 175.

145 "Underwear": Guevara, *Guerrilla Warfare*, 53. "Create": 7. "Decisive": Debray, *Revolution*, 119.

146 Childs, "Historical Critique."

147 Congo: Guevara, *African Dream* ("parasitic": 26; "drinking": 28; "running": 49; "rifle," "perspective," "truck": 26; "poorest": 226-27; "runs": 135); Anderson, *Che*; Hoare, *Mercenary*; Kelly, *America's Tyrant*; Schatzberg, *Mobutu*; Taibo, *Guevara*; Gleijeses, *Conflicting*, 101–23.

148 Bolivia: Guevara, *Bolivian Diary*, 144 ("nonexistent"), 248 ("effectiveness"); James, *Bolivian Diaries*; Guevara, *Guerrilla Warfare*, 10–11 ("reformer," "countryside," "full help"), 8 ("vote"), 116 ("secrecy"); Salmon, *Defeat of Che* (peak strength: 71; Shelton: 86; "bandits": 168); Villegas, *Pombo* ("torrential": 141); Debray, *Praised Be*, 104 ("murderous"); Rojo, *My Friend*; NSA/DCG (esp. "Activities of 2nd Ranger Battalion," Nov. 28, 1967; "Debriefing of Felix Rodriguez," June 3, 1975); LBJ/CSP; Castro, *Revolution*, 136–46; Wright, *Era*, 68 (billion dollars; expectations), 8–87; Anderson, *Che*, 637–710 ("mess": 705; "shoot": 710); Taibo, *Guevara*, 472–562 (100 Rangers: 548; "shoot": 561); Rodriguez, *Shadow* ("tattered": 10; "courage": 11); Ryan, *Fall* (Korea, Laos: 90); Gary Prado interview, HIA/GAG, box 12, file 28.

149 Casey, *Afterlife*.

150 Latin insurgents: Wright, *Era*; Wickham-Crowley, *Guerrillas* ("glorious": 31); Ratliff, *Castroism*; Scheina, *Latin America's Wars*, vol. 2; Castro, *Revolution*; Gott, *Rural Guerrilla*; Kohl, *Urban Guerrilla*.

151 Guevara, *Guerrilla Warfare*, 7.

152 "Ennobles": Marighella, *Minimanual*, 20. See also Flynn, *Brazil*; Skidmore, *Military Rule*; Williams, "Carlos Marighela"; *New York Times Magazine*, Nov. 15, 1970.

153 Nicaragua: Wickham-Crowley, *Guerrillas*, 7, 271–81; Kagan, *Twilight*; Kinzer, *Blood*.

154 Marchak, *God's Assassins*; Timerman, *Prisoner*.

155 Sanford, *Buried*; Commission, "Memory."

156 Boot, "Miracle."

157 Burleigh, *Blood*, ch. 6.

158 Gero, *Flights*, 8.

159 Andrew, *Sword*, 380–82; Andrew, *World*, 246–55.

160 Entebbe: Betser, *Soldier* ("surprise": 328; "shattered": 329); Maj. Gen. (ret.) Uri Sagi and Maj Gen. (ret.) Ephraim Sneh, part of the rescue team, interviews with author, March 1, 2011; Dunstan, *Lightning*; Pedahzur, *Secret Services*, 53–62; Netanyahu, *Entebbe*; Ben-Porat, *Rescue*; Williams, *Diary*; Rabin, *Memoirs* (15 or 20: 287); Peres, *Battling*; Kurzman, *Soldier*; McRaven, *Spec Ops*; Harclerode, *Secret*; Follain, *Jackal*, 107 (kill Jews); Thomas, *Gideon's Spies*, 142–45; Katz, *Elite*; Stevenson, *90 Minutes*; Williamson, *Counterstrike*; Klein, *Striking*, 205–8 (chocolates); *New York Times*, Sept. 13, 1972 ("six million Jews");

161 Wolf, *Face*, 279.

162 Sixties radicals: Gitlin, *Sixties*; Suri, *Power*; Berman, *Utopias*.

163 Weathermen: Varon, *War Home*; Stern, *With*.

164 SLA: Graebner, *Patty's* ("insect": 15); Hearst, *Secret*; Payne, *SLA*; *Los Angeles Times*, May 18, 1994.

165 RAF: Aust, *Baader-Meinhof* (total killed); Varon, *War Home*; Meinhof, *Everybody*; Baumann, *How*; Cockburn, *One Point*, 1–6 (nuclear munitions); Andrew, *Mitrohkin Archive*, 511–12 (East German support); Carr, *Infernal*, 138 ("six"); Wolf, *Man*. The 2008 German film *The Baader-Meinhof Complex* also presents an accurate portrayal of the group's rise and fall.

166 Arafat: Rubin, *Arafat* ("Tom and Jerry": 224; mattress: 39); Walker, *Arafat* ("activity": 11; Algeria: 31; Beetle: 37; "richest": 130); Abu Iyad, *My Home* ("discreet": 29; "unprepared": 81); Sayigh, *Struggle*; Hart, *Arafat*; Morris, *Victims* (1948–56 deaths: 270; parcel bomb: 288; Karameh: 268–69; "fascist": 78; refuge in Israel: 80); *Time*, Dec. 13, 1968 ("Viet Cong"; "everyone"); Strong, "Playboy Interview" ("I fought"; "big lie"); Black, *Secret Wars*, 279 ("relentless"); Yaari, *Strike*; Raviv, *Every Spy*, 163 (bed still warm); Abu-Sharif, *Tried* (use of permits to recruit informers: 151); Byman, *Price*; Friedman, *From* ("dashing": 107); *New York Times*, Nov. 12, 2004 (2,000 killed); Allman, "Road" (shaving, Rolex, "bric-a-brac").

167 Pedahzur, *Secret Services*, 26–28; Morris, *Victims*, 288; Byman, *Price*, 25.

168 Black September: Dobson, *Black September*; Walker, *Arafat* (U.S., Saudi threats: 101–2); Klein, *Striking*; Jonas, *Vengeance*; Black, *Secret Wars*; Pedahzur, *Secret Services*, 40–46; Abu Iyad, *My Home* ("butchers": 97); Raviv, *Prince*, 184–94; Abu-Sharif, *Tried*.

169 Lebanon: Schiff, *Lebanon War*; Rabinovich, *War*; Sayigh, *Struggle*, 522–43; Rubin, *Arafat* (suicide: 88; "Fiji": 93); Morris, *Victims* (650 dead: 558); Cobban, *Palestinian*; Byman, *Price* (15,000 strong: 67).

170 First Intifada: Morris, *Victims*; Black, *Secret Wars*; King, *Revolution*; "Fatalities" (casualties); "China: Tiananmen" (Tiananmen Square deaths); Catignani, *Intifadas*; Peretz, *Intifada* (18,000 arrests: 64); Sayigh, *Struggle*, 607–37; Raviv, *Prince*, 379–404; Yigal Hankin, interview with author, Feb. 28, 2011 ("pants down"); Byman, *Price* (600 killed: 73).

171 Author's meeting with Arafat: *Wall Street Journal*, Dec. 14, 1998.

172 Byman, *Price*, 104.

173 Schweitzer, "Suicide Bombing."

174 Second Intifada: Eiland, "Second Intifada" (March toll, "continue"); Schweitzer, "Suicide Bombing" (attacks in 2002; attacks and attempted attacks in 2009); *PLO: Captured Documents*; Morris, *Victims*; "Intifada Toll" (casualties); Catignani, *Intifadas*; Byman, *Price* (casualties: 152–54); Lt. Gen. (ret.) Moshe "Bogie" Ya'alon ("safe havens," 2010 attacks), Brig. Gen. (ret.) Yossi Kuperwasser ("like Gaza"), Brig. Gen. Noam Tibon, Brig. Gen. (ret.) Michael Herzog ("clueless"), interviews with author, Feb. 27–March 3, 2011.

175 Abu Iyad, *My Home*, 34.

176 Merari, *Terrorism*, 107.

177 Gorenberg, "Mahatma."

178 "Intifada Toll."

BOOK VIII: GOD'S KILLERS: THE RISE OF RADICAL ISLAM

1 Origins of jihadism: Kepel, *Jihad*; Stout, *Terrorist Perspectives*; Wright, *Looming*; Habeck, *Knowing*; Sivan, *Radical Islam*.

2 Hostage crisis: Bowden, *Guests*; Coughlin, *Ghost*; Rubin, *Anti-American*, 107 ("damn"); Bill, *Eagle*, 295–304; and hostages' memoirs (e.g., Queen, *Inside*; Koob, *Guest*; Kennedy, *Ayatollah*; Daugherty, *Shadow*).

3 Mecca: Trofimov, *Siege* ("cinemas": 31; "heretical": 32; 1,000 lives: 225); Coll, *Ghost Wars*, 28 ("dissolute"); Lacey, *Inside*, 16–36; Wright, *Sacred Rage* (dog food: 155); Bergen, *Holy War*, 59 ("riyalpolitik").

4 Islamabad: Trofimov, *Siege*, 109–16 ("magnificent": 116); Coll, *Ghost Wars*, 29-37; Sullivan, *Under Siege*, 71–89; *Washington Post*, Nov. 27, 1994; *Time*, Dec. 3. 1979.

5 Invasion of Afghanistan: Lyakhovskiy, "Soviet Invasion" (80 percent outside control: 4; vodka: 50; "alive": 57; "soaked": 65); Grau, "Take-Down"; CWIHP/SIA; Mitrokhin, "KGB"; Tanner, *Afghanistan*, 235–38; Feifer, *Gamble*, 55–85; Girardet, *Afghanistan*, 114 (mosques closed); Helsinki Watch, "Tears"; Kalinovsky, *Goodbye*, 16–54; Tanner, *Afghanistan*, 231 (flag), 235 (ammunition, batteries); Urban, *War*, 27–50; Rubin, *Fragmentation*, 111–22; Cordovez, *Out*, 13–49; Russian General Staff, *War*, 11–12; Mendelson, *Changing Course*, 39–64. Lyakhovskiy, "Soviet Invasion," 64, reports five KGB men killed in the palace assault along with five other Red Army soldiers; Mitrokhin, "KGB," 97–98, claims, "Over 100 of the KGB were killed."

6 The official figure for Soviet fatalities during the entire war was 13,833. The real figure was closer to 26,000. See Russian General Staff, *War*, 43.

7 Massoud: Girardet, *Afghanistan*, 30 ("wasps"), 83 ("trenches"); Russian General Staff, *War*, 74–83; Coll, *Ghost Wars*, 107–24 (Massoud background); Feifer, *Gamble*; *Washington Post*, Oct. 17, 1983 ("blue-green"), Oct. 18, 1983 ("30 followers"; Volga sedan); Grad, *Massoud* (American Revolution: 29; "energy": 104; "compassion": 120; "washed": 20; food: 199; "toes": 18; chess: 30; "cool": 105; "smiling": 244); *Christian Science Monitor*, June 22, 1982 ("vantage point," machine-gun position), June 28,

1982 ("caves"); Gall, *Russian Lines*; Tanner, *Afghanistan*, 251–52, 257–61; Urban, *War*, 101–5; Kaplan, *Soldiers*, xv ("ornery"), xix ("greatest"); Roy, *Afghanistan*, 72–75; Bergen, *Osama bin Laden*, xxii ("fragility"); Junger, *Fire*, 199–222; Rowan, *Trail*; former CIA officer Reuel Gerecht, email to author, April 27, 2012 (forgotten French).

8 Russian General Staff, *War*, 91.

9 Abuses: Helsinki Watch, "Tears" ("conceivable": 4; "shocks": 10; 200 killed: 35; strafed: 54; toy mines: 60; mosques: 82).

10 $3 billion: Westad, *Cold War*, 350. Advisers: Kalinovsky, "Blind." Hospitals: Feifer, *Gamble*, 146.

11 Troop strength, casualties: Rubin, *Fragmentation*, 1, 131–33; Feifer, *Gamble*, 255; Girardet, *Afghanistan*, 53–54; Kaplan, *Soldiers*, 11, 18; Russian General Staff, *War*, 88.

12 Red Army: Feifer, *Gamble* (diseases: 142; rotten potatoes: 179; "dedy": 142); Borovik, *Hidden War* ("caught": 185; "blood": 183; "animal": 186); Heinamaa, *Soldiers' Story*, 26 ("slaughtered," "shoot"), 16 ("jackals," "moral"), 26 ("destroy"); Yousaf, *Bear Trap*, 54–56; Russian General Staff, *War*, 302 (hospitalized); *Christian Science Monitor*, June 28, 1982 ("imperialism"); Alexievich, *Zinky Boys*; Tamarov, *Afghanistan*.

13 Yousaf, *Bear Trap*, 49.

14 Kaplan, *Soldiers*, 16.

15 Ibid., 69.

16 Reuel Gerecht, email to author, April 27, 2012.

17 Coll, *Ghost Wars*, 153.

18 U.S. aid: Lundberg, "Covert Action"; Coll, *Ghost Wars*, 147–53 (aid spending: 151); Feifer, *Gamble* ($30 million: 130); Crile, *Charlie Wilson's War*, 419 ("directly"); Russian General Staff, *War*, 222 ("appreciable"); Cordovez, *Out*, 194–201; Yousaf, *Bear Trap*, 174–89; Gates, *Shadows*, 348–50; Tanner, *Afghanistan*, 267 (270 shot down); Westad, *Cold War*, 355–56; Bearden, *Main Enemy*, 207–54; Mendelson, *Changing Course*, 95–100; Michael Pillsbury, email to author, Oct. 27, 2010; globalsecurity .com (Hind specs).

19 Cordovez, *Out*, 202; Kalinovsky, *Goodbye*, 84.

20 "chilly": Westad, *Cold War*, 377. 11:55: *New York Times*, Feb. 16, 1989.

21 Rise of Taliban: Rashid, *Taliban*; Goodson, *Endless War*; Tanner, *Afghanistan*.

22 Beirut bombing: Geraghty, *Peacekeepers* (quiet, "shards": 91; "gone": 92; "mangled": 99; PET: 185-186); Hammel, *Root* ("presence": 38; "bright": 295); Dolphin, *24 MAU* (youthful: 19); Wright, *Sacred Rage* ("roar": 70); U.S. Commission, "Report."

23 Hezbollah origins: Jaber, *Hezbollah*; Norton, *Hezbollah* (PLO training: 32); Cambanis, *Privilege*; Nasr, *Revival*, 142–43; Coughlin, *Ghost*, 210–18; Qassem, *Hizbullah;* Harik, *Hezbollah*; Norton, *Amal*; Baer, *No Evil*, 130–31 (PLO connection); Wright, *Sacred Rage*; Byman, *Price*, 209–21.

24 Mughniyeh: Hammel, *Root*, 432 ("Castro"); *Independent*, Feb. 23, 2010 (killed settler, plastic surgery); Jaber, *Hezbollah*, 115–20; Diaz, *Lightning*, 61–68; Bergman, *Secret War* ("creative": 67); *New York Times*, Sept. 2, 2008 (museum).

25 Norton, *Amal*, 170–71.

26 Nasr, *Revival*, 132.

27 Suicide bombers: Cambanis, *Privilege*, 9 (loves"); Nasrallah, *Voice*, 206 ("fearful"); Pape, *Dying*; Pedahzur, *Suicide*; Bloom, *Kill*.
28 Nasrallah, *Voice*, 54.
29 Hostages: Ranstorp, *Hizb'allah* (100 seized: 1); Coughlin, *Hostage*; Baer, *No Evil*.
30 Nasrallah, *Voice*, 54.
31 Bergman, *Secret War*, 78.
32 Morris, *Victims*, 558.
33 "Find": Norton, *Hezbollah*, 39. "Entity": Nasrallah, *Voice*, 95.
34 Khobar: Clarke, *All Enemies*, 114; National Commission, "9/11 Report," 60.
35 Training Al Qaeda: National Commission, "9/11 Report," 68; Bergen, *Osama bin Laden*, 143; Wright, *Tower*, 173–74.
36 Nasrallah: Cambanis, *Privilege*, 180 (humor), 188 (son's death); Nasrallah, *Voice*.
37 $100 million: Cambanis, *Privilege*, 15; Norton, *Hezbollah*, 110.
38 Exum, "Explaining Victory," 152.
39 Luft, "Israel's Security Zone."
40 Exum, "Explaining Victory," 154–55.
41 "Victory": Nasrallah, *Voice*, 233. "Cobwebs": Harel, *34 Days*, 38.
42 Hoffman, "Conflict."
43 Mansoor, *Hybrid*.
44 Second Lebanon War: Based on the author's visits to Israel in August 2006 and February 2011, which included interviews with Israeli soldiers and policymakers while the war was going on and afterward, and to Lebanon in 2009. See also Harel, *34 Days* ("scalded": vii); Boot, "Second Lebanon War"; Biddle, *Lebanon Campaign*; Cambanis, *Privilege* (human shields: 89, 91); Cordesman, *Lessons* (15,000 troops: 5); "Winograd Commission Final Report"; Exum, "Assessment" (decentralized); Exum, "Explaining Victory" (from local areas: 88); Nasrallah, *Voice*, 393 (never expected); Arkin, *Divining* (100 buildings: xx; ambulances: 50; 12,000 bombs: 64; 15,000 Hezbollah fighters: 74); Byman, *Price*, 251–65.
45 *New York Times*, Oct. 6, 2010.
46 "Ending": Nasrallah, *Voice*, 63. "A-Team": Richard Armitage, CBS News, April 18, 2003.
47 Evans, *Algeria*, xiv.
48 Chechnya: Babchenko, *Soldier's War*; Smith, *Allah's Mountains* (casualties: xviii); Hughes, *Chechnya*; Politkovskaya, *Hell*; Akhmadov, *Struggle*; Goode, "Force."
49 http://www.pbs.org/newshour/terrorism/international/fatwa_1998.html.
50 Nexis/Lexis.
51 http://www.pbs.org/newshour/terrorism/international/fatwa_1996.html.
52 Ibid.
53 Young Bin Laden: Bergen, *Osama bin Laden* (TV: 14, 21; "model": 17; *Jihad* magazine: 33; height: 182; "flame": 75; "sand": 168; "components": 116; "bureaucratic": 402; questionnaire: 402–7; "Big Satan": 197); Bergen, *Longest War*; Bergen, *Holy War*; Bin Laden, *Growing Up* (learned English: 108; "good if Islam": 50; "corrupted": 43; no toys: 43; no drugs: 60; no laughter: 62; "crisp": 27; "women": 84; BBC: 199); Wright,

Tower; National Commission, *Report* ($30 million a year: 170; cost of 9/11: 172); Coll, *Bin Ladens* ($1 million/year: 351); Bin Laden, *Inside*; Stout, *Perspectives*, 19 (caliphate), 124 (guerrilla history); *Time*, Jan. 11, 1999 ("cowardly"); *Independent*, March 22, 1997 ("paper tiger"); Nasiri, *Jihad* (weapons training: 142); Benjamin, *Sacred Terror*; Bin Laden, *Messages*; Ibrahim, *Al Qaeda*; Cullison, "Hard Drive"; Randal, *Osama*; Cronin, *Terrorism*, 276 (cost of bombings); Scheuer, *Osama bin Laden*; Kepel, *Own Words*; Richardson, *Terrorists*, 88 (3 R's); Bin Laden to Zawahiri, 2002, Harmony Database, CTC, AFGP-2002-600321 ("media war").

54 9/11: In addition to the sources previously cited for Bin Laden, especially the *9/11 Commission Report*, see Bernstein, *Blue*, and McDermott, *Perfect*.

55 $500 billion: Bergen, *Longest War*, 91. Bankrupt America: Bin Laden, *Growing Up*, 177.

56 Bergen, *Osama*, 322.

57 Waterboarded 183 times: Bergen, *Longest War*, 115. 800 at Gitmo: 106. 28 interrogated: 111. For the debate over such measures, compare Mayer's *Dark Side* with Yoo's *War*.

58 Lacey, *Global Jihad*, 40.

59 Jenkins, *Go Nuclear?*, 101.

60 Najaf bomb: *Washington Post*, Aug. 30, 2003; *Independent*, Aug. 30 (crater); *Los Angeles Times*, Aug. 30 ("reeked").

61 Zarqawi: Weaver, "Zarqawi"; Bergen, *Osama bin Laden*; Bergen, *Longest War*; *Time*, June 11, 2006; *New York Times*, July 13, 2004; Michael, "Legend"; Napoleoni, *Insurgent*; Brisard, *Zarqawi* ("burn": 97).

62 More suicide attacks: Moghadam, *Globalization*, 41, 251. "By April": Bergen, *Longest War*, 167.

63 Pape, *Dying*, 23.

64 Fishman, *Bleedout*, 6.

65 Zarqawi letter, 2004, at www.globalsecurity.org.

66 Zawahiri to Zarqawi, July 9, 2005, at www.globalsecurity.org.

67 Bahney, "Economic Analysis"; Fishman, *Bombers*.

68 Bowden, "Ploy"; Alexander, *Break*.

69 Based on the U.S. military's official database published by WikiLeaks. See *Guardian*, Oct. 23, 2010.

70 Bergen, *Longest War*, 169.

71 McWilliams, *Awakening*, 2.46.

72 Boot, "Vietnam War."

73 Petraeus: Based on the author's numerous conversations and emails with Petraeus since 2003 and on Cloud, *Fourth Star* (Bigeard: 37, 64); Bowden, "Professor" and "Winning Streak"; Broadwell, *All In*; Giron, "General Motors"; Petraeus, "American Military" ("unavoidable": 309; "prepared": 307); Robinson, *Tell Me*; Gericke, *Petraeus*; Sennott, "Good Soldier"; Coll, "Dilemma."

74 "Guerrilla war": *New York Times*, June 28, 2003. "Dependency": CNN.com, Sept. 10, 2003. "Dead-enders": Bergen, *Longest War*, 158.

75 Boot, "Reconstructing Iraq."
76 *Washington Post*, May 16, 2003.
77 Petraeus, email to author, Aug. 7, 2011.
78 O'Hanlon, "Iraq Index."
79 Cloud, *Fourth Star*, 181.
80 Petraeus, "Surge of Ideas" ("pasture," "zone," 1.5 million).
81 "Objective": U.S. Army, *Counterinsurgency*, 37. "Unity": 39. "Environment": 40. "Political": 39. "Appropriate: 45. "Weapons": 49. "Protect": 48. "Humanely": 245.
82 Petraeus, email to author, Aug. 7, 2011.
83 Petraeus, email to author, Jan. 4, 2011.
84 Petraeus, "Guidance."
85 Petraeus, email to author, Aug. 7, 2011.
86 www.icasualties.org.
87 Figures based on the *Guardian*, Oct. 23, 2010, and the Brookings Iraq Index: www.brookings.edu/iraqindex.
88 The surge: Primarily based on the author's eight visits to Iraq since 2003, which included extensive conversations with Iraqi and American leaders, including Petraeus, Odierno, and Crocker, as well as "battlefield circulations," before, during, and after the surge. See also Ricks, *Gamble*; Robinson, *Ends*; Cloud, *Fourth Star*; West, *Strongest Tribe*; McWilliams, *Anbar Awakening*; Kagan, *Surge*.
89 Hafez, *Suicide Bombers*, 243–49.
90 http://pewglobal.org/database/.
91 *Time*, Jan. 11, 1999.
92 Boot, "Treading Softly."

EPILOGUE: MEETING IN MARJAH

1 Based on the author's personal observations.
2 Santayana, *Soliloquies*, 102.

IMPLICATIONS: TWELVE ARTICLES

1 Heilbrunn, *Partisan*.
2 Brig. Gen. Noam Tibon, interview with author, Feb. 27, 2011.
3 Kalyvas, *Logic*, 171.
4 Luttwak, "Dead End"; Merom, *Democracies Lose*.
5 Berman, "Hearts and Minds."
6 Kalyvas, *Logic*, 119.
7 Sheehan, *Shining Lie*, 67.
8 Truong Chinh, *Writings*, 102.
9 Thompson, *Communist Insurgency*, 169.
10 Vann, "Memorandum for the Record," March 16, 1966, AHEC/JPVP.
11 Templer to Lyttelton, Dec. 22, 1953, TEMP.

ACKNOWLEDGMENTS

1 The Council on Foreign Relations (CFR) is an independent, nonpartisan membership organization, think tank, and publisher dedicated to being a resource for its members, government officials, business executives, journalists, educators and students, civic and religious leaders, and other interested citizens in order to help them better understand the world and the foreign policy choices facing the United States and other countries. Founded in 1921, CFR carries out its mission by maintaining a diverse membership with special programs to promote interest and develop expertise in the next generation of foreign policy leaders; convening meetings at its headquarters in New York and in Washington, D.C., and other cities where senior government officials, members of Congress, global leaders, and prominent thinkers come together with CFR members to discuss and debate major international issues; supporting a Studies Program that fosters independent research, enabling CFR scholars to produce articles, reports, and books and hold round tables that analyze foreign policy issues and make concrete policy recommendations; publishing *Foreign Affairs*, the preeminent journal on international affairs and U.S. foreign policy; sponsoring Independent Task Forces that produce reports with both findings and policy prescriptions on the most important foreign policy topics; and providing up-to-date information and analysis about world events and American foreign policy on its website, www.cfr.org.

The Council on Foreign Relations takes no institutional positions on policy issues and has no affiliation with the U.S. government. All views expressed in its publications and on its website are the sole responsibility of the author or authors.

BIBLIOGRAPHY

Newspaper articles, emails, and author interviews are cited only in the endnotes.

ARCHIVES

AHEC: Army Heritage and Education Center, Carlisle, Pennsylvania.
CAP: Creighton Abrams Papers.
CKP: Crook-Kennon Papers.
JPVP: John P. Vann Papers.
MACV: MACV Command Historian's Collection.
NAM: Nelson A. Miles Papers.

AP: *The Papers of John Adams Digital Edition*. University of Virginia Press, Charlottesville.

ATA: Letter Books of Amos Tappan Akerman. Alderman Library, University of Virginia, Charlottesville.

BSC: John Brown/Boyd S. Stutler Collection, West Virginia Division of Culture and History, Charleston.

CAM: Churchill College Archives, University of Cambridge.
CHUR: Winston Churchill Papers, Chartwell Trust.
DEAK: William Deakin Papers.

CSR: Colonial and State Records of North Carolina, University Library, University of North Carolina, Chapel Hill.

CTC: Combatting Terrorism Center, U.S. Military Academy, West Point.

CWIHP: Cold War International History Project, Woodrow Wilson International Center for Scholars, Washington.

SIA: Soviet Invasion of Afghanistan.

VW: The Vietnam (Indochina) Wars.

DPC: Douglas Pike Collection, Vietnam Center and Archive, Texas Tech University, Lubbock.

FMP: Francis Marion Papers, South Caroliniana Library, University of South Carolina, Columbia.

GCP: George Crook Papers, Special Collections and University Archives, University of Oregon, Eugene.

HCP: Henry Clinton Papers, William L. Clements Library, University of Michigan, Ann Arbor.

HIA: Hoover Institution Archives, Stanford University.

ACW: Albert C. Wedemeyer Papers.

EETS: Earl E. T. Smith Papers.

EGL: Edward G. Lansdale Papers.

GAG: Georgie Anne Geyer Papers.

NW: Nym Wales Papers.

HMP: Herbert L. Matthews Papers, Rare Book and Manuscript Library, Columbia University, New York.

IWM: Imperial War Museum, London.

ACP: A. C. Simonds Papers.

FGP: F. G. Peake Papers.

FTB: F. T. Birkinshaw Papers.

LFMS: Letters from Field Marshal Viscount Slim to Lt. Col. H. R. K. Gibbs.

LTEL: Letters from T. E. Lawrence to C. P. Robertson.

MT: Michael Tutton Papers.

NMC: Nevil Macready correspondence with Henry Wilson.

OWP: Orde Wingate Papers.

RDJ: R. D. Jeune Papers.

TWB: T. W. Beaumont Papers.

KSH: Kansas Historical Society, Topeka.

JBP: John Brown Papers.

BBJ: "The Battle of Black Jack," by G. W. E. Griffith (Vol. XVI).

WJB: "With John Brown in Kansas," by August Bondi (Vol. VIII).

LBJ: Lyndon Baines Johnson Presidential Library, Austin, Tex.

B1967: "The Battleground in 1967." Memorandum by Ed Lansdale, Nov. 11, 1966 (Doc. 096c, Memos to the President).

CSP: "Cuban Subversive Policy and the Bolivian Guerrilla Episode." CIA Intelligence Report, May 1968 (National Security File, Box 19).

LOH: Edward Lansdale Oral History Interview.

POL: H. C. Lodge to President, Aug. 3, 1965 (Doc. 094a, Memos to the President).

LFM: Letters of General Francis Marion, Wisconsin Historical Society, Madison.

LTOH: Luis Taruc Oral History, Bentley Historical Library, University of Michigan, Ann Arbor.

NA: National Archives, Kew, England.

AAD: Abrahim Akavia Diary (WO 217/37).

AC: "Afghanistan: Extracts from the Correspondence in India Subsequent to the Insurrection of November, 1841" (PRO 30/12/33/6).

ADM: Admiralty records, Oct.–Dec. 1827 (FO 78/162).

AT: "South Africa: Report on Working of Armoured Trains" (WO 108/414).

BRIAM: Records of the British Advisory Mission, Saigon (FO 371/170100-170102).

BLOCK: "Role of Engineers, Ch. 14: Blockhousing" (WO 108/295).

CIR: "Correspondence Respecting Circassia: 1855–57" (FO 881/1443)

CIRE: "Papers Respecting the Settlement of Circassian Emigrants in Turkey," June 4, 1864 (FO 881/1259).

DRA: "Defense of the Realm Act 1914 and Restoration of Order in Ireland 1920" (WO 35/66).

IBR: "A Report on the Intelligence Branch of the Chief of Police, Dublin Castle, from May 1920 to July 1921" (WO 35/214).

IRE: Military Operations and Inquiries in Ireland (WO 35/88B)

RBJ: Reports on the Blockade of Jellabad (PRO 30/12/32/15).

SAD: South Africa Dispatches (WO 108/380).

TITO: "Establishment of Communications with Tito and Mihailovic" (HS 5/966).

NAI: National Archives of Ireland, Dublin.

BCB: Bernard C. Byrne Witness Statement (WS 631).

CD: Charles Dalton Witness Statement (WS 434).

DB: Dan Breen Witness Statement (WS 1739).

JJS: James J. Slattery Witness Statement (WS 445).

JB: Joseph Byrne Witness Statement (WS 461).

JL: Joe Leonard Witness Statement (WS 547).

PL: Patrick Lawson Witness Statement (WS 667).

PM: Patrick McCree Witness Statement (WS 413).

VB: Vincent Byrne Witness Statement (WS 423).

WJS: William James Stapleton Witness Statement (WS 822).

NARA: U.S. National Archives and Records Administration, Washington and College Park, Md.

CCH: Dispatches from U.S. consuls in Cap Haïtien, Haiti, 1791–1906 (RG 59, M9).

CREST: CIA Records Search Tool.

DOJ-SC: Department of Justice, Source Chronological Files, 1871–1874 (RG 60).

DOJ-LS: Letters Sent by the Department of Justice, 1818–1904 (RG 60, M699).

DS: General Records of the Department of State, Central Decimal File (RG 59).

LM: Letters Relating to Lewis Merrill, Adjutant General's Office, Letters Received, 1863–1870 (RG 94, M1064).

MAAGV-OM: Military Assistance Advisory Group Vietnam, Adjutant General, Security Classified Outgoing Messages (RG 472).

MAAGV-MAR: Military Assistance Advisory Group Vietnam, Adjutant General, Monthly Activity Reports (RG 472).

OSS: OSS Classified Sources and Methods Files (RG 226).

RPY: Records of the Post of Yorkville, S.C., 1871–1877 (RG 393, Part V).

NLI: National Library of Ireland, Dublin.

PBP: Piaras Béaslaí Papers (MSS 33).

KK: Correspondence between Michael Collins and Kitty Kiernan (MSS 31).

MCP: Michael Collins Papers (MSS 40).

VBP: Vincent Byrne Papers (MSS 36).

NSA: National Security Archive, Washington.

DCG. The Death of Che Guevara: Declassified.

RSC: Rendition in the Southern Cone.

OWA: Orde Wingate Archive, Steve Forbes Churchill Collection, New York.

TEMP: Gerald Templer Papers. Private collection of the Templer family, Salisbury, England.

WP: *The Papers of George Washington Digital Edition*. University of Virginia Press, Charlottesville.

RW: Revolutionary War.

CS: Colonial Series.

PUBLICATIONS

Abba, Giuseppe Cesare. *The Diary of One of Garibaldi's Thousand*. London: Oxford University Press, 1962.

Abdullah, King of Jordan. *Memoirs of King Abdullah of Transjordan*. London: Philosophical Library, 1950.

Abu Iyad. *My Home, My Land: A Narrative of the Palestinian Struggle*. New York: Times Books, 1981.

Abu-Sharif, Bassam, and Uzi Mahnaimi. *Tried by Fire: The Searing True Story of Two Men at the Heart of the Struggle between the Arabs and the Jews*. London: Little, Brown, 1995.

Adams, John. *The Works of John Adams, Second President of the United States*. 10 vols. Boston: Little, Brown, 1856.

Adams, Michael. "Too Dumb to Take Cover: American Myths of the Redcoat Soldier." *Bulletin of the Military Historical Society*, 2000.

Addington, Larry H. *The Patterns of War since the Eighteenth Century*. Bloomington: Indiana University Press, 1994.

"Adventures of a Foreigner in Greece." *London Magazine*, 1826–27.

Aieneias the Tactician. *How to Survive under Siege*. London: Bristol Classic Press, 2003.

Ainley, Henry. *In Order to Die*. London: Burke, 1955.

Akhmadov, Ilyas, and Miriam Lanskoy *The Chechen Struggle: Independence Won and Lost*. New York: Palgrave Macmillan, 2010.

Aleshire, Peter. *The Fox and the Whirlwind: General George Crook and Geronimo. A Paired Biography*. New York: John Wiley, 2000.

Alexander, Don W. *Rod of Iron: French Counterinsurgency Policy in Aragon during the Peninsular War*. Wilmington: Scholarly Resources, 1985.

Alexander, Grand Duke of Russia. *Once a Grand Duke*. New York: Farrar & Rinehart, 1932.

Alexander, Larry. *Shadows in the Jungle: The Alamo Scouts behind Japanese Lines in World War II*. New York: New American Library, 2009.

Alexander, Martin S., and J. F. V. Keiger. *France and the Algerian War, 1954–62: Strategy, Operations, and Diplomacy*. London: Frank Cass, 2002.

Alexander, Matthew, with John R. Bruning. *How to Break a Terrorist*. New York: Free Press, 2008.

Alexievich, Svetlana. *Zinky Boys: Soviet Voices from the Afghanistan War*. New York: W. W. Norton, 1992.

Alleg, Henri. *The Question*. Lincoln: University of Nebraska Press, 2006.

Allen, Louis. *Burma: The Longest War, 1941–45*. London: J. M. Dent, 1984.

Allen, W. E. D. *Guerrilla War in Abyssinia*. New York: Penguin, 1943.

Allen, W. E. D., and Paul Muratoff. *Caucasian Battlefields: A History of the Wars on the Turco-Caucasian Border, 1828–1921*. Cambridge: Cambridge University Press, 1953.

Allman, T. D. "On the Road with Arafat." *Vanity Fair*, February 1989.

Ambrose, Stephen E. *Crazy Horse and Custer: The Parallel Lives of Two American Warriors*. Garden City: Anchor Books, 1975.

Amery, L. S., ed. *The Times History of the War in South Africa, 1899–1902*. 7 vols. London: Sampson Low, 1900–09.

Ammianus Marcellinus. *The Roman History of Ammianus Marcellinus*. London: George Bell, 1894.

Anderson, David. *Histories of the Hanged: The Dirty War in Kenya and the End of Empire*. New York: W. W. Norton, 2005.

Anderson, David L. *Trapped by Success: The Eisenhower Administration and Vietnam, 1953–1961*. New York: Columbia University Press, 1991.

Anderson, Fred. *Crucible of War: The Seven Years' War and the Fate of Empire in British North America, 1754–1766*. New York: Alfred A. Knopf, 2000.

Anderson, Jon Lee. *Che Guevara: A Revolutionary Life*. New York: Grove Press, 2010.

Andrew, Christopher. *Her Majesty's Secret Service: The Making of the British Intelligence Community*. New York: Viking, 1986.

Andrew, Christopher, and Vasili Mitrohkin. *The Mitrokhin Archive: The KGB in Europe and the West*. London: Penguin, 1999.

———. *The Sword and the Shield: The Mitrokhin Archive and the Secret History of the KGB*. New York: Basic Books, 1999.

———. *The World Was Going Our Way: The KGB and the Battle for the Third World.* New York: Basic Books, 2005.

Andrews, C. S. *Dublin Made Me.* Dublin: Lilliput Press, 2001.

Andrist, Ralph K. *The Long Death: The Last Days of the Plains Indian.* New York: Macmillan, 1964.

Ang, Cheng Guan. *The Vietnam War from the Other Side: The Vietnamese Communists' Perspective.* London: Routledge Curzon, 2002.

Anglim, Simon. "Orde Wingate in the Sudan, 1928–1933: Formative Experiences of the Chindit Commander." *RUSI Journal*, June 2003.

Appian. *Roman History.* 4 vols. Cambridge: Harvard University Press, 1913.

———. *Wars of the Romans in Iberia.* Warminster: Aris & Phillips, 2000.

Argenti, Philip P. *The Massacres of Chios Described in Contemporary Diplomatic Reports.* London: John Lane, 1932.

Arkin, William M. *Divining Victory: Airpower in the 2006 Israel-Hezballah War.* Montgomery: Air University Press, 2007.

Arkless, David C. *The Secret War: Dhofar 1971/1972.* London: William Kimber, 1988.

Arkush, Elizabeth N., and Mark W. Allen. *The Archaeology of Warfare: Prehistories of Raiding and Conquest.* Gainesville: University Press of Florida, 2006.

Arnold, James R. *Jungle of Snakes: A Century of Counterinsurgency Warfare from the Philippines to Iraq.* New York: Bloomsbury, 2009.

Arrian. *The Campaigns of Alexander.* London: Penguin, 1971.

Ascher, Abraham. *P. A. Stolypin: The Search for Stability in Late Imperial Russia.* Stanford: Stanford University Press, 2001.

Asprey, Robert B. *War in the Shadows: The Guerrilla in History.* New York: William Morrow, 1994.

Asselin, Pierre. "Le Duan, the American War, and the Creation of an Independent Vietnamese State." *Journal of American-East Asian Relations*, Spring–Summer 2001.

Assemblée Generale St. Domingue. *A Particular Account of the Insurrection of the Negroes of St. Domingo, Begun in August, 1791.*

Astin, A. E. *Scipio Aemilianus.* Oxford: Clarendon Press, 1967.

Atkinson, Rick. "The Single Most Effective Weapon against Our Deployed Forces." *Washington Post*, September 30, 2007.

Atlay, J. B. "Tarleton of the Legion." *Cornhill Magazine*, August 1905.

Auguste, Claude B., and Marcel B. Auguste. *L'expedition Leclerc 1801–1804.* Port au Prince: Imprimerie Henri Deschamps, 1985.

Aussaresses, Paul. *The Battle of the Casbah: Terrorism and Counter-Terrorism in Algeria, 1955–1957.* New York: Enigma, 2006.

Aust, Stefan. *Baader-Meinhof: The Inside Story of the RAF.* Oxford: Oxford University Press, 2008.

Avrich, Paul. *Anarchist Portraits.* Princeton: Princeton University Press, 1988.

———. *The Russian Anarchists.* Princeton: Princeton University Press, 1967.

———. *Sacco and Vanzetti: The Anarchist Background*. Princeton: Princeton University Press, 1991.

Babchenko, Arkaday. *One Soldier's War*. New York: Grove Press, 2009.

Baddeley, John F. *The Russian Conquest of the Caucasus*. New York: Longmans, Green, 1908.

Baer, Robert. *See No Evil: The True Story of a Ground Soldier in the CIA's War on Terrorism*. New York: Crown, 2002.

Baggaley, James. *A Chindit Story*. London: Souvenir Press, 1954.

Bahney, Benjamin, et al. "An Economic Analysis of the Financial Records of al-Qaida in Iraq." Santa Monica: RAND, 2010.

Bain, Joseph, ed. *Calendar of Documents relating to Scotland, Preserved in Her Majesty's Public Record Office*. 4 vols. Edinburgh: Neill, 1881–88.

Bakunin, Mikhail. *Bakunin on Anarchism*. Montreal: Black Rose Books, 1980.

Balakian, Peter. *The Burning Tigris: The Armenian Genocide and America's Response*. New York: HarperCollins, 2003.

Balderston, Marion, and David Syrett, eds. *The Lost War: Letters from British Officers during the American Revolution*. New York: Horizon Press, 1975.

Band, Claire and William. *Two Years with the Chinese Communists*. New Haven: Yale University Press, 1948.

Ban Gu. *The History of the Former Han Dynasty*. 2 vols. Baltimore: Waverly Press, 1938–55.

Barber, Noel. *The War of the Running Dogs: The Malayan Emergency: 1948–1960*. New York: Weybright and Talley, 1971.

Barber, Richard, ed. *The Life and Campaigns of the Black Prince*. Woodbridge: Boydell Press, 1979.

Barbour, John. *The Bruce: Being the Metrical History of Robert Bruce, King of Scots, Compiled AD 1365*. Glasgow: Gowans and Gray, 1907.

Barfield, Thomas J. *The Perilous Frontier: Nomadic Empires and China, 221 BC to AD 1757*. Cambridge: Blackwell, 1989.

Barker, John. *The British in Boston: Being the Diary of Lieutenant John Barker of the King's Own Regiment from November 15, 1774, to May 31, 1776*. Cambridge: Harvard University Press, 1924.

Barnard, Sandy. *A Hoosier Quaker Goes to War: The Life & Death of Major Joel H. Elliott, 7th Cavalry*. Wake Forest: AST Press, 2010.

Barnett, Louise. *Touched by Fire: The Life, Death, and Myth Afterlife of George Armstrong Custer*. Lincoln: University of Nebraska Press, 2006.

Barnitz, Albert. *Life in Custer's Cavalry: Diaries and Letters of Albert and Jennie Barnitz, 1867–1868*. New Haven: Yale University Press, 1977.

Barr, James. *Setting the Desert on Fire: T. E. Lawrence and Britain's Secret War in Arabia, 1916–1918*. New York: W. W. Norton, 2008.

Barrett, David D. *Dixie Mission: The United States Army Observer Group in Yan'an, 1944*. Berkeley: Center for Chinese Studies, University of California, 1970.

Barrett, Thomas M. "The Remaking of the Lion of Dagestan: Shamil in Captivity." *Russian Review,* July 1994.

Barron, Evan Macleod. *The Scottish War of Independence*. New York: Barnes & Noble Books, 1997.

Barrow, G. W. S. *Robert Bruce and the Community of the Realm of Scotland.* Edinburgh: Edinburgh University Press, 2005.

Barry, Tom. *Guerilla Days in Ireland: A Firsthand Account of the Black and Tan War (1919–1921).* New York: Devin-Adair, 1956.

Bartlett, W. B. *Assassins: The Story of Medieval Islam's Secret Sect.* Gloucestershire: Sutton, 2001.

Barton, E. C. *Let the Boy Win His Spurs: An Autobiography.* London: Research Publishing, 1976.

Bass, Gary J. *Freedom's Battle: The Origins of Humanitarian Intervention.* New York: Alfred A. Knopf, 2008.

Bass, Robert D. *Gamecock: The Life and Campaigns of General Thomas Sumter.* New York: Holt, Rinehart and Winston, 1961.

———. *The Green Dragoon: The Lives of Banastre Tarleton and Mary Robinson.* Orangeburg: Sandlapper, 1973.

———. *Swamp Fox: The Life and Campaigns of General Francis Marion.* Orangeburg: Sandlapper, 1974.

Batista, Fulgencio. *Cuba Betrayed.* New York: Vantage Press, 1962.

"Battle of Malaya: Smiling Tiger." *Time,* December 15, 1952.

Baumann, Bommi. *How It All Began: The Personal Account of a West German Urban Guerrilla.* Vancouver: Arsenal Pulp Press, 2006.

Bayly, C. A., and Eugenio F. Biagini. *Giuseppe Mazzini and the Globalization of Democratic Nationalism, 1830–1920.* Oxford: Oxford University Press, 2008.

Bayly, Christopher, and Tim Harper. *Forgotten Armies: The Fall of British Asia, 1941–1945.* Cambridge: Harvard University Press, 2005.

———. *Forgotten Wars: Freedom and Revolution in Southeast Asia.* Cambridge: Harvard University Press, 2007.

Beard, John Relly. *Toussaint L'Ouverture: Biography and Autobiography.* Boston: James Redpath, 1863.

Bearden, Milt, and James Risen. *The Main Enemy: The Inside Story of the CIA's Final Showdown with the KGB.* New York: Random House, 2003.

Beckett, Ian F. W. *Modern Insurgencies and Counter-Insurgencies: Guerrillas and Their Opponents since 1750.* London: Routledge, 2001.

Beevor, Antony, and Artemis Cooper. *Paris after the Liberation, 1944–1949.* London: Penguin, 1994.

Begin, Menachem. *The Revolt: The Story of the Irgun.* Bnei-Brak, Israel: Steimazky Group, 2002.

Behr, Edward. *The Algerian Problem.* Harmondsworth: Penguin, 1961.

Bell, David A. *The First Total War: Napoleon's Europe and the Birth of Warfare as We Know It.* Boston: Houghton Mifflin, 2007.

Bell, J. Bowyer. *Terror Out of Zion: The Fight for Israeli Independence.* New Brunswick: Transaction, 1996.

Bell, Madison Smartt. *Toussaint Louverture: A Biography.* New York: Pantheon Books, 2007.

Benjamin, Daniel, and Steven Simon. *The Age of Sacred Terror: Radical Islam's War against America.* New York: Random House, 2003.

Bennett, Rab. *Under the Shadow of the Swastika: The Moral Dilemmas of Resistance and Collaboration in Hitler's Europe.* New York: New York University Press, 1999.

Ben-Porat, Yeshayahu, Eitan Haber, and Zeev Schiff. *Entebbe Rescue.* New York: Delacorte Press, 1977.

Benton, Gregor. *Mountain Fires: The Red Army's Three-Year War in South China, 1934–1938.* Berkeley: University of California Press, 1992.

Benton, Gregor, and Lin Chun, eds. *Was Mao Really a Monster? The Academic Response to Chang and Halliday's Mao: The Unknown Story.* London: Routledge, 2010.

Berenbaum, Michael, ed. *A Mosaic of Victims: Non-Jews Persecuted and Murdered by the Nazis.* New York: New York University Press, 1990.

Bergen, Peter L. *Holy War, Inc.: Inside the Secret World of Osama bin Laden.* New York: Simon & Schuster, 2002.

———. *The Longest War: America and al-Qaeda since 9/11.* New York: Free Press, 2011.

———. *The Osama bin Laden I Know: An Oral History of Al Qaeda's Leader.* New York: Free Press, 2006.

Berger, Carl. *Broadsides and Bayonets: The Propaganda War of the American Revolution.* San Rafael: Presidio Press, 1976.

Bergère, Marie-Claire. *Shanghai: China's Gateway to Modernity.* Stanford: Stanford University Press, 2009.

Bergman, Jay. *Vera Zasulich: A Biography.* Stanford: Stanford University Press, 1983.

Bergman, Ronen. *The Secret War with Iran.* New York: Free Press, 2007.

Bergot, Erwan. *Bigeard.* Paris: Perrin, 1988.

Berman, Eli, Jacob N. Shapiro, and Joseph H. Felton. "Can Hearts and Minds Be Bought? The Economics of Counterinsurgency in Iraq." National Bureau of Economic Research, December 2009.

Berman, Larry. *No Peace, No Honor: Nixon, Kissinger, and the Betrayal of Vietnam.* New York: Touchstone, 2001.

Bernstein, Richard. *Out of the Blue: The Story of September 11, 2001, from Jihad to Ground Zero.* New York: Times Books, 2003.

Bethel, Nicholas. *The Palestine Triangle: The Struggle for the Holy Land, 1935–1948.* New York: G. P. Putnam's Sons, 1979.

Betser, Moshe, with Robert Rosenberg. *Secret Soldier: The Autobiography of Israel's Greatest Commando.* London: Simon & Schuster, 1996.

The Bible: Authorized King James Version. Oxford: Oxford University Press, 1998.

Biddle, Stephen, and Jeffrey A. Friedman. *The 2006 Lebanon Campaign and the Future of Warfare: Implications for Army and Defense Policy.* Carlisle: Institute for Strategic Studies, 2008.

Bidwell, Robin. *Morocco under Colonial Rule: French Administration of Tribal Areas, 1912–1956*. London: Frank Cass, 1973.

Bierman, John, and Colin Smith. *Fire in the Night: Wingate of Burma, Ethiopia, and Zion.* New York: Random House, 1999.

Bigeard, Marcel. *Pour une parcelle de gloire*. Paris: Plon, 1975.

Bill, James A. *The Eagle and the Lion: The Tragedy of American-Iranian Relations*. New Haven: Yale University Press, 1988.

Billias, George Athan, ed. *George Washington's Generals and Opponents: Their Exploits and Leadership.* New York: Da Capo Press, 1994.

Bingham, D. A., ed. *A Selection from the Letters and Despatches of the First Napoleon. With Explanatory Notes*. 3 vols. London: Chapman and Hall, 1884.

Bin Laden, Carmen. *Inside the Kingdom: My Life in Saudi Arabia*. New York: Warner Books, 2004.

Bin Laden, Najwa and Omar. *Growing Up bin Laden: Osama's Wife and Son Take Us into Their Secret World*. New York: St. Martin's Griffith, 2009.

Bin Laden, Osama. *Messages to the World: The Statements of Osama bin Laden*. London: Verso, 2005.

Birnbaum, Louis. *Red Dawn at Lexington*. Boston: Houghton Mifflin, 1986.

Birtle, Andrew J. *U.S. Army Counterinsurgency and Contingency Operations Doctrine, 1860–1941*. Washington, D.C.: Center of Military History, U.S. Army, 1998.

Black, Ian, and Benny Morris. *Israel's Secret Wars: A History of Israel's Intelligence Services*. New York: Grove Press, 1991.

Blake, Christopher. *A View from Within: The Last Years of British Rule in South-East Asia*. Somerset: Mendip, 1990.

Blanch, Leslie. *The Sabres of Paradise: Conquest and Vengeance in the Caucasus*. London: Tauris Parke, 2006.

Blaufarb, Douglas S. *The Counterinsurgency Era: U.S. Doctrine and Performance, 1950 to the Present*. New York: Free Press, 1977.

Blaze, Elzéar. *Captain Blaze: Life in Napoleon's Army.* N.p.: Leonaur, 2007.

Blind Harry. *The History of the Life, Adventures, and Heroic Actions of the Celebrated Sir William Wallace*. New York: William W. Crawford, 1820.

Blood, Bindon. *Four Score Years and Ten: Sir Bindon Blood's Reminiscences.* London: G. Bell, 1933.

Bloom, James J. *The Jewish Revolts against Rome, A.D. 66–135: A Military Analysis.* Jefferson: McFarland, 2010.

Bloom, Mia. *Dying to Kill: The Allure of Suicide Terror.* New York: Columbia University Press, 2005.

Bocca, Geoffrey. *The Secret Army.* Englewood Cliffs: Prentice-Hall, 1968.

Bodard, Lucien. *The Quicksand War: Prelude to Vietnam.* Boston: Atlantic Monthly Press, 1967.

Bohning, Don. *The Castro Obsession: U.S. Covert Operations against Cuba, 1959–1965.* Washington: Potomac Books, 2005.

Bolívar, Simón. *Selected Writings of Bolivar.* 2 vols. New York: Colonial Press, 1951.

Bookchin, Murray. *The Spanish Anarchists: The Heroic Years, 1868–1936*. New York: Free Life Editions, 1977.

Boot, Max. "Reconstructing Iraq: With the Marines in the South and the 101st Airborne in the North." *Weekly Standard*, September 15, 2003.

———. *The Savage Wars of Peace: Small Wars and the Rise of American Power.* New York: Basic Books, 2002.

———. "The Second Lebanon War." *Weekly Standard*, September 4, 2006.

———. *War Made New: Technology, Warfare, and the Course of History, 1500 to Today.* New York: Gotham Books, 2006.

Boot, Max, and Richard W. Bennet. "The Colombian Miracle." *Weekly Standard*, December 7, 2009.

———. "Treading Softly in the Philippines." *Weekly Standard*, January 5, 2009.

Borchgrave, Arnaud de. "The Great Stand: Unforgettable Dienbienphu." *Newsweek*, May 17, 1954.

Borovik, Artyom. *The Hidden War: A Russian Journalist's Account of the Soviet War in Afghanistan.* New York: Grove Press, 1990.

Boteler, Alexander. "Recollections of the John Brown Raid by a Virginian Who Witnessed the Fight." *Century Magazine*, July 1883.

Bourke, John G. *An Apache Campaign in the Sierra Madre*. New York: Charles Scribner's Sons, 1886.

———. *On the Border with Crook*. New York: Charles Scribner's Sons, 1892.

Bourrienne, Louis Antoine Fauvelet de. *Memoirs of Napoleon Bonaparte.* 3 vols. New York: Charles Scribner's Sons, 1895.

Bowden, Brett, and Michael T. Davis. *Terror: From Tyrannicide to Terrorism.* St. Lucia: University of Queensland Press, 2008.

Bowden, Mark. "David Petraeus's Winning Streak." *Vanity Fair* Web Exclusive, March 30, 2010.

———. *Guests of the Ayatollah: The First Battle in America's War with Militant Islam.* New York: Grove Press, 2006.

———. "The Ploy." *Atlantic*, May 2007.

———. "The Professor of War." *Vanity Fair*, May 2010.

Bower, Walter. *A History Book for Scots: Selections from Scotichronicon.* Edinburgh: Mercat Press, 1998.

Bradford, Alfred S. *With Arrow, Sword, and Spear: A History of Warfare in the Ancient World*. Westport: Praeger, 2001.

Bradford, William. *Of Plymouth Plantation, 1620–1647.* New York: Alfred A. Knopf, 1952.

Bradley, James E. *Popular Politics and the American Revolution in England: Petitions, the Crown, and Public Opinion*. Macon: Mercer University Press, 1986.

Braestrup, Peter. *Big Story: How the American Press and Television Reported and Interpreted the Crisis of Tet 1968 in Vietnam and Washington.* New Haven: Yale University Press, 1983.

Branch, Daniel. *Defeating Mau Mau, Creating Kenya: Counterinsurgency, Civil War and Decolonization*. Cambridge: Cambridge University Press, 2009.

Brandt, Heinrich von. *In the Legions of Napoleon: The Memoirs of a Polish Officer in Spain and Russia, 1808–1813*. London: Greenhill, 1999.

Braun, Otto. *A Comintern Agent in China, 1932–1939*. Stanford: Stanford University Press, 1982.

Bray, N. N. E. *Shifting Sands*. London: Unicorn Press, 1934.

Breen, Dan. *My Fight for Irish Freedom*. Dublin: Anvil Books, 1981.

Brewer, David. *The Greek War of Independence: The Struggle for Freedom from Ottoman Oppression and the Birth of the Modern Greek Nation*. Woodstock: Overlook Press, 2003.

Brewster, Charles. "Battle of the Washita." *National Tribune*, August 22, 1901.

Bridgman, Edward Payson, and Luke Fisher Parsons. *With John Brown in Kansas: The Battle of Osawatomie*. Madison: J. N. Davidson, 1915.

Bright, John. *A History of Israel*. 4th ed. Louisville: Westminster John Knox Press, 2000.

Brill, Charles J. *Custer, Black Kettle, and the Fight on the Washita*. Norman: University of Oklahoma Press, 2002.

Brisard, Jean-Charles. *Zarqawi: The New Face of Al Qaeda*. Cambridge: Polity Press, 2005.

Broadwell, Paula, with Vernon Loeb. *All In: The Education of General David Petraeus*. New York: Penguin, 2013.

Brocheux, Pierre. *Ho Chi Minh: A Biography*. Cambridge: Cambridge University Press, 2007.

Broers, Michael. *Europe under Napoleon, 1799–1815*. London: Arnold, 1996.

Brooks, Jeffrey. *When Russia Learned to Read: Literacy and Popular Literature, 1861–1917*. Princeton: Princeton University Press, 1985.

Brousse, Paul. "La propagande par le fait." *Bulletin de la Fédération Jurassienne*, August 5, 1877.

Brown, Dee. *Bury My Heart at Wounded Knee: An Indian History of the American West*. New York: Holt, Rinehart & Winston, 1970.

Brown, George Washington. *The Truth at Last: Reminiscences of Old John Brown*. Rockford: Abraham E. Smith, 1880.

Brown, Malcolm, ed. *T. E. Lawrence: The Selected Letters*. New York: W. W. Norton, 1989.

———. *T. E. Lawrence in War and Peace: An Anthology of the Military Writings of Lawrence of Arabia*. London: Greenhill Books, 2005.

Bruce, Anthony. *The Last Crusade: The Palestine Campaign in the First World War*. London: John Murray, 2002.

Brumwell, Stephen. *White Devil: A True Story of War, Savagery, and Vengeance in Colonial America*. New York: Da Capo, 2004.

Buchanan, John. *The Road to Guilford Courthouse: The American Revolution in the Carolinas*. New York: John Wiley, 1997.

Budiansky, Stephen. *The Bloody Shirt: Terror after Appomattox*. New York: Viking, 2008.

Bui Diem, with David Chanoff. *In the Jaws of History*. Bloomington: Indiana University Press, 1999.

Burchett, W. G. *North of the Seventeenth Parallel*. Hanoi: Red River Publishing, 1957.

———. *Wingate Adventure*. Melbourne: F. W. Cheshire, 1944.

Burke, Edmund. *Select Works*. Edited by E. J. Payne. Oxford: Clarendon Press, 1904.

Burleigh, Michael. *Blood and Rage: A Cultural History of Terrorism*. New York: Harper, 2009.

Burnes, Alexander. *Cabool: A Personal Narrative of a Journey to, and Residence in, That City*. 2nd ed. London: John Murray, 1843.

Butterworth, Alex. *The World That Never Was: A True Story of Dreamers, Schemers, Anarchists, and Secret Agents*. New York: Pantheon, 2010.

Byas, Hugh. *Government by Assassination*. New York: Alfred A. Knopf, 1942.

Byford-Jones, W. *Grivas and the Story of EOKA*. London: Robert Hale, 1959.

Byman, Daniel. *A High Price: The Triumphs and Failures of Israeli Counterterrorism*. Oxford: Oxford University Press, 2011.

Caesar, Julius. *The Gallic War*. Oxford and New York: Oxford University Press, 1996.

Callwell, C. E. *Field-Marshal Sir Henry Wilson: His Life and Diaries*. 2 vols. New York: Charles Scribner's Sons, 1927.

———. *Small Wars: Their Principles and Practice*. 3rd ed. Lincoln: University of Nebraska Press, 1996.

Calvert, Michael. *Fighting Mad: One Man's Guerilla War*. South Yorkshire: Pen & Sword Books, 2004.

———. *Prisoners of Hope*. London: Corgi Books, 1973.

Cambanis, Thanassis. *A Privilege to Die: Inside Hezbollah's Legions and Their Endless War against Israel*. New York: Free Press, 2010.

Campbell, Bruce. *The SA Generals and the Rise of Nazism*. Lexington: University Press of Kentucky, 1998.

Campbell, Bruce M. S., ed. *Before the Black Death: Studies in the "Crisis" of the Early Fourteenth Century*. Manchester: Manchester University Press, 1991.

———. "Benchmarking Medieval Economic Development: England, Wales, Scotland, and Ireland, circa 1290." *Economic History Review*, 2008.

Campbell, J. B. *The Roman Army, 31 BC–AD 337*. New York: Routledge, 1994.

Campbell, Mavis C. *The Maroons of Jamaica, 1655–1796: A History of Resistance, Collaboration, and Betrayal*. Granby: Bergin & Garvey, 1988.

Cancian, Mark F. "The Wehrmacht in Yugoslavia: Lessons of the Past?" *Parameters*, Autumn 1993.

Carr, Caleb. *The Lessons of Terror*. New York: Random House, 2002.

Carr, Matthew. *The Infernal Machine: A History of Terrorism*. New York: New Press, 2006.

Carr, Reg. *Anarchism in France: The Case of Octave Mirbeau*. Montreal: McGill-Queen's University Press, 1977.

Carton, Evan. *Patriotic Treason: John Brown and the Soul of America*. New York: Free Press, 2006.

Casey, Michael. *Che's Afterlife: The Legacy of an Image*. New York: Vintage, 2009.
Cassius Dio. *Roman History*. 9 vols. Cambridge: Harvard University Press, 1927.
Castañeda, Jorge G. *Compañero: The Life and Death of Che Guevara*. New York: Vintage Books, 1998.
Castro, Daniel, ed. *Revolution and Revolutionaries: Guerrilla Movements in Latin America*. Wilmington: Scholarly Resources, 1999.
Castro, Fidel. *The Prison Letters of Fidel Castro*. New York: Nation Books, 2007.
———. *Revolutionary Struggle, 1947–1958*. Vol. 1 of *Selected Works of Fidel Castro*. Edited by Rolando E. Bonachea and Nelson P. Valdés. Cambridge: MIT Press, 1972.
Castro, Fidel, and Ignacio Ramonet. *Fidel Castro: My Life—A Spoken Autobiography*. New York: Scribner, 2009.
Casuso, Teresa. *Cuba and Castro*. New York: Random House, 1961.
Catignani, Sergio. *Israeli Counter-Insurgency and the Intifadas: Dilemmas of a Conventional Army*. New York: Routledge, 2008.
Chaliand, Gerard, and Arnaud Blin, eds. *The History of Terrorism from Antiquity to Al Qaeda*. Berkeley: University of California Press, 2007.
Chambers, Jennie. "What a School-Girl Saw of John Brown's Raid." *Harper's Monthly Magazine*, January 1902.
Champlain, Samuel de. *The Works of Samuel de Champlain*. 6 vols. Toronto: Champlain Society, 1922–36.
Chang, Chun-shu. *The Rise of the Chinese Empire*. 2 vols. Ann Arbor: University of Michigan Press, 2007.
Chang, Jung, and Jon Halliday. *Mao: The Unknown Story*. New York: Alfred A. Knopf, 2005.
Chang, Kia-Ngau. *Last Chance in Manchuria: The Diary of Chang Kia-Ngau*. Stanford: Hoover Institution Press, 1989.
Chang, Kuo-tao. *The Rise of the Chinese Communist Party, 1921–1938*. 2 vols. Lawrence: University Press of Kansas, 1971.
Chazotte, Pierre Etienne. *The Black Rebellion in Haiti: The Experience of One Who Was Present during Four Years of Tumult and Massacre*. Philadelphia: Privately Printed, 1927.
Chen Jian. "China and the First Indo-China War." *China Quarterly*, March 1993.
Ch'en, Jerome. *Mao and the Chinese Revolution*. London: Oxford University Press, 1965.
Childs, John. *Warfare in the Seventeenth Century*. London: Cassell, 2003.
Childs, Matt D. "An Historical Critique of the Emergence and Evolution of Ernesto Che Guevara's *Foco* Theory." *Journal of Latin American Studies*, October 1995.
"China: Tiananmen Legacy Defies Olympic Gloss." *Human Rights Watch*, June 1, 2007.
Chinnery, Philip D. *March of Die*. Shrewsbury: Airlife, 1997.
Chin Peng. *Alias Chin Peng: My Side of History*. Singapore: Media Masters, 2003.
The Chronicle of Lanercost. Glasgow: James Maclehose, 1913.

Churchill, Charles Henry. *The Life of Abdel Kader, Ex-Sultan of the Arabs of Algeria.* London: Chapman and Hall, 1867.

Churchill, Winston. *Blood, Toil, Tears and Sweat: The Speeches of Winston Churchill.* Boston: Houghton Mifflin, 1989.

———. *The Second World War: Closing the Ring.* Boston: Houghton Mifflin, 1951.

———. *The Story of the Malakand Field Force: An Episode of Frontier War.* Champaign: Bookjungle, n.d.

———. *The World Crisis: The Aftermath.* London: Thornton Butterworth, 1929.

———. *Young Winston's Wars: The Original Dispatches of Winston S. Churchill, War Correspondent, 1897–1900.* New York: Viking, 1972.

Clark, Dora Mae. *British Opinion and the American Revolution.* New Haven: Yale University Press, 1930.

Clark, Michael. *Algeria in Turmoil.* New York: Grosset & Dunlap, 1960.

Clark, Ransom. *Narrative of Ransom Clark, the Only Survivor of Major Dade's Command in Florida.* Binghamton: Johnson and Marble, 1839.

Clarke, Dudley. *Seven Assignments.* London: Jonathan Cape, 1948.

Clarke, Richard A. *Against All Enemies: Inside America's War on Terror.* New York: Free Press, 2004.

Clausewitz, Karl von. *On War.* In *The Book of War,* ed. Caleb Carr. New York: Modern Library, 2000.

Clifford, Nicholas R. *Spoilt Children of Empire: Westerners in Shanghai and the Chinese Revolution of the 1920s.* Hanover: Middlebury College Press, 1991.

Cline, Lawrence E. "Pseudo Operations and Counterinsurgency: Lessons from Other Countries." Carlisle: Strategic Studies Institute, U.S. Army War College, June 2005.

Clinton, Henry. *The American Rebellion: Sir Henry Clinton's Narrative of His Campaigns, 1775–1782.* New Haven: Yale University Press, 1954.

Cloake, John. *Templer: Tiger of Malaya: The Life of Field Marshal Sir Gerald Templer.* London: Harrap, 1985.

Clodfelter, Michael. *Vietnam in Military Statistics: A History of the Indochina Wars, 1772–1991.* Jefferson: McFarland, 1995.

———. *Warfare and Armed Conflicts: A Statistical Encyclopedia of Casualty and Other Figures, 1494–2007.* 3rd ed. Jefferson: McFarland, 2008.

Cloud, David, and Greg Jaffe. *The Fourth Star: Four Generals and Their Epic Struggle for the Future of the United States Army.* New York: Three Rivers Press, 2009.

Clutterbuck, Richard L. *The Long Long War: Counterinsurgency in Malaya and Vietnam.* New York: Frederick A. Praeger, 1966.

Coates, John. *Suppressing Insurgency: An Analysis of the Malayan Emergency, 1948–1954.* Boulder: Westview Press, 1992.

Cobban, Helena. *The Palestinian Liberation Organization: People, Power, and Politics.* Cambridge: Cambridge University Press, 1984.

Cockburn, Andrew and Leslie. *One Point Safe.* New York: Doubleday, 1997.

Codrington, Edward. *Memoir of the Life of Admiral Sir Edward Codrington.* London: Longmans, Green, 1873.

Cohen, Alain. *David Galula: The French Officer Who Defined the Art of Counterinsurgency.* Westport: Praeger, 2012.

Cohen, Eliot A. *Commandos and Politicians: Elite Military Units in Modern Democracies.* Cambridge: Center for International Affairs, Harvard University, 1978.

Colby, William, with James McCargar. *Lost Victory: A First-Hand Account of America's Sixteen-Year Involvement in Vietnam.* Chicago: Contemporary Books, 1989.

Coll, Steve. *The Bin Ladens: Oil, Money, Terrorism and the Secret Saudi World.* London: Penguin, 2008.

———. "The General's Dilemma." *New Yorker,* September 8, 2008.

———. *Ghost Wars: The Secret History of the CIA, Afghanistan, and bin Laden, from the Soviet Invasion to September 10, 2001.* New York: Penguin, 2004.

Colletta, Pietro. *History of the Kingdom of Naples, 1734–1825.* Edinburgh: T. Constable, 1858.

Colley, Linda. *Captives: Britain, Empire and the World, 1600–1850.* London: Jonathan Cape, 2002.

Collins, Peter, ed. *Nationalism and Unionism: Conflict in Ireland, 1885–1921.* Belfast: Institute of Irish Studies, Queen's University, 1994.

Commission for Historical Clarification, Conclusions and Recommendations. "Guatemala: Memory of Silence." http://shr.aaas.org/guatemala/ceh/report/ english/toc .html.

The Conduct of Anti-Terrorist Operations in Malaya. St. Petersburg: Hailer Publishing, 2006.

Connable, Ben, and Martin C. Libicki. *How Insurgencies End.* Santa Monica: RAND, 2010.

Connelly, Matthew. *A Diplomatic Revolution: Algeria's Fight for Independence and the Origins of the Post–Cold War Era.* Oxford: Oxford University Press, 2002.

Connelly, Owen. *The Gentle Bonaparte: A Biography of Joseph, Napoleon's Elder Brother.* New York: Macmillan, 1968.

Conrad, Joseph. *The Secret Agent: A Simple Tale.* New York: Signet Classics, 2007.

Conway, Stephen. *The British Isles and the War of American Independence.* Oxford: Oxford University Press, 2000.

———. "To Subdue America: British Army Officers and the Conduct of the Revolutionary War." *William and Mary Quarterly,* July 1986.

Coogan, Tim Pat. *Michael Collins: The Man Who Made Ireland.* New York: Palgrave, 2002.

Cook, Sherburne F. "Interracial Warfare and Population Decline among the New England Indians." *Ethnohistory,* Winter 1973.

Cooper, Matthew. *The Nazi War against Soviet Partisans, 1941–1944.* New York: Stein and Day, 1979.

Cordesman, Anthony H. *Lessons of the 2006 Israeli-Hezbollah War.* Washington: Center for Strategic and International Studies, 2007.

Cordovez, Diego, and Selig S. Harrison. *Out of Afghanistan: The Inside Story of the Soviet Withdrawal.* New York: Oxford University Press, 1995.

Cornwallis, Charles. *Correspondence of Charles, First Marquis Cornwallis.* 3 vols. London: John Murray, 1859.

Corum, James S., and Wray J. Johnson. *Airpower in Small Wars: Fighting Insurgents and Terrorists.* Lawrence: University Press of Kansas, 2003.

Cosmo, Nicola Di. *Ancient China and Its Enemies: The Rise of Nomadic Power in East Asian History.* Cambridge: Cambridge University Press, 2004.

———. *Warfare in Inner Asian History (500–1800).* Leiden, Netherlands: Brill, 2002.

Coughlin, Con. *Hostage: The Complete Story of the Lebanon Captives.* London: Little, Brown, 1992.

———. *Khomeini's Ghost: The Iranian Revolution and the Rise of Militant Islam.* New York: Ecco, 2010.

Courtois, Stephane, et al. *The Black Book of Communism: Crimes, Terror, Repression.* Cambridge: Harvard University Press, 1999.

Cozzens, Peter, ed. *Eyewitnesses to the Indian Wars, 1865–1890.* Vol. 1, *The Struggle for Apacheria.* Mechanicsburg: Stackpole, 2001.

———. Vol. 2, *The Wars for the Pacific Northwest.* Mechanicsburg: Stackpole, 2002.

———. Vol. 3, *Conquering the Southern Plains.* Mechanicsburg: Stackpole, 2003.

———. Vol. 4, *The Long War for the Northern Plains.* Mechanicsburg: Stackpole, 2004.

———. Vol. 5, *The Army and the Indian.* Mechanicsburg: Stackpole, 2005.

Crawford, Oliver. *The Door Marked Malaya.* London: Rupert Hart-Davis, 1958.

Crawshaw, Nancy. *The Cyprus Revolt: An Account of the Struggle for Union with Greece.* London: George Allen & Unwin, 1978.

Crile, George. *Charlie Wilson's War.* New York: Grove Press, 2003.

Cronin, Audrey Kurth. *How Terrorism Ends: Understanding the Decline and Demise of Terrorist Campaigns.* Princeton: Princeton University Press, 2009.

Crook, George. "The Apache Problem." *Journal of the Military Service Institution,* 1886.

———. *General George Crook: His Autobiography.* Norman: University of Oklahoma Press, 1946.

Crossman, R. H. S. "The Ethics of Terrorism." *New Statesman and Nation,* December 15, 1956.

Crowley, Roger, *1453: The Holy War for Constantinople and the Clash of Islam and the West.* New York: Hyperion, 2005.

Crozier, F. P. *Ireland For Ever.* London: Jonathan Cape, 1932.

Cruickshank, Charles. *SOE in the Far East.* Oxford: Oxford University Press, 1983.

Cullison, Alan. "Inside Al-Qaeda's Hard Drive." *Atlantic Monthly,* September 2004.

Cuneo, John R. *Robert Rogers of the Rangers.* New York: Richardson & Steirman, 1987.

Currey, Cecil B. *The Unquiet American.* Washington: Brassey's, 1998.

———. *Victory at Any Cost: The Genius of Viet Nam's Gen. Vo Nguyen Giap.* Washington: Potomac Books, 1999.

Curtius Rufus, Quintus. *The History of Alexander.* London: Penguin, 1984.

Custer, George A. *Wild Life on the Plains and Horrors of Indian Warfare*. Brandon: Sidney M. Southard, 1884.

Daftary, Farhad. *The Assassin Legends: Myths of the Isma'ilis*. London: I. B. Tauris, 2008.

Daingerfield, John E. P. "John Brown at Harper's Ferry." *Century Magazine*, June 1885.

Dalloz, Jacques. *The War in Indo-China, 1945–54*. Dublin: Gill and Macmillan, 1990.

Dalton, Charles. *With the Dublin Brigade (1917–1921)*. London: Peter Davies, 1929.

Daly, Jonathan W. *Autocracy under Siege: Security Police and Opposition in Russia, 1866–1905*. DeKalb: Northern Illinois University Press, 1998.

———. *The Watchful State: Security Police and Opposition in Russia, 1906–1917*. DeKalb: Northern Illinois University Press, 2004.

Dandolo, Emilio. *The Italian Volunteers and the Lombard Rifle Brigade*. London: Longman, 1851.

Danziger, Raphael. *Abd al-Qadir and the Algerians: Resistance to the French and Internal Consolidation*. New York: Holmes & Meir, 1977.

Dash, Mike. *Thug: The True Story of India's Murderous Cult*. London: Granta Books, 2005.

Daugherty, William. *In the Shadow of the Ayatollah: A CIA Hostage in Iran*. Annapolis: Naval Institute Press, 2001.

Davidson, Philip. *Propaganda and the American Revolution, 1763–1783*. Chapel Hill: University of North Carolina Press, 1941.

Davidson, Phillip B. *Vietnam at War: The History, 1946–1975*. New York: Oxford University Press, 1991.

Davis, David Brion. *Inhuman Bondage: The Rise and Fall of Slavery in the New World*. Oxford: Oxford University Press, 2006.

Davis, John A. *Naples and Napoleon: Southern Italy and the European Revolutions, 1780–1860*. Oxford: Oxford University Press, 2006.

Davis, Mike. *Buda's Wagon: A Brief History of the Car Bomb*. London: Verso, 2007.

Dayan, Moshe. *Moshe Dayan: Story of My Life*. New York: William Morrow, 1976.

Deakin, F. W. D. *The Embattled Mountain*. New York: Oxford University Press, 1971.

Debray, Régis. *Praised Be Our Lords: A Political Education*. London: Verso, 2007.

———. *Revolution in the Revolution? Armed Struggle and Political Struggle in Latin America*. Westport: Greenwood Press, 1980.

Dedijer, Vladimir. *The Road to Sarajevo*. New York: Simon & Schuster, 1966.

———. *Tito Speaks: His Self Portrait and Struggle with Stalin*. London: Weidenfeld & Nicolson, 1953.

———. *The War Diaries of Vladimir Dedijer*. 3 vols. Ann Arbor: University of Michigan Press, 1990.

Deflem, Mathieu. "Wild Beasts without Nationality: The Uncertain Origins of Interpol, 1898–1910." In *The Handbook of Transnational Crime and Justice*, ed. Philip Reichel. Thousand Oaks: Sage Publications, 2005.

De Lon, Roy Stanley. "Stalin and Social Democracy, 1905–1922: The Political Diaries of David A. Sagirashvili." Ph.D. diss., Georgetown University, 1974.

DeMontravel, Peter D. *A Hero to His Fighting Men: Nelson A. Miles, 1839–1925*. Kent: Kent State University Press, 1998.

DePalma, Anthony. *The Man Who Invented Fidel: Cuba, Castro, and Herbert L. Matthews of the New York Times*. New York: PublicAffairs, 2006.

Deutscher, Isaac. *Stalin: A Political Biography*. New York: Oxford University Press, 1967.

De Wet, Christiaan Rudolf. *Three Years' War*. New York: Charles Scribner's Sons, 1902.

Diamond, Jared. "Vengeance Is Ours: What Can Tribal Societies Tell Us about Our Need to Get Even?" *New Yorker*, April 21, 2008.

Diaz, Tom, and Barbara Newman. *Lightning out of Lebanon: Hezbollah Terrorists on American Soil*. New York: Ballantine, 2005.

Di Cosmo, Nicola. *Ancient China and Its Enemies: The Rise of Nomadic Power in East Asian History*. Cambridge: Cambridge University Press, 2002.

Dikotter, Frank. *The Age of Openness: China before Mao*. Berkeley: University of California Press, 2008.

Dine, Philip. *Images of the Algerian War: French Fiction and Film, 1954–1992*. Oxford: Clarendon Press, 1994.

Dinh Van Ty. "The Brigade of Iron Horses." *Vietnamese Studies*, 1975.

Diodorus of Sicily. *The Historical Library of Diodorus the Silician in Fifteen Books*. 2 vols. London: J. Davis, 1814.

Djilas, Milovan. *Tito: The Story from the Inside*. New York: Harcourt Brace Jovanovich, 1980.

———. *Wartime*. New York: Harcourt Brace Jovanovich, 1977.

Djordjevic, Dimitrije, and Stephen Fischer-Galati. *The Balkan Revolutionary Tradition*. New York: Columbia University Press, 1981.

Dobson, Christopher. *Black September: Its Short, Violent History*. London: Robert Hale, 1975.

Dodds-Parker, Douglas. *Setting Europe Ablaze: Some Account of Ungentlemanly Warfare*. Surrey: Springwood Books, 1983.

Dolphin, Glenn E. *24 MAU:1983: A Marine Looks Back at the Peacekeeping Mission to Beirut, Lebanon*. Baltimore: PublishAmerica, 2005.

Dong, Stella. *Shanghai: The Rise and Fall of a Decadent City*. New York: William Morrow, 2000.

Dostoevsky, Fyodor. *Demons*. New York: Everyman's Library, 2000.

Doyle, Arthur Conan. *The Great Boer War*. New York: McClure, Phillips, 1902.

Doyle, William. *The Oxford History of the French Revolution*. 2nd ed. Oxford: Oxford University Press, 2002.

Drake, James D. *King Philip's War: Civil War in New England, 1675–1676*. Amherst: University of Massachusetts Press, 1999.

Drea, Edward J. *Japan's Imperial Army: Its Rise and Fall, 1853–1945*. Lawrence: University of Kansas Press, 2009.

Dubois, Laurent. *Avengers of the New World: The Story of the Haitian Revolution*. Cambridge: Belknap Press of Harvard University Press, 2004.

Dubois, Laurent, and John D. Garrigus, eds. *Slave Revolution in the Caribbean, 1789–1804: A Brief History with Documents*. Boston: Bedford/St. Martin's, 2006.

Dubroca, Louis. *The Life of Toussaint Louverture, Chief of the French Rebels in St. Domingo*. London: H. D. Symonds, 1802.

Duff, Douglas V. *Sword for Hire: The Sage of a Modern Free-Companion*. London: John Murray, 1934.

Duffy, Christopher. *The Military Experience in the Age of Reason*. Hertfordshire: Wordsworth Editions, 1998.

Duffy, Michael. *Soldiers, Sugar, and Seapower: The British Expeditions to the West Indies and the War against Revolutionary France*. Oxford: Clarendon Press, 1987.

Dugdale, Blanche. *Baffy: The Diaries of Blanche Dugdal, 1936–1947*. London: Valentine, Mitchell, 1973.

Duiker, William J. *The Communist Road to Power in Vietnam*. 2nd ed. Boulder: Westview Press, 1996.

———. *Ho Chi Minh: A Life*. New York: Hyperion, 2000.

Duncan, Donald. *The New Legions*. New York: Pocket Books, 1967.

Dunlop, John B. *Russia Confronts Chechnya: Roots of a Separatist Conflict*. Cambridge: Cambridge University Press, 1998.

Dunlop, Richard. *Behind Japanese Lines: With the OSS in Burma*. Chicago: Rand McNally, 1979.

Dunstan, Simon. *Israel's Lightning Strike: The Raid on Entebbe 1976*. New York: Osprey, 2009.

Dupree, Louis. *Afghanistan*. Princeton: Princeton University Press, 1973.

Durnford-Slater, John. *Commando: Memoirs of a Fighting Commando in World War Two*. London: Greenhill Books, 2002.

Earle, Edward Mead, ed. *Makers of Modern Strategy: Military Thought from Machiavelli to Hitler*. Princeton: Princeton University Press, 1952.

Eastman, Lloyd E. *Seeds of Destruction: Nationalist China in War and Revolution, 1937–1949*. Stanford: Stanford University Press, 1984.

Edwards, Bryan. *An Historical Survey of the French Colony in the Island of St. Domingo*. London: John Stockdale, 1797.

———. *The History, Civil and Commercial, of the British West Indies*. 5 vols. London: T. Miller, 1819.

Eiland, Giora. "The IDF in the Second Intifada." *Strategic Assessment*, October 2010.

Elkins, Caroline. *Imperial Reckoning: The Untold Story of Britain's Gulag in Kenya*. New York: Henry Holt, 2005.

Elliott, Duong Van Mai. *The Sacred Willow: Four Generations in the Life of a Vietnamese Family*. New York: Oxford University Press, 1999.

Elliott, Marianne. *Wolfe Tone: Prophet of Irish Independence*. New Haven: Yale University Press, 1989.

Ellis, John. *From the Barrel of a Gun: A History of Guerrilla, Revolutionary and Counter-Insurgency Warfare, from the Romans to the Present*. London: Greenhill Books, 1995.

Elphinstone, Monstuart. *An Account of the Kingdom of Caubul, and Its Dependencies in Persia, Tartary, and India*. London: Longman, Hurst, 1815.

Emerson, William. *Diaries and Letters of William Emerson, 1743–1776: Minister of the Church in Concord, Chaplain of the Revolutionary Army*. N.p., 1972.

English, Richard. *Armed Struggle: The History of the IRA*. Oxford: Oxford University Press, 2005.

———. *Irish Freedom: The History of Nationalism in Ireland*. London: Pan Books, 2007.

Epple, Jess C. *Custer's Battle of the Washita and a History of the Plains Indian Tribes*. New York: Exposition Press, 1970.

Esdaile, Charles J. *Fighting Napoleon: Guerrillas, Bandits and Adventurers in Spain, 1808–1814*. New Haven: Yale University Press, 2004.

———. *The Peninsular War: A New History*. Houndmills: Palgrave Macmillan, 2003.

———, ed. *Popular Resistance in the French Wars: Patriots, Partisans and Land Pirates*. Houndmills: Palgrave Macmillan, 2005.

Espoz y Mina, Francisco. *Breve extracto de la vida del General Mina*. London: Taylor and Hessey, 1825.

Eusebius. *The Ecclesiastical History of Eusebius Pamphilus*. London: Henry G. Bohn, 1851.

Evans, Martin. *The Memory of Resistance: French Opposition to the Algerian War (1954–1962)*. Oxford: Berg, 1997.

Evans, Martin, and John Phillips. *Algeria: Anger of the Dispossessed*. New Haven: Yale University Press, 2007.

Evans, Richard J. *The Coming of the Third Reich*. New York: Penguin, 2004.

Evelyn, William Glanville. *Memoir and Letters of Captain W. Glanville Evelyn, of the 4th Regiment ("King's Own"), from North America, 1774–1776*. Oxford: James Parker, 1879.

Ewald, Johann von. *Diary of the American War: A Hessian Journal*. New Haven: Yale University Press, 1979.

———. *Treatise on Partisan Warfare*. New York: Greenwood Press, 1991.

Exum, Andrew. "Hizballah at War: A Military Assessment." Washington Institute for Near East Policy, December 2006.

———. "Hizballah at War: Explaining Victory through the Comprehensive Approach to Conflict." Ph.D diss., King's College, 2010.

Eyck, F. Gunther. *Loyal Rebels: Andreas Hofer and the Tyrolean Uprising of 1809*. Lanham: University Press of America, 1986.

Eyre, Vincent. *The Military Operations at Cabul*. London: John Murray, 1843.

Fall, Bernard B. *Hell in a Very Small Place: The Siege of Dien Bien Phu*. New York: Da Capo Press, 2002.

———. *Street without Joy*. Mechanicsburg: Stackpole Books, 1994.

Farmer, Malcolm F. "The Origins of Weapons Systems." *Current Anthropology* (December 1994).

Farrokh, Kaveh. *Shadows in the Desert: Ancient Persia at War*. Oxford: Osprey, 2007.

Farwell, Byron. *The Great Anglo-Boer War*. New York: W. W. Norton, 1976.

"Fatalities in the First Intifada." B'Tselem [http://www.btselem.org/english/statistics/first_Intifada_Tables.asp].

Fausz, J. Frederick. "The 'Barbarous Massacre' Reconsidered: The Powhatan Uprising of 1622 and the Historians." *Explorations in Ethnic Studies*, 1978.

Feifer, Gregory. *The Great Gamble: The Soviet War in Afghanistan*. New York: Harper-Collins, 2009.

Fellman, Michael. *Inside War: The Guerrilla Conflict in Missouri during the American Civil War*. Oxford: Oxford University Press, 1990.

Feraoun, Mouloud. *Journal, 1955–1962: Reflections on the French-Algerian War*. Lincoln: University of Nebraska Press, 2000.

Fergusson, Bernard. *Beyond the Chindwin: An Account of Number Five Column of the Wingate Expedition into Burma 1943*. South Yorkshire: Pen & Sword Military, 2009.

———. *The Trumpet in the Hall, 1930–1958*. London: Collins, 1970.

———. *The Wild Green Earth*. London: Collins, 1946.

Ferling, John. *Almost a Miracle: The American Victory in the War of Independence*. Oxford: Oxford University Press, 2007.

Ferrill, Arther. *The Origins of War: From the Stone Age to Alexander the Great*. Boulder: Westview Press, 1997.

Fick, Carolyn E. *The Making of Haiti: The Saint Domingue Revolution from Below*. Knoxville: University of Tennessee Press, 1990.

Figes, Orlando. *Natasha's Dance: A Cultural History of Russia*. New York: Metropolitan Books, 2002.

———. *A People's Tragedy: A History of the Russian Revolution*. New York: Viking, 1996.

Figner, Vera. *Memoirs of a Revolutionist*. DeKalb: Northern Illinois University Press, 1991.

Finerty, John Frederick. *War-Path and Bivouac, or, The Conquest of the Sioux*. Chicago: Donohue and Henneberry, 1890.

Finlay, George. *History of the Greek Revolution*. 2 vols. Edinburgh: William Blackwood and Sons, 1861.

Finley, Milton. *The Most Monstrous of Wars: The Napoleonic Guerrilla War in Southern Italy, 1806–1811*. Columbia: University of South Carolina Press, 1994.

Fischer, David Hackett. *Champlain's Dream*. New York: Simon & Schuster, 2008.

———. *Paul Revere's Ride*. New York: Oxford University Press, 1994.

———. *Washington's Crossing*. Oxford: Oxford University Press, 2004.

Fisher, Andrew. *William Wallace*. Edinburgh: Birlinn, 2007.

Fishman, Brian, ed. *Bombers, Bank Accounts, & Bleedout: Al Qaeda's Road in and out of Iraq*. West Point: Combating Terrorism Center, 2008.

Fitzgibbon, Maurice. *Arts under Arms: A University Man in Khaki*. London: Longmans, Green, 1901.

Fleming, Walter. *A Documentary History of Reconstruction*. 2 vols. Cleveland: Arthur H. Clark, 1906–07.

Florus, Publius Annius. *Epitome of Roman History*. In *Sallust, Florus, and Velleius Paterculus*. London: George Bell, 1889.

Flynn, Peter. *Brazil: A Political Analysis*. London: Ernest Benn, 1978.

Follain, John. *Jackal: The Complete Story of the Legendary Terrorist, Carlos the Jackal*. New York: Arcade, 2011.

Foner, Eric. *Reconstruction: America's Unfinished Revolution, 1863–1877*. New York: Perennial Classics, 1989.

Foot, M. R. D. *Resistance: European Resistance to Nazism, 1940–1945*. New York: McGraw-Hill, 1977.

———. *SOE: The Special Operations Executive, 1940–1946*. London: Pimlico, 1999.

———. *War and Society: Historical Essays in Honour and Memory of J. R. Western, 1928–1971*. New York: Barnes & Noble Books, 1973.

———. "Was S.O.E. Any Good?" *Journal of Contemporary History*, January 1981.

Footman, David. *The Alexander Conspiracy: A Life of A. I. Zhelyabov*. LaSalle: Library Press, 1968.

Forbes, Charles Stuart. *The Campaigns of Garibaldi in the Two Sicilies: A Personal Narrative*. Edinburgh: William Blackwood, 1861.

Forman, Harrison. *Report from Red China*. New York: Henry Holt, 1945.

Foy, Michael T. *Michael Collins's Intelligence War: The Struggle between the British and the IRA, 1919–1921*. Gloucestershire: Sutton Publishing, 2006.

Franklin, Benjamin. *Autobiography of Benjamin Franklin*. New York: Henry Holt, 1916.

Franklin, John Hope, and Alfred A. Moss Jr. *From Slavery to Freedom: A History of African Americans*. 7th ed. New York: McGraw-Hill, 1994.

Franqui, Carlos. *Diary of the Cuban Revolution*. New York: Viking, 1980.

Fraser, Antonia. *Faith and Treason: The Story of the Gunpowder Plot*. New York: Doubleday, 1996.

Fraser, Flora. *Pauline Bonaparte: Venus of Empire*. New York: Alfred A. Knopf, 2009.

Fraser, Ronald. *Napoleon's Cursed War: Popular Resistance in the Spanish Peninsular War*. London: Verso, 2008.

Frayne, Douglas. *The Royal Inscriptions of Mesopotamia, Early Periods*. Vol. 2, *Sargonic and Gutian Periods (2334–2113 BC)*. Toronto: University of Toronto Press, 1993.

Freedman, Lawrence. *Kennedy's Wars: Berlin, Cuba, Laos, and Vietnam*. New York: Oxford University Press, 2000.

French, David. *The British Way in Counter-Insurgency, 1945–1967*. New York: Oford University Press, 2012.

Friedman, Jeffrey A. "The Strategy Trap and the American Indian Wars." Harvard Kennedy School, February 2011.

Friedman, Thomas L. *From Beirut to Jerusalem*. New York: Anchor Books, 1990.

Froissart, Jean. *Chronicles*. London: Penguin, 1978.

Fromkin, David. *A Peace to End All Peace: The Fall of the Ottoman Empire and the Creation of the Modern Middle East*. New York: Henry Holt, 2010.

Frontinus, Sextus Julius. *Strategematicon*. London: Thomas Goddard, 1811.

Fuller, J. F. C. *The Generalship of Alexander the Great.* Hertfordshire: Wordsworth, 1998.

———. *The Last of the Gentlemen's Wars: A Subaltern's Journal of the War in South Africa, 1890–1902*. London: Faber and Faber, 1937.

Gabriel, Richard A. *The Military History of Ancient Israel.* Westport: Praeger, 2003.

Gadea, Hilda. *My Life with Che: The Making of a Revolutionary.* New York: Palgrave Macmillan, 2008.

Gage, Beverly. *The Day Wall Street Exploded: A Story of America in the First Age of Terror.* New York: Oxford University Press, 2010.

Gage, Thomas. *The Correspondence of General Thomas Gage with the Secretaries of State, 1763–1775*. 2 vols. New Haven: Yale University Press, 1931.

Gale, John. *Clean Young Englishman.* New York: Coward-McCann, 1965.

Gall, Sandy. *Behind Russian Lines: An Afghan Journal.* New York: St. Martin's Press, 1983.

Galula, David. *Counterinsurgency Warfare: Theory and Practice.* New York: Frederick A. Praeger, 2005.

———. *Pacification in Algeria, 1956–1958*. Santa Monica: RAND, 2006.

Galvin, John R. *The Minute Men: The First Fight: Myths & Realities of the American Revolution*. Washington: Pergamon-Brassey's, 1989.

Gammer, Moshe. *The Lone Wolf and the Bear: Three Centuries of Chechen Defiance of Russian Rule*. Pittsburgh: University of Pittsburgh Press, 2006.

———. *Muslim Resistance to the Tsar: Shamil and the Conquest of Chechnia and Daghestan*. Abingdon: Frank Cass, 2005.

Gann, L. H., and Peter Duignan, eds. *African Proconsuls: European Governors in Africa.* New York: Free Press, 1978.

Gao Wenqian. *Zhou Enlai, the Last Perfect Revolutionary: A Biography.* New York: PublicAffairs, 2007.

Gardiner, Ian. *In the Service of the Sultan: A First Hand Account of the Dhofar Insurgency.* Barnsley: Pen & Sword Military, 2006.

Garibaldi, Giuseppe. *Autobiography of Giuseppe Garibaldi*. 3 vols. London: Walter Smith and Innes, 1889.

———. *Garibaldi: An Autobiography.* Edited by Alexandre Dumas. London: Routledge, Warne, and Routledge, 1861.

———. *My Life*. London: Hesperus Classics, 2004.

Gat, Azar. *War in Human Civilization.* Oxford: Oxford University Press, 2006.

Gates, David. *The Spanish Ulcer: A History of the Peninsular War.* New York: Da Capo Press, 1986.

Gates, Robert M. *From the Shadows: The Ultimate Insider's Story of Five Presidents and How They Won the Cold War.* New York: Simon & Schuster, 1996.

Gatewood, Charles B. *Lt. Charles Gatewood and His Apache Wars Memoir.* Lincoln: University of Nebraska Press, 2005.

Gaulle, Charles de. *Memoirs of Hope: Renewal and Endeavour.* New York: Simon & Schuster, 1971.

Geggus, David Patrick. *Haitian Revolutionary Studies*. Bloomington: Indiana University Press, 2002.

———. *Slavery, War, and Revolution: The British Occupation of Saint Domingue, 1793–1798*. Oxford: Clarendon Press, 1982.

———. "Toussaint Louverture and the Haitian Revolution." In *Profiles of Revolutionaries in Atlantic History, 1700–1850*, ed. R. William Weisberger, Dennis P. Hupchick, and David L. Anderson. Boulder: Social Science Monographs, 2007.

Geifman, Anna. *Death Orders: The Vanguard of Modern Terrorism in Revolutionary Russia*. Santa Barbara: Praeger, 2010.

———. *Entangled in Terror: The Azef Affair and the Russian Revolution*. Wilmington: Scholarly Resources, 2000.

———. *Thou Shalt Kill: Revolutionary Terrorism in Russia, 1894–1917*. Princeton: Princeton University Press, 1993.

Geraghty, Timothy J. *Peacekeepers at War: Beirut 1983—The Marine Commander Tells His Story*. Washington: Potomac Books, 2009.

Geraghty, Tony. *The Irish War: The Military History of a Domestic Conflict*. London: HarperCollins, 1998.

Gericke, Bradley T. *David Petraeus: A Biography*. Santa Barbara: Greenwood, 2011.

Gero, David. *Flights of Terror: Aerial Hijack and Sabotage since 1930*. Sparkford: Haynes Publishing, 2009.

Gerolymatos, André. *The Balkan Wars: Conquest, Revolution and Retribution, from the Ottoman Era to the Twentieth Century and Beyond*. New York: Basic Books, 2002.

Geronimo. *Geronimo: His Own Story. As Told to S. M. Barrett*. New York: Meridian, 1996.

Gershovich, Moshe. *French Military Rule in Morocco: Colonialism and Its Consequences*. London: Frank Cass, 2000.

Geyer, Georgie Anne. *Guerrilla Prince: The Untold Story of Fidel Castro*. Kansas City: Andrews McNeel, 2001.

Giap, Vo Nguyen. *Dien Bien Phu: Rendezvous with History*. Hanoi: Gioi Publishers, 2004.

———. *People's War, People's Army: The Viet Cong Insurrection Manual for Underdeveloped Countries*. Honolulu: University Press of the Pacific, 2001.

———. *Unforgettable Days*. Hanoi: Foreign Languages Publishing House, 1975.

Gibbon, Edward. *The Decline and Fall of the Roman Empire*. 6 vols. Boston: Phillips, Sampson, 1852.

Gibson, James William. *The Perfect War: Technowar in Vietnam*. New York: Atlantic Monthly Press, 2000.

Gilbert, Martin. *Winston S. Churchill*. Vol. 4, *1916–1922: The Stricken World*. Boston: Houghton Mifflin, 1975.

Gildea, Robert. *France since 1945*. Oxford: Oxford University Press, 2002.

Gillette, William. *Retreat from Reconstruction, 1869–1879*. Baton Rouge and London: Louisiana State University Press, 1979.

Gilmour, David. *The Long Recessional: The Imperial Life of Rudyard Kipling.* New York: Farrar, Straus and Giroux, 2002.

Girard, Philippe R. *Paradise Lost: Haiti's Tumultuous Journey from Pearl of the Caribbean to Third World Hot Spot.* New York: Palgrave Macmillan, 2005.

Girardet, Edward R. *Afghanistan: The Soviet War.* New York: St. Martin's Press, 1985.

Giron, Arthur E. "The General Motors." *Runner's World,* December 3, 2007.

Gitlin, Todd. *The Sixties: Years of Hope, Days of Rage.* New York: Bantam Books, 1993.

Gleeson, James. *Bloody Sunday: How Michael Collins's Agents Assassinated Britain's Secret Service in Dublin on November 21, 1920.* Guilford: Lyons Press, 2004.

Gleig, Robert George. *Sale's Brigade in Afghanistan, with an Account of the Seizure and Defence of Jellalabad.* London: John Murray, 1879.

Gleijeses, Piero. *Conflicting Missions: Havana, Washington, and Africa, 1959–1976.* Chapel Hill: University of North Carolina Press, 2002.

Godfrey, E. S. *An Account of Custer's Last Campaign and the Battle of the Little Big Horn.* Palo Alto: Lewis Osborne, 1968.

———. "Some Reminiscences, Including the Washita Battle." *Cavalry Journal,* October 1928.

Goldsworthy, Adrian. *How Rome Fell: Death of a Superpower.* New Haven: Yale University Press, 2009.

———. *Roman Warfare.* London: Phoenix, 2007.

Golway, Terry. *Irish Rebel: John Devoy and America's Fight for Ireland's Freedom.* New York: St. Martin's Press, 1998.

Goode, Steven M. "A Historical Basis for Force Requirements in Counterinsurgency." *Parameters,* Winter 2009–10.

Goodman, Martin. *Rome and Jerusalem: The Clash of Ancient Civilizations.* New York: Alfred A. Knopf, 2007.

———. *The Ruling Class of Judaea: The Origins of the Jewish Revolt against Rome, A.D. 66–70.* Cambridge: Cambridge University Press, 1987.

Goodson, Larry P. *Afghanistan's Endless War: State Failure, Regional Politics, and the Rise of the Taliban.* Seattle: University of Washington Press, 2001.

Goodwin, Jan. *Caught in the Crossfire.* New York: E. P. Dutton,1987.

Gordon, Andrew. *A Modern History of Japan from Togukawa Times to the Present.* New York: Oxford University Press, 2003.

Gordon, James. *History of the Rebellion in Ireland in the Year 1798.* London: T. Hurst, 1803.

Gordon, John W. *The Other Desert War: British Special Forces in North Africa, 1940–1943.* New York: Greenwood Press, 1987.

———. *South Carolina and the American Revolution: A Battlefield History.* Columbia: South Carolina University Press, 2003.

Gordon, Thomas. *History of the Greek Revolution.* 2 vols. Edinburgh: William Blackwood, 1844.

Gorenberg, Gershom. "The Missing Mahatma: Searching for a Gandhi or a Martin Luther King in the West Bank." *Weekly Standard,* April 6, 2009.

Gortzak, Yoav. "Using Indigenous Forces in Counterinsurgency Operations: The French in Algeria, 1954–1962." *Journal of Strategic Studies*, 2009.

Gott, Richard. *Rural Guerrillas in Latin America*. Middlesex: Penguin, 1973.

Grad, Marcela. *Massoud: An Intimate Portrait of the Legendary Afghan Leader*. St. Louis: Webster University Press, 2009.

Graebner, William. *Patty's Got a Gun: Patricia Hearst in 1970s America*. Chicago: University of Chicago Press, 2008.

Graff, David A., and Robin Higham, eds. *A Military History of China*. Boulder: Westview Press, 2001.

Granado, Alberto. *Traveling with Che Guevara: The Making of a Revolutionary*. New York: Newmarket Press, 2004.

Grandmaison, Thomas August Le Roy de. *La petite guerre; ou, Traité du service des troupes légères en campagne*. Paris: n.p., 1756.

Grant, Ulysses S. *Personal Memoirs*. New York: Modern Library, 1999.

Grau, Lester W. "The Take-Down of Kabul: An Effective Coup de Main." Leavenworth: Combat Studies Institute, October 2002.

Grauwin, Paul. *Doctor at Dienbienphu*. New York: John Day, 1955.

Gray, John S. *Centennial Campaign: The Sioux War of 1876*. Ft. Collins: Old Army Press, 1976.

———. *Custer's Last Campaign: Mitch Boyer and the Little Bighorn Reconstructed*. Lincoln: University of Nebraska Press, 1991.

Great Britain. Parliament. *Hansard's Parliamentary Debates*. London: H. M. Stationery Office, 1803–.

———. *Parliamentary Register; or, History of the Proceedings and Debates of the House of Commons*. 17 vols. London: John Stockdale, 1802.

Green, Israel. "The Capture of John Brown." *North American Review*, December 1885.

Green, Peter. *Alexander of Macedon, 356–323 B.C.: A Historical Biography*. Berkeley: University of California Press, 1991.

Green, Philip James. *Sketches of the War in Greece*. London: Thomas Hurst, 1827.

Greenberg, Lawrence M. *The Hukbalahap Insurrection: A Case Study of a Successful Anti-Insurgency Operation in the Philippines, 1946–1955*. Washington: U.S. Army Center of Military History, 1987.

Greene, Graham. *The Quiet American*. New York: Penguin, 2004.

Greene, Jerome A. *Battles and Skirmishes of the Great Sioux War, 1876–1877*. Norman: University of Oklahoma Press, 1993.

———. *Lakota and Cheyenne: Indian Views of the Great Sioux War, 1876–1877*. Norman: University of Oklahoma Press, 1994.

———. *Morning Star Dawn: The Powder River Expedition and the Northern Cheyennes, 1876*. Norman: University of Oklahoma Press, 2003.

———. *Washita: The U.S. Army and the Southern Cheyennes, 1867–1869*. Norman: University of Oklahoma Press, 2008.

———. *Yellowstone Command: Colonel Nelson A. Miles and the Great Sioux War, 1876–1877*. Lincoln: University of Nebraska Press, 1991.

Greene, Jerome A., and Douglas D. Scott. *Finding Sand Creek: History, Archeology, and the 1864 Massacre Site*. Norman: University of Oklahoma Press, 2006.

Greene, Nathanael. *The Papers of General Nathanael Greene*. 13 vols. Chapel Hill: University of North Carolina Press, 1976–2005.

Greer, Herb. *A Scattering of Dust*. London: Hutchinson, 1962.

Gregorie, Anne King. *Thomas Sumter*. Columbia: R. L. Bryan, 1931.

Grenier, John. *The First Way of War: American War Making on the Frontier*. New York: Cambridge University Press, 2005.

Griffin, Patricia E. *The Chinese Communist Treatment of Counter-Revolutionaries, 1924–1949*. Princeton: Princeton University Press, 1976.

Griffith, Kenneth, and Timothy E. O'Grady. *Curious Journey: An Oral History of Ireland's Unfinished Revolution*. London: Hutchinson, 1982.

Grimal, Henri. *Decolonization: The British, French, Dutch, and Belgian Empires, 1919–1963*. Boulder: Westview Press, 1978.

Grimsley, Mark. *The Hard Hand of War: Union Military Policy toward Southern Civilians, 1861–1865*. Cambridge: Cambridge University Press, 1995.

Grivas, George. *The Memoirs of General Grivas*. New York: Frederick A. Praeger, 1965.

Gross, Feliks. *Violence in Politics: Terror and Political Assassination in Eastern Europe and Russia*. The Hague: Mouton, 1972.

Grousset, René. *The Empire of the Steppes: A History of Central Asia*. Translated by Naomi Walford. New Brunswick: Rutgers University Press, 1970.

Gruber, Ira D. *The Howe Brothers and the American Revolution*. New York: Atheneum, 1972.

Guerin, Daniel. *No Gods, No Masters: An Anthology of Anarchism*. 4 vols. Edinburgh: AK Press, 1998.

Guevara, Ernesto "Che." *The African Dream: The Diaries of the Revolutionary War in the Congo*. New York: Grove Press, 1999.

———. *Back on the Road: A Journey through Latin America*. New York: Grove Press, 2000.

———. *The Bolivian Diary*. Melbourne: Ocean Press, 2006.

———. *Guerrilla Warfare*. Lincoln: University of Nebraska Press, 1961.

———. *The Motorcycle Diaries: Notes on a Latin American Journey*. Melbourne: Ocean Press, 2003.

———. *Reminiscences of the Cuban Revolutionary War*. Melbourne: Ocean Press, 2006.

Guilaine, Jean, and Jean Zammit. *The Origins of War: Violence in Prehistory*. Malden: Blackwell, 2005.

Guillermaz, Jacques. *A History of the Chinese Communist Party, 1921–1949*. New York: Random House, 1972.

Habeck, Mary R. *Knowing the Enemy: Jihadist Ideology and the War on Terror*. New Haven: Yale University Press, 2006.

Hackett, John, ed. *Warfare in the Ancient World*. New York: Facts on File, 1989.

Hafez, Mohammed M. *Suicide Bombers in Iraq: The Strategy and Ideology of Martyrdom*. Washington: U.S. Institute of Peace Press, 2007.

Hahn, Steven. *A Nation under Our Feet: Black Political Struggles in the Rural South from Slavery to the Great Migration*. Cambridge: Harvard University Press, 2003.

Haile Sellassie I. *My Life and Ethiopia's Progress.* 2 vols. East Lansing: Michigan State University Press, 1994.

Halevi, Yossi Klein, and Michael B. Oren. "Center Right: Israel's Unexpected Victory over Terrorism." *New Republic*, September 27, 2004.

Hall, John. *That Bloody Woman: The Turbulent Life of Emily Hobhouse, Cornwall's Forgotten Heroine*. Cornwall: Truran Books, 2008.

Hallo, William W., and J. J. A. Van Dijk. *The Exaltation of Inanna*. New Haven: Yale University Press, 1968.

Hamblin, William J. *Warfare in the Ancient Near East to 1600 BC: Holy Warriors at the Dawn of History.* London: Routledge, 2006.

Hamilton, Ian. *The Commander.* London: Hollis & Carter, 1957.

Hammel, Eric. *The Root: The Marines in Beirut, August 1982–February 1984*. St. Paul, Minn.: Zenith Books, 2005.

Hanna, Henry Bathurst. *The Second Afghan War, 1878-79-80: Its Causes, Its Conduct, Its Consequences*. Westminster: Archibald Constable, 1904.

Hanson, Victor Davis. *Carnage and Culture: Landmark Battles in the Rise of Western Power.* New York: Doubleday, 2001.

———. *Makers of Ancient Strategy: From the Persian Wars to the Fall of Rome*. Princeton: Princeton University Press, 2010.

———. *A War like No Other: How the Athenians and Spartans Fought the Peloponnesian War.* New York: Random House, 2006.

Harclerode, Peter. *Secret Soldiers: Special Forces in the War against Terrorism*. London: Cassell, 2000.

Hardorff, Richard G. *Washita Memories: Eyewitness Accounts of Custer's Attack on Black Kettle's Village*. Norman: University of Oklahoma Press, 2006.

Hardy, Grant, and Anne Behnke Kinney. *The Establishment of the Han Empire and Imperial China*. Westport: Greenwood Press, 2005.

Harel, Amos, and Avi Issacharoff. *34 Days: Israel, Hezbollah, and the War in Lebanon*. New York: Palgrave Macmillan, 2008.

Harik, Judith Palmer. *Hezbollah: The Changing Face of Terrorism*. London: I. B. Tauris, 2007.

Harper, T. N. *The End of Empire and the Making of Malaya*. Cambridge: Cambridge University Press, 1999.

Harris, Walter B. *Morocco That Was*. Westport: Negro Universities Press, 1970.

Harrison, Margaret H. *Captain of the Andes: The Life of Don José de San Martín, Liberator of Argentina, Chile, and Peru*. New York: Richard R. Smith, 1943.

Hart, Alan. *Arafat: A Political Biography*. Bloomington: Indiana University Press,1989.

Hart, Peter. *The I.R.A. and Its Enemies: Violence and Community in Cork, 1916–1923*. Oxford: Oxford University Press, 2000.

———. *The I.R.A. at War, 1916–1923*. Oxford: Oxford University Press, 2003.

———. *Mick: The Real Michael Collins*. London: Macmillan, 2005.

———, ed. *British Intelligence in Ireland, 1920–21: The Final Reports*. Cork: Cork University Press, 1921.

Hartford, Kathleen, and Steve M. Goldstein. eds. *Single Sparks: China's Rural Revolutions*. Armonk: M. E. Sharpe, 1989.

Hartigan, Richard Shelly. *Lieber's Code and the Law of War*. Chicago: Precedent, 1983.

Hassal, Mary. *Secret History; or, The Horrors of St. Domingo*. Freeport: Books for Libraries Press, 1971.

Hassrick, Royal B. *The Sioux: Life and Customs of a Warrior Society*. Norman: University of Oklahoma Press, 1964.

Hatch, Thom. *Black Kettle: The Cheyenne Chief Who Sought Peace But Found War*. Hoboken: John Wiley, 2004.

Hatley, Paul Buchanan. "Prolonging the Inevitable: The Franc-Tireur and the German Army in the Franco-German War of 1870–1871." Ph.D. diss., Kansas State University, 1997.

Haukelid, Knut. *Skies against the Atom*. London: W. Kimber, 1954.

Havelock, Henry. *Narrative of the War in Afghanistan in 1838–1839*. 2 vols. London: Henry Colburn, 1840.

Hawes, Stephen, and Ralph White, eds. *Resistance in Europe, 1939–1945*. London: Allen Lane, 1975.

Hay, Alice Ivy. *There Was a Man of Genius: Letters to My Grandson Orde Jonathan Wingate*. London: Neville Spearman, 1963.

Hayes, John H., and Sara R. Mandell. *The Jewish People in Classical Antiquity: From Alexander to Bar Kochba*. Louisville: Westminster John Knox Press, 1998.

Headrick, Daniel R. *The Tools of Empire: Technology and European Imperialism in the Nineteenth Century*. New York: Oxford University Press, 1981.

Hearn, Chester G. *The Maccabees: The Years before Herod*. Baltimore: PublishAmerica, 2003.

Hearst, Patty. *Every Secret Thing*. Garden City: Doubleday, 1982.

Heath, William. *Memoirs of Major General William Heath*. New York: William Abbatt, 1901.

Heather, Peter. *The Fall of the Roman Empire: A New History of Rome and the Barbarians*. Oxford: Oxford University Press, 2006.

Heehs, Peter. "Terrorism in India during the Freedom Struggle." *Historian*, Spring 1993.

Heer, Hannes, and Klaus Naumann, eds. *War of Extermination: The German Military in World War II, 1941–1944*. New York: Berghahn Books, 2000.

Heilbrunn, Otto. *Partisan Warfare*. New York: Frederick A. Praeger, 1967.

Heinamaa, Anna, Maija Leppanen, and Yuri Yurchenko. *The Soldiers' Story: Soviet Veterans Remember the Afghan War*. Berkeley: University of California Press, 1994.

Heinl, Robert Debs, and Nancy Gordon Heinl. *Written in Blood: The Story of the Haitian People, 1492–1995*. Lanham: University Press of America, 2005.

Helsinki Watch. "Tears, Blood and Cries: Human Rights in Afghanistan since the Invasion, 1979–1984." New York, December 1984.

Henige, David. *Numbers from Nowhere: The American Indian Contact Population Debate*. Norman: University of Oklahoma Press, 1998.

Henissart, Paul. *Wolves in the City: The Death of French Algeria*. New York: Simon & Schuster, 1970.

Henniker, M. C. A. *Red Shadow over Malaya*. Edinburgh: William Blackwood, 1955.

Hensman, Howard. *The Afghan War of 1879–80*. London: W. H. Allen, 1881.

Herodotus. *The Histories*. New York: Everyman's Library, 1997.

Hibbert, Christopher. *Garibaldi: Hero of Italian Unification*. New York: Palgrave Macmillan, 2008.

Hildermeier, Manfred. *The Russian Socialist Revolutionary Party before the First World War*. New York: St. Martin's Press, 2000.

Hildinger, Erik. *Warriors of the Steppe: A Military History of Central Asia, 500 B.C. to 1700 A.D.* New York: Da Capo Press, 2001.

Hilsman, Roger. *American Guerrilla: My War behind Japanese Lines*. Washington: Brassey's, 1990.

———. *To Move a Nation: The Politics of Foreign Policy in the Administration of John F. Kennedy*. Garden City: Doubleday, 1967.

Hinchcliffe, Peter, John T. Ducker, and Maria Holt. *Without Glory in Arabia: The British Retreat from Aden*. London: I. B. Tauris, 2006.

Hingley, Ronald. *Nihilists: Russian Radicals and Revolutionaries in the Reign of Alexander II (1855–81)*. New York: Delacorte Press, 1967.

Hinton, Richard J. *John Brown and His Men, with Some Accounts of the Roads They Traveled to Reach Harper's Ferry*. Rev. ed. New York: Funk and Wagnalls, 1894.

Hoare, Mike. *Congo Mercenary*. London: Robert Hale, 1967.

Hobhouse, Emily. *The Brunt of the War and Where It Fell*. London: Methuen, 1902.

———. *Report to the Committee of the Distress Fund for South African Women and Children*. London: Friars, 1901.

Hobsbawm, Eric. *Bandits*. Rev. ed. New York: New Press, 2000.

Ho Chi Minh. *Ho Chi Minh on Revolution*. New York: Signet Books, 1968.

———. *Selected Writings (1920–1969)*. Honolulu: University Press of the Pacific, 2001.

Hodgson, Marshall G. S. *The Secret Order of the Assassins: The Struggle of the Early Nizari Ismailis against the Islamic World*. Philadelphia: University of Pennsylvania Press, 2005.

Hoe, Alan, and Eric Morris. *Re-enter the SAS: The Special Air Service and the Malayan Emergency*. London: Leo Cooper, 1994.

Hoffman, Bruce. *Inside Terrorism*. New York: Columbia University Press, 1998.

Hoffman, Frank G. "Conflict in the 21st Century: The Rise of Hybrid Wars." Arlington: Potomac Institute for Policy Studies, December 2007.

Hoffman, Ronald, Thad W. Tate, and Peter J. Albert, eds. *An Uncivil War: The Southern Backcountry during the American Revolution*. Charlottesville: University Press of Virginia, 1985.

Hoig, Stan. *The Battle of the Washita: Custer's Campaign against the Cheyenne*. Norman: University of Oklahoma Press, 1979.

———. *Sand Creek Massacre*. Norman: University of Oklahoma Press, 1974.

Hoisington, William, Jr. *Lyautey and the French Conquest of Morocco*. New York: St. Martin's Press, 1995.

Holland Robert. *Britain and the Revolt in Cyprus, 1954–1959*. Oxford: Clarendon Press, 1998.

Holland, Tom. *Persian Fire: The First World Empire and the Battle for the West*. New York: Anchor Books, 2007.

———. *Rubicon: The Last Years of the Roman Republic*. New York: Anchor Books, 2005.

Holt, Frank L. *Into the Land of Bones: Alexander the Great in Afghanistan*. Berkeley: University of California Press, 2005.

Hopkinson, Michael. *The Irish War of Independence*. Montreal: McGill-Queen's University Press, 2002.

Hopkirk, J. G. *An Account of the Insurrection in St. Domingo Begun in August 1791*. Edinburgh: William Blackwood, 1833.

Horgan, John. *Sean Lemass: The Enigmatic Patriot*. Dublin: Gill & Macmillan, 1997.

Horne, Alistair. *The Fall of Paris: The Siege and the Commune, 1870–71*. London: Penguin, 2007.

———. *A Savage War of Peace: Algeria, 1954–1962*. New York: Viking, 1977.

Horne, James. *A Land as God Made It: Jamestown and the Birth of America*. New York: Basic Books, 2005.

Horne, John, and Alan Kramer. *German Atrocities, 1914: A History of Denial*. New Haven: Yale University Press, 2001.

Horry, Peter, and Mason Locke Meems. *The Life of General Francis Marion*. Winston-Salem: John F. Blair, 2000.

Howard, Michael. *The Franco-Prussian War*. London: Routledge, 2006.

Howard, Thomas Phipps. *The Haitian Journal of Lieutenant Howard, York Hussars, 1796–1798*. Knoxville: University of Tennessee Press, 1985.

Howarth, David. *The Greek Adventure: Lord Byron and Other Eccentrics in the War of Independence*. New York: Atheneum, 1976.

Howarth, Patrick. *Attila, King of the Huns: The Man and the Myth*. New York: Carroll & Graf, 2001.

Howe, Samuel Gridley. *Letters and Journals of Samuel Gridley Howe during the Greek Revolution*. London: John Lane, 1909.

Hsiung, James C., and Steven I. Levine, eds. *China's Bitter Victory: The War with Japan, 1937–1945*. Armonk: M. E. Sharpe, 1992.

Hudson, Charles. *History of the Town of Lexington*. 2 vols. Boston: Houghton Mifflin, 1913.

Hughes, Geraint. "A 'Model Campaign' Reappraised: The Counter-Insurgency War in Dhofar, Oman, 1965–1975." *Journal of Strategic Studies*, April 2009.

Hughes, James. *Chechnya: From Nationalism to Jihad*. Philadelphia: University of Pennsylvania Press, 2007.

Hull, Isabel V. *Absolute Destruction: Military Culture and the Practices of War in Imperial Germany*. Ithaca: Cornell University Press, 2005.

Hunt, Ray C., and Bernard Norling. *Behind Japanese Lines: An American Guerrilla in the Philippines.* New York: Pocket Books, 1986.

Hutton, Andrew. *The Custer Reader.* Lincoln: University of Nebraska Press, 1992.

———. *Soldiers West: Biographies from the Military Frontier.* Lincoln: University of Nebraska Press, 1987.

Hyam, Ronald. *Britain's Declining Empire: The Road to Decolonization, 1918–1968.* Cambridge: Cambridge University Press, 2006.

Ibrahim, Raymond, ed. *The Al Qaeda Reader.* New York: Broadway Books, 2007.

Intelligence Branch, Army Headquarters, India. *The Second Afghan War 1878–80: Official Account.* London: John Murray, 1908.

"Intercepted Letters of the Soldiery in Boston." *Historical Collections of the Essex Institute* (1861).

"Intifada Toll 2000–2005." *BBC*, February 8, 2005.

Isaac, Benjamin. *The Limits of Empire: The Roman Army in the East.* Oxford: Clarendon Press, 1990.

Isaacson, Walter. *Benjamin Franklin: An American Life.* New York: Simon & Schuster, 2003.

Jaber, Hala. *Hezbollah: Born with a Vengeance.* New York: Columbia University Press, 1997.

Jackson, Julian. *France: The Dark Years, 1940–1944.* Oxford: Oxford University Press, 2001.

Jacob, William. *Travels in the South of Spain in Letters Written A.D. 1809 and 1810.* London: J. Johnson, 1811.

Jacobsen, Mark. "Only by the Sword: British Counter-Insurgency in Iraq, 1920." *Small Wars & Insurgencies*, August 1991.

James, Daniel, ed. *The Complete Bolivian Diaries of Che Guevara and Other Captured Documents.* New York: Cooper Square Press, 2000.

James, Lionel ("The Intelligence Officer"). *On the Heels of De Wet.* Edinburgh: William Blackwood, 1902.

James, Richard Rhodes. *Chindit.* London: John Murray, 1980.

James, William Dobein. *A Sketch of the Life of Brig. Gen. Francis Marion and a History of His Brigade.* Dodo Press, 2007.

Jarvis, C. S. *Arab Command: The Biography of Lieutenant-Colonel F. W. Peake Pasha.* London: Hutchinson, 1942.

Jeney, M. de. *Partisan; ou, l'art de faire la petite guerre.* London: R. Griffiths, 1760.

Jenkins, Brian Michael. *Will Terrorists Go Nuclear?* Amherst: Prometheus Books, 2008.

Jensen, Richard Bach. "The International Campaign against Anarchist Terrorism, 1880–1930s." *Terrorism and Political Violence*, 2009.

———. "Rifles and Dynamite: Anarchist Terrorism in Nineteenth Century Europe." *Terrorism and Political Violence*, 2004.

Jocelyn, Ed, and Andrew McEwen. *The Long March: The True Story behind the Legendary Journey That Made Mao's China.* London: Constable, 2006.

John of Fordun. *Chronicle of the Scottish Nation*. 2 vols. Burnham on Sea: Llanerch, 1993.

Joll, James. *The Anarchists*. Boston: Little, Brown, 1964.

Jomini, Antoine-Henri. *The Art of War*. Mineola: Dover, 2007.

Jonas, George. *Vengeance: The True Story of an Israeli Counter-Terrorist Team*. New York: Simon & Schuster, 2005.

Jones, A. H. M. *The Later Roman Empire 284–602: A Social, Economic, and Administrative Survey*. 2 vols. Norman: University of Oklahoma Press, 1964.

Jones, Howard. *Death of a Generation: How the Assassination of Diem and JFK Prolonged the Vietnam War*. New York: Oxford University Press, 2003.

Jordanes. *The Origins and Deeds of the Goths*. Princeton: Princeton University Press, 1908.

Josephus. *The New Complete Works of Josephus*. Grand Rapids: Kregel Publications, 1999.

"Journal of Lieutenant Thomas Anderson of the Delaware Regiment, 1780–1782." *Historical Magazine*, 1867.

Judd, Denis, and Keith Surridge. *The Boer War*. New York: Palgrave Macmillan, 2003.

Junger, Sebastian. *Fire*. New York: W. W. Norton, 2001.

Juvaini, Ala-ad-Din Ata-Malik. *The History of the World Conqueror*. 2 vols. Cambridge: Harvard University Press, 1958.

Kagan, Kimberly. *The Surge: A Military History*. New York: Encounter, 2009.

Kagan, Robert. *A Twilight Struggle: American Power and Nicaragua, 1977–1990*. New York: Free Press, 1996.

Kalinovsky, Artemy. "The Blind Leading the Blind: Soviet Advisers, Counter-Insurgency and Nation-Building in Afghanistan." Washington: Woodrow Wilson Center for Scholars, January 2010.

———. *A Long Goodbye: The Soviet Withdrawal from Afghanistan*. Cambridge: Harvard University Press, 2011.

Kalyvas, Stathis N. *The Logic of Violence in Civil War*. Cambridge: Cambridge University Press, 2006.

Kaplan, Robert D. *Soldiers of God: With Islamic Warriors in Afghanistan and Pakistan*. New York: Vintage Books, 2001.

Karnow, Stanley. *Vietnam: A History*. New York: Penguin, 1983.

Katz, Samuel M. *The Elite: The True Story of Israel's Secret Counterterrorist Unit*. New York: Pocket Books, 1992.

Kavanagh, Sean. "The Irish Volunteers' Intelligence Organisation." *Capuchin Annual* (1969).

Kaye, John William. *History of the War in Afghanistan*. 3 vols. London: Richard Bentley, 1851.

Kedward, Roderick. *The Anarchists: The Men Who Shocked an Era*. New York: American Heritage Press, 1971.

Kee, Robert. *The Green Flag: A History of Irish Nationalism*. London: Penguin, 2000.

Keegan, John. *A History of Warfare*. New York: Alfred A. Knopf, 1993.

Keeley, Lawrence H. *War before Civilization: The Myth of the Peaceful Savage*. New York: Oxford University Press, 1996.

Keim, DeBenneville R. *Sheridan's Troopers on the Borders: A Winter Campaign on the Plains*. London: George Routledge, 1885.

Kelly, Sean. *America's Tyrant: The CIA and Mobutu of Zaire*. Washington: American University Press, 1993.

Kennan, George. "The Russian Penal Code." *Century Magazine*, April 1888.

———. *Siberia and the Exile System*. 2 vols. London: James S. Osgood, 1891.

Kenneally, Ian. *The Paper Wall: Newspapers and Propaganda in Ireland, 1919–1921*. Cork: Collins Press, 2008.

Kennedy, Hugh. *The Armies of the Caliphs: Military and Society in Early Islamic States*. New York: Routledge, 2001.

———. *The Great Arab Conquests: How the Spread of Islam Changed the World We Live In*. New York: Da Capo Press, 2007.

———. *Mongols, Huns and Vikings*. London: Cassell, 2002.

Kennedy, Moorhead. *The Ayatollah in the Cathedral*. New York: Hill and Wang, 1986.

Kennedy, Paul. *The Rise and Fall of the Great Powers: Economic Change and Military Conflict from 1500 to 2000*. New York: Vintage, 1989.

Kennedy, Robert M. *German Antiguerrilla Operations in the Balkans (1941–1944)*. Washington: Center of Military History, U.S. Army, 1989.

Kepel, Gilles. *Jihad: The Trail of Political Islam*. Cambridge: Harvard University Press, 2002.

Kepel, Gilles, and Jean-Pierre Milelli, eds. *Al Qaeda in Its Own Words*. Cambridge: Harvard University Press, 2008.

Kerkvliet, Benedict J. *The Huk Rebellion: A Study of Peasant Revolt in the Philippines*. Lanham: Rowman & Littlefield, 2002.

Kershaw, Ian. *Hitler, 1889–1936: Hubris*. New York: W. W. Norton, 1998.

Ketchum, Richard M. *Victory at Yorktown: The Campaign That Won the Revolution*. New York: Henry Holt, 2004.

Kettle, Michael. *De Gaulle and Algeria, 1940–1960: From Mers El-Kebir to the Algiers Barricades*. London: Quarter Books, 1993.

Kierman, Frank A., Jr. *Chinese Ways in Warfare*. Cambridge: Harvard University Press, 1974.

Kimball, Jeffrey. *The Vietnam War Files: Uncovering the Secret History of Nixon-Era Strategy*. Lawrence: University Press of Kansas, 2004.

King, Charles. *The Ghost of Freedom: A History of the Caucasus*. Oxford: Oxford University Press, 2008.

King, Mary Elizabeth. *A Quiet Revolution: The First Palestinian Intifada and Nonviolent Resistance*. New York: Nation Books, 2007.

King-Clark, Robert. *Free for a Blast*. London: Grenville Publishing, 1988.

Kingsbury, Susan Myra, ed. *Records of the Virginia Company, 1606–26*. 4 vols. Washington: Government Printing Office, 1906–35.

Kinzer, Stephen. *Blood of Brothers: Life and War in Nicaragua*. New York: G. P. Putnam's Sons, 1991.

Kipling, Rudyard. *Complete Verse: Definitive Edition*. New York: Anchor Books, 1989.

Kirby, S. Woodburn. *The War against Japan*. 4 vols. London: Her Majesty's Stationery Office, 1958–65.

Kiser, John W. *Commander of the Faithful: The Life and Times of Emir Abd el-Kader*. Rhinebeck: Monkfish, 2008.

Kissinger, Henry. *Ending the Vietnam War*. New York: Simon & Schuster, 2003.

Kitson, Frank. *Gangs and Counter-Gangs*. London: Barrie and Rockliff, 1960.

———. *Low Intensity Operations: Subversion, Insurgency, and Peacekeeping*. St. Petersburg: Hailer, 2006.

Klein, Aaron. J. *Striking Back: The 1972 Munich Olympics Massacre and Israel's Deadly Response*. New York: Random House, 2007.

Kohl, James, and John Litt. *Urban Guerrilla Warfare in Latin America*. Cambridge: MIT Press, 1974.

Koob, Kathryn. *Guest of the Revolution*. Nashville: Thomas Nelson, 1982.

Kopperman, Paul E. *Braddock at the Monongahela*. Pittsburgh: University of Pittsburgh Press, 1977.

Kousser, J. Morgan, and James M. McPherson. *Region, Race, and Reconstruction: Essays in Honor of C. Vann Woodward*. New York: Oxford University Press, 1982.

Krepinevich, Andrew F. *The Army and Vietnam*. Baltimore: Johns Hopkins University Press, 1986.

Kropotkin, Peter. *Memoirs of a Revolutionist*. Boston: Houghton Mifflin, 1899.

Krueger, Alan B. *What Makes a Terrorist: Economics and the Roots of Terrorism*. Princeton: Princeton University Press, 2007.

Kuo, Warren. *Analytical History of Chinese Communist Party*. Taipei: Institute of International Relations, 1966.

Kupperman, Karen Ordahl. *The Jamestown Project*. Cambridge: Harvard University Press, 2007.

Kurapovna, Marcia Christoff. *Shadows on the Mountain: The Allies, the Resistance, and the Rivalries That Doomed WWII Yugoslavia*. New York: John Wiley, 2010.

Kurzman, Dan. *Soldier of Peace: The Life of Yitzhak Rabin*. New York: HarperCollins, 1998.

Kwasny, Mark W. *Washington's Partisan War, 1775–1783*. Kent: Kent State University Press, 1996.

Kynaston, David. *Austerity Britain, 1945–51*. London: Bloomsbury, 2007.

Lacey, Jim. *A Terrorist's Call to Global Jihad: Deciphering Abu Musab al-Suri's Islamic Jihad Manifesto*. Annapolis: Naval Institute Press, 2008.

Lacey, Robert. *Inside the Kingdom: Kings, Clerics, Modernists, Terrorists, and the Struggle for Saudi Arabia*. New York: Penguin, 2009.

Lachica, Eduardo. *The Huks: Philippine Agrarian Society in Revolt*. New York: Praeger, 1971.

Lacroix, Pamphile. *La révolution de Häiti*. Paris: Karthala, 1995.

Lamson, Peggy. *The Glorious Failure: Black Congressman Robert Brown Elliott and the Reconstruction in South Carolina.* New York: W. W. Norton, 1973.

Land, Isaac, ed. *Enemies of Humanity: The Nineteenth-Century War on Terrorism.* Houndmills: Palgrave Macmillan, 2008.

Langlais, Pierre. *Dien Bien Phu.* Paris: Presses Pocket, 1963.

Lansdale, Edward G. *In the Midst of Wars: An American's Mission to Southeast Asia.* New York: Fordham University Press, 1991.

———. "Viet Nam: Do We Understand Revolution?" *Foreign Affairs,* October 1964.

Lapham, Robert, and Bernard Norling. *Lapham's Raiders: Guerrillas in the Philippines, 1942–1945.* Lexington: University Press of Kentucky, 1996.

Laqueur, Walter. *Guerrilla Warfare: A Historical and Critical Study.* New Brunswick: Transaction, 2005.

———. *A History of Terrorism.* New Brunswick: Transaction, 2002.

Larteguy, Jean. *The Centurions.* New York: E. P. Dutton, 1962.

———. *The Praetorians.* St. Petersburg: Hailer, 2005.

Lauchlan, Iain. *Russian Hide-and-Seek: The Tsarist Secret Police in St. Petersburg, 1906–1914.* Helsinki: SKS-FLS, 2002.

Lawrence, Mark Atwood, and Fredrik Logevall. *The First Vietnam War: Colonial Conflict and Cold War Crisis.* Cambridge: Harvard University Press, 2007.

Lawrence, T. E. *Seven Pillars of Wisdom: A Triumph.* New York: Anchor Books, 1991.

———. *T. E. Lawrence to His Biographer, Liddell Hart.* London: Faber and Faber, 1938.

Lazreg, Marnia. *Torture and the Twilight of Empire: From Algiers to Baghdad.* Princeton: Princeton University Press, 2008.

Leach, Douglas Edward. *Flintlocks and Tomahawks: New England in King Philip's War.* East Orleans: Parnassus Imprints, 1992.

LeBlanc, Steven A., with Katherine E. Register. *Constant Battles: The Myth of the Peaceful, Noble Savage.* New York: St. Martin's Press, 2003.

Leclerc, Charles Victor Emmanuel. *Lettres du général Leclerc, commandant en chef de l'armée de Saint-Domingue en 1802.* Paris: Societé de l'histoire des colonies françaises, 1937.

Lederer, William J., and Eugene Burdick. *The Ugly American.* New York: W. W. Norton, 1999.

Lee, Charles. *The Lee Papers, 1754–1811.* 4 vols. New York: New York Historical Society, 1872–75.

Lee, Henry. *Memoirs of the War in the Southern Department of the United States.* New York: University Publishing, 1869.

Leebaert, Derek. *To Dare and to Conquer: Special Operations and the Destiny of Nations, from Achilles to Al Qaeda.* New York: Little, Brown, 2006.

Léger, Jacques Nicolas. *Haiti, Her History and Her Detractors.* New York: Neale Publishing, 1907.

Lepore, Jill. *The Name of War: King Philip's War and the Origins of American Identity.* New York: Alfred A. Knopf, 1998.

Lermontov, Mikhail. *A Hero of Our Time.* New York: Penguin, 2001.

Lester, J. C., and D. L. Wilson. *Ku Klux Klan: Its Origins, Growth and Disbandment.* New York: Neale Publishing, 1905.

Leulliette, Pierre. *St. Michael and the Dragon: Memoirs of a Paratrooper.* Boston: Houghton Mifflin, 1964.

Levick, Barbara. *Vespasian*. London: Routledge, 1999.

Levine, Steven I. *Anvil of Victory: The Communist Revolution in Manchuria, 1945–1948.* New York: Columbia University Press, 1987.

Lewin, Ronald. *The Chief: Field Marshal Lord Wavell, Commander-in-Chief and Viceroy, 1939–1947.* New York: Farrar Straus Giroux, 1980.

Lewis, Bernard. *The Assassins: A Radical Sect in Islam.* New York: Basic Books, 1967.

Lewis, Brian. "The Legend of Sargon: A Study of the Akkadian Text and the Tale of the Hero Who Was Exposed at Birth." Ph.D. diss., New York University, 1976.

Lewis, Mark Edward. *The Early Chinese Empires: Qin and Han.* Cambridge: Harvard University Press, 2007.

Li, Zhisui. *The Private Life of Chairman Mao.* New York: Random House, 1994.

Liang, Hsi-Huey. *The Rise of Modern Police and the European State System from Metternich to the Second World War.* Cambridge: Cambridge University Press, 1992.

Liddell Hart, Basil H. *Lawrence of Arabia.* New York: Da Capo Press, 1935.

———. *Strategy.* New York: Plume, 1991.

Lieber, Francis. *Instructions for the Government of Armies of the United States in the Field.* Washington: Government Printing Office, 1898.

Lieven, Dominic. *Russia against Napoleon: The True Story of the Campaigns of War and Peace.* New York: Viking, 2009.

The Life, Trial, and Execution of Captain John Brown, Known as "Old Brown of Ossawotomie." New York: Robert M. De Witt, 1859.

Liman Sanders, Otto von. *Five Years in Turkey.* Annapolis: U.S. Naval Institute, 1928.

Lincoln, Charles H., ed. *Narratives of the Indian Wars, 1675–1699.* New York: Charles Scribner's Sons, 1913.

Lincoln, W. Bruce. *The Romanovs: Autocrats of All the Russias.* New York: Doubleday, 1981.

Lindsay, Franklin. *Beacons in the Night: With the OSS and Tito's Partisans in Wartime Yugoslavia.* Stanford: Stanford University Press, 1993.

Lister, Jeremy. *Concord Fight: Being so Much of the Narrative of Ensign Jeremy Lister of the 10th Regiment of Foot as Pertains to His Services on the 19th of April, 1775.* Cambridge: Harvard University Press, 1931.

Liverani, Mario, ed. *Akkad, the First World Empire: Structure, Ideology, Traditions.* Padova: Sargon, 1993.

Livy. *The History of Rome, Books Thirty-Seven to the End.* London: Bell, 1888.

Loewe, Michael. *Everyday Life in Early Imperial China.* Indianapolis: Hackett, 2005.

Lonergan, Walter F. *Forty Years of Paris.* London: T. Fisher Unwin, 1907.

Longworth, Philip. *The Cossacks.* New York: Holt, Rinehart, and Winston, 1969.

———. *Russia: The Once and Future Empire from Pre-History to Putin.* New York: St. Martin's Press, 2005.

Lorge, Peter. *War, Politics, and Society in Early Modern China, 900–1795*. London and New York: Routledge, 2005.

Louverture, Toussaint. *The Haitian Revolution*. London: Verso, 2008.

———. *Memoir of General Touissant Louverture, Written by Himself.* In John Reilly Beard, *Toussaint L'Ouverture: Biography and Autobiography*. Boston: James Redpath, 1863.

Low, Charles Rathbone. *The Life and Correspondence of Field-Marshall Sir George Pollock*. London: W. H. Allen, 1873.

Lucas, James. *Kommando: German Special Forces of World War Two.* New York: St. Martin's Press, 1985.

Luft, Gal. "Israel's Security Zone in Lebanon—A 'Tragedy'?" *Middle East Quarterly*, September 2000.

Lundberg, Kirsten. "Politics of a Covert Action: The U.S., the Mujahideen, and the Stinger Missile." Case Study C15-99-1546.0. John F. Kennedy School of Government, Harvard, 1999.

Lunt, James D. *Bokhara Burnes*. London: Faber, 1969.

Lutnick, Solomon. *The American Revolution and the British Press, 1775–1783*. Colombia: University of Missouri Press, 1967.

Luttwak, Edward N. "Dead End: Counterinsurgency Warfare as Military Malpractice." *Harper's Magazine*, February 2007.

Lyakhovskiy, Aleksandr Antonovich. "Inside the Soviet Invasion of Afghanistan and the Seizure of Kabul, December 1979." Working Paper no. 55. Washington: Woodrow Wilson International Center for Scholars, January 2007.

Lyall, Jason, and Isaiah Wilson III. "Rage against the Machines: Explaining Outcomes in Counterinsurgency Wars." *International Organization*. Winter 2009.

Lyautey, Hubert. "Du rôle social de l'officier." *Revue des Deux Mondes*, March–April 1891.

———. "Du rôle colonial de l'armée." *Revue des Deux Mondes*, January 15, 1900.

———. *Lettres du Tonkin et de Madagascar (1894–1899)*. 2 vols. Paris: Armand Colin, 1920.

Lynn, John A., ed. *Acta of the XXVIIIth Congress of the International Commission of Military History.* Chicago: McCormack Foundation, 2003.

Lyttelton, Oliver. *The Memoirs of Lord Chandos: An Unexpected View from the Summit.* New York: New American Library, 1963.

Macdonald, Peter. *Giap: The Victor in Vietnam*. New York: W. W. Norton, 1993.

Mack, John E. *A Prince of Our Disorder: The Life of T. E. Lawrence.* Cambridge: Harvard University Press, 1998.

Mackay, Christopher S. *Ancient Rome: A Military and Political History.* Cambridge: Cambridge University Press, 2004.

Mackay, Donald. *The Malayan Emergency, 1948–60: The Domino That Stood.* London: Brassey's, 1997.

Mackay, James. *William Wallace: Brave Heart*. Edinburgh: Mainstream Publishing, 1995.

Mackenzie, Frederick. *Diary of Frederick Mackenzie.* 2 vols. Cambridge: Harvard University Press, 1930.

Mackenzie, William. *The Secret History of S.O.E.: Special Operations Executive 1940–1945.* London: St. Ermin's Press, 2000.

Mackesy, Piers. *The War for America, 1775–1783.* Lincoln: University of Nebraska Press, 1993.

Mackey, Robert R. *The Uncivil War: Irregular Warfare in the Upper South, 1861–1865.* Norman: University of Oklahoma Press, 2004.

Mack Smith, Denis. *Garibaldi: A Great Life in Brief.* Westport: Greenwood Press, 1956.

———. *Mazzini.* New Haven: Yale University Press, 1994.

Maclean, Fitzroy. *Disputed Barricade: The Life and Times of Josip Broz-Tito, Marshal of Jugoslavia.* London: J. Cape, 1957.

———. *Eastern Approaches.* London: Penguin, 1991.

Macready, Nevil. *Annals of an Active Life.* 2 vols. London: Hutchinson, 1924.

Macrory, Patrick. *Retreat from Kabul.* Guilford: Lyons Press, 2002.

Madden, Thomas F. *Empires of Trust: How Rome Built—and America Is Building—a New World.* New York: Dutton, 2008.

Mahon, John K. *History of the Second Seminole War, 1835–1842.* Rev. ed. Gainesville: University Presses of Florida, 1989.

Malato, Charles. "Some Anarchist Portraits." *Fortnightly Review,* September 1, 1894.

Malone, Patrick M. *The Skulking Way of War: Technology and Tactics among the New England Indians.* Lanham: Madison Books, 1991.

Man, John. *Attila: The Barbarian King Who Challenged Rome.* New York: Thomas Dunne, 2005.

Mann, Charles C. *1491: New Revelations of the Americas before Columbus.* New York: Alfred A. Knopf, 2003.

Mansoor, Peter, and Williamson Murray, eds. *Hybrid Warfare: The Struggle of Military Forces to Adapt to Complex Opponents from the Ancient World to the Present.* Cambridge: Cambridge University Press, 2012.

Mao Zedong. *Aspects of China's Anti-Japanese Struggle.* Bombay: People's Publishing House, 1948.

———. *On Guerrilla Warfare.* 2nd ed. Baltimore: Nautical & Aviation Publishing, 1992.

———. *Selected Military Writings of Mao Zedong.* Peking: Foreign Languages Press, 1968.

Marchak, Patricia. *God's Assassins: State Terrorism in Argentina in the 1970s.* Montreal: McGill-Queen's University Press, 1999.

Marighella, Carlos. *Minimanual of the Urban Guerrilla.* St. Petersburg: Red and Black, 2008.

Mario, Alberto. *The Red Shirt: Episodes.* London: Smith, Elder, 1865.

Marks, Steven G. *How Russia Shaped the Modern World.* Princeton: Princeton University Press, 2003.

Marlowe, Ann. *David Galula: His Life and Intellectual Context*. Carlisle: Strategic Studies Institute, 2010.

Marshall, Peter. *Demanding the Impossible: A History of Anarchism*. London: Harper Perennial, 2008.

Marshman, John Clark. *Memoirs of Major-General Sir Henry Havelock*. New York: Longmans, Green, 1909.

Martin, A. C. *The Concentration Camps 1900–1902: Facts, Figures, and Fables*. Cape Town: Howard Timmins, 1957.

Martinez, J. Michael. *Carpetbaggers, Cavalry, and the Ku Klux Klan*. Lanham: Rowman & Littlefield, 2007.

Martinez, Manuel F. *Magsaysay: The People's President*. Makati City: Salesiana, 2005.

Massu, Jacques. *La vraie bataille d'Alger*. Paris: Plon, 1971.

Masters, John. *Bugles and a Tiger: My Life in the Gurkhas*. London: Cassell, 2004.

———. *The Road Past Mandalay*. London: Cassell, 2003.

Matthews, Herbert L. *The Cuban Story*. New York: George Braziller, 1961.

Matyszak, Philip. *The Enemies of Rome: From Hannibal to Attila the Hun*. London: Thames & Hudson, 2004.

Maurice, Frederick, et al. *History of the War in South Africa, 1899–1902*. 4 vols. London: Hurst and Blackett, 1906–10.

Maurice's Strategikon: Handbook of Byzantine Military Strategy. Philadelphia: University of Pennsylvania Press, 1984.

Maurois, André. *Marshal Lyautey*. London: John Lane, 1931.

Maxwell, Gavin. *Lords of the Atlas: The Rise and Fall of the House of Glaoua, 1893–1956*. London: Longmans, 1966.

May, Timothy. *The Mongol Art of War: Chinggis Khan and the Mongol Military System*. Yardley: Westholme, 2007.

Mayer, Jane. *The Dark Side: The Inside Story of How the War on Terror Turned into a War on American Ideals*. New York: Doubleday, 2008.

Mazower, Mark. *Hitler's Empire: How the Nazis Ruled Europe*. New York: Penguin, 2008.

Mazzini, Giuseppe. *Life and Writings of Joseph Mazzini*. 6 vols. London: Smith, Elder, 1890.

McClain, James L. *Japan: A Modern History*. New York: W. W. Norton, 2002.

McClintock, Michael. *Instruments of Statecraft: U.S. Guerrilla Warfare, Counterinsurgency, and Counter-terrorism, 1940–1990*. New York: Pantheon, 1992.

McCrady, Edward. *The History of South Carolina in the Revolution, 1775–1783*. 2 vols. New York: Macmillan, 1902.

McDermott, Terry. *Perfect Soldiers: The Hijackers: Who They Were, Why They Did It*. New York: HarperCollins, 2005.

McKenzie, Steven L. *King David: A Biography*. Oxford: Oxford University Press, 2000.

McMahon, Robert J. *Colonialism and Cold War: The United States and the Struggle for Indonesian Independence, 1945–49*. Ithaca: Cornell University Press, 1981.

McNamee, Colm. *Robert Bruce: Our Most Valiant Prince, King and Lord.* Edinburgh: Birlinn, 2006.

McPherson, James. *Battle Cry of Freedom: The Civil War Era.* Oxford: Oxford University Press, 1988.

McRaven, William. H. *Spec Ops: Case Studies in Special Operations Warfare.* San Marin: Presidio, 1995.

McWilliams, Timothy, Kurtis P. Wheeler, and Gary Montgomery, eds. *Al-Anbar Awakening.* Vol. 1, *American Perspectives.* Quantico: Marine Corps University, 2009.

———, eds. *Al-Anbar Awakening.* Vol. 2, *Iraqi Perspectives.* Quantico: Marine Corps University, 2009.

Meador, Betty De Shong. *Inanna, Lady of Largest Heart: Poems of the Sumerian High Priestess Enheduanna.* Austin: University of Texas Press, 2000.

Meinhof, Ulrike. *Everybody Talks about the Weather . . . We Don't.* New York: Seven Stories Press, 2008.

Melena, Elpis. *Garibaldi: Recollections of His Public and Private Life.* London: Trubner, 1887.

———. *Recollections of General Garibaldi.* London: Saunders, Otley, 1861.

Mellick, Andrew D. *The Story of an Old Farm; or, Life in New Jersey in the Eighteenth Century.* Somerville: Unionist-Gazette, 1889.

Mendelson, Sarah E. *Changing Course: Ideas, Politics, and the Soviet Withdrawal from Afghanistan.* Princeton: Princeton University Press, 1998.

Méneval, Claude-François. *Memoirs Illustrating the History of Napoleon I from 1802 to 1815.* 3 vols. New York: D. Appleton, 1894.

Merari, Ariel, and Shlomo Elad. *The International Dimension of Palestinian Terrorism.* Boulder: Westview Press, 1986.

Merom, Gil. *How Democracies Lose Small Wars.* Cambridge: Cambridge University Press, 2003.

Merriman, John. *The Dynamite Club: How a Bombing in Fin-de-Siècle Paris Ignited the Age of Modern Terror.* Boston: Houghton Mifflin Harcourt, 2009.

Michael, George. "The Legend and Legacy of Abu Musab al-Zarqawi." *Defence Studies,* September 2007.

Michino, Gregory F. *Lakota Noon: The Indian Narrative of Custer's Defeat.* Missoula: Mountain Press, 1997.

Middlekauff, Robert. *The Glorious Cause: The American Revolution, 1763–1789.* Oxford: Oxford University Press, 2005.

Miles, Nelson A. *Personal Recollections and Observations of General Nelson A. Miles.* Chicago: Werner, 1896.

———. *Serving the Republic: Memoirs of the Civil and Military Life of Nelson A. Miles, Lieutenant General, United States Army.* New York: Harper & Brothers, 1911.

Miller, Harry. *The Communist Menace in Malaya.* New York: Frederick A. Praeger, 1954.

Milner, Alfred. *The Milner Papers: South Africa, 1897–1905.* 2 vols. London: Cassell, 1933.

Milner, Joe. *To Blazes with Glory: A Chindit's War.* Devon: Lazarus Press, 1995.

Miot de Mélito, André François. *Memoirs of Count Miot de Melito.* New York: Scribner, 1881.

Missall, John, and Mary Lou Missall. *The Seminole Wars: America's Longest Indian Conflict.* Gainesville: University Press of Florida, 2004.

Mitchell, Stephen. *A History of the Later Roman Empire, AD 284–641.* Malden: Blackwell, 2007.

Mitnick, Barbara J., ed. *New Jersey in the American Revolution.* New Brunswick: Rivergate Books, 2005.

Mitrokhin, Vasiliy. "The KGB in Afghanistan." Working Paper no. 40. Washington: Woodrow Wilson International Center for Scholars, July 2009.

Mockaitis, Thomas R. *British Counterinsurgency, 1919–60.* London: Macmillan, 1990.

Mockler, Anthony. *Haile Selassie's War: The Italian-Ethiopian Campaign, 1935–1941.* New York: Random House, 1984.

Moghadam, Asif. *The Globalization of Martyrdom: Al Qaeda, Salafi Jihad, and the Diffusion of Suicide Attacks.* Baltimore: Johns Hopkins University Press, 2008.

Moloney, Ed. *The Secret History of the IRA.* New York: W. W. Norton, 2002.

Montanus, Paul D. "A Failed Counterinsurgency Strategy: The British Southern Campaign, 1780–1781. Are There Lessons for Today?" Carlisle: U.S. Army War College, 2005.

Montefiore, Simon Sebag. *Young Stalin.* New York: Alfred A. Knopf, 2007.

Montmorency, Hervey de. *Sword and Stirrup: Memoires of an Adventurous Life.* London: G. Bell, 1936.

Moore, Harold G., and Joseph L. Galloway. *We Were Soldiers Once . . . and Young.* New York: Ballantine, 2004.

Moore, Rayburn S. "John Brown's Raid at Harpers Ferry: An Eyewitness Account by Charles White." *Virginia Magazine of History and Biography,* October 1959.

Moran, Charles. *Churchill Taken from the Diaries of Lord Moran: The Struggle for Survival, 1940–1965.* Boston: Houghton Mifflin, 1966.

Morgan, Edmund S. *American Heroes: Profiles of Men and Women Who Shaped Early America.* New York: W. W. Norton, 2009.

Morgan, Ted. *My Battle of Algiers: A Memoir.* Washington, D.C.: Smithsonian Books, 2006.

———. *Valley of Death: The Tragedy at Dien Bien Phu That Led America into the Vietnam War.* New York: Random House, 2010.

Morris, Benny. *1948: A History of the First Arab-Israeli War.* New Haven: Yale University Press, 2008.

———. *Righteous Victims: A History of the Zionist-Arab Conflict, 1881–2001.* New York: Vintage Books, 2001.

Morris, Donald R. *The Washing of the Spears: A History of the Rise of the Zulu Nation under Shaka and Its Fall in the Zulu War of 1879.* New York: Simon & Schuster, 1965.

Mortimer, Gavin. *Stirling's Men: The Inside History of the SAS in World War II.* London: Weidenfeld & Nicolson, 2004.

Mosely, Leonard. *Gideon Goes to War.* New York: Charles Scribner's Sons, 1955.

———. *The Glorious Fault: The Life of Lord Curzon.* New York: Harcourt Brace, 1960.

Moss, W. Stanley. *Ill Met by Moonlight.* London: Harrap, 1950.

Most, Johann. *Science of Revolutionary Warfare.* El Dorado: Desert Publications, 1978.

Moultrie, William. *Memoirs of the American Revolution, So Far as It Related to the States of North and South Carolina, and Georgia.* New York: David Longworth, 1802.

Moyar, Mark. *Triumph Forsaken: The Vietnam War, 1954–1965.* Cambridge: Cambridge University Press, 2006.

Muenchhausen, Friedrich von. *At General Howe's Side, 1776–1778: The Diary of General William Howe's Aide to Camp, Captain Friedrich von Muenchhausen.* Monmouth Beach: Philip Freneau Press, 1974.

Mundy, Rodney. *H.M.S. Hannibal at Palermo and Naples, during the Italian Revolution, 1859–1861.* London: John Murray, 1863.

Murray, W. H. *Rob Roy MacGregor: His Life and Times.* Edinburgh: Canongate Press, 1993.

Nagl, John A. *Learning to Eat Soup with a Knife: Counterinsurgency Lessons from Malaya and Vietnam.* Chicago: University of Chicago Press, 2005.

Naimark, Norman M. *Terrorists and Social Democrats: The Russian Revolutionary Movement under Alexander III.* Cambridge: Harvard University Press, 1983.

Napoleon I. *The Confidential Correspondence of Napoleon Bonaparte with His Brother Joseph, Sometime King of Spain.* 2 vols. New York: D. Appleton, 1856.

———. *Correspondance de Napoléon Ier: publiée par ordre de l'empereur Napoléon III.* 32 vols. Paris: Henri Plon, J. Dumaine, 1858–70.

Napoleoni, Loretta. *Insurgent Iraq: Al Zarqawi and the New Generation.* New York: Seven Stories Press, 2005.

Nashel, Jonathan. *Edward Lansdale's Cold War.* Amherst: University of Massachusetts Press, 2005.

Nasr, Vali. *The Shia Revival: How Conflicts within Islam Will Shape the Future.* New York: W. W. Norton, 2007.

Nasrallah, Hassan. *Voice of Hezbollah: The Statements of Sayyed Hassan Nasrallah.* London: Verso, 2007.

National Commission on Terrorist Attacks upon the United States. *The 9/11 Commission Report.* New York: W. W. Norton, n.d.

Neill, Edward D. *Memoir of Rev. Patrick Copland: A Chapter of the English Colonization of America.* New York: Charles Scribner, 1871.

Neligan, David. *The Spy in the Castle.* London: MacGibbon & Kee, 1968.

Netanyahu, Iddo. *Entebbe: The Jonathan Netanyahu Story: A Defining Moment in the War on Terrorism.* Green Forest: Balfour Books, 2003.

Neumann, Sigmund. *The Future in Perspective.* New York: G. P. Putnam's Sons, 1946.

Nguyen, Tien Hung, and Jerrold L. Schecter. *The Palace File.* New York: Harper & Row, 1986.

Nikolaejewsky, Boris. *Aseff the Spy: Russian Terrorist and Police Stool.* Hattiesburg, Miss.: Academic International, 1969.

Norris, J. A. *The First Afghan War, 1838–1842*. Cambridge: Cambridge University Press, 1967.

Norton, Augustus Richard. *Amal and the Shi'a: Struggle for the Soul of Lebanon*. Austin: University of Texas Press, 1987.

———. *Hezbollah: A Short History*. Princeton: Princeton University Press, 2007.

Oates, Stephen B. *To Purge This Land with Blood: A Biography of John Brown*. Amherst: University of Massachusetts Press, 1984.

O'Ballance, Edgar. *The Algerian Insurrection, 1954–62*. Hamden: Archon Books, 1967.

Oberdorfer, Dan. *Tet!* New York: Doubleday, 1971.

O'Connell, Robert L. *Of Arms and Men: A History of War, Weapons, and Aggression*. New York: Oxford University Press, 1989.

Ogburn, Charlton, Jr. *The Marauders*. New York: Harper & Brothers, 1956.

O'Hanlon, Michael, and Ian Livingston. "Iraq Index: Tracking Variables of Reconstruction and Security in Post-Saddam Iraq." www.brookings.edu/iraqindex.

Oliver, H. *The International Anarchist Movement in Late Victorian London*. New York: St. Martin's Press, 1983.

O'Malley, Ernie. *On Another Man's Wounds: A Personal History of Ireland's War of Independence*. Boulder: Roberts Rinehart, 1999.

Oman, Charles. *A History of the Peninsular War*. 7 vols. Oxford: Clarendon Press, 1902.

Omissi, David E. *Air Power and Colonial Control: The Royal Air Force, 1919–1939*. Manchester: Manchester University Press, 1990.

O'Neil, Bard E. *Insurgency and Terrorism: From Revolution to Apocalypse*. Washington: Potomac Books, 2005.

Oren, Michael. "Orde Wingate: Friend under Fire." *Azure*, Winter 2001.

Orwell, George. *The Collected Essays, Journalism & Letters*. 4 vols. Boston: Nonpareil Books, 2000.

Osanka, Franklin Mark, ed. *Modern Guerrilla Warfare: Fighting Communist Guerrilla Movements, 1941–1961*. New York: Free Press, 1962.

Ossoli, Margert Fuller. *Memoirs of Margaret Fuller Ossoli*. 2 vols. Boston: Phillips, Sampson, 1852.

Ott, Thomas O. *The Haitian Revolution, 1789–1804*. Knoxville: University of Tennessee Press, 1973.

Owings, W. A. Dolph, Elizabeth Pribic, and Nikola Pribic, eds. *The Sarajevo Trial*. 2 vols. Chapel Hill: Documentary Publications, 1984.

Pachonski, Jan, and Reuel K. Wilson. *Poland's Caribbean Tragedy: A Study of Polish Legions in the Haitian War of Independence, 1802–1803*. New York: Columbia University Press, 1986.

Pakenham, Thomas. *The Boer War*. New York: Avon Books, 1979.

———. *The Scramble for Africa*. New York: Avon Books, 1991.

Palij, Michael. *The Anarchism of Nestor Makhno, 1981–1921: An Aspect of the Ukrainian Revolution*. Seattle: University of Washington Press, 1976.

Pan Ku. *The History of the Former Han Dynasty*. 3 vols. New York: American Council of Learned Societies, 1938–55.

Pape, Robert A. *Dying to Win: The Strategic Logic of Suicide Terrorism*. New York: Random House, 2006.

Papen, Franz von. *Memoirs*. London: Andre Deutsch, 1952.

Paret, Peter. *French Revolutionary Warfare from Indochina to Algeria*. New York: Frederick A. Praeger, 1964.

———. *Internal War and Pacification: The Vendée, 1789–1796*. Princeton: Center of International Studies, 1961.

Paret, Peter, with Gordon A. Craig and Felix Gilbert, eds. *Makers of Modern Strategy: From Machiavelli to the Nuclear Age*. Princeton: Princeton University Press, 1986.

Parham, Althea de Puech, ed. *My Odyssey: Experiences of a Young Refugee from Two Revolutions by a Creole of Saint Domingue*. Baton Rouge: Louisiana State University Press, 1959.

Park, Thomas, and Aomar Boum. *Historical Dictionary of Morocco*. Lanham: Rowman & Littlefield, 2006.

Parker, Geoffrey, ed. *The Cambridge Illustrated History of Warfare: The Triumph of the West*. Cambridge: Cambridge University Press, 2004.

Parkman, Francis. *France and England in North America*. 2 vols. New York: Library of America, 1983.

Paroulakis, Peter H. *The Greek War of Independence*. Darwin: Hellenic International Press, 2000.

Parris, John. *The Lion of Caprera: A Biography of Giuseppe Garibaldi*. New York: David McKay, 1962.

Patti, Archimedes L. A. *Why Viet Nam? Prelude to America's Albatross*. Berkeley: University of California Press, 1980.

Pavlowitch, Stevan K. *Hitler's New Disorder: The Second World War in Yugoslavia*. New York: Columbia University Press, 2008.

Payne, Leslie. *The Life and Death of the SLA*. New York: Ballantine, 1976.

Peckham, Howard H., ed. *Sources of American Independence: Selected Manuscripts from the Collections of the William L. Clements Library*. 2 vols. Chicago: University of Chicago Press, 1978.

———. *Toll of Independence: Engagements and Battle Casualties of the American Revolution*. Chicago: University of Chicago Press, 1974.

Pedahzur, Ami. *The Israeli Secret Services and the Struggle against Terrorism*. New York: Columbia University Press, 2009.

———. *Suicide Terrorism*. Malden: Polity Press, 2008.

Peers, C. J. *Soldiers of the Dragon: Chinese Armies, 1500 BC–AD 1840*. Oxford: Osprey, 2006.

Peers, William R., and Dean Brelis. *Behind the Burma Road: The Story of America's Most Successful Guerrilla Force*. Boston: Atlantic Monthly Press, 1963.

Peng Dehuai. *Memoirs of a Chinese Marshal*. Beijing: Foreign Languages Press, 1984.

Pennell, C. R. *A Country with a Government and a Flag: "The Rif War" in Morocco, 1921–1926*. Cambridgeshire: Middle East and North African Studies Press, 1986.

Pennell, E. R. and J. *The Life of James McNeill Whistler.* 2 vols. London: William Heinemann, 1908.

Percy, Hugh Earl. *Letters of Hugh Earl Percy from Boston and New York, 1774–1776.* Boston: Charles E. Goodspeed, 1902.

Perdue, Peter. *China Marches West: The Qing Conquest of Central Eurasia.* Cambridge: Harvard University Press, 2005.

Peres, Shimon. *Battling for Peace: A Memoir.* New York: Random House, 1995.

Peretz, Don. *Intifada: The Palestinian Uprising.* Boulder: Westview Press, 1990.

Perez, Faustino. "Granma Voyage Began Revolutionary War." Radio address, Dec. 2, 1958. http://www.themilitant.com/1996/6013/6013_25.html.

Perowne, Stewart. *The Life and Times of Herod the Great.* London: Hodder and Stoughton, 1956.

Peterson, J. E. *Oman's Insurgencies: The Sultanate's Struggle for Supremacy.* London: SAQI, 2007.

Petraeus, David H. "The American Military and the Lessons of Vietnam." Ph.D. diss., Princeton University, 1987.

———. "Counterinsurgency Guidance." *Military Review,* September/October 2008.

———. "The Surge of Ideas: COINdinistas and Change in the U.S. Army in 2006." Speech to the American Enterprise Institute, May 6, 2010.

Pettifer, James, ed. *The New Macedonian Question.* London: Macmillan, 1999.

Phillips, Rufus. *Why Vietnam Matters: An Eyewitness Account of Lessons Not Learned.* Annapolis: Naval Institute Press, 2008.

Phillipps, L. March. *With Rimington.* London: Edward Arnold, 1901.

Pienaar, Philip. *With Steyn and De Wet.* London: Methuen, 1902.

Pieragostini, Karl. *Britain, Aden, and South Arabia: Abandoning Empire.* New York: St. Martin's Press, 1991.

Pike, Douglas. *PAVN: People's Army of Vietnam.* Novato: Presidio Press, 1986.

Pioneer. *The Risings on the North-West Frontier, 1897–1898.* Allahabad: Pioneer Press, 1898.

Pipes, Richard. *The Degaev Affair: Terror and Treason in Tsarist Russia.* New Haven: Yale University Press, 2003.

———. *Russia under the Old Regime.* New York: Penguin, 1995.

Playfair, I. S. O. *The Mediterranean and the Middle East.* Vol. 1, *The Early Successes against Italy (to May 1941).* London: Her Majesty's Stationery Office, 1954.

PLO: Captured Documents. Philadelphia: Pavilion Press, 2004.

Plutarch. *Plutarch's Lives.* 2 vols. New York: Modern Library, 2001.

Politkovskaya, Anna. *A Small Corner of Hell: Dispatches from Chechnya.* Chicago: University of Chicago Press, 2003.

Polk, William R. *Violent Politics: A History of Insurgency, Terrorism, and Guerrilla War, from the American Revolution to Iraq.* New York: HarperCollins, 2007.

Polybius. *The Histories.* 6 vols. Cambridge: Harvard University Press, 1922–27.

Pomper, Philip. *Lenin's Brother: The Origins of the October Revolution.* New York: W. W. Norton, 2010.

Popkin, Jeremy D. *Facing Racial Revolution: Eyewitness Accounts of the Haitian Insurrection*. Chicago: University of Chicago Press, 2007.

Porch, Douglas. *The Conquest of Morocco*. New York: Farrar, Straus and Giroux, 2005.

———. *The Conquest of the Sahara*. New York: Farrar, Straus and Giroux, 2005.

———. *The French Foreign Legion: A Complete History of the Legendary Fighting Force*. New York: HarperPerennial, 1991.

———. *The French Secret Services: From the Dreyfus Affair to the Gulf War*. New York: Farrar, Straus and Giroux, 1995.

Pownall, Henry. *Chief of Staff: The Diaries of Lieutenant General Sir Henry Pownall*. Edited by Brian Bond. 2 vols. London: L. Cooper, 1972–74.

Prestwich, Michael. *Edward I*. New Haven: Yale University Press, 1988.

Price, David A. *Love and Hate in Jamestown: John Smith, Pocahantas, and the Heart of a New Nation*. New York: Alfred A. Knopf, 2003.

Price, Jonathan J. *Jerusalem under Siege: The Collapse of the Jewish State, 66–70 C.E.* Leiden: E. J. Brill, 1992.

Price, Richard, ed. *Maroon Societies: Rebel Slave Communities in the Americas*. Garden City: Anchor Books, 1973.

Priscus. "Priscus at the Court of Attila." Fragment 8. http://www.ucalgary.ca/~vandersp/Courses/texts/prisfr8.html.

Puls, Mark. *Samuel Adams: Father of the American Revolution*. New York: Palgrave Macmillan, 2006.

Qarakhi, Muhammad Tahir al-. *The Shining of Daghestani Swords in Certain Campaigns of Shamil*. In *Russian-Muslim Confrontation in the Caucasus: Alternative Visions of the Conflict between Imam Shamil and the Russians, 1830–1859*, ed. Thomas Sanders, Ernest Tucker, and Gary Hamburg. London: RoutledgeCurzon, 2004.

Qassem, Naim. *Hizbullah: The Story from Within*. London: Saqi, 2007.

Queen, Richard, with Patricia Hass. *Inside and Out: Hostage to Iran, Hostage to Myself*. New York: G. P. Putnam's Sons, 1981.

Quinn-Judge, Sophie. *Ho Chi Minh: The Missing Years, 1919–1941*. Berkeley: University of California Press, 2002.

Quirk, Robert E. *Fidel Castro*. New York: W. W. Norton, 1993.

Rabin, Yitzhak. *The Rabin Memoirs*. Berkeley: University of California Press, 1996.

Rabinovich, Itamar. *The War for Lebanon, 1970–1985*. Ithaca: Cornell University Press, 1985.

Rable, George C. *But There Was No Peace: The Role of Violence in the Politics of Reconstruction*. Athens: University of Georgia Press, 2007.

Radzinsky, Edvard. *Alexander II: The Last Great Tsar*. New York: Free Press, 2005.

Rainsford, Marcus. *An Historical Account of the Black Empire of Hayti*. London: James Cundee, 1805.

Raj, J. J., Jr. *The War Years and After: A Personal Account of Historical Relevance*. Selangor Darul Ehsan, Malaysia: Pelanduk Publications, 1993.

Ramakrishna, Kumar. *Emergency Propaganda: The Winning of Malayan Hearts and Minds, 1948–1958*. Richmond: Curzon, 2002.

———. "'Transmogrifying' Malaya: The Impact of Sir Gerald Templer (1952–54)." *Journal of Southeast Asian Studies*, February 2001.

Randal, Jonathan. *Osama: The Making of a Terrorist*. New York: Vintage Books, 2004.

Rankin, Hugh F. *Francis Marion: The Swamp Fox*. New York: Crowell, 1973.

Ranstorp, Magnus. *Hizb'allah in Lebanon: The Politics of the Western Hostage Crisis*. New York: St. Martin's Press, 1997.

Rapoport, David C. "Fear and Trembling: Terrorism in Three Religious Traditions." *American Political Science Review*, September 1984.

———. "The Fourth Wave: September 11 in the History of Terrorism." *Current History*, December 2001.

Rashid, Ahmed. *Taliban: Militant Islam, Oil, and Fundamentalism in Central Asia*. New Haven: Yale University Press, 2010.

Ratliff, William E. *Castroism and Communism in Latin America, 1959–1976: The Varieties of Marxist-Leninist Experience*. Washington: AEI-Hoover, 1976.

Raviv, Dan, and Yossi Melman. *Every Spy a Prince: The Complete History of Israel's Intelligence Community*. Boston: Houghton Mifflin, 1990.

Reich, Walter. *Origins of Terrorism: Psychologies, Ideologies, Theologies, States of Mind*. Washington: Woodrow Wilson Center Press, 1998.

Reitz, Deneys. *Commando: A Boer Journal of the Boer War*. London: Faber and Faber, 1929.

Rejali, Darius. *Torture and Democracy*. Princeton: Princeton University Press, 2007.

Remington, Frederic. *John Ermine of the Yellowstone*. New York: Macmillan, 1913.

Renehan, Edward J., Jr. *The Secret Six: The True Tale of the Men Who Conspired with John Brown*. New York: Crown Publishers, 1995.

Revere, Paul. *Paul Revere's Three Accounts of His Famous Ride*. Boston: Massachusetts Historical Society, 1968.

Reynolds, David S. *John Brown, Abolitionist: The Man Who Killed Slavery, Sparked the Civil War, and Seeded Civil Rights*. New York: Vintage Books, 2006.

Riall, Lucy. *Garibaldi: Invention of a Hero*. New Haven: Yale University Press, 2007.

Richardson, John S. *The Romans in Spain*. Oxford: Blackwell Publishers, 1996.

Richardson, Louise. *What Terrorists Want*. New York: Random House, 2006.

Richardson, Peter. *Herod: King of the Jews and Friend of the Romans*. Columbia: University of South Carolina Press, 1996.

Ricks, Thomas E. *The Gamble: General David Petraeus and the American Military Adventure in Iraq, 2006–2008*. New York: Penguin, 2009.

Ridley, Jasper. *Garibaldi*. London: Phoenix Press, 2001.

Rittenberg, Sidney, and Amanda Bennett. *The Man Who Stayed Behind*. Durham: Duke University Press, 2001.

Roberts, David. *Once They Moved like the Wind: Cochise, Geronimo, and the Apache Wars*. New York: Simon & Schuster, 1993.

Roberts, Frederick Sleigh. *Forty-One Years in India*. 2 vols. New York: Longmans, Green, 1898.

Roberts, Walter R. *Tito, Mihailovic, and the Allies, 1941–1945*. New Brunswick: Rutgers University Press, 1973.

Robinson, Charles M., III. *A Good Year to Die: The Story of the Great Sioux War*. New York: Random House, 1995.

Robinson, J. B. Perry. *Transformation in Malaya*. London: Secker & Warburg, 1956.

Robinson, Linda. *Tell Me How This Ends: General David Petraeus and the Search for a Way out of Iraq*. New York: PublicAffairs, 2008.

Robson, Brian. *Crisis on the Frontier: The Third Afghan War and the Campaign in Waziristan, 1919–1920*. Gloucestershire: Spellmount, 2007.

———. *The Road to Kabul: The Second Afghan War, 1878–1881*. Gloucestershire: Spellmount, 2007.

Rocca, Jean Albert de. *Memoirs of the War of the French in Spain*. London: John Murray, 1815.

Rodriguez, Felix I., and John Weisman. *Shadow Warrior*. New York: Simon & Schuster, 1989.

Rogers, Robert. *Journals of Major Robert Rogers*. Albany: Joel Munsell's Sons, 1883.

Rojo, Ricardo. *My Friend Che*. New York: Grove Press, 1968.

Rolls, S. C. *Steel Chariots in the Desert*. London: Jonathan Cape, 1937.

Rolo, Charles J. *Wingate's Raiders: An Account of the Fabulous Adventure That Raised the Curtain on the Battle for Burma*. New York: Viking, 1944.

Romanus, Charles F., and Riley Sunderland. *Stillwell's Command Problems*. Washington: Department of the Army, 1956.

Rooney, David. *Wingate and the Chindits: Redressing the Balance*. London: Cassell, 1994.

Roosevelt, Theodore. *Letters and Speeches*. New York: Library of America, 2004.

Rootham, Jasper. *Miss Fire: The Chronicle of a British Mission to Mihailovich, 1943–1944*. London: Chatto & Windus, 1946.

Ros, Martin. *Night of Fire: The Black Napoleon and the Battle for Haiti*. New York: Da Capo Press, 1994.

Rosenbaum, Naomi. "Success in Foreign Policy: The British in Cyprus, 1878–1960." *Canadian Journal of Political Science*, December 1970.

Rosengarten, John G. "John Brown's Raid: How I Got into It, and How I Got out of It." *Atlantic Monthly*, June 1865.

Rosenthal, Eric. *General de Wet: A Biography*. Cape Town: Simondium Publishers, 1968.

Ross, John F. *War on the Run: The Epic Story of Robert Rogers and the Conquest of America's First Frontier*. New York: Bantam Books, 2009.

Ross, Michael. *Banners of the King: The War of the Vendée, 1793–4*. New York: Hippocrene Books, 1975.

Rosslyn, Earl of. *Twice Captured: A Record of Adventure during the Boer War*. London: William Blackwood, 1900.

Rountree, Helen C. *Pocahontas's People: The Powhatan Indians of Virginia through Four Centuries.* Norman: University of Oklahoma Press, 1990.

———. *The Powhatan Indians of Virginia: Their Traditional Culture.* Norman: University of Oklahoma Press, 1989.

Rowan, A. R. *On the Trail of a Lion: Ahmed Shah Massoud, Oil, Politics, and Terror.* Oakville: Mosaic Press, 2006.

Rowlandson, Mary. *Narrative of the Captivity and Removes of Mrs. Mary Rowlandson.* 5th ed. Lancaster: Carter, Andrews, 1828.

Roy, Jules. *The Battle of Dienbienphu.* New York: Carroll & Graf, 2002.

———. *The War in Algeria.* New York: Grove Press, 1961.

Roy, Olivier. *Afghanistan: From Holy War to Civil War.* Princeton: Darwin Press, 1995.

Rozema, Vicki. *Voices from the Trail of Tears.* Winston-Salem: John F. Blair, 2003.

Rubin, Barnett R. *The Fragmentation of Afghanistan: State Formation and Collapse in the International System.* New Haven: Yale University Press, 1995.

Rubin, Barry, and Judith Colp Rubin, eds. *Anti-American Terrorism and the Middle East: A Documentary Reader.* New York: Oxford University Press, 2004.

———. *Yasir Arafat: A Political Biography.* Oxford: Oxford University Press, 2005.

Rubin, Hyman. *South Carolina Scalawags.* Columbia: University of South Carolina Press, 2006.

Ruchames, Louis, ed. *A John Brown Reader.* London: Abelard-Schuman, 1959.

Rudorff, Raymond. *Belle Epoque: Paris in the Nineties.* London: Hamish Hamilton, 1972.

———. *War to the Death: The Sieges of Saragossa, 1808–1809.* South Yorkshire: Pen & Sword Military, 2006.

Russell, Peter E. "Redcoats in the Wilderness: British Officers and Irregular Warfare in Europe and America, 1740 to 1760." *William and Mary Quarterly,* October 1978.

Russian General Staff. *The Soviet-Afghan War: How a Superpower Fought and Lost.* Edited by Lester W. Grau and Michael A. Gress. Lawrence: University Press of Kansas, 2002.

Ruud, Charles A., and Sergei A. Stepanov. *Fontanka 16: The Tsars' Secret Police.* Montreal: McGill-Queen's University Press, 1999.

Ryan, Henry Butterfield. *The Fall of Che Guevara: A Story of Soldiers, Spies, and Diplomats.* New York: Oxford University Press, 1998.

Ryan, Meda. *The Real Chief: Liam Lynch.* Cork: Mercier Press, 2005.

Ryan, Nigel. *A Hitch or Two in Afghanistan: A Journey behind Russian Lines.* London: Weidenfeld & Nicolson, 1983.

Sadler, John. *Border Fury: England and Scotland at War, 1296–1568.* New York: Longman, 2006.

Saggs, H. W. F. *The Might That Was Assyria.* London: Sidgwick & Jackson, 1984.

Saich, Tony. *The Rise to Power of the Chinese Communist Party.* Armonk: M. E. Sharpe, 1996.

Saich, Tony, and Hans van de Ven, eds. *New Perspectives on the Chinese Communist Revolution.* Armonk: M. E. Sharpe, 1995.

Sainteny, Jean. *Ho Chi Minh and His Vietnam: A Personal Memoir.* Chicago: Cowles, 1972.

Sale, Florentia. *A Journal of the First Afghan War.* Oxford: Oxford University Press, 2002.

Salisbury, Harrison. *The Long March: The Untold Story.* New York: McGraw-Hill, 1985.

Salmon, Gary Prado. *The Defeat of Che Guevara: Military Responses to Guerrilla Challenge in Bolivia.* New York: Praeger, 1987.

Sampson, Victor, and Ian Hamilton. *Anti-Commando.* London: Faber and Faber, 1931.

Sanford, Victoria. *Buried Secrets: Truth and Human Rights in Guatemala.* New York: Palgrave Macmillan, 2003.

Santayana, George. *Soliloquies in England and Later Soliloquies.* New York: Scribner's, 1922.

Sasson, Jack M., eds. *Civilizations of the Ancient Near East.* 4 vols. Peabody: Hendrickson, 2006.

Saville, Lord, William Hoyt, and John Toohey. *Report of the Blood Sunday Inquiry.* http://www.bloody-sunday-inquiry.org/.

Savinkov, Boris. *Memoirs of a Terrorist.* New York: Albert & Charles Boni, 1931.

Sawyer, Ralph D., ed. *The Seven Military Classics of Ancient China.* New York: Basic Books, 1993.

Sayigh, Yezid. *Armed Struggle and the Search for State: The Palestinian National Movement, 1949–1993.* Oxford: Clarendon Press, 1997.

Schaff, Philip, and Henry Wace, eds. *A Select Library of Nicene and Post-Nicene Fathers of the Christian Church.* Vol. 6, *Saint Jerome: Letters and Select Works.* New York: Christian Literature Company, 1893.

Schatzberg, Michael G. *Mobutu or Chaos? The United States and Zaire, 1960–1990.* Lanham: University Press of America, 1991.

Scheidel, Walter, Ian Morris, and Richard P. Saller, eds. *The Cambridge Economic History of the Greco-Roman World.* Cambridge: Cambridge University Press, 2008.

Scheina, Robert L. *Latin America's Wars.* 2 vols. Washington: Brassey's, 2003.

Scheuer, Michael. *Osama bin Laden.* Oxford: Oxford University Press, 2011.

Schiff, Ze'ev, and Ehud Ya'ari. *Israel's Lebanon War.* New York: Simon & Schuster, 1984.

Schikkerling, Roland William. *Commando Courageous: A Boer's Diary.* Johannesburg: Hugh Keartland, 1964.

Schiller, Friedrich. *History of the Thirty Years' War.* London: Bell and Daldy, 1873.

Schlesinger, Arthur M., Jr. *A Thousand Days: John F. Kennedy in the White House.* Boston: Houghton Mifflin, 1965.

Schoenburn, David. *As France Goes.* New York: Harper & Brothers, 1957.

Schofield, Victoria. *Afghan Frontier: Feuding and Fighting in Central Asia.* London: Tauris Parke, 2003.

Scholl-Latour, Peter. *Death in the Ricefields: An Eyewitness Account of Vietnam's Three Wars, 1945–1979.* New York: St. Martin's Press, 1979.

Schram, Stuart R. *Mao's Road to Power: Revolutionary Writings, 1912–1949*. 7 vols. Armonk: M. E. Sharpe, 1992–.

Schultz, Eric B., and Michael J. Tougias. *King Philip's War: The History and Legacy of America's Forgotten Conflict*. Woodstock: Countryman Press, 1999.

Schwartz, Maria Esperanza von. *Recollections of General Garibaldi; or, Travels from Rome to Lucerne*. London: Saunders, Otley, 1861.

Schweitzer, Yoram. "The Rise and Fall of Suicide Bombing in the Second Intifada." *Strategic Assessment*, October 2010.

Scirocco, Alfonso. *Garibaldi: Citizen of the World*. Princeton: Princeton University Press, 2007.

Scolnic, Benjamin Edidin. *Thy Brother's Blood: The Maccabees and Dynastic Morality in the Hellenistic World*. Lanham: University Press of America, 2008.

Scott, Douglas D., Richard A. Fox Jr., Melissa A. Connor, and Dick Harmon. *Archaeological Perspectives on the Battle of the Little Bighorn*. Norman: University of Oklahoma Press, 1989.

Scott, Ronald McNair. *Robert the Bruce: King of Scots*. New York: Carroll & Graff, 1996.

Scotti, Anthony J., Jr. *Brutal Virtue: The Myth and Reality of Banastre Tarleton*. Westminster, Md.: Heritage Books, 1995.

Secher, Reynald. *A French Genocide: The Vendée*. Notre Dame: University of Notre Dame Press, 2003.

Sefton, James E. *The United States Army and Reconstruction, 1865–1877*. Baton Rouge: Louisiana State University Press, 1967.

Sennott, Charles M. "The Good Soldier." *Men's Journal*, June 2008.

Serge, Victor. *Memoirs of a Revolutionary, 1901–1941*. London: Oxford University Press, 1963.

Sergeant, Harriet. *Shanghai: Collision Point of Culture, 1918–1939*. New York: Crown, 1990.

Servan-Schreiber, Jean-Jacques. *Lieutenant in Algeria*. New York: Alfred A. Knopf, 1957.

Seth, Ronald. *The Russian Terrorists: The Story of the Narodniki*. London: Barrie and Rockliff, 1966.

Seton-Watson, Hugh. *The Russian Empire, 1801–1917*. Oxford: Oxford University Press, 1967.

Shanks, Hershel, ed. *Ancient Israel: A Short History from Abraham to the Roman Destruction of the Temple*. Englewood Cliffs: Prentice-Hall, 1988.

Shaw, Brent D., ed. *Spartacus and the Slave Wars: A Brief History with Documents*. Boston: Bedford/St. Martin's, 2001.

Shea, William L. *The Virginia Militia in the Seventeenth Century*. Baton Rouge: Louisiana State University Press, 1983.

Sheehan, Neil. *A Bright Shining Lie: John Paul Vann and America in Vietnam*. New York: Random House, 1988.

Sheehan, William. *British Voices from the Irish War of Independence, 1918–1921: The Words of British Servicemen Who Were There.* Cork: Collins Press, 2005.

Shelley, Percy Bysshe. *Hellas: A Lyrical Drama.* London: Shelley Society, 1886.

Sherer, Moyle. *Military Memoirs of Field Marshal the Duke of Wellington.* 2 vols. London: Longman, 1830.

Sherry, Norman. *The Life of Graham Greene.* Vol. 2, *1939–1955.* New York: Viking, 1994.

Shirer, William L. *The Rise and Fall of the Third Reich: A History of Nazi Germany.* New York: Simon & Schuster, 1960.

Shirreff, David. *Bare Feet and Bandoliers: Wingate, Sandford, the Patriots and the Part They Played in the Liberation of Ethiopia.* London: Radcliffe Press, 1995.

Short, Anthony. *In Pursuit of Mountain Rats: The Communist Insurrection in Malaya.* Singapore: Cultured Lotus, 2000.

Short, K. R. M. *The Dynamite War: Irish-American Bombers in Victorian Britain.* Dublin: Gill and Macmillan, 1979.

Short, Philip. *Mao: A Life.* New York: Henry Holt, 1999.

Shotwell, James T. *At the Paris Peace Conference.* New York: Macmillan, 1937.

Showalter, Dennis. *The Wars of German Unification.* London: Hodder Arnold, 2004.

Shy, John. *A People Numerous and Armed: Reflections on the Military Struggle for American Independence.* Ann Arbor: University of Michigan Press, 1990.

Siao-yu. *Mao Tse-tung and I Were Beggers.* Syracuse: Syracuse University Press, 1959.

Siljak, Ana. *Angel of Vengeance: The "Girl Assassin," the Governor of St. Petersburg, and Russia's Revolutionary World.* New York: St. Martin's Press, 2008.

Sima, Qian. *Records of the Grand Historian: Han Dynasty.* 2 vols. Hong Kong: Columbia University Press, 1993.

Simpson, Howard R. *Dien Bien Phu: The Epic Battle America Forgot.* Washington: Brassey's, 1994.

———. *Tiger in the Barbed Wire: An American in Vietnam, 1952–1991.* Washington: Brassey's, 1992.

Sims, William Gilmore. *The Life of Francis Marion: The True Story of South Carolina's Swamp Fox.* Charleston: History Press, 2007.

Singer, Barnett, and John Langdon. *Cultured Force: Makers and Defenders of the French Colonial Empire.* Madison: University of Wisconsin Press, 2004.

Sinor, Denis, ed. *The Cambridge History of Early Inner Asia.* Cambridge: Cambridge University Press, 1990.

Sivan, Emmanuel. *Radical Islam: Medieval Theology and Modern Politics.* New Haven: Yale University Press, 1990.

Skidmore, Thomas E. *The Politics of Military Rule in Brazil, 1964–85.* New York: Oxford University Press, 1988.

Slatta, Richard W., and Jane Lucas De Grummond. *Simon Bolivar's Quest for Glory.* College Station: Texas A&M University Press, 2003.

Slepyan, Kenneth. *Stalin's Guerrillas: Soviet Partisans in World War II.* Lawrence: University Press of Kansas, 2006.

Slim, William. *Defeat into Victory: Battling Japan in Burma and India, 1942–1945*. New York: Cooper Square Press, 2000.

Smedley, Agnes. *The Great Road: The Life and Times of Chu Teh*. New York: Monthly Review Press, 2009.

Smith, David James. *One Morning in Sarajevo: 28 June 1914*. London: Phoenix, 2009.

Smith, Harvey, et al. *Area Handbook for South Vietnam*: Washington: Government Printing Office, 1967.

Smith, John. *The Generall Historie of New England, Virginia, and the Summer Isles*. 2 vols. New York: Macmillan, 1907.

Smith, Richard Harris. *OSS: The Secret History of America's First Central Intelligence Agency*. Guilford: Lyons Press, 2005.

Smith, Samuel Abbott. *West Cambridge on the Nineteenth of April, 1775*. Boston: Alfred Mudge, 1864.

Smith, Sebastian. *Allah's Mountains: The Battle for Chechnya*. New York: Tauris Parke, 2009.

Smuts, Jan Christian. *Memoirs of the Boer War*. Johannesburg: Jonathan Ball Publishing, 1994.

———. *Selections from the Smuts Papers*. Vol. 1, *June 1886–May 1902*. Edited by W. K. Hancock and Jean van der Poel. Cambridge: Cambridge University Press, 2007.

Smuts, J. C. *Jan Christian Smuts: A Biography*. New York: William Morrow, 1952.

Snell, Daniel C. *Life in the Ancient Near East, 3100–332 B.C.E.* New Haven: Yale University Press, 1997.

Snow, Dean R., and Kim M. Lanphear. "European Contact and Indian Depopulation in the Northeast: The Timing of the First Epidemics." *Ethnohistory*, Winter 1988.

Snow, Edgar. *Red Star over China*. New York: Grove Press, 1968.

Snow, Helen Foster. *The Chinese Communists: Sketches and Autobiographies of the Old Guard*. Westport: Greenwood Press, 1972.

Somerville, Thomas. *My Own Life and Times, 1741–1814*. Edinburgh: Edmonston & Douglas, 1861.

Sorenson, Theodore C. *Kennedy*. New York: Harper & Row, 1965.

Sorley, Lewis. *A Better War: The Unexamined Victories and Final Tragedy of America's Last Years in Vietnam*. New York: Harcourt Brace, 1999.

———. *Westmoreland: The General Who Lost Vietnam*. Boston: Houghton Mifflin Harcourt, 2011.

Soucek, Svat. *A History of Inner Asia*. Cambridge: Cambridge University Press, 2000.

Southey, Robert. *History of the Peninsular War*. 6 vols. London: John Murray, 1828.

Spalinger, Anthony John. *War in Ancient Egypt: The New Kingdom*. Malden: Blackwell, 2005.

Spence, Jonathan D. *Mao Zedong: A Life*. New York: Penguin, 1999.

Spencer, John H. *Ethiopia at Bay: A Personal Account of the Haile Selassie Years*. Algonac: Reference Publications, 1984.

Spotts, David L. *Campaigning with Custer and the Nineteenth Kansas Volunteer Cavalry on the Washita Campaign, 1868–'69*. New York: Argonaut Press, 1965.

Sprague, John T. *The Origins, Progress, and Conclusion of the Florida War*. New York: D. Appleton, 1848.

Spring, Matthew H. *With Zeal and with Bayonets Only: The British Army on Campaign in North America, 1775–1783*. Norman: University of Oklahoma Press, 2008.

Stapleton, William J. "Michael Collins's Squad." *Capuchin Annual* (1970).

Starkey, Armstrong. *European and Native American Warfare, 1675–1815*. Norman: University of Oklahoma Press, 1998.

Starobin, Joseph R. *Eyewitness in Indo-China*. New York: Greenwood Press, 1954.

St. Clair, Arthur. *A Narrative of the Manner in Which the Campaign against the Indians . . . Was Conducted*. Philadelphia: Jane Aiken, 1812.

St. Clair, William. *That Greece Might Still Be Free: The Philhellenes in the War of Independence*. Cambridge: OpenBook, 2008.

Steele, Ian K. *Warpaths: Invasions of North America*. New York: Oxford University Press, 1994.

Stein, Aurel. *On Alexander's Track to the Indus: Personal Narrative of Explorations on the North-West Frontier of India*. Chicago: Ares Publishers, 1974.

Stepniak (Sergei Kravchinski). *Underground Russia: Revolutionary Profiles and Sketches from Life*. London: Smith, Elder, 1883.

Stern, Susan. *With the Weathermen: The Personal Journal of a Revolutionary Woman*. New Brunswick: Rutgers University Press, 2007.

Stevenson, William. *90 Minutes at Entebbe*. New York: Bantam, 1976,

Stewart, Brian. *Smashing Terrorism in the Malayan Emergency: The Vital Contribution of the Police*. Selangor Darul Ehsan: Pelanduk Publications, 2004.

Stewart, Jules. *Crimson Snow: Britain's First Disaster in Afghanistan*. Gloucestershire: Sutton, 2008.

Stibbe, Philip. *Return Via Rangoon: A Young Chindit Survives the Jungle and Japanese Captivity*. London: Leo Cooper, 1994.

Stiles, Ezra. *The Literary Diary of Ezra Stiles*. Edited by Franklin Bowditch Dexter. 3 vols. New York: C. Scribner's Sons, 1901.

Stilwell, Joseph W. *The Stilwell Papers*. New York: William Sloane Associates, 1948.

Stirling, W. F. *Safety Last*. London: Hollis and Carter, 1953.

Stockwell, A. J., ed. *British Documents on the End of Empire*. Ser. B, vol. 3, *Malaya*, pt. 2, *The Communist Insurrection, 1948–1953*. London: Her Majesty's Stationery Office, 1995.

Stoddard, Lothrop. *The French Revolution in San Domingo*. Boston: Houghton Mifflin, 1914.

Stoll, Ira. *Samuel Adams: A Life*. New York: Free Press, 2008.

Storss, Ronald. *The Memoirs of Sir Ronald Storss*. New York: G. P. Putnam's Sons, 1937.

Stout, Mark E., et al., eds. *The Terrorist Perspectives Project: Strategic and Operational Views of Al Qaeda and Associated Movements*. Annapolis: Naval Institute Press, 2008.

Strauss, Barry. *The Spartacus War*. London: Simon & Schuster, 2009.

Strong, Morgan. "Playboy Interview: Yasir Arafat." *Playboy*, September 1988.

Strother, D. H. "The Late Invasion of Harper's Ferry." *Harper's Weekly*, November 5, 1859.

Stryker, William, ed. *Documents relating to the Revolutionary History of the State of New Jersey*. Vol. 1, *1776–1777*. Trenton: John L. Murphy, 1903.

Stubbs, Richard. *Hearts and Minds in Guerrilla Warfare: The Malayan Emergency, 1948–1960*. Singapore: Oxford University Press, 1989.

Sturgis, Mark. *The Last Days of Dublin Castle: The Mark Sturgis Diaries*. Dublin: Irish Academic Press, 1999.

Suchet, Louis-Gabriel. *Memoirs of the War in Spain, from 1808 to 1814*. 2 vols. London: Henry Colburn, 1829.

Suetonius. *The Twelve Caesars*. London: Penguin, 1979.

Sullivan, Joseph G., ed. *Embassies under Siege: Personal Accounts by Diplomats on the Front Lines*. Washington: Brassey's, 1995.

Sumida, Jon Tetsuro. *Decoding Clausewitz: A New Approach to On War*. Lawrence: University Press of Kansas, 2008.

Summers, Harry G. *On Strategy: A Critical Analysis of the Vietnam War*. New York: Dell, 1984.

Sun Shuyun. *The Long March: The True History of Communist China's Founding Myth*. New York: Doubleday, 2006.

Suri, Jeremi. *Power and Protest: Global Revolution and the Rise of Détente*. Cambridge: Harvard University Press, 2003.

Sutherland, William, and Richard Pope. *Late News of the Excursions and Ravages of the King's Troops, on the Nineteenth of April 1775*. Cambridge: Press at Harvard College, 1927.

Sweig, Julia E. *Inside the Cuban Revolution: Fidel Castro and the Urban Underground*. Cambridge: Harvard University Press, 2002.

Swinson, Arthur. *North-West Frontier: People and Events, 1839–1847*. London: Hutchinson, 1967.

Sykes, Christopher. *Orde Wingate: A Biography*. Cleveland: World, 1959.

Szulc, Tad. *Fidel: A Critical Portrait*. New York: Avon, 1986.

Tabachnick, David Edward, and Toivo Koivukoski. *Enduring Empire: Ancient Lessons for Global Politics*. Toronto: University of Toronto Press, 2010.

Taber, Robert. *War of the Flea*. Washington: Potomac Books, 2002.

Tacitus. *The Agricola and The Germania*. London: Penguin, 1970.

———. *The Annals & The Histories*. New York: Modern Library, 2002.

Taibo, Paco Igancio. *Guevara, Also Known as Che*. New York: St. Martin's Press, 1997.

Tamarov, Vladislav. *Afghanistan: A Russian Soldier's Story*. Berkeley: Ten Speed Press, 2001.

Tanner, Stephen. *Afghanistan: A Military History from Alexander the Great to the Fall of the Taliban*. New York: Da Capo Press, 2002.

Tarleton, Banastre. *A History of the Campaigns of 1780 and 1781 in the Southern Provinces of North American*. London: T. Cadell, 1787.

Taruc, Luis. *He Who Rides the Tiger: The Story of an Asian Guerrilla Leader.* New York: Frederick A. Praeger, 1967.

Tattersall, Ian. *The World from Beginnings to 4000 BCE.* New York: Oxford University Press, 2008.

Taylor, Alan. *American Colonies: The Settling of North America.* New York: Penguin, 2002.

Taylor, Jay. *The Generalissimo: Chiang Kai-shek and the Struggle for Modern China.* Cambridge: Harvard University Press, 2009.

Taylor, Maxwell D. *The Uncertain Trumpet.* New York: Harper & Brothers, 1960.

Terrill, Ross. *Mao: A Biography.* New York: Harper Colophon, 1980.

Thesiger, Wilfred. *The Life of My Choice.* New York: W. W. Norton, 1987.

Thomas, Gordon. *Gideon's Spies: The Secret History of the Mossad.* New York: St. Martin's Griffin, 2009.

Thomas, Hugh. *Cuba, or the Pursuit of Freedom.* New York: Da Capo Press, 1998.

Thomas, Lowell. *With Lawrence in Arabia.* London: Prion, 2002.

Thomas, S. Bernard. *Season of High Adventure: Edgar Snow in China.* Berkeley: University of California Press, 1996.

Thompson, E. A. *The Huns.* Oxford: Blackwell, 1996.

Thompson, J. Lee. *Forgotten Patriot: A Life of Alfred, Viscount Milner, of St. James's and Cape Town, 1854–1925.* Madison: Fairleigh Dickinson University Press, 2007.

Thompson, Julian. *The Imperial War Museum Book of War behind Enemy Lines.* London: Sidgwick & Jackson, 1998.

Thompson, Robert. *Defeating Communist Insurgency: The Lessons of Malaya and Vietnam.* St. Petersburg: Hailer, 2005.

———. *Make for the Hills: Memories of Far Eastern Wars.* London: Leo Cooper, 1989.

Thompson, Virginia. *French Indo-China.* London: George Allen & Unwin, 1937.

Thoreau, Henry David. *The Writings of Henry David Thoreau.* 11 vols. Boston: Houghton Mifflin, 1893.

Thornton, John K. *Warfare in Atlantic Africa, 1500–1800.* London: UCL Press, 1999.

Thrapp, Dan L. *The Conquest of Apacheria.* Norman: University of Oklahoma Press, 1967.

Thucydides. *History of the Peloponnesian War.* Harmondsworth: Penguin, 1986.

Tilman, Robert O. "The Non-Lessons of the Malayan Emergency." *Asian Survey*, August 1966.

Timerman, Jacobo. *Prisoner Without a Name, Cell Without a Number.* New York: Alfred A. Knopf, 1981.

Toland, John. *The Rising Sun: The Decline and Fall of the Japanese Empire, 1936–1945.* New York: Modern Library, 2003.

Tolstoy, Leo. *The Cossacks.* New York: Modern Library, 2006.

———. *Hadji Murad.* New York: Cosimo Classics, 2006.

———. *Sevastapol and Other Military Tales.* New York: Funk & Wagnall, 1903.

Tomasevich, Jozo. *War and Revolution in Yugoslavia, 1941–1945: Occupation and Collaboration.* Stanford: Stanford University Press, 2001.

———. *War and Revolution in Yugoslavia, 1941–1945: The Chetniks.* Stanford: Stanford University Press, 1975.

Tone, John Lawrence. *The Fatal Knot: The Guerrilla War in Navarre and the Defeat of Napoleon in Spain.* Chapel Hill: University of North Carolina Press, 1994.

Tourtellot, Arthur Bernon. *Lexington and Concord: The Beginning of the War of the American Revolution.* New York: W. W. Norton, 1959.

Towill, Bill. *A Chindit's Chronicle.* San Jose: Authors Choice Press, 2000.

Trelawny, E. J. *Recollections of the Last Days of Shelley and Byron.* Boston: Ticknor and Fields, 1859.

Trelease, Allen W. *White Terror: The Ku Klux Klan Conspiracy and Southern Reconstruction.* Baton Rouge: Louisiana State University Press, 1999.

Trevelyan, George Macaulay. *Garibaldi and the Thousand.* London: Longmans, Green, 1912.

———. *Garibaldi and the Making of Italy, June–November 1860.* New York: Longmans, Green, 1928.

———. *Garibaldi's Defence of the Roman Republic.* London: Longmans, Green, 1907.

———. "The War-Journals of 'Garibaldi's Englishman.'" *Cornhill Magazine,* January, June 1908.

Trevelyan, George Otto. *The American Revolution.* 14 vols. New York: Longmans, Green, 1915.

Trigger, Bruce G. *The Children of Aataentsic: A History of the Huron People to 1660.* Montreal: McGill-Queen's Press, 1987.

Trigger, Bruce G., and Wilcomb E. Washburn, eds. *The Cambridge History of the Native Peoples of the Americas.* Vol. 1, *North America,* pts. 1 and 2. Cambridge: Cambridge University Press, 1996.

Trinquier, Roger. *Les Maquis d'Indochine, 1952–1954.* Paris: SPL, 1976.

———. *Modern Warfare: A French View of Counterinsurgency.* Westport: Praeger, 2006.

———. *Le temps perdu.* Paris: Albin Michel, 1978.

Trofimov, Yaroslav. *The Siege of Mecca.* New York: Doubleday, 2007.

Trotsky, Leon. *Against Individual Terrorism.* New York: Pathfinder Press, 1980.

Truong Chinh. *Selected Writings.* Hanoi: Gioi, 1994.

Tulloch, Derek. *Wingate in Peace and War.* London: Macdonald, 1972.

Ulam, Adam B. *In the Name of the People: Prophets and Conspirators in Prerevolutionary Russia.* New York: Viking, 1977.

Ulloa, Marie-Pierre. *Francis Jeanson: A Dissident Intellectual from the French Resistance to the Algerian War.* Stanford: Stanford University Press, 2007.

Underhill, John. *Newes from America; or, A New and Experimentall Discoverie of New England.* London: Peter Cole, 1638.

Urban, Mark. *War in Afghanistan.* New York: St. Martin's Press, 1990.

U.S. Army and Marine Corps. *Counterinsurgency Field Manual.* Chicago: University of Chicago Press, 2007.

U.S. Commission on Beirut International Airport Terrorist Act. "Report of the DOD

Commission on Beirut International Airport Terrorist Act, October 23, 1983." Washington, December 20, 1983.

U.S. Commissioner of Indian Affairs. *Report of the Commissioner of Indian Affairs for the Year 1866*. Washington: Government Printing Office, 1866.

U.S. Congress. *Report of the Joint Special Committee Appointed under Joint Resolution of March 3, 1865*. Washington: Government Printing Office, 1867.

U.S. Congress. *Report of the Joint Select Committee on the Condition of Affairs in the Late Insurrectionary States* [KKK Report]. 13 vols. Washington: Government Printing Office, 1872.

U.S. Department of Defense. *The Pentagon Papers: The Senator Gravel Edition*. 5 vols. Boston: Beacon Press, 1971.

———. *United States–Vietnam Relations, 1945–1967: Study Prepared by the Department of Defense*. 12 vols. Washington: Government Printing Office, 1971.

U.S. Department of State. *Foreign Relations of the United States*. Washington: Government Printing Office, various dates.

U.S. House of Representatives. *Report of the Special Committee Appointed to Investigate the Troubles in Kansas*. Washington: Cornelius Wendell, 1856.

U.S. Secretary of the Interior. *Annual Report of the Secretary of the Interior on the Operations of the Department for the Year 1873*. Washington: Government Printing Office, 1873.

U.S. Senate. *South Carolina in 1876: Testimony as to the Denial of the Elective Franchise in South Carolina*. 3 vols. Washington: Government Printing Office, 1877.

U.S. Superintendent of Census. *The Statistics of the Population of the United States . . . Compiled from the Returns of the Ninth Census, June 1, 1870*. Washington: Government Printing Office, 1872.

Utley, Robert M. *Cavalier in Buckskins: George Armstrong Custer and the Western Military Frontier*. Norman: University of Oklahoma Press, 1988.

———. *Frontier Regulars: The United States Army and the Indian, 1866–1891*. Lincoln: University of Nebraska Press, 1973.

———. *Frontiersmen in Blue: The United States Army and the Indian, 1848–1865*. Lincoln: University of Nebraska Press, 1967.

Utley, Robert M., and Wilcomb E. Washburn. *Indian Wars*. Boston: Houghton Mifflin, 2002.

Uyar, Mesut, and Edward J. Erickson. *A Military History of the Ottomans: From Osman to Ataturk*. Santa Barbara: ABC Clio, 2009.

Valeriano, Napoleon D., and Charles T. R. Bohannan. *Counter-Guerrilla Operations: The Philippine Experience*. New York: Frederick A. Praeger, 1962.

Valerio, Anthony. *Anita Garibaldi: A Biography*. Westport: Praeger, 2001.

Vandervort, Bruce. *Indians Wars of Mexico, Canada, and the United States, 1812–1900*. New York: Routledge, 2006.

Van Wagner, R. D. *1st Air Commando Group: Any Place, Any Time, Any Where*. Montgomery: Air Command and Staff College, 1986.

Varon, Jeremy. *Bringing the War Home: The Weather Underground, the Red Army*

Faction, and Revolutionary Violence in the Sixties and Seventies. Berkeley: University of California Press, 2004.

Vaughan, Alden T. "'Expulsion of the Salvages': English Policy and the Virginia Massacre of 1622." *William and Mary Quarterly*, January 1978.

Vaughan, Charles Richard. *Narrative of the Siege of Zaragoza*. London: W. Flint, 1809.

Vecchj, Candido Augusto. *Garibaldi at Caprera*. London: Macmillan, 1862.

Venturi, Franco. *Roots of Revolution: A History of the Populist and Social Movements in Nineteenth-Century Russia*. Chicago: University of Chicago Press, 1960.

Vernadsky, George, Ralph T. Fisher Jr., Alan D. Ferguson, and Andrew Lossky, eds. *A Source Book for Russian History from Early Times to 1917*. 3 vols. New Haven: Yale University Press, 1972.

Verney, John. *Going to the Wars: A Journey in Various Directions*. London: Collins, 1955.

Victoria, Queen. *The Letters of Queen Victoria, Third Series*. 3 vols. London: John Murray, 1932.

Villard, Oswald Garrison. *John Brown, 1850–1859: A Biography Fifty Years After*. Boston: Houghton Mifflin, 1910.

Villegas, Harry. *Pombo, a Man of Che's Guerrilla: With Che Guevara in Bolivia, 1966–68*. New York: Pathfinder, 1997.

Vizetelly, Ernest Alfred. *The Anarchists, Their Faith and Their Record*. London: John Lane, 1911.

Volckmann, R. W. *We Remained: Three Years behind the Enemy Lines in the Philippines*. New York: W. W. Norton, 1954.

Vuckovich, Zvonimir. *A Balkan Tragedy: Yugoslavia, 1941–1946: Memoirs of a Guerrilla Fighter*. New York: Columbia University Press, 2004.

Waldron, Arthur. "China's New Remembering of World War II: The Case of Zhang Zizhong." *Modern Asian Studies*, October 1996.

———. *From War to Nationalism: China's Turning Point, 1924–1925*. Cambridge: Cambridge University Press, 1995.

———. *The Great Wall of China: From History to Myth*. Cambridge: Cambridge University Press, 1998.

Walker, Jonathan. *Aden Insurgency: The Savage War in South Arabia, 1962–1967*. Staplehurst: Spellmount, 2005.

Walker, Tony, and Andrew Gowers. *Arafat: The Biography*. London: Virgin Books, 2003.

Wall, Irwin M. *France, the United States, and the Algerian War*. Berkeley: University of California Press, 2001.

Waller, John H. *Beyond the Khyber Pass: The Road to British Disaster in the First Afghan War*. Austin: University of Texas Press, 1993.

Walsh, Robert. *A Residence at Constantinople*. 2 vols. London: Frederick Westley and A. H. Davis, 1836.

Warburton, Robert. *Eighteen Years in the Khyber, 1879–1898*. London: John Murray, 1900.

Waring, Alice Noble. *The Fighting Elder: Andrew Pickens (1739–1817)*. Columbia: University of South Carolina Press, 1962.

Watts, Dale E. "How Bloody Was Bleeding Kansas? Political Killing in Kansas Territory, 1854–1861." *Kansas History: A Journal of the Central Plains*, Summer 1995.

Wavell, Archibald. *The Good Soldier*. London: Macmillan, 1948.

Wawro, Geoffrey. *The Franco-Prussian War: The German Conquest of France in 1870–1871*. Cambridge: Cambridge University Press, 2003.

Weatherford, Jack. *Genghis Khan and the Making of the Modern World*. New York: Three Rivers Press, 2004.

Weaver, Mary Anne. "Inventing Zarqawi." *Atlantic Monthly*, July/August 2006.

Weber, Eugen. *France: Fin de Siècle*. Cambridge: Harvard University Press, 1986.

Weigley, Russell F. *The Age of Battles: The Quest for Decisive Warfare from Breitenfeld to Waterloo*. Bloomington: Indiana University Press, 1991.

Weiner, Tim. *Legacy of Ashes: The History of the CIA*. New York: Doubleday, 2007.

Weinstein, Jeremy M. *Inside Rebellion: The Politics of Insurgent Violence*. Cambridge: Cambridge University Press, 2007.

Weizmann, Chaim. *Trial and Error: The Autobiography*. New York: Harper & Brothers, 1949.

Wellington, Arthur Wellesley, Duke of, *Despatches, Correspondence, and Memoranda of Field Marshal Arthur Duke of Wellington, K.G.* 8 vols. London: John Murray, 1867–80.

———. *The Dispatches of Field Marshal the Duke of Wellington . . . From 1799 to 1818*. 13 vols. London: John Murray, 1834–39.

Wert, Jeffrey D. *Custer: The Controversial Life of George Armstrong Custer*. New York: Simon & Schuster, 1996.

West, Bing. *The Strongest Tribe: War, Politics, and the Endgame in Iraq*. New York: Random House, 2008.

West, Jerry L. *The Reconstruction Ku Klux Klan in York County, South Carolina, 1865–1877*. Jefferson: McFarland, 2002.

West, Richard. *Tito and the Rise and Fall of Yugoslavia*. New York: Carroll & Graf, 1994.

Westad, Odd Arne. *Decisive Encounters: The Chinese Civil War, 1946–1950*. Stanford: Stanford University Press, 2003.

———. *The Global Cold War*. Cambridge: Cambridge University Press, 2007.

Westenholz, Joan Goodnick. *Legends of the Kings of Akkade: The Texts*. Winona Lake: Eisenbrauns, 1997.

Westmoreland, William C. *A Soldier Reports*. New York: Da Capo Press, 1989.

Wickham-Crowley, Timothy P. *Guerrillas and Revolutions in Latin America*. Princeton: Princeton University Press, 1992.

Wickwire, Franklin and Mary. *Cornwallis: The American Adventure*. Boston: Houghton Mifflin, 1970.

———. *Cornwallis and the War of Independence*. London: Faber and Faber, 1971.

Willard, Margaret Wheeler, ed. *Letters on the American Revolution, 1774–1776*. Port Washington: Kennikat Press, 1925.

Williams, John W. "Carlos Marighela: The Father of Urban Guerrilla Warfare." *Terrorism*, 1989.

Williams, Louis. "Entebbe Diary." *IDF Journal*, 2004.

Williamson, Hugh Ross. *The Gunpowder Plot*. London: Faber and Faber, 1951.

Williamson, Joel. *After Slavery: The Negro in South Carolina during Reconstruction, 1861–1877*. Chapel Hill: University of North Carolina Press, 1965.

Williamson, Tony. *Counterstrike Entebbe*. London: Collins, 1976.

Wilson, David K. *The Southern Strategy: Britain's Conquest of South Caroline and Georgia, 1775–1780*. Columbia: University of South Carolina Press, 2005.

Wilson, Dick. *The Long March 1935: The Epic of Chinese Communism's Survival*. New York: Viking, 1971.

———. *Mao Zedong in the Scales of History*. Cambridge: Cambridge University Press, 1977.

Wilson, H. W. *After Pretoria: The Guerilla War*. 2 vols. London: Amalgamated Press, 1902.

Wilson, James. *The Earth Shall Weep: A History of Native America*. New York: Atlantic Monthly Press, 1999.

Wilson, Jeremy. *Lawrence of Arabia: The Authorized Biography of T. E. Lawrence*. New York: Atheneum, 1990.

Windrow, Martin. *The Last Valley: Dien Bien Phu and the French Defeat in Vietnam*. New York: Da Capo Press, 2004.

———. *Our Friends Beneath the Sands: The Foreign Legion in France's Colonial Conquests, 1870–1935*. London: Weidenfeld & Nicolson, 2010.

Winnington-Ingram, H. F. *Hearts of Oak*. London: W. H. Allen, 1889.

"Winograd Commission Final Report." January 30, 2008. http://www.cfr.org/israel/winograd-commission-final-report/p15385.

Winter, Ormonde. *Winter's Tale: An Autobiography*. London: Richards Press, 1955.

Winterton, Earl. *Fifty Tumultuous Years*. London: Hutchinson, 1955.

Witte, Sergei. *The Memoirs of Count Witte*. Garden City: Doubleday, Page, 1921.

Wolf, Markus. *Man without a Face: The Autobiography of Communism's Greatest Spymaster*. New York: Times Books, 1997.

Wolfe, Tom. *Radical Chic & Mau-Mauing the Flak Catchers*. New York: Farrar, Straus and Giroux, 1970.

Wolpert, Stanley. *Shameful Flight: The Last Years of the British Empire in India*. Oxford: Oxford University Press, 2006.

Woodcock, Caroline. *An Officer's Wife in Ireland*. London: Parkgate, 1994.

Woodhouse, C. M. *The Battle of Navarino*. London: Hodder and Stoughton, 1965.

———. *The Struggle for Greece, 1941–1949*. Lanham: Ivan R. Dee, 2003.

Woodward, David R. *Hell in the Holy Land: World War I in the Middle East*. Lexington: University Press of Kentucky, 2006.

Woolman, David S. *Rebels in the Rif: Abd el Krim and the Rif Rebellion*. Stanford: Stanford University Press, 1968.

Woolf, Greg. *Becoming Roman: The Origins of Provincial Civilization in Gaul*. Cambridge: Cambridge University Press, 1998.

Woolf, Stuart. *Napoleon's Integration of Europe*. London: Routledge, 1991.

Wooster, Robert. *Nelson A. Miles and the Twilight of the Frontier Army.* Lincoln: University of Nebraska Press, 1993.

Worthington, Ian. *Alexander the Great, Man and God.* Harlow: Pearson Longman, 2004.

Wright, David Curtis. "The Hsiung-nu-Hun Equation Revisited." *Eurasian Studies Yearbook*, 1997.

Wright, Lawrence. *The Looming Tower: Al-Qaeda and the Road to 9/11.* New York: Alfred A. Knopf, 2007.

Wright, Robin. *Sacred Rage: The Wrath of Militant Islam.* New York: Simon & Schuster, 2001.

Wright, Thomas C. *Latin America in the Era of the Cuban Revolution.* Westport: Praeger, 2001.

Wynter, H. W. *Special Forces in the Desert War, 1940–1943.* London: Public Record Office, 2001.

Xenophon. *Cyropaedia.* 2 vols. London: William Heinemann, 1914.

Yaari, Ehud. *Strike Terror: The Story of Fatah.* New York: Sabra Books, 1970.

Yadin, Yigael. *The Art of Warfare in Biblical Lands.* New York: McGraw-Hill, 1963.

———. *Bar-Kokhba: The Rediscovery of the Legendary Hero of the Second Jewish Revolt against Rome.* New York: Random House, 1971.

———. *Masada: Herod's Fortress and the Zealots' Last Stand.* London: Weidenfeld & Nicolson, 1966.

Yang, Benjamin. *From Revolution to Politics: Chinese Communists on the Long March.* Boulder: Westview Press, 1990.

Year Book 1898: City of Charleston. Charleston: Lucas & Richardson, n.d.

Yeatman, Ted P. *Frank and Jesse James: The Story behind the Legend.* Nashville: Cumberland, 2000.

Yenne, Bill. *Indian Wars: The Campaign for the American West.* Yardley: Westholme, 2006.

———. *Sitting Bull.* Yardley: Westholme, 2008.

Yoo, John. *War by Other Means: An Insider's Account of the War on Terror.* New York: Atlantic Monthly Press, 2006.

Young, Hubert. *The Independent Arab.* London: John Murray, 1933.

Young, Peter. *Commando.* New York: Ballantine, 1969.

Yousaf, Mohammad, and Mark Adkin. *Afghanistan—The Bear Trap: The Defeat of a Superpower.* Havertown: Casemate, 2001.

Yu, Ying-shih. *Trade and Expansion in Han China: A Study in the Structure of Sino-Barbarian Economic Relations.* Berkeley: University of California Press, 1967.

Zamoyski, Adam. *Moscow 1812: Napoleon's Fatal March.* New York: HarperCollins, 2004.

Zayyat, Montasser. *The Road to Al-Qaeda: The Story of bin Laden's Right-Hand Man.* London: Pluto Press, 2004.

Zelkina, Anna. *In Quest for God and Freedom: The Sufi Response to the Russian Advance in the North Caucasus.* London: Hurst, 2000.

Zhai, Qiang. *China and the Vietnam Wars, 1950–1975.* Chapel Hill: University of North Carolina Press, 2000.

Zimmerman, William. *A Popular History of Germany: From the Earliest Period to the Present Day.* 4 vols. New York: Henry J. Johnson, 1878.

Zips, Werner. *Black Rebels: African-Caribbean Freedom Fighters in Jamaica.* Princeton: Markus Wiener, 1999.

Zuckerman, Frederic S. *The Tsarist Secret Police Abroad: Policing Europe in a Modernising World.* Houndmills: Palgrave Macmillan, 2003.

———. *The Tsarist Secret Police in Russian Society, 1880–1917.* New York: New York University Press, 1996.

Zuczek, Richard. *State of Rebellion: Reconstruction in South Carolina.* Columbia: University of South Carolina Press, 1996.

INDEX

Page numbers in italics refer to maps.